HUMAN RESOU[RCE]
MANAGEMENT [IN]
IRELAND

THIRD EDITION

Patrick Gunnigle, Noreen Heraty
& Michael J. Morley

GILL & MACMILLAN

Gill & Macmillan
Hume Avenue
Park West
Dublin 12
with associated companies throughout the world
www.gillmacmillan.ie

© 2006 Patrick Gunnigle, Noreen Heraty & Michael J. Morley

ISBN–13: 978 0 7171 3933 0
ISBN–10: 0 7171 3933 6

Index compiled by Cover to Cover
Print origination in Ireland by
Carrigboy Typesetting Services, Co. Cork

The paper used in this book is made from the wood pulp of managed forests.
For every tree felled, at least one is planted, thereby renewing natural resources.

Contents

Foreword

Iwelcome the new edition of *Human Resource Management in Ireland*. This latest edition continues the fine tradition started in 1990 with the publication of the first in-depth book on the topic, entitled *Personnel Management in Ireland: Practice, Trends and Developments*. Since then, there have been comprehensive revisions in 1997 and 2002.

The human resource management function has grown dramatically over the sixteen years since *Personnel Management in Ireland* was first published. Today organisations are increasingly looking to their people as the critical source of competitive advantage. The challenge for HR professionals is to demonstrate that the HR function has the capacity to add real strategic value. A sound theoretical base underpinning HR activities is essential if this is to be achieved.

The team at the University of Limerick has played a pioneering role in the development of HR theory and practice in Ireland and are now our most influential thought leaders in this area. This fact is recognised by the Chartered Institute of Personnel and Development (CIPD) which awarded 'Centre of Excellence' status to the University of Limerick, the only third-level institution in Ireland to gain such recognition and just one of a very small number of centres to be so honoured internationally.

The unique feature of this excellent publication is that while it provides an accessible text for Irish students – based on Irish research data – it is also grounded in developments on the international stage. The book is essential reading on University and Institute of Technology courses, and on programmes leading to CIPD accreditation. Furthermore, the comprehensive and up-to-date treatment of the subject matter makes it an ideal source of reference material for HR professionals, consultants and others with responsibility for the management and development of people.

This revised edition offers an insightful analysis of the most important developments in Irish employment relations including the recent 'right to bargain' legislation and the growth in non-union employment relations. It considers the implications for HRM of labour shortages and the growth in the number of foreign nationals working in Ireland. It provides a comprehensive examination of the links between business strategy, HRM and organisation performance, including Irish research evidence on the nature and extent of strategic human resource management. The implications of 9/11, the dot.com downturn, the growth of the service sector, the competitive pressures on manufacturing and the relentless spread of globalisation are all critically examined. A particularly useful feature of the book is that the sections on employment law, recruitment and selection, reward management and performance management systems incorporate research evidence of practices in many Irish organisations. The book also contains a most interesting evaluation of 'best practice' human resource management.

Once again I highly commend the authors for providing us with such a scholarly, yet accessible and practical, text on the complex issue of managing people at work. I am confident that this new edition will build on the success of previous editions. Students and practitioners alike shall find much to interest and reward them in *Human Resource Management in Ireland*, 3rd edition.

Michael McDonnell BBS, MSc, Chartered Fellow, CIPD
Director, Chartered Institute of Personnel and Development (CIPD) in Ireland.
President, European Association of Personnel Management (EAPM).

Acknowledgments

In helping us complete this text, we would like to acknowledge the help and contribution of a number of individuals and organisations. We would especially like to thank Dr Edel Conway, Dublin City University and Dr Margaret Heffernan, NUI Galway, who provided invaluable material, advice and assistance on HRM, strategy and performance. Various external organisations and individuals provided data and assistance. In particular we would like to thank the following:

- Brian Sheehan, Tony Dobbins & Colman Higgins, *Industrial Relations News*
- Michael McDonnell and Wendy Sullivan, Chartered Institute of Personnel & Development in Ireland
- Dr Gerard McMahon, Dublin Institute of Technology
- Teresa Brannick, Smurfit Graduate School of Business, University College Dublin
- Declan Morrin and Larry O'Grady, Labour Relations Commission
- Labour Market Section, Central Statistics Office,
- Veronica Gallagher, Irish Business & Employers Confederation
- John O'Hagan, Department of Enterprise, Trade and Employment
- Jan Boud, Irish Congress of Trade Unions
- Dr Tony Dundon, National University of Ireland, Galway
- Professor Aidan Kelly, University College Dublin, who provided the initial encouragement for developing an Irish HRM textbook many years ago.

Colleagues at the University of Limerick were most helpful and supportive of our efforts. In particular we would like to acknowledge the help of Dr Michelle O'Sullivan, for her extensive research assistance on the employee relations chapters.

Anthony McDonnell, Christine Cross, Claire Murphy, David Collings, Daryl D'Art, Emma Parkinson, Jill Pearson, Juliet MacMahon, Joe Wallace, Jonathan Lavelle, Patrick Flood, Pauline Devaney, Sarah Moore, Sarah MacCurtain, Tom Garavan and Tom Turner all helped in various ways, not least through their own research and publications. We would also like to thank our Business Studies Librarian, Aoife Geraghty, and all the Library staff, University of Limerick, for their assistance.

We would also like to mention the contribution of Marion O'Brien, Aoileann O'Donnell and Emma Farrell of Gill & Macmillan and Jane Rogers, for helping to bring this work to fruition.

Finally, we would like to mention our families – Theresa, Eoin, Sean and Tadhg (Gunnigle) and Oisín, Alannah, Óran and Fionnán (Morley).

PG, NH, MM January 2006

Support Material for
Human Resource Management in Ireland, 3rd ed.
by Patrick Gunnigle, Noreen Heraty & Michael J. Morley

Dynamic and easy to use, online support material for this book is available at *www.gillmacmillan.ie*.

*Provides **lecturers** with:*
- PowerPoint slides
- Web links
- Questions with suggested answers
- Extra case studies

To access lecturer support material on our secure site:
1) Go to *www.gillmacmillan.ie/lecturers*
2) Logon using your username and password. If you don't have a password, register online and we will email your password to you.

*Provides **students** with:*
- Web links
- Questions with suggested answers
- Extra case studies

To access student support material
1) Go to *www.gillmacmillan.ie/student*
2) Click on the link for student support material

1

Human Resource Management in Ireland: an Introduction

P eople are the lifeblood of organisations. An organisation's workforce represents one of its most potent and valuable resources. Consequently, the extent to which an organisation's workforce is managed effectively is a critical element in improving and sustaining organisational performance. Indeed, it is widely argued that effective workforce management is one of the pivotal factors that characterises high-performing organisations (Boxall and Purcell 2003; Huselid 1995; Tiernan *et al.* 2001). However, the challenge is also great. Workforce management is one of the most difficult aspects of organisational management. This difficulty largely stems from the fact that people are inherently different. Managing an organisation's workforce means dealing with people who differ physically and psychologically. This is the essence of *human resource management* (HRM): that aspect of organisational management concerned with the management of an organisation's workforce.

This chapter provides an historical overview of the field of HRM. The objective is to place HRM in Ireland within a national and international setting, and thus allow an evaluation of HRM in the context of broader contemporary developments in the field. It also explores the concept of *human resource management* as it emerged as a distinctive approach to workforce management in the US in the 1980s, contrasts this with what was then viewed as 'traditional' personnel management, and assesses the implications for HRM practice in Ireland.

THE HISTORICAL DEVELOPMENT OF HRM

Early Days: The Emergence of the HR Role

The origins of what we now term HRM lie in the dramatic changes brought about by the industrial revolution, which had its roots in eighteenth-century Britain but later spread to Europe and North America (see Niven 1967). A central element of this was the growth of the 'factory system', whereby owners of capital employed large numbers of wage labourers to produce standardised goods in larger quantities for bigger markets. Such developments had dramatic effects on the organisation of work. From the owner's perspective, the new factory employees required direction, equipment had to be maintained, production

1

controlled and goods distributed and sold. Here we have many of the key elements of modern management: the need to plan, organise, direct and control the use of equipment, capital, materials and employees within organisations. This early phase of industrial society was characterised by extremely poor working conditions for the bulk of the new 'factory' labour. Workers themselves could do little to improve their position since they had little economic or political power. It was not until the growth of organised labour through the trade union movement, and of political influence resulting from mass enfranchisement, that concerns of workers could command the attention and action of employers and, indeed, governments.

We can point to two important developments in the late nineteenth and early twentieth century which critically impacted upon the development and evolution of HRM, particularly in regard to the emergence of the specialist HR function. These were (i) the welfare tradition and (ii) scientific management (see Niven 1967; Foley and Gunnigle 1994).

THE WELFARE TRADITION

The origins of modern HRM are generally traced back to what has become known as the welfare tradition, which developed in a few large companies in Britain during the late nineteenth and early twentieth centuries. In the early stages of industrialisation, many factory owners regarded their labour force in largely instrumental terms. Working conditions were poor and employees enjoyed few of the benefits we now associate with employment such as sick pay, pensions, and basic health, safety and welfare provisions (Niven 1967). The welfare tradition refers to a series of voluntary initiatives undertaken in certain companies to improve the conditions of factory workers, particularly in relation to pay, working hours and health and safety.

This phase is particularly important in the development of HRM as it was characterised by the appointment of welfare officers who are seen as the forerunners of the modern HR practitioner. Welfare officers first emerged in the mainly Quaker-owned firms in the food and confectionery industry in Britain in the late 1800s. These progressive employers, often influenced by their religious beliefs, undertook various initiatives to improve working conditions in their factories. A common aspect of this approach involved the appointment of so-called 'welfare officers'. The early 1900s saw the appointment of welfare officers in Irish companies, such as Jacobs and Maguire & Paterson in Dublin (Byrne 1988).

The First World War added some impetus to the welfare movement in Britain because of the need to accelerate factory production. However, large-scale unemployment and depression in the post-war period meant that initiatives in the area of welfare and HR work were abandoned in many organisations. In 1919 the Welfare Workers' Institute, founded in Britain in 1913 as the Welfare Workers' Association, had a membership of 700. By 1927, when it had been renamed the Institute of Industrial Welfare Workers, its membership had fallen to 420 (Farnham 1984).

Despite such oscillation in the significance of the welfare tradition, its influence on contemporary HR practice is enduring. Welfare has been inextricably linked with a 'caring' approach to employees, dealing with issues such as health, working conditions and personal problems. This is very much in evidence in modern HRM practice in areas such as counselling, employee assistance programmes, and occupational health and safety provision. On a rather different level, the welfare tradition has been a source of some confusion about the position of the HR practitioner in the managerial hierarchy. Early welfare officers occupied a semi-independent position in the factory system, with employees the main beneficiaries of their work. This led to the so-called 'middle man' perception of the welfare role, with employees seeing them as the representatives of worker interests. However, it is clearly apparent that modern HR practitioners operate as an integral part of the management team and represent employers' as opposed to workers' interests.

SCIENTIFIC MANAGEMENT

Another important early influence on the emergence of HRM was the advent of scientific management and what became known as 'Taylorism'. As the welfare tradition succumbed in the face of economic depression, Taylorism and its associated notions of labour efficiency became an increasingly popular managerial approach. By the early years of the twentieth century, improvements in technology coupled with increases in company size and complexity forced employers to investigate new ways of improving industrial performance. In the US, F. W. Taylor led the way by pointing to the efficiency and profitability benefits to be gained through greater standardisation of work systems and methods.

Based on his research at the Bethlehem Steel Company (1900–11), Taylor encouraged employers to adopt more systematic approaches to job design, employment and payment systems (Taylor 1947). Such scientific management approaches were widely adopted in both the US and Britain in the inter-war years. Particular emphasis was placed on job analysis, time and motion studies, and the creation of incentive bonus schemes, thereby extending the work of the emerging HR function. Scientific management led to a shift in the emphasis of HR away from the employee-oriented 'caring/do-gooding' agenda of the welfare tradition and towards the more managerial 'efficiency/profitability' agenda of the work study officer. From the HR perspective, the spread of scientific management placed greater weight on the careful selection and systematic training of employees. Associated with this trend was an increased attention to job design, working conditions and payment systems. HR also took responsibility for much of the research and administration required to underpin such initiatives.

Despite extensive criticism, the principles of Taylorism had, and continue to have, a profound impact on management practice. Probably its most significant legacy is the notion that work *planning* (seen as a management task) should be separated from work *doing* (seen as a worker task). This separation delineated the primary role of management as that of establishing work standards, procedures and methods. Such approaches to work organisation were dominated by a desire to maximise the productive efficiency of the company's technical resources. Management's role was to ensure that other organisational resources, including employees, were organised in such a way as to facilitate the optimal utilisation of the technical system.

This efficiency approach, based on Taylorist principles, has been a characteristic of employers' approaches to job design since the early years of the twentieth century. It advocated the breaking down of jobs into simple, repetitive, measurable tasks requiring skills that could be easily acquired through systematic job training. Taylorism helped improve efficiency and promoted a systematic approach to selection, training, work measurement and payment. However, it is also seen as the source of many of the problems associated with industrial work, such as high levels of labour turnover and absenteeism, and low levels of employee motivation (see, for example, Mowday *et al.* 1982; Steers and Mowday 1987). Indeed, the growth of the behavioural science movement (discussed below) can be traced to criticisms of Taylorism and to suggestions that improvements in organisational effectiveness could be achieved through greater attention to workers' needs and, particularly, by providing workers with more challenging jobs and an improved work environment.

The Behavioural Science Movement

The emergence of the behavioural sciences gave a major impetus to HRM by establishing a body of knowledge to underpin many aspects of HR work such as selection, training, motivation, industrial relations and payment systems. It also served to focus attention on some of the problems created by work organisation in the large factories of the new industrial era, such as monotony and low morale.

The emergence of the behavioural science movement is most commonly associated with the work of Elton Mayo and of Roethlisberger and Dickson (see Roethlisberger and Dickson 1939). Based on their studies of worker productivity, it was suggested that employee behaviour and performance was influenced by motivation and needs as well as by working conditions and payment practices. This research highlighted the importance of social factors, group dynamics, and employee motivation in affecting both individual performance and organisational effectiveness. Although this work has been the subject of methodological criticisms (see Carey 1967), it had an important influence on management practice, particularly in the sphere of HRM. Its major contribution was possibly the stimulation of interest in applying behavioural science principles to the study of organisational and worker behaviour. Subsequent work on the application of the behavioural sciences to the study of organisations has helped inform our understanding of organisational functioning and, particularly, of workers' motivation. Indeed, much of the subsequent research in this field has focused on investigating employees' motivation and attempting to reconcile employers' and workers' needs through appropriate organisation structures, work systems and managerial styles. We consider this literature in chapter 6, which deals with employee motivation and the design of work.

Industrial Relations as a Key HR Activity

A particularly significant development affecting the nature of HRM and the role of the emerging HR function was the growing significance of industrial relations. The growth of an industrial relations emphasis in HR work was a direct result of the increasing influence of trade unions. In Ireland, the trade union movement had become well established in the early 1900s in industries in the major cities of Dublin, Belfast and Cork (McNamara *et al.* 1988). A particularly important development during this period was the emergence of the 'new unionism', which primarily sought to organise unskilled workers.

In Ireland, the growth in influence and power of the 'new unionism' was most visibly manifested in the activity of Jim Larkin and the Irish Transport and General Workers' Union (ITGWU). A period of conflict between employer and worker interests came to a head in the 'Dublin lockout' of 1913 (see Yeates 2000). Gradually, trenchant employer opposition to trade unions gave way to reluctant acceptance of their role and legitimacy. Roche and Larragy (1989) estimate that union membership rose from 110,000 in 1914 to 250,000 in 1920 leading Roche (1997a:54) to label this period the 'first phase of rapid mass union membership growth in Ireland'. An important outcome of this turbulent period was that it served to accelerate the organisation of employees into trade unions and employers into employers' associations and thus placed an increased emphasis on *industrial relations* as an important aspect of workforce management (Gunnigle and Flood 1990).

The period from the early 1920s saw a reversal in the fortunes of unions. Membership fell in the face of economic recession and external competition as the Government pursued an open economy policy. This reflected developments in Britain where economic depression after the First World War saw a re-emergence of autocratic management styles. A combination of factors, particularly low pay and poor working conditions, contributed to high levels of industrial conflict culminating in the General Strike of 1926 in Britain. During this period workers and their trade unions became increasingly suspicious of management motives in introducing welfare initiatives in the workplace. Trade unions became quite anti-welfare, viewing this as an employer strategy to prevent workers from joining trade unions.

With a growth in industrial employment in Ireland, union membership increased steadily during the 1930s and collective bargaining became more widespread. In certain organisations this period saw the establishment of a personnel function, with the emphasis on *industrial relations* rather than welfare. Employers were forced to accommodate the reality of organised labour and responded through multi-employer bargaining via employers' associations, and by the employment of 'labour relations officers' to deal with industrial relations (and certain other HR matters) at workplace level.

A related and important factor contributing to the growth in significance of industrial relations was the nature of pay bargaining. During the Second World War wages were controlled under the Emergency Powers Orders. The rescinding of these in 1946 marked the start of a new era for industrial relations with the establishment of the Labour Court. The removal of the Emergency Powers Orders and the negotiation of a general pay increase for unionised employees constituted what became known as the first *wage round* (see Nevin 1963; McCarthy *et al.* 1975; O'Brien 1989). A wage round was essentially a period of intensive collective bargaining between employers and trade unions occurring at regular intervals and resulting in a similar general wage increase for unionised employees (Wallace *et al.* 2004).

The nature of collective bargaining in the immediate postwar period had important implications for the development of HRM in Ireland. Growth in the size and complexity of organisations demanded greater specialisation and knowledge in workforce management, particularly in the area of industrial relations. In the public sector and among some larger private companies these needs were achieved through the establishment of specialist 'personnel' departments, whose key activity was industrial relations (O'Mahony 1958). By the 1960s, levels of unionisation among manual workers had increased significantly and *shop stewards* began to emerge as important players in regard to workplace-level industrial relations (Roche and Larragy 1989; Marsh 1973). This situation was accentuated by the growth in white-collar trade unionisation from the 1960s (Bain 1970; Kelly 1975). The decade of the 1960s was also characterised by a marked increase in levels of industrial conflict.

A further development contributing to the increasing significance of industrial relations as a critical concern in HRM was the onset of the *national wage agreement* era in 1970. The negotiation of the first national wage agreement marked a transformation from the rather unclear system of wage rounds, which had existed since the end of the war. An important effect of national wage agreements was to move major pay bargaining issues away from the level of the enterprise. This development was initially seen as freeing management from complex negotiations with trade unions and giving them more certainty in corporate planning. However, the reality was somewhat different. At a time of relative economic prosperity and substantial growth in union membership, the key workplace role for trade unions, namely pay bargaining, was removed. With the expectation that pay increases would be derived by means of national agreements, trade unions increasingly focused their attention on matters that could be negotiated at local (workplace) level such as employment conditions, pay anomalies and productivity deals. Indeed, far from eliminating local bargaining, national agreements merely changed their focus, and the period saw the negotiation of various types of productivity deals. These became an important means by which trade unions could gain pay increases above the stated maxima laid down in national wage agreements. The emphasis on industrial relations therefore continued to expand during the national wage agreement era.

For the HR function, industrial relations remained a priority with HR ('personnel') practitioners heavily involved in workplace bargaining with trade unions. Industrial harmony was the objective, and industrial relations specialists, through their negotiating, inter-personal and procedural skills, had responsibility for its achievement. Increased industrial unrest from the mid-1960s to the end of the 1970s served to confirm industrial relations as a key concern of employers. It gave the emerging HR function a central management role. HR departments, whose major responsibility was industrial relations, became established in most medium and larger organisations. The Donovan Report in Britain (1968) was also influential in encouraging collective bargaining, the adoption of comprehensive industrial relations procedures and greater specialisation in industrial relations management.

Increased Government intervention in the management sphere since the 1970s has also had a significant influence on the HR function. As discussed above, this was particularly evident in the area of centralised pay bargaining. The early seventies also witnessed the introduction of an unprecedented wave of *employment legislation*, which was to impinge on the industrial scene and significantly impacted upon the role of the HR practitioner. This legislation primarily focused on extending the individual employment rights of workers in areas such as dismissals and equality. Key legislation approved in this period included the Unfair Dismissals Act 1977, the Anti-Discrimination (Pay) Act 1974, the Employment Equality Act 1977, and a number of Redundancy Acts. Clearly, organisations had to come to grips with the application of such legislation and much of this responsibility was assumed by the emerging HR function. HR practitioners were expected to provide expert advice and guidance on the new legislation and to oversee its implementation in the workplace. Chapters 11, 12 and 13 of this text review employee relations issues in Ireland.

The Multinational Influence

The attraction of foreign direct investment (FDI) by multinational corporations (MNCs) has been a cornerstone of Irish Government policy for over four decades. The economic significance of the FDI sector in the Irish economy is highlighted by the fact that employment in the sector accounts for some 50 per cent of manufacturing employment, compared to an average of 19 per cent for the eleven other European Union (EU) member states for which the OECD presents data (Barry 2002). There are now over 1,000 foreign MNCs employing almost 130,000 people operating in Ireland.[1] OECD data show a three-fold increase in FDI inflows to Ireland during the 1990s (OECD 2000). It is reported that MNCs contribute approximately 55 per cent of manufactured output and a staggering 75 per cent of industrial exports (O'Higgins 2002; Tansey 1998). The key areas of MNC activity are electronics and engineering, pharmaceuticals and healthcare, software and internationally traded services, as outlined in table 1.1. The United States is by some

---

1. This figure is derived from data supplied by IDA Ireland and based on the Forfas Annual Employment Surveys. It includes only firms supported by IDA Ireland and is thus likely to understate the level of MNC activity. Clearly a number of MNCs operate in Ireland but do not benefit from aid from our industrial promotions agencies. This would particularly apply to firms in retail, catering and consultancy (e.g. Lidl, Homebase and McDonalds).

way Ireland's largest source of FDI, accounting for just under half of all foreign-owned firms in the country and employing just under 90,000 people (see table 1.2). US FDI into Ireland increased five-fold during the 1990s (OECD 1999).

Table 1.1 Foreign direct investment by sector (employment in IDA-supported companies 1998–2003)

SECTOR	1998	2000	2002	2003
Electronic and Engineering	60,645	70,771	60,282	56,894
International Financial Services	27,047	40,497	42,762	43,394
Pharmaceutical and Healthcare	16,047	17,837	18,996	19,463
Miscellaneous Industry	14,015	11,719	9,964	9,242
Total	**177,754**	**140,824**	**132,004**	**128,993**

Source: IDA Ireland 2002, 2003

Table 1.2 Foreign direct investment by ownership (number of firms) 2001–2003

	2001	2002	2003
US	518 (42.3%)	507 (46.2%)	489 (46.4%)
Germany	164 (13.4%)	148 (13.5%)	149 (14.1%)
UK	162 (13.2%)	132 (12.0%)	118 (11.2%)
Rest of Europe	274 (22.4%)	211 (19.2%)	214 (20.3%)
Far East/Asia Pacific	55 (4.5%)	38 (3.5%)	44 (4.2%)
Rest of the world	52 (4.2%)	62 (5.6%)	40 (3.8%)
Total	**1,225**	**1,098**	**1,054**

Source: IDA Ireland 2002, 2003

The main contributory factors used to explain Ireland's high level of inward FDI include the level of tax on company profits (corporation tax), grants and other forms of financial incentive, labour quality and supply, and particular aspects of the Irish business climate (cf. Jacobsen and Andreosso 1990). Both Barry (2002) and Gunnigle & McGuire (2001) point to the critical significance of Ireland's low corporate tax regime in attracting US FDI. Barry (2002) finds that the effective tax on profits from US MNCs in Ireland was 6 per cent, while the comparative figures for Germany, Spain and the UK were 29 per cent, 25 per cent and 19 per cent respectively. Labour supply and quality have also been identified as a positive influence in attracting FDI, particularly the comparatively young age profile of the Irish labour force and the high level of educational attainment among younger age cohorts (cf. Tansey 1998). High levels of labour flexibility and a comparatively less regulated industrial relations and HR environment also emerge as factors favourably impacting on FDI, as does the use of English as first language, and Ireland's membership of the EU (Hannigan 2000; Barry 2002).

Given the significance of multinational companies in Ireland it is hardly surprising that they have had an important impact on the development of HRM. MNCs have been to the fore in developing comprehensive policies and procedures across various aspects of HRM, and in giving a greater impetus to the role of the specialist HR function (HR department).

A particularly important legacy of MNC investment has been the diffusion of new HR techniques. In areas such as selection testing, training methods, reward systems and communications, MNCs have been to the fore in introducing new developments and methods. We have evidence, for example, that MNCs have also been associated with innovation in areas of high-performance work systems (Mooney 1988), performance-related pay (Gunnigle, Turner and D'Art 1998) and with enhancing the status of the specialist HR function (Gunnigle 1998a). At a general level, the effect of MNCs has been to contribute to establishing HRM as a more central component of the management process. MNCs, particularly those of US origin, have also been to the fore in avoiding trade union recognition in their Irish facilities. This trend appears to have taken root during the early 1980s and has increasingly become commonplace among American and other foreign-owned MNCs (cf. Gunnigle 1995; Wallace 2003).

The impact of MNCs on HRM in Ireland is considered throughout this text, with particular mention of their impact on employee relations in chapter 12.

HRM Education

Another important factor that has contributed to the growth and expansion of the HR role is a progressively increasing emphasis on the professional education of HR practitioners since the 1970s. Clearly, increasing specialisation in the HR sphere required commensurate growth in the education and training of HR specialists. Many of the newer multinational and larger indigenous organisations emphasised the appointment of qualified and experienced HR practitioners. While the origins of formal courses in aspects of HRM can be traced back to the 1940s, the most significant developments have taken place since the 1960s.

The establishment of AnCO as the national training agency in 1967 added impetus to the development of the HR role through increased emphasis on training and development. In the 1970s the first courses leading to membership of the then Institute of Personnel Management (now the Chartered Institute of Personnel and Development) were offered at centres in Dublin and Limerick. Since then, full- and part-time undergraduate and postgraduate programmes have been established at most universities and a large number of other institutes of higher education. In 2004, courses leading to various categories of membership of the CIPD were available at fifteen centres throughout the Republic of Ireland.

We also find that courses in HRM, organisation behaviour and/or employment relations form part of most undergraduate programmes in business and related disciplines. There are also a number of specialist HRM master's programmes on offer, while HRM is generally a core module in MBA programmes. Thus, there has been a progressive increase in formal education of HR practitioners, which has served to enhance the status and competencies available across the broad field of HRM.

This growth in HR education has occurred in parallel with growth in membership of the CIPD in the UK and Ireland. The CIPD is the professional body for HR practitioners in Ireland and the UK. It began its life in the UK in 1913 as the Welfare Workers' Association, operated for many years as the Institute of Personnel Management (IPM) and became the Institute of Personnel and Development (IPD) in 1994 – the name being a derivative, resulting from the merger between the Institute of Personnel Management and the Institute of Training and Development in the UK. It was granted a Royal Charter in July 2000 in acknowledgement of its role as the major management association in the HR field. The resulting change in title to CIPD reflects this change in status. Membership of the CIPD in the UK and Ireland in late 2004 was just over 114,000. In Ireland membership has increased dramatically: from a base of just fourteen registered members in 1937, membership passed the 1,000 mark in 1987 and by late 2004 there were over 4,500 CIPD members in Ireland.

RETRENCHMENT AND RE-DEFINITION

In evaluating the development of HRM in Ireland, it is clear that increased industrialisation, foreign direct investment and commercial activity since the 1960s have contributed to the establishment of HR as a discrete management function. By the late 1970s the HRM role was firmly established in most of the larger Irish organisations. HR or 'personnel' departments operated as a distinct management function with responsibility for a well-defined range of HR activities, with particular focus on industrial relations.

However, the 1980s heralded a period of major change for HRM. A depressed economic climate, together with increased competitive pressures, led to a slump in business activity for most of the decade. These developments helped to change both the focus of HRM and the nature of HR activities. Competitive pressures combined to set new priorities, forcing the HR function to act under tighter cost controls and to undertake a wider range of activities (Berridge 1992; Tyson 1987; Foley and Gunnigle 1994). The recessional climate reduced the need for many hitherto 'core' activities such as recruitment and, particularly, industrial relations. The harsher economic atmosphere of the 1980s dramatically changed the industrial relations environment. An economic context characterised by widespread redundancies and high unemployment significantly altered the bargaining environment with adverse consequences for trade unions. Increasingly employers sought to address issues such as payment structures and levels of wage increases, the extent of demarcation and restrictive work practices, and generally to reclaim managerial prerogative, which they felt had been eroded by trade unions heretofore.

Restrictive trade union legislation in Britain and hard-line management approaches in many firms indicated a more offensive approach to dealings with trade unions. This was reflected in the adverse outcomes for trade unions to strikes by miners in Britain and air traffic controllers in the US in the early 1980s. Trade unions were in retreat and membership began to fall in many developed economies. In Ireland trade union membership fell significantly throughout the 1980s and industrial unrest also declined from the highs of the 1970s (see chapter 13 for greater detail).

At the same time increased market competition forced many organisations to seek new means of establishing competitive advantage. One apparent source of such improvements lay in the better utilisation of human resources. Some organisations began to investigate different approaches to workforce management, particularly in areas such as work organisation and job design, reward systems, employee relations and training and development.

However, the most widely debated development over the period was the emergence of what became known as *human resource management*. In this text we use the term 'human resource management' (HRM) in a generic fashion to encompass all aspects of workforce management in organisations. HRM has indeed become the umbrella term for what was formerly known as 'personnel management'. From an academic perspective, HRM has also become the umbrella discipline encompassing research and education in the fields of industrial relations, personnel management, organisational behaviour and human resource development.

This was not always the case. The use of the term 'human resource management' only came into popular usage in the early 1980s. In its initial conception, HRM essentially referred to the development of a more integrated and strategic approach to workforce management. It had its roots in the US, which has traditionally been receptive to the application of organisational psychology and behavioural science principles in an attempt to improve organisation performance (Beaumont 1993). We now consider this development.

THE DISTINCTIVE CONCEPT OF HRM AS IT EMERGED IN THE US IN THE 1980s

While in this text we use the term *human resource management* in generic terms to encompass that aspect of organisational management that is concerned with the management of an organisation's workforce, it originally entered the management vocabulary as a term which described a distinctive and seemingly novel approach to workforce management. Here we briefly review the emergence of HRM as the field has developed in the US since the early 1980s.

In the earlier sections of this chapter we noted the growing interest in more closely aligning business strategy and HRM. Indeed, many commentators have identified HRM as a neglected area of strategic management and one with a potentially crucial role to play with regard to strategy implementation, especially in the area of organisation change (McGrath and Geaney 1998; Beer *et al.* 1984; Fombrun *et al.* 1984). Above we noted that the 1980s was a period of reappraisal for the personnel/HR field. Increased competitive pressures forced many organisations to review their approach to workforce management. A key development was the emergence of *human resource management* as a distinctive approach to workforce management. HRM was seen by many as a new development that contrasted with 'traditional' *personnel management.* Its apparently proactive stance was viewed as a major departure from the traditionally reactive 'industrial relations' focus associated with established approaches to 'personnel management'.

> The new approaches . . . which adopted a managerialist rather than a pluralist stance, the restructuring possibilities, and the reduction in trade union power and influence were the backdrop to what is now perceived as a new paradigm on which to base employment relationships. In the eyes of some commentators, human resource management (HRM) came to represent the new paradigm, and the critical distinction drawn was the notion that HRM placed initiatives on people management at the strategic heart of the business . . . The new flexibility agreements, new working practices, reorganisations, de-layering activities, the flatter organisations, direct communications with the workforce, and stronger corporate cultures . . . could be understood as a new, more coherent approach . . . If this was propaganda, it was propaganda that managers themselves started to believe as the 1980s came to a close.
>
> Tyson, Witcher and Doherty (1994)

The conception of human resource management as a distinctive approach to workforce management and the associated emphasis on a greater role for HRM stems from two contrasting sources in the US literature. The first source emanates from the 'human resource' literature and is based on the 'human capital approach' of the Harvard Business School (HBS) model (Beer *et al.* 1984, 1985). This focused on the individual employee as the key organisational resource that management must nurture and develop to maximise its contribution to the organisation. It encouraged employers to deploy a coherent range of pro-employee HR policies to ensure the attraction, retention and development of committed, high-performing employees. This model is thus the basis for the 'soft' or benign approach to human resource management, whereby senior management acknowledge that people are the organisation's 'most valuable' resource.

The second literature source advocating increased strategic consideration of HRM comes from the broader business strategy literature, specifically the work of Fombrun (see, for example, Fombrun *et al.* 1984). This approach posited that organisational performance can be substantially improved by integrating HRM considerations into strategic decision-making to ensure that HR policies complement business strategy. In contrast to the HBS model, this approach does not prescribe either a 'hard' or 'soft' approach to workforce management. Rather, it was grounded on contingency principles, arguing that top management adopt the policies that best 'fit' the firm's business strategy and context. However, because its focus is overtly managerial, encouraging employers to employ the HR policies that will yield the best returns in terms of organisational performance, it has tended to become associated with the concept of 'hard' HRM (see figure 1.1)

Figure 1.1 Hard and soft HRM

Human Resource Management	*Human Resource* **Management**
HR Strategy as:	**HR Strategy as:**
Series of policy choices	Fit to corporate/business strategy
• Total HR/management philosophy	Emphasis on alignment and coherence
• General management perspective	Key to strategy implementation
• Multiple stakeholders	
• Evaluation through commitment, competence, congruence and cost effectiveness	
Primary emphasis on management philosophy (approach to HRM)	*HR as source of competitive advantage*

The Harvard Business School (HBS) model presents a broad causal map of the determinants and consequences of HRM policy choices as outlined in figure 1.1. HRM is described as 'involving all management decisions and actions that affect the nature of the relationship between the organisation and its employees – its human resources'. Thus, those in top management, and particularly the chief executive, are seen as having the primary responsibility for aligning business strategy and HRM. Four key components comprise the HBS model: (i) stakeholder interests; (ii) HRM policy choice; (iii) HRM outcomes and (iv) long-term consequences.

Presented as an open systems perspective 'in that HRM policy choices can affect each of the other components and be affected by them' (Lundy and Cowling 1996, 51), the central contention is that HR outcomes are affected by policy choices made in four key areas: (i) reward systems; (ii) human resource flows; (iii) work systems and (iv) employee influence. Each of these policy areas is seen as a key element of strategic choice, which profoundly impacts upon employee behaviour and attitude towards the organisation. Strategic choice in these areas is influenced by broader contextual factors (situational constraints and stakeholder interests). Decisions made in these policy areas are seen as affecting HR outcomes in the areas of employee commitment, congruence of employee and management interests, employee competence, and cost effectiveness. These outcomes are also seen as having broader long-term consequences for individual employee wellbeing, organisational effectiveness and societal wellbeing.

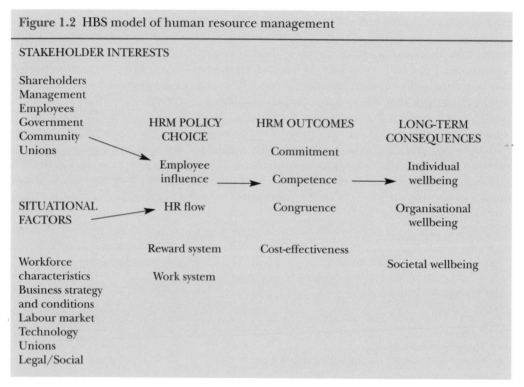

Figure 1.2 HBS model of human resource management

Source: Beer *et al.* (1984).

On this side of the Atlantic, Guest's (1987) 'hard-soft, tight-loose' framework of HRM is possibly the most widely referenced (see figure 1.3). The 'hard-soft' dimension refers to a continuum ranging from a resource-based ('soft') managerial perspective, characterised by benign pro-employee policies, to a more calculated ('hard') management perspective

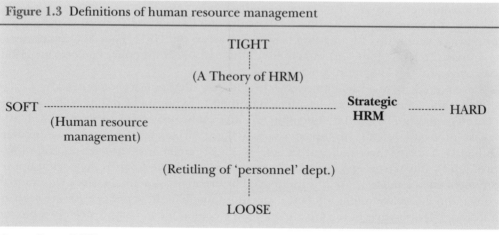

Figure 1.3 Definitions of human resource management

Source: Guest (1987).

where policy choice is driven by the need to complement business strategy and meet financial criteria. The 'tight-loose' dimension refers to a continuum ranging from, at one extreme, HRM merely involving a retitling of traditional personnel management ('loose') with no real change in HR practice, to, at the other extreme, HRM becoming a clearly defined and articulated approach to workforce management with an explicit and strong ('tight') theoretical underpinning.

Guest then proceeded to develop a more full-blown theory of HRM as outlined in figure 1.4. He argued that firms would be more successful if they pursued four key HRM goals: (i) strategic integration; (ii) employee commitment; (iii) flexibility; and (iv) quality. He suggested that these HRM goals can be optimally achieved through coherent HRM policy choices in the areas of organisation and job design, management of change, recruitment, selection and socialisation, appraisal, training and development, rewards and communications. Guest identified five necessary conditions for the effective operation of HRM:

1. *Corporate leadership*, to ensure that the values inherent in HRM are championed and implemented.
2. *Strategic vision*, to ensure the integration of HRM as a major component of the corporate strategy.
3. *Technological/production feasibility* – Guest warned that heavy investment in short-cycle, repetitive production assembly-line equipment mitigates against the job design principles and autonomous teamworking necessary for HRM.
4. *Employee relations feasibility* – he suggested that multi-union status, low-trust management-employee relations and an adversarial employee relations orientation mitigate against the implementation of HRM.
5. *Management capacity* to implement appropriate policies.

Figure 1.4 A theory of human resource management

HRM POLICIES	HR OUTCOMES	ORGANISATIONAL OUTCOMES
Org./Job design		High job performance
Management of change	Strategic integration	High problem-solving, change and innovation
Recruitment, selection and socialisation	Commitment	
Appraisal, training, development	Flexibility/ adaptability	High cost-effectiveness
Reward systems	Quality	Low turnover, absence, grievances
Communications		
	LEADERSHIP/CULTURE/STRATEGY	

Source: Guest (1987, 516).

Contrasting HRM and Personnel Management

When HRM is contrasted with what might be termed traditional personnel management, a number of key differences do emerge as outlined by Guest (1987), see figure 1.5. First, it is argued that workforce management considerations are fully integrated with strategic decision-making in the HRM model, whereas in the traditional personnel model the 'personnel' input is less pronounced and issue-specific. A second contrast is that HRM is seen as essentially proactive and long-term, while the traditional personnel management approach is more reactive and adopts a shorter-term perspective. In terms of the desired mode of psychological contract, HRM is seen as facilitating employee commitment, while the traditional personnel management model is more in terms of managerial control over employees (Walton 1985). In regard to employee relations, HRM is viewed as essentially unitarist in perspective, seeing no conflict of interests between employers and employees. In contrast, 'traditional' personnel management is grounded in the pluralist tradition involving acceptance that a conflict of interest exists between employers and workers. A related factor is that HRM is seen as focusing on relations between (line) management and the individual worker, while the traditional model is seen as operating primarily through collectivist relations between management and employee representatives (normally trade unions). Another area of contrast is that HRM is seen as operating most effectively in organic, fluid company structures, while 'personnel management' is felt to characterise more bureaucratic organisation structures. HRM is seen to operate primarily through line management, while in the traditional personnel management model primary responsibility is vested in the specialist personnel function.

The final perceived difference is that HRM is seen as essentially focused on maximising the HR contribution to overall company effectiveness, while personnel management

Figure 1.5 Personnel management and HRM compared

	Traditional Personnel Management	HRM
Input into corporate planning	Issue specific	Integrated
Time and planning perspective	Short-term; reactive; marginal	Long-term; proactive; strategic
Psychological contract	Compliance	Commitment
Employee relations	Pluralist; collective Low trust; adversarial	Unitarist, individual High trust
Organisation structures/ systems	Bureaucratic, mechanistic; centralised; formally defined roles	Organic, fluid; devolved; flexible roles
Principal delivery mechanism	Specialist personnel management function	Line management
Aims	Maximise cost-effectiveness	Maximise HR utilisation

Source. Adapted from Guest (1987).

focuses on the more limited goal of improving cost-effectiveness. Despite these argued contrasts between HRM and traditional personnel management, Guest cautions that this does not necessarily imply that HRM is better than 'traditional' personnel management. Rather, he suggests a contingency approach whereby either a HRM or traditional personnel management approach may be best suited to particular oganisational contexts.

Since its emergence HRM has been a source of intense debate, with respect to its theoretical pedigree, empirical foundations, and practical implications. Several authors have identified a number of inherent contradictions and inconsistencies in HRM, particularly the 'soft' variant advocated by the Harvard Business School model (Legge 1989, 2005; Keenoy 1990; Blyton and Turnbull 1992). For example, Legge (2005) highlights the apparent paradox between the traditional commodity status of labour under the capitalist framework and the essentially unitarist perspective of HRM, which sees no inherent conflict of interests between management and employees. It has been widely accepted that in the capitalist framework there is an inherent conflict of interest between management and employees over the price of labour. Indeed, this conflict of interest is the very basis of the pluralist perspective. However, the HRM perspective appears to ignore the 'inherency' of a conflict of interests, but rather focuses on the achievement of congruence of management and employee interests and on achieving high levels of employee commitment (Walton 1985, Flood 1989). This focus on employee commitment not only seems incongruent with the pluralist perspective of the organisation but also appears to conflict with another basic tenet of HRM, namely that HR policies should 'fit' with business strategy. Clearly, many decisions that complement business strategy may not develop employee commitment. If, for example, an organisation's business strategy is to maximise short-term returns to shareholders, this may well involve decisions that do not develop employee commitment; for example, replacing labour with technology, contracting out certain tasks and/or making employees redundant. A related issue on this theme is the suggestion that HRM involves the simultaneous achievement of higher levels of individualism and teamwork. These twin goals clearly have tremendous potential for conflict. For example, performance-related pay based on individual employee performance may indeed conflict with teamwork, as can individual communications/negotiations (see chapters 6 and 11).

High levels of flexibility are seen as a core objective of HRM. Guest (1987) suggests that increased flexibility involves the creation of structural mechanisms in organisations to ensure responsiveness to changing environmental conditions. This suggests high levels of functional (ability to deploy personnel across a range of different job tasks), numerical (ability to take on and shed labour in line with business demand) and financial (ability to link wages to the labour market context and to evaluations of individual performance) flexibility. However, several authors have noted the difficulties in achieving congruence in different flexibility forms, viz. numerical, functional and financial. It is clearly difficult to achieve high levels of functional flexibility (e.g. multi-skilling) where employees have a tenuous relationship with the organisation, for example as a result of attempts to improve numerical flexibility (Blyton and Morris 1992; Gunnigle 1992b).

Another contradiction in the HRM argument that HR policies must be internally consistent arises in relation to job security. A prominent theme in the extant literature is that for HRM to be effective, management must provide implicit job tenure guarantees for employees (Beer *et al.* 1984, Guest 1987, 1989; Walton 1985). For example, Guest (1989) argues that job tenure commitments are a 'necessary' precondition in achieving a 'mutuality of management and employee interests', which he suggests is a key policy goal of HRM. However, it is patently evident that increased competitive pressures can make job security increasingly difficult to achieve. Indeed, job security may itself be incompatible with broader business goals attributed to HRM, such as increased flexibility in responding to market changes. In practice, it would appear that some organisations seek to achieve such flexibility by policies that actually reduce the likelihood of job tenure commitments – for example, using temporary workers. On the issue of the practicability of achieving a 'fit' between business strategy and HRM policies (e.g. job tenure commitments), Blyton and Turnbull (1992, 10) comment:

> This is particularly problematic in highly competitive or recessionary conditions where the 'needs of the business' are likely to undermine any internal 'fit' with ('soft') HRM values: shedding labour for example will severely challenge, if not destroy, an organisation's HRM image of caring for the needs and security of its employees.

Another apparent inconsistency in HRM is the focus on achieving greater individualism in management-employee relations. As we have seen, employee relations in the Republic of Ireland have been characterised by extensive reliance on collectivism as manifested in, for example, relatively high levels of trade union density and low-trust management-employee relations (Whelan 1982). The 'soft' HRM approach, as outlined by the HBS model and Guest, places the managerial emphasis on achieving high-trust relations between management and employees, and appears to have a preference for pursuing this goal in a non-union environment. Within the 'soft' HRM model, high-trust relations are pursued through managerial initiatives to increase individual employee involvement and motivation, and the adoption of techniques such as performance appraisal and performance-related pay. Thus, such organisations attempt to create close management-employee ties and break down the traditional management-worker dichotomy, of which collective bargaining is seen as the principal manifestation. Again, this is is indicative of a unitarist management perspective:

> HRM values are unitarist to the extent that they assume no underlying and inevitable differences of interest between management and workers . . . HRM values are essentially individualistic in that they emphasise the individual-organisation linkage in preference to operating through group and representative mechanisms . . . These values . . . leave little scope for collective arrangements and assume little need for collective bargaining. HRM therefore poses a considerable threat to traditional industrial relations and more particularly trade unionism.
>
> Guest (1989, 43)

Although over two decades have now passed since the articulation of this particular comprehension of HRM, the implications for practice remain unclear. Some contributors argue that HRM merely involved a re-titling exercise, or 'old wine in new bottles', with little substantive change in HR practice (Armstrong 1987; Keenoy 1990; D'Art 2002). Others have argued, however, that the emergence of (strategic) HRM involves a complete re-orientation of the HR role and function in organisations (Beer *et al.* 1984; Storey 1992). More recently, however, this rhetoric versus reality debate has effectively been overtaken by a new debate focused on establishing the causal relationship between HRM practice and organisation performance, sometimes labeled the 'black box' question (Boxall and Purcell 2003, see also Huselid 1995; Pfeffer, 1994, 1998a). The emergence of HRM and its linkages with strategy and performance are considered in detail in chapter 3. Below we briefly review contemporary developments in HRM, particularly those impacting on the Irish context.

CONTEMPORARY DEVELOPMENTS

When we consider the exceptionally high levels of economic growth and employment creation from the early 1990s, it is sometimes difficult to appreciate the pessimism that characterised the Irish economy for much of the 1980s. Economic growth during the first half of the decade was extremely low, unemployment and inflation rose steadily, and the country's fiscal debt was unsustainable. Substantial employment decline was recorded during this period when unemployment rose from less than 8 per cent to almost 20 per cent of the labour force and resulted in the resumption of large-scale emigration (Tansey 1998). As public debt and unemployment reached record proportions, the economy became locked in deep recession. A quote from *The Economist* (1988, 1) captures the situation in which the Irish economy found itself:

> . . . the country was on the skids. In four years its national debt had doubled. As a proportion of Gross Domestic Product, Ireland's debt was the biggest in Europe. Servicing costs were gobbling one third of annual tax revenue and 90 per cent of the revenue from income tax. Real interest rates of 10 per cent were driving business to despair. A panicky flight of capital had begun. The International Monetary Fund [IMF] expected a call for help.

As we now know, IMF intervention was not called for. By 1987, there was a political and societal agreement that fundamental initiatives were needed to to tackle the problems facing the country, but there also appeared to be limited support for a replication of the Thatcherite policies employed in the UK during the 1980s (Wallace *et al.* 2004). Rather, the Government embraced fiscal rectitude, encompassing severe cutbacks in public expenditure, and social partnership, as twin strategies designed to turn the economy around. These, together with a confluence of favourable developments in both the domestic and the Irish economy, have since contributed to a remarkable transformation in Ireland's economic fortunes. Indeed, the Irish economy has now recovered to such an extent that by the late 1990s it was widely heralded as a model of effective economic management. Expansive growth in the Irish economy characterised this period. From the mid-1990s to the turn of the millennium, gross domestic product (GDP) growth rates averaged over 9 per cent a year or almost four times the EU average. Ireland became the OECD's fastest growing economy with levels of economic performance at or above the levels of the world's high-growth economies.

From an HR perspective it is clear that industrial relations played a key role in this transformation. In 1987 the first of a series of centrally negotiated accords (the *Programme for National Recovery* 1987–91) was agreed by the 'social partners', principally government, employers and trade unions. Since then five further agreements have been concluded. While opinion varies on the relative contribution of centralised bargaining to Ireland's economic transformation, there is widespread consensus that they played an important role. In particular, they are seen to have contributed to low levels of wage inflation, (Tansey 1998, Walsh 1999), reductions in personal taxation and low levels of industrial conflict (Roche 1997a). These issues are covered in greater depth in chapter 13.

In terms of international competitiveness, the 2000 *World Competitiveness Report* (www.imd.ch) ranked Ireland as the fifth most competitive world economy, up from tenth in 1997, achieving particularly strong scores in areas such as education, government and technological capacity. However, the downturn in the US economy after 9/11 (see below), and cost and infrastructure issues at home, have led more recently to a fall in the country's rankings. Nevertheless, the 2004 report ranked Ireland as the tenth most competitive world economy (up from eleventh in 2003).

The transformation from a comparatively poor and under-developed economy in the late 1950s to one characterised by industrial expansion and strong economic growth involved major changes in the structural distribution of employment and in the nature and operation of the labour market (see chapter 4 for greater detail). This primarily involved a progressive decline in agricultural and traditional industrial employment, and a dramatic rise in the service sector, particularly private services. Between 1980 and 1996, Irish non-agricultural employment growth of 26 per cent exceeded that of the EU (7 per cent) and the US (15 per cent).

Of the current labour force of almost 1.9 million, some 6.4 per cent are employed in agriculture, 27.4 per cent in industry and the remaining 66.2 per cent in services. Over recent years, the largest share of employment creation was accounted for by the growth in the services sector. Unemployment, a traditional bugbear and the cause of large-scale emigration from the country over many decades, has also fallen significantly. In 1986 unemployment levels were 18 per cent or almost one in five of the workforce. In 2004 the equivalent figure was just over 4 per cent, or less than one in twenty.

From an HRM perspective, the arrival of the 'Celtic tiger' brought very different challenges. Probably the most pressing of these concerns the 'attraction and retention' of workers. Rapidly falling unemployment levels, combined with increased demand for labour, made for a very tight labour market. Employers were increasingly forced to compete for new workers and sought to develop innovative means of retaining current employees. Related issues include pressures from workers and trade unions for better reward packages. We saw some increased activity in the areas of HR development and reward strategies as organisations sought both to enhance the capacity of their workforce and to improve performance and competitiveness.

More recently a number of developments, particularly the so-called *dot.com* downturn and the aftermath of *9/11* (2001), have clearly impacted on the Irish economy and indeed HRM. Given Ireland's reliance on FDI, especially by American MNCs, it was predictable that these events would have important knock-on effects in Ireland. Post-2001 we saw a fall in the level of FDI into Ireland and increasing economic difficulties for some MNCs operating in Ireland. This was particularly evident in the information and communications technology (ICT) sector, where the level of job losses and company closures increased significantly in 2001 and 2002. These included the closure of both Motorola and Gateway's Dublin plants, involving a gross loss of almost 1,700 jobs. Indigenous ICT firms suffered particularly badly. Many of these had grown quickly on the back of sales either into the US or to US subsidiaries in Ireland. Casualties included Ebeon and one of Ireland's real success stories in the sector, Baltimore Technologies. IDA Ireland (2003) estimate that employment in the ICT sector fell by over 5 per cent in 2002, which represents quite a credible performance in the circumstances. Indeed, certain firms, such as Dell Computers, appear to have weathered the downturn quite well. We have also seen some important new investments, such as MBNA, eBay and Google. In 2003 Intel, one of the flagships of FDI in Ireland, completed its state-of-the-art fabrication plant ('Fab 24') involving an investment of more than €2.2 billion. This development was widely seen at the time as a vote of confidence both in the future of the ICT sector globally, and in Ireland as a location for

FDI. Overall, IDA Ireland noted a slowing of job losses in 2002 (down from 17,800 in 2001 to 14,700 in 2002) while new FDI increased by one third, with the pharmaceutical/ healthcare sector representing the strongest growth area and the internationally traded services sector also performing quite well.

Climbing the Value Chain?

We have already outlined Ireland's adoption of 'industrialisation by invitation' from the early 1960s. Much of this investment focused on high-volume, low-cost manufacturing attracted to Ireland by the financial incentives, low corporation tax and low labour costs. As the economy developed and costs increased, many of the firms in this wave of FDI closed and/or moved production to lower-cost locations, particularly Asia and, more recently, Central and Eastern Europe. While the past fifteen years has seen a major increase in FDI into Ireland, we have also witnessed a trend of firms transferring all or some of their operations abroad. Given increasing competition between nations for FDI and the accelerating costs of doing business here, it is clear that Ireland will find it much more difficult to attract new FDI start-ups from abroad. As a result the country's industrial promotions strategy has changed in two very significant regards:

1. The emphasis in industrial development has shifted somewhat from one of attracting new greenfield start-ups towards the retention of existing MNCs through helping Irish subsidiaries move up their corporation's respective 'value chain' (i.e. attract higher-order products or services and develop greater capacity in research and development).
2. Greater emphasis on achieving a regional balance in the spatial distribution of FDI (essentially encouraging FDI projects to locate outside of Dublin and major industrial centres and into more economically disadvantaged regions, ideally on a clustered basis).

These changes reflect a significant HRM dimension. It is clear that Ireland's recent economic development has meant that labour costs have risen significantly. Consequently, it is now accepted that if Ireland is to retain its position as a leading European location for FDI, then it must seek to attract higher-order production or service activities which are less reliant on low labour costs. As noted above, labour availability has also become more problematic as unemployment has fallen from close to 20 per cent in the mid-1980s to its current level of approximately 4.5 per cent. Combined with the difficult economic climate post-9/11, this has accelerated the decline of low-margin manufacturing Ireland. As also noted above, employment in the MNC sector fell for the second consecutive year in 2002 (by 2.2 per cent – an improvement on the 2001 decline of 2.7 per cent (IDA Ireland 2001, 2002)).

While the ICT sector has had a difficult time (employment fell by 5 per cent in 2002), other sectors, notably healthcare and pharmaceuticals, fared much better (employment levels grew by about 4 per cent in 2002). A particular example is Abbott Ireland, whose expansion over the recent past appears to reflect well on the policy changes highlighted above, both in the Irish subsidiary's success in attracting 'higher-order' investment and in aiding employment growth in less developed regions (the Midlands and Northwest). The healthcare and pharmaceuticals sector form a key part of the IDA Ireland's policy of deepening the roots of existing MNC investment through the attraction of higher-order activities. The most high-profile example is probably Wyeth Medica, which in 2001 established its new 'bio-technology campus' in Dublin, lauded as 'the largest ever single-site biotechnology facility in the world', involving an investment of $1.4 billion by the parent company, American Home Products Corporation (IDA Ireland 2001, 1).

Growth in the Service Sector

Changes in the structural distribution of employment in the Irish economy have important implications for HRM (see chapter 4 for greater detail). Of particular note is the growth in employment in the service sector. As alluded to above, the structure of the labour market changed drastically since independence. In 1926 agriculture accounted for 54 per cent of total employment, while today the equivalent figure is just over 6 per cent (Haughton 2000; O'Sullivan 2005). Thus Ireland has followed the pattern of other developed countries with employment in primary sectors (agriculture, fishing, etc.) being gradually superseded by employment in industry, with that, in turn, being superseded by employment in services. By far the most marked development over the recent past is the dramatic growth in employment in the services sector, which increased by a staggering 70 per cent between 1993 and 2004 (O'Sullivan 2005). In 1990 the services sector accounted for 57 per cent of total employment while the equivalent figure in 2004 was 66 per cent. The HR implications of this change are addressed throughout this text. Of particular note has been its contribution to the increased diversity in employment forms and increased levels of female participation in the labour force. There is little doubt that increased employment in the service sector has involved a growth in diversity in employment forms, specifically a growth in atypical or non-standard employment forms (i.e. any form of employment that deviates from the full-time, permanent format, including self-employment, temporary and part-time work). A National Economic and Social Forum (1995) report identified the principal characteristics of services employment as involving a relatively high proportion of female, part-time, temporary and self-employed workers. Wallace and Clifford (1998, 9) attribute the high proportion of part-time working, and other forms of atypical employment forms in services, to 'demands for greater flexibility arising from the sectoral shifts from traditional manufacturing and agriculture to services employment'. Data from the Central Statistics Office indicated that in 2000 some 30 per cent of female employees worked part-time (compared to 7 per cent of males), of whom 27 per cent worked in the services sector (O'Sullivan 2005) Other HR implications of these developments in the Irish labour market are addressed later in the text, notably the changing migration patterns (chapter 4), training and development aspects (chapters 9 and 10) and employee relations implications (chapters 11 and 12).

CONCLUSION

These various historical developments provide a context for our treatment of each major area of HR activity addressed throughout the text. In the next chapter we move beyond our historical review to consider HRM practice in organisations.

2

Human Resource Management in Practice

T his chapter explores the nature of HRM in practice and identifies key human resource (HR) activities within organisations. We place particular focus on the issue of HR policy choice in an attempt to explain the evident variation that exists in organisational approaches to HRM.

THE NATURE OF HRM

During discussions with a class of mature students taking an introductory HRM course, a number of class members suggested that 'personnel' did not really operate in their organisations since they had 'no personnel department'. This interpretation of HRM as being the responsibility of HR specialists is a common, if flawed, conception. HRM is concerned with the management of an organisation's workforce. Thus conceived, it is a *generalist* responsibility, which constitutes an important aspect of the job of everyone with managerial responsibilities. It incorporates all policies and practices involving workforce management and is therefore an inherent aspect of the management process. All organisations have important HR responsibilities, with the deployment, development, motivation and reward of employees representing core HR activities.

However, HRM may also be seen as a *specialist* management function. In this context, certain HR activities are seen as the responsibility of HR specialists who have particular responsibility for developing and deploying their organisation's HR strategies, policies and practices. Even where a specialist function exists, line management will continue to play a central role in operational day-to-day HR activities, such as recruitment or on-the-job training. The key role of the specialist HR function is to provide adequate assistance, advice and administrative support. However, it may play more of an executive role by taking direct responsibility for certain activities. Common examples might include collective bargaining with trade unions or approving promotion decisions.

This conception of HRM in *generalist* and *specialist* terms is important. It recognises that HRM is a key responsibility of all managers. It also recognises that in some, mostly larger, organisations HR specialists are employed to undertake particular aspects of the HR role. Thus, although HR involves managers at all levels in the organisation's hierarchy, it is useful to consider the respective roles of three critical layers: top or senior management; line management; and the specialist HR function.

At the highest level of organisational decision-making, HRM involves *senior management* developing the organisation's HR philosophy and strategy. Senior management may comprise the owner or manager of a small retail store or the corporate board of directors of a multinational corporation. At an operational level, HRM primarily involves *line management* undertaking the day-to-day operational activities of HR: communicating with employees, monitoring performance, handling employee grievances, etc. In most larger organisations one generally finds a *specialist HRM function*. This involves the employment of one or more HR specialists who together may constitute an HRM department. The primary role of the specialist function is to help devise and execute the organisation's HR strategies and policies (Cole 1988). It also undertakes specialist tasks and acts as a source of expert advice and guidance to line and top management.

HRM Activities

If we accept that HRM is concerned with the management of an organisation's workforce, it is clear that the range of HR activities that may be undertaken by an organisation is extensive. Many of these are basic activities common to all types of organisation, such as recruiting and rewarding workers. Certain HR activities may only be appropriate in particular organisational contexts and require more specialist skills. Examples might include the administration of job evaluation schemes or negotiating collective agreements with trade unions. Other HR activities may be more optional in character and their incidence related to preferred managerial approaches or styles. Examples of these might include the operation of profit sharing schemes or the establishment of employee assistance programmes. Since there is a wide range of HR activities that may be undertaken in an organisation, it is clear that the nature of HRM may differ considerably between organisations.

At a general level it is possible to identify critical HRM activities that are shared by all types of organisation. Possibly the most comprehensive attempt to chart these activities was that undertaken by the Personnel Standards Lead Body (1993) in the United Kingdom, which identified the following core activities:

1. *Strategy and Organisation*
   This involves: contributing to organisational strategy, organisation structure and processes; influencing culture and values; and developing personnel/HR strategies and policies.

2. *Employee Resourcing*
   Incorporates human resource planning; recruitment and selection; deployment and termination of employment.

3. *Employee Development*
   Includes training and development; management development; career development and performance management.

4. *Reward Management*
   Incorporates the selection of reward strategies and administration of payment and benefit systems.

5. *Employee Relations*
Includes: industrial relations; employee involvement and participation; communication; health, safety and welfare; and employee services.

6. *Employment and Personnel/HR Administration*
Incorporating administration of employees' records; employment policies and practices; working conditions; and personnel/HR information systems.

The Impact of Scale

A useful approach in considering the nature of HRM is to reflect on the extent and variation of HRM activities as organisational scale increases.

In *smaller organisations* responsibility for all HR matters normally rests with line management (Gunnigle and Brady 1984). For obvious financial and structural reasons, such organisations would not normally employ a HR specialist. Nevertheless, effective HRM remains a vital consideration. Since payroll may be one of the largest ongoing costs in small firms, performance and profitability can often be increased by better human resource utilisation (Gunnigle 1989; McMahon 1994). Indeed, poor recruitment or inadequate training can have a proportionately more serious effect in smaller organisations than in their larger counterparts. Of course, the nature of HRM is made potentially simpler in small firms due to the scale of operations, which eases the burden of communications and reduces the level of administrative support required.

In the majority of small companies, HRM will be concerned with basic activities essential to the effective running of the organisation. For such organisations, key HR activities incorporate: human resource planning; recruitment and selection; training and development; reward management; employee relations; health, safety and welfare; and administrative support.

When we consider larger organisations we find that the increase in scale normally renders the HRM process more complex. It expands the range of HRM activities and increases the complexity of HR administration. Normally there is also greater formality and sophistication in HR policies and procedures. However, while such changes simply affect the nature of the HRM process, the basic objectives and activities remain the same.

A common response of many larger Irish organisations is to have a specialist HR department that co-ordinates HR activities and carries out much of the administrative work (Shivanath 1987; Foley and Gunnigle 1994; Monks 1992). Such specialist departments may comprise one or two individuals with general responsibility for HR matters. Alternatively, very large organisations may employ an extensive HR department characterised by a high degree of task specialisation as outlined in figure 2.1.

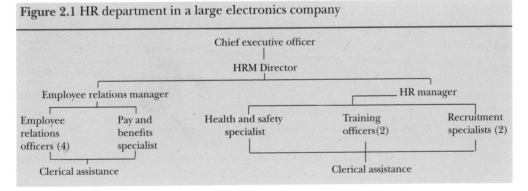

Figure 2.1 HR department in a large electronics company

23

It is apparent that increases in the size and complexity of organisations result in specialisation and formalisation in the conduct of HR activities. One also finds that the specialist HR function takes responsibility for a larger range of activities. However, the key role of top management in deciding on the overall HR approach, and of line management in carrying out a range of operational HR tasks, should remain intact.

The specialist HR function normally operates in a *staff* capacity. This means that its primary role is to provide assistance and advice to line management (at all levels) in undertaking their HR responsibilities.

STRATEGY, POLICY AND PRACTICE IN HRM

The study of *business strategy* has achieved increasing prominence as organisations seek to adapt to a changing business environment (see chapter 3). Business strategy is concerned with policy decisions affecting the entire organisation, the main objective being to best position the organisation to deal effectively with its environment. Strategic decisions are long-term in nature, affect the future of the organisation, and serve to guide subsequent decision-making at lower levels. The central tenet of business strategy was that organisations should incorporate human resource considerations into strategic decision-making, establish a corporate human resource philosophy and develop a complementary and coherent set of HR strategies and policies to improve HR utilisation (Guest 1987; Beer *et al.* 1984).

In recent years, the HRM literature has placed an ever-increasing emphasis on the need to align HRM with overall business strategy (cf. Beer *et al.* 1984; Fombrun *et al.* 1984). It is further argued that a well-aligned business and HR strategy can contribute to improvements in firm performance (cf. Schuler 1987, Schuler and Jackson 1987a; Huselid 1995; Boxall and Purcell 2003). This proposed link between business strategy, HRM strategies and HR activities is illustrated summarily in figure 2.2. The linkages between strategy, HRM and performance are treated in depth in chapter 3.

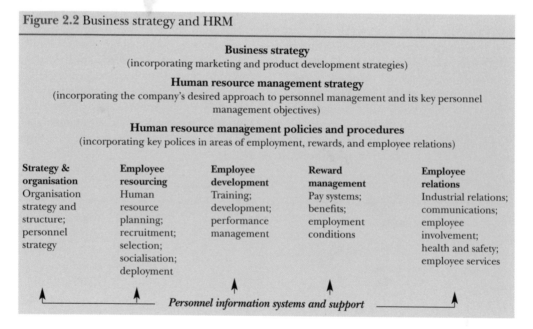

Figure 2.2 Business strategy and HRM

Business strategy
(incorporating marketing and product development strategies)

Human resource management strategy
(incorporating the company's desired approach to personnel management and its key personnel management objectives)

Human resource management policies and procedures
(incorporating key polices in areas of employment, rewards, and employee relations)

Strategy & organisation	Employee resourcing	Employee development	Reward management	Employee relations
Organisation strategy and structure; personnel strategy	Human resource planning; recruitment; selection; socialisation; deployment	Training; development; performance management	Pay systems; benefits; employment conditions	Industrial relations; communications; employee involvement; health and safety; employee services

Personnel information systems and support

HRM Strategy

An HRM strategy incorporates an organisation's basic philosophy, overall approach and long-term objectives in managing human resources. It forms the basis for the subsequent development of more explicit HR policies and procedures in critical areas of workforce management, such as employee selection and reward management. The responsibility for developing HR strategy rests primarily with top management, aided, as appropriate, by the specialist HR function. HR strategies are often expressed in the form of general statements outlining critical organisational beliefs and values concerning HRM. Table 2.1 outlines examples of such statements from two companies.

Table 2.1 Statements of corporate beliefs in HRM

Company 1: Key beliefs in managing people
- To treat each employee with dignity, as an individual.
- To maintain an open atmosphere where direct communications with employees affords the opportunity to contribute to the maximum of their potential and fosters unity of purpose.
- To provide personal opportunities for training and development to ensure the most capable and most efficient workforce.
- To respect senior service.
- To compensate fairly by salary, benefits and incentives.
- To promote on the basis of capability.

Company 2: Core values and beliefs about how employees should be managed (selection)
- *Employment:* Employees are recruited and promoted on merit and we believe in maximum openness in competition and appointments. We respect our employees and value each as an individual. All employees have equal opportunity for development and advancement according to their qualifications, abilities and the needs of the business. We seek to use individual talents and skills to the best advantage of the person and the company.
- *Pay and conditions:* We have pay and conditions of employment designed to attract the right people, motivate employees, stimulate quality work and reflect performance, while taking account of national economic circumstances and policy. We try always to be fair and equitable in the treatment of individuals and in responding to their needs.

The examples in table 2.1 are explicit indications of particular espoused organisational strategies in HRM. However, in practice one finds that a majority of companies do not have such explicit statements. Data generated from the Cranfield-University of Limerick (CUL) study of HR practice in Irish organisations found that approximately four in every ten firms had a written HR strategy (Gunnigle, Morley, Clifford and Turner 1997). This study focused on larger firms (i.e. those with fifty or more employees). Clearly the incidence of formal HR strategies is likely to be much lower among smaller organisations. Does this imply that such organisations do not have an HR strategy? Generally not. Virtually every organisation has a philosophy and broad approach concerning how it views and manages its workforce. While this may not necessarily be written, it can be inferred from how employees are treated and rewarded within the organisation. In such situations the organisation's HR philosophy is implicit rather than explicit in nature.

HRM Policies

Of course, broad HR strategies and related HR philosophy statements expressing corporate beliefs and values are likely to be ineffective unless they are implemented in the day-to-day practice of HRM. To effectively bridge the gap between espoused beliefs and workplace practice, organisations may develop HR policies in key activity areas of HRM such as recruitment, rewards and employee relations. The primary role of such policies is to guide managers in the execution of their HRM responsibilities. They also act as an important yardstick for workers in outlining the standards and approaches they should expect from the organisation, and the norms the organisation expects from its workforce. Examples of HR policy statements are outlined in table 2.2.

Table 2.2 HR policy statements (indicative)

Company 1: Policy statement on promotion and development
This company encourages everyone to prepare for career enhancement thorough its educational assistance and training programmes. It is our policy to promote from within whenever suitable and experienced candidates are available.

Company 2: Policy statement on employment equality
It is our policy to ensure that all employees are afforded equal treatment irrespective of their sex, marital or parental status, race or religion. This company ensures equal access to employment, training, development and promotion solely based on essential job requirements and the individual's ability and fitness for work.

Company 3: Policy statement on pay and employment conditions
It is our policy to provide pay and terms of employment, which are competitive with the top quartile of comparable firms in our industrial segment.

Company 4: Policy statement on employee relations
We seek to develop good relations with employees and their trade unions. Where difficulties arise, the company will seek to resolve these quickly and as close to the workplace as possible. The company is committed to adherence to agreed procedures in the resolution of employee relations' difficulties.

HRM Procedures

Policy statements, therefore, establish the limits within which managers, supervisors and team leaders execute their various operational HRM responsibilities. To aid this process further, organisations very often have a set of HRM procedures that comprise detailed statements to guide managers and workers in the implementation of policies. These procedures normally embrace detailed statements covering a range of operational HR activities and some examples are outlined in table 2.3. The specialist HR function normally plays a key role in developing HR policies and procedures. They also provide support and direction to line managers in the implementation of procedures through advice, guidance and administrative assistance.

Table 2.3 HRM procedures (indicative)

Company 1: Procedure on educational assistance
To help personal development and maintain the company's competitive position, all relevant educational courses or parts thereof, which have been successfully completed and are appropriate to your career will be paid for by the company. All such courses must be approved, prior to the commencement of the course, by your department manager and the Human Resource Manager in order to be considered for reimbursement. Application forms are available from the Human Resource Department.

➤➤

Table 2.3 HRM procedures (indicative) *(contd.)*

Company 2: Procedure on probationary period
The first six months of your employment will be considered a probationary period. During this time, your supervisor will assess your suitability for the job. He/she will sit down with you and discuss your performance after one month, after three months and, again, after six months service. You will be given every opportunity and assistance to make a success of your new position. Within this time the company shall have the sole and absolute right of deciding on your suitability for continued employment. Your employment may be terminated by the company at any time during this period without recourse to the disciplinary or grievance procedure.

HRM POLICY CHOICE: VARIATIONS IN STRATEGY, POLICY AND PRACTICE IN HRM

The preceding discussion alluded to the fact that in practice one finds immense variation between organisations in their approach to workforce management. This is manifested in differing HRM strategies, policies and procedures and may be attributed to the differential impact of factors in the external or internal environment of organisations. Purcell (1987) notes the tendency to identify and contrast prominent organisations according to their 'employment policies and practices'. While many of these differences are due to external environmental factors, such as product market performance, Purcell also identifies *strategic choice* (exercised by senior management) as a key factor explaining differences in organisational approaches to HRM (cf. Beer *et al.* 1984; Kochan *et al.* 1986).

Strategic choice addresses the extent to which management (i) possess and (ii) exercise choice in developing their HRM strategies, policies and procedures. This implies that senior managements possess some room for manoeuvre, and while environmental factors may constrain the range of choice, they retain considerable power in making decisions on 'appropriate' HR styles and policies. Senior management can therefore use their resources and power to make strategic choices, which both influence environmental factors and affect particular management approaches or 'styles'. Thus, organisational approaches to HRM are often evaluated in terms of the interplay between environmental factors, managerial ideology and values and strategic choice:

> Choice should be viewed as both a cause and a consequence of environmental influences, that is, managements have some influence over the kind of markets in which they choose to operate, and in some cases over the structure of the market itself, as well as having some choice over the way in which they respond to environmental pressures.
>
> Marchington and Parker (1990, 99)

The interplay of such factors will normally lead to consequential variations in patterns of HRM.

The Context for Choice: Variation in Organisational Approaches to HRM

In order to identify and explain variations in organisational approaches to HRM it is necessary to examine the interplay between a diverse range of external and internal factors that influence and constrain managerial choice and practice in the sphere of workforce management. A particular focus of such analysis is the external environment (such as product and labour markets), management values and business strategy as key factors impacting on organisational approaches to HRM.

It is argued that changes in environmental conditions influence decisions on business strategy and ultimately HRM (Kochan *et al.* 1986). Such decisions will be conditioned by managerial values and constrained by historical factors and current organisational practice in HRM. Figure 2.3 presents a framework for evaluating variation in organisational approaches to HRM. This framework is further discussed below.

Figure 2.3 HRM policy choice: context and variation

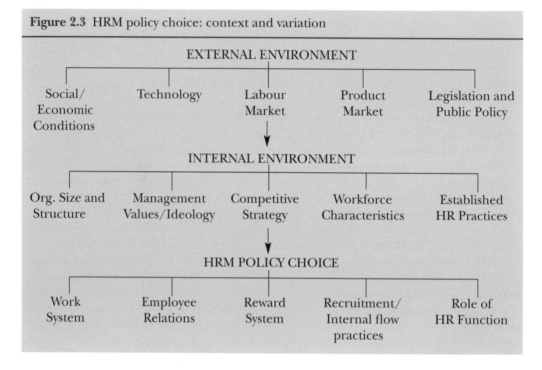

The External Environment

Trends in the socio-economic context, such as *levels of economic performance* and *cultural norms and values*, will impact upon business strategy and management practice. Economic performance and public policy, as manifested levels of economic activity, state intervention and approaches to organised labour, clearly exert a significant impact on management approaches to HRM (Wallace *et al.* 2004). Although economic activity in Ireland remained depressed for much of the 1980s, the opposite has been the case for the past several years. Economic growth has created a boom in business activity across almost all sectors of the economy. Labour shortages and pressures for increased output are just some of the spin-offs with important implications for HRM. At the same time we have seen increased competition in certain sectors (such as telecommunications) and also some difficulties in certain sectors (such the ICT sector since 2001). Increased competitive pressures tend to encourage a greater focus on reducing labour costs and improve labour productivity.

Broader *social changes* in areas such as education, living standards and class mobility also exert significant influence on HRM. Higher education levels can contribute to increased worker expectations in relation to rewards, working conditions and opportunities for personal development.

Developments in *technology* are another key external environmental factor influencing approaches to HRM. Technology, seen in generic terms as the equipment used to perform particular tasks, and the way in which it is organised, has a major influence on approaches to workforce management (Beer *et al.* 1984). We noted in chapter 1 that Guest (1987) identified technological/production feasibility as a requisite condition for the successful implementation of more 'strategic' HRM approaches, suggesting that large-scale investment in short-cycle, repetitive, assembly-line technology mitigates against the job design and autonomous teamworking principles characteristic of 'strategic' HRM. Technology also affects cost structure, and consequently impacts upon important aspects of HRM, such as reward systems. Boxall and Purcell (2003) suggest that in labour-intensive sectors, where wage costs are high, organisations may be more constrained in developing employee-oriented or 'soft' HRM styles. However, in capital-intensive sectors, where labour constitutes a small proportion of total costs, organisations may have greater scope to adopt such approaches, incorporating, for example, attractive reward and employee development policies. Technological developments may also impact directly on job content and lead to changes in the competencies required to carry out particular tasks effectively. These issues are addressed in greater detail in chapter 6 (specifically concerning the issues of work systems and job design).

The *labour market* exerts possibly the most profound influence on HRM, especially in the areas of recruitment, training and reward systems. Looking at the Irish labour market, the most notable development has been the huge growth in employment levels since the early 1990s and the resultant decline in unemployment (from almost 20 per cent at one stage in the 1980s to current levels of approximately 4.5 per cent). An associated and significant development has been the change in the sectoral distribution of employment, encompassing a progressive decline in agricultural employment and growth in industrial and – particularly – service sector employment. This means that the Irish labour market has been transformed from significant over-supply to one characterised by very limited labour availability, and indeed labour shortages in certain sectors. This has meant that 'dipping' into the external labour market is no longer a ready option for many employers. Such conditions increase the onus on organisations to 'grow' capacity from within (e.g. by investing more in training and development), to develop HR policies to attract and retain workers, or to develop new sources of labour supply. Lower unemployment also tends to exert upward pressure on wages and fringe benefits, and can also impact on other aspects of HRM such as labour turnover and power relations in collective bargaining. Other notable developments in employment structure include the increased feminisation of the workforce (higher female participation, see chapter 4), the growth of atypical employment forms and increased immigration.

Product market performance is also a significant influence on strategic decision-making and organisational approaches to HRM. It is clear that favourable market conditions such as high market share and high margins allow organisations greater scope to adopt 'soft' HRM approaches, such as high pay and attractive fringe benefits. Thus, organisations that operate from a strong product market position (e.g. high market share, growing market, stable demand) have greater scope to adopt sophisticated HR policies such as employee development, job tenure commitments and elaborate management-employee communications. We can point to some particular instances from the Irish ICT sector during the 1998–2000 period. For example, one of Ebeon's HR policies (in response to recruitment difficulties) was the use of 'referral bonuses', whereby an IR£3,500 (about €4,450) bonus was offered to employees for each successful hire. Lucky employees who managed ten successful hires received a BMW 3 Series! In contrast, firms experiencing high levels of market pressure (contracting market share; intense price competition) may have considerably less scope for choice and be forced to adopt a more traditional cost reduction and labour control approach. High-volume, low-margin garment manufacture provides a particular example here. Some years ago we witnessed the closure of Fruit of the Loom's operations in Donegal and Derry, and the loss of a huge number of jobs to Morocco's lower cost base. The characteristics of an organisation's product market will be influenced by a variety of factors such as the cost of entry, nature of competition, technology and the customer base (see chapter 3 for more detail).

There are a number of important aspects of *public policy* that impact on HRM in Ireland, most particularly in the areas of employee relations and employment law. In regard to employee relations the traditional approach of Irish Governments was grounded in the 'voluntarist' tradition. This meant that the state intervened to only a minimal degree in management-employee relations, allowing employers and employees (and their representative institutions) considerable scope to determine the terms of their relationship in regard to pay increases, working conditions and the extent of consultation rights afforded to employees (cf. Hillery 1994). However, this approach has been considerably diluted over recent years as we have seen greater state intervention in industrial relations and the enactment of a broad range of legislation dealing with employment issues. Recent Governments have also been strong advocates of centralised agreements on pay and other aspects of social and economic policy, involving negotiations with the main employer and trade union federations. The issue of trade union recognition has also emerged as an area of considerable debate over the past two decades as an increasing number of organisations have chosen to pursue a non-union strategy. This is evident not only among high profile multinational corporations (MNCs) such as Intel and Hewlett Packard but also in a number of indigenous firms, most notably Ryanair (see also chapter 11 for greater detail). In the area of employment law, the period since the 1970s has witnessed the passing of several important acts, particularly in the area of individual employment rights (e.g. unfair dismissal), while more recently we have seen an increase in legislation dealing with atypical employment forms, such as the Protection of Employees (Part-Time Work) Act 2001 and the Protection of Employees (Fixed Term Work) Act 2003. A particularly important influence in the area of employment legislation is the impact of the European Union (EU). The 1987 Single European Act, aimed at strengthening economic cohesion, placed a strong emphasis on integrating social policy throughout the EU (Hourihan 1997). In 1989 a Charter of Fundamental Social Rights of Workers (the *Social Charter*) was signed by all member states except the United Kingdom. The Social Charter and attendant Social Action Programme comprised forty-nine legally binding directives and recommendations (see chapter 11 on employee relations and chapter 14 on employment law). A final important aspect of public policy relates to approaches to industrial development. Since the turn of the 1960s Irish Government policy has been to actively encourage foreign direct investment in Ireland. In our earlier historical review we noted the extensive role that multinational companies (MNCs) play in the Irish economy. Ireland's strong public policy stance on promoting MNC investment has significantly shaped the development of HRM in the country.

We noted earlier that MNCs have been an important source of innovation in HRM, particularly in the application of new HR approaches and in expanding the role of the specialist HRM function. However, it is also clear that MNCs have posed particular and unique challenges in the sphere of employee relations, particularly in their ability to switch the locus of production and in the increasing trend of trade union avoidance.

THE INTERNAL ENVIRONMENT

While factors in the external environment impact on management practice and decisions, it is largely factors in the *internal environment* that shape the unique organisational responses to such external factors.

Organisation structure and size are clearly important factors impacting upon HRM. Irish organisations are generally smaller in scale and employee numbers than their counterparts in countries such as the UK or Germany. Numerous studies have noted that trade union recognition and greater specialisation in HRM are positively related to organisation size (Brown 1981; Purcell and Sisson 1983; Thomason 1984). In the Irish context, Gunnigle and Brady (1984) found that management in smaller organisations veer towards a unitarist frame of reference and adopt less formality in employee relations than their counterparts in larger organisations. In relation to organisation structure, Purcell (1989) argues that senior management in highly diversified organisations is primarily concerned with financial issues, with the consequence that HRM considerations are not a concern of corporate decision-makers, but rather an operational concern of management at the business-unit level. A corollary of this argument is that 'core business' organisations, whose operation relies on a narrow product range, are more likely to integrate HRM issues into strategic planning, whereas highly diversified organisations are more likely to adopt differing HR strategies and policies suited to the needs of different constituent businesses and establishments (Wallace *et al.* 2004).

Several writers identify the locus of HR strategy formulation as a key issue in influencing the nature of establishment-level HRM (Purcell and Sisson 1983; Kochan *et al.* 1986). For example, Poole (1986) argues that, in the employee relations sphere, the growth of large multinational enterprises presents management with the opportunity to develop policies at corporate level, 'where they are relatively unrestricted by intervention by Government or plant-level agreements with labour'. Of course the scope of such unfettered management prerogative is dependent both on public policy (which may, for example, place constraints on management decisions) and the distribution of power between the various parties in employee relations.

Managerial values and ideology are also seen as having a significant influence on variations in organisational approaches to HRM. Management values and ideology incorporate the deeply held beliefs of senior management, which guide decisions on various aspects of workforce management. They are particularly important in interpreting developments in the external and internal environment, and making decisions about the organisation's overall approach to workforce management. Clearly, all organisations are characterised by particular values and philosophies on workforce management and employee relations. As discussed earlier, such values/ideology may be explicit in some organisations, as demonstrated in statements of corporate mission or philosophy. In others, they may be implicit and, therefore, must be inferred from management practice in areas such as supervisory style, reward systems and communications. Two cases may be highlighted to emphasise the key role of management values in impacting upon HRM at organisation level (Wallace *et al.* 2004). First, in a number of organisations we can point to the key role of influential founders in determining their organisation's corporate values and general HRM approach. Prominent international examples include Marks and Spencer, Hewlett Packard and Dell Computers. The influence of entrepreneurial founders is also prominent in Irish indigenous firms, and the particular HR approaches adopted by organisations such as Dunnes Stores, Superquinn (at least up to 2005) and Ryanair seem to be heavily influenced by the values and philosophy of their respective founders and/or chief executives. A second instance of the impact of managerial values on HRM relates to the notion that managerial ideology is related to broader ethnic and cultural values. Of particular significance is the suggestion that in the sphere of employee relations (see chapter 11), managerial opposition to pluralism (i.e. accepting that a conflict of interest exists between employers and workers) and particularly to trade unions is characteristic of the value system of American managers, whereas certain HRM-type approaches, which emphasise individual (rather than collective) management-employee relations, direct communications and merit-based rewards, are very much in line with this value system (Bendix 1956; Kochan *et al.* 1986). This interpretation is very significant in Ireland, where our economy is heavily dependent on foreign investment and where the bulk of such investment is American. In analysing the broad links between ideology and management practice, Poole (1986) finds support for the suggestion that managerial ideologies differ between countries, particularly in relation to the achievement of control over labour. In the US context, he argues that the influence of values and ideologies are most obviously manifest in trade union avoidance practices, a pronounced 'unitary' perspective and deployment of sophisticated HRM approaches. Both Poole and Kochan *et al.* (1986) note that while managerial preferences have fluctuated over time, many US employers have embraced a non-union approach against a more general trend in the developed world towards a tacit acceptance of trade unions.

Looking specifically at the Irish context, we find that a traditional criticism of business culture in Ireland is that it has not always encouraged enterprise and innovation. This trait was attributed to Ireland's relatively late independence, which created what some have termed a 'dependence mentality'. However, this culture would seem to have been effectively laid to rest over recent decades. Levels of productivity and export performance have increased dramatically and compare very favourably with international standards. Indeed, studies have noted the flexibility of the Irish workforce and the relevance of coherent and strong corporate culture formation (Kakabadse 1990; Tiernan *et al.* 2001).

Another internal factor impacting upon HRM is an organisation's *competitive strategy*, which is concerned with achieving sustainable competitive advantage in a particular industry or industry segment. The notion of competitive advantage is primarily associated with the work of Michael Porter (1980, 1985) and encompasses the means (i.e. competitive strategies) by which competing firms seek to gain market advantage over one another. This is normally achieved by an organisation either pricing its product or service more competitively or, alternatively, differentiating it from competitors along some dimension that will make it more attractive for customers (such as added features, or better reliability). Porter maintains that the organisation's choice of strategy helps define its overall approach to market competition and thus establishes the context for policies and actions in other key areas of organisational management, such as HRM. In particular, several commentators have argued that different business strategies require particular HR strategy configurations and that HR specialists can play an important role in effectively aligning HRM and competitive strategy (Schuler 1992; Schuler and Jackson 1987a, 1987b). These issues are treated in greater detail in chapter 3.

Other important internal factors that influence organisational approaches to HRM include *workforce profile* and *established HRM practices and traditions*. These factors will be particularly important in impacting upon the efficacy of organisation change initiatives, such as those aimed at developing particular employee competencies. Clearly particular workforces will be characterised by a specific age and skill profile. An ageing workforce may require training in areas such as new technology, while a younger workforce may have very different requirements, such as a need for experiential placements in different areas of the organisation to build understanding and competence. Past practice also impacts on the viability of certain change initiatives. For example, many organisations have experimented with job re-design initiatives. However, the research evidence indicates that employees may not necessarily react positively to such initiatives (Hackman and Oldham 1980; Tiernan *et al.* 2001). Rather it appears that employees who were characterised by a strong desire for achievement, responsibility and autonomy were most positively disposed to, and motivated by, such initiatives. Such employee characteristics may in turn have been conditioned by past practice in HRM. For example, if individual initiative has traditionally been stifled by, for example, restrictive job design, it may be difficult effectively to implement a comprehensive job enrichment and internal promotion/development policy. These issues are addressed in more detail in chapter 6, which deals with employee motivation and the design of work.

Key Areas of HR Policy Choice

The above discussions have outlined the major factors that help explain variation in organisational approaches to HRM. The manifestations of such variation will be evident in key areas of HR policy choice, particularly the work system, employee relations, rewards, recruitment and internal flow policies and the role of the specialist HR function.

The *work system* incorporates the way various organisational tasks are structured and affects issues such as organisational structure and job design. Decisions on the work system are primarily a managerial responsibility. The approach chosen is a valuable indicator of management beliefs regarding HRM. Traditional approaches to the organisation of work have been dominated by a desire to maintain control over the work process whilst maximising the productive efficiency of the organisation's technical resources. Thus choices on the organisation of work and the design of jobs were often seen as determined primarily by the technical system. Management's role was to ensure that other resources, including employees, were organised in such a way as to facilitate the optimal utilisation of the technical system. This approach often resulted in bureaucratic structures, elaborate procedures and systems, top-down supervisory control and limited employee involvement. It also encouraged the fragmentation of jobs into simple, repetitive and measurable tasks, which gave post-holders little autonomy. In contrast, it appears that the increased emphasis on improving quality, service and overall competitiveness has led to work redesign initiatives aimed at restructuring work systems to increase employee autonomy, motivation and performance (Beer *et al.* 1984; Tiernan *et al.* 2001; Walton 1985). Much of this focus has been on restructuring organisations and jobs to give greater scope for intrinsic motivation and employee involvement, through, inter alia, providing more defined, challenging jobs within a more organic, flexible organisational structure. At the same time we also find evidence of the adoption of 'harder' approaches as evidenced by job and work design initiatives, which seek to tightly prescribe performance targets and objectives, intensify the pace of work and more closely monitor employee performance (Gunnigle 1995).

A second important area of HR policy choice is *employee relations*. This involves issues such as collective bargaining, communications, grievance handling, dispute resolution and discipline administration. It may also encompass related areas such as health, safety, welfare and employee services. Traditionally the emphasis in most larger organisations was on 'industrial relations', which focused primarily on collective bargaining between employers and trade unions. However, over recent decades we have seen some shift towards a more individualistic approach to workforce management and the pursuit of a non-union strategy by organisations. A major difference here is that terms and conditions of employment (e.g. pay increases) would be determined by individual contracting (individual worker and management) as opposed to collective bargaining. Another important aspect relates to management-employee communications. Differences in managerial approach tend to focus on the range of communication mechanisms used and the extent to which these operate in a top-down fashion vis-à-vis their capacity to facilitate upward communications.

An organisation's *reward system* is a critical indicator of organisational approaches to HRM. High or low pay, the range of fringe benefits and the mechanism for determining reward levels provide valuable insights into an organisation's general approach to HRM. Significant considerations in the design of reward systems are the role of pay, the degree to which pay increases are based on measures of employee performance, and the compatibility of the reward system with business strategy and other areas of HR activity, such as recruitment. In the Irish context basic pay levels have traditionally been based on the 'going rate' concept, namely that the appropriate pay level for a particular occupation is largely determined by the normal rate paid for that job in other organisations and/or sectors. Pay increases in recent years have, in most instances, been determined at national level through centralised agreements. These apply to almost all unionised employees but may also influence the level of pay increases in non-union firms. Increases for managerial and other professional and technical categories are generally agreed at enterprise level. This may normally occur as a result of periodic performance reviews based on a range of criteria such as individual performance, department or company performance and comparisons with pay increases in other organisations. An interesting trend in the Irish context is the growing utilisation of performance-related pay (PRP) based on formal reviews (appraisals) of individual employee performance. The area of reward systems is addressed comprehensively in chapter 7.

Another important area of HR policy choice is *recruitment and internal flow practices*. This area incorporates the nature and sophistication of recruitment and employment practices. The latter dimension embodies the management and deployment of workers once they have taken up employment and incorporates key HR issues such as employee development, succession planning, appraisal and career counselling. In this broad area we can again point to some significant developments in the Irish context. First, economic growth and high levels of job creation over the recent past has meant that firms have found it increasingly difficult to fill vacant positions. This clearly encouraged employers to place a greater emphasis on sourcing and retaining labour. It also led to increased 'poaching' of employees, particular in areas of the labour market characterised by skill shortages. Another element has been an increase in the use of performance management techniques, particularly performance appraisal. An important issue for organisations is the relative emphasis placed on using either internal or external labour market sources; in other words whether vacancies are normally filled from the current pool of workers within the organisation or by sourcing labour from outside the organisation.

THE SPECIALIST HR FUNCTION
A particularly significant aspect of HR policy choice concerns the role of the specialist HR function. For example, it is suggested that an essential feature of 'strategic' HRM is that the major responsibility for HR be assumed by line managers (Beer *et al.* 1984). However, Guest (1987) notes 'the well-established professional structure of HRM' in Britain, where 'professional' HR specialists undertake responsibility for a range of HR issues and possess valued expertise in core HR areas such as selection, training, pay and employee relations.

It would seem that the issue of whether HR issues are best managed by a specialist HR function or by line managers is a matter of emphasis since, in most larger organisations, both will be involved in various aspects of HRM practice. For example, the 'professional' HRM model involves a major role for the HR function in handling HR activities, with a heavy reliance on systems and procedures, particular in the area of employee relations. Guest (1987) suggests that this approach is most appropriate in stable, bureaucratic organisations. On the other hand, we have already noted that more contemporary approaches place a greater emphasis on the role of line management in HR activities and greater top management involvement in developing HR strategies and policies. Recognising the considerable differences that may arise in the role that the HR function may play in organisations, Tyson and Fell (1986) developed three broad typologies of the HR function, as outlined in table 2.4 (also see Tyson 1987).

Table 2.4 Models of the specialist HR function

1. Administrative/support role: Within this model personnel management is a low-level activity operating in a clerical support mode to the line management. It is responsible for basic administration and welfare provision.

2. Systems/reactive role: Within this model personnel management is a high-level function with a key role in handling industrial relations and in developing policies and procedures in other core areas. The role is largely reactive, dealing with the personnel management implications of business decisions. This model incorporates a strong 'policing' component, where the personnel department is concerned with securing adherence to agreed systems and procedures.

3. Business manager role: Within this model personnel management is a top-level management function involved in establishing and adjusting corporate objectives and developing strategic personnel policies designed to facilitate the achievement of long-term business goals. Personnel management considerations are recognised as an integral component of corporate success, with the personnel director optimally placed to assess how the company's human resources can best contribute to this goal. Routine personnel activities are delegated, allowing senior practitioners to adopt a broad strategic outlook.

An early Irish study by Shivanath (1987) considered the relevance of Tyson's role models for HRM practice in a cross-section of large organisations (see also Monks 1993). In relation to the *administrative and support* model, the survey evidence found that the vast majority of Irish HR practitioners were not limited to this role. While HR departments were, of necessity, concerned with routine clerical and administrative tasks, these were generally delegated, allowing senior practitioners to deal with more strategic matters. The description of the HR practitioner within the *systems and reactive* model seemed most accurately to reflect the roles of the majority of Irish practitioners. Employee relations was identified by the bulk of respondents as the most crucial area of their work. The study also found that the *business manager model* was prominent in a number of organisations.

In a similar vein, but using a two-dimensional model, Storey (1992) categorises the HR function along (i) strategic/tactical and (ii) interventionary/non-interventionary continua as outlined in figure 2.4. The 'tactical/strategic' dimension measures the level at which the HR function operates in making decisions or providing support in organisations. This provides a useful addition to the Tyson model as it points out that the HR function may act at a strategic level, but in an advisory capacity, and thus may exhibit the strategic input of the business manager model but with the discretion of an administrative/support model. Turning to the 'interventionary/non-interventionary' dimension, this raises a key issue in the HR literature, namely the suggestion that the HR function is adopting a less 'hands on' approach in the management of the employment relationship. Whether or not this approach is a result of a conscious policy decision, there is certainly an evident trend towards reassessing the level of intervention that HR departments engage in. Consequently, this dimension represents an informative measure of the role of the HR function in organisations. Storey (1992) uses this two-dimensional model to produce a categorisation of four HRM function types:

1. advisors
2. handmaidens
3. regulators
4. change-makers.

Advisors essentially provide support to line and general management. While this function is carried out at a strategic level it is reactive and non-interventionary, providing specialist skills but in a consultancy capacity.

Handmaidens represent a 'subservient, attendant relationship' with HR operating in a low-level, non-interventionary capacity reacting to the needs of line managers in response to day-to-day operational problems. Storey suggests that this HR type is indicative of a clerical and welfare role and characteristic of firms where the HR presence had been depleted or reduced.

Regulators operate in an interventionary mode, but rarely at the level of strategy formulation. This approach is representative of a traditional 'industrial relations' orientation with the senior HR practitioner responsible for devising and negotiating policies and procedures to ensure the smooth operation of the organisation (similar to Tyson and Fell's (1986) 'systems/reactive' category). The rationale behind this category is that even when line managers wish to undertake this role, many are not competent enough or are not trained adequately to do so. In this model the HR contribution is significant at an operational level (in ensuring the smooth running of the organisation) rather than at a strategic level.

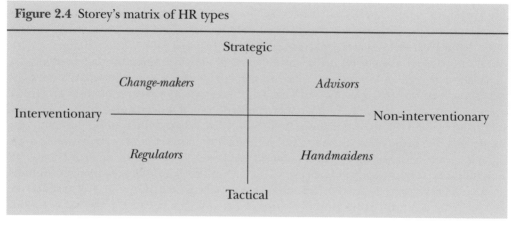

Figure 2.4 Storey's matrix of HR types

Source: Storey (1992).

Change-makers act as specialists and are highly interventionist and strategic in perspective. This represents the highest level of the operation for the HR function (similar to Tyson and Fell's (1986) 'business manager'). Senior HR practitioners are aware of both the 'soft' and 'hard' elements of HR practice. The two roles may exist in part side by side: the calculated, quantitative, rational approach of the business-oriented specialist and the 'softer' approach of realising the full potential of the 'human' side of the organisation.

DISCUSSION

There is little doubt that 'traditional' approaches to HRM and employee relations in Ireland have been increasingly challenged over recent decades. There is also general agreement that the main sources of such challenge originate outside the sphere of HRM itself (Beaumont 1995b) and can be traced to changes in the broader business environment (see, for example, Sparrow and Hiltrop 1994). In the Irish context, Roche and Gunnigle (1997, 445–6) identify a number of developments in the wider business context as the source of significant change in HRM management in Ireland, such as:

- the globalisation of competition in product, service and capital markets;
- improved communications and transport infrastructures;
- greater liberalisation of world trade;
- more intense price competition;
- competitive strategies based on quality, product innovation and price;
- diffusion of new production techniques to reduce cycle time, control costs and improve quality;
- growth of, and competition from, emerging economies;
- increased product and service customisation;
- changes in the public/semi-state sector.

Changes in the global business environment tend to have particularly significant implications for Ireland due to our high level of dependence on multinational investment and international trade. The impact of increased competitive pressures has been to focus attention on cost, product innovation and quality as factors impacting on competitive positioning and to create a 'flexibility imperative', whereby companies have to be increasingly responsive to consumer demand on dimensions such as customisation, delivery and support services. These competitive challenges are increasingly penetrating the state-owned sector. A major reason for this development is the erosion of state monopolies as a result of developments at European Union level.

An early example of a state company having to deal with increased competitiveness was Aer Lingus. Deregulation in the airline industry meant that the company was faced with increased competition on key routes. Resultant restructuring led to significant changes in employment numbers, employment patterns and reward systems. The ESB is currently grappling with EU-sponsored initiatives aimed at deregulating the electricity and telecommunications markets. Such changes are likely to have profound effects on HRM strategies, policies and practices in these companies.

In the Irish context we find evidence of both 'continuity and change' in HRM (Monks 1992, 1993; Gunnigle *et al.* 1994; Turner and Morley 1995; Gunnigle, Morley and Turner 1997). The continuity dimension is evident in the fact that the core HRM activity areas (recruitment, development, employee relations etc.) have remained more or less constant. We can similarly note the continuing presence of a specialist HR function in Irish organisations and an ongoing emphasis on employee relations as a key aspect of the HR role. However, we can also point to important areas of change in HRM. Thus, while the core areas of HRM have remained fairly constant, practice within specific areas (e.g. recruitment and selection) has undergone considerable change. In Ireland, as elsewhere, these changes are driven by developments in technology, expansion of the services sector, strong economic growth, greater female participation, inward migration, and changes in social and political life.

Given these developments it is hardly surprising that there remain numerous variants of HRM in practice (Keenoy 1990). Thus, Gunnigle (1998a: 17) argues that 'contingency approaches are now the order of the day', with the role of HR function influenced by a variety of factors as discussed in this chapter. To aid analysis it is useful to outline four typologies of HRM:

1. the high-commitment model
2. the transaction cost model
3. the traditional adversarial model
4. the partnership model.

See Table 2.5.

Table 2.5 Typologies of HRM in Ireland

High-commitment HR
Generally associated with a 'soft' HRM style, this was the first personnel/HR function type model seriously to challenge 'industrial relations orthodoxy' in Ireland. It is characterised by a resource perspective of employees incorporating the view that there is an organisational pay-off, in performance terms, from a combination of 'sophisticated' HR and IR policies designed to develop employee commitment and emphasise the mutuality of management and employee interests. In this model, the HR function is high-powered and well-resourced, with a significant change agent role. This model appears to characterise core business organisations whose competitive strategy is based on a product differentiation/premium price approach, often on a 'first to market' basis. Such organisations may employ significant numbers of highly trained technical and engineering staffs whose development and retention are critical to organisational success. This model generally relies on a *union substitution* premise, although organisations with union recognition, but where the union role is somewhat peripheral, also fall within this category.

Transaction Cost HR
While the commitment model has received much attention, its viability has increasingly come under scrutiny in recent years. In particular, exemplars of the commitment model (e.g. Digital and IBM) experienced intense competitive pressures from low-cost producers, with some going out of business. The transaction cost model places the emphasis on minimising personnel costs. Thus, outsourcing becomes an important strategy, particularly in using contracted labour and other forms of 'atypical' employment. This approach is also associated with intensification in the pace of work and increasing workload and employee flexibility. This model may rely on a union suppression premise: it is often linked to the (management) suggestion that unions inhibit the development of flexibility levels required to ensure competitiveness. In this typology the key role of the HR function is cost-effective labour supply. The role is essentially reactive: dealing with the operational workforce management consequences of a low-cost competitive strategy.

Traditional Adversarial HR
This approach equates to the 'industrial relations orthodoxy' mentioned above (and discussed in greater detail in chapter 1) and, as we have seen, was traditionally the dominant type of HR

function in larger organisations in Ireland. It is grounded in low-trust management-employee relations and primary reliance on adversarial collective bargaining and equates to Tyson's systems/reactive manager typology.

Partnership HR
The development of union-management partnerships has been the focus of much recent debate in Ireland (see chapters 12 and 13). The rationale for partnership is based on so-called 'mutual gains' principles whereby workers and trade unions actively pursue, *with* management, solutions to business problems and appropriate work re-organisation in return for greater involvement in both. Within this typology, the HR function becomes an important strategic lever in developing the partnership agenda. It also assumes an important role in implementing a range of HR and IR policy initiatives to underpin this new orientation: specifically in areas such as reward systems, management-employee communications, job design and employee development.

In the international sphere too, it is clear that many organisations are currently investigating and experimenting with different approaches to workforce management. In particular, attention has increasingly focused on so-called 'strategic' forms of HRM, particularly on developing coherent linkages between HRM practice and business strategy, with the goal of improving organisation performance. We pursue this theme in the next chapter.

3

Strategy, Performance and Human Resource Management

INTRODUCTION

One of the most notable characteristics of management literature over the past two decades has been the increased interest in achieving a closer alignment between business strategy and human resource management (HRM), and more recently in evaluating the impact, if any, of HRM practice on organisation performance (*see* Fombrun *et al.* 1984; Schuler 1987, 1992; Huselid 1995; Guest 1997; O'Brien 1998; Purcell *et al.* 2003). Indeed, there are many who take the view that this desire to bring about the alignment of business strategy and people management policies and practices provided the wellspring for both the transition from personnel management to HRM in the first instance, and the more recent evolution towards 'strategic' HRM, with its distinct focus on improving performance. However, there are others who take the view that we would do well to exercise caution in assuming any automatic connection between HRM and organisation performance, particularly in light of ongoing methodological limitations (see Wall and Wood, 2005).

The concept of strategic HRM refers to the development of a strategic corporate approach to workforce management, whereby HRM considerations become integral to strategic decision-making as organisations seek to establish a corporate HR philosophy and strategy that complements their business strategy (*see* Fombrun *et al.* 1984; Buller and Napier 1993; Guest 1987; Mayrhofer *et al.* 2000; Purcell 2004). Referred to as 'matching' by Boxall (1992), and often alluding to the messages advanced in the resource-based view of the firm (Barney 1995), and human capital accumulation theory (Garavan *et al.* 2001), its core objective is the alignment of business strategy, organisational configuration and HR policies and practices in order to achieve valuable, rare and less imitable sources of competitive advantage. Though complex, it is, as Monks (2001) notes, a literature that is now well established.

It also seems likely that this strategic focus will continue, since HRM considerations have been a neglected area within strategic management thinking generally (*see* Fombrun *et al.* 1984). Arguably, part of this prediction is based on the premise that this field is, at present, characterised by a serious hiatus. For example, Beattie and McDougall (1998) note that much of the literature in the field is 'either normative (written mainly by those in consultancy roles), or conceptual (written by academics)', and, in their view, there have been few attempts to integrate the conceptual with the normative in the HRM literature. Similarly, Ferris *et al.* (1999) point to the gap between the science and the practice of HRM in this area. They refer to Buckley *et al.* (1998), who characterise the hiatus as 'a disconnect', noting that:

> It is a disconnect in that scientists and practitioners seem to have segregated along these lines. This is a relatively recent phenomenon because until the relatively recent past, the study of HRM was problem driven (e.g. the Hawthorne studies are a shining example of significant scientist/practitioner collaboration). Our zest to develop a theory of HRM may have been instrumental in driving a wedge between scientists and practitioner . . . managers are relatively familiar with the research in HRM, but they fail to see many practical implications coming from said research.

Thus, despite an extensive and growing body of literature addressing the concepts of strategy and a strategic approach to HRM, there remains limited consensus as to the substance, nature and implications of these concepts. Indeed, Mayrhofer *et al.* (2000) note that 'some of this literature [strategy in HRM] is flawed by rather simplistic notions of strategy, while more of it points to the complex, multidimensional nature of the concept of strategy'. Here they quote Mintzberg (1988), who notes that strategy has been used in at least five different ways, namely as a plan, a ploy, a pattern, a position and a perspective. It would seem that diversity of meaning continues to be the order of the day. Chadwick and Cappelli (1999) argued more recently that scholars have varying goals with respect to their particular research in the strategic HRM area, with the result that there is considerable variation in the use of the term 'strategic'. Similarly, Luoma (2000) notes that:

> The concepts of strategy and HRM are both somewhat ambiguous. What is the outcome when we put these two together? The result is a strict definition of strategic HRM or a more general idea of valuing people as key elements in a company's business – or something in between . . . It all depends on the way we view these terms.

Consequently, many methodological problems arise when seeking to unearth the linkages between business strategy and HRM because of the differences in meaning associated with the concept of 'business strategy', not to mention 'HRM strategy', the nature of HRM itself and the highly problematic notion of 'integration' and 'measurement' (Tyson *et al.* 1994; Buller and Napier 1993; Whittington 1993; Tyson 1992; Blyton and Turnbull 1992, 1994; Gunnigle, Morley, Clifford and Turner 1997; Delery and Doty 1996; Guest 2001a).

This chapter considers the debate on linking decisions in the HRM sphere with broader decisions on business strategy, and focuses on the link between HRM practice and organisation performance. It attempts to synthesise key aspects of the debate on the relationship between business strategy and HRM and examines efforts at integrating evolving strategy and HRM initiatives. It considers the nature of strategic management with a particular emphasis on competitive strategy at the level of the enterprise.

THE CONCEPT OF STRATEGIC MANAGEMENT

There is extensive literature on the concept of business strategy with the consequence, according to Lundy and Cowling (1996, 16), that anyone trying to reach some understanding of the current state of knowledge of the strategy process will likely experience 'perplexity'. Numerous writers dealing with managerial and business decision-making have used the term 'strategy' to describe a particular set of choices taken over a period of time to achieve given business objectives. Thus, *strategic management* is concerned with policy decisions affecting the entire organisation, with the overall objective being to best position the organisation to deal effectively with its environment. This conception of strategic management implies that in an organisational setting there is a hierarchy of decision choices and that key decisions on business strategy will steer more specific operational decisions on short-term problems and issues (Thurley and Wood 1983).

Some evaluations of strategic management have attempted to identify the various components of the strategy concept, and the levels and types of strategy that may occur. Hofer and Schendel (1978) identify three levels of strategy: corporate, business and functional levels. *Corporate level strategy* is essentially concerned with the question 'what business should we be in?' *Business level (competitive) strategy* addresses the question, 'how do we compete in this business?' Finally, *functional level strategy* focuses on how the activities of particular functions (such as HRM) come together to support the business level strategy. These differing strategy levels are illustrated in figure 3.1.

Figure 3.1 Levels of strategic decision-making

CORPORATE STRATEGY
(what business should we be in?)

BUSINESS/COMPETITIVE STRATEGY
(how to establish and sustain competitive advantage)

FUNCTIONAL STRATEGY
(contribution of various functional parts of the organisation), e.g.:
Marketing
Operations/Production
Finance
HRM

In addition to identifying different levels of strategy, Hofer and Schendel (1978) found it useful to distinguish between strategy process and content. *Strategy process* concerns the activities involved in the formation of a strategy. These activities include analysing competitors and scanning the environment to identify threats and opportunities. *Strategy content*, on the other hand, refers to the actual policies chosen by the organisation and the methods and activities used to implement these policies.

While these distinctions help to clarify the concept of strategic management, there remains some difficulty in relation to analysing the strategy concept in such a way that it reflects the reality of organisational life/activities. For example, there is an inherent assumption that an organisation's strategy is formed after key organisational leaders have formally analysed all relevant information, developed a number of possible options and rationally chosen the option that maximises organisational performance. In addition, it is often assumed that implementing these strategic policies is not problematic because there is goal congruity between the parties. Consequently decisions made by top managers will be followed by individuals and groups at lower levels with little resistance.

Clearly, such assumptions run contrary to evidence on the realities of actual practice in regard to organisational decision-making and implementation. Recognising these difficulties, Mintzberg (1978, 1987) distinguished between '*realised*' and '*unrealised*' *strategies*, and between '*intended*' and '*emergent*' *strategies*. 'Deliberate' strategies are those that are both intended and realised in the organisation. This is the concept of business strategy that appears most frequently in the literature. In addition to deliberate strategies, there may be intended strategies that for some reason are never implemented. These are 'unrealised' strategies. Finally, according to Mintzberg, realised strategies (patterns of decisions) may 'emerge' without the conscious intentions of the strategists. These are termed 'emergent' strategies. Mintzberg's categorisation goes beyond that of a deliberate strategy (in the sense of the traditional planning-oriented view of the term) to that of an emergent strategy, which is conceived as patterned responses that may not have been planned by the actors and may develop in an incremental and opportunistic manner. Strategies can therefore develop in an organisation without being consciously intended. Indeed, Mintzberg suggests that for a strategy to have been intended exactly as realised would be a 'tall order'.

STRATEGIC DECISION-MAKING AND HUMAN RESOURCE MANAGEMENT

Despite these complexities we have seen an ever-increasing emphasis on strategic management as organisations strive to accommodate an increasingly turbulent and competitive business environment. We noted earlier that strategic management is concerned with long-term policy decisions affecting the future of the organisation. Strategic decision-making incorporates strategy formulation, strategy implementation, and evaluation and control; it emphasises the monitoring and evaluation of environmental opportunities and constraints, as well as the strengths and weaknesses of the organisation. Corporate, business and functional strategy represent different levels of strategic decision-making. Each level involves decisions that are strategic in nature. However, some commentators have persuasively argued that decisions at higher levels, such as those at corporate or business unit level, will guide subsequent decisions on functional strategy.

Boxall and Purcell (2003) emphasise this point by differentiating between *upstream* and *downstream* strategic decisions. Upstream or first-order decisions concern the long-term direction and nature of the organisation. Downstream decisions deal with the implications of first-order decisions for organisational structure (a downstream decision). Purcell argues that HR policy choices are made in the context of downstream strategic decisions on organisational structure. Such choices are strategic in nature since they establish the basic approach to workforce management. However, Purcell's argument suggests that HR policy choices are third-order strategic decisions since they will be heavily influenced by first- and second-order decisions and by broader environmental factors (see figure 3.2). Using British data Purcell examined how trends in first- and second-order strategy, particularly diversification and decentralisation, affect management decision-making. He identified the growth in size and influence of the diversified firm as giving greater prominence to decision-making at the corporate level. Within this business form, portfolio planning is commonly used to evaluate the performance of constituent business units and aid resource allocation and investment/divestment decisions. Within the portfolio planning approach to corporate strategy, the organisation is seen as a collection of different businesses that should pursue different strategies to suit particular market conditions. This implies that different functional strategies, including HRM, need to be applied at the business unit level to suit particular business strategies. Key decisions on resource allocation (first-order decisions) are taken at corporate level and it is the responsibility of business unit managers to deal with the implications of such decisions and take appropriate operational decisions to satisfy corporate requirements. Thus, first-order decisions, while not necessarily incorporating HRM considerations, significantly influence HR policy and practice within particular business units.

Figure 3.2 Upstream and downstream strategic decision-making

	UPSTREAM	
FIRST-ORDER	Long-term direction of the firm	E
	Scope of activities, markets, location	N
		V
		I
SECOND-ORDER	Internal operating procedures	R
	Relationships between parts of the	O
	organisation	N
		M
		E
THIRD-ORDER	(e.g.) Strategic choice in HRM	N
		T
	DOWNSTREAM	

Source: Purcell (1989).

This somewhat pessimistic view of HR's influence on the strategy process has been counterbalanced somewhat by more recent work, particularly that of a number of US researchers. In particular, commentators have argued that over more recent years the influence of HR considerations on strategy development has increased and that the distinction between corporate, competitive and HR strategy has blurred (Barney 1991; Ulrich 1997; Pfeffer 1998a, 1998b; Snell 2005). For example, as Snell (2005) and others have argued, in the current era of increased competition and globalisation, many of the traditional sources of competitive advantage, such as barriers to entry (e.g. monopolies), technology and access to capital, have become less important, with the result that HR and HR processes can emerge as key sources of competitive advantage (*see also* Pfeffer 1994, 1998a).

Much of this recent focus, which posits HR as a key potential source of competitive advantage and thus potentially the critical component in overall strategy development, draws on the influence of the resource-based view (RBV) of the firm. This perspective is grounded in the economics and strategy literature (*see* Penrose 1959) and distinguishes between 'physical' and 'human' resources. In regard to the latter, a basic assumption of the RBV is that different firms possess bundles of different human resources and utilise different HR processes that give rise to differing HR capabilities. HR proponents of the RBV argue that HR capabilities provide a key potential source of competitive advantage (cf. Barney 1991, 1997). For example, Flood *et al.* (1997) argue that the top management team represents one particular source of competitive advantage. Also, the increased emphasis on 'knowledge stocks' (*see* Snell 2005) represents another potential source of competitive advantage:

> With rare exceptions, the economic and producing power of the firm lies more in its intellectual and service capabilities than in its hard assets – land, plant and equipment . . . Virtually all public and private enterprises – including most successful corporations – are becoming dominantly repositories and coordinators of intellect.
>
> Quinn (1992, 241)

While perspectives vary, there is little doubt that the relationship between HRM and performance has become an dominant issue in the field (Guest 1997; Boxall and Purcell 2003). Indeed, identifying the means and extent to which firms can lever HR capacity to impact positively on performance has become the essence of what is now popularly known as 'strategic HRM'. We have seen a large number of studies examine the relationship between HR practices and selected measures of performance, such as profits, sales and quality, to this end (Ichniowski 1992; Huselid 1995; MacDuffie 1995; Snell and Youndt 1995; Wright and Snell 1998; Godard and Delaney 2000). We can categorise most of this work into two 'schools', namely (i) the 'best fit' (or contingency) school (*see also* O'Brien 1998; Boxall and Purcell 2000); and (ii) the 'best practice' (or universalistic) school. We now consider each in turn.

'Best Fit' HRM

The essence of the 'best fit' approach is that the optimal HR strategy is one that 'fits' the organisation's overall business strategy. The primary emphasis is on achieving 'vertical' fit, i.e. the chosen HRM approach should complement the overall business strategy:

> . . . there should be vertical linkage between HR practices and processes and the organisational strategy of the firm.
>
> Stiles and Kulvisaechana (2003, 13)

Harvard academic Michael Porter's work on competitive strategy provided much of the basis for subsequent research on linking HR strategy with business or competitive strategy (Porter 1980, 1985, 1987, 1990). The research on competitive advantage focuses primarily on identifying those factors that allow an organisation to differentiate its product or service from its competitors to increase market share. Porter (1980, 1985) argues that the focus of strategic decision-making should be on the development of appropriate competitive strategies at the level of individual business units. *Competitive strategy* is concerned with achieving sustainable competitive advantage in particular industries or industry segments. Price and quality are common mechanisms by which organisations attempt to achieve competitive advantage. Porter's key legacy has probably been his three generic strategies for achieving competitive advantage, namely *cost leadership, differentiation* and *focus* (Porter 1985).

Cost leadership (sometimes called *cost reduction*) involves positioning the organisation as a low-cost producer of a standard 'no frills' product or service for either a broad or a focused market. To succeed with a cost leadership strategy it is suggested that the firm must become the cost leader and not one of several firms pursuing this strategy. Cost leadership requires an emphasis on tight managerial controls, low overheads, economies of scale and a dedication to achieving productive efficiency.

On the other hand, a *differentiation* (sometimes called *product innovation*) strategy requires that an organisation's product or service becomes unique in some dimension that is valued by the buyer, to the extent that the buyer is willing to pay a premium price. The basis for a differentiation strategy may be the product or service itself or other aspects such as delivery or after-sales service.

The third generic competitive strategy, *focus*, involves choosing a narrow market segment and serving this through either a low-cost or a differentiation focus.

Porter's approach is essentially contingency-based: a particular organisation's choice of competitive strategy (cost leadership, differentiation or focus) is seen as determining the context for downstream policies and actions in each key functional area, such as HRM. Thus each generic strategy warrants different skills and requirements for success. Of particular significance from an HR perspective is the need to match selection, workforce profile and employee relations practice with the chosen competitive strategy. He further contends that different organisational cultures are implied in each strategy and that HR policy choice is a key influence in establishing and maintaining 'appropriate' corporate cultures. In the *differentiation* strategy, it is suggested that culture might serve to encourage innovation, individuality and risk-taking; in *cost leadership*, culture might encourage frugality, discipline and attention to detail. In line with contingency theory, Porter argues there is no such thing as a good or bad culture. Rather, he suggests that culture is a means of achieving competitive advantage and should match the competitive strategy: culture is a means to an end, not an end in itself. Another commonly espoused argument for achieving best fit on this dimension is that organisations will experience severe problems in strategy implementation if it is not effectively linked with appropriate HR policy choices (Galbraith and Nathanson 1978; Fombrun *et al.* 1984; Fombrun 1986; Tomlinson 1993; O'Brien 1998).

Horwitz (1999) notes that 'best fit' HRM models may also distinguish between external (or 'vertical') fit and internal (or 'horizontal') fit. As noted above, external fit is concerned with achieving optimal 'fit' between an organisation's business strategy and/or life-cycle stage and its HRM strategy, policies and practices (*cf.* Beaumont 1993; O'Brien 1998). On the other hand, internal fit involves ensuring that policy and practice in each key area of HRM activity (e.g. recruitment, rewards or employee relations) is mutually complimentary:

> The notion of external fit deals with how an organisation mobilises its resources to compete in the external environment. Internal fit usually concerns implementing espoused strategic goals and policies, and the degree of alignment between stated intent (vision and mission), actual behaviour and policy performance at operational level.

Since the early 1980s numerous authors have developed models of 'best fit' strategy-HRM linkages. While some of these have focused on the link between an organisation's stage of development (growth, maturity, decline, etc.,) and HRM, by far the most influential have been those focused on promoting fit between the firm's competitive strategy and HRM (Lengnick-Hall and Lengnick-Hall 1988; Sisson and Storey 2000). We now briefly consider some of the most prominent best-fit HRM models.

SCHULER'S 'STRATEGY – EMPLOYEE BEHAVIOUR' MODEL
Some of the most extensive work on linking business strategy and HRM has been conducted by Randall Schuler and his colleagues in the US and argues that business strategies are most effective when they are systematically co-ordinated with HRM practices (Schuler 1989, 1992, 1995; Schuler and Jackson 1987a, 1987b, 1996; Schuler *et al.* 1987). Of particular note is the suggestion that the key focus of HRM should be to develop

Figure 3.3 Linking business strategy and HRM

BUSINESS STRATEGY	HR STRATEGY	DESIRED EMPLOYEE BEHAVIOURS		HRM POLICY AND ACTIVITY FOCUS
Cost Reduction	Utilisation	Relatively repetive and predictable behaviour	Recruitment	Explicit job analysis Mostly internal recruitment/labour market focus
		Mostly short-term focus High concern for quantity	Appraisal	Short term focus; individual criteria; results oriented criteria
		Moderate concern for quality	Rewards	Hierarchical pay, few incentives
		Major emphasis on results	Training and Development	Narrow career paths; limited training
		Comfortable with stability	Employee Relations	Little employment security; low employee participation; 'traditional' industrial relations
Differentiation	Facilitation	Long term focus	Recruitment	Implicit job analysis; external recruitment/labour market focus
		Creative job behaviour High level of independent co-operative behaviour	Appraisal	Long term focus; process and results criteria; some group criteria
		Moderate concern for quality	Rewards	Egalitarian pay; numerous incentives
		Moderate concern for quantity	Training and Development	Broad career paths; extensive training
		Equal concern for focus and results Tolerance of ambiguity	Employee Relations	High employee participation; co-operative labour management relations; some employment security
Focus	Accumulation	Relatively predictable and repetitive behaviour	Recruitment	Explicit job analysis; some external recruitment
		Long/medium term focus High concern for quality	Appraisal	Long term focus; process and results criteria; some group criteria
		Moderate concern for quantity	Rewards	Egalitarian pay; numerous incentives
		Concern for process and results	Training and Development	Broad career paths; extensive training and development
		Commitment to organisation goals	Employee Relations	High employee participation; co-operative labour management relations; some employment security

Source: Adapted from Schuler (1987, 1989, 1996); Schuler and Jackson (1987a and b).

employee behaviours that 'fit' the organisation's chosen competitive strategy (*cf.* Schuler 1987, 1989; Schuler and Jackson 1987a). Utilising Porter's generic competitive strategies, this approach argues that firms should deploy HRM policies and practices that develop and reinforce employee behaviours best suited to achieving the chosen competitive strategy (cost leadership, differentiation or focus) (*cf.* Boxall and Purcell 2000). Thus, for a chosen competitive strategy to be successful, it has to be supported by particular patterns of employee behaviour, which can be shaped by the organisation's HR strategies, policies and practices: see figure 3.3.

This model identifies three alternative HRM strategy types (*accumulation, utilisation* and *facilitation*), each designed to develop particular employee behaviour patterns to facilitate the achievement of the chosen competitive strategy. Thus, firms following a 'focus' competitive strategy require an 'accumulation' HRM strategy, which emphasises careful selection based on personality rather than technical fit, and an emphasis on training, egalitarian pay structures and lifetime employment. Organisations following a 'cost-reduction' competitive strategy require a HRM 'utilisation' strategy, based on selecting individuals on the basis of technical ability and emphasising cost minimisation in terms of training, etc. Organisations following a 'differentiation' strategy require a 'facilitation' HRM strategy, focused on the ability of individuals to work together via cross-functional work teams and the use of job rotation and career planning to help foster a collaborative work climate. This competitive strategy employee behaviour-HR policy model is outlined in figure 3.3.

FOMBRUN'S 'STRATEGY IMPLEMENTATION' MODEL

In a similar vein, Fombrum and his colleagues developed a model linking strategy, organisation structure and HRM (Fombrun *et al.* 1984). Suggesting that the integration of HRM considerations into strategic decision-making represents 'a true frontier' in workforce management, they caution that while many organisations wish to include HR issues in strategic decision-making, the traditional approach has been to consider these issues only after strategic decisions have been taken. They also observe that often the major emphasis in strategic planning has been on strategy formulation, with very little thought being given to strategy implementation, sometimes resulting in the failure of strategic planning at the operational level. This lack of attention to strategy implementation is seen as a major challenge to organisations, and provides a potentially central role for HRM in ensuring that employees work to make strategies happen. Thus a key plank of the Fombrum model is that HRM plays a crucial role in effective strategy implementation, providing the key to implementing strategic choice and to achieving better alignment between strategic direction and HRM policy and practice. This view is echoed in the work of Butler (1988) and Purcell (1989). As we have seen, Purcell (1989) views HRM as an important 'downstream' strategic choice which helps with the implementation of 'upstream' strategic decisions on competitive strategy.

The model proposed by Fombrun and his colleagues posits strategic management consideration of three key issues (Fombrun *et al.* 1984):

- *Mission and strategy*: identification of an organisation's purpose and plan for how this can be achieved.
- *Formal structure*: for the organisation of people and tasks to achieve mission and strategy.
- *HRM systems*: recruitment, development, evaluation and reward of employees.

This framework is represented in figure 3.4 and is seen to differ from traditional approaches to strategic management by incorporating HRM considerations as an integral component of strategic decision-making. Fombrun *et al.* (1984) further suggest that an organisation's HRM approach tends to reflect managerial assumptions about employees and 'appropriate' workforce management practices. Fombrun (1986) identifies four key aspects of organisational approaches to workforce management that give valuable insights into the managerial approach to employees:

1. *The nature of the psychological contract.* This may vary from, at one extreme, a managerial perspective that views employees in instrumental terms and emphasises high levels of control of both employees and the work environment to, at the other extreme, an approach that sees employees as able and committed beings who should be afforded challenging and meaningful work in an agreeable work environment.
2. *Level of employee involvement.* Organisational approaches may vary from those with high levels of employee involvement in decision-making to those where decisions are solely a management prerogative.
3. *Internal/external labour market.* This addresses the relative emphasis on internal versus external recruitment and related differences in emphasis on employee development.
4. *Performance evaluation.* This factor addresses the relevant managerial emphasis on group versus individual performance evaluation.

He further argues that HRM systems need to become more flexible so as to 'fit' strategic choice. Four key areas of HRM are identified where management should ensure their respective approach fits the chosen competitive strategy, namely: (a) selection/promotion/ placement; (b) appraisal; (c) rewards; and (d) employee development. His model evaluates each of these in relation to its strategy fit.

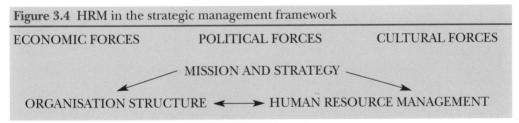

Figure 3.4 HRM in the strategic management framework

ECONOMIC FORCES   POLITICAL FORCES   CULTURAL FORCES

MISSION AND STRATEGY

ORGANISATION STRUCTURE ⟷ HUMAN RESOURCE MANAGEMENT

Source: Adapted from Fombrun *et al.* (1984).

MILES AND SNOW'S STRATEGY-HR FIT MODEL

Another commonly used competitive strategy typology is that of Miles and Snow (1978, 1984), who advance three generic strategy types, namely 'defenders', 'prospectors' and 'analysers'. *Defenders* seek stability by producing only a limited set of products directed at a narrow segment of the total potential market. *Prospectors* are almost the opposite: their strength is in finding and exploiting new product and market opportunities. *Analysers* try to capitalise on the best of both: they seek to minimise risk and maximise opportunity for profit. The strategy here is to move into new products or new markets only after viability has been proven by prospectors. Miles and Snow argue that successful organisations pursue a consistent strategy that is aligned with and supported by complementary organisational structures and management practices, including HRM. They also suggest that organisations that do not possess this *environment-strategy-structure* alignment (*reactors*) are not as successful as the other three categories. Difficulties in developing appropriate HRM policies are seen as a major barrier to the effective strategy implementation.

Miles and Snow (1984) suggest that these three basic types of strategic behaviour can be associated with particular HRM configurations as outlined in figure 3.5. Three specific case study examples are used to illustrate strategy-HRM 'fit', namely a defender (Lincoln Electric), a prospector (Hewlett Packard) and an analyser (Texas Instruments).

Figure 3.5 Linking business strategy and HR policy

	STRATEGIC TYPE		
	DEFENDER	*PROSPECTOR*	*ANALYSER*
PRODUCT and MARKET STRATEGY	Limited, stable product line Predictable markets	Broad, changing product line Changing markets	Stable and changing product lines Predictable and changing markets
RESEARCH and DEVELOPMENT	Narrow; product improvement	Broad; new product development	Focused; 'second to market'
MARKETING	Sales emphasis	Market research emphasis	Extensive marketing campaigns
HR STRATEGY	Maintenance	Entrepreneurial	Co-ordination
RECRUITMENT and SELECTION	'Make'; internal	'Buy'; external	'Make and Buy'; mixed
MANPOWER and PLANNING	Formal, extensive	Informal, limited	Formal, extensive
TRAINING and DEVELOPMENT	Extensive; skill building	Limited; skill acquisition	Extensive; skill building
APPRAISAL	Process-oriented; identify training needs; individual/ group performance evaluation	Results-oriented; identify staffing needs; corporate/division performance evaluation	Process-oriented; identify training and staffing needs; individual/group/ divisional performance evaluation
REWARDS	Based on level in hierarchy; internal equity; pay-oriented	Based on performance; external equity; incentive-oriented	Mostly based on level in hierarchy; internal and external comparisons; pay and incentive-oriented

Source: Adapted from Miles and Snow (1984).

In *defender* organisations, the emphasis is on building the organisation's HR capacity through recruitment at entry levels and internal promotion. The key HR activities are: selection, placement, training, development, appraisal, and ensuring a fit between the reward system and job design. Defender organisations are characterised as lean and hard-working, and demand predictable, planned HR policies and regular maintenance of these policies.

Prospector organisations experience rapid change demanding considerable HR re-deployment. The major HR focus is on sourcing and deploying high-quality personnel. The HR management objective is entrepreneurial, acquiring and developing critical staff. There is little opportunity for long-term planning or sophisticated HRM techniques.

In *analyser* organisations, the emphasis is on developing appropriate organisational structures and management approach with the HRM focus on co-ordinating policies and allocating personnel optimally across the organisation.

Criticisms of 'Best Fit'

Despite the advances that models have brought, there remain numerous criticisms of 'best fit' approaches.

First, and most significantly, commentators point to the lack of sophistication in identifying and describing 'strategy' (Ferris *et al.* 1999; Boxall and Purcell 2000). Ferris *et al.* (1999) find that linking HRM with business strategy remains 'troublesome', principally because of the measures of strategy used in the studies to date. In their review they plausibly note that:

> Recent conceptual pieces have been critical of researchers in this area, suggesting that they have incorporated antiquated notions of firm strategy. Most studies have utilised such typologies as those of Porter (1980) or Miles and Snow (1978). These generic categorisations have little in common with the realities of the modern competitive environment with which organisations are confronted. First, categorisations are exclusive, assuming that organisations pursue a certain strategic goal while ignoring other strategic concerns. Second, they depict the competitive environment, and consequently organisational strategy, as being static instead of dynamic.

In light of this, they suggest that future tests of the HRM-strategy relationship must view strategy along a broader continuum involving a broader range of strategic factors and must conceptualise it as a dynamic, rather than as a static, phenomenon. Finally they suggest that the almost exclusive focus on deliberate or intended strategy, to the detriment of the emergent or realised strategy, remains problematic. It, they suggest, represents a 'flawed reality' in the context of the omnipresent unstable, dynamic environments that we have all become accustomed to. As Marchington and Grugulis (2002, 209–10) observe:

> organisations are dynamic and complex, and typically operate in multiple product markets, whereas the contingency models rely on examining links between two sets of static variables – for example, product market and HR practice which are not static in reality.

There is also evidence that some of the most successful firms are those that compete simultaneously on each of the competitive strategy dimensions, namely low cost, high quality and innovation (*see* Cronshaw *et al.*, 1994). A plausible Irish example here is Dunnes

Stores. Once heralded as one of the 'kings' of low cost ('Dunnes Stores' better value beats them all!'), it now competes much more aggressively in other dimensions, particularly on quality and product range.

It would also appear that the 'best fit' literature overestimates the power of management and the extent of management prerogative in choosing the most 'appropriate' HR policies. Boxall and Purcell (2000) note the need for organisations to comply with prevailing traditions and legal requirements. For example, a particular firm's preferred HR approach may be to avoid trade unions and collective bargaining, but local tradition and legislation may require such firms to engage in such activity. Similarly, particular labour or product market conditions may force firms to employ policies that they would not ideally choose, or indeed 'fit' with their particular business strategy. For example, labour shortages among particular employee categories may lead some firms to provide special incentives and HR policies to attract and retain such employees (see chapter 5), even though such polices may be out of line with their preferred HR approach and with policies pertaining to other employee categories.

There are other criticisms associated with specific 'best fit' models. For example, Hendry and Pettigrew (1992) question the validity of life cycle-based models that suggest that different types of HR practices are appropriate for different life cycle stages (growth, maturity, decline etc.): they argue that the idea of organisations moving from one predictable stage to another is debatable. More generally, a number of commentators have noted that a focus on fit with strategy is but one possible contingency, and that several other variables may be considered (Conway and McMackin 1997). For example, Datta *et al.* (2005) find evidence to suggest that the link between HR systems and productivity is influenced by particular industry characteristics (such as capital intensity, nature of regulation, growth etc.).

UNIVERSAL OR 'BEST PRACTICE' HRM

The term 'best practice' is much used in the contemporary vocabulary of management. It is generally taken to involve the identification of the 'best way' of undertaking a particular management function or task and ensuring this 'best way' is applied in all instances, regardless of context (Gooderham *et al.*, 2004; Boxall and Purcell 2000; Brewster *et al.* 2000)). With regard to HRM, it posits that if organisations adopt a set of best HR practices they will reap returns in terms of enhanced performance:

> Proponents of the universalistic [best practice] perspective . . . contend that there is one 'best' way to manage human resources in firms. In this stream of work . . . [HRM] is viewed as the implementation of a set of high performance work practices . . . to motivate and facilitate worker contribution to organization success
>
> Harrell-Cook (2002, 33)

The 'best practice' school thus rejects contingency approaches ('best fit') and encourages organisations to adopt particular HR practices in areas such as employee selection, rewards, development and involvement. The primary emphasis is on achieving 'horizontal' fit, i.e. practice across different HR areas (selection, training, rewards, etc.,) should be consistent and complementary.

While best practice HRM is most often associated with the work of Pfeffer (1994, 1998a, 1998b) (see discussion below), its roots can be traced back somewhat further. The Harvard Business School (HBS) model (Beer *et al.* 1984, *see* chapter 1) encouraged top management teams to deploy a set of 'pro-employee' policies in four key areas of HRM (namely rewards, HR flows, work systems and employee involvement), suggesting that this would yield both tangible benefits for the firm (high commitment, enhanced competencies, better employee relations and greater cost-effectiveness), and longer-term benefits in terms of employee wellbeing, organisational effectiveness and societal wellbeing. This model has formed the basis for what is sometimes termed 'soft' HRM, whereby senior management recognise that people are the organisation's 'most valuable' resource and deploy a set of employee-oriented policies to nurture and develop this resource. Similarly, Arthur (1992, 1994) found that HR approaches focused on increasing employee commitment (i.e. high levels of training and employee participation, good rewards and decentralised decision-making) led to higher performance, while HR approaches focused on control, efficiency and reduced employee discretion were associated with high labour turnover and poor performance.

Over the recent past we have witnessed an upsurge in interest in the idea of 'best practice' HRM, led in large measure by Pfeffer's (1994, 1998a) identification of 'best' HRM practices which, he argues, can enhance performance (e.g. higher profits, greater sales etc.) regardless of the basis upon which firms seek to compete. He further contends that the benefits can be even more pronounced when complementary sets of HR practices ('HR bundles') are used together (*see also* Wood 1999). Pfeffer (1998a, 1998b) identifies seven specific HRM practices, which, when used together, will, he argues, lead to higher revenue, profits, market value and organisational survival (*see also* Huselid 1995; Pfeffer and Viega 1999). These seven key HRM practices are outlined in table 3.1.

Table 3.1 Pfeffer's seven key HRM practices

1. *Employment security*	Viewed as fundamental to securing employee commitment, ensuring employees continue to contribute to improved productivity, promoting long-term thinking and generally underpinning the other HR practices.
2. *Targeted selection*	Focus on selective hiring of outstanding people to ensure the organisation has the competencies to build effectiveness and performance.
3. *Workplace teams and decentralisation*	Utilisation of self-managed teams and decentralisation in decision-making. This is viewed as an important means of pooling ideas and process improvement and also as a way of reducing layers of hierarchy.
4. *High pay contingent on organisational performance*	Focus on 'above the norm' compensation and performance-related rewards to 'incentivise' superior performance.
5. *Employee training*	Strong focus on training to ensure employees have the capability to deal proactively with workplace challenges.
6. *Reduction of status differentials*	Emphasis on developing an egalitarian workplace and removal of status differentials (e.g. differing benefits such as healthcare or differing control mechanisms such as 'clocking in'). Seen as important in promoting a more open management style.
7. *Business information-sharing with employees*	Focus on sharing business and financial information. Seen as important means of developing employee commitment and trust. Provides employees with adequate context for decision-making in teams.

Pfeffer's work draws on a comparatively small number of case studies to establish his argument that HRM practice leads to superior organisational performance and even sustained competitive advantage. This work has also been closely linked with the concept of high-performance work systems (HPWS) and with the work practices and HR policies used in a number of 'high-tech' US companies (*see* Walton 1985; Lawler 1986). Pfeffer's approach might be best labelled as a 'pure' best practice perspective (universalism), and differs from the more empirical HPWS studies by Arthur (1992, 1994), and others (see discussion below). While Pfeffer's work is essentially prescriptive, arguing that a standard set of HR practices should be adopted by firms in general, many of the HPWS studies considered the impact of strategy and other variables, in their search for an optimal 'bundling' of HR practices.

While a precise definition of a HPWS is difficult to come by, it is based on the premise that organisation performance can be improved through the use of particular practices, notably employee participation, teamworking and communications, all designed to develop high levels of employee commitment, involvement and flexibility (*see* MacDuffie 1995; Applebaum and Batt 1994; Applebaum *et al.* 2000). Over recent years a number of studies have investigated what have been variously labelled as 'high-performance', 'high-commitment' or 'high-involvement' work systems (Edwards and Wright 2001; Roche 1999; Wood and de Menezes 1998). Much of this research has focused on the impact of HRM on bottom line performance, and has sought to advance knowledge by providing more precise quantitative estimates of HRM effects (cf. Arthur 1992, 1994; Huselid 1995; MacDuffie 1995; Delaney and Huselid 1996; Delery and Doty 1996; Huselid and Becker 1996; Ichniowski *et al.* 1996; Wood 1995; Wood and Albanese 1995).

One of the more influential of these studies is that of Huselid (1995) whose work points to a positive causal link between particular 'bundles' of HR practice and organisation performance (as measured by productivity, employee turnover and financial performance). The essence of Huselid's work is that particular 'high-performance' HR practices (including comprehensive employee recruitment and selection procedures, 'incentive' compensation and performance management systems, and extensive employee involvement and training) positively impact on the bottom line. Drawing on data from a large-scale survey of US firms, Huselid (1995, 667) found a strong positive relationship between high-performance work practices and firm performance:

> Prior work in both the academic and popular press has argued that the use of High Performance Work Practices will be reflected in better firm performance. This study provides broad evidence in support of these assertions. Across a wider range of industries and firm sizes, I found considerable support for the hypothesis that investments in such practices are associated with lower employee turnover and greater productivity and corporate financial performance

These findings are quite emphatic. Huselid (ibid., 667) finds evidence of strong and positive linkages between HR practices and organisation performance. Indeed, he goes on to calculate the dimensions of such linkages and argues that the 'magnitude of the returns for investments in high performance work practices is substantial':

> A one standard deviation increase in such practices is associated with a relative 7.05 per cent decrease in turnover and, on a per employee basis, $27,044 more in sales and $18,641 and $3,814 more in market value and profits, respectively. These

internally consistent and economically and statistically significant values suggest that firms can indeed obtain substantial financial benefits from investing in the practices studied . . .

Huselid (1995, 667)

Criticisms of 'Best Practice'

The best practice and HPWS models as advocated by Pfeffer, Huselid and others essentially suggest that firms should deploy bundles of sophisticated, high-cost and highly integrated HRM polices and practices designed to develop organisational and HR capabilities to compete on the basis of productivity, quality and service (cf. Nolan and O'Donnell 1995; Ulrich 1997). However, it is clear that the high costs associated with this approach make it 'far from fashionable' (Marchington and Grugulis 2002, 191). We now briefly consider some of the major criticisms of the 'best practice' school (*see also* Wood 1999; Boxall and Purcell 2000; Lewin 2001; Marchington and Grugulis 2002).

A first and important criticism of best practice approaches is the problem of definition. As numerous sources observe, there is no uniform definition of HPWS (*see* Lewin 2001). There are different views on whether the degree of emphasis on individual performance-related pay is consistent with a corresponding emphasis placed on teamwork (Arthur 1994; Huselid 1995; Pfeffer 1994). Some authors emphasise the use of internal promotions (e.g. Huselid 1995; Pfeffer 1994), while others argue that this leads to a more inflexible HR system and greater bureaucracy, intense unionisation and lower levels of productivity (Arthur 1994; Ichniowski *et al.* 1996).Thus, different proponents of best practice tend to proffer different lists of what constitutes HPWS (*see* Becker and Gerhart 1996).

Second, much of this research suffers from particular methodological flaws (*see* Lewin 2001). Of particular note here is the over-sampling of manufacturing (and consequently under-representation of the services sector), over-reliance on snapshot surveys and the limited number of longitudinal and case-based studies. A notable exception in this latter regard is MacDuffie's study of the impact of HR policies on performance in the international automobile sector (MacDuffie 1995; Pil and MacDuffie 1996). Other concerns relate to difficulties with the particular measures of organisation performance used (see below) and concerns about causality. This latter concern was mentioned in chapter 1: is it that certain HRM practices lead to organisational success or that organisational success gives firms the wherewithal to deploy certain HRM practices? Finally, it appears that many of the best practice studies, such as Huselid (1995), rely on single or, at most, two respondents. More often than not, this tends to be the HR practitioner. However, Purcell (1999) suggests that HR specialists 'have neither detailed knowledge about competitive strategies nor the proportion of sales which are derived from these strategies', and argues that 'considerable caution is needed when interpreting conclusions from these quantitative studies'.

Third, this stream of research tends to focus exclusively on the impact of HRM on performance while excluding the role of other key functional areas such as marketing, production/operations, or finance. Lewin (2001) notes this shortfall and points out that some US scholars in these different functional areas have found that marketing, finance, operations and practices in other areas can significantly impact on business performance. One must therefore be sceptical of HRM research that does not consider or control for such effects.

Fourth, there remain deep-set concerns about the measures of organisational performance used in many of the studies. We noted earlier the impact of Huselid's work, which found that certain ('high-performance') HR practices had a predictable and demonstrable impact on bottom line measures of firm performance, namely financial turnover, sales, market value and profitability (Huselid 1995). However, case study evidence from the UK on the impact of HRM on performance found that none of the HR directors interviewed were particularly concerned about demonstrating any links between HR interventions and profitability or shareholder value (cf. Purcell 2004). This finding is not as remarkable as it may first appear. Measures such as profitability are lag indicators and can be impacted upon by numerous factors, many of which are beyond the realm of management control, such as currency movements, commodity prices and developments in the international economy and international affairs. One might consider, for example, the impact of 9/11 or the dot.com downturn on Irish enterprises in the tourism and ICT sectors. Purcell (2004, 17) argues that the connection between HRM and such lag measures are 'too stretched or distant with too many other variables influencing profit' to be a useful measure. However, this did not mean that these managers were not concerned with the impact of HR on performance – quite the contrary. They paid considerable attention to the role HR played in improving performance but did so using 'lead indicators', which focused on more immediate measures of HR performance. Three principal measures were used: (a) labour market measures such as labour turnover, labour retention, absenteeism and accident rates; (b) employee satisfaction measures, which were often linked to opinion survey findings; and (c) operational measures, such as down time, scrap levels, time delays and customer retention.

Fifth, as with our earlier critique (chapter 1) of the emergence of HRM as a distinctive concept in the US in the 1980s, best practice HRM has been widely criticised for its unitarist underpinnings. This criticism begs the question 'best for whom?'. While proponents such as Pfeffer largely fudge this issue, it is clear that, in this tranche of literature, decisions on what constitutes 'best practice' is managerially driven with little attention afforded to employee voice. This is a particularly important criticism from an European and Irish perspective, given that best practice often ignores the role of independent employee representation and the role of joint regulation:

> In all of the persuasive rhetoric on 'best practice' HRM, one element is noticeable by its absence – independent employee voice. Not only is this apparent at the workplace, since Pfeffer's notion of employee involvement is based on economic efficiency and problem solving rather than industrial democracy . . . there is no sense that employees are active participants in the employment relationship whose frames of reference may differ from those espoused by their managers.
>
> Marchington and Grugulis (2002, 17)

Finally, as Lewin (2001) notes, best practice or HPWS research focuses exclusively on 'high-involvement' approaches with little or no consideration of the role and impact of 'low-involvement' work systems. This is all the more surprising given widespread international evidence that ever greater demands are being placed on employees, and that employer power and prerogative in the workplace is increasing (*see* Sparrow and Hiltrop 1994). In her analysis of the impact of the introduction of new production techniques (*Just in Time* (JIT) and *Statistical Process Control* (SPC)) on employees, Klein (1989, 60) found that these do not necessarily make for an empowered workforce:

> In Japan . . . where JIT and SPC have been used most comprehensively, employees are routinely organised into teams, but their involvement in workplace reform is

typically restricted to suggestions for process improvement through structured quality control circles or *kaizen* groups. Individual Japanese workers have unprecedented responsibility. Yet it is hard to think of them exercising genuine autonomy, that is, in the sense of independent self-management.

Marchington and Grugulis (1999, 3) are equally cautious in their critique of Pfeffer's (1998b) seven best HR practices. In regard to 'workplace teams and decentralisation' they comment:

> we argue that HR practices – such as teamworking – which appear superficially attractive may not offer universal benefits and empowerment but actually lead to work intensification and more insidious forms of control; in other words, quite different and more worrying interpretations from that which is portrayed in the 'upbeat' literature – such as that by Pfeffer.

Lewin (2001) notes the increased incidence of part-time, temporary and contract employment, and outsourcing, and the fact that these may often be associated with the growth and diffusion of 'low-involvement' work systems. He further notes the now common distinction between 'core' and 'peripheral' employees and the fact that while core employees are most likely to be covered by high-involvement work systems, the opposite is likely to be the case for peripheral categories – who are more likely be covered by low-involvement work systems. The lack of emphasis on the deployment and impact of low-involvement work systems (e.g. outsourcing, contract working) on performance thus represents an important deficit in the extant research.

BEYOND BEST FIT AND BEST PRACTICE: NEW AND EMERGING MODELS

While criticisms of HRM's links with strategy and impact on bottom line performance are well founded, such work has nevertheless advanced knowledge in this key area. For example, although there has been some considerable criticism of Huselid's work (*see* Purcell 1999) and one may justifiably harbour reservations about some of the findings on impact of HRM practices on bottom line performance – especially the apparent precision of the financial benefits outlined above – an important contribution of the work of Huselid and others is that it demonstrates the potential for performance improvement to be gained from using particular 'bundles' of HR practices. This contribution should not be overstated however. While research points to the potential performance benefits which may accrue from investment in HR, such benefits are not universally applicable. Work by writers such as MacDuffie (1995) and Marchington and Grugulis (2002) suggests that 'best practice' HRM may lead to performance improvements only where employees have specific and much needed skills/knowledge that take time to develop and nurture, and where the rewards for such HR investment outweigh the costs:

> Innovative human resource practices are likely to contribute to improved economic performance only when three conditions are met: when employees possess knowledge and skills that managers lack; when employees are motivated to apply this skill and knowledge through discretionary effort; and when the firm's business or production strategy can only be achieved when employees contribute such discretionary effort.
>
> MacDuffie (1995, 199)

As alluded to earlier, a related and important implication of this work is that it is the *linkages* between different HRM practices that are important, rather than the implementation of a specific and isolated HR practice. Thus, it is the so called 'bundling' of HR practices that have the potential to yield gains in organisational performance. As Guest (1998, 65) comments:

> One thing is clear from all of the research: there is no value in investing heavily in specific practices. Performance-related pay, psychometric tests in selection or extensive training will not in themselves bring bottom-line results. The key lies in having the right 'bundle' of practices and the challenge for personnel managers is to find it.

However, Becker *et al.* (1997, 43) warn about the adoption of possible 'deadly combinations' that may develop within firms when HR practices are utilised that:

> . . . might well make sense in isolation but when evaluated within the context of other HRM practices deployed throughout the firm are a recipe for disaster. Simple examples can be found in firms that invest in sophisticated performance management systems only to adopt compensation policies that provide for little meaningful economic distinction between high and low performing employees; or firms that encourage employees to work together in teams, but then provide raises based on individual contributions.

Boxall and Purcell's (2003) work on linking HRM to business performance seems to meet many of these caveats: see figure 3.6. This starts by positing two broad goals for business firms: (a) securing viability with adequate profitability; and (b) achieving some form of

Figure 3.6 Linking HR goals, non-HR goals and business goals

Critical HR Goals
Desired types & levels of:
• Labour Productivity (Cost Effectiveness)
• Organisational Flexibility
• Social Legitimacy (employment citizenship)

Ultimate Business Goals
• Viability with adequate returns to shareholders
• Sustained Competitive Advantage?

Critical Non-HR Goals:
Desired outcomes for:
• Sales
• Market Share
• Return on Capital Employed
• Social Legitimacy (environmental impacts)
• etc.

Source: Boxall and Purcell 2003, 7

sustained competitive advantage. It follows that firms will seek to use their human and other resources to achieve these business goals. In the HR sphere, Boxall and Purcell (ibid., 8) identify three 'critical HR goals' or 'performance domains', namely: (a) labour productivity; (b) organisational flexibility; and (c) social legitimacy. They argue that an 'outstanding mix of outcomes' in all three domains makes for 'superior performance in HRM' and (most likely) sustained competitive advantage. We now consider each of these in turn.

Labour productivity, i.e. the value of labour outputs in relation to the cost of labour inputs. This domain represents the key measure of cost effectiveness and the 'touchstone against which every new HR policy ought to be evaluated: will it make labour more productive and will its costs, or the investment it implies, be justified?' (ibid., 8). Such evaluation applies both at the level of individual HR practices (e.g. evaluating the costs and benefits of introducing a particular HR intervention, such as formal performance appraisal) and in regard to the firm's overall approach to HR (is the overall approach giving adequate returns in terms of productivity?). As mentioned earlier, expensive 'soft' HRM approaches (high levels of rewards, training, etc.) may be appropriate for organisations in capital-intensive 'high-tech' environments where labour represents a low proportion of overall costs. A particular example relates to certain firms in the pharmaceutical sector in Ireland that are involved in the production of premium price drugs, where it is critical to maintain continuity of supply (e.g. Pfizer, Merck). The opposite may be the case among many small firms acting as sub-suppliers to major multinationals or in sectors characterised by intense price competition, where labour represents a high proportion of total costs (e.g. apparel manufacture).

Organisational flexibility, i.e. an organisation's capacity to change. Here, Boxall and Purcell distinguish between two types of flexibility, namely 'short-run responsiveness' and 'long-run agility'. Short-run responsiveness incorporates the various forms of flexibility discussed in chapter 1, namely functional (ability to deploy personnel across a range of different job tasks), numerical (ability to take on and shed labour in line with business demand) and financial (ability to link wages to the labour market context and to evaluations of individual performance) flexibility. Long-run agility refers to an organisation's ability to cope effectively with developments in the business environment. This is an altogether more 'woolly' but nevertheless critical HR concern, addressing the extent to which organisations have the capacity to deal with changes in the environment. There is clearly great potential for conflict between short-run responsiveness and long-run agility. For example, firms may shed key personnel during a business downturn and consequently lose valuable knowledge and skills that may be required to deal with longer-term changes in its competitive environment.

Social legitimacy. While the previous two HR performance domains focus on bottom line performance, Boxall and Purcell argue that firms must also concern themselves with their standing as an employer, or what they term 'employment citizenship'. This will focus in large measure on how firms behave with regard to prevailing social norms and Government regulation of employment practice and conditions. However, 'employment citizenship' is only one element of social legitimacy, which also embraces other aspects of social standing – the impact on the environment and general corporate social responsibility. This is in line with Elkington's (1997) concept of a 'triple bottom line' – namely that firms must be concerned with their performance with reference to financial, environmental and social criteria. It also resonates with Kaplan and Norton's (1996) 'balanced score card', which identifies three key stakeholders in organisations, namely shareholders, customers and employees. In Ireland and internationally, it is clear that firms vary in their approach to employment citizenship. While some clearly aspire to becoming 'employers of choice' in their particular region or labour market, others will seek to comply minimally or to apply standards below those provided for by legislation or social norms. The alleged mistreatment of migrant workers by Gama Construction and Irish Ferries in 2005 provide some Irish examples in this regard. Internationally, considerable concern has been raised in regard to employment standards in sectors such as textiles and footwear manufacture in many low-wage countries, in regard to both multinational subsidiaries and local firms.

Boxall and Purcell's (2003) work illustrates the importance of 'bundling' HR practices mentioned earlier. Seeking to improve performance in a key domain (e.g. labour productivity) is likely to involve interventions across a number of HR activity areas, such as training, motivation or rewards. However, it is clear that performance in other domains (e.g. flexibility) will require interventions in some similar areas (e.g. training). Thus, the co-ordination of HR interventions represents a key challenge in ensuring HR contributes to organisation performance.

A related and critical consideration raised by Boxall and Purcell (ibid., 14) is the inevitability of what they term 'strategic tensions' in regard to HR performance. They identify three major areas where this may arise, namely labour scarcity, motivation and change.

To perform well in regard to labour productivity and flexibility, one would expect an organisation to attract and develop highly skilled and competent employees. However, as noted in chapter 1, certain categories of employee may be in scarce supply, for example, highly qualified information technology or health care workers. As a result, firms may be forced to compete aggressively for such labour. Inevitably, some firms will be more successful than others. In Ireland, you will often find that certain large, successful multi-nationals have the financial resources to provide rewards, training and other incentives necessary to attract such staff. However, others, particular smaller firms, may not have such capacity and consequently suffer from problems of labour quality and retention:

> The goals of securing reasonable productivity . . . and building some capacity for development . . . are seriously compromised if the firm cannot make competitive job offers. It then struggles to build capabilities . . . In the extreme, the tension associated with labour scarcity can become a full blown 'capability crisis', compromising productivity and profitability and threatening the firm's reputation and viability.
>
> Boxall and Purcell (2003, 14)

The second area of strategic tension, namely worker motivation, addresses potential trade-offs between employer (and managerial) interests vis-à-vis employee interests. Addressing such tensions often falls within the area of employee relations, and what has been termed the 'wage-effort' bargain. It addresses how employers and workers behave towards each other in the workplace. Will employees work to the best of their ability and deliver on criteria such as productivity and flexibility? Will employers provide satisfactory working conditions and an environment that ensures a favourable work experience for employees? We find numerous examples of situations where such aspirations are not met. For example, there is considerable evidence that demands on employees in many firms have increased over recent decades, notably in regard to increasing work loads and intensification in the pace of work (Wilkinson *et al.* 1997; D'Art and Turner 2002; Heffernan and Dundon 2004).

A key area where conflicts of interest often arise is in regard to the distribution of profits, with employees seeking a greater share based on their contribution to performance and employers seeking to satisfy other 'constituencies', notably shareholders, senior management and re-investment.

The final area of strategic tension in HR identified by Boxall and Purcell (ibid.) relates to organisation change. They specifically note, first, the potential for conflict between improving performance in regard to productivity and flexibility, and second, the need to achieve a balance between the long-run and short-run capacity of the organisation to deal with change. The former issue was raised in chapter 1 pertaining to our discussion of some of the paradoxes in the concept and of HRM as it developed in the US in the 1980s. There we noted that attempts, for example, to ensure numerical flexibility may detrimentally impact the firm's capacity to improve productivity. A common means of achieving numerical flexibility is to employ a higher proportion of workers on a temporary or contract basis, allowing the firm lay off such workers more easily. However, the more tenuous nature of such contracts, and the higher level of labour turnover entailed, increases the difficulty in achieving the levels of workforce competency and commitment necessary to deal with longer-term competitive challenges:

> . . . suppose a firm decides to place most of its operating staff on temporary contracts to provide for short-term flexibility . . . This reduces the level of fixed cost but is likely to create problems with employee turnover . . . Over time, the firm is likely to find that it fails to build the kind of learning process that underpins long-term growth.
>
> Boxall and Purcell (2003, 17)

Of course, firms who utilise only permanent contracts may face the opposite challenge. In periods of slack demand, the costs of maintaining full employment may become unsustainable and threaten the financial viability of the organisation. Achieving a balance between these competing tensions is clearly the key – but difficult – challenge for firms and their HR specialists.

RECENT EVIDENCE
Moving beyond models of linkages between HRM and organisation performance, we now consider some recent research evidence in the area.

On this side of the Atlantic, John Purcell and colleagues at the University of Bath have again been to the fore. Over recent years their work for the Chartered Institute of Personnel and Development (CIPD) has involved case study analyses of the association between HR policies and performance outcomes, and provides some important insights on the impact of HRM on firm performance (Hutchinson and Purcell 2003; Purcell *et al.* 2003; Purcell 2004). This research draws on two important ideas in the literature: (i) the *resource-based view of the firm* and its implications for HRM; and (ii) the idea of *discretionary employee behaviour* and how this can be 'triggered'. We briefly consider each in turn before examining the findings of Purcell's recent work.

The Resource-Based View of the Firm, Human Capital and HRM
Much of the contemporary discourse on HRM's impact on performance draws on recent work on the resource-based view of the firm (RBV) to identify internal sources of sustained competitive advantage. As mentioned earlier, the RBV has its origins in the economics and strategy literature (*see* Penrose 1959; Wernerfelt 1984; Barney 1991; Wright and McMahon

1992). Initially, conceptions of strategy were based on best 'positioning' the firm to deal with competitive challenges at the level of the industry (e.g. SWOT analysis [strengths, weaknesses, opportunities, threats]), and choosing an appropriate competitive strategy (e.g. choosing between Porter's generic strategies – 'cost leadership', 'differentiation' and 'focus'). In contrast, the RBV focuses on the link between strategy and a firm's *internal resources* (physical, capital and human). In the RBV, the sources of competitive advantage are the valuable and sometimes intangible resources and competencies within a firm, such as skill pools, reputation and networks. Clearly human resources have the potential to be one such source. However, to provide sustained competitive advantage these resources must meet a number of criteria, notably: (i) they must add positive value; (ii) they must be rare; (iii) they should be inimitable, or extremely difficult to imitate; and (iv) it should not be possible for competitors to substitute them with another resource (for more detailed discussion, see Wright and McMahon 1992).

Using the RBV, we have seen a growing body of evidence that links the development of *human capital* to improved organisation performance (Barney 1991, 1997; Wright *et al.* 2001). This stress on human capital development reflects the RBV that market value depends more on intangible than tangible resources:

> The issue of what contributes to competitive advantage has seen . . . a shift away from external positioning in the industry and the relative balance of competitive forces, towards an acknowledgement that internal resources be viewed as crucial to sustained effectiveness . . . Competitive advantage is dependent not, as traditionally assumed, on such bases as natural resources, technology, or economies of scale, since these are increasingly easy to imitate. Rather competitive advantage is, according to the RBV, dependent on the valuable, rare and hard to imitate resources that reside within the organisation. Human capital in a real sense is an 'invisible asset'.
>
> Stiles and Kulvisaechana (2003, 3–4)

Drawing on some of the insights provided by the RBV, Purcell and his team's case study investigations (Hutchinson and Purcell 2003; Purcell *et al.* 2003; Purcell 2004) explore what they term 'HR advantage'. In so doing they employ Boxall's (1996) distinction between *Human Capital Advantage* and *Organisation Process Advantage*, namely the idea that both people and processes can aid firm performance. Thus, it is important not only to choose, develop and reward people effectively but also to deploy effective systems and ways of working (e.g. supervisory style, mechanisms for involvement and participation etc.). Stiles and Kulvisaechana (2003) make a similar distinction in cautioning that identifying and developing human capital is not in itself sufficient to achieve competitive advantage. Rather they argue (ibid., 5) that organisations must also possess strong social capital and organisation capital (see figure 3.7):

> . . . the accumulation of exceptionally talented individuals is not enough . . . There must also be a desire on the part of individuals to invest their skills and expertise in the organisation and in their position. In other words, individuals must commit or engage with the organisation if effective utilisation of human capital is to happen. In addition, therefore, to human capital, there must also be *social* and *organisational* (or structural) capital.

Figure 3.7 Human, social and organisational capital

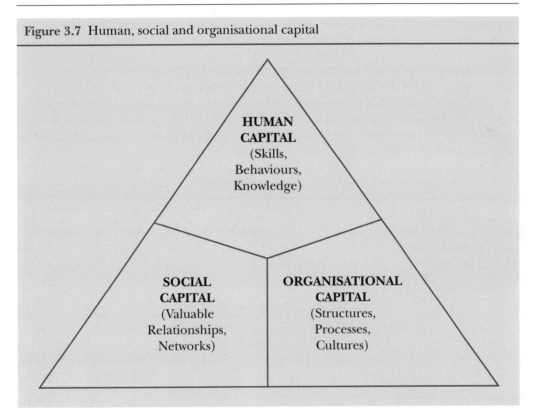

Discretionary Employee Behaviour

The idea of discretionary employee behaviour relates to the need to identify how and why workers might be encouraged to work at levels of performance above and beyond what might be considered average or acceptable:

> We argued that something must persuade, induce, cajole, or encourage employees to do more or do things better or more innovatively both individually and in working with others than they otherwise would, or were doing in the past. This extra behaviour was discretionary in the sense that it is neither compulsory, nor could be forced. It had to be given.
>
> Purcell (2004, 3)

Consequently, a key challenge for management is to facilitate or 'trigger' such behaviour. The work of Applebaum *et al.* (2000) contends that worker performance is dependent on three key factors: worker *ability* (A), worker *motivation* (M), and adequate *opportunity* (O) to perform. This is generally expressed by the equation:

$$P = f (A, M, O), \text{ where } P = \text{Performance}$$

Thus, superior worker performance is most likely to occur where workers have: (i) the requisite ability ('they *can do* the job because they possess the necessary knowledge and skills'); (ii) the requisite motivation ('they *will do* the job because they are adequately incentivised'); and (iii) an adequate and supportive working environment ('e.g. functioning technology and the opportunity to be heard when problems occur' (Purcell 2004, 4)).

THE UNIVERSITY OF BATH 'PEOPLE AND PERFORMANCE' MODEL
Using the P = f (A, M, O) equation, Purcell and his University of Bath team identified some eleven HR policy areas that they considered important in impacting on performance (see figure 3.8). They used this model in examining each of their twelve case study firms, a number of which were selected because of their reputation as innovators in HRM. The principal findings of this study are discussed below.

Figure 3.8 The University of Bath *people and performance* model

= Key HR Policy Areas

The first key finding was that a clear and shared sense of an organisation's *mission, values and culture* was important. This was termed the 'Big Idea' or 'a clear sense of mission underpinned by values and a culture expressing what the firm is and its relationship with its customers and employees' (Purcell 2004, 7) and was seen as a key element to 'inform and enthuse' HR policy and practice. This might differ between organisations, e.g. in Jaguar the big idea was 'quality', while in Selfridges it was being 'friendly, aspirational and bold'. Six of the twelve companies studied had a 'big idea' and all of these reported higher levels of organisation commitment, a factor widely considered critical in contributing to performance (*see* Applebaum *et al.* 2000; Barney 1997; Coyle-Shapiro *et al.* 2004).

A second important finding of the Bath University research was the critical role played by *front line managers* (FLMs), e.g. supervisors, team/section leaders etc., in bridging the gap 'between espoused and enacted policies' and thus in 'bringing HR policies to life' (Purcell 2004, 11; *see also* Hutchinson and Purcell 2003):

> ... the really important finding was that the employees' experience of HR policy and practice was strongly mediated by the way front line managers (FLMs) sought to implement a given policy, their enthusiasm in doing so (what we call 'enacted') and their wider role in leading a team or section and in controlling things like quality, lateness and absence.

We noted in chapters 1 and 2 how this role has become even more important over recent years due to (a) the greater emphasis on returning more HR responsibilities to line managers and (b) the fact that the employment relationship has become increasingly individualised (e.g. more focus on individual performance reviews, development, mentoring, etc). Again, it was the impact of a worker's relationship with their FLM which was found to impact strongly on levels of commitment, job satisfaction and motivation:

> The higher employees rate FLMs in terms of the way they manage people: the more committed and satisfied those employees will be and the higher their levels of (self reported) job discretion.
>
> Hutchinson and Purcell (2003, 14)

Another important finding from the Bath University team's research was that the *impact of HR policies varied between different occupational categories.* Their research focused on three such categories, 'professionals', 'front line managers' and 'workers' (cf. Hutchinson and Purcell, 2003; Purcell *et al.* 2003). A summary of the preferences of these categories and the HR factors positively and negatively impacting on their commitment to the organisation are summarised in table 3.2 and box 3.1.

Table 3.2 HR policies positively and negatively linked to organisation commitment

	Positive	**Negative**
Professional workers	• Communication • Reward/recognition • Appraisal • Effort • Relationship with managers • Career opportunity	• Poor management leadership • Lack of job challenge • Unsatisfactory work/life balance • Poor employee relations climate
Front line managers	• Relationship with manager • Career opportunities • Work/life balance • Openness • Job security	• Low job satisfaction (esp. career opportunities) • Dissatisfied with training • Lack of openness
Workers	• Communication • Rewards and recognition • Openness	• Dissatisfied with career opportunities • Poor job security • Low job satisfaction (job challenge and influence)

Box 3.1 Different HR bundles for different occupational categories

Professionals want excellent communication about all aspects of the business with good rewards and recognition for good work. They want to know how well they are doing, enjoy working hard but need to get on with their boss and want some hope of career progression whether in the firm or in their profession. What seems to destroy commitment is poor leadership and a lack of respect from managers, boring work, lack of support to help them achieve a work/life balance, no opportunity to gain more money through better performance, and working in a place with an 'us' and 'them' atmosphere.

Front line managers: What is really important is having a good positive working relationship with their boss and senior managers generally. This includes being able to talk about problems (openness). If they feel secure in their jobs, find the firm helps them achieve a work life balance and they believe they are not stuck for ever in their current job they are more likely to be positive about their employer and show commitment. What destroys commitment is where front line managers find little job satisfaction, have inappropriate or no training and cannot talk about personal problems with their managers.

Workers value communication, want praise and reward (we were often told in answer to a general question about what else the organisation could do to encourage people to improve their performance 'if only someone would say thank you sometimes') and work in an open environment, able to discuss grievances and personal problems. The destroyers of commitment were working in boring jobs with little opportunity to influence how the job was done, feeling insecure and the lack of any hope for future betterment or change.

Source: Purcell (2004, 16–17)

The final important finding from the University of Bath research was that *dissatisfaction with existing policies is a more powerful demotivator than an absence of policies.* The clear message here is that if management are to employ a particular HR policy it is critical to get this right.

Human Capital and Competitive Advantage: The Idea of HR 'Configurations'
In the US a number of studies have examined the impact of different bundles of HR practices on performance, with the goal of identifying HR 'configurations' that are both internally consistent and aligned with the organisation's strategy and environment (Becker and Huselid 1998, Edwards and Wright 2001). This perspective suggests that 'best fit' and 'best practice' approaches do not necessarily conflict, but can be employed concurrently, albeit at different levels of the HR system (Becker and Gerhart 1996). First, it posits that different firms require different 'configurations' of HR practices to meet their specific needs. Second, it suggests that different HR configurations may be used for different employee categories within the same organisation. As we will see below, commentators such as Snell (2005) argue that more costly 'best practice' approaches may be used for highly 'valued' categories (e.g. research and development personnel), while a more cost-control and 'minimalist' HR approach may be used among certain other categories (e.g. general operators).

The 'configurational' approach fits neatly with the RBV of the firm (Barney 1995), which argues that a properly developed HR system can create a unique and somewhat invisible asset to an organisation, making it difficult for competitors to imitate. Much of the recent work using the RBV has focused on developing *human capital*, specifically in identifying and developing *knowledge stocks* and *knowledge flows* (Conner and Prahalad 1996; Lepak and Snell 1999, 2002). *Knowledge stocks* are the codified knowledge that an organisation possesses, such as cumulative experience and contextual information, expert insights, intelligence on competitors, business and process knowledge etc. *Knowledge flows* incorporate the way knowledge grows, travels and is stored within organisations (from and to management, between staff, through planned interventions e.g. training, projects, directives and through common sources, e.g. data or knowledge bases). Recent HR research has sought to identify the means by which HR strategy and policy can guide the process by which organisations develop and deploy human, social, and organisational capital to enhance competitiveness (Lepak and Snell 1999, 2002; Snell 2005).

While acknowledging that the 'people are our most important asset' mantra is quite hollow in light of the historical evidence and that HR remains a low-priority activity in many firms, Snell (2005, 2) argues that the distinction between HR and competitive strategy has currently begun to blur:

> If the competitive potential of a firm rests in its intellectual activities, then what people know and how they behave become the *sine qua non* of strategic management. In other words, neither the formation nor implementation of strategies can be separated from how people are managed.

As a consequence, Snell (2005, 3) suggests that HR may act as a 'catalyst for strategic capability'. This means that HR is no longer something that comes after and needs to accommodate strategic planning but rather that:

> strategic planning is now increasingly viewed as resulting from the capabilities available through a firm's human resources. In this era of competitive potential, HR is perhaps becoming more important for propelling strategy than ever before. And we are seeing the first instances where heads of HR are being promoted to CEOs of companies.

However, he also cautions that assuming this new position poses particular and significant challenges for the HR community. First, he points to the *complexity of managing human assets*. In particular he argues that much of the work on developing 'best practice' HR interventions has tended to view an organisation's workforce as one large monolith to be addressed by generic HR practices rather than as comprising different groups and individuals for whom differing HR approaches may be appropriate(cf. Lepak and Snell 1999, 2002). This resonates with the 'configurational' perspective outlined above, and also with Boxall and Purcell's (2003) argument that different bundles of HR practices may be appropriate to different occupational categories.

Second, Snell (ibid., 3) argues that *HR strategy needs to extend beyond a focus on human capital* to incorporate consideration of other knowledge-based assets which are significant 'for organizational learning, innovation, and strategic capability' and that we need to explore their links with strategy.

Rather than assuming that one single HR system is appropriate for all of an organisation's workforce, Lepak and Snell (1999) advocate what they term an HR 'architecture', which demonstrates how an organisation's portfolio of human capital differs and suggests differing HR strategies and modes of employment contract for different employee categories. Initially, their architecture was based on the premise that a firm's human capital may be evaluated on two dimensions, namely its *strategic value* and its *uniqueness*. The 'strategic value' dimension is mainly grounded in the RBV, while the 'uniqueness' dimension is based on transaction cost economics. As the *strategic value* and *uniqueness* of human capital varies among different types of employees, so too, it is argued, should the types of HR systems and employment contracts deployed. Using the dimensions of human capital *strategic value* and *human capital uniqueness*, Lepak and Snell (1999) propose four HR configurations: commitment; collaboration; market-based; and compliance, see figure 3.9 and box 2.2.

Figure 3.9 Mapping human capital

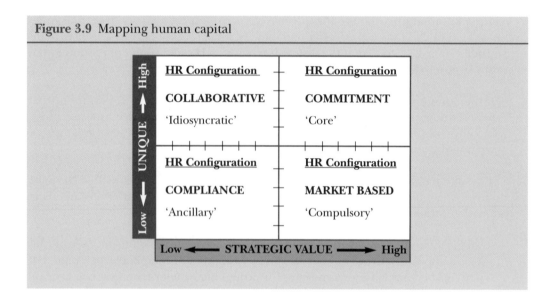

Box 2.2 Four HR configurations

Commitment (high uniqueness, high strategic value). This approach is deemed appropriate for 'core' employees who possess high levels of skills and knowledge and who are of high strategic value to their organisation. The HR mode proposed is a classic 'soft' HRM configuration (internal labour market/employee development/high commitment focus). The focus is on attracting and developing the 'best' and ensuring a positive work experience and reward structure to ensure they are committed and stay with the organisation.

Collaboration (high uniqueness, low strategic value). In contrast, one may also find employment ('idiosyncratic') categories or individuals who possess highly specialised skills and knowledge and skills that are critical to the organisation but that provide little value to the customer (e.g. information technology specialists). Here, Lepak and Snell (1999) advocate human capital 'alliances' and a variable range of HR systems. While we find a strong emphasis on recruitment and selection, the overall HR approach will depend on how difficult it is to find such people, and whether their input is required over the long or short term. Where the relationship is short term, there may be little or no scope for employee involvement, but where it is more long term there will likely be a much greater focus on their immersion into company culture and eliciting their commitment and involvement in decision making.

Market-based (low uniqueness, high strategic value). Here the argument is that where qualified ('compulsory') workers are available in the labour market it makes sense for management to recruit such people directly as opposed to incurring unnecessary expenditure in developing these resources internally. From an HR perspective, there is an emphasis on good selection but less focus on employee development, involvement and retention. Indeed, turnover among such categories may provide the organisation with the numerical flexibility in dealing with changes in the business environment.

Compliance (low uniqueness, low strategic value). This approach is deemed appropriate among ('ancillary') employment categories, which are necessary but who add little value to customers and who can be easily sourced from the external labour market. The organisation focus is on acquiring such workers at the lowest costs, and once recruited, to engage in minimal levels of HR investment. Thus, while basic recruitment and reward practices will be in place, there is little or no emphasis on employee involvement or development. The mode of employment relationship is one characterised by compliance. Workers are expected to follow clear rules and procedures and achieve pre-ordained standards.

Source: Lepak and Snell (1999)

This approach suggests that different types of employment contract may be used for different categories of workers and that HR investment should be directed at those categories most likely to create competitive advantage for the firm. More recent empirical investigation has shed further light on the utility of this HR architecture (see figure 3.10). Based on a study of 148 firms, Lepak and Snell (2002) found that each cell in the matrix differs in terms of employment modes, employment relationships and HR practices. Their approach employed two further dimensions, namely the nature of the employment contract (either predominantly 'relational' (soft) or 'transactional' (hard)), and the extent to which employees were 'internalised' into the organisation (secure employment, high levels of employee development) or 'externalised' (contract or casual employment, no employee development): see figure 3.10.

Figure 3.10 Detailed human capital (HC) architecture

This analysis suggests that categories with a high strategic value tend to be 'internalised' into the organisation (secure employment, high levels of employee development etc.) and tend to have commitment-based 'relational' connections to their firms. A similar pattern applies to many 'idiosyncratic' employee categories. In contrast, ancillary contract employee categories had transactional connections to their firm and were largely managed using a compliance-based HR system.

While a key proposition from this research is that different employees and employee categories possessing different portfolios of human capital tend to be managed in different ways, one should not 'pigeon-hole' particular jobs or skill portfolios. It all depends on how particular employees are viewed and used within the firm:

> No job or skill area is inherently associated with one cell in the matrix or another. In fact, a skill set such as sales, production, or engineering could show up in any one of the cells depending on how it is used strategically. This is a critical point for HR strategy: A particular type of human capital may be core for one firm, but ancillary for another. It all depends on how the firm competes.
>
> Snell (2005, 6)

A further area of investigation concerns how differing combinations of these four HR configurations impact on organisation performance. A study by Lepak *et al.* (2003) examined their impact on two measures of performance, namely 'return on equity' and 'market to book' (i.e. the market value of a firm divided by capital invested). The results indicated that organisations that used both core and contract workers had higher levels of performance than those that used only one or neither of these employment modes.

CONCLUSION

Strategic human resource management has proliferated in much of the current HR literature (Ferris *et al.* 1999), but, as Luoma (2000) notes, while it is often said that a company's HRM practices should fall in line with the strategy of the company, and while nobody denies the importance of such a connection, the deeper nature of this relationship remains comparatively unexplored. This is a complex area, built upon diverse literatures, beset by definitional disagreements and characterised by empirics derived from differing notions of what should be measured or, indeed, what is worth measuring. This chapter has attempted to explore core aspects of this literature and unearth some of the linkages between business strategy, HRM and firm performance. It will be evident to the reader that, conceptually and empirically, some difficulties remain. None the less, some significant progress has also been made in strategy-HRM-performance links and the signs are that this will remain a significant line of enquiry in the years ahead. In the Irish context there has been limited investigation of these issues, although recent work by researchers at Dublin City University and the National University of Ireland, Galway, goes some way towards providing important insights on the experience of strategic HRM in Ireland (Monks and McMackin 2001; Conway 2003, 2004; Conway and McMackin 1997; Heffernan 2004; Heffernan and Dundon 2004). For example, recent work by Conway (2003) and Heffernan (2004) address an important gap in this field, namely how employees experience HRM practice, and the impact of HRM practice on employee attitudes and commitment.

In evaluating current developments, we often run the danger of confusing prominent exemplars of 'soft' HRM with the widespread pervasiveness of such approaches. As we have seen, much of the evidence and support for strategic HRM emanates from the US.

However, the context of such developments in the US is considerably different from Ireland and it seems inappropriate simply to extrapolate from the US experience and infer similar trends here. Differences in cultural and political traditions, industrial and employment structure, employee relations institutions and practice are just some of the unique factors influencing approaches to HRM in the Republic of Ireland. As Gooderham *et al.* (2004, 17) suggest, 'clearly the practice of HRM cannot be divorced from its institutional context'.

Most of the remaining chapters in this text consider theory and practice in the main activity areas of HRM. However, the next chapter deals with a key contextual/institutional backdrop for HRM practice, namely the labour market.

4

Human Resource Management and the Labour Market

As we have seen from discussion in the first three chapters, the central issue for human resource management remains the development of policies and practices that allow for the most effective utilisation of the organisation's human capital – its employees. Successive studies have sought to identify key indicators of strategic practice in an effort to prescribe a set of core managerial principles upon which effective human resource management might be based (Lepak and Snell 2002; Way and Johnson 2001; Storey 1995; Guest 1989; Beer *et al.* 1984). However, we have also seen that HRM is contextually bound: that is, it is both influenced and constrained by its environment for business. One critical component of this environment concerns the labour market to which HR practices are directed.

Elliott (1990, 3) defines the labour market as the context within which the buyers and sellers of labour come together to determine the pricing and allocation of labour services. He further suggests that, of the many markets that exist in a modern economy, the market for labour is the most important one. It is from selling their services in this market that most families derive their income; it is also in this market that they spend the largest part of their waking hours. When not working, many individuals devote a large part of the remaining time to acquiring the skills necessary for effective performance in this market. The education and training individuals undertake during their lives is chiefly designed to equip them with skills that enhance their performance in the labour market. The link, then, between human resource management and the labour market is clearly demonstrated, particularly where HRM is concerned with managing this labour in the most effective means possible.

This chapter will examine the operation of HRM within the context of the labour market. Various theories of the labour market are examined and the link between labour market theories and human resource management is discussed. Rather than ascribing an ideal version of HRM, labour market theories serve to explain why individual organisations may vary the nature of their human resource policies in line with the prevailing economic climate in which they find themselves operating. Core features of labour market operations are then outlined and, finally, a summative account of the Irish labour market is presented.

THEORIES OF THE LABOUR MARKET AND HRM

The labour market comprises all the buyers and sellers of labour, the buyers being the employers and the sellers being the workers. It has long been recognised, however, that labour markets differ from other markets in the economic system. Marshall (1928) held that labour differed from other commodities because workers are inseparable from the services that they provide, that is, they carry their history, their culture and their social norms into their place of work. Similarly, Keynes (1936) recognised that the employment relationship differs from other contractual relationships because of its frequently long and indeterminable duration, which provides time for customs and norms, particularly those concerned with fairness, to build up around it. Marsden (1986) notes that several economists have attempted to develop economic theory in such a way as to take account of such influences. While accepting that pressures of supply and demand, of competition and of substitution are active in the labour market, they feel that customs, social norms, group pressures and institutional rules are also active in shaping wage structures, labour mobility patterns and other aspects of labour market behaviour.

In a broad sense, the behaviour of labour markets can perhaps be best understood by reflecting on the overlap between the three social sciences of labour economics, industrial relations and industrial sociology. Each of these different disciplines makes, to some extent, different predictions about human behaviour under similar circumstances, and stresses different causes for observed patterns of behaviour. Thus, while labour economics examines the behaviour of employers and employees in response to the general incentives of wages, prices, profits and non-pecuniary aspects of the employment relationship, such as working conditions, the greater part of industrial relations and industrial sociology deals with group activities, the internal dynamics of organisations, social norms and the processes of rule-making both within and outside the organisation. It is for this reason that there is no one single theory of the labour market, but rather a number of differentiated and often competing approaches. Three of the most prevalent perspectives will be examined here:

1. The competitive approach, relating to a market approach to demand and supply.
2. The institutional approach, referring to the critical role of institutions as the determinants of labour market operation.
3. The normative or radical approach, focusing on the traditional class struggle between owners of production and the workers.

We shall now have a look at each of these theories and identify how each might account for how HRM is enacted.

The Competitive Model of the Labour Market

In the standard competitive model of the labour market, derived from neo-classical economics, it is presumed that individuals are rational economic maximisers: that is, they make rational choices to maximise the economic benefit to themselves. It is assumed that individuals have a set of preferences and will organise their time and effort so that they will achieve the highest rate of return possible to themselves. In the context of employment, an individual will weigh up the marginal benefits of working as opposed to not working and thus will take into account factors such as wages, time, leisure and so forth when making the decision to work. In this manner the equilibrium wage and the associated level of employment are determined by the intersection of labour supply and labour demand. This intersection produces a market-clearing wage with the result that, at that wage, the quantity of labour willingly supplied exactly equals the quantity of labour willingly demanded.

Marsden (1986) and Beardwell and Holden (2001) identify a number of key assumptions that underpin this model of the labour market.

- The labour market is comprised of a large number of employers and employees each with their own set of preferences based on utility or wealth maximisation.
- All other forms of labour market organisation develop out of competitive conditions.
- There are no constraints on entry to the labour market, that is, that new organisations and new workers can enter the labour market at any time.
- Jobs in most organisations can be done by a fairly large number of workers provided they have the appropriate skills – in its most extreme form (homogenous labour) all jobs can be done by all workers.
- The organisation can be treated as a transmission mechanism between markets, that is, in-house training and work experience are of equal benefit to all firms and are thus transferable.
- The only cost to the organisation of hiring labour is the wage, thus there is no marginal gain in retaining existing workers rather than hiring new ones.
- There is perfect information. All workers and all organisations know the state of the market and are instantly aware of any changes in the market.
- Technology is the chief link in the derived demand for labour since it determines the skills that will be required from the labour market and the elasticities of substitution between different factors of production.

In the competitive model, adjustments to changes in product markets or production methods are made through the price mechanism: that is, as costs increase, the price of labour decreases. In this way both employers and employees are price takers – organisations will only employ as many individuals as is economically viable, bearing in mind the law of diminishing marginal returns. Workers will choose to work where the cost of not working (or leisure) outweighs the benefits of being employed. In such a scenario, unemployment does not exist since wages are flexibly adjusted in line with labour supply.

HRM from a Competitive Perspective

The competitive model assumes that, as organisations face increased competition in their product markets, they will continually seek new and better ways of reducing costs. Within this perspective, one can argue that the primary goal of HRM is cost minimisation and, particularly, the reduction of labour costs. Given the existence of wage rigidities implicit in the model, one would expect that organisations would seek to reduce such wage rigidities by implementing structures and systems that allow for the more flexible deployment of labour. There are two particular labour pools associated with the competitive model – the unskilled labour market and the skilled labour market.

Taking the unskilled labour market first, the model assumes that labour turnover is high and that the wage rate tends towards the market rate. Since there is a ready supply of unskilled labour available in the external labour market, it is relatively easy and cost-efficient to hire such employees. Furthermore, as these employees do not have specific job knowledge or training, it is assumed that they will only leave the organisation when higher wages are offered elsewhere. For this reason, organisations will accept high levels of labour turnover since it is relatively easy to replace such workers and the costs of replacement are lower than the costs of providing incentives to retain them. Within such a scenario, it is unlikely that companies would adopt a 'soft' HRM approach.

The competitive model also envisages a second labour pool of skilled workers. In this instance structured internal labour markets will exist since, as organisations contribute to the costs of training employees, they will have a vested interest in retaining them. In this situation, it is more cost-effective to develop structured, internal labour markets that typically provide employment security, progressive wage increases based on tenure and opportunities for internal promotion, rather than the costly alternative of recruiting and training.

The competitive model therefore suggests two possible scenarios that HRM might enact. The first scenario envisages a 'no frills' employment strategy, which offers low-skilled work, little if any training, and pays the market rate for labour. The second scenario suggests the development of structured internal labour markets for skilled employment, which may be linked to functional and financial flexibility. In both cases, the primary driver of HRM policies is cost minimisation.

The Institutional Model of the Labour Market

The debate over the validity of economic theories of the labour market has raged over the last number of years with many sceptics arguing that organisational and institutional factors and social norms have a greater influence on the behaviour of labour markets than pure labour market economics. Specifically, the tendency of employees to collectively represent themselves through the operation of trade unions has, in many organisations, led to a situation where the managerial prerogative to manage has been much diluted.

Perhaps the key variable that serves to differentiate the institutional model from the neo-classical model is that institutionalists do not concur that individuals behave independently of others. Rather, they perceive that individuals formulate choices and preferences with reference to perceived choices and preferences made by others. Similarly, organisations make choices based on the actions of their competitors and other organisations. In this way the notion of perceived equity and fairness enters into the equation. Moreover, organisations are to some degree constrained by the choices made by other organisations operating in a given product and service market. Beardwell and Holden (1997) further suggest that goals other than profit maximisation may be pursued, i.e. market share, organisational growth or a target rate of return on capital present within the organisation. Institutionalists place a considerable emphasis on the role of group norms, customs and collective power in shaping labour market conditions such as wage rigidities, structured internal labour markets and efficiency wages.

HRM from an Institutional Perspective

The institutional perspective focuses on the process by which the employment relationship is regulated and, in particular, highlights the role played by various interest groups in the development of employment strategies and policies. While the competitive model focuses particularly on cost reduction, the institutional model is more concerned with reducing inefficiencies in the utilisation of labour. Specifically, it suggests that the actors in the labour process play a significant role in determining labour efficiency and advocates the use of various HRM policies that seek to alter the nature of power within organisations. In practice, then, the institutional approach would perceive that the central role of HRM is to develop a unitarist perspective of the firm whereby policies are introduced that seek to co-opt employees into the managerial vision of the organisation. One might therefore expect some elements of 'soft' HRM to be in evidence (such as employee involvement, total quality management (TQM), single union agreements) in exchange for greater flexibility and productivity agreements. Two scenarios are possible within the institutional framework – the first might involve the co-opting of unions in order to secure agreement through participative decision-making, while the second scenario might result in greater individualising of the employment relationship as a means of marginalising trade union power and influence. In any event, the dominant ethos espoused by the institutional model is the modification of existing power structures, through changing existing norms and behaviour patterns, in order to reduce inefficiencies.

The Radical Model of the Labour Market

The radical approach is based on the traditional class struggle between workers and capital as reflected in the work of, among others, Marx and Engels. Within a social change paradigm, Marxism has been concerned with the conditions under which the working class could develop sufficient unity and consciousness to challenge and then replace capitalism. Here capitalism is essentially viewed in pejorative terms. Thompson (1983), for example, argues that the capitalist labour process is subject to a number of identifiable tendencies, whose critical features are deskilling, fragmentation of tasks, hierarchical organisation, the division between mental and manual work, and the struggle to establish the most effective means to control labour. Similarly, Braverman (1974) argues that deskilling is an inherent tendency of the capitalist labour process and that Taylorism, or scientific management, was an effort to relieve workers of their job autonomy and craft knowledge. Hence, the radical perspective envisages an inevitable conflict between workers and managers, as the owners of production, where the division of labour is perceived as a means of constraining workers' power while greater specialisation of tasks serves to subordinate the worker.

From this perspective, the workers' capacity to resist exploitation and alienation lies in the development of collective representation through trade union organisation. Resistance to specialisation and standardisation is not limited to the jobs that workers do but rather extends to forms of work organisation and work structuring that are seen to segment the workforce and workforce solidarity. Hence the adoption of elements of workforce flexibility that results in the creation of core and periphery labour markets is seen as a covert managerial technique to exploit labour further.

HRM from a Radical Perspective

The radical approach also focuses on organisational processes of regulating the employment relationship, but it differs from the institutional approach in that it presumes that all managerial activities are geared towards the creation of greater profits at the expense of the workers. In particular, HRM policies are viewed as deliberate means of exploiting labour and weakening the collective power of employees. Within this framework, the adoption of, for example, the core/periphery employment model, is seen to be a particular example of a divide and conquer policy, where management co-opt a select number of core workers (who receive all the attendant benefits of security, training promotions, incentives), at the expense of the majority, for whom flexibility results in increased work intensification, greater direct control, diminished employment security and possibly lower pay.

The radical perspective views all policies and strategies that seek to individualise the employment relationship as further evidence of management's covert objective to reduce collective resistance. Within such an organisation, the purpose of HRM, from the radical perspective, is not the reduction of costs or inefficiencies, but rather the exploitation of labour through the extension of managerial control over the employment relationship.

We have seen that it is possible to ascribe a set of HR practices associated with each labour market perspective. However, it is recognised that perspectives, by their very nature, offer but a partial or uni-dimensional view of their subject matter – the reality of labour market functioning is altogether more complex than any of these perspectives might suggest. To this end, the next section explores some of the core idiosyncrasies of labour markets today.

KEY LABOUR MARKET CHARACTERISTICS

Outside of pure prescriptions or theories of labour market functioning exist a number of core realities or features of labour markets that shape the way they operate in practice, and subsequently influence or constrain the range of choices available to those engaging and managing human resources.

Unemployment

A notable feature of most labour markets is some element of unemployment and, contrary to the presumptions of the competitive model, not all of those who are seeking employment can find it. Labour is not homogenous – rather it is highly differentiated – and so it is a remarkable peculiarity of labour markets that unemployment can exist alongside wage inflation and job vacancies.

Wage Rigidities

One of the key presumptions underpinning competitive models of labour markets is that wages can be flexibly adjusted in line with demand for labour, that is, that organisations can reduce wages as their demand for labour falls. In fact, wages are more likely to move upwards more readily than they move downwards, and this downward wage rigidity is often offered as a critical explanation for the nature and extent of high levels of unemployment. More often, organisations resort to recruitment freezes (see for example the cutback in recruitment in the public sector in Ireland in the early 1990s), reductions in overtime, and ultimately lay-offs or redundancy as short-term reactions to decreased demand for labour. Wage levels are also externally influenced by social partnership agreements, Joint Industrial Councils, Government interventions and so forth.

Occupational Segregation

Mainstream neo-classical theory usually starts from the presumption of an otherwise homogenous market divided up only by the technical limitations on the substitutability of different skills and abilities, and possibly by the constraints imposed by the need to certify the quality of skills. Here, the labour market is structured into sub-markets by restrictions on the substitutability between different kinds of labour. While competition between workers in different sub-markets may be very limited, each sub-market itself remains a zone of competition, in which normal market relationships apply. Institutional writers have argued that institutional rules, such as demarcation and apprenticeship rules, arising out of collective bargaining and company recruitment practices, can also play a major role in defining the limits of sub-markets.

Two discrete types of labour market can be said to exist – labour markets for unskilled or casual labour, and occupational labour markets involving transferable skills. In other words, in the context of rational choice, individual workers seeking to maximise their net advantages will focus on searching for information about advantages in other firms and on obtaining access to different occupational labour markets through investment in education and training (typically associated with generic and transferable skills).

Internal Labour Markets

Doeringer and Piore (1971) define internal labour markets (ILMs) as internal administrative units within which the pricing and allocation of labour are governed by a set of administrative rules and procedures. Both human capital theory (Becker 1964) and transaction cost theory (Nordhaug 1994; Rao 2002; Williamson and Masten 1999) offer a useful distinction between what are termed specific (idiosyncratic) or non-transferable knowledge and skills, for which there is no market outside of the employing firm, and general, non-specific knowledge and skills that can be applied in any organisational context. Nordhaug (2004) notes that whereas general skills and knowledge can be sold in external labour markets, firm specific competencies are valuable to one firm only. From an organisational perspective, investment in general (transferable) skills is a rather more risky venture since these skills are valuable to most organisations and so the potential loss of their investment through labour turnover is high (employees with transferable skills are highly employable and can easily move from one firm to another).

Investment in specific skills might well be the preferred option for organisations since these skills are not readily transferable and it can facilitate the development of highly valuable firm-specific human capital (*see* chapter 10 for further discussion of this concept). However, specific skills investment can reduce employee mobility which may neither be in the interests of the national economy nor of the individual employee – individual workers are more likely to be interested in the acquisition of more general skills that will improve their employability.

The development of structured internal labour markets can thus be seen as one means of managing these competing interests. Here a system of job hierarchies is designed that provides mobility chains or career progression up through the organisation hierarchy. Formal patterns of progression between jobs are regulated through rules and customs and provide a sense of stability within organisations. Labour mechanisms working within internal labour markets are governed by administrative rules, rather than open market competition, and adjustments within these markets are typically through management-driven techniques such as job evaluation, job design, wage and salary administration and so forth. Here, the use of human resource policies can have the cumulative effect of building barriers to labour mobility since accumulated rights are inextricably linked with tenure.

Structured internal labour markets can be a useful mechanism of managing the costs of investment in firm specific skills or 'human capital'. ILMs are seen to determine wage and employment structures different from, but within the constraints set by, competitive market forces. Williamson (1978) argues that ILMs are developed less to reduce the costs of investing in training, but rather that the offer of more stable employment and of internal labour market conditions creates a situation in which it is in the workers' own self-interest to promote the longer-term prosperity of the firm and hence to adopt a co-operative attitude. Nordhaug (2004) similarly posits that both the organisation and the employee with specific knowledge and skills will be interested in an extended contractual relationship that is seen to be of mutual benefit.

Flexibility and Alternative Forms of Engagement

The notion of labour market flexibility within organisations emerged as a key debate in the HRM literature sometime during the mid-1980s. Set against the backdrop of global recession, many of the arguments for labour market flexibility called for structural changes to both the design of organisations and work to overcome 'institutional rigidities' (Boyer

1988); to offset competitive pressures and low productivity (Sparrow and Hiltrop 1994); or to manage the shift towards service sector employment (Morley 1994). The basic premise underpinning these arguments was that organisations could pursue two opposing strategies of labour market utilisation or engagement, either relying heavily on the external labour market and low levels of employee involvement, or favouring internal mobility and the development of multiple skills among existing employees.

To date, the flexibility debate has focused on the contribution that various employment strategies might make, both to organisational adaptability and performance and increased opportunities for employees (Brewster *et al.* 1993; Marginson 1991; Berg 1989; Gunnigle and Daly 1992). These adaptability and performance improvements and increased employee opportunities are seen to be brought about through the development of numerical, pay/cost and functional flexibility (Atkinson 1984; Curson 1986; Pollert 1988 and 1991; Green *et al.* 1993).

The flexible firm model as originally advanced by Atkinson (see figure 4.1) involves a reorganisation of firms' internal labour markets and their division into separate components, in which the worker's experience and the employer's expectations of him/her are increasingly differentiated (Atkinson and Meager 1986). This hierarchical restructuring allows radically different employment policies to be pursued for different groups of workers. Within this framework, the 'core' is composed of full-time staff, enjoying relatively secure challenging jobs with good pay and employment conditions. Two sets of 'periphery' workers can be created: the first set is highly skilled, often technical or professional employees who are contracted into the organisation on fixed-term contracts and who enjoy relatively good conditions of employment. The second 'periphery' is composed of an

Figure 4.1 The flexible firm

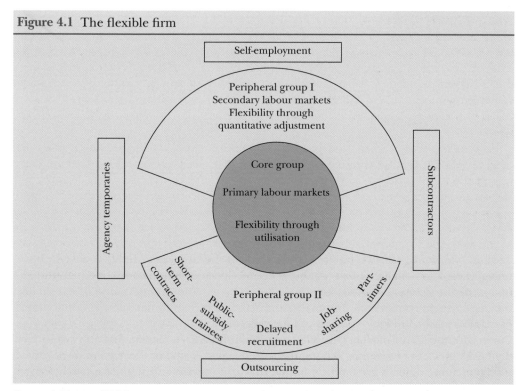

Source: Atkinson (1984).

amalgam of temporary, part-time and contract groups with less favourable pay and employment conditions and less job security or training and promotion opportunities.

The flexible firm scenario suggests an attempt by organisations to increase flexibility in three key areas.

1. *Numerical flexibility*, incorporating the use of non-standard employment forms, which allows the organisation to hire and/or shed labour flexibly in line with business demands.
2. *Financial/pay flexibility* whereby pay rates are linked to labour and product market conditions and pay increases for individual employees are variable and contingent upon performance.
3. *Functional flexibility*, incorporating multi-skilling, which is defined as the expansion of skills within a workforce or the ability of organisations to reorganise the competencies associated with jobs so that the job holder is willing and able to deploy such competencies across a broader range of skills.

Despite concerns regarding the utility of the flexible firm model, the debate concerning labour market segmentation and alternative forms of engagement continues. Drawing on the theoretical frameworks of transaction cost economics (Klein *et al.* 1978), human capital theory (Becker 1964; Flamholtz and Lacey 1981), and the resource-based view of the firm (Barney 1991; Prahalad and Hamel 1990), Lepak and Snell (1999, 2002) have developed a human resource architecture that depicts four particular modes of employee engagement: internal development, acquisition, contracting and alliance (see figure 4.2).

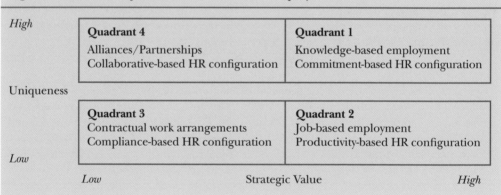

Figure 4.2 Human capital Characteristics and Employment Modes

High		
	Quadrant 4 Alliances/Partnerships Collaborative-based HR configuration	**Quadrant 1** Knowledge-based employment Commitment-based HR configuration
Uniqueness		
	Quadrant 3 Contractual work arrangements Compliance-based HR configuration	**Quadrant 2** Job-based employment Productivity-based HR configuration
Low		
	Low Strategic Value High	

Source: Lepak and Snell 2002

This architecture (adapted by them from their earlier model in 1999) is based on the recognition that not all employees possess knowledge and skills that are of equal strategic importance and so organisations make decisions on whether to internalise or externalise the employment relationship. Internalisation refers to the continual internal development of employees who are felt to possess unique skills and capabilities that are highly valued by the organisation and not readily available from outside it. Externalisation refers to a deliberate strategy of sourcing skills and competencies outside of the organisation – these skills and competencies are neither unique nor firm-specific and so they are rather more readily available in the external labour market. Snell *et al.* (1996, 65) note that:

If the types and levels of skills are not equally distributed, such that some firms can acquire the talent they need and others cannot, then (*ceteris paribus*) that form of human capital can be a source of sustained competitive advantage.

Lepak and Snell (1999) suggest that a strong internalisation focus might be reflected in jobs that are rather loosely defined to allow for change, in extensive training opportunities including career development and mentoring arrangements, skills-based payment systems and developmental performance appraisal systems. Indeed this combination of HR practices is similar to those depicted in the high-performance work systems literature (Huselid 1995; Lawler *et al.* 1995).

More generally, the extant literature on alternative forms of engagement depicts a number of specific scenarios. It is argued that competitive pressures are increasingly forcing organisations to increase their capacity to employ or shed labour more rapidly in order to achieve a better fit between workforce size and fluctuations in the demand for goods and services (Marginson 1991; Berg 1989; Boyer 1988). Consequently, non-standard employment in the form of temporary and casual workers, fixed-term contracts, home working and subcontracting is seen to follow (Brewster *et al.* 1993; Hegewisch and Bruegel 1992; McGregor and Sproull 1992; Blackwell 1990; Meulders and Tytgat 1989; Lane 1988). Functional flexibility concerned with the relaxing of demarcation lines and the adoption of broader job descriptions (Hunter and McInnes 1992; Blyton and Morris 1991) is also seen as a mechanism for achieving greater organisational adaptability. Finally, while some research does suggest that flexibility is on the increase, this may simply be occurring in reaction to depressed labour and product market conditions, rather than as a systematically planned emergence of the totally flexible firm. However, such apparently expedient responses to environmental conditions may well be sustained when the environment changes, as organisations become more anxious to retain the advantages of certain flexibility forms (Hakim 1991).

Criticisms of the flexibility scenario are widespread. Pollert (1991) cautioned that prophesies of a 'new' or 'radical break' in the nature and the 'future' of work have driven the whole flexibility debate into a 'post-industrial futurology', one in which new types of work, and new employment relations are being heralded as the novel and indeed path-breaking developments of the new era. Indeed, despite some evidence of growing reliance on non-standard workers, it is not at all clear that employers are deliberately moving into flexible employment practices for the long-term strategic reasons that Atkinson identified.

This debate on alternative forms of engagement has found new resonance in recent research agendas dedicated to promoting work/life balance and reducing work/family conflict. The issue of balancing work and non-work aspects of life is one that is receiving increasing attention across most industrialised economies today, and is fast defining the labour market scene (Hyman and Summers 2004). It is included here in our review of labour market functioning since it has considerable implications for the nature of the employment relationship. Subsumed under the various headings of work/life balance, work/family conflict, flexibility in work arrangements, family-friendly work practices, the debate on how to achieve balance between work and out of work commitments has escalated in the past years or more, both at national policy level and at the level of the organisation (Morley 2004; Hyman and Summers, 2004; Poelmans *et al.* 2003; Guest 2003). For example, in the EU context, Morley (2004) notes that policy initiatives aimed at national governments and ultimately at employers designed to support and encourage the reconciliation of work and family demands have emerged as a key plank of the Union's equal opportunities remit. Under Equal Opportunities guidelines, member states and the social partners have been required to implement and promote a range of family-friendly work initiatives. At the level of the organisation, Harker (1996) notes that family-friendly policies are designed to fulfill several interlinked objectives, including enabling people to fulfill work and family demands, promoting gender equality and the sharing of responsibilities, and balancing the needs of employees and their employers. However, as Hardy and Adnett (2002, 164) note, the slow growth of family-friendly practices suggests that there are market failures in their provision and implementation.

Elloy and Smith (2003) suggest that families operate as social systems with an inter-relationship between work and non-work roles so that tensions in one are inevitably transferred to the other. Radical changes in work have significant repercussions on the family, and indeed the community, with an increasingly knowledge-based and flexible labour market making greater demands on families (Carnoy 1999). Jacobs and Gerson (2001) note that debates on the growth of work-family conflict increasingly tend to centre on employed parents and dual-career couples. However, as their research suggests, the shift from the sole male breadwinner to dual-income couples, along with single parent households, has created a substantial and growing concern to balance the demands of work and family. Regardless of differences in family structure, there is a common wish on the part of the working population at all levels to reduce the separation between family and work and to find the possibility of achieving a better balance between working life, family obligations, leisure and socialising (Papalexandris and Kramar 1997, 582). As a consequence, the concept of the family-friendly workplace, defined as 'one which recognizes the non-workplace family responsibilities of its employees and develops and implements policies that allow employees to simultaneously fulfill work and family responsibilities' (Strachan and Burgess 1998, 251) has received increasing attention.

Guest (2001) identifies a set of factors that have brought the issue of work/life balance into sharp relief and these are summarily presented here:

1. The perceived intensification of work in recent years – including pace of change, demands for timely responses and demand for constant availability.
2. A growing concern that the quality of home and community life is deriorating – quality time being eroded by longer hours at work, exhaustion, increased shift and weekend work and exacerbated by increased female employment.
3. Changing attitudes and values of workers – the new generation of worker whose psychological contract does not extend to include unlimited commitment to the organisation, and who is interested in life outside of work.

Poelmans and Sahibzada (2004) caution of the necessity to develop a thorough under-standing of the context in which work/family policies and culture are embedded, noting that at each step of the decision-making process, the human resource manager is confronted with reaching a decision regarding work/family policies and culture that not only meets the needs of the organisation, but the individual employee as well. An Employment in Europe (2003) survey, in a commentary on flexibility, security and quality in work, called for:

> . . . the availability of attractive work, offering suitable working time arrangements, possibilities to reconcile work and family life, and opportunities for skills upgrading and career advancement. In addition to financial incentives, career advancement and

other quality elements, working time flexibility and job security are for many people key inducements to take up work and to stay in the labour market.

In Ireland, the current proportion of part-time work is 12.3 per cent, indicating that part-time working is still less prevalent here than in many other EU member states. In 1996, for example, almost 70 per cent of women workers in the Netherlands, and 45 per cent of those in the UK, were working part-time. However, since 1993, the unprecedented growth in the Irish economy has resulted in the creation of mainly full-time jobs. This about-turn may be as a result of the expansion of manufacturing employment and the current 'boom' being experienced in the building and construction industry. Overall, the increased propensity towards part-time employment may be indicative of increased flexibility in the Irish labour market. However, it remains exceptionally low by EU standards and there remains continued scope for an upward trend to continue. Temporary work, as a proportion of overall employment, currently stands at just 7 per cent.

PROFILE OF THE IRISH LABOUR MARKET

An editorial in *The Economist* in May 1997 suggested that foreign companies cite a number of specific attractions for choosing Ireland as a European base. These include the combination of having English as the spoken language, a recognised pro-European outlook, and a well-educated workforce, particularly at the upper end. Over the past decade the Irish workforce has become increasingly better educated and a higher proportion of young people are remaining in further education and training. Arguably, these and related labour market characteristics have significant explanatory power in accounting for the recent and sustained success of Irish economy; some of these are examined in detail here.

Population

In 2005, Ireland's population crossed the 4 million threshold, which is its highest level since the census of 1871 when a figure of 3.8 million was recorded (though still significantly down from its original pre-famine (1841) level of 6.5 million).

Table 4.1 Average annual births, deaths, natural increases and estimated net migration for each intercensal period 1926–2002 (000s)

Period	Total births	Total deaths	Natural increase	Change in population	Estimated net migration
1926–36	58	42	16	0	–17
1936–46	60	43	17	–1	–19
1946–51	66	40	26	1	–24
1951–56	63	34	27	–12	–39
1956–61	61	33	26	–16	–42
1961–66	63	33	29	13	–16
1966–71	63	33	30	19	–11
1971–79	69	33	35	49	14
1979–81	73	33	40	38	–3
1981–86	67	33	34	19	–14
1986–91	56	32	24	-3	–27
1991–96	50	31	18	20	2
1996–2002	54	31	23	49	26

Source: CSO 2004b

Growth in the Irish population is attributable both to natural increases (more births than deaths) and to net migration in more recent years (inward as opposed to outward migration). A number of specific features are worth highlighting here. Census figures show that the population aged 15–64 has increased year on year over the past thirty years from 1,626,000 in 1961 to 2,590,000 in 2002 (CSO 2004a). Highest recorded growth rates occurred between 1991 and 2001, and this is attributed both to the 'maturation' of the baby boomers of the 1970s and early 1980s, and the fact that there were fewer people retiring from the labour force overall (many of this age cohort had emigrated from Ireland in the depression of the 1940s).

Since the mid-1990s the average annual birth rate has increased substantially from a low of 48,000 in 1994 to 61,500 in 2003. Although Ireland continues to have a higher birth rate than most other EU countries (1.99 as opposed to 1.6) it is not expected to continue to rise into the future.

Ireland has a relatively young population; the most populous age group remains 24–44. This suggests that the proportion of the population that comprises the labour force (aged 16–65) will continue to expand in the medium term as those currently of school-going age enter the labour market and the average age of the population is increasing. However, the Irish population is starting to age and, if the Irish birth rate continues to decline overall (as it is expected to), there will be an appreciable impact on the dependency ratio (the proportion of the population who are economically dependent on the labour force). For example, the older population (aged 65+) is expected to increase (CSO 2004b) very dramatically from a figure of 430,000 in 2001 to more than 1.1 million by 2036. In 2001, the young population (under 14) was almost double the old population – it is predicted that will be completely reversed by 2036 (750,000 young people compared with 1.1 million aged 65 and over). This is unlikely to have any impact in the short term but, as the average age of the working-age population moves closer to the 60s, and with net migration inflows diversifying the characteristics of the active labour market, then this will have significant implications for human resource policies, particularly in terms of succession planning, training and retraining, rewards and so forth. Indeed, there appears to be growing discussion, particularly at national policy level, with respect to pushing out the retirement age from 65 to 70 – this again will likely impact HR policy development in terms of engagement and knowledge development.

Migration
Migration, understood as the difference between emigration from and immigration to Ireland, and the performance of Ireland's labour market are inextricably linked; this relationship has been particularly evident in recent years. Net outward migration has traditionally constituted an integral feature of the Irish labour market. More than 1.2 million people have left Ireland since the foundation of the state in 1921. While the 1970s witnessed a periodical reversal of this trend, net emigration resumed through the 1980s, rising from 9,000 in 1984 to 46,000 in 1989. However, this situation has reversed since then, leading Cross and Turner (2005) to suggest that the dramatic economic growth and expansion of employment in the late 1990s has changed Ireland from a country of emigration to one of net immigration.

Migration flows can be grouped into three key periods. The first period spans 1986–90 when approximately 160,000 more people left the country than entered it. Net outflows peaked at 40,000 per annum in 1988 and 1989. The second period was 1991–5, when 1,600 more people entered Ireland than left it. Recession in the world economy, particularly in the US and the UK, stemmed the outflow in the early 1990s, and the commencement of the upswing in the Irish economic environment reduced the numbers migrating abroad. The final period represents the years since 1996, which have witnessed historically large net inward migration. Net inflows averaged about 20,000 per annum until 1999 and increased substantially thereafter. Immigration reached a high of 41,000 in 2002 before declining to close to 32,000 in 2004 (CSO, 2004b). Analysis of migration flows in recent years suggests that a considerable proportion of this initial net migration comprised Irish citizens who emigrated some years earlier, and workers from the UK. For example, during the period 1996–2000, 100,000 Irish persons returned to Ireland (accounting for close to half of all immigrants), while UK nationals accounted for nearly one fifth of inflows. The greatest proportion of more recent immigration is comprised of both EU (non-UK) and non-EU citizens. Cross and Turner (2005) note that non-Irish nationals represented 5.8 per cent of the Irish population in the 2002 census (CSO 2004a). Back in 1998, Sweeney (1998) suggested that many of those seeking work in Ireland may also be seeking that 'quality of life' which has often been cited as compensation for lower living standards. He indicates that this ephemeral 'quality of life' – meaning the good social life, proximity to countryside and local amenities – is often given as the reason for staying in a country that traditionally offered few opportunities for well-qualified people to change jobs. However, it is increasingly apparent that many of those who come to Ireland today are economic migrants seeking better work opportunities and asylum seekers/refugees seeking a fresh start.

Recent CSO (2004) estimates predict an average annual net inflow of 22,500 people until 2036 – this would be consistent with the Irish economy and the labour market continuing to perform strongly into the longer term. Even with modest performance, i.e. in line with average EU growth rates, it is predicted that Ireland will need an average annual net inflow of 11,000 over the period.

The Irish Labour Force

While aggregate changes in the Irish labour force over the past fifteen years have at times been erratic, the overall trend has been upward. There was an average annual gain of 43,500 in the labour force between 1991 and 2004. If migration remains high, it is predicted that the Irish labour force will grow by approximately 38,000 people each year until 2036.

Overall labour force participation rates have continued to improve in recent years and in 2004 stood at 60 per cent. Most of the increases in the labour force in the 1990s have been attributed to increased 'domestic labour' supply, supplemented by net immigration. Since 2000, increased participation levels are accounted for principally by immigration: between 1999 and 2004, 25 per cent of the growth in the labour force was accounted for by immigrant, non-national workers. Female participation rates continue to grow (though marginally), and overall female labour force participation has risen from 34.1 per cent of the 15–64 age cohort in 1992 to 49.4 per cent in 2004. Female labour force participation has been more rapid than male labour force growth over the last number of years, although these growth rates have started to converge more recently. Male participation rates exceed EU rates and have increased relatively little for most age groups over the last number of years. In 1989, the male participation rate was 69.4 per cent, while in 2005 it was 70.9 per cent. Analysis by FÁS (2000, 2005) suggests that the overall relatively small increase reflects the fact that participation rates of males in the 30–44 age cohort have been in excess of 90 per cent for the last number of years. There has been and remains little

Table 4.2 Persons aged 15 years and over classified by sex and principal economic status (000s)

Sex and economic status	1999	2000	2001	2002	2003	2004	2005
Males							
At work	917.8	960.3	991.5	999.8	1,008.2	1,038.5	1,080.6
Unemployed	89.8	75.0	67.6	80.4	80.5	81.1	77.1
Student	173.0	171.8	172.2	177.5	182.6	179.0	176.8
On home duties	9.2	8.7	5.4	5.9	5.3	4.5	5.1
Retired	185.5	187.8	195.6	196.8	202.4	206.9	208.7
Other	56.7	54.2	55.9	61.7	70.7	68.7	72.5
Total	**1,431.9**	**1,457.8**	**1,488.2**	**1,522.1**	**1,549.8**	**1,578.7**	**1,620.9**
Females							
At work	595.8	629.7	662.1	696.7	709.8	731.9	776.8
Unemployed	35.1	34.3	31.6	34.3	33.1	31.6	32.5
Student	186.2	194.1	195.9	195.2	199.0	198.4	193.6
On home duties	570.5	558.1	551.9	546.9	555.2	551.9	539.4
Retired	61.4	60.8	61.1	64.4	65.0	70.3	72.2
Other	30.2	26.7	28.8	30.1	33.2	37.9	42.1
Total	**1,479.2**	**1,503.7**	**1,531.5**	**1,567.7**	**1,595.3**	**1,621.9**	**1,656.6**
All persons							
At work	1,513.6	1,590.0	1,653.5	1,696.5	1,718.0	1,770.4	1857.4
Unemployed	124.8	109.3	99.2	114.7	113.6	112.6	109.7
Student	359.2	365.9	368.1	372.7	381.6	377.4	370.4
On home duties	579.7	566.8	557.4	552.8	560.5	556.4	544.6
Retired	246.9	248.6	256.7	261.2	267.4	277.2	280.9
Other	86.9	80.9	84.8	91.9	103.9	106.6	114.6
Total	**2,911.1**	**2,961.5**	**3,019.7**	**3,089.8**	**3,145.1**	**3,200.6**	**3,277.4**

Source: CSO

scope for participation to increase further for these particular groups. Efforts to improve overall participation rates continues, however. Speculation on the causes of the overall increased female participation has focused on factors such as smaller family size, changing structure of employment demand, institutional factors and improvements in educational attainment. FÁS (1998) notes the emergence of changes in the occupational pattern of women's jobs in Ireland, where within the professional occupations, for example, women's share has increased most rapidly in the business professions and (from a much smaller base) in engineering and science. Their share has also risen, but more slowly, in education and has declined sharply among religious professionals. However, while female participation continues to increase in Ireland, recent labour market analysis by FÁS (2004) suggests that there remains some scope for increased participation in the labour force by females, particularly women aged forty and over. Participation rates among the age group 40–59 are considerably lower than the average EU rate. The EU has set a target to achieve a 70 per cent employment rate over the next few years and seeks to improve female participation rates overall. This will inevitably feed into the work/life balance debate.

Employment and Occupational Trends

Overall employment growth has slowed down during the past couple of years, though, at 2.4 per cent in 2004, it is still strong by European standards. However, it is less impressive than the heady heights attained towards the close of the 1990s. Between 1995 and 2005 employment grew by over 50 per cent and, at the end of October 2005, the standardised unemployment rate in Ireland was 4.4 per cent. Employment growth has been spread across most sectors of the Irish economy, though the figures in table 4.3 affirm the continuing trend of significant services sector growth in the years 1998–2005.

Table 4.3 Employment and unemployment (ILO) (000s)

Economic Sector (NACE Rev.1)	March –May 1998	March –May 1999	March –May 2000	March –May 2001	March –May 2002	March –May 2003	March –May 2004	March –May 2005
Agriculture, Forestry & Fishing	136.0	137.3	132.9	122.5	124.0	116.6	117.0	113.7
Other Production Industries	302.4	307.7	309.5	318.1	305.0	306.1	300.6	294.2
Construction	126.1	142.1	166.2	180.0	182.2	191.4	206.0	242.2
Wholesale & Retail Trade	211.1	222.5	235.2	247.8	246.8	251.6	260.2	266.9
Hotels and Restaurants	97.8	102.0	108.1	103.8	104.2	114.4	107.8	111.0
Transport, Storage & Communication	87.0	96.2	101.3	111.1	111.7	112.1	113.2	118.2
Financial & Other Business Services	171.1	194.6	210.8	217.1	228.9	227.1	237.0	257.1
Public Administration & Defence	70.9	74.5	78.4	81.3	90.6	92.4	89.5	98.2
Education	93.3	100.6	102.8	103.8	111.3	116.1	117.9	123.1
Health	113.9	120.3	133.0	144.0	159.3	169.9	177.0	188.0
Other Services	84.5	91.4	93.3	92.4	99.8	95.7	110.0	116.4
Total in Employment	**1,494.0**	**1,589.1**	**1,671.4**	**1,721.9**	**1,763.9**	**1,793.4**	**1,836.2**	**1,929.2**
Total Unemployed	126.4	96.9	74.5	65.1	77.0	82.1	84.2	85.6
Total Labour Force	**1,620.4**	**1,685.9**	**1,745.9**	**1,787.0**	**1,840.9**	**1,875.5**	**1,920.3**	**2,014.8**
Not in Labour Force	1,246.8	1,225.1	1,215.6	1,232.6	1,248.9	1,269.6	1,280.3	1,262.6
Population 15 Years & Over	2,867.3	2,911.1	2,961.5	3,019.7	3,089.8	3,145.1	3,200.6	3,277.4

Source: CSO

Employment trends are inexorably linked with the occupational structure of the labour market which tends to be associated with technological developments, product market variations, sectoral composition, and the general nature of employment practices (in terms of work structuring, composition of employment, flexibility and so forth). In 1997 a report on occupational employment forecasts to 2003 was completed jointly by FÁS and the ESRI (Duggan *et al.* 1997). This was in an effort to determine the changing pattern of occupational segregation in the Irish labour market and to identify possible variations in skill requirements across fourteen broadly identified occupational classifications. Over the period 1997–2003 they predicted significant changes in broad occupational groupings, which would have an appreciable impact on the distribution of overall employment. Their data predicted that agricultural employment would continue to fall over the intervening years to 2003 and that the largest increases in employment would occur in managerial and professional occupations (categorised in the report as those workers who hold degree-level qualifications). Strong growth was also forecast for associate professions (diploma/sub-degree qualification level), for sales and personal services-type employment, and for clerical work. Projected growth was also featured for skilled manual workers (both those involved in maintenance and those in core production). The forecasts indicated, however, that jobs that do not require prior specialised qualifications, and that rely more on on-the-job training, or are unskilled, are less likely to experience the same level of growth as those occupations that are qualification based and driven.

Recent survey data affirm this trend of growth in professional, managerial and skilled occupation categories (see tables 4.4 and 4.5).

Table 4.4 Main categories of employment

	1973	1978	1983	1988	1993	1998	2003
Agriculture	255,000	226,000	189,000	170,600	149,700	136,000	116,000
Industry	335,000	350,000	331,000	310,200	324,300	428,400	497,500
Services	477,000	534,000	604,000	629,800	709,200	929,600	1,179,300
Total	**1,067,000**	**1,110,000**	**1,124,000**	**1,110,700**	**1,183,100**	**1,494,000**	**1,793,400**

Source: CSO (2004)

Table 4.5 Persons in employment (ILO) classified by sex and occupation

Broad occupational group	March –May 2001	March –May 2002	March –May 2003	March –May 2004	March –May 2005
Males					
1. Managers and administrators	222.7	227.1	224.3	227.1	218.6
2. Professional	96.0	99.3	107.5	108.4	112.5
3. Associate professional and technical	66.6	65.2	70.2	72.3	70.9
4. Clerical and secretarial	51.7	54.1	51.0	53.1	58.7
5. Craft and related	219.2	213.4	228.4	231.3	260.1
6. Personal and protective service	68.2	72.1	73.7	72.8	73.4
7. Sales	55.3	54.6	54.6	59.0	63.0
8. Plant and machine operatives	147.2	144.5	138.0	130.3	138.0
9. Other	92.3	97.4	93.3	111.0	114.9
Total males	**1,019.0**	**1,027.7**	**1,040.9**	**1,065.2**	**1,110.1**
Females					
1. Managers and administrators	87.0	86.9	92.6	92.1	98.1
2. Professional	77.2	90.2	93.3	103.0	106.1
3. Associate professional and technical	81.6	90.4	94.7	94.8	100.5
4. Clerical and secretarial	160.7	170.6	165.9	167.6	177.7
5. Craft and related	14.3	12.0	13.6	12.4	11.7
6. Personal and protective service	96.5	96.5	109.9	112.6	125.0
7. Sales	86.1	89.7	91.6	93.3	101.4
8. Plant and machine operatives	45.7	40.3	35.7	29.1	29.7
9. Other	53.7	59.5	55.0	66.1	68.9
Total females	**702.8**	**736.1**	**752.5**	**771.0**	**819.1**

Table 4.5 Persons in employment (ILO) classified by sex and occupation *(contd.)*

Broad occupational group	March –May 2001	March –May 2002	March –May 2003	March –May 2004	March –May 2005
All persons					
1. Managers and administrators	309.7	314.1	316.9	319.2	316.7
2. Professional	173.2	189.5	200.8	211.4	218.6
3. Associate professional and technical	148.2	155.6	164.9	167.1	171.5
4. Clerical and secretarial	212.4	224.7	216.9	220.7	236.3
5. Craft and related	233.5	225.4	242.1	243.6	271.9
6. Personal and protective service	164.6	168.6	183.6	185.4	198.4
7. Sales	141.4	144.3	146.2	152.3	164.4
8. Plant and machine operatives	192.9	184.8	173.7	159.4	167.7
9. Other	146.1	156.9	148.3	177.0	183.7
Total persons	**1,721.9**	**1,763.9**	**1,793.4**	**1,836.2**	**1,929.2**

Source: CSO/Quarterly National Householder Surveys

There is evidence to suggest that female participation in employment is extending out from the traditional occupations of clerical work and health associated professions and into more business and commercial professions where they have been, and continue to remain, under-represented. Sexton *et al.* (2001) predicted that female employment will continue to rise over the next number of years by as much as 35 per cent, which represents a rate of expansion more than double that forecast for men.

Participation in Education

The Irish education system has undergone significant change in the past thirty years due, in no small part, to the strongly interventionist role adopted by the Irish state in pursuit of economic development from the early 1960s onwards. In recognition of the fundamental value of a good education system to the economic and social development of a nation, free second-level education was introduced in 1966, and compulsory schooling was extended from fourteen to fifteen years of age.

Following the publication of the White Paper on Education (1995), which echoed a persistent concern regarding the general suitability of the Leaving Certificate cycle for all students, a decision was taken to restructure the Leaving Certificate programme into three components: the established Leaving Certificate programme; the Leaving Certificate Applied Programme; and the Leaving Certificate Vocations Programme. However, the majority of senior cycle students continue to follow the mainstream Leaving Certificate Programme, which retains an emphasis on general academic education and continues to prepare students for entry to the labour market or to third level education.

Participation at third level is determined by a points system based on Leaving Certificate examination results and, while entry to some programmes of study is more difficult in terms of the number of points required, in general demand for third level education far outstrips the limited supply of places available at third level institutions. This high demand has led to the relatively recent addition of a further tier to the educational system. Private commercial colleges (post-Leaving Certificate colleges) now also provide a range of State certified programmes in a number of disciplines, as well as their other programmes, many of which are not State certified. The total number of full-time students at third level has increased significantly over the last number of years (in excess of 40 per cent since 1990) and a number of factors are seen to have contributed to this general upsurge in participation. These include the provision of post-Leaving Certificate courses; the abolition of fees for undergraduate students in publicly-funded third level colleges in 1995, which provided wider access to third level education; greater investment in education and increased number of third level places.

The past thirty years have been marked by increased expenditure on education, coupled with greater numbers in education and higher participation rates (see table 4.6). Young people are staying in the education system for longer across all levels of education, and, in a comparison of those who have completed third level education in the OECD countries, it would appear that Ireland fares positively against many of her EU counterparts. Here again there is evidence of increased participation among the younger age categories, perhaps as a result of the policy changes discussed earlier.

Table 4.6 Persons, males and females aged 15 years and over classified by highest level of education completed, 2002

		Persons	**Males**	**Females**
Total aged 15 years and over		3,089,775	1,522,120	1,567,655
Total whose full-time education has ceased		2,622,458	1,299,346	1,323,112
Highest level of education completed	Primary (including no formal education)	552,220	287,337	264,883
	Lower secondary	565,433	292,951	272,482
	Upper secondary	724,099	350,724	373,375
	Third Level — Non-degree	250,429	113,447	136,982
	Third Level — Degree or higher	396,408	192,314	204,094
	Not stated	133,869	62,573	71,296
Total whose full-time education has not ceased		467,317	222,774	244,543
Economic status	Total at school, university etc.	350,774	166,155	184,619
	Other	116,543	56,619	59,924

Source: CSO, 2004

Today, with close to one million students participating in education in Ireland, there is little room for complacency in relation either to Ireland's educational system or indeed to educational participation rates more generally. The link between education and employment – the attainment of educational qualifications critically impacting upon one's ability to successfully gain and retain employment – is well documented. The 1997 OECD report on education argued that many of the benefits of education cannot be quantified and that social cohesion, rather than narrow economic gain, is the greatest prize for societies in which all citizens use learning to become more effective participants in democratic, civil and economic processes. Indicators from the OECD (2005) education report associate higher levels of education with higher earnings, a lower chance of unemployment and more skills that yield social advantage. This link is evidenced in the most recent Irish labour force survey, which suggests that individuals who possess no post-primary qualification are six times more likely to be unemployed than are those with a third level qualification. In the case of those who do find employment, the remuneration they receive is very often far lower than those with higher qualifications. Education and earnings are thus positively linked, and so the earnings advantage of increased education would appear to outweigh the costs of acquiring it. Greater discussion on lifelong learning and adult education is presented in chapter 9.

This chapter has sought to provide some insight into how labour markets function and how this might likely shape the nature of HRM in organisations. The Irish labour market has undergone considerable change in recent years and, in association with considerable capital investment in the Irish labour market, this has resulted in sustained employment creation combined with falling rates of unemployment and an appreciable rise in the overall standard of living. The demographic profile of the Irish population is favourably disposed towards high labour market participation, and it is unlikely, in the short term at least, that Ireland will experience the level of ageing of the labour force that is being evidenced in many EU countries. More recently, however, educational attainment and human capital investment are being viewed as critical determinants of positive economic growth and development.

Tansey (1998) indicates that each step up the educational ladder yields a significantly positive rate of return in terms of higher lifetime earnings, thus the benefits of increased educational attainment are spread across the whole of the economy in terms of increased productivity, increased employment and a widened tax base for the state. The educational profile of the Irish labour force has changed considerably over the last number of years, particularly as a result of direct policy intervention to widen the provision and scope of second and third level education. Today the quality of the Irish labour force compares very favourably with those of other EU and OECD countries, particularly with respect to those holding a third level qualification, though less so for older worker cohorts.

Projections of occupational trends over the next five years suggest that unskilled and semi-skilled jobs will be displaced and that educational attainment and qualifications will increasingly become the criteria upon which employability is determined. There is thus a considerable danger that those who drop out of the education system before completing their formal education will become increasingly marginalised and unemployable.

As business becomes increasingly knowledge-based, there is considerable pressure on the organisation to ensure that its internal capability can match external environmental requirements. The onus is increasingly being placed on the HR function or practitioner to ensure that the firm's labour pool has both the skills and abilities to meet organisational requirements, and furthermore, the capacity to deal with possible changes that the external environment might demand. The following chapters explore these and other issues in greater detail.

5

Human Resource Planning, Recruitment and Selection

The issue of how to ensure that the best (most effective) people work for them is something that all organisations wrestle with. In recent times, the significance of changes in business and social environments have prompted many organisations to reconsider the *modus operandi* of their human resource management policies and practices. Both Millmore (2003) and Thomas and Ray (2000) argue that the ability to attract, hire, retain and develop the most capable talent is the single most important determinant of an organisation's strategic effectiveness.

Moreover, labour shortages in specific labour markets throughout Europe have led to increased attention being focused on how best to attract prospective applicants (Barber 1998; Breaugh and Starke 2000; Highhouse and Hoffman 2001). Selecting individuals with good technical skills is no longer sufficient to ensure effective job performance. Increasingly, employers are seeking people who have good interpersonal abilities, congruent values and beliefs and, more importantly, good development potential. Graves and Karren (1996) suggest that employees must be able to work as team members, have knowledge of automated process and be IT literate, be flexible enough to manage varied workloads and be able to cope with changes as they occur. The question for most organisations is how to find the 'right' candidate with the required knowledge as quickly as possible at the lowest costs possible – what Heraty and Morley (1998a) refer to as 'the search for good-fit'.

Human resource management encapsulates a number or a bundle of core activities that, in practice, are interdependent and occur simultaneously, but which are presented here separately to aid our understanding of each distinct activity. The initial activity depicts the organisation determining the nature and calibre of employees required for effective functioning (*human resource planning* phase), and for establishing the employment relationship (*recruitment and selection* phase) and the psychological contract.

Once the employment relationship has been established, the concern shifts to identifying a range of procedures and practices that facilitate the retention and development of those recruited. Here issues to be addressed include designing an effective system of work (*job design*); determining the scope of the effort-reward bargain (*reward practices*); monitoring performance (*performance appraisal and management*); facilitating performance improvement and learning (*employee development*); and finally, managing the employment relationship (*employee relations*). Clearly, then, there is considerable interplay between each of these activity areas to ensure the creation and development of an effective workforce. Indeed, Legge (1995) notes that the integration and internal consistency of HR systems is a critical determinant of organisational success. In this chapter, however, we will concentrate on the initial phases of human resource planning, recruitment and selection.

THE PURPOSE OF HUMAN RESOURCE PLANNING

Accepting that human resources are potentially the most valuable resource available to an organisation is one thing – recognising how highly differentiated, complex and unpredictable they are is quite another! Beardwell and Holden (1997) argue that where organisations fail to place and direct human resources in the right areas of the business, at the right time, and at the right cost, serious inefficiencies are likely to arise, creating considerable operational difficulties and likely business failure. It stands to reason, then, that human resource management can only be truly effective where human resource actions and activities are linked with strategic business issues or priorities (Bechet and Walker 1995; Bratton and Gold 1999; Tansey 1998; Grundy 1997; Gubman 2004). This necessitates that human resource considerations be integrated into the strategic planning process. Rothwell (1995) suggests that formalised human resource planning represents a bridging mechanism that allows corporate plans to be translated into actionable human resource requirements. This, Millmore (2003) argues, requires a capacity to anticipate those human resource require-ments that are necessary to ensure the successful implementation of the strategic plan. Human resource planning can thus be perceived as a critical element of an effective management system since it involves forecasting human resource needs for the organisation and developing appropriate plans as required to achieve these needs.

At its most basic level human resource planning is concerned with ensuring that the organisation employs the right quantity of people with the necessary knowledge, skills and attitudes (KSAs) that are required for effective organisational functioning – both now and for the future. Reilly (1996) describes human resource planning as a process in which an organisation attempts to estimate the demand for labour and evaluate the size, nature and sources of supply that will be required to meet that demand. For many organisations this constitutes a difficult process since planning, by its nature, is fraught with considerable tensions and unpredictability.

Arguably, shrinking organisational size, structural delayering and frequent restructuring has reduced some of the onerous demands on, or even requirements for, organisational human resource planning systems. However, Lundy and Cowling (1996) dismiss this perception. They argue that, rather than nullifying the requirement for careful human resource planning, new developments in the form of flatter organisation, or high-performance work systems, have actually attached increased importance to the process to facilitate the emergence of more flexible planning scenarios. Many of the arguments in favour of human resource planning proposed initially by Walker (1980) remain highly relevant in today's competitive business environment:

- Facilitating in the reduction of human resource costs through the anticipation of shortages or surpluses of human resources, which can be corrected before they become unmanageable and expensive.
- Providing a basis for planning employee development to make optimum use of workers' aptitudes, and to facilitate career development.

- Improving the overall business planning process.
- Providing equal opportunities for all categories of employees (taking into account the diverse nature of the labour market both external and internal to the organisation).
- Promoting greater awareness of the critical importance of having well-integrated human resource management policies and activities throughout all levels of the organisation.

In calculating the additional unnecessary costs of poor recruitment and selection, Hacker (1997) documents the costs of a poor hiring decision as re-advertising, training a replacement, potential customer loss, decreased productivity, low employee morale. Although difficult to calculate accurately, and accepting that there is considerable variability within sectors, it is estimated that the costs involved for the average job can be as high as €7,000, especially if you cost time. There are, however, other implications of poor decision-making, and Sandico and Kleiner (1999) make an interesting observation here:

> The obvious bad hires are the ones who leave the job soon after they are hired. Other poor hires are not as apparent because the problem does not become noticeable until later: they are the clock-watchers, the incapables who get their work done by others, or the marginal workers who have found a way to beat the system. These are the 'false positive' employees – the people who were hired but should not have been.

Ross (1981) cautions that because human resource planning is future oriented, there must be an explicit link coupling human resource planning with other organisational functions such as strategic planning, economic and market forecasting and investment planning. Human resource planning is based on identified future plans of the organisation and involves major policy decisions that can only be taken by top management. At the operational level, human resource planning involves catering for the human resource implications of operational business decisions such as the termination of a particular product line. These operational plans may then form the basis for short-term action plans in a range of HR areas from recruitment to termination. These may encompass the design of training programmes to upgrade operator skills, recruitment schedules for graduate trainees and forecasts of salary budgets for the next quarter.

Thus, human resource planning facilitates organisational functioning by evaluating current human resource utilisation and the human resource implications of change. Effective human resource planning helps avoid major discontinuities in human resource availability. It helps determine future HR strategies, anticipate human resource-related problems and take positive action to ensure that adequate human resources are employed and effectively deployed throughout the organisation. It is a central component of a proactive role whereby HR practitioners can make a valuable contribution to strategic decision-making.

THE HUMAN RESOURCE PLANNING PROCESS
Human resource planning has traditionally started from the premise that a balance needs to be achieved between the supply of and demand for human resources. The central assumption underpinning models of human resource planning is that demand for labour is derived from corporate plans, while labour supply is derived either internally – from current stocks of employees (internal labour market (ILM)), or externally – from potential employees in the external labour market (Taylor 1998; Bratton and Gold 1999; Iles 1999).

It is the balancing of demand for, and supply of, human resources that leads to the development of plans related to the other core functional activities of HR management. A model of the human resource planning process is depicted in figure 5.1.

The planning process outlined in figure 5.1 identifies four key stages in the human resource planning process: stocktaking; forecasting; planning; and implementing. As indicated at the start of this chapter, all of these stages are interlinked and thus form a cycle whereby human resource planning affects, and is affected by, the range of human resource policy choices that the organisation has available to it. Hendry (1995) advocated this view of HR planning as a cycle of events, arguing that change can be initiated at any point in the cycle (responding to external market fluctuations, for example) and so the HR plan is more flexible as a result.

Figure 5.1 Human resource planning process

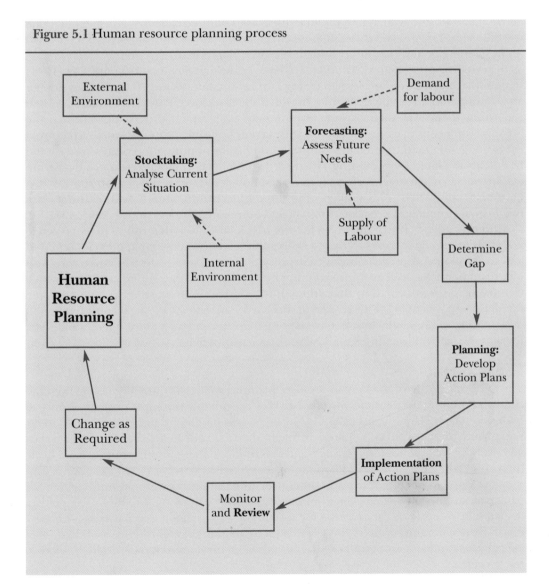

STOCKTAKING

The first stage in the development of human resource plans involves the identification of a range of variables that impact upon organisational operations. The model depicts two particular categories of influencers: the external environment within which the organisation operates, and the internal organisational environment itself. In the first chapters of this text, much of the discussion focused on external factors that impact upon organisational functioning (such as Government policies, economic considerations and product market conditions) while, internally, the link between business planning and HR management was explicated. In addition to this, chapter 4 outlined particular labour market considerations that have relevance to the operation of HR management; while chapter 14 details aspects of the legislative environment that directly affect the employment relationship. These are some of the key issues that impact on human resource management decision and so, rather than reiterate the discussions of these chapters, it is suggested that you take some time to read through these chapters so that you have a more contextualised understanding of how they affect human resource planning.

In reviewing approaches to human resource planning, Sisson and Timperley (1994) suggest that stocktaking involves analysing current human resources, that is, developing an accurate human resource profile, in which the workforce is evaluated and classified according to factors such as age, experience, skills and abilities. Specifically, the organisation needs to gather details on the current skills mix of its workforce in terms of education level, training level, job knowledge and ability. Information of this kind should be readily available from existing HR records, which will include reference data from employees' curricula vitae, performance reviews, job descriptions and any job analyses that have been conducted. This skills profile should be read in tandem with existing work practices, technological processes utilised, and corporate business strategy employed.

Moreover, Mayo (1991) advocates the use of job analysis to determine the knowledge and skills required for each job type; a skills audit to identify core competencies required and to develop a skills inventory of current employees; and a performance review to identify potential as well as future training needs. This provides the organisation with a rich database of information that allows it to evaluate both existing human resource capability and potential for development. Resource capability is a critical consideration in determining the strategic direction of the organisation, and, at a more operational level, impacts the types of learning and development activities that may be provided.

FORECASTING

The forecasting stage of the human resource planning model involves forecasting both the supply of labour and demand for labour. This is probably the most difficult aspect of human resource planning, because it requires the organisation to make predictions about how many employees will be required for the future (demand analysis based on past trends and likely future business functioning); and determining where future employees are likely to be sourced (supply analysis). Planning by nature relies heavily on past experience and the development of certain hypotheses concerning the future, and given the mercurial nature of the current business environment, it is hardly surprising that forecasting either demand for, or supply of labour, is highly speculative at best. It is a useful process, however, for it forces organisations to be ever vigilant to market conditions and customer expectations and at least more prepared to meet the inevitable changes that are around the corner.

Forecasting Demand for Labour

As indicated earlier, a preliminary step in developing human resource plans involves the identification of clearly defined organisational objectives, which indicate strategic purpose and direction. These may then be supplemented by more detailed operational plans that outline the role of each function in facilitating the achievement of strategic goals. Demand for labour can only be forecast with any degree of accuracy in the very short term and that, while most managers will be aware of what their current requirements are, the issue of predicting requirements for the future is far more problematic.

However difficult the process, and imprecise the results, some forecasting is required in order that the organisation can make more informed decisions. Sisson and Timperley (1994) suggest that demand forecasting involves determining the general pattern of trading and production, product demand, technology and administrative changes, capital investment plans, market strategies, acquisitions, divestments, mergers, product diversification and centralisation-decentralisation. Coupled with these demand factors, one can also argue that an organisation's demand for labour will also be affected by current legislative provisions; prevailing economic climate, and the range of flexible choices available to organisations (refer back to chapter 4 for specific examples). Mayo (1991) further suggests that knowledge of the following aspects of organisational functioning will facilitate improved demand forecasting:

- Changes in requirements for management, geographically or in 'new business areas'.
- New subsets of the organisation that may be required as the plan progresses, and those that will no longer be required.
- Changes in the number of particular types of jobs.
- The knowledge, skills, attitudes and experiences that will be required for particular types of job.
- Requirements for joint ventures and collaborative management.
- Changes needed in career structures.

Forecasting Supply of Labour

INTERNAL SUPPLY

The forecasting of internal labour supply constituted the central preoccupation of human resource planning throughout the 1960s and 1970s and resulted in the development of a number of mathematical models to predict labour attrition in a given time period (Armstrong 1992). Sisson and Timperley (1994) provide a summary of the various types of models developed:

- 'Renewal' or 'pull' models, where people are assumed to be 'pulled through' as a vacancy occurs through wastage or promotion and where vacancies in any grade are defined by outflows (wastage or promotion).
- 'Linear programming' models for recruitment and deployment.
- 'Camel' models based on assessing promotion chances in a hierarchy, using age distribution and estimates about the future size of the human resource system.
- 'Markov' or 'push' models that are based on predictable wastage patterns that are determined by length of service and an individual's career.

Lundy and Cowling (1996) suggest that such quantitative approaches to the internal supply of human resources have focused on three key supply indices, namely wastage, absenteeism and the age profile of the workforce.

WASTAGE/LABOUR TURNOVER
In any given year, it is expected that a certain number of people will inevitably leave the organisation and will need to be replaced in order to maintain production or service. This is known as natural wastage or attrition and is typically referred to as labour turnover. Employees may leave an organisation for many reasons such as retirement, seeking better opportunities elsewhere, dissatisfaction with the job, unrealistic/unmet job expectations, retirement, redundancy, dismissal and so forth. The ability, therefore, to predict a rate of labour turnover is an important aspect of human resource planning. It can facilitate the creation of HR policies that seek to improve retention rates, particularly for those employees whom the organisation has a vested interest in retaining (i.e. those who are efficient and/or highly knowledgeable of the organisation (with valuable tacit knowledge), those who are difficult to replace or those in whom the organisation has invested considerable training).

Measuring labour turnover is therefore a necessary prelude to planning and remedial action. One of the simplest methods of calculating wastage is through a turnover analysis:

$$\frac{\text{Number of employees who leave in one year}}{\text{Average number employed in the past year}} \times 100 = \%$$

Turnover rates will clearly vary within industries, within organisations, and even between jobs, and so it is difficult to establish an 'acceptable' rate of annual turnover. A recent CIPD survey on recruitment and retention (2004) suggests an average turnover rate of 15.7 per cent for Ireland (the comparable figure for the UK is 16.1 per cent), and, combined across both countries, reported the highest levels of turnover in personal services employment including call centres (50.9 per cent)and hotel, catering and leisure (45.7 per cent). Some time ago, Beardwell and Holden (1997) suggested that a turnover rate of 25 per cent is perfectly respectable in modern large-scale organisations, but that anything approaching 30–35 per cent should give some cause for concern. While the turnover index has the advantage of being easy to calculate, and gives some indication of whether losses are high or low, it is a relatively crude measure, because it does not provide details on the types of employees who are leaving, or in which departments most losses are occurring.

A calculation of the labour stability index can provide additional information about labour turnover. This stability index is calculated as:

$$\frac{\text{Number of employees with more than one year's service}}{\text{Total number employed one year ago}} \times 100 = \%$$

The stability index provides details on whether the organisation is retaining experienced employees since it calculates and emphasises those who stay with the organisation. However, indices alone will not provide specific details on why the organisation is experiencing particular levels of wastage and thus many organisations are adopting the use of the 'exit interview' to help explain turnover. While there is inevitable variability in how organisations design their exit interviews, the purpose of such interviews is to provide details on why an employee has chosen to leave the organisation. It may ask the employee to rate the organisation against a list of predetermined criteria, such as attractiveness of reward package, satisfaction with job, supervisory arrangements and so forth. Combined with turnover and stability indices, the information received from the exit interviews can provide some useful indicators of potential problems with respect to various personnel procedures and practices.

Many years ago, Hill and Trist (1955), in conjunction with the Tavistock Institute (UK), conducted a number of landmark studies of labour turnover and developed what has become known as the 'survival curve' (see figure 5.2). The evidence from their studies suggested that the propensity to quit employment is highest during the early stages of employment but this tapers away as employees settle down in the organisation.

Figure 5.2 The survival curve

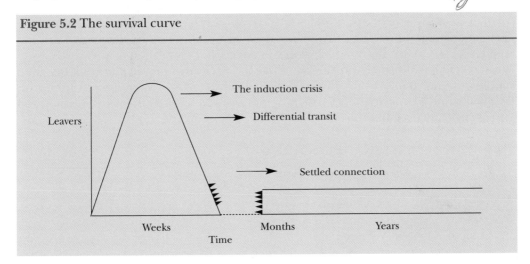

Hill and Trist explained the survival curve in terms of a social process that involves three distinct phases. The first phase they labelled the '*induction crisis*', at which time wastage/turnover is very high. Many reasons have been cited for the existence of the induction crisis and generally it is thought to be associated with some of the following:

- New employees find that the job is not what they imagined it would be i.e. they had unmet expectations – perhaps as a result of the job advertisement and/or selection interview.
- New employees find that they are unhappy with some aspect of the work environment, i.e. they find it difficult to adjust to or settle into working in the organisation.
- Some new employees find alternative work elsewhere that is perceived to be more attractive, i.e. they have applied for a number of jobs and take the first one available until something more 'suitable' comes along.

The period of time covered by the induction crisis can vary considerably between organisations and between job categories, and in some cases can last up to two years. However, it is generally assumed to reach its peak after the first six weeks of employment. The second period is termed the '*differential transit*' where, as the employee begins to feel more comfortable in his/her position and settles into company life, the likelihood of suddenly leaving begins to decrease. The final stage is called '*settled connection*' and Hill and

Trist (1955) suggest that employees who remain with the organisation for this period of time tend to be viewed as 'quasi-permanent'. At this stage there is a perceived greater incentive in staying with the organisation rather than leaving to go elsewhere. The survival curve is, in many ways, indicative rather than definitive and, while it does not take into account personal motivation or career expectations, it suggests that there are inherent predictabilities in the process, which allow organisations to forecast wastage with some reliability.

Absenteeism

When forecasting the likely number of people who will be required over the next period, organisations also take account of their current levels of absenteeism and likely future trends. Absenteeism is taken to mean all absence from work other than paid holidays. Seminal work by Steers and Rhodes (1978) on developing a model of employees' attendance suggests, among other things, that an employee's attendance at work is a function of two particular variables: ability to attend and motivation to attend. Ability to attend is chiefly concerned with illness or some incapacity that prevents an employee from attending work – in most cases this is involuntary absenteeism. Motivation to attend, on the other hand, is explicitly linked with the employee's feelings about the organisation and the job itself, and whether the employee feels a pressure to attend work (see figure 5.3).

Figure 5.3 A model of employee absenteeism

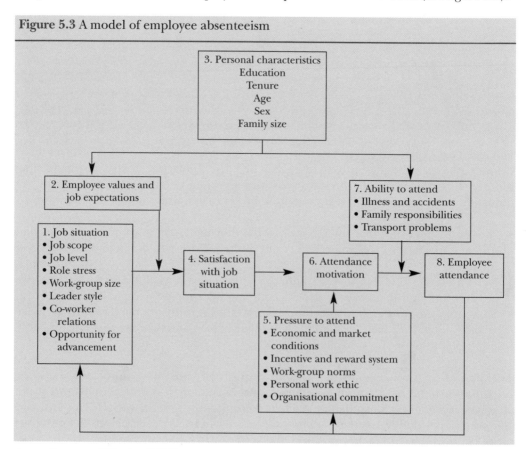

Source: Steers and Rhodes (1978).

Steers and Rhodes found a clear correlation between absenteeism trends and labour turnover trends. Here, when employees are unhappy with their work situation (for whatever reason) and would like to leave but are unable to find alternative work, absenteeism rates tend to increase. However, when alternative work is more readily available, absenteeism rates decrease and labour turnover becomes more frequent.

At the organisational level, information on absenteeism is typically gathered from attendance sheets, time cards, medical records and other HR data. The most common formula used to calculate absenteeism is as follows:

$$\frac{\text{Total absence (days/hours) in a particular time period}}{\text{Total possible time (days/hours)}} \times 100 = \%$$

This index calculates the percentage of the total time available in a specified period that has been lost because of absence. Absenteeism costs organisations in terms of paying workers for work not done, in paying for substitute workers, in downtime due to inexperience or increased stress levels resulting from one worker doing the work of two. Cowling and Walters (1990) suggest that there is a significant correlation between the nature of the job and absenteeism, pointing to job satisfaction as an important component of motivation to attend.

According to a recent report by the Small Firms Association (SFA) (reported in IRN 5/09/2002) the Irish national average rate of absenteeism is 3.4 per cent, or 7.8 working days. This rate is reported higher in larger firms (4.6 per cent or 10.5 working days), while for small firms the average falls to 2.6 per cent or 5.9 working days. A more recent study (2004) by IBEC, the employer's confederation, suggests that 14 million working days are lost each year in Ireland due to absenteeism, giving an estimated total annual cost of €1.5 billion to business, and €882 per employee. This estimated annual cost of €882 per employee closely mirrors the CIPD (UK) survey finding of an average annual cost of €841 per employee, but is slightly higher than a Confederation of British Industry (CBI) survey finding of €706 per employee.

Interestingly, however, recent data from a European survey suggest that Ireland's rate of absenteeism, caused by illness, is actually among the lowest among European Union member states (see box 5.1).

Box 5.1 Work attendance in Ireland

Irish rank second in EU in work attendance
Extract from *The Irish Times* 16 September 2004

The Republic has the second-lowest rate of sickness behind Greece in the European Union, according to a new survey published today.

The Third European Survey on Working Conditions monitored employee sick days in the 15 members of the European Union in 2000.

The rates are defined as the proportion of the employed national workforce who had taken at least one day off work in the previous 12 months because of sickness or occupational injury.

Greece had the lowest rate of absenteeism with 6.7 per cent followed by Ireland with 8.3 per cent and Portugal with 8.4 per cent.

The countries with the highest rates were Finland with 24 per cent, The Netherlands with 20.3 per cent and Germany with 18.3 per cent. The average for all the countries was 14.5 per cent.

It is clearly important, therefore, that organisations maintain accurate records of absenteeism and plot absenteeism on a regular basis to discover any upward trends. High levels of absenteeism might point to inconsistencies between HR activities and thus might require an organisation to rethink its strategy in respect to, for example, selection, supervision, job design, performance appraisal, discipline, rewards or development.

AGE ANALYSIS

The third supply index that an organisation might wish to examine is the age distribution of each category of employee to determine, for example, imminent retirement patterns, plan recruitment policies, and identify career and succession paths for those with future potential within the organisation. Lundy and Cowling (1996) suggest that plotting the age structure of a workforce throws into sharp relief whether, for example, a large proportion of employees are reaching retirement age, or whether the cadre of key executives is young and likely to be jostling each other for promotion in the near future.

A predominantly 'mature' age profile would suggest the need for a strong recruitment drive to fill the vacancies left by those about to retire. A predominantly 'middle-aged' workforce might indicate potential (or existing) bottlenecks in the promotion system, which, if unresolved, can create dissatisfaction and possible absenteeism or turnover problems (this can also be a feature of a young age profile). An age distribution that is heavily weighted at the young end and at the 'mature' end might lead to complications in terms of engendering cultural norms and cohesive group dynamics. A balanced mix of ages is, of course the ideal scenario where the organisation can develop and structure its internal labour market around progressive succession planning and ensuring the sharing of valuable tacit knowledge.

External Supply

Chapter four drew attention to the importance of external labour market trends and the changing demography of the labour force. In terms of human resource planning, the organisation will be particularly interested in, for example: current levels of unemployment (most especially in the local geographic area); the changing structure of the workforce and its effects on recruitment and supply (i.e. the increasing propensity to complete third level education leads to fewer school leavers entering the labour force); the trend towards flexible employment choices with the concomitant increase in female participation rates; and the current levels of education and training provision that determine the skills mix of the external labour market. All of these factors serve to determine the outcome of the essential 'make or buy' question: that is, is it more effective to source prospective employees outside of the organisation ('buy' decision) or should the organisation develop its own internal labour market ('make' decision)? These decisions are made in view of forecasted labour demand, strategic corporate plans and external environmental considerations.

PLANNING

Once the organisation has forecasted likely demand for, and supply of, labour it can then estimate whether there are any imbalances between the two, that is, whether the organisation is faced with a labour shortage or a labour surplus. Where a shortage exists, or is predicted to occur, the organisation can decide to plan for recruitment or retraining as appropriate. A labour surplus requires that an organisation make plans for redundancy, redeployment, retraining, or perhaps lay-off or short-time. Regardless of the particular options open to it, the organisation's eventual decision will have consequences for the general nature of employee relations, the structuring of work, the reward package offer and the structure of its internal labour market. For this reason the organisation needs to carefully weigh the attendant costs and benefits of whichever strategy it decides to employ.

IMPLEMENTATION

On completion of the human resource plans, the organisation operationalises its decision and the cycle is once again set in motion. Since both internal and external environments are subject to considerable change over time, it is advised that human resource plans are monitored and reviewed on a regular basis and amended or redirected as required.

The human resource planning process identifies a range of options that are available to an organisation depending on whether it forecasts a shortage or surplus of labour occurring in the future. The remainder of this chapter explores the process of recruitment and selection as a response to a perceived shortfall in required human resources.

RECRUITMENT AND SELECTION

Much of the literature on HRM has emphasised the necessity for recruiting and selecting employees who are committed to the goals of the organisation. It suggests that the profitability and even the survival of an enterprise usually depend upon the calibre of the workforce (Schuler and Jackson 1999; Ulrich 1997; Storey 1992) and that human resources represent a critical means of achieving competitiveness (Snell 2005; Cappelli 1999; Prahalad and Hamel 1990). It has been argued that the recruitment and selection decisions are the most important of all decisions that managers have to make since they are a prerequisite to the development of an effective workforce, while the costs of ineffectual commercial viability can often be attributed to decades of ineffective recruitment and selection methods (Russo *et al.* 1995; Redman and Mathews 1995; McMahon 1988; Plumbley 1985; Smith and Robertson 1986; Lewis 1984).

Terpstra (1996) indicates that, as companies downsize, 'de-layer' (reduce hierarchy) and try to boost productivity with fewer people, those who remain are being asked to assume more tasks, roles and responsibilities. He suggests that, as this trend continues, companies will be asking fewer employees to know, do, change and interact more. Thus interest is increasingly focused on identifying the recruiting sources that are most likely to yield high-quality employees and the selection methods that best predict future job performance. Organisations can be said to deal with two different kinds of uncertainty – uncertainty about job demands and uncertainty about candidates' suitability. Job analysis seeks to cope with the first while selection deals with the second.

The recruitment and selection process is essentially concerned with finding, assessing and engaging new employees. As such, its focus is on matching the capabilities and inclinations of prospective candidates against the demands and rewards inherent in a given job (Plumbley 1985; Herriot 1989; Heraty *et al.* 1994; Heraty and Morley 1998). Montgomery (1996, 94) highlights this notion of fit as the key to job success:

> Think back in your career and ask yourself, of all the people you know who failed in a job and were terminated, how many of them failed because they lacked the right educational degree, the right job experience, or the right industry background? In all likelihood, most of them failed because of inadequate interpersonal skills, an inability to communicate, or because they just didn't fit in with the culture; in other words – bad chemistry!

There are two distinct phases involved in this matching process; that of recruitment which is concerned with attracting a group of potential candidates to apply for a given vacancy, followed by selection, which denotes the process of choosing the most suitable candidate from a pool of candidates identified through recruitment. The recruitment and selection process is outlined in figure 5.4.

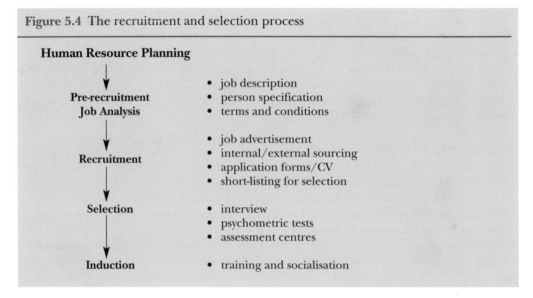

Figure 5.4 The recruitment and selection process

Human Resource Planning

Pre-recruitment
Job Analysis
- job description
- person specification
- terms and conditions

Recruitment
- job advertisement
- internal/external sourcing
- application forms/CV
- short-listing for selection

Selection
- interview
- psychometric tests
- assessment centres

Induction
- training and socialisation

The Job Analysis Phase

When an organisation makes the decision to fill an existing vacancy through recruitment, the first stage in the process involves conducting a comprehensive job analysis. This may already have been conducted through the human resource planning process, particularly where recruitment is a relatively frequent occurrence. Schneider and Schmitt (1986) define job analysis as a means of identifying the human behaviour necessary for adequate job performance; in other words, it provides an indication of the knowledge, skills and attitudes (KSAs) about all kinds of work activity. Based on the identification of such behaviours, theories about the kinds of people that the job requires, in terms of knowledge skills and abilities, can be formulated and procedures for the identification of such people can be developed. While a number of different methods of job analysis have been developed over the years, many of which involve considerable statistical modelling, figure 5.5 outlines nine of the most common job analysis techniques that are used by organisations today.

A job analysis has a variety of uses that extends beyond the selection process. Among others, it can be used for promotion and career development purposes, for job transfers, for learning and training programmes, for salary review, for work restructuring and for the introduction of new technology. Once a job analysis has been conducted, the organisation has a clear indication of the particular requirements of the job, and where that job fits into the overall organisational structure. The job analysis then forms the basis for developing three critical recruitment and selection tools namely the *job description*, the *person specification* and the *terms and conditions of employment*.

JOB DESCRIPTION

In the past, there was a tendency to couch job descriptions in vague or loose terms to allow for any changes that might occur in the main job purpose over time. Furthermore, in many organisations, job descriptions were discussed in general terms at the selection interview but were not formally recorded or written down. This practice has largely dissipated in recent years, particularly since the Terms of Employment (Information) Act 1994/2001.

Figure 5.5 Advantages and disadvantages of nine methods of job analysis

1. Questionnaire method

Advantages	Good for producing quantitative information and can produce objective and generalisable results; cheap.
Disadvantages	Substantial sample needed; substantial foreknowledge needed to be able to construct questionnaire; respondents must be able and willing to give accurate replies.

2. Check-list method
Similar to questionnaire method, but, since responses are either 'yes' or 'no', the results may be cruder or require larger sample; they tend to require fewer subjective judgments.

3. Individual interviews

Advantages	Very flexible; can provide detailed information; easy to organise and prepare.
Disadvantages	Time-consuming; expensive; difficult to analyse.

4. Observation interviews
Similar to individual interviews but give additional information, for example visual or auditory information; these contextual clues make it more difficult for the analyst to be misled; the methods may expose both the analyst and the worker to increased safety hazards.

5. Group interviews
Similar to the individual interview but less time-consuming for the analyst, and some claim that richer information is obtained, since interviewees stimulate each other's thought. They are more difficult to organise, and there is the danger that a group is over-influenced by one person.

6. Expert analysis

Advantages	Quick, cheap, and can be used for jobs that do not yet exist. Can avoid restrictive practices.
Disadvantages	The experts may not be true experts, and an unrealistic analysis may result.

7. Diary method

Advantages	Cheap, flexible, and requires little advance preparation. Useful for non-manual tasks, where observation is of limited value. Can also be used in jobs requiring a wide variety of tasks.
Disadvantages	Needs co-operation from respondents; tendency to keep incomplete logs, so frequent but minor items are often omitted.

8. Work participation method

Advantages	Can produce very realistic analyses.
Disadvantages	Expensive, time-consuming, and can only be used for jobs requiring short training and no safety hazards.

9. Critical incident method

Advantages	Focuses on the aspects of a job that are crucial to success.
Disadvantages	Often produces incomplete data that is difficult to analyse.

Source: Smith and Robertson (1993).

The Act requires all employers to furnish their employees with written details of the terms and conditions pertaining to their employment, or to refer such employees to where their job details are specified (i.e. company handbook or notice board). For this reason organisations are paying careful notice to the development of job description that are up-to-date, complete and inclusive of most job requirements. While job descriptions vary according to job classification or type, they typically conform to a relatively set framework (figure 5.6).

Figure 5.6 Elements of a job description

Job title
Department
Location
Reports to
Purpose
Main tasks
Liaison and main contacts
Staff responsibilities
Special features
Rewards and conditions

The job description is essentially a broad statement of the purpose, scope, duties and responsibilities that are attached to the job, and as such is the basis for the contract of employment. Furthermore, since job advertisements normally detail the job description, it is critically important that organisations have a precise understanding of the nature of the job vacancy and that this realistic preview of the job then be used to attract the most suitable candidates. Russo *et al.* (1995) suggest that an effective job description could include information on the following:

- *Job identification*: in particular job title, department, division, company name and location.
- *Relationship with others*: notable vertical relationships (supervision and monitoring) or horizontal relationships (liaison with others, co-operation).
- *Job content*: especially the actual tasks of the job, the level of responsibility of the task, frequencies of performance, the importance of the task.
- *Working conditions*: for instance physical environment (noise, heat), social environment (working in a group, night shift), monetary environment (salary, fringe benefits).
- *Performance standards/objectives*: expressed in quantitative terms (i.e. level of output or sales, time limits to be met), or in qualitative terms (i.e. maintenance of a quality standard within a group).
- *Human requirements*: such as physical and psychological characteristics of the job holder/applicant that would comply with the demands of the job (person specification).
- *Other important information*: for example, training and career opportunities, firm's performance in its market (image-related information).

PERSON SPECIFICATION
Once the job description has been drawn up, the organisation can then develop a person specification. The person specification essentially describes the ideal person for the job

and thus provides a detailed description of the qualifications, knowledge, specific skills and aptitudes, experience and personal attributes that are required to do the job effectively. The person specification has a number of very important functions within the recruitment and selection process: not only does it describe the person required for the job, it also helps in deciding where the organisation should concentrate its search and advertising efforts, i.e. level of experience and/or qualification can be used as a guide on whether to advertise nationally or target graduate career fairs. The person specification can also facilitate systematic short-listing and will (should) form the basis upon which selection criteria are determined. It is therefore of critical importance that the person specification exactly matches the job description so that the most suitable potential job candidates can be attracted for selection.

Since, by their nature, personnel specifications describe the ideal candidate or jobholder, it is advisable to further differentiate between characteristics/requirements that are absolutely *essential* to perform the job, and those that are *desirable* (would be useful/nice to have but are not essential). This process is particularly useful as it helps in determining overall candidate suitability when the eventual selection is made. Both Rodger (1952) and Munro-Fraser (1954) have developed somewhat similar categorisations that are deemed useful for specifying some personal characteristics that can aid effective recruitment and selection. Both of these schemes are detailed in table 5.1.

Table 5.1 Person specification categories

Rodger (1952)
- Physical make-up: physique, health, appearance, speech
- Attainments: education, training, experience
- General intelligence: fundamental intellectual capacity
- Special aptitudes: dexterity, numeracy, verbal, other
- Interests: leisure, intellectual, practical, physical, social, artistic
- Disposition: acceptability, interaction, impact on fellow-workers and management, dependability, stability
- Circumstances: domestic, family, mobility, flexibility

Munro-Fraser (1954)
- Impact on others: first impressions, appearance, verbal ability
- Qualifications: education, training, experience
- Innate abilities: comprehension and capacity, conceptual ability, aptitude, intelligence
- Motivation: objectives, commitment, ambition, initiative
- Emotional adjustment: coping with stress, working with others

Both of the frameworks outlined in table 5.1 are useful in that they establish general guidelines around which the person specification can be built. However, it is important to note that the research underpinning the development of these frameworks was completed many years ago and at a time where the regulatory environment for employment was considerably different from what it is today. For this reason, these schemes are useful as indicators of some categories that can be used, but they are heavily reliant on personal judgement to determine the kinds of human qualities associated with successful performance and so are neither politically nor socially neutral. Moreover, it is not recommended that issues associated with physical ability, or personal/family circumstances be included in general use. The organisation must be ever vigilant to ensure that the person specification is not discriminatory in any way (the relevant equality legislation is discussed fully in chapter fourteen). Using the frameworks outlined above, figure 5.7 illustrates a sample person specification that might be used for a position as an HR officer.

Figure 5.7 Sample person specification – HR officer

	Essential requirements	Desirable requirements
Education	Degree/diploma in business studies or related discipline	Specialisation in personnel/HRM or training; membership of CIPD
Experience	One year's experience in computerised HR department with knowledge of selection, reward systems, and training	Two or more years experience at HR/training officer level in a manufacturing environment
Skills	Computer literate in use of excel, access, CBT; interviewing skills; negotiation skills	Knowledge of dedicated HR software packages; French language fluency
Motivation	Ambitious to succeed in HR; commitment to continuous professional development	Ability to motivate and influence others
Disposition/ Circumstances	Outgoing personality; ability to work as team member; adaptable	Flexibility in working patterns; available to travel abroad as required

The characteristics specified in figure 5.7 can be weighted if required, e.g. for a graduate position, greater importance might be attached to educational attainments and skills rather than work experience, which a graduate might not yet have gained. By attaching weights to the various criteria outlined, the process of eventual selection is facilitated, particularly where two or more candidates appear to be similarly suitable. A clear focus on the job content will indicate the types of behaviours that are required to do the job, and these behaviours can also be weighted to differentiate between candidates.

In summary then, a person specification must meet four particular requirements:

1. It must relate to a particular job and thus closely match the job description.
2. It must be specific and detail exactly what is required to complete the job effectively i.e. 'extensive management experience' gives no indication of the quantity or quality of experience that is deemed necessary for the job.
3. It must allow the organisation to differentiate between individual applicants and so ideally, the specification should be weighted or scaled to facilitate an accurate measurement of individual characteristics.
4. It must allow the organisation to assess whether a candidate meets the specification, i.e. all of the characteristics specified must be capable of being measured and assessed. As an example, many person specifications require individuals who are 'highly motivated' yet motivation is inherently difficult to assess, particularly in an interview. We shall return to this later in the chapter.

TERMS AND CONDITIONS

While often included in the job description, in practice the terms and conditions of employment refer specifically to the effort-reward relationship and so include details on the hours to be worked, methods of payment, job entitlements (holidays, bonuses, allowances) and other attendant benefits. Since terms and conditions are often the most visible attributes of the job, they play an important role in the attraction of suitable candidates. Furthermore, as with person specifications, care must be taken to ensure that the terms and conditions of employment meet the requirement of the various employment law statutes (refer to chapter fourteen for details on relevant employment legislation).

The Recruitment Phase

Once the job analysis stage has been completed, the organisation begins the process of recruitment to attract suitable candidates for the particular vacancy. Anderson and Shackleton (1986) indicate that the quality of new recruits depends upon an organisation's recruitment practices, and that the relative effectiveness of the selection phase is inherently dependent upon the calibre of candidates attracted. Indeed Smith, Gregg and Andrews (1989) argue that the more effectively the recruitment stage is carried out the less important the actual selection process becomes. Recruitment can be seen to have three important functions:

1. To attract a pool of suitable applicants for the vacancy.
2. To deter unsuitable candidates from applying.
3. To create a positive image of the company.

The decision to recruit will normally involve the development of a job advertisement. This job advertisement should include the job description, person specification and details on the terms and conditions of employment. It is probably the most effective tool available, if completed correctly, to meet the three key objectives outlined above. The advertisement itself should be striking enough to be noticed and the key information pertaining to the job should dominate so that it will attract those who might be suitable for the position.

Perhaps the most immediate decision facing recruiters is whether to recruit internally from those already employed by the organisation, or to source the external labour market. The decision to access the internal labour market brings with it a number of distinct advantages. It is cost-effective, both in terms of eliminating the need for external advertising or sourcing and also in terms of reducing the induction or settling in period. It is also considered to be good HR practice, as not only may current employees view it as a positive motivator, but also the quality of the internal labour market is continuously upgraded and maintained through high-quality recruitment, selection, promotion, career development and multi-skilling. However, the organisation limits its potential range of candidates by drawing solely from the internal labour market, and often, the introduction of 'new blood' can provide a rewarding stimulus and facilitate organisational dynamics.

There are a number of alternative recruitment methods available to an organisation, the more salient of which are described briefly in table 5.2.

Table 5.2 Recruitment methods

Method	Comments	Advantages	Disadvantages
1. Internal: existing employees	Internal advertising may be requirement for some companies under union-negotiated agreements.		
1.1 Self-applicants		Inexpensive, quick. Motivation factor.	Can be indirectly discriminatory. No new talent into company.
1.2 Supervisor/manager recommendations		Know applicant's strengths, weaknesses and behaviour well.	Records of existing and acquired skills and experience need constant updating.
1.3 Succession planning		Training and development already in place, therefore succession smoother.	Information may be subject to bias.
2. Using existing contacts			
2.1 Unsolicited enquiries	Write-ins, personal enquiries on spec. NB: Should be handled courteously or may affect success of other external methods.	Less expensive. Know applicants are already interested.	Needs system implementation to cope. Need to review 'hold' file after certain period (six months?). May be indirectly discriminatory.
2.2 Previous applicants	Retain forms of unsuccessful applicants for given period and assess against new vacancies as they arise.	Can enhance company image if handled well. May speed process considerably.	As 2.1.
2.3 Previous employees	Particularly retired, or others leaving to unpaid job (e.g. new mothers or carers for elderly or ill dependants) in the 'would re-employ' category.	By changing terms of employment (especially by increasing flexibility or reducing hours). Could re-attract to part-time, flexible or temporary working to meet peak organisational demands. Known work behaviour.	Inbuilt flexibility requirement for employee not always feasible in given situations. Requirements for peaks of job may be outside remit of person.

Table 5.2 Recruitment methods *(contd.)*

Method	Comments	Advantages	Disadvantages
2.4 Existing employee contacts	Existing employees encourage family, friends or contacts to apply for vacancies.	Employee may well know others with similar skills, knowledge, and attitudes. May have passed on knowledge of culture and job requirements.	May well be indirectly discriminatory if not combined with other methods. May be 'weaker' employees who recommend, whose attitudes etc. company does not wish to have reinforced through peer recruitment.
3. External contacts			
3.1 Union referrals	Register kept by union of members seeking employment. Usual in some sectors (e.g. printing) where closed shop and/or custom-and-practice arrangements are traditional.	Confidence in skills. Cost.	Indirectly discriminatory. Overlooks those in work.
3.2 Professional referrals	Registers as above, particularly for professions, e.g. lawyers, doctors, accountants, engineers, linguists.	As 3.1.	As 3.1.
3.3 Employment exchange	Government provision. Network covering most towns and cities, acting as agents for and employees. Particularly concerned with manual and junior positions.	Variety of free services, which can be provided at national level. Speed. Perceived as potential employers service within a secure, non-profit-making framework. Extremely valuable if effort made to cultivate contact.	Unemployed rather than employed are registered, reinforcing labour exchange stereotype. As with all agencies results reflect quality of job description supplied.
3.4 Out-placement consultants	Providing practical help to redundant employees, enforced early retirees, etc.	Actively seeking to place, and may provide training required.	Available when recruitment needs reduce, and vice versa, reflecting economic situation.
3.5 Private selection consultants—local	Deal mainly with clerical, junior administration, shop staff, etc.	Reduce administration for employer. 'Normal' method in many places.	Employer pays for recruits. No guarantee against recruit leaving quickly. Some poor practice has led to employer distrust on occasions.

➥

Table 5.2 Recruitment methods *(contd.)*

Method	Comments	Advantages	Disadvantages
3.6 Management selection	Usually recruitment plus initial stages of selection of managerial, professional and specialist staff.	Specialist knowledge, objectivity, selection skills (especially when unusual recruitment need for company).	Payment by employer. May lack cultural awareness of company. Exclusion of internal applicants.
3.7 Search consultants ('headhunters')	Informal network of contacts keeping track of those likely to be in constant demand, especially senior management. Promising candidates sought out and approached directly.	Possibility of joining can be discussed without commitment. Concentrates on those in employment.	Potential candidates outside head-hunters network excluded. Recruit may be headhunted again by same consultant! Cost (because labour intensive).
3.8 Schools and career service	Guidance and some testing of young people under 18. In-depth knowledge of potential applicants.	Useful source of 'raw' recruits to be developed by the company. Can assist in image enhancement. Cost.	Some 'guidance' of higher quality than other methods. Possibility of indirect discrimination if recruitment concentrated on one or two institutions.
3.9 Colleges	Recruitment of college leavers after conclusion of variety of courses. Tendency to recruit in local colleges in catchment area.	Work experience placements offer opportunity to preview. Increased employer impact on training provided, which can be very work-specific.	Tends to be once-yearly process. Recruits lack experience. Possible indirect discrimination.
3.10 Universities	Traditional 'milk round' by large national and international employers. Ad hoc enquiries by leavers. Frequently appointment boards provide full-time careers advisory service.	Can build strong relationship with those offering specialisms, prestige, etc. Sandwich and other work placements offer opportunity to preview potential.	Travel and accommodation costs can be high. Takes recruiters away from company for long periods.
3.11 Government training schemes	Government-funded initiatives aimed at specific skill shortages and/or disadvantaged groups.	Many skills provided at Government cost can be integrated with on-the-job experience. Opportunity to preview before offering permanent employment. Financial incentives.	Perception of 'cheap labour' can reduce company image unless well managed. Administration heavy. Training commitment required.

Table 5.2 Recruitment methods *(contd.)*

Method	Comments	Advantages	Disadvantages
3.12 Temporary agencies	Provision of short- or longer-term cover (an alternative to recruiting permanent employees).	Provide cover for coping with unexpected absence (e.g. illness), peaks in work loads, one-off or temporary requirement for skills (installation of new, specialist machinery), or transitional developments in work organisation.	Time scale often makes integration into company culture difficult. Quality can vary. Cost.
4. Advertising, media	An overlap between advertising and previous methods discussed frequently exists. Recruitment agencies can provide external expertise.		Essential for monitoring cost-effectiveness.
4.1 Press	Local and national papers, trade and professional journals.	Expensive, especially television and national press. Must be aimed at identified groups.	Only reach those using that medium.
4.2 Television	Includes teletext (Aertel) and view-data (Minitel).	Can provide non-recruitment advantages through increased customer awareness. Sound and vision used.	
4.3 Radio	Local, occasional national broadcasts.	Cheaper than television.	
4.4 Cinema		May be useful for 17 to 25-year-old groups, where several recruits needed; targets likely to have some prior knowledge.	

The choice of recruitment method is often determined by the nature of the position being advertised and whether the skills required for the job are in short supply or otherwise. Thus, for entry-level jobs, for example, it may be sufficient to advertise in local papers or to allow news of the position to be spread by word of mouth. However, where the position requires considerable experience and/or qualifications of a particular type, the organisation might have to consider recruitment at national level or beyond, through the newspaper media, trade and professional journals, or employ the services of recruitment agencies or consultants.

Concomitant with decisions on the choice of recruitment method, the organisation must take account of the application process for vacancies. The most common methods involve the application form or the curriculum vitae (CV). The CV is probably the most common method of job application and it generally tends to conform to a set standard: name, contact address, contact telephone number/email, education and achievements, employment history, professional associations and references. Most CVs are accompanied by a covering letter that seeks to 'sell' the applicant's suitability for the position. Increasingly, however, organisations are developing in-house application forms that seek to elicit job-specific information in a uniform fashion that can enable comparisons to be made between separate applications. Application forms elicit much the same information as is generally presented in a CV, but they also require the applicant to supply additional information in support of his/her application. In practical terms this requires the applicant to again 'sell' his/her skills and highlight the positive contribution he/she could make to the organisation. A relatively recent innovation in the recruitment arena is *e-recruiting*.

E-RECRUITING

Web-based recruitment and early-stage pre-screening of applicants are now a reality across Europe with the more technologically advanced European Community countries leading the way in these developments. In an *Irish Times* special feature on web recruitment (McMahon 2001) it was estimated that over 300 million people worldwide and close to one million people in Ireland were online. Today, with the increasing investment in technology and broadband, it is estimated that at least half of all Irish households are linked to the Internet. If we consider that the Internet is a very recent phenomenon – it only dates back to the late 1980s – it is easy to see that its use will become an ever more pervasive feature of everyday life, which will inevitably change the way individuals and organisations do business. Already we are seeing evidence of this in the recruitment sphere. Thomas and Ray (2000) comment that recent strong economic growth in many countries has produced a demand for both a quality and quantity of employees that local or regional labour markets have not been able to satisfy. For many companies, online recruiting has represented one response to their staffing challenge and they are seeking to utilise one or more of the major techniques available to them for recruitment purposes: general commercial sites, specialised job sites, chat rooms or newsgroups and company websites.

- *General job sites* are commercial, all-purpose sites such as www.monster.com and www.careermosaic.com (worldwide) or (in Ireland) www.irishjobs.ie, www.loadzajobs.ie and www.jobfinder.ie – these services are often offered free to applicants but charge employers a fee, depending on the type of subscription.
- *Specialised job sites* come in many forms (e.g. www.jobtrack.com) and can include newspaper classified ads reproduced on the websites (i.e. from *The Irish Times*), or professional associations can host their own careers pages or vacancy slots (the Academy of Management in the US regularly advertises lectureship/research positions).
- *Chatrooms and newsgroups* vary considerably and allow a ready access to a specialist audience, e.g. HRNet, which is a newsgroup for HR professionals.
- A *company web page* uses the firm's own web page as a recruiting tool – here the marginal costs are low and the company can control the content and provide any amount of information it feels is relevant to attract candidates. One downside is that only those who are already familiar with the company name or what it stands for (brand) are likely to be viewing the jobs pages.

A survey by Internet Business Network (1999) indicated that up to two-thirds of visitors to commercial job sites are not actively seeking employment, whereas individuals who consciously seek out company websites are more likely to be actively seeking jobs.

For the most part, convenience and speed are the two distinct advantages offered by the Internet. E-recruiting lowers recruiting costs and levels the playing field. Menagh (1999) suggest that e-recruiting may cost less than half the outlay on conventional advertising; it is faster and reaches more applicants than more conventional forms of recruitment. However, it does require that other organisational systems be in place to support it (i.e. to screen and short-list applications efficiently).

Those attracted to the net tend to be relatively well educated and computer literate (Thomas and Ray 2000), so e-recruitment is particularly useful for graduate recruitment. However, e-recruiting has a limited ability to attract some types of job seeker: it might not be able to target, for example, the local labour market or those with no Internet access.

SCREENING AND SHORT-LISTING

Once applications have been received, organisations must devise means of analysing their contents and suitability for selection. In this respect the person specification becomes an invaluable tool for identifying suitable and unsuitable applicants. Dale (1995) suggests that there is an inherent tendency to compare applicants against each other rather than against the job requirements, and the biases and heuristics of the short-lister provide the underlying rationale that determines suitability. Using the example of a vacancy for an office manager, she identifies a short-listing matrix, based on the person specification, that can facilitate more informed decisions (see table 5.3).

Table 5.3 Short-listing matrix for position of office manager

Criteria	Candidate			
	1	2	3	4
Attainment				
Successful completion of further education course	Yes	Yes	Yes	Yes
Some job-related management training	Yes	No evidence	No evidence	Yes
Experience				
IT office applications	No evidence	Yes	No evidence	Yes
Customer service	Yes	Yes	Yes	Yes
Staff training and supervision	Yes	No evidence	No evidence	Yes
Record maintenance	No evidence	Yes	Yes	Yes
Abilities				
Communication skills	Untidy application	Yes	Application badly produced	Yes

●→

Table 5.3 Short-listing matrix for position of office manager *(contd.)*

Criteria	Candidate			
Leadership skills	Trainer with no supervisory responsibilities	No evidence	No evidence	Yes
Planning and organisation	Poor organisation of information on form	No evidence	Application badly produced	?
Training and instructional skills	Yes	No evidence	No evidence	Yes
Aptitudes				
Customer-focused	No evidence	Yes	No evidence	Yes
Accuracy	No evidence	?	Application badly produced	Yes
Concern for quality	Untidy application	Yes	Application badly produced	Yes
Interests				
Involved with people	Yes	Solitary interests	No evidence	Yes
Learning and self-development	No evidence	Yes	No evidence	Yes

Source: Dale (1995).

The matrix can be used as a means of eliminating applicants who fail to achieve the minimum essential criteria as set down in the job description and person specification. Individuals are scored according to how well they meet the particular job and behavioural requirements (rather than on how they appeal to the individual doing the short list) and those who score lowest are dropped from the process. The short-listing matrix will only work effectively where there is a well-detailed, measurable job description – incomplete or inaccurate information will render the process largely redundant. Those who score high on the short-listing matrix are deemed more likely to be suitable and they can then be progressed to the next phase, i.e. selection.

The Selection Phase

Personnel selection has generally been regarded as an applied area with a heavy emphasis on predictive efficiency (Iles 1999). Traditionally, the primary goal was to develop selection instruments that would be useful for predicting candidates' future work performance. However, we are increasingly understanding selection from a social process perspective. Here selection is seen as a negotiation process between the employer and candidate and so studies are now focusing upon applicant attitudes and the impact of selection procedures (Iles and Robertson 1997), applicant decision-making in competitive labour market conditions (Anderson *et al.* 2001), and the generation of a viable psychological contract between employers and employees (Herriot 1989). In sum, the selection decision remains a difficult one. Dale (1995) proposes that:

Most mistakes are caused by the fact that managers generally give little thought to the critical nature of the decisions. Employers are surprised and disappointed when an appointment fails, and often the person appointed is blamed rather than recognising the weaknesses in the process and methodology . . . even the soundest of techniques and best practice (in selection) contain scope for error. Some of this is due to the methods themselves, but the main source is the frailty of the human decision-makers.

There are a number of alternative selection techniques that can be used to determine the suitability of a job applicant. Before these are discussed, however, it is important to understand terms such as 'suitability', 'validity' and 'reliability' as they apply to the selection decision.

Suitability is largely determined by the nature of the job and the responsibilities that are attached to it and how well the candidate's knowledge, skills and abilities match these job requirements (Adkins *et al.* 1994). While the job description and person specification will largely determine specific job criteria, one can distinguish four generic criteria that can help to evaluate the relative suitability of an applicant.

1. The organisation requires an individual who has the capacity to perform the tasks associated with a position to an acceptable standard. Previous work experience, educational attainments, and the skills' profile of the applicant will all provide a reasonable indication of work ability.
2. The organisation requires an individual who has the ability to develop new knowledge and skills and can 'grow' with the job. Increasingly, as the nature of work changes and becomes more demanding, there is a strong orientation towards continuous development and competency upgrading. An individual's previous history of skills development and educational and training records can provide some useful indicators in this respect.
3. The organisation requires an individual who will 'fit' into the organisation's culture and has the capacity to work effectively within its structures and systems. The extent to which an individual will 'fit' into the organisation is largely indeterminable, but some inference may be drawn from experiences in previous work environments and a determination of his/her ambitions and expectations.
4. The organisation requires an individual who will work productively, is intrinsically motivated and can establish co-operative relationships with other workers. While past behaviour is not the most reliable predictor of future intent, organisations typically conduct reference checks to establish some idea of previous work behaviour.

Validity, in terms of the selection decision, refers to the extent to which the selection method used measures what it is supposed to measure. Thus, can the organisation be assured (in so far as is possible) that there are no intervening factors or biases that are distorting the result that has been achieved? Reliability, on the other hand, refers to whether the same selection decision reached would again be reached if other individuals made it, i.e. it is consistent. To illustrate the relevance of both validity and reliability it is useful to take the example of the selection interview. If the interview is a valid selection technique it should predict, with a high degree of accuracy, the expected work behaviour of a job applicant (validity). If it is a reliable selection technique, regardless of who makes the selection decision, the end result will be the same, i.e. if five managers were independently asked to interview and choose between a number of candidates, they would all choose the same candidate.

There are a considerable number of alternative techniques available that can aid the selection decision, and several research studies on the reliability, validity and utility of these different methods (Gatewood and Fields 1998; Terpstra *et al.* 1999). Guion (1998) contends that many people use specific selection instruments, simply because they prefer them, or always have used them, and not because of any empirical evidence of their utility and that, for similar reasons, other selection instruments are never used, despite evidence of their predictive value. Gilliland (1993) suggests the use of organisational justice theory as a means of understanding applicants' reactions to selection procedures and proposes that four procedural justice dimensions may form the basis for fairness reactions:

1. Perceived job relatedness
2. Opportunity to demonstrate one's ability
3. Interpersonal treatment
4. The propriety of the questions

Studies have found that the predictive validity of the structured interview is quite high (Campion *et al.* 1988; Wiesner and Cronshaw 1988); that cognitive ability tests are among the most valid predictors available to organisations; that work samples and assessment centres are highly valid selection devices (Hunter and Hunter 1984; Reilly and Warech 1993). The sole selection device that appears to have limited usefulness is the unstructured interview. Selection affects the emergence of a psychological contract between employees and organisations, therefore organisations should be just as much concerned with the social validity of a selection method (its acceptability to the candidate) as with its predictive ability.

Newell (2000) cautions that while attempts have been made to improve the selection process through developing a more systematic approach, it could be argued that some of the current trends in organisations (with their emphasis on sharing and creating knowledge) make the 'best practices' model somewhat problematic. She particularly notes that:

- Best practices associated with a thorough job analysis and person specification may be difficult or inappropriate, particularly where the job requires flexibility and there is no fixed job role *per se.*
- Best practice tends to highlight the importance of 'fit' with the current organisational culture, yet many jobs call for innovative and creative individuals – this may be counter to the prevailing culture.
- Issues surrounding diversity should be taken into account in terms of the selection techniques applied, to ensure no disadvantage to particular groups of individuals.

Individuals tend to assume that a device that is widely used must be valid and it is perhaps for this reason that the interview continues to enjoy considerable popularity across organisations. For many jobs, organisations utilise a series of interviews ranging from the initial meeting through to the second and often third interview. While interviews can either be conducted on a one-to-one basis or be panel-based, the principles underpinning effective interviewing apply to both (these are discussed in the following pages). Anderson and Shackleton (1993) provide an interesting comparison of some of the more commonly used selection techniques (see tables 5.4 and 5.5). However, they describe the selection interview separately since the interview forms the basis of almost all selection decisions, and they suggest that the techniques outlined in table 5.5 should, in fact, be used to augment the interview decision.

Table 5.4 Different functions of the interview

Interview function	Appropriate stage in selection procedure	Interview functioning	Interviewer's objectives	Interviewee's objectives
1. Mutual preview	Phase I/II. Early stages of selection procedure probably following initial screening of written applications but preceding administration of main assessment techniques.	Informal, open-ended discussion to explain selection procedures and to offer career guidance counselling to interviewee by providing detailed and realistic job preview (RJP).	• To meet and 'set the scene' for applicant. • To inform applicants of company's selection procedure.	• To establish what will be involved at each stage in selection procedure. • To visit company 'on site'. • To obtain preview of job to allow self-assessment and self-selection.
2. Assessment	Phase II, one of a battery of candidate assessment techniques.	Formal, structured interaction guided by detailed job analysis and pre-formulated strategy.	• To record answers to critical incident-type questions. • To probe and feed back results of other selection methods (particularly testing).	• To survive! • To obtain feedback and ensure accuracy of results of other methods.
3. Negotiation	Phase III. Final stage of selection procedure, immediately before, or after, offer of employment has been made.	Negotiation of outstanding points of difference, both interviewer and interviewee-directed and led.	• To ensure acceptance of job offer. • To facilitate job role transition. • To identify follow-up personnel procedures.	• To discuss contractual and non-contractual terms and conditions. • To facilitate job role transition. • To initiate the job change process.

Source: Anderson and Shackelton (1993).

Table 5.5 Main techniques of candidate assessment

Technique	Description	'Fit' with interview	Contribution to selection system
Psychometric testing	Standardised test of performance attitudes or personality. Major types: • cognitive ability • personality • attitudes and values • career choice and guidance	Can precede or follow interview stage. Results can form basis of further interview questions, or interview can be used to feed back test results. Personality tests are particularly useful in this respect and can facilitate probing questions at interview.	*Ability tests* • High predictive accuracy for aspects of cognitive ability. • 'Normed' results allow candidate to be compared with many similar people. Longer-term relevance, i.e. job role may change over time; ability remains relatively constant. *Personality tests*

Table 5.5 Main techniques of candidate assessment *(contd.)*

Technique	Description	'Fit' with interview	Contribution to selection system
			• Indications of inter-personal or managerial style that can be followed up at interview and/or compared with exercises in an AC. • 'Faking' scales built in to tests may detect high level of impression manage-ment and biasing of self-presentation.
Work examples	Pre-designed and constructed samples of work performance designed to tap aspects of critical job performance usually monitored and observed by trained experts, who rate candidates on job-relevant dimensions.	Usually following initial interview and often conducted as part of an AC. Can therefore provide dynamic and highly job-relevant data for discussion at follow-up interview stage.	• High predictive accuracy. Directly relevant job tasks as samples of future behaviour. • Rated by observers on critical dimensions of job performance, some-times identical to those used for staff appraisal. • If constructed properly can add a sample of directly relevant candidate behaviour on segments of the job itself.
Assessment centres (ACs)	Multiple-method design, usually incorporating testing, interviews, and work sample exercises, where candidates are tested by observers on job-relevant dimensions. Can last from one to five days.	Usually the final stage of assessment to reach outcome decisions. Because of cost of running ACs interviews usually conducted as integral part of an AC.	• All the above, as well as: • Opportunity to observe candidates over longer period in formal and informal situations. • Multiple assessments by several assessors over several exercises can eliminate some individual biases associated with one-to-one interviews (see chapter 3).
Reference letter	Varies from very brief factual check (e.g. 'Did candidate hold this position between these dates, as claimed?') to extensive rating of abilities, personality, and attitude to work.	Commonly used as final check on candidate after conditional offer of employment has been made. Interview can throw up specific issues to be checked with previous employers by reference letter.	• Best used as factual check only. • Most appropriate as final check: references taken up with existing employer before offer of employment will not be popular with candidates!

Source: Anderson and Shackleton (1993).

THE EFFICIENCY OF THE SELECTION INTERVIEW

Over the years considerable research concerning both the validity and reliability of the selection interview has been undertaken, often with conflicting results (Anderson 1992; Hunter and Hunter 1984; Wiesner and Cronshaw 1988). In reviewing this body of research, Anderson and Shackleton (1993) suggest that, in terms of validity and reliability, the overall efficiency of selection interview decisions has, in fact, been much maligned in recent years and they highlight a number of points that merit attention.

- Interviews can be much more accurate than many recruiters may believe.
- Structured interviews that are built around a pre-planned format are more valid and reliable than unstructured, non-directed conversations (Wiesner and Cronshaw 1988).
- Interviews are significantly more accurate if based upon detailed job analysis techniques, where the interview decision reached is based on the application of both the job description and person specification.
- The interview is an appropriate and fairly reliable method for assessing job-relevant social skills (Wagner 1949; Avery *et al.* 1987).
- Interviewer accuracy varies and recruitment decisions should always be validated, that is, interviewers should check their decisions against subsequent job performance.

A well-structured interview can provide very useful information on the individual's job experience, job knowledge, cognitive ability, and social/behavioural skills that, when combined, can be used to determine person-organisation fit.

Errors and Biases in Selection

While the central question of whether 'interviewers are born, not made' remains unanswered, there is considerable evidence to suggest that the process of interviewing is all too often subject to a number of underlying biases and errors that adversely affect the selection decision (Anderson and Shackleton 1993; Wareing and Stockdale 1987; Macon and Dipboye 1988; Anderson 1992; Dale 1995). While it is untrue to suggest that all interviews are biased or error-prone, based on existing research Anderson and Shackleton (1993) have classified some of the more common errors and biases, a number of which are considered below.

- Expectancy effect – interviewers can form either a positive or negative impression of a candidate based on the biographical information from the application form/CV and this tends to have a bearing on all subsequent decisions (often termed gut instinct or snap decision).
- Information-seeking bias – based on their initial expectations, interviewers can actively seek information that will confirm this initial expectation.
- Primacy effect – interviewers may form impressions about a candidate's personality within the first five minutes of meeting him/her and tend to be more influenced by what is said early in the interview.
- Stereotyping – stereotypes can often be ascribed to particular groups of individuals, may be based on gender, race, family circumstances etc., and decisions based on stereotypes may be in breach of the current equality legislation.
- Horns/halo effect – based on information received an interviewer may rate a candidate either universally favourably or universally unfavourably. Furthermore, negative information tends to be more influential than positive information, and thus, even

where there is a balance between positive and negative information, the overall impression will tend to be negative.

- Contrast and quota effects – interviewer decisions can be inherently affected by decisions made about earlier candidates, and pre-set selection quotas. Thus, where a number of candidates have been selected for interview, those who are interviewed later are invariably compared with those who went before them (rather then being assessed specifically against pre-determined criteria).

However rigorous the process, interviewing remains essentially a selective process and thus the interviewer needs to ensure that, as far as is possible, the errors or biases described above are eliminated from the process. The operation of panel interviews or successive

---

Table 5.6 Types of interview questions

1. **Direct or closed**
These have the effect of yielding short answers such as 'yes,' 'no,' or 'sometimes': 'How did you travel?'
Note: They are useful for the purpose of getting facts, but too much use leads to a staccato interview, and a short one if the applicant is nervous.

2. **Leading**
These lead the interviewee to give the answer the interviewer expects or wants to hear: 'We are always in flux. You do like change, don't you?'
Note: There is no value in this type of question, unless the interviewers have self-deception in mind. Most interviewees would follow the lead.

3. **Topic-changing**
Moving the interview on to a new topic: 'Thanks for the information on your qualifications. Would you tell me how you chose your career route?'
Note: These questions are helpful in creating a smooth flow during the interview and are important to control your timing as you move through your interview plan.

4. **Probing and developing**
These enquire more fully into a particular area, or encourage building on an answer already given: 'Why did you say you prefer jobs that involve travel?'
Note: These questions are very important in seeking specific evidence and testing the interviewee's knowledge, experience, feelings and attitudes.

5. **Open-ended**
These encourage full answers: 'Would you tell me about how you spend your leisure time?' 'Why did you apply for this particular job?'
Note: These types of questions are very useful in getting the person talking and involved in the interview. Here the interviewee is given the opportunity to answer at length and to choose what to talk about.

6. **Reflecting back**
Reflecting back to the person what he/she has said by restating it is a question: 'Promotion is very important to you, then?' 'Are you saying you're frightened by computers?'
Note: These types of questions are important in making sure that your understanding of the information supplied is clear and accurate. It also shows that you are listening and interested in what the interviewee is saying.

7. **Command questions**
These are really statements that act as questions e.g. 'tell me about that', or 'give me an example . . .'
Note: These statements are especially useful in getting the interviewee to provide additional information on specific areas that may be required for the job. They can be quite authoritative in tone, so it's probably best to combine them with other types of question.

Overall: The most effective interview is likely to combine the range of question types and in the appropriate order and thus highlighting the importance of preparing for the interview in advance, and indeed effective training in how to interview.

Source: adapted from Evenden and Anderson (1992).

interviews can obviate many of the inherent problems associated with interviewing and can facilitate greater validity and reliability in the final decision analysis. Furthermore, attention to effective interpersonal interaction such as active listening and attendant non-verbal behaviour; competent questioning; and a facilitative interview environment (free from noise and other distractions) can further ensure that the interview is as productive as possible. Evenden and Anderson (1992) suggest that the choice of questions, and appropriate use of them, can ensure greater balance and flow to the interview itself (see table 5.6).

Testing

The use of selection tests can be used to improve the validity and reliability of the selection process, but are not used alone. Rather they tend to be used in tandem with other selection techniques, such as the interview. While a range of tests is available, the most commonly used tests, for selection purposes, include cognitive ability tests, personality tests, and performance or work sample tests. A range of cognitive tests has been designed and standardised; they are primarily used to measure an applicant's capability to perform a job (i.e. measure mathematical reasoning for IT software/programming jobs) and they have a fairly high predictive ability. Personality tests are designed to measure personality dimensions such as extroversion, conscientiousness, emotional stability, openness to new experiences and ability to get on with others and while some have high predictive ability, over-reliance on their outcomes is not advised. Performance or work sample tests require job applicants to perform some of the tasks that make up the job being applied for. They provide a fairly immediate assessment of the skills and abilities of the applicant, e.g. a computer technician asked to diagnose a problem with a server; an artist asked to provide a portfolio or produce a sketch.

Placement, Induction and Follow-up

When the selection decision is made, a job offer is made to the chosen candidate and the unsuccessful applicants are notified. Where the selection process involved a number of internal applicants, due care should be taken in communicating the selection decision to them, particularly if they have been unsuccessful. A letter of offer can constitute a legally binding document since it usually forms part of a legal contract of employment. When the offer has been accepted, it is customary to offer a period of induction for the successful candidate, which is designed to facilitate the smooth transition to work in the organisation. Induction periods vary from company to company and can last as long as three months. It is similarly common to find that the new recruit is 'on probation' for the first three months of employment to determine whether the events work out as expected (this largely depends on the job position and can be as long as twelve months in some cases).

As discussed earlier in this chapter, labour turnover tends to be highest during the induction period and thus organisations can reduce the induction crisis through a carefully managed socialisation process. This can involve furnishing the new employee with a company manual, explaining the nature of the business in greater detail, outlining the structure and hierarchy of the organisation, and providing a liaison to 'show him/her the ropes' as it were. (Coaching, mentoring, facilitation, training and development, as socialisation techniques, are further discussed in chapter ten.) Positive reinforcement and feedback are critical considerations throughout the induction period. They can be facilitated by some form of interim performance appraisal, and can aid in the establishment of behaviour norms that are desired by the organisation.

RECRUITMENT AND SELECTION IN IRELAND

With respect to the current state of play in recruitment and selection in Ireland, the 1999/2000 round of the Cranet E./University of Limerick Survey is instructive. In the survey, questions in the area of recruitment and selection focused on whether respondents were experiencing difficulties in staff recruitment and retention, the methods employed in recruitment and retention, how managerial vacancies were filled and the selection methods most commonly employed.

Turning to the issue of difficulties in recruitment and retention, which is an indicator of the current state of the labour market, the 1995 round of the survey reported that some two-thirds of Irish organisations had a staff turnover level of 5 per cent or less. The situation was somewhat different in the 1999 survey and was reflected in the number of organisations reporting difficulties in recruitment and retention, as shown in figure 5.8.

Across the employee grades of manual, clerical, professional, information technology and managerial a large number of respondents reported that they were experiencing problems in this area. The most profound difficulties lay in attracting and keeping professional and IT staff, which can be attributed to skills shortages in these areas concomitant with strong growth in the IT sector in Ireland as a result of direct foreign investment.

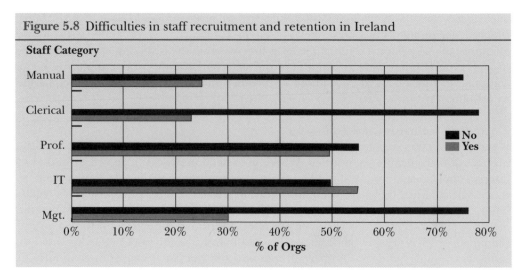

Figure 5.8 Difficulties in staff recruitment and retention in Ireland

Source: Cranet E./University of Limerick Survey (1999).

In response to the problems of recruitment and retention respondents were asked what methods, if any, they had adopted in relation to this area. The most common method found was to increase pay and benefits, quoted by 56 per cent of respondents. Retraining of existing employees was a method adopted by 53 per cent of respondents. The impetus for this arguably stemmed from either the need to meet the development requirements of employees to aid retention or from the need to look to internal recruitment as a means of filling hard to fill vacancies (see figure 5.9).

The filling of managerial vacancies is an important area of recruitment, and may have significant implications for organisational performance and the managing of human resources within a firm. The 1999 survey found that most Irish organisations chose to

Figure 5.9 Methods adopted in relation to recruitment and retention

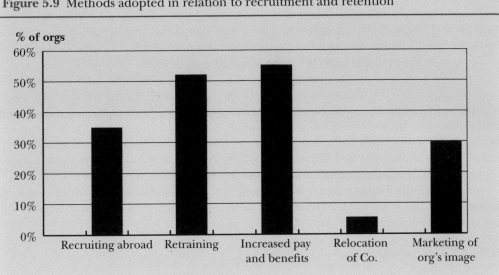

Source: Cranet E./University of Limerick Survey (1999).

recruit internally for all levels of management. However, other methods such as recruitment agencies, advertisements etc. are still commonly used, particularly in the recruitment of senior managers (see figure 5.10).

Figure 5.10 Filling of managerial vacancies

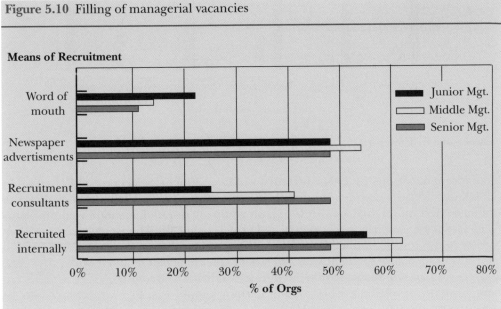

Source: Cranet E./University of Limerick Survey (1999).

As identified earlier, selection tools available to organisations range from the more traditional methods of interviews, application forms and references, through to the more sophisticated techniques such as psychometric tests and assessment centres. The selection methods used can determine whether or not the right person is matched to the right job, which in turn has knock-on effects for the firm's performance.

The data generated by the Cranet E./University of Limerick survey indicates that less use is being made of what are considered the more 'sophisticated' selection techniques. The picture emerging from the data suggests that the application form, the interview panel and reference checks remain the most commonly used selection methods, while more sophisticated and reliable techniques such as psychometric testing and assessment centres are used in a smaller number of cases. The 1999/2000 data reveal that interview panels, one-to-one interviews and application forms still remain the most popular methods of selection, with application forms being used in every appointment by 56 per cent of respondents. Reference checks are also used by 73 per cent of companies in all appointments (see figure 5.11).

Figure 5.11 Selection methods used in Ireland

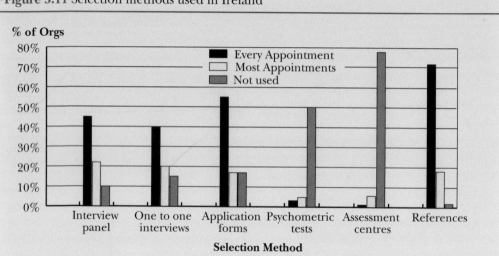

Source: Cranet E./University of Limerick Survey (1999).

More recent data from the 2004 CIPD survey of Recruitment, Selection and Retention in the UK and Ireland supports the trends in recruitment and selection depicted by the Cranet data. It found that two-thirds of Irish company respondents indicated problems filling vacancies, especially at managerial and professional level. The average length of time such vacancies remain unfilled is reported at about 9–10 weeks and companies in Ireland cited a lack of available specialist skills and lack of applicants with required work experience as the key reasons for their recruitment difficulties. In such circumstances, companies are most likely to redistribute work among existing employees. From reported costs of recruitment, the CIPD estimates the average cost of recruiting for the 'typical' job in Ireland to be €2,100, and about twice that for managerial/professional positions – the figures are about the same for the UK.

Recruiting nationally through newspaper advertising remains the most p.
recruitment strategy (86 per cent), although 77 per cent of respondents indicate tha
also operate a policy of advertising internally. Interestingly, in light of the discussion
recruitment earlier, 66 per cent of Irish companies report that they also use their own
page to highlight vacancies.

Consistent with the Cranet data, the CIPD survey highlights that the most popu
selection method in Ireland remains the interview. Significant and escalating proble
with retention are reported in the survey and here Irish respondents (similarly to their U
counterparts) cite better opportunities elsewhere, career and development issues as con
reasons for their turnover rates. Interestingly, and reflecting our discussion earlier, th
survey indicates that one in five new employees still leave the organisation within the first
six months, and, even more significantly, 50 per cent of those who leave do so within the
first two years. Irish companies indicate that their prime response to retention difficulties
has been to improve communication/involvement (47 per cent) and learning and
development opportunities (44 per cent). It is important to note, however, that annual
turnover rates (15.9 per cent for Ireland; 16.1 per cent for the UK) are not considered by
respondents to be adversely reflecting their overall performance.

Back in 1997, the CIPD's Recruitment Forum (Kilibarda and Fonda 1997) highlighted
a number of common failings in the recruitment and selection process. Included among
these failings were:

- No obvious link with HR strategy, resourcing strategy and broader business and
  organisational goals.
- A lack of job analysis and, therefore, inappropriate job descriptions and person
  specifications.
- Important details missing from recruitment advertising.
- Little use of referencing for short-listing.
- An unclear use of structured interview design and application.
- An insufficient use of occupational psychology, where psychometric testing is employed,
  together with a lack of feedback and counselling.
- An increasing use of invalid prediction methods.
- A lack of widespread monitoring and lack of remedial action in those organisations that
  did monitor recruitment.
- A lack of validation of situation specific selection procedures.

These inconsistencies can be used as a checklist for organisations today as they strive to
ensure that the time and costs associated with recruitment and selection result in positive
outcomes for the parties concerned.

In summary, this chapter has focused on human resource planning, recruitment a
selection. The nature of the human resource planning process in terms of stocktaki
forecasting, planning and implementation was set down and the benefits of engagin
the HR planning process were presented. With respect to the recruitment process
analysis and the general advantages and disadvantages attached to it were outlined
nature of the job description and the person specification were presented an
importance of outlining the terms and conditions attached to the job vacanc
discussed. The large array of recruitment options available to an organisation an
particular advantages and disadvantages were also presented. The selection optic

errors and biases commonly associated with different approaches were set down. Finally, current practices in Ireland as revealed by the 1999–2000 round of the Cranet E./University of Limerick survey and the CIPD survey (2004) were presented.

The chapter has presented a phased understanding of the HR planning and recruitment and selection process. However, as with any planning process, the dynamic interplay between all aspects and all pieces of information of the process cannot be underestimated. Indeed, as Newell (2000) has highlighted, our traditional understanding of recruitment and person-job fit is being challenged by the dynamic environment now confronting many firms. She notes that:

> The traditional view of selection and assessment presents a very static picture of the job. It underestimates the degree of change within organisations. Jobs continuously change in response to changes in the environment so that the 'square hole' today may well be the round hole next year, requiring very different knowledge, skills and attitudes. This view also presents a static view of the individual. It overestimates the personal criteria that influence job criteria and underestimates the role of situational demands. Recognising the dynamic nature of jobs and the interactions between the individual and the situation is imperative if organisations are going to achieve long-term sustainability within this knowledge-intensive age.

Nowhere is this more compelling than in the Irish labour market today.

6

Employee Motivation and the Design of Work

In 1971 Thomas Fitzgerald, writing in the *Harvard Business Review*, argued that motivation theory does not work and we should discard the dismal vocabulary of motives, motivators and motivation, and think about becoming a society of persons. His argument was based on the premise that the proposed remedies advanced by prominent motivation theorists were inadequate; because the seriousness of the motivation problem had been underestimated, and in some respects misunderstood; and because the problem of employees' motivation is rooted in certain fundamental conditions of industrial society and its solution requires costly and extensive changes in our interdependent, closely linked systems. Truth, he argued, is sometimes damaged in the process of analysis and reconstruction, and concepts can easily become more real than the reality from which they were cut.

> When transplanted from the laboratory, the language of motivation may become subtly elitist by suggesting that the employee resembles a captive rodent in a training box equipped with levers, trick doors, food pellets, and electric grids . . . When a man gets up in the morning, we can say that this act is a conditioned response to the stimulus of an alarm, but that doesn't tell us anything important.
>
> Fitzgerald (1971, 12)

More than thirty-five years later, the vocabulary prevails, promulgating concepts such as needs, wants and desires as central aspects of the human condition. However, it is recognised that effective management depends on a knowledge and understanding of human motivation that goes beyond any 'common sense conventional wisdom' (Litwin and Stringer 1968). While motivation, as a concept, is a complex phenomenon, 'frequently used', according to George and Jones (1992), 'but often poorly understood', any management practices that wish to make inroads in this area must be based on systematic knowledge about motivational processes that have *relevance* to the individual and the workplace. Managers confronted with organisational ills such as persistent absenteeism and turnover, low morale, expressed job dissatisfaction, poor job and organisational commitment and unacceptable quality, productivity and performance want, as Herzberg (1968) put it 'the surest and least circumlocuted way of getting someone to do something'.

In this chapter we explore the concept of motivation and examine the relationship between motivational processes and – that other important organisational factor – job design. Linking both motivation and job design helps to establish the important of job context in generating goal-directed behaviour and to avoid the mistaken belief that motivation is the only important determinant of work performance (Griffin and McMahan 1994). Definitional aspects of the concept are considered and the scope of motivation is examined. Various content and process theories of motivation are presented and evaluated. The main job design schools of thought are synthesised in an attempt to maximise our understanding of the main issues involved and to give a flavour of the interdependent, symbiotic nature of both motivation and job design as potential mechanisms for the delivery of sustained performance. This is considered important against the backdrop of a situation where, as Martin (2001) notes, 'increasingly the formal design of jobs is being seen as a means of improving levels of employees' motivation, quality and commitment to the objectives of the organisation'.

MOTIVATION: ROLE AND DEFINITION

Motivation at work has been the focus of sustained attention since the emergence of industrial society as a result of the industrial revolution. Steers and Porter (1987) advance a number of factors that account for the status of motivation as a crucial point of interest. First, they suggest that managers and organisational researchers cannot avoid a concern for the major behavioural requirements of the organisation. The necessity of attracting the right calibre of employee and engaging them in such a way as to ensure high performance remains a central concern of the productive process and productive effort. Second, they argue that the all-encompassing nature of the concept itself has resulted in it remaining as a central line of inquiry. As a complex phenomenon it impacts upon a large number of factors and any worthwhile understanding of organisations requires a deal of attention to be focused on this collection of factors and how they combine to create certain outcomes. Third, competitive trends in the business environment, coupled with increased business regulation, has forced organisations to seek out any mechanisms which might improve organisational *effectiveness* and *efficiency*. The ability to direct employees' efforts towards these twin goals of effectiveness and efficiency are seen as crucial. A fourth reason for the sustained interest in motivation concerns the issue of technological advancement, which is particularly evident in the job design debate. An organisation must continually ensure that its workforce is capable and willing to use advanced manufacturing technologies to achieve organisational goals. A final reason, according to Steers and Porter (1987), centres on the issue of planning horizons. Taking a longer-term perspective of the human resource in an attempt to build up a pool of well-skilled enthusiastic employees has brought the concept of motivation centrestage. Dessler (2001) highlights that it remains a central plank of current management practice and spans the range of techniques used in building a performance-oriented organisation. These include the use of performance-related pay, merit pay, on the spot rewards, skill-based pay, recognition, job redesign, empowerment, and the use of goal setting methods, of positive reinforcement and lifelong learning.

Nevertheless it is an extremely difficult area in which to apply accurate measurement. Furnham (1997, 293) notes that there are major problems in measuring job motivation. Asking people, he notes, is problematic, both because some people find it very difficult to report their motives accurately as they do not have sufficient insight into themselves, as well as the fact that there are pressures put on people to give socially desirable, rather than truthful answers. Furnham suggests that it is equally difficult to try and infer motivation from actual behaviour, 'because although it is true that efficient performance is a function of hard work, it may be impaired by a range of other activities such as the group norm of production, machine breakdown, or the non-delivery of crucial items'. He goes on to note that:

> Measuring job motivation, involvement and commitment is not very problematic in terms of theory. The major problem lies in either people dissimulating their answers (usually lying about how motivated they are to get the job, and demotivated they are on the job) or not being able to report on their motivational patterns accurately. Motivation is complex and many workers are unable to articulate what features of their job are motivating or not.
>
> Furnham (1997, 295)

However, despite such quantification difficulties, or perhaps because of them, motivation remains a central area of inquiry. The study of motivation at work has and continues to be largely based on analysing employees' behaviour at work and thus motivation theory is essentially concerned with explaining why people behave as they do, or why people choose different forms of behaviour in order to achieve different ends.

Figure 6.1 Elements of work motivation

Element	Definition	Example
Direction of Behaviour	Which behaviours does a person choose to perform in an organisation?	Does an engineer take the time and effort to convince sceptical superiors of the need to change the design specifications for a new product to lower production costs?
Level of Effort	How hard does a person work to perform a chosen behaviour?	Does an engineer prepare a report outlining problems with the original specification, or does he/she casually mention the issue when bumping into a supervisor in the hall and hope that the supervisor will take the advice on faith?
Level of Persistence	When faced with obstacles, roadblocks, and stone walls, how hard does a person keep trying to perform a chosen behaviour successfully?	When the supervisor disagrees with the engineer and indicates that a change in specifications is a waste of time, does the engineer persist in trying to get the change implemented or give up despite his/her strong belief in the need for a change?

Source: George and Jones (2001).

Westwood (1992) notes that the concept of motivation is comprised of seven key features.

- It is an internal state experienced by the individual. While it is subject to external contextual influences, an individual's motivational state develops within and is unique to oneself.

- The individual experiences a motivational state in a way that gives rise to a desire, intention or pressure to act.
- Motivation brings with it an element of choice, i.e. the individual experiencing a state of arousal as a result of an internal or external stimulus responds through choosing to act in a way and at a level of intensity that they determine.
- Action and performance are, in part, a function of motivation.
- Motivation is a multifaceted phenomenon best characterised as a complex process with multiple elements and the possibility of multiple determinants, options and outcomes.
- Individuals differ in terms of their motivational state and the factors that affect the motivational state of an individual is variable across time and situations.

Traditional approaches to employees' motivation have relied heavily on extrinsic factors, particularly pay. However, the motivation of individual employees and perceived job satisfaction will be influenced by a myriad of factors. Some will be related to individual employees and their personal characteristics. Others, such as supervisory relations or discretion, will stem either from the working environment or the job itself.

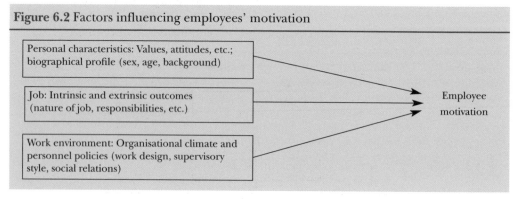

Figure 6.2 Factors influencing employees' motivation

Source: Gunnigle and Flood (1990).

In relation to individual factors, it is important that organisations select employees whose motives and work values 'fit' the organisational environment, management approach and reward package. On the other hand, the organisational climate, management style, and design of work should facilitate good performance by providing adequate opportunity for employees to satisfy their varying needs. Management must be keenly aware of the need to motivate employees through both extrinsic and intrinsic outcomes. Extrinsic outcomes are tangible and visible and include things such as a pay increase or a company car. Intrinsic outcomes relate to the satisfaction of personal wants and desires and include elements such as increased autonomy, responsibility and feedback.

However, there is no simple answer to the crucial question: How do you motivate people? Herzberg (1968) perhaps best demonstrates the complexity attached to this question:

> What is the simplest, surest, and most direct way of getting someone to do something? Ask him? But if he responds that he does not want to do it, then that calls for a psychological consultation to determine the reason for his obstinacy. Tell him? His response shows that he does not understand you, and now an expert in

communication methods has to be brought in to show you how to get through to him. Give him a monetary incentive? I do not need to remind the reader of the complexity and difficulty involved in setting up and administering an incentive system. Show him? This means a costly training programme.

This remains a vital area of inquiry in an attempt to achieve and maintain high levels of motivation, especially in competitive industry, primarily because, according to Pettinger (1994):

> There is a correlation between organisations that go to a lot of trouble to motivate their staff, and profitable business performance . . . The ability to gain the commitment and motivation of staff in organisations has been recognised as important in certain sectors of the business sphere. It is now more universally accepted as a critical business and organisational activity, and one that has highly profitable returns and implications for the extent of the returns on investment that is made in the human resource.

The word *motivation* was originally derived from the Latin word *movere*, meaning to move. Modern interpretation of motivation is somewhat more all-encompassing, expressing various understandings about how we view people and organisations. Thus while Vroom (1964) conceptualises motivation as a process governing choices made by persons or lower organisms among alternative forms of voluntary activity, DuBrin (1978) suggests that motivation centres on the expenditure of effort toward achieving an objective the organisation wants accomplished. Arnold *et al.* (1995), using a mechanical analogy, suggest that the motive force gets a machine started and keeps it going and argue that motivation concerns the factors that push or pull us to behave in certain ways. Bennet (1991) suggests that an employee's motivation to work consists of all the drives, forces and influences – conscious or unconscious – that cause the employee to want to achieve certain aims.

Most of the early work on motivation was centred on getting more out of the employee, although many of the theorists were also concerned with finding an answer to the problem that was consistent with the essential dignity and independence of the individual. Motivation theory bases its analysis of employees' performance on how work and its rewards satisfy individual employees' needs. Numerous theories have been developed over the years to aid management in identifying employees' motives and needs, the most influential of which will be discussed here.

Motivation theory bases its analysis of worker performance on how work and its rewards satisfy the individual employees' needs. The general conclusion is that if these needs are satisfied employees will be motivated to work at high-performance levels but, if not, their performance will be less than satisfactory. Of course motivation is only one factor affecting performance. Other factors, particularly technology, training, and individual ability, will have a major influence on performance levels.

A central management concern is how to get employees to perform at the height of their abilities. If this can be achieved, management will have gone a long way towards creating a successful organisation. The understanding of human needs at work and the creation of a working environment that satisfies those needs is a key task of senior management.

When discussing motivation theory, it is useful to distinguish between content and process models of motivation as they differ in their relative focus. Content models focus on the wants and needs that individuals are trying to satisfy or achieve within the situation, or *what* motivates human behaviour. They are dedicated to an exploration of individual needs, wants, desires and aspirations. The content approaches discussed here are the *hierarchy of needs theory, ERG theory, acquired needs theory* and *dual-factor theory*. Process models attempt to show how the external context drives individuals to behave in a particular fashion and how managers can change the situation to better link need satisfaction to performance, or how the content of motivation influences behaviour. The process approaches discussed here are *theory X, theory Y, expectancy theory* and *equity theory*.

Maslow's Hierarchy of Needs

Maslow, who was a clinical psychologist, suggested that human motivation was dependent on the desire to satisfy various levels of need. Maslow's *hierarchy of needs* is perhaps the most publicised theory of motivation. It seeks to explain different types and levels of motivation, which are important to individuals at different times. It is based on the principle of the existence of a series of needs that range from basic instinctive needs for sustenance and security to higher-order needs, such as self-esteem and the need for self-actualisation. Lower-order or fundamental needs, according to this theory, must be satisfied before higher-order needs can be set in motion and dealt with.

Figure 6.3 Maslow's Hierarchy of Needs

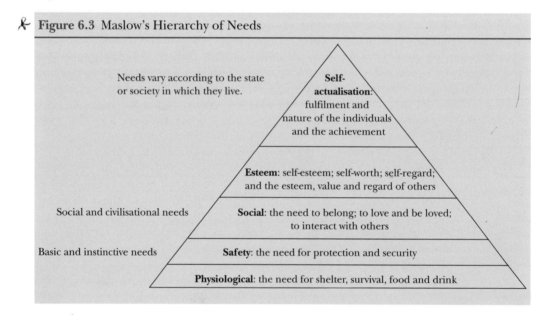

Source: Maslow (1943).

Maslow suggests that there are five levels of need, ranked in the order shown, as this is the order in which they will likely be activated by the individual in order to satisfy them. The chronological order of needs from the lowest to the highest order is important. First, it suggests that it is the next unachieved level that acts as the prime motivator. Thus people without the basic necessities of life such as food and shelter will be motivated by basic physiological and, later, security needs. Only when these have been satisfied will higher-order needs become important. And, then, only when all the lower-order needs are satisfied, do higher level needs act as a motivator – first esteem needs and ultimately self-actualisation.

The second inference arising from this ascending order of needs is that once a particular need category is satisfied it ceases to have a major impact on motivation. Thus any level of needs only motivates while it remains unachieved. Once achieved it is the next level in the hierarchy that dominates the individual's priorities.

Physiological needs include such elements as food, shelter, clothing and heat. These basic needs must be satisfied for the person to survive. In modern society it is employment and the income it generates that allows the individual to satisfy such needs.

Safety needs refer to things such as security at home, tenure at work and protection against reduced living standards. Only when physiological needs have been satisfied will the individual concentrate on safety needs.

Social or love needs refer to people's desire for affection and the need to feel wanted. Our need for association, for acceptance by others and for friendship, companionship and love might also be included here.

Esteem needs cover one's desire for self-esteem and self-confidence and also one's need for recognition, authority and influence over others. Self-actualisation refers to the need for self-fulfilment, self-realisation, personal development and fulfilment of the creative faculties (see figure 6.3).

Hierarchy of needs theory states that a need that is unsatisfied activates seeking or searching behaviour. Thus the individual who is hungry will search for food and the one who is unloved will seek to be loved. Once this seeking behaviour is fulfilled or satisfied, it no longer acts as a primary motivator: needs that are satisfied no longer motivate. This clearly illustrates the rationale for arranging these needs in a hierarchy. The sequential ascending order implies that it is the next unachieved level that acts as the prime motivator. However, need propensity means that higher-order needs cannot become an active motivating force until the preceding lower-order need is satisfied. However, individuals will

---

Figure 6.4 The self-actualising person

1. Perceives people and events accurately, without undue interference from their own preconceptions.
2. Accepts self and others, including imperfections, but seeks improvement where possible.
3. Is spontaneous, especially in their thoughts and feelings.
4. Focuses on problems outside self, rather than being insecure and introspective.
5. Is detached, so that they are not unduly thrown off course by awkward events.
6. Is autonomous, and remains true to self despite pressure to conform.
7. Appreciates good and beautiful things, even if they are familiar.
8. Has peak experiences of intense positive emotions of a sometimes mystical quality.
9. Has close relationships, but only with a few carefully chosen people.
10. Respects others, avoids making fun of people, and evaluates them according to their inner qualities rather than race or class.
11. Has firm moral standards and sense of right and wrong, though these may be different from many other people.
12. Is creative; this is perhaps the most fundamental aspect of self-actualisation and is seen as the result of the other aspects listed above. By being open-minded and open to their experience the self-actualising person sees things in novel ways and can draw novel conclusions from established information.

Source: Sugarman (1986).

seek growth when it is feasible to do so and have an innate desire to ascend the hierarchy. Self-actualisation is the climax of personal growth. Maslow (1943) describes it as the desire for self-fulfilment. The desire to become more and more what one is, to become everything that one is capable of becoming.

Maslow's theory has been the subject of much interpretation and criticism. First, Maslow's work was based on general studies of human behaviour and motivation and, as such, was not directly associated with matters central to the workplace. Arising from this, the theory is extremely difficult to apply because of the illusive nature of the needs identified, particularly in the context of the workplace. Researchers have also found little support for the concept of exclusive pre-potency. A more realistic scenario is that individuals have several active needs at the same time, which implies that lower-order needs are not always satisfied before one concentrates on higher-order needs. Another criticism of this approach is that career advancement may be the true factor underlying changes in need deficiencies. Research demonstrates that as managers advance in organisations their lower-order needs diminish. Simultaneously, they experience an increased desire to satisfy higher-order needs. Finally, it has also been suggested that the theory attempts to demonstrate an imputed rationality in human actions that may not necessarily exist. The conceptualisation of our needs in such a logical, sequential fashion, while useful as a frame of reference to which we can all compare ourselves, has not resulted in convincing evidence among researchers.

Other inconsistencies that research has thrown up include the fact that needs do not often group together in the ways predicted, the restricting of the concept of a need to a purely biological phenomenon remains problematic and needs, while often generally described, are done so with insufficient precision.

Overall, Maslow's hierarchy of needs appears to be a convenient way of classifying needs, but it has limited utility in explaining work behaviour. Its primary value has been the fact that it highlights in a general way the importance of human needs.

Existence-Relatedness-Growth (ERG) Theory
ERG theory, as developed by Alderfer (1972), reduces Maslow's fivefold needs category into a threefold taxonomy. A second major difference, stemming from criticisms of Maslow's approach, is that less emphasis is placed on a hierarchical order of lower- and higher-order needs, implying that all needs levels may be influential at the same time.

Figure 6.5 Existence-Relatedness-Growth theory

Existence	←——→	Relatedness	←——→	Growth
Physiological and material needs		Social, interpersonal and friendship needs		Personal growth, development, self-respect

Source: Alderfer (1972).

Another important variation is the proposition that an already satisfied lower-order need may be reactivated as a motivator when a higher-order need cannot be satisfied. Thus an employee who has satisfied basic material and social needs may be concerned with his personal growth and development (e.g. promotion). If there is no scope for such development he may revert back to a preoccupation with previously satisfied needs (e.g. social or financial). The other implication, referred to above, is that more than one needs category may be important at any one time. Robbins (2001, 161) summarises the contribution of ERG theory in the following way:

> ERG theory argues, like Maslow, that satisfied lower-order needs lead to the desire to satisfy higher-order needs; but multiple needs can be operating as motivators at the same time, and frustration in attempting to satisfy a higher-level need can result in regression to a lower-level need. ERG theory is more consistent with our knowledge of individual differences among people. The evidence demonstrating that people in other cultures rank the need categories differently – for instance, natives of Spain and Japan place social needs before their physiological requirements – would be consistent with ERG theory. Several studies have supported ERG theory, but there is also evidence that it does not work in some organisations. Overall, however, ERG theory represents a more valid version of the need hierarchy.

Acquired Needs Theory

An alternative approach, developed by McClelland (1961), concentrated on identifying motivational differences between individuals as a means of establishing which patterns of motivation led to effective performance and success at work. He distinguishes three basic needs in addition to physical drives:

- Need for achievement [nAch]: desire to consistently want challenging tasks demanding responsibility and application.
- Need for power [nPow]: need for control over people.
- Need for affiliation [nAff]: need for good social and personal relations with people.

McClelland suggested that these needs are acquired and developed over one's life. Depending on which needs are dominant, these will exert varying influences on work performance. People with a high need for achievement tend to have a strong motivation to take on challenging tasks and do them better. This, combined with a moderate to high need for power and a lower need for affiliation, has been suggested as a good indicator of success in senior management (McClelland and Boyatzis 1982). An important implication of this approach is that, if such needs are acquired, then they may be developed through appropriate environmental conditions that facilitate the emergence of the desired needs profile.

McGregor's Theory X, Theory Y

Unlike previous approaches that concentrated on analysing the motivations of people at work, McGregor (1960) examined managerial assumptions about employees and the resultant implications of such assumptions for managerial approaches to issues like control, job design and remuneration systems. He identified two very differing sets of assumptions about employees' behaviour and motivation which were termed theory X and theory Y.

Approaches by organisations to workforce management differ considerably and these two contrasting frameworks are useful in helping to analyse and explain management styles. Both classifications represent extreme styles and approaches to people management. In practice, organisations may adopt elements of both approaches, but often with a particular leaning that indicates a preference for one or other approach.

Traditional autocratic management approaches were clearly based on theory X assumptions. Despite considerable academic and practical support it would seem that

Figure 6.6 Theory X, theory Y

THEORY X	THEORY Y
Employees are inherently lazy, dislike work will do as little as possible.	Employees like work and want to undertake challenging tasks.
Consequently, workers need to be corrected, controlled and directed to exert adequate effort.	If the work itself and the organisational environment is appropriate, employees will work willingly without need for coercion or control.
Most employees dislike responsibility and prefer direction.	People are motivated by needs for respect, esteem, recognition and self-fulfilment.
Employees want only security and material rewards.	People at work want responsibility. The majority of workers are imaginative and creative and can exercise ingenuity at work.

Source: Gunnigle and Flood (1990).

theory Y does not have the whole-hearted backing of many senior managers. Consequently its application has often been restricted to once-off initiatives designed to deal with particular problems or issues rather than reflecting a change in corporate approaches to the way employees are managed.

Dual-Factor Theory

Herzberg (1968) was equally concerned about the impact of work and job design on motivation. He saw the key to improving employees' motivation in terms of job satisfaction. Herzberg felt that by identifying the factors at work that produced the greatest levels of satisfaction (or dissatisfaction) it would be possible to design jobs that provided job satisfaction, thereby encouraging higher levels of performance. His approach concentrated on identifying which factors contributed most to employees' satisfaction at work (called 'motivator' factors). He also sought to identify those factors that influenced levels of employees' dissatisfaction ('maintenance/hygiene' factors). Herzberg concluded that these two sets of factors were inherently different in terms of their impact on motivation and performance.

A central aspect of Herzberg's dual-factor theory is that only by varying motivator factors can management improve performance and motivation. Varying maintenance factors will reduce levels of dissatisfaction but will never act as a motivator.

The implication here is that management can only stimulate employees' motivation by designing jobs to incorporate the motivator factors (i.e. jobs that encourage and facilitate responsibility, advancement and recognition). Herzberg believed that high levels of job satisfaction could be achieved by altering job content to allow for personal growth and development while also ensuring that the job context (pay, working conditions etc.) were appropriate. This process became known as job enrichment (see job design).

Herzberg's approach has gained considerable recognition, particularly for differentiating between the impact of intrinsic and extrinsic factors on employees' motivation. Criticisms have tended to focus on its reliability of application to all types of jobs (not just professional/white collar) and the view of job satisfaction as being almost synonymous with motivation.

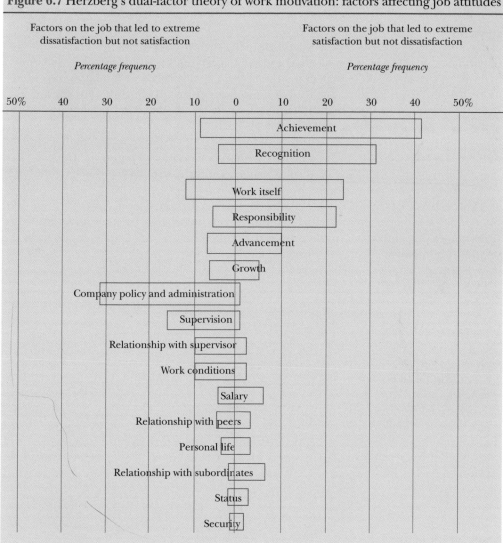

Figure 6.7 Herzberg's dual-factor theory of work motivation: factors affecting job attitudes

Factors on the job that led to extreme dissatisfaction but not satisfaction

Factors on the job that led to extreme satisfaction but not dissatisfaction

Percentage frequency

Percentage frequency

50% 40 30 20 10 0 10 20 30 40 50%

Achievement

Recognition

Work itself

Responsibility

Advancement

Growth

Company policy and administration

Supervision

Relationship with supervisor

Work conditions

Salary

Relationship with peers

Personal life

Relationship with subordinates

Status

Security

Source: Herzberg (1968).

Expectancy Theory

Most of the approaches discussed above represent attempts to identify a general set of employees' needs, which cause workers to behave in a certain way. The belief is that by identifying such needs management can provide for their ease of achievement, thus facilitating improved performance. Many of these approaches rank such motives or goals in a hierarchical order with self-actualisation as the ultimate motivator.

However, most managers will probably point out that employees differ markedly in terms of motivation. One may find two employees, similar in terms of age, sex and background, one of whom will strive to achieve high-performance levels, undertake additional tasks etc., while the other is content to get by doing the minimum acceptable to the organisation.

How does one explain such variations? One approach that avoids attempts to find a definitive set of employees' motives, but seeks to explain individual differences in terms of goals, motives and behaviour, is expectancy theory. Associated with Vroom (1964), expectancy theory focuses on the relationship between the effort put into the completion of particular activities by the individual and the expectations concerning the actual reward that will accrue as a result of expending the effort. Expectancy theory attempts to combine individual and organisational factors that impact on this causal effort/reward relationship. Broadly, this theory argues that individuals base decisions about their behaviour on the expectation that one or another alternative behaviour is more likely to lead to needed or desired outcomes. The relationship between one's behaviour and particular desired outcomes is affected by individual factors such as personality, perception, motives, skills and abilities, and by organisational factors such as culture, structure and managerial style (the context in which one is operating).

Thus, expectancy theory avoids attempts to isolate a definitive set of employees' motives, but rather seeks to explain individual differences in terms of goals, motives and behaviours. It postulates that employees' motivation is dependent on how the employer perceives the relationship between effort, performance and outcomes.

Figure 6.8 Expectancy theory

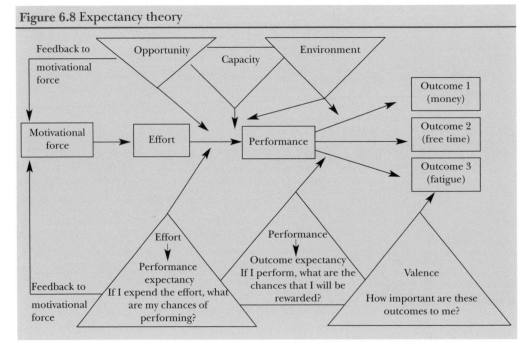

Source: Umstot (1988).

Mabey and Salaman (1995, 191) note that expectancy theory has been developed from Vroom's early specifications to be expressed very clearly as a combination of three factors, namely expectancy, instrumentality and valence.

Expectancy is the probability assigned by the individual that work effort will be followed by a given level of achieved task performance (value = 0 to 1). It refers to the perceived probability that a particular level of effort will lead to desired performance levels. If the desired outcome (e.g. bonus pay) demands a given level of performance (production goals), the individual employee must believe that level is achievable or he will not expend the necessary effort. (If I tried, would I be able to perform the action I am considering?)

Instrumentality is the probability assigned by the individual that a given level of achieved task performance will lead to various work outcomes (rewards) (value = 0 to 1). Thus expectancy theory suggests that employees' decisions on how they perform are based upon their perception of desired outcomes, whether performance targets are achievable and an evaluation of the likelihood that by achieving these targets they will realise their desired outcomes. (Would performing the action lead to identifiable outcomes?)

Valence is the value attached by the individual to various work outcomes (rewards) (value = -1 to +1). It is thus a measure of the strength of attraction that a particular outcome or reward has for the individual employee. (How much do I value these outcomes?)

The motivational appeal of a given work path is drastically reduced whenever any one or more of the factors approaches the value of zero. Thus the model suggests that the individual's level of effort (motivation) is not simply a function of rewards. The individual must feel that they have the ability to perform the task (expectancy), that this performance will impact on the reward and that this reward is actually valued. Only if all conditions are satisfied will employees be motivated to exert greater effort in the performance of a job. It is critical that individuals can see a connection between effort and reward and that the reward offered by the organisation will satisfy employees' needs. However, there is no simple formula, since individuals possess different preferences for outcomes and have different understandings of the relationship between effort and reward. They may well be motivated in very different ways. Among the criticisms levelled at the theory are the difficulties associated with testing the theory empirically, and the fact that it assumes a type of rationality with respect to how the individual thinks and behaves, which may not exist. This approach suggests that employees will expend a high level of effort if they believe this will result in performance levels that will be rewarded by valued outcomes. These valued outcomes may vary between individuals. One may value money, another promotion, and yet another recognition. However, it is not only the outcome that is important, but also the belief that valued outcomes can be achieved through improved effort and performance.

In relation to the implications of expectancy theory for management, Vroom (1964) suggests that managers must seek to understand the goals and motives of individual employees, ensure these are clearly and positively linked to desired performance levels which in turn are achievable from the employee's perspective. Lawler (1978) goes a little further and highlights specific areas for management action:

- Need to establish what are valued outcomes.
- Need to specify desired and achievable performance levels.
- Ensure there is a clear link between effort, performance and desired outcomes.
- Ensure adequate variation of outcomes available.
- Ensure equity and fairness for the individual employee.

Expectancy theory does not attempt to identify a universal set of motivational factors. Rather it highlights the importance of a range of potential motivational factors. These may be either intrinsic or extrinsic. Intrinsic outcomes are those originating from doing the job (sense of achievement, satisfaction) while extrinsic outcomes are those provided by other people, particularly management, and include pay and promotion.

Equity Theory

The concept of a fair day's work for a fair day's pay is often utilised to express how the parties to the labour process wish to perceive the employment relationship. Equity theory, sometimes referred to as justice theory, resembles expectancy theory in that it sets down the individual's cognitive process that determines whether or not he/she will engage in the effort-reward bargain within the framework of the social exchange process.

Developed by Adams (1965), the equity theory of motivation is based on the comparison between two variables: inputs and outcomes. 'Inputs' refers to what the individual brings to his/her employment and includes things such as effort, experience and skills. 'Outcomes' describes the range of factors the employee receives in return for his/her inputs, i.e. pay, recognition, fringe benefits and status symbols. Adams suggests that individual expectations about equity correlation between inputs and outcomes are learned during the process of socialisation in the home or at work and through comparison with the inputs and outcomes of others. Adams (1965) suggests that individuals can:

- change inputs, i.e. can reduce effort if underpaid;
- try to change their outcomes, i.e. ask for a pay rise or promotion;
- psychologically distort their own ratios by rationalising differences in inputs and outcomes;
- change the reference group to which they compare themselves in order to restore equity.

Huseman *et al.* (1987) enumerate the core propositions of equity theory as follows:

1. Individuals evaluate their relationships with others by assessing the ratio of their outcomes from, and inputs to, the relationship against the outcome-input ratio of another comparable individual.
2. If the outcome-input ratios of the individual and the comparable other are deemed to be unequal, then inequity exists.
3. The greater the inequity the individual perceives (in the form of either over-reward or under-reward), the more distress the individual experiences.
4. The greater the distress an individual experiences, the harder he/she will work to restore equity. Among the possible equity restoration techniques the individual might use are: distorting inputs or outcomes; disregarding the comparable other and referring to a new one; or terminating the relationship.

Thus, employees will formulate a ratio between their inputs and outcomes and will compare this ratio with the perceived ratios of inputs and outcomes of other people in the same or a similar situation. If these two ratios are not equal then the individual will take action in an attempt to restore a sense of equity.

Considerable research interest has been generated in testing the relationships advanced by Adams, particularly those relationships that focus on employees' reactions to pay.

Overall, the research highlights support for Adams' theory about employees' reactions to wage inequities. Mowday concludes that the research support for the theory appears to be strongest for predictions about under-payment inequity. Furthermore, equity theory appears to offer a useful approach to understanding a wide variety of social relationships, which may occur in the workplace.

Table 6.1 Equity theory research on employees' reactions to pay

Study	Equity condition	Method of induction	Task	Dependent variables	Results
Adams (1963)	Overpayment; hourly and piece rate	Qualifications	Interviewing	Productivity, work quality	Hourly overpaid subjects produced greater quantity; piece-rate overpaid subjects produced higher quality and lower quantity than equitably paid subjects
Adams and Jacobsen (1964)	Overpayment; piece rate	Qualifications	Proof-reading	Productivity, work quality	Overpaid subjects produced less quantity of higher quality
Adams and Rosenbaum (1962)	Overpayment; hourly and piece rate	Qualifications	Interviewing	Productivity	Hourly overpaid subjects produced more quantity, while piece-rate overpaid subjects produced less quantity
Anderson and Shelly (1967)	Overpayment; hourly	Qualifications, importance of task	Proof-reading	Productivity, work quality	No differences were found between groups
Andrews (1967)	Overpayment and under-payment; piece rate	Circumstances, previous wage experiences	Interviewing, data checking	Productivity, work quality	Overpaid subjects produced higher quality and under-paid subjects produced greater quantity and lower quality
Arrowood (1961)	Overpayment; hourly	Qualifications, work returned	Interviewing	Productivity	Overpaid subjects had higher productivity
Evans and Simmons (1969)	Overpayment and under-payment; hourly	Competence, authority	Proof-reading	Productivity, work quality	Underpaid subjects produced more of poorer quality in competence condition; no difference found in other conditions
Friedman and Goodman (1967)	Overpayment; hourly	Qualifications	Interviewing	Productivity	Qualifications induction did not affect productivity; when subjects were classified by perceived qualifications, unqualified subjects produced less than qualified subjects
Goodman and Friedman (1968)	Overpayment and under-payment; hourly	Qualifications, quantity v. quality emphasis	Questionnaire coding	Productivity, work quality	Overpaid subjects produced more than equitably paid subjects; emphasis on quantity v. quality affected performance
Goodman and Friedman (1969)	Overpayment; piece rate	Qualifications, quantity v. quality emphasis	Questionnaire scoring	Productivity, work quality	Overpaid subjects increased productivity or work quality, depending on induction

Table 6.1 Equity theory research on employees' reactions to pay *(contd.)*

Study	Equity condition	Method of induction	Task	Dependent variables	Results
Lawler (1968b)	Overpayment; hourly	Qualifications, circumstances	Interviewing	Productivity, work quality	Overpaid (unqualified) subjects produced more of lower quality; subjects overpaid by circumstances did not
Lawler, Koplin, Young and Fadem (1968)	Overpayment; piece rate	Qualifications	Interviewing	Productivity, work quality	Overpaid subjects produced less of higher quality in initial work session; in later sessions subject's perceived qualifications and productivity increased; the need for money was related to productivity for both groups
Lawler and O'Gara (1967)	Underpayment; piece rate	Circumstances	Interviewing	Productivity, work quality	Underpaid subjects produced more of lower quality and perceived their job as more interesting but less important and more complex
Pritchard, Dunnette and Jorgenson (1972)	Overpayment and under-payment; hourly and piece rate	Circumstances, actual change in payment	Clerical task	Performance satisfaction	Circumstances induction did not result in performance differences for piece rate, but some support was found for hourly overpay and under-pay Changes in pay rate supported hourly predictions; some support found for piece rate overpayment prediction but not for underpayment
Valenzi and Andrews (1971)	Overpayment and under-payment; hourly	Circumstances	Clerical task	Productivity, work quality	No significant differences found between conditions; 27% of underpaid subjects quit; no subjects in other conditions quit
Wiener (1970)	Overpayment; hourly	Qualifications, inputs v. outcomes, ego-oriented v. task-oriented	Word manipulation		Outcome-overpayment subjects produced more; input-overpaid subjects produced more only on ego-oriented task
Wood and Lawler (1970)	Overpayment; piece rate	Qualifications	Reading	Amount of time reading, quality	Overpaid subjects produced less, but this could not be attributed to striving for higher quality

Source: Mowday (1987).

WORK DESIGN

The nature of work organisation and design will significantly influence the degree to which work is intrinsically satisfying for employees and promotes high levels of motivation. Indeed, early concern with job design, according to Brooks (1999), focused almost exclusively on attempts to improve individual motivation and it remains the case that organisations should carefully consider their approach to work design and choose the approach that best suits their particular needs.

The study of individual tasks in organisations has long been accorded a high degree of importance in organisation and management literature and theory. Investigation in the area has attempted to describe strategies for changing or refining jobs so as to enhance variables such as effort, performance, motivation, satisfaction, commitment, absenteeism and so forth. Historically and presently the focus within job design has been on results and outcomes (Janson 1979). There is a body of opinion that sees at least some of the roots of the industrial and indeed social problems of modern societies in the nature of poorly structured work (Kopelman 1985). The central view of the various schools of thought, according to Kelly (1980), is that the organisation of work on the basis of task fragmentation is counterproductive. It is suggested that the situation can be remedied by reversing the division of labour and meeting the social needs of individuals at work, as well as the economic needs of employers. The central issue therefore, in Lupton's (1976) words, is 'how to design for best fit'. Over the years the field of job design has been characterised by shifts from one theoretical perspective to another. According to Griffin (1987), the primary shifts have been from task specialisation (e.g. Taylor 1911), to job enlargement (e.g. Walker and Guest 1952), to job enrichment (e.g. Herzberg 1968), to socio-technical systems theory and the quality of working life (QWL) movement (e.g. Cherns and Davis 1975) to high-performance work design (e.g. Hackman 1987; Buchanan and McCalman 1989; Morley 1994).

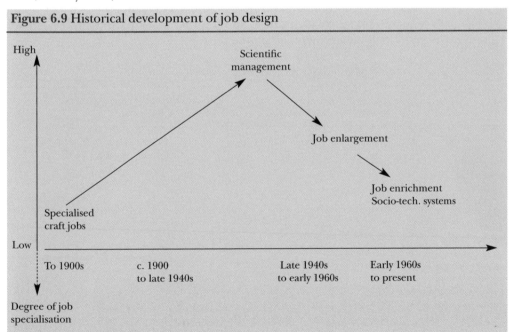

Figure 6.9 Historical development of job design

Source: Adapted from Moorhead and Griffin (1989).

145

Broadly conceived, work organisational design refers to the way the various tasks in the organisation are structured and carried out. It reflects the interaction of management style, the technical system, human resources and the organisation's products or services. Davis (1966) defines the process of job design as that which is concerned with the '. . . specification of the contents, methods, and relationships of jobs in order to satisfy technological and organisational requirements, as well as the social and personal requirements of the job holder'. Concurring with this definition, the following table demonstrates that the reasons that employers restructure jobs are a mix of improving productivity, reducing or eliminating organisational problems and providing satisfying work for employees.

Cherns and Davis (1975) identify three parties with an explicit interest in job restructuring, employees' motivation and satisfaction and work performance. The first, they claim, is labour, primarily represented by unions and other organised bodies. Unions are seen to be interested in 'the conditions of work, learning and adaptability, reward and satisfaction, and future structures of formal relationships with management'. The second party to the process is management; they are interested in the efficient use of their human resources through the development of appropriate work methods. Finally there is the state. Government is seen to be concerned with matters related to labour and management because of the integral part they play in the successful running of the economy. Manpower planning, training and education, income policy, unemployment and the enhancement of industrial democracy projects are, argue Cherns and Davis (1975), typically regulated by the institutions of the state.

The design of individual jobs is seen to impact particularly upon employees since it influences job content, employees' discretion, degree of task fragmentation and the role of supervision. Decisions on the organisation of work are primarily a management responsibility and the particular approach chosen will be a good indicator of corporate beliefs about how employees should be managed and jobs structured, and about the role of supervision. It will also reflect the organisation's approach to many aspects of personnel management as manifested through attitudes to recruitment, employees' development, motivation, rewards and management/employee relations.

Table 6.2 Reasons for introducing job changes

	Birchall and Wild		Reif and Schonerbek		Total
	Blue-collar	*White-collar*	*Blue-collar*	*White-collar*	
System output					
Productivity	12	9			21
Costs	5	3	21		29
Quality	7	5	13		25
Down time	1				1
Inventories	1				1
Skills	2	2			4
Flexibility	3	3			6
Specialisation			14		14
System changes					
Introduction of automated equipment	2	1			3
Introduction of new plant	3	2			5

Table 6.2 Reasons for introducing job changes *(contd.)*

	Birchall and Wild		Reif and Schonerbek		Total
	Blue-collar	*White-collar*	*Blue-collar*	*White-collar*	
Personnel problems					
Labour turnover	6	5		6	17
Absenteeism	4	1			5
Attract labour	1				1
Improve labour relations	2	2			4
Concern for employee					
Worker morale	10	7	15		32
To give meaning to work	4	4			8
Monotony			11		11
Eliminate social problems	3				3
Others	8	3	4	6	21
Total	74	47	78	12	211

Source: Birchall (1975).

Task Specialisation

Kopelman (1985) notes that task specialisation, task standardisation and work simplification are three of the key implementing concepts of what is often referred to as the classical approach to job design. Variously referred to as task specialisation, scientific management or Taylorism, the traditional approach to the organisation of work was dominated by a desire to maximise the productive efficiency of the organisation's technical resources. Choices on the organisation of work and the design of jobs were seen as determined by the technical system. Management's role was to ensure that other organisational resources, including employees, were organised in such a way as to facilitate the optimal utilisation of the technical system. This efficiency approach is based on scientific management principles and has been a characteristic of employer approaches to job design since the turn of the century. Jobs were broken down into simple, repetitive, measurable tasks whose skills could be easily acquired through systematic job training.

Figure 6.10 Traditional approach to job design

Characteristics	Outcomes
Bureaucratic organisation structure	Tight supervisory control
Top-down supervisory control	Minimal need for employee discretion
Work planning separated from execution	Work measurement
Task fragmentation	Reliance on rules and procedures
Fixed job definitions	Job specialisation
Individual payment by results	Reduced job flexibility
	Short training time
	Little employee influence on job or work organisation

The rationale for this approach to work and job design was based on 'technological determinism', where the organisation's technical resources were seen as a given constraint and the other inputs, including employees, had to accommodate the technical system. It also reflected managerial assumptions about people at work. Close supervision, work measurement and other types of controls indicate a belief about employees akin to McGregor's theory X. It suggests that employees need to be coerced to work productively and that this is best achieved by routine, standardised tasks.

Figure 6.11 The three main objectives of Taylorism

High productivity: through the identification of the best way of doing each task and of applying the use of monetary incentives workers would be encouraged to produce efficiently. This would benefit both company and employee financially and in other ways.

Standardisation of work activity: through the application of work-study techniques the best way would be identified and each employee would be carefully selected to match the needs of the task. This would standardise both work activity across employees and the performance they achieved (through the application of incentive payments).

Discipline at work: he also attempted to introduce an improved hierarchical approach to authority, which would allow the decisions of managers to be effectively cascaded throughout the organisation. This would allow a more effective control of workforce activity, channelling it in the desired directions, which the scientific management designed jobs would then convert into a highly cost-effective output.

Source: Martin (2001).

This traditional model of job design has undoubtedly brought positive benefits to many organisations. It helped improve efficiency and promoted a systematic approach to selection, training, work measurement and payment systems. However, it has also led to numerous problems such as high levels of labour turnover and absenteeism and low motivation. Thus short-term efficiency benefits were often superseded by long-term reductions in organisational effectiveness. Many behavioural scientists argued that the effectiveness of organisations could be increased by recognising employees' abilities and giving them challenging, meaningful jobs within a co-operative working environment. The consequence, according to Newell (1995, 22) in her treatise on the 'healthy organisation' was that:

> Taylor had a limited perspective on human needs and motivation. He saw a worker as no different from a machine. With a machine, output depends on the amount of fuel put in. Likewise, with a worker, output was seen to depend on the amount of fuel put in: however in this case the fuel needed was money. No account was taken of the individual's psychological needs for interesting work with some degree of challenge and autonomy. Nor was account taken of the psychosocial needs of workers for friendship and support. Indeed, Taylor explicitly tried to prevent the formation of work groups, seeing these as a potential threat to managerial control, and so to efficiency.

More recently the increased emphases on improving quality, service and overall competitiveness have led to the emergence of other schools of thought aimed at restructuring work systems to increase employee motivation, commitment and performance. Much of the focus of work of the successors to task specialisation has been on the restructuring of jobs to incorporate greater scope for intrinsic motivation. Subsequent schools questioned traditional management assumptions about why employees worked. The traditional approach saw employees as essentially instrumental in their attitudes to work. Jobs were seen as a means to an end and it was these extrinsic rewards that motivated employees. Consequently employers created work systems with closely circumscribed jobs, supervised work and rewarded quantifiable performance.

Job Enlargement

Regalia (1995, 13) suggests that, in the European context at least, there is no doubt that demands for greater employee say and participation in the organisation of their work as well as worker commitment and interest in productive goals have had a long history. Job enlargement and job enrichment as alternative mechanisms of work structuring differ in their relative emphases; the former makes one's job 'bigger', while the latter adds some element to the job that is dedicated to increasing the employees' psychological growth. Job enlargement grew from the arguments of humanitarians in the 1950s that production methods prevalent at the time created poor working conditions that led to high levels of job dissatisfaction. The proposed solution was job enlargement, which, when introduced, would lead to more variety and less routine work. This assumption was drawn upon by Walker and Guest (1952) in their study of automobile assembly lines. They studied 180 workers and identified six main characteristics of mass production technology: (i) repetitiveness, (ii) low skill requirement, (iii) mechanically paced work, (iv) little alteration of tools or methods, (v) low requirement for mental attention and (vi) minute sub-division of product.

In concluding that the solution to eliminating the ills of mass-production technology lay in job enlargement, their proposals have generated some debate. The disputed issues centre on meaning and methodology. Walker and Guest viewed job enlargement as 'the combination of more than two tasks into one'. However, this did not in any way distinguish it from 'job extension', which could possibly be nothing more than the addition of more meaningless tasks (Wall 1982). It has been argued that there is no explicit theory on which the concept of job enlargement can become a model of job restructuring. There is no motivation theory, according to Buchanan (1979), on which job enlargement stands. Aldag and Brief (1979) note that job enlargement experiments failed to use a conceptual framework of how the structuring of jobs should be actually executed. Furthermore, Buchanan (1979) argues that job enlargement studies have largely ignored external variables and people's differing attitudes towards work.

Job Enrichment

Largely attributed to Herzberg (1968) job enrichment was developed for the advancement of the dual-factor theory of work motivation. The job enrichment approach suggested that employees gain most satisfaction from the work itself and it was intrinsic outcomes arising from work which motivated employees to perform well in their jobs. In his celebrated article 'One more time: how do you motivate employees?' Herzberg establishes the concept of vertical loading as a means of moving away from the addition of 'one meaningless task to the existing (meaningless) one'. Vertical loading, dedicated to the addition of more challenging dimensions to the job remains the mainstay of job enrichment.

Figure 6.12 Principles of vertical job loading

Principle	Motivators involved
A. Removing some controls while retaining accountability	Responsibility and personal achievement
B. Increasing the accountability of people for their own work	Responsibility and recognition
C. Giving a person a complete natural unit of work (module, division, area, etc.)	Responsibility, achievement, and recognition
D. Granting additional authority to an employee in their activity; job freedom	Responsibility, achievement, and recognition
E. Making periodic reports directly available to the worker rather than to the supervisor	Internal recognition
F. Introducing new and more difficult tasks not previously handled	Growth and learning
G. Assigning people specific or specialised tasks, enabling them to become experts	Responsibility, growth, and advancement

Source: Herzberg (1968).

In a similar treatise of intrinsic outcomes and job satisfaction, Hackman and Oldham (1980) enumerate three basic conditions necessary for promoting job satisfaction and employees' motivation.

- Work should be *meaningful* for the doer.
- Doers should have *responsibility* for the results.
- Doers should get *feedback* on the results.

This approach suggested that it was the design of work and not the characteristics of the employee that had the greatest impact on employees' motivation. Hackman and Oldham identified five 'core job characteristics' that needed to be incorporated into job design to increase meaningfulness, responsibility and feedback.

1. Skill variety: extent to which jobs draw on a range of different skills and abilities.
2. Task identity: extent to which a job requires completion of a whole, identifiable piece of work.
3. Task significance: extent to which a job substantially impacts on the work or lives of others either within or outside the organisation.
4. Autonomy: freedom, independence and discretion afforded to the job holder.
5. Feedback: degree to which the job holder receives information on their level of performance, effectiveness, etc.

Having identified the factors necessary to promote satisfaction and intrinsic motivation, the next stage is to incorporate these characteristics into jobs through various job redesign strategies. Hackman and Oldham suggest five implementation strategies to increase task variety, significance and identity, and create opportunities for greater autonomy and feedback.

1. Form natural work groups: arrange tasks together to form an identifiable, meaningful cycle of work for employees, e.g. responsibility for single product rather than small components.
2. Combine tasks: group tasks together to form complete jobs.
3. Establish client relationships: establish personal contact between employees and the end user/client.
4. Vertically load jobs: many traditional approaches to job design separate planning and controlling (management functions) from executing (employee's function). Vertically loading jobs means integrating the planning, controlling and executing functions and giving the responsibility to employees (e.g. responsibility for materials, quality, deadlines and budgetary control).
5. Open feedback channels: ensure maximum communication of job results (e.g. service standards, faults, wastage, market performance and costs).

Figure 6.13 Designing enriched jobs

How does management enrich an employee's job? The following points, which we have just alluded to in the text, are derived from the application of the Job Characteristics Model and they seek to specify the types of changes in jobs that are most likely to lead to improving their motivation potential score.

Combine Tasks: Management should seek to take existing and fractionalised tasks and put them back together to form a new and larger module of work. This effort increases both skill variety and task identity.

Create Natural Work Units: The creation of natural work units means that the tasks that an employee does form an identifiable and meaningful whole. This increases employees' ownership of the work and improves the likelihood that employees will view their work as meaningful and important rather than irrelevant and boring.

Establish Client Relationships: The client is the user of the product or service that the employee works on (and may be an internal customer within the organisation or an external one beyond the organisation). Wherever possible, managers should try to establish direct relationships between workers and their clients. This has the impact of increasing skill variety, autonomy, and feedback for the employee.

Expand Jobs Vertically: Vertical expansion gives employees responsibilities and control that were formally reserved for management. In particular it seeks to close the gap between the 'doing' and the 'controlling' aspects of the job, and it increases employees' autonomy.

Open Feedback Channels: By increasing feedback, employees not only learn how well they are performing their jobs, but also whether their performance is improving, deteriorating, or remaining at a constant level. Ideally, this feedback about performance should be received directly as the employee does the job, rather than from management on an occasional basis.

Source: Hackman (1977).

Figure 6.14 Model of job characteristics

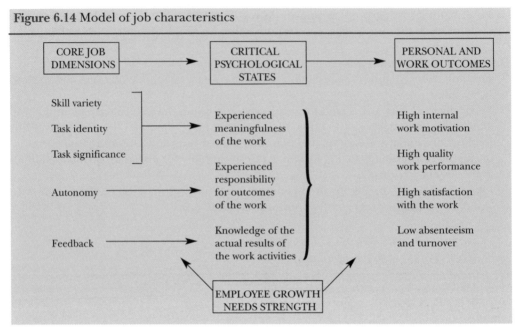

Source: Hackman and Oldham (1980).

Having proved to be 'by far the most popular approach to task design' (Roberts and Glick 1981), the espoused advantages of redesigning jobs along the lines of Hackman and Oldham's job characteristics model have been summarised thus:

> By redesigning jobs to increase variety, identity, significance, autonomy and feedback, the psychological experience of working is changed . . . individuals experience the work as more meaningful, they feel more responsible for the results, and they know more about the results of their efforts. These psychological changes lead to many improved work outcomes, which have been observed following the redesign of work.
>
> Beer *et al.* (1985, 576–7)

Hackman and Oldham thus argued that changes have positive long-term benefits for both the organisation and the individual employee, such as increased motivation and improved performance. However, their theory also posits that not all workers are expected to respond favourably to job enrichment initiatives (Hackman *et al.* 1975) 'Employee growth needs strength' is considered the most important source of variation in this respect: only those workers with a strong desire for achievement, responsibility and autonomy will be motivated by increased intrinsic satisfaction and hence motivated to perform better (see figure 6.16). For other workers, these changes may be a source of anxiety and lead to resentment and opposition to job redesign and other changes in the work system.

The utility of job enrichment has been tested in a variety of work contexts such as banking, medicine and telecommunications. In evaluating the results, Schermerhorn *et al.* (1985, 213) conclude that while the results have been promising, further research is necessary to refine and support the concept.

At the moment, researchers generally feel that job enrichment is not a universal panacea for job performance and satisfaction problems. They also recognise that job enrichment can fail when job requirements are increased beyond the level of individual capabilities and/or interests.

In the Irish context, support for the job enrichment approach is to be found in Blennerhassett's study of motivation among civil service executives (Blennerhassett 1983). This study found that respondents identified the work itself as the most important potential source of job satisfaction and motivation. However, Blennerhassett also found that respondents rated their jobs very poorly on the core job characteristics of skill variety, identity, significance etc. and generally felt their jobs allowed little scope for satisfaction, motivation or involvement. Since the study population was executive and higher executive officers, these findings raise serious question marks about the design of jobs in the civil service, and possibly beyond.

The 'Quality of Working Life' Movement

While job enrichment has the potential to positively impact on how employees experience work, its focus on job content has certain limitations. Clearly, many factors beyond job content impact on how employees experience work, such as working conditions, employees' involvement and autonomy, work intensity and the nature of supervision. The 'quality of working life' (QWL) approach has its origins in the US during the 1960s and 1970s (see, for example, Walton 1973; Skrovan 1983). Focusing on the overall quality of employees' experiences in the workplace, it embraces both job design and broader issues such as autonomy, employees' participation, justice, working conditions and job security as critical factors impacting on the quality of working life. A particular stimulus for the QWL approach was a desire to improve the quality of working life for employees by avoiding what were seen as characteristics of a low quality of working life (Morley *et al.* 1998). Figure 6.15 summarises some of the main characteristics of low and high quality working life as identified in the extant literature (see for example Steers and Porter 1987; Schermerhorn *et al.* 1985; Schuler and Jackson 1996).

Figure 6.15 High and low quality working life: indicative characteristics

Low Quality of Working Life	*High Quality of Working Life*
• Jobs characterised by low levels of task significance, variety, identity and feedback	• Adequate and fair reward systems
• No or little employee involvement	• Safe and healthy working conditions
• Top-down communications	• Opportunity to use personal capabilities
• Inequitable reward systems	• Opportunity for personal growth and development
• Inadequate job definition	• Integration into social system of organisation
• Poor employment conditions/Hire and fire approach	• High labour standards/employee rights
• Discriminatory HR policies	• Pride in relevance and value of work
• Low job security	• Balance between work and non-work roles

Source: Morley, Moore, Heraty and Gunnigle (1998).

Beyond the job enrichment initiatives mentioned earlier, the QWL movement seeks to increase employees' influence and involvement in work organisation and job design. Again, this challenges some traditional management assumptions about employees. It involves recognising that employees can and want to make a positive input into organisational decision-making. It assumes that such involvement is valued by employees and results in increased commitment, responsibility and performance.

Increased employee influence in work system design also addresses the issue of employee supervision as an aspect of the management role. If employees are to be involved in making decisions about the organisation of work and responsible for the subsequent execution of such decisions, much of the 'control' aspect is removed from the supervisory role. It necessitates a change in attitude to workforce management. Supervisors become less concerned with monitoring and controlling employees' performance and more involved in advising and facilitating employees in carrying out their jobs.

This approach requires high levels of commitment and trust from both management and employees. Management must feel confident that employees have the required competence and will use their greater levels of influence positively and to the benefit of the organisation. Employees must be happy that their increased commitment and sense of responsibility will not be abused or exploited by employers.

There are various mechanisms available to encourage increased levels of employees' participation in the design and operation of work systems. Possibly the best known approach is quality circles. These are small groups of employees and managers who meet together regularly to consider means of improving quality, productivity or other aspects of work organisation. They are seen as having played an important role in the success of Japanese organisations and have been successfully applied in Western economies including Ireland.

There are numerous other participative and consultative mechanisms that may be established and can work effectively in the appropriate organisational environment. Creating such an environment has become an important concern for organisations. Past experience in applying various techniques to improve employees' motivation and involvement has demonstrated that these operate best where there is a change in the overall corporate approach. The issue for senior management is how to create a corporate culture whose values, beliefs and practices establish an organisational environment within which employees are highly committed to and work towards the achievement of business goals.

High-Performance Work Systems (HPWS)

Commentators such as Buchanan and McCalman (1989) suggest that the heretofore limited impact of job design theories is a weakness that needs to be remedied. 'It (job design) has tended to be regarded as an isolated management technique aimed at local organisational problems and at individual jobs rather than realising that it must form part of the whole company philosophy, through all levels, if it is to be really successful'. The motive behind high-performance work systems (HPWS) is rooted in the desire and the need to improve the overall competitive position of the organisation. As Buchanan and McCalman comment, 'the new strategic imperatives require new work organisation strategies'.

The notion of HPWS is very much associated with the new high-tech companies of the 1980s, and especially those that located to greenfield sites in attempts to establish a fundamentally different type of organisation and organisation culture. The essence of HPWS appears to lie in the adoption of a culture of continuous improvement and innovation at all levels in the organisation and the implementation of a range of work and human resource practices to sustain and develop this culture; in particular team-working, quality consciousness and flexibility (Morley *et al.* 1998). They are also felt to reflect an increased management emphasis on developing broadly defined, challenging jobs within more organic, flexible organisation structures:

> The high-performance work organisation has a distinctive structure which is designed to provide employees with skills, incentives, information and decision making responsibilities that will lead to improved organisational performance and facilitate innovation . . . The main aim is to generate high levels of commitment and involvement of employees and managers.
>
> Tiernan *et al.* (1996, 113)

High-performance work systems are thus seen as embracing much more than a change in the nature of jobs. Rather, they appear to embrace fundamentally different assumptions about organisational structure and orientation, so that all aspects of organisational management are altered to embrace a new culture designed to improve performance and responsiveness through developing a more committed, flexible and skilled workforce (see for example, Buchanan 1994).

As a means of distinguishing high-performance work design from previous movements Mooney (1988) draws upon the differences between system and value changes within organisations. As the concept implies, a system change simply encompasses changes of methodology or ritual, he argues. Many of the previous job design schools were built on principle. On the other hand, value changes, according to Mooney, run deeper, involving a re-focus on fundamental business tenets. Thus, while the HPWS school involves system changes to accompany the new emphasis, they are driven and sustained by value changes dedicated to the creation of a new order in workplace relations, and a revised understanding of them.

As noted earlier, a primary driver of HPWS is increased pressure on organisations to improve organisational competitiveness. This indeed may explain its prevalence in high-technology sectors, especially electronics and software, which tend to be characterised by high levels of market volatility and product innovation. In relating the experience of the Digital Equipment Corporation (possibly the most prominent early exemplar of high-performance work systems), Perry (1984, 191) notes how the company's Connecticut (Enfield) plant sought to respond to increased competition and product change.

> The goal at Enfield was flexibility: the capacity to respond quickly and effectively to an uncertain environment. Traditional ways of handling uncertainty had included the introduction of new procedures, changing the structure, employing more people, and tightening management controls. These strategies simply increased overheads, increased the complexity of the organisation and generated more uncertainty. To deal with these issues, management decided to introduce a more participative style of decision-making, multi-skilled operating teams, an innovative rewards system, and systematic career planning and development. The plant manager's review of these changes revealed: a 40 per cent reduction in product manufacturing time; a sharp increase in inventory turnover; a reduction in the level of management hierarchy to three; a 38 per cent reduction in standard costs; a 40 per cent reduction in overhead and equivalent output, with half the people and half the space.
>
> Buchanan (1994, 102)
> [Summary of a more detailed review by Perry (1984)]

HPWS are also closely linked to the idea of benchmarking performance against external standards: the idea that organisational performance should be disaggregated and compared to valid external standards such as cycle time, re-work, labour costs and productivity (Vaill 1982). The external comparators may be other similar companies or simply other plants with the organisation's portfolio. The growth of total quality management and, particularly, quality accreditation schemes have been an important catalyst in this regard. For example, companies who trade internationally often seek to achieve ISO 9000, which is a worldwide standard. In Ireland the Quality Mark Scheme, introduced in 1982, is an increasingly important goal.

Clearly, an important dimension of HPWS entails the development of new or different approaches to the management of employees as well as in regard to the structure of jobs and systems. These themes pervade both what is termed the high-performance literature (Vaill 1982; Perry 1984; Lawler 1986; Buchanan and McCalman 1989), and indeed the excellence literature (Peters and Waterman 1982; Moss Kanter 1983; Quinn Mills 1991). Almost all contributors highlight the need to empower employees in an attempt to make the organisation more effective. While commentators may differ on detail, there is overwhelming support for the use of team-based work systems as a means of developing a highly skilled, flexible and motivated workforce within a leaner, flatter, more responsive organisation structure.

In evaluating the impact of HPWS, it is necessary to consider the extent to which this development represents a fundamentally new approach to the design of jobs and work systems. Huczynski and Buchanan (1991) address this issue and identify the following distinctions between the high-performance work systems (HPWS) approach of the 1990s and the quality of work life (QWL) approach of the 1960s and 1970s:

1. *More strategic focus*: it is argued that the HPWS approach seeks to improve organisational competitiveness through increased flexibility and quality, while the QWL approach primarily concentrated on achieving reductions in absenteeism and turnover.
2. *Focus on performance rather than job experience*: the HPWS approach has a strong focus on performance criteria; increased employee autonomy is seen as leading to increased employee competence and skills, better decision-making, greater flexibility and adaptability and better use of technology. In contrast, the major rationale of the QWL approach was based on improving the job experience of employees; increased autonomy was seen as leading to increased worker satisfaction and a better job experience.
3. *Major change in management style*: the HPWS approach is seen as requiring a fundamental overhaul of management style, requiring major cultural change and redefinition of the role of management, from top management down. The QWL approach appeared to be more limited, involving only a re-orientation in the role of first line supervisors.
4. *Long term comprehensive strategy*: the HPWS approach is seen as a major change initiative affecting the whole organisation and involving a long-term commitment by all parties. The QWL approach tended to be more of a 'quick fix applied to isolated and problematic work groups' (Huczynski and Buchanan 1991, 86).
5. *Representative of strategic human resource management*: consistent with the argument that the 1980s and 1990s witnessed a move from 'reactive/operational' personnel management to 'strategic' human resource management (HRM), it is argued that HPWS is a key element of strategic HRM while QWL is more of a personnel administration technique.

Figure 6.16 Organisational characteristics of high-performance, high-involvement work systems

Organisational Structure	Flat and lean Enterprise-oriented Team-based Participative structure; councils, fora
Job Design	Job enrichment Autonomous teams/work groups
Information System	Open flow Work/job focus Decentralised – team/group-based Participatively established goals/standards
Career System	Career tracks/ladders/counselling Open job posting
Selection	'Realistic' job preview Team/group-based Potential- and process-skill-oriented
Training	Strong commitment and investment Peer training 'Economic' education Interpersonal skills
Reward System	Open Skill-based Gain-sharing/share ownership Flexible benefits All salary/egalitarian
Personnel Policies	Employment tenure commitments Participatively established through representative group(s)
Physical Layout	Based on organisational structure Egalitarian Safe and pleasant

Source: Adapted from Lawler (1982).

In Ireland, the first prominent examples of organisations that sought to develop high-performance work systems along the lines described above came from the ranks of firms that had previously experimented with such systems elsewhere. These were mostly US high-tech companies such as Digital, Apple and Amdahl. More recently we have seen greater diversity in the range of companies undertaking such initiatives. One of the mostly widely quoted examples is that of Bord na Mona (see O'Connor 1995; Magee 1991). Here we find a semi-state company that, by the 1980s, faced severe competitive problems, particularly in relation to (high) costs, (poor) productivity and a pressing need to improve quality, performance and employee relations (Magee 1991). In an attempt to deal with these issues, the company undertook a number of radical initiatives. First, a new multi-disciplinary and team-based management structure was established. The initial challenge was to reduce costs, which was addressed by a major redundancy programme that saw 2500 workers (out of approximately 5000) leave the company. After this, management initiated a more fundamental overhaul:

> It was recognised by everyone concerned . . . that cost-cutting through redundancy would not be enough. We had to change our work practices at the same time. We knew that a fundamental restructuring of how we did our business had to be undertaken to create flexibility in adapting to changing markets, to improve productivity and to improve our competitive position. After extensive negotiation, the 'enterprise scheme' was introduced with the full agreement and co-operation of all parties. The Bord na Mona enterprise scheme allows our staff to form their own autonomous enterprise units, which are team-based and where the unit's earnings are directly related to performance and productivity. *Our workers have become their own bosses.*
>
> O'Connor (1995, 116)

The introduction of autonomous work groups (AWGs) meant that instead of working in isolation, the workers became team members. Leaders were selected for these AWGs, which then assumed responsibility and authority for the completion of tasks (Tiernan *et al.* 1996). In addition to the establishment of AWGs, Bord na Mona also reduced the number of levels in the management hierarchy. It seems that the results of these various changes have been extremely positive. Edward O'Connor, then managing director of the company, summed up the experience as follows:

> The spirit of enterprise this has brought into Bord na Mona has increased productivity per workers in a way that is truly amazing. Our productivity has increased by 75 per cent. Our people now make their own decisions and take their own risks. The series of work groups or enterprise units that have been set up have different structures, but essentially Bord na Mona supplies them with services and they produce quality peat, at a price that is agreed in advance. These are people who, formerly, did what they were told to do, got paid whether or not peat was produced, whether the sun shone all summer or whether it rained all the time . . . The new work practices and systems we have introduced amount to nothing less than a fundamental restructuring of the organisation.
>
> O'Connor (1995, 117)

In evaluating the impact of HPWS, an issue of particular significance is their effect on the work experience of employees. It is particularly important to address the coupling of initiatives to improve direct employee involvement with the application of management techniques designed to improve quality and productivity, especially just in time (JIT) and statistical process control (SPC) systems. Just in time (JIT) approaches focus on reducing waste, with particular emphasis on eliminating inventories (of materials, work in progress and finished goods). Statistical process control (SPC) approaches seek to apply rigorous statistical analysis of quality and performance levels to improve performance.

The introduction of these initiatives is generally rooted in the premise that increased direct employee involvement and autonomy is consistent with the use of JIT, SPC or related techniques. Indeed the arguments that direct employee involvement/autonomy mutually complements the use of SPC and JIT is often a key selling point in encouraging employees (and their trade unions) to co-operate in the introduction of such approaches. However, this is not necessarily the case. In her incisive review of the implications of techniques such as JIT and SPC for employees and their work experience, Klein (1989, 60) argues that such changes in production systems do not necessarily make for a more empowered workforce.

> In Japan . . . where JIT and SPC have been used most comprehensively, employees are routinely organised into teams, but their involvement in workplace reform is typically restricted to suggestions for process improvement through structured quality control circles or kaizen groups. Individual Japanese workers have unprecedented responsibility. Yet it is hard to think of them exercising genuine autonomy, that is, in the sense of independent self-management.

Using examples from both the US and Japan, Klein argues that increased pressures and constraints on workers are a common by-product of such manufacturing reforms. Her analysis challenges the view that high-performance work systems necessarily contribute to an improved work experience for employees. In particular, Klein points to important aspects of the work experience that may regress or be lost as a result of reforms using SPC and JIT.

1. *Individual autonomy* may be reduced due to the elimination of inventories under JIT, resulting in less slack or idle time which in turn limits the opportunity for workers to discuss issues, evaluate changes and make suggestions.
2. *Team autonomy* may be reduced because of the greater interdependency between groups due to the absence of buffer inventories, with resulting work pressures reducing the time available to consider broader changes in the work system.
3. *Ability to influence work methods* may be reduced because SPC sets strict guidelines for working methods and procedures.

However, this analysis does not necessarily mean that high-performance work systems incorporating JIT and SPC cannot positively impact on the job experience of workers. Rather, it points to the fact that these techniques and systems may be applied in different ways. Thus, the issue of management choice is important. Equally important, one could argue, is the role of workers and trade unions in influencing management choice as to the nature of deployment of these new systems. It is plausible to argue that unfettered management prerogative in introducing so called high-performance work systems can contribute to a regression in employment conditions and the work experience of employees.

It would appear that the optimal means of facilitating workers' influence on the application of new work systems is through some combination of direct and indirect participation.

Lean Production

A contemporary development very much associated with HPWS is the focus on lean production. As Legge (2000) notes, lean production systems rest on the principle of eliminating anything that does not add value to the end product. It is, she notes, characterised by the absence of indirect workers, buffer stocks and the re-work typical of mass production, and by the presence of re-skilled, multi-tasked workers using flexible equipment, organised on cellular lines for small-batch, just-in-time, right-first-time production with rapid changeover. Much of the literature in this field emanates from the automobile manufacturing sector and merits brief review here.

In 1990 researchers at the Massachusetts Institute of Technology (MIT) published the results of one of the largest studies undertaken in the automobile or any other industry (Womack, Jones and Roos 1990). The study looked at ninety assembly plants in seventeen countries. It concluded that the industrial world is experiencing the most revolutionary change since the growth of mass production, as Japanese inspired 'lean production techniques begin to replace conventional means of mass production' (*European Industrial Relations Review* 1992, 13).

In its attempt to discern the source of Japanese advantage, the MIT study concluded that their success was due primarily to what they termed 'lean production'. This term was used to indicate that it involved using 'less' of almost everything when compared to mass production: half the human effort, half the manufacturing space, half the investment in tools and half the engineering effort (Womack, Jones and Roos 1990). Additional advantages noted in the study included the need to carry lower inventory (less than half of that associated with conventional mass production), a lower level of defects and greater product variety. The development of lean production is attributed to Eiji Toyota, and the MIT study identified the main characteristics of lean production or 'Toyotism' as follows:

- Workers are organised into teams with a leader who, unlike the mass-production fore-man, undertakes assembly work and fills in for absent workers. Teams are given responsibility for the functions previously carried out by indirect workers such as simple machine maintenance, quality control, materials ordering and clearing up the work area.
- There is a 'zero defect' approach to production, involving an effective system for immediately detecting defects and problems, and tracing them to their root cause to make sure they do not recur. As the process is perfected, almost no 'rework' is necessary.
- 'Lean' product development techniques, involving strong design team leadership, personnel continuity of development teams, and an emphasis on communications and 'simultaneous development', drastically reduce the time and effort involved in manufacturing.
- Production in small batches, in order to eliminate the costs of high inventories of finished parts required by mass production systems. Cars are built to specific order, with the assistance of flexible machinery, and parts are delivered on a just-in-time basis.
- An absence of vertical integration. Instead, production of parts and components is rationalised in a hierarchy of suppliers. Thus, 'first tier' suppliers are responsible for working as an integral part of the development team, while 'second tier' suppliers are responsible for making the components required for the first tier supplier.

In evaluating the job experience of workers under lean production we find some divided opinions. The authors of the MIT study argue that while lean production requires very high effort levels from workers, it represents a more positive work experience than conventional mass production. The essence of the MIT argument is that lean production contrasts the 'mind-numbing stress' of mass production by providing workers with the skills to exercise greater control over their work environment.

However, in a review based on the experiences of the Swedish automobile industry, Berggren (1990) challenges the MIT argument that lean production is fundamentally different to mass production. This study compares Japanese lean production systems with Swedish 'whole car' manufacturing systems. Berggren argues that lean production essentially represents another stage in the evolution of mass production, since it entails many of the core characteristics of that system: pre-defined work processes, short job cycles, repetitive tasks and intense supervision. He also points to the intense demands which lean production places on workers in areas such as working time, flexibility, effort levels and attendance. Based on his research of five Swedish plants with different work systems, Berggren concludes that the further one moves away from assembly line work systems towards 'whole car systems' the greater the improvements in terms of the job experience of workers (on dimensions such as job satisfaction, challenge, stress and employee involvement).

This chapter has explored the principles of motivation and work design. Definitions were set down and the pedigree of both concepts in the management cannon were established. In relation to motivation, hierarchy of needs theory, ERG theory, acquired needs theory and dual-factor theory were all examined under the umbrella of content approaches to understanding motivation at work. Theory X, theory Y, expectancy theory and equity theory, as process theories of motivation, were also examined. Finally, the importance of work organisation and job design as a critical determinant of employee satisfaction and motivation at work has been presented and the various schools of thought have been synthesised.

The issues raised in this chapter are related to broader corporate choices about the nature and role of the organisation. Employee performance will be influenced by a variety of factors relating to both the individual and the work context. The work environment is seen as particularly important. As information technology becomes more flexible in its application, employers have possibly greater scope to introduce changes in work organisation. Apart from the necessity for management commitment and positive beliefs about people at work, these changes have broader implications for other HRM policy choices. In particular it is important that any changes in work organisation complement decisions taken in other HR areas, especially in human resource planning, selection, employee development, employee relations and remuneration.

Decisions on work organisation and job design represent a critical aspect of human resource management in organisations. They influence key areas such as organisational structure, management style, employees' motivation and reward systems. While environmental factors exercise a key influence, top management still retain considerable discretion in making choices on the nature of work systems. Indeed, the growth in sophistication and flexibility of information technology may allow employers greater scope to introduce changes in work organisations.

Employees' selection and development are particularly significant since corporate choices on work and job design need to dovetail with workforce needs and motives. The degree of congruence between the work system, job design and employees' needs will be a major influence on employee relations.

7

Reward
Management

Understanding the construct of reward systems, its impact upon the organisation's structure, system, strategies and employees, has been an area of continued intrigue (Werner and Ward 2004), and in today's business environment, its importance should not be underestimated. It has been highlighted (Morley and McCarthy 1999) that the quantity of evidence on the apparent significance of reward policies and practices and their links to organisational outcomes, though controversial, is beginning to grow. This is largely as a result of the recognition that compensation practices must be relevant in a world where there is increasing competition and awareness of the contribution of the human asset to overall organisational performance (Gerhart and Rynes 2003; Miller and Lee 2001; Morley *et al.* 2001; Benchley 2001; Bloom and Milkovich 1998).

Reward management has become especially important in helping to attract and retain employees and also in influencing performance and behaviour at work (Allen 2001; Stredwick 2000). As Sanfilippo and Weigman (1991) put it, 'in the 1990s there is a recognition that compensation practices must be relevant to a world where there is unrelenting competition at every level and more awareness that labour productivity is a key dimension of making a profit'. While Lawler (2000) in his treatise on 'Rewarding Excellence' argues that strategic success is heavily dependent on how well the organisation's reward systems support the organisation's strategic intent. Viewed in this way, it becomes obvious that *pay, incentives* and *benefits* are of central importance to employees and organisations alike. Subsumed under the label 'reward management' are numerous objectives relating to human resource plans and business strategies, high-performance and continuous improvement, the satisfaction of individual needs and wants, cultural maintenance and the promotion of teamwork. High or low pay, the nature of incentives and the range of fringe benefits in existence provide a valuable insight into the corporate approach to human resources. How the reward package is structured and applied may have a major impact on employee performance and it represents 'a major mediating mechanism between the requirements of those planning the organisation and the desires and interests of the employees' (Bowey 1975, 57).

This chapter explores the concept of reward management. Pay, incentives and benefits as possible components of the overall reward package are defined and the objectives and scope of reward management are examined. During the course of the chapter, it will become obvious to the reader that the management of rewards is more than just direct wages and salaries paid. Additional direct payments in the form of bonuses and other incentives are used extensively. A growing cost for many employers is employees' benefits, which represent indirect reward because employees receive the value of the benefits without getting direct cash payments (Mathis and Jackson 1994). The reward package is often one of the largest costs faced by employers with many having labour costs as high as 50 per cent of all operating costs. It will also become clear that although the total cost of a reward system is reasonably straightforward to calculate, the value derived by employers and employees is much more difficult to identify and quantify. In order to help clarify where added value might accrue, issues in the design of an effective reward system are considered and the meaning, purpose and methods of job evaluation are set down. The choice of pay, incentive and fringe benefits available to an organisation are presented and examined. Finally, the debate on pay as a motivator is briefly examined.

THE SCOPE OF REWARD MANAGEMENT

As with the design of the work system, an organisation's reward system is a powerful indicator of its philosophy and approach to people management. Three aspects of the reward package are worth distinguishing at the outset, namely *pay*, *incentives* and *benefits*. Pay refers to the basic wage or salary that an employee receives. An incentive refers to the rewarding of an employee for effort that results in higher performance that goes beyond normal performance expectations. Benefits refer to indirect rewards such as health insurance cover and pension entitlements associated with organisational membership. In relation to incentive schemes that emphasise differential rewards based on performance as a means of increasing motivation, it is not axiomatic that higher motivation will follow. Such schemes have numerous drawbacks in terms of design, operation and negative side effects. For this and other reasons many organisations use standard pay rates that do not vary according to performance. In establishing a remuneration system an organisation must weigh up the motivational aspects of a performance-related scheme against its drawbacks in terms of operational and other difficulties. It must be established in the context of the organisation's strategic needs and manpower profile, and be part of the overall human resource approach encompassing other motivational factors appropriate to the organisation and relevant to the workforce.

Schuler (1995) outlines a number of core objectives underlying an organisation's reward package.

- It serves to attract potential employees: in conjunction with the organisation's human resource plan and its recruitment and selection efforts, the reward package and its mix of pay, incentives and benefits serves to attract suitable employees.
- It assists in retaining good employees: unless the reward package is perceived as internally equitable and externally competitive, good employees may potentially leave.
- It should serve to motivate employees: the reward package can assist in the quest for high-performance by linking rewards to performance i.e. having an incentive element.
- It contributes to human resource and strategic business plans: an organisation may want to create a rewarding and supportive climate, or it may want to be an attractive place to work so that it can attract the best applicants. The reward package can assist these plans and also further other organisational objectives such as rapid growth, survival or innovation.

Thus the reward package is important to the organisation because it helps to attract and retain employees and influence performance and behaviour at work, though the extent to which reward management actually achieves performance improvements remains somewhat disputed (Smith 1992). Concomitantly it is important to employees because it provides the means to satisfy basic needs and may also allow them to satisfy less tangible desires for personal growth and satisfaction.

Figure 7.1 Components of the reward package

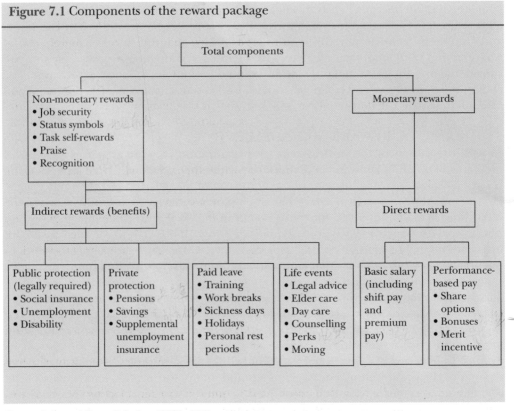

Source: Adapted from Schuler (1995, 384).

Overall, regardless of how it is constituted, and clearly employers do have choices in this area, the reward package is centrally important to the organisation. It serves to attract potential employees, something that may be more or less difficult, depending on the nature of the external labour market. In conjunction with the organisation's human resource plan and its recruitment and selection activities, the reward package and its mix of pay, incentives and benefits serves to attract suitable employees. It also assists in the retention of good employees, provided that the reward package is perceived to be both internally equitable and externally competitive. In relation to internal equity, rewards must be seen as fair when compared to others in the organisation. The criteria for the allocation of rewards should be equitable and clear and should be relatively easily understood. These should be communicated and accepted by all parties and applied consistently throughout the organisation. In terms of external competitiveness, the package must be seen as fair when compared to those offered for comparable work outside the organisation. More broadly, it constitutes a core aspect of the human resource and business planning process.

Concomitantly, it is important to employees because it provides the means to satisfy basic needs for survival, security and may also allow them to satisfy less tangible desires for personal growth and satisfaction.

TOWARDS AN EFFECTIVE REWARD SYSTEM

Important considerations in the design of an organisation's reward system will be the relative emphasis on extrinsic versus intrinsic rewards, the role of pay and whether it is contingent upon individuals' performances and its compatibility with the organisation's business goals and other human resource policies. This latter issue is particularly significant since the organisation's reward system must complement overall business objectives and other human resource policy choices. Decisions on the organisation's cost structure and market strategy will influence the reward strategy. A high-volume, low-cost strategy may constrain the organisation's ability to provide expansive rewards. On the other hand a product innovation strategy may require a comprehensive reward system that attracts and retains high calibre staff. The reward system must also 'fit' with other HR decisions. Recruitment and selection will provide a particular workforce profile and the reward system must cater for their various needs. The reward system also complements HR practices in areas like employee development and promotion.

The design and implementation of an effective reward system has proven a difficult task for many organisations. Beer *et al.* (1985) suggest that many employee grievances and criticisms of reward systems actually mask more fundamental employee relations problems. Because extrinsic rewards are a tangible outcome of an employee's relationship with an organisation, they are an obvious target for discontent within the employment relationship. Dissatisfaction with elements of this relationship, such as the supervisory style or opportunities for personal development, may manifest themselves in dissatisfaction with aspects of the reward system. Consequently, organisations experiencing problems with their reward system should examine decisions taken on other human resource policy issues, such as selection, employee relations or work design, rather than making piecemeal changes to the compensation package.

Another potential problem concerns suggestions that pay should be contingent on individual performance. Support for contingent payment systems is based on the concept that it is fair and logical to reward individual employees differentially, based on some measure of performance. While this principle is rarely a source of contention, problems may arise in attempting to develop reliable and acceptable mechanisms for evaluating employee performance. These include the limited criteria used (e.g. work-study), inconsistency of application (e.g. performance appraisal), or bias and inequity in employees' evaluations. A more fundamental issue may be resentment towards the exercise of managerial control via performance measurement and reward distribution, which is inherent in many 'reward-for-performance' approaches.

In attempting to develop an effective reward system, Lawler (1977) highlights the following essential characteristics.

- Reward level: the reward package must satisfy basic needs for survival, security and self-development.
- Individuality: apart from satisfying basic needs the reward system must be flexible enough to meet the varying individual needs of the organisation's employees.
- Internal equity: rewards must be seen as fair when compared to others in the organisation; criteria for the allocation of rewards should be equitable and clear; these should be

communicated and accepted by all parties and applied consistently throughout the organisation.

- External equity: rewards must be seen as fair when compared to those offered for comparable work outside the organisation.
- Trust: management and employees must believe in the reward system; employees accepting that certain rewards will be forthcoming when the relevant criteria are met; management trusting that employees will perform at an appropriate level in return for such rewards.

Thus the objectives of an effective reward system encapsulate the identification of prevailing market trends, balancing individual and groups needs with organisational needs and/or constraints, ensuring fairness and equity, inducing and rewarding higher levels of performance and working within the law.

DETERMINING THE RELATIVE VALUE OF JOBS

Of primary importance is the establishment of basic pay levels for various jobs. Here again the organisation must be aware of the need to establish pay equity. This initially applies to *external comparisons* with pay levels in other organisations. Comparable pay rates influence an organisation's ability to attract and retain employees. Suitable comparable organisations should be chosen to maintain pay competitiveness while keeping wage costs at reasonable levels. Pay levels will be influenced by factors in the broader business environment such as:

- Economic climate: here factors like levels of inflation, disposable income and industrial activity will exert both direct and indirect influences on payment levels by affecting employment levels, demand, consumer price indices, etc.
- Labour market: the state of the labour market will be influenced by general economic factors. It will also depend on labour supply and demand for certain skills and local factors like the level of company closures, emigration, etc. Information on local and national pay rates may be obtained through wage surveys of comparable organisations.
- Government policy: Government will exert considerable influence on pay levels both indirectly (fiscal policy) and directly through what it pays its own employees (state, semi-state sector), national pay guidelines, minimum pay levels (Joint Labour Committees), and legislation (e.g. equal pay).
- Trade unions: through collective bargaining trade unions will seek to improve or, at least, maintain their members' earning levels. Such claims will generally be based on comparability, differentials and cost of living increases.

They will also depend on factors relating to the organisation itself. Managerial philosophy and style in managing employees will impact upon approaches to the supervision, development and payment of employees. The organisation's competitive position will influence its ability to reward employees. These factors help determine the organisation's position as a low, high or average payer, which in turn will influence the choice of comparable organisations for pay purposes.

Organisations must also strive to maintain *internal equity* in determining differential pay rates for various jobs. The establishment of an internal pay structure involves deciding the relative value of jobs within an organisation and results in the creation of a hierarchy of job grades. The perceived equity of internal job grades will impact upon employees' performance and commitment. Grading can equally be a source of grievance and conflict, which requires careful handling.

Establishing fair and consistent pay rates and differentials between jobs is an important step in developing an effective compensation system. Management will want to ensure that jobs that contribute most to the organisation are rewarded appropriately. They will also be keen to ensure that conflict over pay and job grading is kept to a minimum by establishing an equitable and consistent system for grading jobs and determining differentials. Aspirations for pay equity can be partially satisfied by ensuring pay rates are competitive in comparison with other organisations. Before this, however, the organisation should establish an acceptable mechanism for internally grading and evaluating jobs.

The initial stage in establishing the relative worth of jobs is an analysis of job content. This will often be achieved through systematic job analysis that should provide detailed information on the duties, demands, responsibilities and skills of the various jobs in the organisation. Such information may then be used to establish the organisation's grading structure and decide related pay levels through some method of job evaluation.

Approaches to Job Evaluation

Job evaluation is often described as being concerned solely with the techniques used to establish the comparative worth of jobs within an organisation, but is also, according to Armstrong and Baron (1995) about making decisions on what people should be paid for the work they do. It is a technique for determining the relative worth of jobs within an organisation so that differential rewards may be given to jobs of different worth. It operates by examining job content and placing jobs in a hierarchy according to their contribution to the attainment of corporate objectives. Fowler (1996) notes that:

> Selecting the right job evaluation system is crucial if the resulting pay frameworks are to be consistent with an organisation's structure, style and values. There is no one best scheme. Each organisation needs to assess its own requirements and set these against the range of available methods.

Armstrong and Baron (1995) cite the following key purposes of job evaluation:

- to provide a rational basis for the design and maintenance of an equitable and defensible pay structure;
- to help in the management of the relativity existing between jobs within the organisation;
- to enable consistent decisions to be made on grading and rates of pay;
- to establish the extent to which there is comparable worth between jobs so that equal pay can be provided for work of equal value.

Job evaluation schemes are commonly classified into *non-analytical schemes* and *analytical schemes*. Non-analytical schemes involve the making of comparisons between whole jobs without analysing them into their constituent parts or elements. Among the main schemes here are *job ranking, job classification* and *paired comparison*. Analytical schemes involve jobs being broken down into a number of critical factors that are then analysed and compared, using a quantitative measure. Among the main analytical methods are *points rating, Hay method* and more recently, *competence-based* job evaluation.

We now turn to a description of the non-analytical and analytical schemes mentioned.

Job Ranking

Ranking is the simplest method of job evaluation and according to Armstrong and Baron (1995) 'is almost intuitive'. It aims to judge each job as a whole and determine its place in a job hierarchy by comparing one job with another and arranging them in perceived order of importance, their difficulty, or their value to the organisation. No attempt is made to quantify judgements. A ranking table is then drawn up and the jobs thus ranked are arranged into grades. Pay levels are then agreed for each grade. Sometimes a single factor such as skill is used; alternatively a list of factors such as skill, responsibility, complexity and physical demands is used. Armstrong and Baron (1995) list the following advantages and disadvantages of job ranking.

Advantages

- It is in accord with how people instinctively value jobs.
- It is simple and easily understood.
- It is quick and cheap to implement, as long as agreement can be reached on the rank order of the jobs without too much argument.
- It is a way of checking the results of more sophisticated methods to indicate the extent to which the hierarchies produced are felt fair – but this may simply reproduce the existing hierarchy and fail to eliminate the gender bias.

Disadvantages

- There are no defined standards for judging relative worth – and therefore no rationale to defend the rank order – it is simply a matter of opinion.
- Ranking is not acceptable as a method of determining comparable worth in equal-value cases.
- Evaluators need an overall knowledge of every job to be evaluated, and ranking may be more difficult when a large number of jobs are under consideration.
- It may be difficult, if not impossible, to produce a felt-fair ranking for jobs in widely different functions, when the demands made upon them vary significantly.
- The division of the rank order into grades is likely to be somewhat arbitrary.

Overall, job ranking as a method of job evaluation is most useful for small organisations with a limited range of jobs to evaluate.

Job Classification

Job classification is more complex than job ranking in that classes or grades are established and the jobs are then placed into the grades. Thus, it begins, not by ranking jobs, but by agreeing a grading structure. Initially the number of job grades and particular criteria for these grades are agreed, so that for each job grade there is a broad description of its key characteristics. The number of grades is usually limited to between four and eight, between each of which there are clear differences in the demands made by any job in its respective grade. In establishing the grades, benchmark jobs considered to be particularly characteristic of each job grade are chosen, and using detailed job descriptions, all other jobs are evaluated by comparison with both the benchmark jobs and the criteria for each job grade. Evaluated jobs are then placed in their appropriate grades. Job classification advantages include:

- Its simplicity and the ease with which it can be understood.
- Greater objectivity than job ranking.
- Standards for making grading decisions are provided in the form of the grade definitions.

Key disadvantages include:

- The basis of the job evaluation is either one factor or an intuitive summary of many factors.
- It is difficult to apply to more complex jobs where duties and skills do not fit neatly into one grade but overlap with other grades.
- It may not be able to cater for a wide range of jobs or for senior jobs where grade descriptions have to be very general.
- Because it is not an analytical system it is not effective as a means of establishing comparable worth and is unacceptable in equal value cases.

Paired Comparison

More sophisticated than the previous two methods, the paired comparison approach is based on the premise that it is more reasonable to compare one job with another than to consider a larger number of jobs together. The method requires the comparison of each job individually with every other job, until one builds up a rank order of jobs. When a job is deemed to be of higher worth than the one to which it is being compared, it is awarded two points. If it is deemed to be of equal worth it receives one point; if it is found to be of less worth it receives no points. The points are then totalled for each job and a rank order is produced.

The main advantage of this approach is that it is easier to compare one job with another at a time, which results in greater overall consistency. The main disadvantages are that it relies on whole or complete job ranking, which is difficult, and there is a limit to the number of jobs that can be ranked.

Points Rating

Points rating is a widely used method of job evaluation. It involves breaking down each job into a number of component job factors and then analysing these separately defined factors, which are assumed to be common to all jobs. Gunnigle and Flood (1990) suggest that it is based on the assumption that the degree to which differences in the job factors arise will accurately reflect the actual difference between total jobs. The selection of the job factors is critical. Benge (1944), who first promulgated the method, suggested that it should be limited to the following five factors, which he believed were the universal factors found in all jobs: skill requirements; mental requirements; physical requirements; responsibility; and working conditions. Each of these job factors may then be broken down into a number of sub-factors. The sub-factors of responsibility might well include financial, quality, equipment and materials, training and others. Once the factors and sub-factors have been agreed, point values are then allocated (see table 7.1).

Table 7.1 Points rating job evaluation

| | LEVEL | | | | |
Factor	1 Minimum	2 Low	3 Moderate	4 High	Total points
Responsibility					
(*a*) Financial	10	20	30	40	
(*b*) Quality	10	20	30	40	
(*c*) Equipment	10	20	30	40	
(*d*) Training	10	20	30	40	
(*e*) Other	10	20	30	40	200
Working conditions					
(*a*) Hazardous	15	30	45	60	
(*b*) Unpleasant	10	20	30	40	100

In the example shown here, responsibility is twice as important as working conditions, while in relation to working conditions, hazardous conditions get more points than those that are simply rated as unpleasant. The various jobs may then be evaluated and placed in their appropriate grades. This can be done by either taking one factor and evaluating its significance in all jobs under consideration, or taking each job and evaluating it in terms of all job factors. The former approach is recommended as it concentrates on the comparable worth of jobs in terms of a specific factor and this information can be brought together at the end to give a total picture of relative job worth.

Among the advantages of points rating are:
- It is systematic and analytical in the sense that it compares jobs on a factor by factor basis.
- The standards of comparison are clearly defined.

Frequently cited disadvantages include:
- It is complex and difficult to understand.
- It can be time-consuming and expensive.
- Although analytical, it still relies on a good deal of subjective judgement.
- It may be impossible to put numerical values on different aspects of jobs, since skills are not always quantifiable in this way, particularly when comparing the skills demanded by jobs of often disparate demands and responsibilities.

Hay Method
The Hay method or plan is one of the most widely used job evaluation methods in the world and is generally classified as a points-factor rating. Traditionally associated with managerial and professional jobs, it is becoming more widely used for technical, clerical and other positions. The method relies on three primary factors, namely know-how, problem solving and accountability (see figure 7.2).

It combines aspects of points rating and factor comparison. Values are established for each job using the factors set out in the table and jobs are compared to one another on each factor. Points-factor schemes of this kind are popular because people generally feel that they work.

Among the frequently quoted advantages are:
- the wide acceptance of the approach;
- evaluators are forced to consider a range of factors and thus avoid over-simplifications;
- a higher level of objectivity than other approaches;
- many external comparisons are available because of the widespread adoption of the method.

Disadvantages include:
- the degree of complexity;
- because of its standardised nature, it may not reflect an organisations real needs;
- despite the impression of objectivity, human judgement is required in the process.

Competence-Based Job Evaluation
Variously referred to as competence-based, skill-based or knowledge-based, the emphasis is on an evaluation of the individual who performs the job and his/her competencies and

Figure 7.2 Primary factors in the Hay method

PROBLEM-SOLVING (MENTAL ACTIVITY)	KNOW-HOW	ACCOUNTABILITY
The amount of original, self-starting thought required by the job for analysis, evaluation, creation, reasoning, and arriving at conclusions.	The total of all knowledge and skills, however acquired, needed for satisfactory job performance (evaluates the job, not the person).	The measured effect of the job on company goals.
Problem-solving has two dimensions:	Know-how has three dimensions:	Accountability has three dimensions:
• The degree of freedom with which the thinking process is used to achieve job objectives without the guidance of standards, precedents, or direction from others.	• The amount of practical, specialised or technical knowledge required.	• Freedom to act, or the relative presence of personal or procedural control and guidance, determined by answering the question, 'How much freedom has the job holder to act independently?' – for example, a plant manager has more freedom than a supervisor under his or her control.
• The type of mental activity involved; the complexity, abstractness or originality of thought required.	• Breadth of management, or the ability to make many activities and functions work well together; the job of company president, for example, has greater breadth than that of a department supervisor.	
	• Requirement for skill in motivating people.	• Dollar magnitude, a measure of the sales, budget, value of purchases, value added or any other significant annual money figure related to the job.
Problem-solving is expressed as a percentage of know-how, for the obvious reason that people think with what they know. The percentage judged to be correct for a job is applied to the know-how point value; the result is the point value given to problem-solving.	Using a chart, a number can be assigned to the level of know-how needed in a job. This number—or point value—indicates the relative importance of know-how in the job being evaluated.	• Impact of the job on dollar magnitude, a determination of whether the job has a primary effect on final results or has instead a sharing, contributory or remote effect.
		Accountability is given a point value independent of the other two factors.

Note: The total evaluation of any job is arrived at by adding the points for problem-solving, know-how, and accountability. The points are not shown here.

Source: Schuler (1995).

performance abilities rather than on job title or grade. Thus if the previously described job evaluation methods had at their core the principle of 'paying for the job', competence-based evaluation has as its central tenet 'pay for the person'. Armstrong and Baron (1995) argue that competence-based job evaluation is growing in importance because much greater significance is now attached to knowledge work in organisations, and more emphasis is being placed on flexibility, multi-skilling individuals and team autonomy and empowerment.

Armstrong and Baron (1995) highlight three approaches to developing competence-based job evaluation:

1. Take an existing analytical scheme and modify the factor plan to make it more competence-related by reference to an existing competence framework.
2. Take existing competence frameworks and adapt them to develop a competence-based scheme.
3. Conduct a special analysis of generic and job specific abilities to produce a competency framework and develop a scheme from this analysis.

Figure 7.3 A comparison of conventional job evaluation and competence-based job evaluation

COMPONENT	SKILL-BASED EVALUATION	JOB-BASED EVALUATION
1. Determination of job worth	Tied to evaluation of skill blocks	Tied to evaluation of total job
2. Pricing	Difficult because overall pay system is tied to market	Easier, because wages are tied to labour market
3. Pay ranges	Extremely broad: one pay range for entire cluster of skills	Variable, depending on type of job and pay grade width
4. Evaluation of performance	Competence tests	Performance appraisal ratings
5. Salary increases	Tied to skill acquisition as measured by competence testing	Tied to seniority, performance appraisal ratings, or actual output
6. Role of training	Essential to attain job flexibility and pay increases for all employees	Necessitated by need rather than desire
7. Advancement opportunities	Greater opportunities: anyone who passes competence test advances	Fewer opportunities: no advancement unless there is a job opening
8. Effect of job change	Pay remains constant unless skill proficiency increases	Pay changed immediately to level associated with new job
9. Pay administration	Difficult, because many aspects of pay plan (training, certification) demand attention	Contingent on complexity of job evaluation and pay allocation plan

Source: Adapted from Schuler (1995).

Among the abilities likely to be examined or considered in any of these approaches are interpersonal and communication skills, reasoning and critical thinking ability, technical and business knowledge, decision-making ability, team working and leadership skills, resource management capabilities and planning, organising and problem- solving abilities. The advantages of competence-based job evaluation include:

- It provides a framework for relevant ongoing employee development.
- It can assist in making the organisation more flexible through an ever-expanding focused skill base.
- There is a clear focus on the person.

The following disadvantages are frequently cited:

- The competence movement has been accused of being vague in its terminology.
- It can be as complex and difficult as any other form of job evaluation.
- It can lead to too much emphasis being placed on the skills and knowledge that the person brings to the job and not enough on the outputs from that job.

Criticisms of Job Evaluation

Fowler (1996) suggests that:

> Job evaluation, once a highly regarded management tool, has come under fire in recent times. Its critics say that because it assesses the job rather than the job holder, it fails to recognise the contribution of the individual. It has also been argued that the detailed job descriptions involved in some schemes serve to inhibit flexibility.

Edwards *et al.* (1995) enumerate a number of weaknesses associated with traditional job evaluation. They suggest that it leads to an inappropriate focus on promotion whereby people are led to believe that a job is more important than the individual in the job. Second, they highlight its inability to reward knowledge workers on the basis that traditional job-based pay systems that reward position in the hierarchy do not work well for knowledge workers whose performance is based on specialised applied learning rather than on general skills. Third, they point to its inability to keep pace with high-speed organisational changes and emergent employee roles.

Gunnigle and Flood (1990) cite the potential for error in human judgements that form a central part of the process as perhaps one of its greatest drawbacks.

> Despite some of the obvious benefits of job evaluation . . . it is not infallible. It attempts to create a consistent and equitable system for grading jobs. However, it depends on the judgement of people with experience and training, requiring them to make decisions in a planned and systematic way, and the results do not guarantee total accuracy.

Choosing and Introducing the Job Evaluation Scheme

Introducing job evaluation will have a tremendous impact on company pay structures and employee relations generally. Therefore any decisions should only be taken after careful deliberation. Fowler (1996) suggests that a job evaluation scheme needs to be determined primarily by setting the characteristics of different methods against the organisation's circumstances and objectives. In this respect he suggests that the following questions are useful:

1. Is the principal aim to meet the requirements of equal pay legislation?
2. How many different jobs are there to be evaluated?
3. How complex is the pay structure?
4. What are the factors or characteristics to which the organisation wishes to allocate monetary value within the pay structure?
5. Is the scheme intended for making market comparisons?
6. Is there an advantage in using a computerised system?

The introduction of job evaluation can be a complex process and thus it is often useful to seek expert advice and guidance at the initial stages. This expert would usually be responsible for advising on the technical aspects of the scheme and assisting with decisions on the type of scheme to use, the establishment and composition of overseeing committees, the training of job analysts and communicating the details of the scheme to all concerned.

In relation to participation, it is suggested that, at all stages in the process, staff should be kept adequately informed. It is vital that those who will be most directly affected by the scheme should know its objectives, its content and how it will operate. Middle management and supervisors are critical here. They will play a vital role in implementing the scheme so it is imperative that they understand it and appreciate their role in its operation.

The Reward Package: Pay and Incentives

Determining the worth of a job and the setting down of basic pay levels are critical aspects of the process of establishing a pay system. Choosing the actual payment system is the other critical aspect.

The choice of system is an important consideration for organisations. It will partially reflect the corporate approach to human resource management and impact on areas such as employee relations, supervisory style and employees' motivation. The particular package offered will be determined by a variety of factors related to the organisation, the general business environment and the workforce. In relation to choices of payment schemes, Mooney (1980) feels these are related to the characteristics of the organisation and product. In particular he identifies the significance of:

1. Company ownership: Mooney feels that a continuing influx of foreign companies will increase the utilisation of performance-related bonus schemes.
2. Size: performance-related schemes are more common in larger organisations, while small firms tend to rely on a flat rate only.
3. Technical system: organisations operating large batch production techniques – which are common in Ireland – are more likely to use performance-related payment systems.
4. Labour costs: Mooney feels this is the most important factor influencing the choice of payment system. Flat-rate-only or company-wide schemes dominate in capital cost-intensive organisations, while individual or group incentive schemes are popular in high labour cost organisations.

Overall, as with other aspects of human resource management, the corporate approach to compensation should complement the organisation's strategic business goals, human resource philosophy and other HR activities.

There are numerous options in the type of pay and incentive and benefits package an organisation might adopt. Armstrong and Murlis (1998) offer some broad distinctions between the main types of compensation systems as follows:

- *Gain sharing schemes*: where the pay of a group of employees is linked to improvements in internal company productivity.
- *Employee stock ownership schemes* (ESOPs): where company stock is offered (at a preferential rate) to certain groups of employees.
- *Profit sharing schemes*: where a part of total pay is provided in the form of a share of profits that have accrued over the pay period.
- *Skill-based pay schemes*: where payment is made on the basis of job-related skills or competencies.

- *Individual incentive schemes*: where employees are rewarded for reaching or exceeding specific established performance criteria. Piece rate schemes are the most obvious form of individual performance-related pay.
- *Group incentive schemes*: where the underlying principles relating to individual schemes are related to team or group incentive plans.

The more common types of payment systems are presented below. Statutory and non-statutory benefits available in Ireland are then considered.

Flat Rate Systems

FLAT RATE ONLY

A traditional approach to reward, flat rate pay schemes pay a person for the time spent on the job and no incentive is provided for actual performance. They are popular because of their simplicity and ease of administration. They are particularly useful for managerial and administrative jobs where specific performance criteria are difficult to establish. They help attract employees to join the organisation, but their motivational potential in encouraging good performance is thought to be limited. In Mooney's (1980) study of wage payment systems in Ireland, he found the flat rate system by far the most popular, particularly for indirect employees. However, he also found that approaches combining the flat rate with incentive payments based on some measure of performance were on the increase.

ANNUAL HOURS CONTRACT

As with the flat-rate-only system, the annual hours contract is based on the premise that one is paid for the time spent on the job. However, in this instance working time is organised on an annual rather than a weekly basis. Thus the annual hours contract will

---

Figure 7.4 Methods for calculating the annual hours contract

There are two ways of calculating the contract, which produce the same result:

(1) Standard working week formula

Calendar year:	52.18 weeks (inc. leap year)
Annual leave:	4 weeks
Public holidays:	1.8 weeks
Average working week:	46.38 weeks × 39 hours
Annual hours:	1,808.82 (net basic working hours)

(2) Annual working formula
In a complete calendar year there are an average of 365.25 days, which comprise 8,766 hours.
Example:
Employee works 39 hours a week.

$$\frac{39 \times 365.25}{7} = 2,035 \text{ hours a year}$$

Less annual and public holidays:	2,035
20 days' annual leave:	7.8 × (20)
9 public holidays:	7.8 × (9)
	− 226.2
Employee available to work:	1,808.8 hours per year

Source: O'Sullivan (1996).

specify the number of hours to be worked in the year rather than the week. Originally developed in Scandinavia, O'Sullivan (1996) notes that it is increasingly being regarded as an important alternative to the standard 39-hour week plus overtime in Ireland.

O'Sullivan cites a number of advantages to be gained from this approach. From the company's perspective, there will often be an improvement in unit costs and productivity, the elimination of large-scale overtime, a closer match between output and demand and a reduction in absenteeism. From the employee's perspective, the benefits include improved basic pay, stability of earnings and increased leisure time. The disadvantages cited by O'Sullivan include the necessity to recoup monies owing to the company if an employee leaves during the year; the necessity for re-organisation and cultural and value changes that are congruent with this approach.

Performance-Based Incentive Systems

Conyon *et al.* (2001) note that performance-related pay systems have emerged as a central theme in contemporary human resource management. They note that there is a widespread belief that the traditional wage–employment relationship, where employees are rewarded simply by straight salaries, is not ideal for a modern competitive economy.

The use of incentives is not a new phenomenon – performance-related pay schemes have formed a significant part of the traditional remuneration package in many organisations. McBeath and Rands (1989) define performance-related pay 'as an intention to pay distinctly more to reward highly effective job performance than you are willing to pay for good solid performance', the objective of which should be to develop a productive, efficient, effective organisation (Hoevemeyer 1989).

Kessler and Purcell (1992) argue that the very mechanics of such schemes involve a fundamental restructuring of the employment relationship, which often results in greater managerial control over staff by isolating the individual from the work group and forcing the personalised design and evaluation of work. Support for performance-based incentive systems is based on the concept that it is fair and logical to reward individual employees differentially, based on some measure, or combination of measures, of performance. 'In fact, the principle of [such] pay is so logical that it seems almost ludicrous to criticise it' (Meyer 1975, 39). Since if 'two individuals are performing the same job and one is substantially more effective than the other, the person with the superior contributions should surely be paid more' (Lowery *et al.* 1996, 27). Bowey and Thorpe (1986) suggest there is a positive correlation between individual performance and incentive payments with improvements in costs and quality. However, they also point to potentially adverse affects on attitudes to work and employee relations. A continuing problem in such approaches is finding an acceptable mechanism to assess equitable and consistent performance. Otherwise performance-based payments can lead to problems as a result of resentment towards managerial control or inequity and inconsistency in performance evaluation. An important factor seems to be the extent of employee involvement with schemes that require extensive consultation; they have greater chances of success. Armstrong and Murlis (1988) outline six factors that underpin such successful systems.

1. An equitable mechanism for performance measurement incorporating performance appraisal.
2. Consistency of rewards among individual employees.
3. Managerial flexibility to link reward decisions to organisational needs to attract and retain employees.

4. Simple to understand and apply.
5. Good basic compensation package.
6. Clearly defined employee development policy.

It is important that management clearly outline key performance criteria and reward employees accordingly. Employee acceptance will depend on perceived equity in performance evaluation. It demands a climate of trust and fairness – the main responsibility for whose development lies with management. In this context, performance-based incentive schemes in an organisational environment will be much more likely to fulfil their core functions.

- To ensure an adequate supply of skilled and trained employees in response to fluctuating labour demands. While choice is more repressed in turbulent economic circumstances, individuals making an employment decision will look not only at the terms of employment, but also at the total remuneration package, including variable and incentive pay.
- To elicit from employees, both individually and collectively, performance which reinforces the strategic direction of the organisation. Thus one of the key underlying assumptions is that pay has the potential to motivate.
- To serve as vehicle for organisational change.

Kelly and Monks (1997), in their trawl of the research literature, discovered that performance-related pay schemes often have the realisation of change objectives at their core.

The growth of performance-based incentive systems in Ireland has been inexorably linked to the broader HRM trend towards relating pay more closely to performance. It is evident that performance-based incentive systems might take a number of forms and the question facing most organisations is not which type of scheme to pick but rather, which package of methods will be most successful in fulfilling the organisation's strategic goals. Morley *et al.* (1999) report that in the area of performance-based incentive pay, Irish private sector organisations were, in recent years, far more likely than formerly to have introduced such schemes for several grades. They found that performance-related pay was the most popular incentive used, with 59 per cent of private and 25 per cent of public sector companies implementing it at managerial level. However, this figure declines rapidly as one descends the hierarchy, a factor that has not changed to any significant degree since the early 1990s. Thus the established practice of differentiating between manual and managerial employees in the application of such performance-based incentive schemes remain very much in evidence. Arguably this may be rationalised in a number of ways. A traditional explanation for such treatment has been the difficulty of disaggregating the impact of the individual's effort and performance on effectiveness at the lower echelons of the organisation, and performance-related pay was thus generally considered to be applicable principally to managerial levels. In recent times, this problem has been overcome in many organisations, by assessing the individual within the confines of his/her particular task or job.

A second explanation is the opposition of trade unions, which may often be opposed to payments based on individual performance, preferring collective increases achieved through management-union negotiations. Grafton (1988) feels that schemes that operate increases in addition to general salary awards are less likely to cause employee opposition as they operate as a discretionary element, which does not cut across the collective bargaining role of the trade union. In an appropriate organisational climate performance-based incentive pay can be effectively used to augment negotiated pay and benefit increases and stimulate improved employee and organisational performance.

The penetration of foreign multinational companies (MNCs), particularly US-owned MNCs, into Irish industrial structures is significant here in accounting for the performance-based incentive pay trend in Ireland. While McMahon *et al.* (1988) feel that MNCs have adapted to accommodate local practices, this need not necessarily result in an abandon-ment of foreign management philosophy, but rather, the pursuit of such within existing frameworks and customs. In the case of US multinationals, successive research has repeatedly emphasised the prevalence of linking pay to a measure of performance (Hay Associates 1975; Locker and Teel 1977; Eichel and Bender 1984). The perceived importance of performance-related schemes amongst US organisations is maintained in their subsidiary plants in the Irish context, with many managerial, professional and clerical employees being covered by such schemes. In more recent years, Britain has also seen a change of emphasis in relation to performance approaches. Much of the effort was traditionally directed at assessing future labour requirements and labour training needs (Gill 1977).

However, more recently, according to Long (1986), there has been a greater emphasis on organisational survival and the assessment of current performance. Such emphasis has resulted in a large growth in performance-related pay as a method of improving such performance.

In the section that follows here, we provide a description of several variants of 'shorter term and longer term' (Fierro 2001) performance-based incentive schemes.

FLAT RATE PLUS INDIVIDUAL PBR SYSTEM

Many commentators suggest that individually rewarding performance has a strong motivational impact. Payment is related to the employee's contribution and required performance levels; related financial rewards are specified and these are achievable immediately after these performance criteria have been met. Despite the popularity that individual PBR schemes have achieved in the recent past they do, according to Appelbaum and Shapiro (1991), potentially have a number of flaws. First, they result in a preoccupation with the task at hand and do not relate individual performance to the larger company objectives. Second, they work against creating a climate of openness, trust, joint problem-solving and commitment to organisational problem-solving. Third, they can divide the workforce into those supporting the plan and those not in favour of the plan, which may create adversarial relationships.

FLAT RATE PLUS GROUP/TEAM-BASED PBR

The greatest problem associated with individual PBR schemes is therefore not that they will not work, but rather that they will focus the attention and effort in a direction that does not aid the achievement of the strategic goals of the organisation. In recognition of these and related problems, many organisations have turned to group/team bonus schemes. Payment systems that pay a flat rate plus an incentive based on group/team or sectional performance are used where it is difficult to measure individual performance or to avoid some of the harmful side-effects of individual-based schemes, while providing some incentive which is related to a measure of performance. Daly (1989) defines Group Bonus Schemes as 'The application of payment by results schemes to a group or team where the bonus payments are divided among team members on a pre-agreed basis.' As with individual schemes there is a wide range of schemes from which an organisation may choose, but Ost (1990) feels that all incentives based on group or team work are subject to a number of guiding premises:

1. They always have one or more explicitly stated unit or firm-level performance goals that can only be achieved through team work.
2. A team-based incentive system always contains a reward component that is contingent on the successful achievement of those goals.
3. The reward must be perceived by the employee as resulting from contributions that he/she has made.
4. The reward must be perceived as a fair reward.
5. The behaviours and the rewards offered must clearly signal what is meant by good performance.

PIECEWORK

Piecework involves payment solely by performance. While it remains popular in specific areas (e.g. seasonal work in agriculture, outworkers) it is unacceptable to many employees and their organisations since it provides no guarantee of a minimum income to satisfy basic requirements for both individual and societal wellbeing.

GAIN-SHARING AND SHARE OWNERSHIP SCHEMES

Gain-sharing and share ownership schemes incorporate arrangements that reward employees for improvements in corporate performance through profit sharing, share ownership or some other compensation mechanism. Gain-sharing schemes differ from more traditional profit sharing arrangements insofar as they link rewards based on corporate performance to changes in managerial philosophy and style, which incorporate greater employee influence, involvement and participation.

The direct effects of such schemes on employee motivation are believed to be poor because of their weak relationship with individual performance and lack of immediacy. However, they are seen as having important long-term benefits in increasing employees' participation, awareness and commitment.

Most gain-sharing schemes involve either profit sharing or employee share ownership. Profit sharing is a scheme under which employees, in addition to their normal remuneration, receive a proportion of the profits of the business. Profit sharing may take a number of forms and it is largely at the discretion of the employer and employees to decide to what measure of profit the incentive should be tied, what percentage should be allocated and how it should be administered to employees.

Employee share ownership schemes involve the allocation of company shares to employees according to an agreed formula. Interest in Ireland in employee share ownership schemes has traditionally been relatively low (Long 1988). The growth, small though it has been, is rooted in the finance acts of 1982–4, which were driven by governmental commitment to 'ensuring the success and efficiency of Irish industry and the prosperity and security of Irish workers for the future', by developing employee shareholding. More recent changes, however, have served further to undermine the already narrow base of share ownership in Ireland. Bertie Ahern, the then Minister for Finance, removed tax incentives for employee share schemes. While resultant action was a dilution rather than removal, employees and employers may be more reluctant to adopt such schemes in what could be described as 'an atmosphere of uncertainty'.

Gain-sharing arrangements incorporating either profit or equity sharing are generally linked to organisational attempts to increase employee involvement and commitment. Armstrong and Murlis (1988) enumerate a number of objectives underlying such schemes:

- to encourage employees to identify themselves more closely with the company by developing a common concern for its progress;
- to stimulate a greater interest among employees in the affairs of the company as a whole;
- to encourage better co-operation between management and employees;
- to recognise that employees of the company have a moral right to share in the profits they helped to produce;
- to demonstrate in practical terms the goodwill of the company to its employees;
- to reward success in businesses where profitability is cyclical.

Such schemes have become particularly popular in Britain and the US and have been linked to corporate successes on such criteria as market share, profitability and quality.

COMPETENCE OR SKILL-BASED PAY

The concept of skill-based pay is not particularly new. However, it has recently been revived in the context of 'a move towards person-based pay, rather than job-based pay as the tasks people do at work change so rapidly' (Sparrow 1996). According to O'Neill and Lander (1994), while relatively limited in application, it has been used for years under names such as pay for knowledge, competency pay, pay for skills and multi-skilled pay. While there may be slight technical differences in these terms they are generally used interchangeably. Skill-based pay is a payment system in which pay progression is linked to the number, kind and depth of skill that individuals develop and use. Ricardo and Pricone (1996) view skill-based pay as an innovative reward system that promotes workforce flexibility by rewarding individuals based on the number, type and depth of skills mastered. Armstrong (1995) highlights that it involves paying for the horizontal acquisition of the skills required to undertake a wider range of tasks, and/or for the vertical development of the skills needed to operate it at a higher level, or the in-depth development of existing skills. In this way competence or skill-based pay is directly linked to competence or skilled-based job evaluation described earlier. In terms of operation, there will usually be a basic job rate for the minimum level of skills. Above this level, individuals will be paid for new skills acquired that assist them in performing their job as individuals or members of a team. O'Neill and Lander (1994) cite four major reasons for the increasing adoption of skill-based pay:

- The need to develop and maintain productive efficiencies through increased output, often combined with a leaner workforce and fewer levels of supervision.
- The need to make more flexible utilisation of the existing workforce to cover absenteeism, turnover and production bottlenecks.
- The need to support new technologies such as computer-aided manufacturing, and new value systems such as total quality management.
- The need to build higher levels of involvement and commitment, increase teamwork, and provide more enriched jobs that provide greater reward opportunities for employees.

BROADBANDING

A concept that is closely related to competence or skill-based pay is broadbanding. Broadbanding has been defined by Tyler (1998) as the elimination of all but a few, usually between three and ten, comprehensive salary bands. It therefore represents a compensation management strategy that involves consolidating several salary grades into fewer, wider pay bands. The bands have minimum and maximum monetary amounts. Stredwick (2000) suggests that broadbanding is emerging as a particular response to the competitive global economy in Europe, and that it generates enhanced flexibility. Similarly, Hequet (1995) claims that broadbanding is one of the fastest growing compensation schemes in the US. He cites a study carried out by the American Compensation Association that found that 78 per cent of the 116 respondents used broadbanding. Merrick (1997) notes an increasing trend towards broadbanding in Europe also. One of the reasons for its growth is the trend towards de-layering and flatter organisational structures (Sheehan 1997). Examples of companies who are using broadbanding in Ireland include IBM and Nortel. Merrick notes that IBM Europe has dedicated itself to replacing its twenty-five traditional grades with ten bands. The IBEC survey reports that 11 per cent of the companies surveyed have skill-based, competency-based or broadbanding pay systems in operation (IBEC 1998).

Overall, it is evident that incentive or performance-based schemes may take a number of forms and the question facing most organisations is not which type of scheme to pick, but rather which package of methods will be most successful in fulfilling the organisation's strategic goals. In implementing incentive schemes Balkin and Gomez-Mejia (1987) highlight a number of issues which must be addressed: the number of different forms to offer, the relative importance of each form and the proportion of the workforce to which each form may be applicable. The responses to these questions will be determined by the objectives of the performance-based incentive system itself and whether the organisation sees enhanced performance, cost containment or employee retention as the overriding objective of the system. It must be realised however that while performance-based incentive schemes represent a potentially effective tool, they are not a panacea for all organisational ills. Incentive schemes will only fulfil their true potential if existing barriers to individual, group and organisational effectiveness have been removed. Such schemes do not represent a mechanism for compensating wage differentials, nor for overcoming inadequacies in the production system.

Performance-based incentive schemes seem to be becoming more popular in Irish organisations, but on a gradual incremental basis. Drawing upon data from the Cranet E./ University of Limerick *Study of HR Practices in Ireland*, we can view some evidence of the increased popularity of incentive schemes in many Irish organisations. There is remarkable consistency between the results from the 1992 round of this survey and the 1995 and 1999/2000 subsequent rounds. The use of profit sharing and share options appears to have changed little during the three rounds of this survey. A higher percentage of respondents report the utilisation of group bonus schemes in the most recent round of the survey, especially for managerial grades and professional and technical grades. Merit or performance-related pay continues to be used primarily among higher-level employee grades, though the 1999/2000 results do show a slight decrease here. The use of merit/PRP for manual grades appears stable.

The growth of incentive schemes in Ireland has been inexorably linked to the trend towards relating pay more closely to performance. However, the take up of incentive schemes is correlated with the organisational ownership. Thus, in the Irish context, US owned organisations on the whole appear far more likely to utilise incentives than their counterparts, particularly Irish indigenous organisations who demonstrate a lower take-up across the range of incentives (Gunnigle *et al.* 1994; Morley *et al.* 1999).

Table 7.2 Use of incentive schemes in Ireland

	Management			Prof/technical			Clerical			Manual		
	1999	1995	1992	1999	1995	1992	1999	1995	1992	1999	1995	1992
Share options	21.5	23.0	22.8	13.9	13.8	13.6	11.2	11.5	9.2	9.0	9.6	8.8
Profit sharing	17.9	19.2	15.8	13.9	13.4	12.3	12.1	12.6	10.5	10.5	10.0	10.1
Group bonus	24.2	21.1	14.9	20.0	15.7	12.7	17.3	16.1	11.0	16.8	15.3	14.0
Merit/PRP	44.4	51.3	49.1	38.6	44.8	42.5	30.0	36.8	29.4	17.7	15.3	13.2

Source: Cranet E./University of Limerick Surveys (1992, 1995, 1999).

THE REWARD PACKAGE: FRINGE BENEFITS

In general, fringe benefits (both statutory and voluntary) are estimated to constitute an additional 25–30 per cent on top of basic weekly pay for manual grades. For clerical, administrative and managerial categories, a figure of 15–35 per cent may be appropriate. However, the percentage add-on is primarily related to the level of fringe benefits voluntarily agreed at company level, particularly items such as company cars, pensions, health insurance cover and sickness benefit, and can, therefore, vary considerably between organisations.

The nature of fringe benefits provided to employees varies considerably between organisations and are normally the result of voluntary agreements either between employees (or their representatives) and management. Some of the more common benefits that are provided include:

- Childcare/crèche facilities.
- Career breaks.
- Additional holidays/pay/bonuses.
- Sick-pay schemes.
- Health insurance.
- Pension schemes.
- Sports and recreation facilities.
- Company cars.

PAY AS A MOTIVATOR

For as long as organisations have existed, rewards have been recognised as a major motivator of employees as well as an important tool and expense for organisations (Werner and Ward 2004). The utility of using pay to motivate and promote performance has been a subject of debate for many years with empirical and theoretical support for both sides of the argument. Most managers instinctively believe that money is a motivator, even though empirical evidence to support this is far from conclusive (Milkovich and Newman 2002; Kelly and Monks 1997; Fowler 1991; Goffee and Scase 1986). Indeed, failure of such schemes, in some instances, to fulfil their potential has been attributed to a flawed theoretical base (Pearse 1987), which in many cases serves to undermine effectiveness by demotivating employees (Sargent 1990). The propensity of pay to motivate has been the subject of much academic debate, which has done little to clarify our thinking, a problem intensified by the fact that empirical evidence has failed to establish a tangible link between incentive pay and enhanced performance (Bevan and Thompson 1992).

Perhaps the key point that may be drawn from the available evidence, both academic and empirical, is that pay is a complex, multi-faceted issue that serves as both a tangible and intangible motivator, offering intrinsic and extrinsic rewards. Thus, the applicability of pay related incentive schemes across a wide range of organisational contexts is difficult to generalise on and is largely dependent on organisational circumstances and prevailing conditions.

Notwithstanding the reservations expressed, however, pay and benefits are increasingly becoming areas of extreme importance in determining the effectiveness of the organisation.

In his treatise on how to motivate employees Herzberg (1968) wrote, a 'KITA', which he suggests stands for a kick in the 'pants', produces movement, but not motivation. Kohn (1993) argues the same is true of rewards. 'Punishment and rewards', he argues, 'are two sides of the same coin. Rewards have a punishment effect because they, like outright punishment, are manipulative. "Do this and you'll get that" is not very different from "Do this or here's what will happen to you".' In the case of incentives, the reward itself may be highly desired, but by making that bonus contingent on certain behaviours, managers manipulate their subordinates, and that experience of being controlled is likely to assume a punitive quality over time.

Herzberg has further argued that just because too little money can irritate and demotivate does not mean that more and more money will bring about increased satisfaction or increased motivation.

Pay is important to employees. It provides the means to live, eat and achieve other personal or family goals. It is a central reason why people hold down and move between jobs. However, a key question is not the importance of financial incentives as such but whether they motivate employees to perform well in their jobs.

Once an employee has been attracted to the organisation and the job the role of money as a motivator is debatable. Clearly money – or the lack of it – can be a source of dissatisfaction and grievance. However, if the employee is reasonably happy with his income, does that income induce him to perform at high levels of performance? Many of the theoretical prescriptions suggest that money is important in satisfying essential lower order needs. Once these are out of the way it is the factors intrinsic to the job that are the prime motivators, especially self-actualisation. Others suggest that money is important at all levels and, as expectancy theory indicates, may be a prime motivator where it is a valued outcome and where there is a strong link between effort, performance and the achievement of greater financial reward.

During the 1960s and 1970s many organisational behaviourists emphasised the importance of job enrichment and organisational development and it became somewhat popular to discount the importance of money as a motivator (Biddle and Evenden 1989). The current emphasis on performance, productivity and cost reduction have tended to focus on primary job values like employment security, benefits and – particularly – the pay package. Most managers will agree that remuneration – especially the money element – has an important role in motivating employees. However, it is only one factor in the total motivational process. Clearly many people are not primarily motivated by money, but by other factors such as promotion prospects, recognition or the job challenge itself. All employees do not have a generalised set of motives. Rather, an organisation's workforce will be comprised of people with varying sets of priorities relating to different situations and work contexts resulting in differing employee motives and goals. These motives and goals will vary both between employees and with individual employees over time. For example, a young single person may prioritise basic income and free time and the job itself may not hold any great interest. Later, that person, now married and with a mortgage, may be more concerned with job security and fringe benefits such as health insurance and pension.

Morley and McCarthy (1999, 381) suggest there are four key issues that should be considered when exploring the extent to which employees are motivated by pay:

1. It is clear that employees must value financial rewards. If people are paid at a very high level, or simply not concerned with financial rewards, higher pay will have little incentive value for employees. At this stage other factors related to the job and work environment must have the potential to motivate employees.
2. If money is a valued reward, employees must believe that good performance will allow them to realise that reward. This suggests that pay should be linked to performance and differences in pay should be large enough adequately to reward high levels of performance. This approach obviously rejects remuneration systems that reward good, average and poor performance equally, such as regular pay increments based on seniority.
3. Equity is an important consideration. Employees must be fairly treated in their work situation, especially in terms of the perceived equity of pay levels and comparisons with fellow employees. They will be keen that rewards (pay, incentives and benefits) adequately reflect their input (effort and skills). Should employees feel they are not being treated fairly on these criteria performance levels may fall.
4. Finally, employees must believe that the performance levels necessary to achieve desired financial rewards are achievable. The required performance criteria and levels should be clearly outlined and communicated to employees.

Organisations must also ensure that employees have the necessary ability, training, resources and opportunity to achieve such performance levels. Otherwise, employees will either not be able, or else not try, to expend the necessary effort.

From the motivational perspective effective payment systems should have the following characteristics:

- Be objectively established.
- Clarify performance levels required and rewards available.
- Reward the achievement of required performance levels adequately and quickly.
- Ensure employees have ability, training resources and opportunity to achieve required performance level(s).
- Recognise that financial incentives are only one source of motivation, and design jobs to ensure employees can satisfy other needs through their work (e.g. achievement, challenge).
- Take regular steps to identify employee needs and ensure these can be satisfied within the organisational environment.

Even where these characteristics are present success is not guaranteed. For example, an incentive scheme based on production figures may be established to encourage employees to achieve high-performance levels. However, unofficial norms established by the work group may dictate 'acceptable' performance levels and ensure this is not exceeded through various social pressures. Equally, such an approach may signal to employees that management are clearly in charge and may either lessen employee feelings of control and competence or encourage conflict over the standards set.

It should always be appreciated that, while pay is an important source of employee motivation, it is not the only one. To motivate effectively, financial incentives should be structured in such a way as to highlight the link between effort, performance and reward: adequately reward good performance and be equitable in the eyes of employees. The remuneration system should be viewed as part of a total motivational process that allows for individual differences and provides motivational opportunities through additional extrinsic and intrinsic factors, particularly self-fulfilment.

This chapter has focused on the area of reward management. An organisation's reward package is seen to consist of pay (base wages), various incentives (performance-related incentives and rewards) and fringe benefits. Organisations will provide various mixes of these three components in order to attract, retain and motivate their employees. While developing an effective reward package can prove a rather difficult task, if the reward package satisfies basic needs as well as being flexible enough to meet individual employee needs and has equity, fairness and trust as its central tenets, it can be effective.

Job evaluation is the most common method of determining the relative worth of jobs and a variety of analytical and non-analytical schemes are available. With the exception of competence-based approaches, job evaluation techniques focus solely on the job, rather than on the individual performing it.

Numerous options are available to organisations in the types of pay, incentive and benefits packages it might adopt. While flat rate systems still prevail, various individual, group and team incentive schemes have grown in popularity in recent years, largely in response to competitive pressures. Additional direct payments in the form of bonuses and other incentives are used extensively.

Turning to the actual payment approaches employed there has been an increase in variable pay in Ireland in recent years. Variable pay subsumes many different types of compensation systems, including bonuses, gainsharing, and profit-sharing, but the defining feature is that rewards must be re-earned each period (Kuhn and Yockey 2003). A total of 41.1 per cent of respondents to the 1999/2000 round of the Cranet E./University of Limerick Survey on HR practices in Ireland reported that they had increased their use of variable pay in the previous three years. Concomitantly, only 1 per cent of respondents reported that they had decreased their use of variable pay during the same period. The general increase is consistent with the European trend and it serves not only to allow employees enjoy periods of success, but also helps spread risk in times of difficulty. Zalusky (1991) suggests, however, that this growth in variable pay is limited as the banks that hold mortgages do not adjust monthly bills to fit changes in workers' income. This is particularly relevant in Ireland, given the open nature of the economy (Foley *et al.* 1996; Morley and McCarthy 1999).

The cost of employee benefits is also on the increase for many employers. These benefits represent a type of indirect reward because employees receive the value of the benefits without getting direct cash payments. More broadly, the complete reward package is now often one of the largest costs faced by employers with many organisations having labour costs at or above 50 per cent of all operating costs (Morley and McCarthy 1999). The recent 'Employee Participation in Organisational Change Survey' reports the findings of an investigation carried out across ten countries of the EU. It is reported that public service organisations have very high labour costs: 40 per cent of the respondents indicated that labour costs constituted over 75 per cent of total costs. Private firms indicated that their labour costs were a smaller proportion of overall costs: 45 per cent reported that labour costs were between 25 and 50 per cent of overall costs (European Foundation for the Improvement of Working and Living Conditions 1999).

8

Managing and Appraising Performance

The management of performance in organisations is clearly a key variable in organisational effectiveness and growth. Designed on the basis of the information needs at senior management as well as operational levels, Simons (1995) notes that performance management has become an essential tool in both the formulation and the implementation of strategy. In view of the strategic pressures driving organisations, it is becoming increasingly evident that organisations will need to carefully monitor performance if they are going to realise improvements in productivity and growth, and to do so through the institutionalisation and consistent application of a 'goals oriented approach' (Scott-Lennon 1995). Nilsson and Rapp (2002) comment that performance management has moved away from its traditional form, with a focus on monetary measures such as return on investment (ROI), and has broadened its scope and gradually become more strategically oriented. They suggest that performance management is required to extend beyond the mere diagnostic use of providing information on the current performance and position of the business in relation to existing strategy; it must also be used interactively to identify needs for strategic change.

Lawler (2003) comments that virtually every organisation has a performance management system that is expected to accomplish a number of important objectives with respect to human capital management. The objectives often include motivating performance, helping individuals develop their skills, building a performance culture, determining who should be promoted, eliminating individuals who are poor performers and helping implement business strategies. He further notes:

> while there is little doubt that a performance management system which can accomplish these objectives can make a very positive contribution to organisational effectiveness, but there is less clarity about what practices make a performance management system effective.
>
> Lawler (2003, 396)

It is precisely this point that is taken up by Latham *et al.* (2005). They note that while the primary purpose of appraising employees is to instil in them the desire for continuous improvement, the outcome of many performance appraisals is frequently a decrease rather than an increase in performance. Among the reasons for this decrease is the belief by employees that they are being incorrectly evaluated by the wrong person; that is, the person who is evaluating them lacks objectivity, and hence is not 'fair', or that the feedback that is given to them is not seen as timely or constructive. Thus, it is not surprising that a performance appraisal often leads to legal challenges for the appraisers and the organisation that employs them.

A performance management system can only be truly effective where it is perceived to be fair by all of those involved in the process (Cook and Crossman 2004; Delery and Doty 1996; Murphy and Cleveland 1991). Pulakos (1997, 291), in her treatise on the 'ratings of job performance', puts it thus:

> Rewarding and promoting effective performance in organisations, as well as identifying ineffective performers for developmental programmes or other personnel actions, are essential to effective human resource management in organisations. The ability to perform these functions relies on assessing employee performance in a fair and accurate manner.

The emphasis in this chapter is thus on exploring the dimensions of performance management and outlining a range of considerations pertaining to the development and operation of effective performance appraisal systems. The chapter concludes with an examination of recent developments in the area of performance management and explores current performance appraisal practices in Ireland.

THE NATURE OF PERFORMANCE MANAGEMENT

The extant literature on managing job performance reveals several terms that are often used interchangeably, such as performance appraisal, performance assessment, performance evaluation and job appraisal. However, in general terms, they are invariably all concerned with measuring an individual's performance in a given job against pre-determined work standards and involve designing a formal system to facilitate observation, monitoring, analysis, feedback and target setting. Armstrong (1995) indicates that performance management, as a concept, emerged in the late 1980s as a result of a growing recognition that a more continuous and integrated approach was needed to manage and reward performance. He further notes that many of the more recent developments in performance appraisal have been absorbed into the concept of performance management, which is 'a much wider, more comprehensive and more natural process of management' (Armstrong 1995, 431).

Sparrow and Hiltrop (1994) suggest that performance management is essentially a strategic management technique that links business objectives and strategies to individual goals, actions, performance appraisal and rewards through a defined process. They further stress that the most important feature of an effective performance management system is its ability to be seen as a method of continuously securing improvements in the performance of teams and individuals against pre-defined business strategies and objectives (Sparrow and Hiltrop 1994, 553). Lockett (1992) indicates that the core objectives of performance management are:

1. The continuous improvement of business performance in terms of customer service, product quality and market leadership.

2. The continuous development of organisational capability through the design of effective production systems, the development of organic structures; the enhancement of employee performance in line with business demands and the expansion of product and service lines.

Philpott and Sheppard (1993), from their analysis of performance management in operation, outline a number of characteristics that are associated with effective and ineffective performance management systems (see table 8.1).

In a similar vein, Fletcher and Williams' (1992, 47) research suggests that, not only were most of the organisations studied a long way from operating sophisticated personnel management, but, for most of them, performance management was synonymous with performance appraisal, or performance related pay, or both. They commented that:

> There is, of course, much more to it than that. The real concept of performance management is associated with an approach to creating a shared vision of the purpose and aims of the organisation, helping each individual employee understand and recognise their part in contributing to them, and in so doing manage and enhance the performance of both individuals and the organisation.

Table 8.1 Characteristics of good and bad performance management systems

Good	Bad
Tailor-made to fit the particular needs and circumstance of the organisation	• Lack of strategic direction, with no clear objectives
• Congruent with the existing culture insofar as they support the achievement of high performance standards but will help to change or reshape that culture if necessary	• Rivalry and territorialism between departments
• Support the achievement of the organisation's mission and the realisation of its values	• Persistent failure to meet objectives and deadlines
• Define the critical success factors which determine organisational and individual performance	• Lack of clear accountabilities and decision-making
• Clarify the principal accountabilities of managers and staff so that they are fully aware of their objectives, the standards of performance expected of them, and the quantitative key performance indicators which will be used to measure their achievements	• Confusion over roles in organisation
	• Middle managers feel unable to influence events
	• Absenteeism, sickness and/or overtime out of control
	• Work-force and middle managers resistant to change
	• High turnover amongst key posts
	• Staff appraisal lacks credibility
• Enable systematic review of performance against agreed criteria in order to establish and act on strengths and weaknesses, identify potential, plan and implement career development and training programmes and provide a basis for motivation through intrinsic and extrinsic rewards	• PRP scheme regarded as ineffective
	• Lack of detailed information on costs and contributions
• Develop PRP systems which provide incentives and rewards as motivators for improved performance	• Poor budgetary control and plan
	• Outdated or inadequate management information systems
• Provide an integrated approach to increasing motivation and commitment, which combines the impact of results-orientated performance appraisal and PRP systems with the actions that management and individual managers can take, such as career development and succession planning programmes to develop attitudes and behaviours which lead to better performance	• Lack of structural career and succession planning process

Source: Philpott and Sheppard (1993). Copyright © L. Philpott and L. Sheppard, 1993. Reprinted with permission.

The various definitions of performance management outlined su...
a management process of linking individual, group and organisati...
the main strategic mission and values. As such it is an organisatio... essentially
concerned with the continuous assessment and review of perfor... ce with
determined strategic objectives. There are a number of marked simil... that is
performance management system and management by objectives (M... st pre-
systems set objectives, require the identification of performance meast... n the
continuous appraisal and feedback. However, Fowler (1991) suggests tha... both
management goes further than MBO, in that it is applied to all staff (not jus... olve
was traditionally the case with MBO). It includes greater qualitative performanc... nce
and focuses more on corporate goals and values than on individual objectives. ... rs,
vein, Armstrong (1995) differentiates performance management from th... r
performance appraisal, indicating that it does not represent an activity that is imp...
managers and that it is primarily owned and driven, not by the personnel departme...
by line managers.

THE PROCESS OF PERFORMANCE MANAGEMENT

A central tenet of effective performance management is that a participative approach ...
taken to the system design. This implies involving all organisational actors in jointly
determining the nature and scope of the system. The system should have the full
commitment of top management, yet not be viewed as a top-down affair (Wright and
Brading 1992). Armstrong (1995) suggests that performance management be regarded as
a flexible process and presents a conceptual framework of the performance management
cycle (see figure 8.1).

Figure 8.1 A conceptual framework for performance management

Source: Armstrong (1995).

This model is based on the premise that all work performance is driven by a range of
corporate strategies and objectives, which are broken down and translated into key
functional or departmental objectives. A performance contract is developed that outlines
the tasks, knowledge, skills and competencies that are required to achieve these key
objectives. Built into the model is the requirement for continuous feedback on
performance, with the possibility of interim reviews. The system further prescribes the

—e formal review per year, when employees and managers constructively
o͵mance and identify a new performance contract. This review typically takes
e͵ annual performance appraisal, which will be described in the next section.
ṯmployee development is an inherent aspect of the process where specific
ḁirements are identified at the review stage, and informal training and learning
ḁching, mentoring and self-development is encouraged throughout the year.
el identifies two further components, namely performance rating and
ḁnce-related-pay. Armstrong suggests that these are not inevitably associated with
ḁance management, *per se*, while Wright and Brading (1992) argue that formal
of performance should be avoided if possible and the focus brought closer to
ḁtive outcomes. However, while there is an increasing tendency to link rewards with
ḁrmance (see chapter 7), it is recommended that decisions on pay be separated from
performance review to facilitate the developmental nature of performance
ḁnagement (Armstrong 1995; Gunnigle and Flood 1990; Evenden and Anderson 1992).

PERFORMANCE APPRAISAL

Grote (1996, ix) notes that over the past fifty years performance appraisal has become such
a commonplace in organisational life that virtually every company has an appraisal system.
Gunnigle and Flood (1990) describe performance appraisal as a systematic approach to
evaluating employee performance, characteristics and/or potential, with a view to assisting
decisions in a wide range of areas such as pay, promotion, employee development and
motivation. Outlining the purpose of performance appraisal, they suggest that the
performance management loop provides the framework within which systematic appraisal
can take place (see figure 8.2).

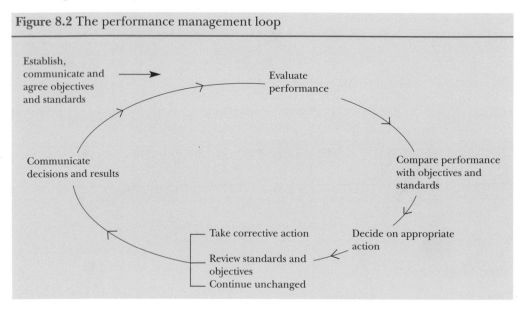

Figure 8.2 The performance management loop

Establish, communicate and agree objectives and standards

Evaluate performance

Communicate decisions and results

Compare performance with objectives and standards

Take corrective action

Decide on appropriate action

Review standards and objectives

Continue unchanged

Appraisal of performance is likely to take place on a daily basis, often very informally, e.g.
through casual meetings, informal discussions between supervisor and staff, team briefings
and so forth. However, the establishment of a formal appraisal system is a necessary
prerequisite to effective performance management since it provides a dedicated period of

time for managers and supervisors to meet with their staff and discuss a range of factors pertaining to work performance.

Table 8.2 Why should you appraise: employer and employee viewpoints

The employer's perspective:
Appraisals are conducted for a number of reasons, not least to help the organisation to:
1. Assess the performance of individuals
2. Set individual objectives
3. Assess how well objectives are being attained
4. Confirm what jobs/tasks are actually being done
5. Determine who should be promoted or transferred
6. Determine who needs training and of what sort
7. Assess who should be considered for advancement

The employee's perspective:
If the process is well handled and the appraisal system is effective, the employee should see the process and its constructive engagement as:
1. A career development exercise
2. A way of assessing career and other wants and needs, and how the organisation can actually provide them
3. A way of clarifying the job, its duties, objectives etc.
4. A way of becoming aware of their own potential, and how that potential can be realised and fulfilled

Source: Hunt (1992).

Similarly, Evenden and Anderson (1992) identify a range of perceived benefits associated with effective performance appraisals, some of which are presented in table 8.3.

Table 8.3 Benefits of performance appraisal

Benefits to managers
- Opportunity to learn about employees' hopes, fears, anxieties and concerns relating to both their present job and their future
- Chance to clarify and reinforce important goals and priorities
- Mechanism for measuring changes in employee work performance
- Opportunity to motivate staff by recognising achievements
- Clarification of overlap or ambiguities that may exist in the work structure

Benefits to employees
- Opportunity to receive feedback on how performance is viewed in the organisation
- Opportunity to communicate views about the job
- Opportunity to discuss career options
- Recognition of tasks carried out well and objectives achieved
- Basis for identifying training and development needs

Benefits to the organisation
- Assistance with succession planning and the identification of future potential
- Facilitation of human resource planning through competency analysis
- Method of ensuring harmony between business objectives and employee performance
- Generally improved communications throughout the organisation
- Opportunity to improve performance

Source: Evenden and Anderson (1992).

The performance appraisal system can be seen to have many interrelated functions including performance evaluation and target setting, the establishment of work standards, identification of skills gaps, and the facilitation of communications and motivation. However, only an effective appraisal system will result in the realisation of many of these outcomes. Hunt (1992, 10) notes that appraisals are characteristically inefficient. Among the reasons for this are: an unclear definition of the appraisee's job; unclear objectives; one or both parties being unaware of the format and aims of the appraisal interview; untrained appraisers and/or appraisees; a high degree of subjectivity surrounding the process; and biased or incomplete data being gathered and used for determining process outcomes. Furthermore, in some cases the process of evaluation can become the overriding consideration of the appraisal process, and often the motivational and developmental aspects are given little consideration. Given that the annual appraisal may represent the only formal meeting the manager or supervisor has with his/her staff (on a one-to-one basis), there is a considerable onus on the manager or supervisor to ensure that adequate attention is paid to all aspects of the appraisal process. However, in spite of their perceived benefits, performance appraisal schemes are not a general panacea for poor management or fundamental weaknesses in the organisation's structure or design, and thus, as indicated earlier, the organisation must take cognisance of the range of policies, systems and procedures that affect work performance.

Randell (1994) suggests that an examination of an organisation's appraisal scheme can show a great deal about how the organisation views its staff and how they should be managed and developed. Adopting the approach that beliefs about human behaviour at work can be broadly classified, he suggests that appraisal systems are developed according to what those who design them view as the causes of work performance:

- Where the past is seen as a reasonable determinant of present and future work behaviour, the performance appraisal scheme will focus on a comprehensive assessment of past strengths and weaknesses. This view is largely connected with reinforcement theories of motivation, whereby good performance is rewarded in the hope that it will be repeated, while poor performance is discouraged or even punished to decrease the likelihood of it occurring in the future.
- Where the 'here and now' is seen as the critical determinant of work behaviour then the appraisal system will focus on factors such as employees' understanding and learning. This approach draws heavily on cognitive psychology and equity theories of motivation where employees' perceptions of the work situation are seen to determine subsequent behaviour.
- Where the 'pull' of future events desired by employees is seen as the prevailing influence on work behaviour, appraisal systems will emphasise rewards and opportunities. This approach draws upon expectancy theories of motivation and focuses on self-fulfilment to encourage desired work behaviour.

There are two underlying principles associated with all three perspectives, namely a desire to add to the individual's capacity for doing an existing job, and a need to maintain and/or improve motivation.

Methods of Performance Appraisal

There is considerable variety in the range of performance appraisal techniques that can be used by organisations. A summarised description of the most commonly used techniques are presented in table 8.4. A number of these techniques will be examined in closer detail.

Table 8.4 Performance appraisal techniques

Method	Characteristics	Strengths	Weaknesses
Rating	Appraiser specifies on a scale to what degree relevant characteristics (normally related to job-related behaviour or personality) are possessed by appraisee	Ease of comparison; range in complexity from very simple to very involved, using descriptions of behaviour or performance	Subjective; personality or behavioural traits difficult to measure
Ranking	Appraiser ranks workers from best to worst, based on specific characteristics or overall job performance	Simple; facilitates comparisons	Little basis for decisions; degrees of difference not specified; subjective
Paired comparison	Two workers compared at a time and decision made on which is superior, resulting in a final ranking order for full group	Ease of decision-making; simple	Difficult with large numbers together with weakness attributed to ranking
Critical incident	Appraiser or supervisor observes incidence of good and bad perform-ance. These are used as a basis for judging and assessing or discussing performance	Job-related; more objective	Needs good observational skills; time-consuming
Free-form	General free-written appraisal by appraiser	Flexible	Subjective; difficulty of comparison
Performance or objectives-oriented systems	Appraiser evaluates degree to which specific job targets or standards have been achieved	Job-related; objective; participative	Needs measurable targets; danger of collusion
Assessment centre	Appraisees undergo a series of assessments (interviews, tests, simulations, etc.) undertaken by trained assessors	Range of dimensions examined; objective	Expensive; not necessarily job-specific
Self-assessment	Appraisees evaluate themselves using a particular format or structure	Participative; facilitates discussion; promotes self-analysis	Danger of lenient tendency; potential source of conflict between appraiser and appraisee

The *free form* appraisal technique is completely unstructured and essentially involves the appraiser writing a narrative discussion of the employee's performance. While it allows considerable discretion to the appraiser, who is not constrained by set criteria, this discretion can result in some inconsistencies and does not allow for effective comparisons.

Rating usually involves the appraiser rating the employee's performance and behaviour against a pre-determined scale. These ratings, based on a sequential scale, can be made against a series of relatively standard headings that tend to include generalised performance characteristics or particular personality traits. Rating scales are often used in conjunction with results-oriented schemes, which measure performance against a set of objectives. In such cases, rating scales are used to indicate the extent to which an employee was successful in achieving the objective. Two examples of the use of rating scales in results-oriented schemes are illustrated in tables 8.5 and 8.6, which contain extracts from performance plans used in a large manufacturing organisation in Ireland.

Table 8.5 Extract from performance appraisal plan for managers – manufacturing firm

Employee name:
Job title:
Appraiser:
Appraisal period:
Date of appraisal:

Section one: this section outlines the key roles and competencies that managers must demonstrate to perform their jobs effectively. Using the rating scale below, evaluate the extent to which the manager named above demonstrates effectiveness in each of the areas identified. Enter N/A for those areas that are not relevant to the manager's current position.

Rating

1. Planning   _____
   - manages systems and processes
   - sets measurable goals and targets
   - assigns tasks responsibly

2. Production   _____
   - motivates others positively
   - demonstrates personal commitment
   - facilitates co-operative environment

3. Teambuilding   _____
   - manages conflict
   - facilitates participation
   - develops interaction

4. Coaching   _____
   - develops others
   - communicates effectively
   - understands interaction

5. Innovation   _____
   - divergent thinking
   - challenges processes
   - stimulates change

Rating scale
1. *Negative results, did not achieve objectives*
2. *Mixed results, achieved some objectives*
3. *Good results, achieved most objectives*
4. *Very good results, achieved all objectives*
5. *Strong results, achieved all and exceeded some objectives*
6. *Excellent results, exceeded most objectives*
7. *Outstanding results, exceeded all objectives*

Table 8.6 Extract from performance appraisal form for employees – manufacturing firm

Employee name:
Job title:
Appraiser:
Appraisal period:
Date of appraisal:

Section one: this section outlines the key roles and competencies that employees must demonstrate to perform their jobs effectively. Using the rating scale below, evaluate the extent to which the employee named above demonstrates effectiveness in each of the areas identified. Enter N/A for those areas that are not relevant to the employee's current position.

1. Quality of work: the extent to which the quality of work is accurate and thorough   _____
2. Dependability: the extent to which the employee can be relied upon to do a good job   _____
3. Judgement: the extent to which the employee makes rational choices   _____
4. Organisation: the extent to which the employee can plan and structure work   _____

5. Communications: the extent to which the employee can transmit and receive information in a comprehensive manner   _____
6. Adaptability: the extent to which the employee can cope with change and uncertainty   _____

Rating scale
1. *Negative results, did not achieve expectations*
2. *Mixed results, achieved some expectations*
3. *Good results, achieved most expectations*
4. *Very good results, achieved all expectations*
5. *Strong results, achieved all and exceeded some expectations*
6. *Excellent results, exceeded most expectations*
7. *Outstanding results, exceeded all expectations*

Armstrong (1995) and Gunnigle and Flood (1990) argue that, while rating scales are a convenient means of comparing employees and arriving at an evaluation, they tend to ignore the complex set of variables that determine work performance, and are a highly subjective method of assessment. Furthermore, it is particularly difficult to achieve any great level of consistency with rating scales because, as indicated, they are highly subjective and some appraisers will be more generous than others, while others will be harder on their staff (Armstrong refers to these as 'the swan effect' and 'the goose effect' respectively). A further problem associated with both rating and ranking methods concerns the error of central tendency, that is, that there is a particular tendency to veer towards the mid-point on such scales and so ascribe average values to performance.

One means of improving consistency might be to require the appraiser to make a forced distribution of assessment that involves plotting overall evaluation against the normal distribution curve. An example of this might be where, if there are twenty employees in a particular department, the overall distribution of performance should appear as follows:

Excellent:	5%
Good:	15%
Average:	60%
Poor:	15%
Unsatisfactory:	5%

While proponents might argue that this type of appraisal puts a rigor and discipline into the performance management system that overcomes the all-too-common leniency tendencies of managers, it does not get away from the fact that there is no rule that suggests that work performance or ability should be normally distributed and, to assume so, ignores the myriad of variables such as culture, production norms, supervisory arrangements and personal motivation that can impact on work performance. Indeed Lawler (2003) refers to many criticisms of the forced distribution approach, including the arguments that it represents an unrealistic mandate, and that it may force managers to make judgments they cannot support with data they do not believe in. Because of this it can lead to decisions that cannot be defended when there is an adverse impact.

An alternative to forced distribution might be the forced choice technique, which seeks to avoid the error of central tendency. Again, appraisers are asked to rate performance against a pre-determined scale, but this technique does not have a middle or average value. An illustration of the forced choice technique is presented in table 8.7.

Table 8.7 Example of forced choice appraisal technique

Criterion	Evaluation choices (tick as appropriate)			
Initiative	Takes responsibility and uses it well	Keen to take on new tasks	Needs direction	No initiative
	——	——	——	——

Results-oriented schemes are based on the underlying principles of management by objectives (MBO) and include the specification of objectives, participation in agreeing objectives, measurement of performance against objectives, and finally feedback and monitoring. In the results-oriented system, performance is measured against previously agreed targets or key result areas. As with MBO, there is a particular requirement for targets to be jointly set between manager and employee to ensure commitment to the process and allow for re-negotiation as required. Hunt (1992) uses the example of targets for a salesperson. They might include the total number of sales, number of new customers, number of repeat customers, average size of orders, proportions of different products sold, plus whatever is deemed to be relevant to the organisation. In this schema, numerical figures can be put side by side with actual performance, and successes and areas for improvement can be straightforwardly determined (see table 8.8).

This type of appraisal scheme requires managers to have a comprehensive understanding of the nature and scope of the employee's job and demands high levels of vigilance in observation, target setting, feedback and future planning. As with all appraisal systems, it is highly dependent on a responsible appraiser. Although a useful technique, it can pose difficulties when the job is subject to considerable variation, or when it is largely dependent on the performance of other jobs. Furthermore, there is a strong emphasis on measurable and quantifiable criteria, which might overshadow more qualitative criteria, such as work behaviour and interaction.

Table 8.8 Performance against previous objectives scheme: sales personnel

Appraisee's name: _____
Position: _____
Appraiser's name: _____
Date: _____
Length of time in the post (years): _____

	TARGET	ACTUAL
Number of customers:	_____	_____
Total value of sales:	_____	_____
Average value of sale per customer:	_____	_____
Number of new contacts:	_____	_____
Number of new customers:	_____	_____
Proportion of contacts turned into customers:	_____	_____
Size of territory:	_____	_____
Number of potential new customers:	_____	_____

Source: Hunt (1992).

When jobs are difficult to quantify in measurable terms, the *critical incident technique* might prove useful. This technique was advanced by Flanagan (1954), who viewed it as a procedure for gathering certain important facts concerning behaviour in defined situations. Anderson and Wilson (1997, 89) define it as a technique consisting of 'a flexible set of procedures for collecting and analysing reports of incidents – instances of actual behaviour – that constitute job performance at various levels of effectiveness'.

This technique requires the appraiser to identify three or four critical components of the job, and assess performance based on how well these tasks were completed. Anderson and Wilson (1997) note that critical incident reports, which are at the core of this technique, are obtained from persons who are in a position to observe those performing the activity in question. They suggest that such critical incident reports include three important pieces of information:

1. A description of the situation that led to the incident.
2. The actions or behaviours of the focal person in the incident.
3. The results or outcomes of those actions.

Based on these three pieces of information, an interpretation of the effectiveness of the actions can be made.

The critical incident technique can be costly to perform, particularly as it may involve considerable observation, which may generate negative feelings from employees who might feel threatened by the process. When the appraisal takes place on an annual basis, it can be difficult to discuss constructively key incidents that took place more then six months ago.

Behaviourally anchored rating scales (BARS), particularly associated with the early work of Smith and Kendall (1963), were developed to reduce rating errors and they include a

Table 8.9 An example of a critical incident report

SITUATION: A contractor was assigned a project that would involve de-terminating and removing several hundred wires, removing the conduit from the gear, relocating the gear, reinstalling the conduit and wire, and finally re-terminating the wire. The work had to begin at 11.00 p.m. on Thanksgiving and it had to be completed by 7.00 a.m. the following day, which seemed nearly impossible.

ACTION: The foreman chose seven of the best wiremen employed by the company to do the work. Through skilful planning and hard work, the crew worked through the night without stopping for a break and got the job done on time and with no problems.

OUTCOME: The customer was extremely impressed that they got such a project completed in such a short amount of time with zero errors. As a result, the customer has chosen this contractor to do almost all of its work.

Source: Anderson and Wilson (1997).

number of performance dimensions that represent major requirements of the actual job, such as teamwork. Armstrong (1995) provides the following example of BARS in operation (see table 8.10).

Table 8.10 Example of BARS

A. Continually contributes new ideas and suggestions. Takes a leading role in group meetings but is tolerant and supportive of colleagues and respects other people's points of view. Keeps everyone informed about own activities and is well aware of what other team members are doing in support of team objectives.
B. Takes a full part in group meetings and contributes useful ideas frequently. Listens to colleagues and keeps them reasonably well informed about own activities while keeping abreast of what they are doing.
C. Delivers opinions and suggestions at group meetings from time to time but is not a major contributor to new thinking or planning activities. Generally receptive to other people's ideas and willing to change own plans to fit in. Does not always keep others properly informed or take sufficient pains to know what they are doing.
D. Tendency to comply passively with other people's suggestions. May withdraw at group meetings, but sometimes shows personal antagonism to others. Not very interested in what others are doing or in keeping them informed.
E. Tendency to go own way without taking much account of the need to make a contribution to team activities. Sometimes uncooperative and unwilling to share information.
F. Generally uncooperative. Goes own way, completely ignoring the wishes of other team members and taking no interest in the achievement of team objectives.

Source: Armstrong (1995).

Pulakos (1997) notes that the development of BARS relies on input from job incumbents and/or their supervisors. These stakeholders, referred to as 'subject matter experts' in the developmental process, are charged with the task of providing the detailed information that is necessary to construct the actual rating scales. These scales, Pulakos notes (1997, 298), are the rating dimensions and the behaviours that define different levels of effectiveness for each performance dimension of the job. With respect to how the relevant behaviours are gathered, she highlights that:

The behaviours are derived from critical incidents [see technique mentioned earlier] ... After the critical incidents are collected from subject matter experts and edited by psychologists, subject matter experts are then asked to sort the critical incidents into dimensions and rate them on an effectiveness rating scale. Often, a 7-point rating scale is used. The percentage of subject matter experts sorting each incident into a particular dimension and the means and standard deviations of the effectiveness ratings for each incident are computed.

One of the main advantages of such an approach is that the behavioural anchors settled on for measurement purposes can be particularly effective for generating comparisons. However, the drawback documented in the literature is that those conducting the appraisal often report difficulties in rating the individual's performance to the specific scale anchors that are generated and used in the rating assessment. By way of example, look at the BARS rating scale shown in table 8.10 and you will get some indication of the potential difficulties that an appraiser might experience in trying to compare the individual's performance to the specific scale anchors illustrated in the table.

360-Degree Feedback

Also known as multi-rater assessment and multi-sourced assessment, 360-degree feedback is a relatively new appraisal technique that has gained popularity in recent years. Ward (1995) and Garavan, Morley and Flynn (1997) suggest that it is designed to provide a complete multi-dimensional overview of an employee's performance. McCarthy and Pearson (2001) define it thus:

> 360-degree, or multi-rater, feedback is the practice of collecting perceptions of an employee's performance from sources such as subordinates/direct reports, peers/colleagues, and supervisors. What makes 360-degree feedback revolutionary is that the perspectives of many stakeholders are included in the evaluation of an employee's performance and workplace behaviour. In traditional appraisal systems, it is only the observations and opinions of the boss that are considered important and are therefore the only source of evaluation included in the appraisal.

Latham *et al.* (2005, 80) note that feedback from multiple sources is blossoming in the workplace and explain its popularity as follows:

> Anyone who has children is aware that how they interact with their grandparents is not necessarily how they interact with their parents, babysitters, or siblings. Moreover, how they behave on the playground is unlikely to yield clues as to how they behave in the classroom, let alone in the home. The answer to 'Who is my child?' is 'All of the above.'

Toegel and Conger (2003), however, sound a note of caution with respect to the recent uptake of 360-degree feedback for assessment purposes. They reflect that the technique was originally designed for developmental purposes, and that its use as an evaluative tool may weaken its developmental potential. While the underlying premise of 360-degree feedback remains sound, they argue that it may be more appropriate to develop separate tools to satisfy multiple requirements.

Nowack (1993) identifies five major reasons for the increasing use of 360-degree inventories as follows:

1. A need for cost-effective alternatives to assessment centres.
2. The increasing availability of assessment software capable of summarising data from multiple sources into customised feedback reports.
3. The need for continuous measurement in continuous-improvement efforts.
4. The need for job-related feedback for employees affected by career plateauing.
5. The need to maximise employees' potentials in the face of technological changes, competitive challenges, and increased workforce diversity.

Waldman *et al.* (1998) add that a further key purpose driving the present spread and use of 360-degree feedback is the legitimate desire to further management or leadership development. In this regard they note that:

> Providing feedback to managers about how they are viewed by direct subordinates, peers, and customers/clients should prompt behaviour change. Many managers have not received as much honest feedback as is necessary for an accurate self-perception.

The appraisal takes into account skills, competencies and work behaviour, and information is typically sourced from records, reports, work colleagues and the individual being appraised. McCarthy and Pearson (2001) observe that, while some organisations restrict the stakeholder groups used in the evaluation process to peers or subordinates, others take a broader approach and include additional raters, such as customers, suppliers, cross-functional team members, managers-once-removed, and subordinates-once-removed. Structured questionnaires are designed and administered to relevant assessors, they are completed anonymously and then returned to the employee. This technique is particularly comprehensive and provides a multi-faceted assessment of work performance, taking into account a range of variables that might not be considered when one manager conducts the appraisal. However, as this technique provides such a broad range of information, there may be a need to train employees in its interpretation and provide counselling where required. Figure 8.3 provides details on companies that use 360-degree feedback.

Most appraisal techniques require some element of target setting for their effective operation. Objectives and target setting can help to provide clarity, realism and precision and allow both parties to focus upon the same criteria during discussion. Evenden and Anderson (1992) suggest that, in order to improve the motivational aspects of appraisal, each job should be broken down into its key areas and then objectives for each area be developed. They describe key areas as the main tasks that need to be done, so that effective contributions can be made to departmental and, through them, company objectives. In identifying targets and objectives, they suggest the use of a few ground rules to facilitate the target-setting process:

*   Should not set too many.
*   Should be set jointly by the manager and employee.
*   Should be related to agreed personal objectives (of employee).
*   Should be revisable and not too rigid.
*   Should be clear, concrete and challenging.
*   Should identify constraints that may affect achievement.
*   Should identify time scales, review dates and milestones on the way.
*   Should link target-setting into the action plans.

Figure 8.3 Who is using 360-degree feedback?

Fifteen years ago, 360-degree feedback was virtually unheard of, but since then it has become extremely popular, especially in the United States. The majority of Fortune 500 companies have embraced it. The Trends in Ireland indicate that 360-degree is also becoming popular here. A survey conducted at the University of Limerick and in conjunction with IMI reports that 43.2 per cent of companies that have introduced competencies also use 360-degree feedback. Organisations such as Allied Irish Banks, Pfizer Tablet Plant, Intel Ireland, Eircom, Boston Scientific, First Active and Ulster Bank Markets all use 360-degree feedback.

Philip Anderson, Head of Management and Staff Development at AIB declares, 'The process has worked very well at the Bank and has been very well received by the management population'. He highlights the importance of follow-up and that feedback recipients at AIB are currently being afforded the opportunity to go through the 360-degree feedback programme a second time. One of the managers who participated in the programme at AIB heralds it as 'one of the best courses I have ever undertaken'. Another forwards that the process 'offered an opportunity to reflect on my areas of strength and weakness and more importantly offered an avenue to address those weaknesses'. In terms of the perceived changes that have resulted from receiving the 'all round' feedback, one manager at AIB asserts, 'the feedback highlighted a couple of areas for attention which improved my focus and commitment. This in turn led me to attaining a highly accomplished performance rating at my annual performance review'.

Pfizer Tablet Plant introduced, from start up, a paperless, face-to-face 360-degree feedback programme. The process differs from the more typical 360-degree feedback approach since feedback is given in a group setting, with a facilitator present and thus, anonymity is not part of the system. The same feedback process is used by all colleagues throughout the plant, no matter what their role. Eileen O'Riordan, Team Development Facilitator with Pfizer, explains, 'The drive in the tablet plant is to improve and develop high performance teamwork. We had to create a process that could only become a reality if teams truly believed they could influence their effectiveness. A 360-degree paperless feedback process provides a much more appropriate way of doing this than more conventional approaches. It is not about dumping your opinion on anyone. It is about development and growth. It is about building mutual support and trust'. One of the feedback recipients at the Tablet Plant claims 'The process is a great learning tool . . . it is honest, open feedback on performance, relationships etc.' Another recipient stated, 'You know that the feedback on performance is genuine, because it's in their own words.'

Source: McCarthy and Pearson (2000).

The Appraisal Interview

Kikoski (1999) suggests that the Achilles heel of the entire appraisal process is the annual performance review interview. Specifically, he notes that line managers are under-prepared to handle the interview and reluctant to give negative feedback, leading to a situation where the people being appraised receive incomplete and inaccurate messages about their performance. Some of the principles of effective interviewing were outlined in chapter 5 (see the section on selection interviewing) and many of these have application here. Of particular importance is the preparation for the interview itself. Most formal appraisal interviews take place once a year, even though there may be ongoing reviews throughout the year. For this reason both managers and employees need to set time aside to think carefully about the appraisal process: the targets that were previously identified; work performance over the period; particular variables that may be affecting successful completion of work tasks; and the range of developmental opportunities that might have application in developing action plans for the future. Adequate notice of the appraisal interview is a major consideration in facilitating thorough preparation. An employee needs to determine not only how he/she has performed over the past year but also what his/her main expectations, in terms of career and skills development, might be. Equally, the manager needs to be assured that he/she is familiar with all aspects of the employee's performance so that constructive, motivational feedback can be provided. A key 'rule of thumb' associated with appraisal interviewing is to focus on behaviour, which the employee can change if required, rather than personality, which is rather more constant and very difficult to modify. It is in this respect that pre-determined key objectives and associated standards and targets come into play.

The appraisal interview is perhaps the most difficult interview that a manager has to conduct, because the twin goals of performance evaluation and motivation facilitation are not necessarily compatible. Evaluation requires a manager to act as 'judge' and yet the developmental aspect demands a more facilitative, 'supportive' approach. When these are combined with the inherent pitfalls that are associated with the interviewing process (see chapter 5), the result can often lead to interaction that is stressful and demanding for both the manager and the employee being appraised.

There are three particular interview styles that are often associated with the appraisal interview: the *tell-and-sell* approach; the *tell-and-listen* approach and the *problem-solving* approach.

The *tell-and-sell* approach is directive and authoritative in nature and involves the manager telling the employee how he/she has evaluated performance, and then attempting to convince the employee of the fairness of the assessment. This approach is invariable uni-directional, from the manager to the employee, and provides very little opportunity for the employee to participate in the evaluation process. The likely response from the employee is a defensive one, and, where he/she has no input into setting action plans for the future, there is likely to be little commitment to follow-up action. Bearing in mind the key perceived benefits of appraisal outlined earlier, it is unlikely that this approach will facilitate their attainment and is thus not recommended as good practice.

The *tell-and-listen* approach is similar in some respects to the one just outlined, but there is some attempt made to involve the employee in the process. In this approach, the manager again communicates his/her evaluation of performance to the employee, and then actively encourages the employee to respond to the evaluation given. However, given the exigencies of human nature (particularly in respect to being told, rather than being asked), it is unlikely that this approach is any more effective than the first one.

The *problem-solving* approach is based on the premise that the appraisal process is one that is jointly conducted by the manager and the employee. Here, the manager first asks the employee to discuss his/her performance against agreed targets and to express any problems that might be affecting work behaviour. Rather than being given an evaluation, the employee is free to comment and highlight particular aspects of performance, and the manager provides feedback on performance. This approach advocates that an evaluation be conducted after the interview has been completed and takes account of the contribution made by the employee towards his/her own evaluation.

Evenden and Anderson (1992) identify a set of guidelines that can facilitate effective appraisal interviewing:

- The interview should commence with a clear statement of the purpose of the meeting, which will ensure both parties are aware of the rationale for the interview.
- The managers should attempt to establish rapport and put the employee at ease. While this is a difficult process and is heavily dependent on the nature of the relationship

between both parties, it can be facilitated by ensuring that adequate notice of the interview has been given to the employee and he/she has had time to prepare for it.

- Discuss the main tasks and responsibilities undertaken by the employee and invite comments. This stage should take account of any self-appraisal that has been conducted and should focus on the objectives and key tasks of the job.
- Ensure that a balanced discussion takes place. The manager is required to praise the employee for good performance, but also to be frank in discussing any perceived weaknesses. As indicated earlier, the focus should be on the attainment of work targets and standards.
- Encourage the employee to talk frankly about any frustration in the job and any problem areas. Questioning style is particularly pertinent here, especially if the employee is unsure about, or unwilling to admit to problems or difficulties.
- Encourage the employee to develop self-analysis and self-discovery, particularly in relation to developing action plans for the future. Greater commitment to new objectives and plans is likely where the employee has an input into determining them.
- Bring the interview to a close with a summary that clarifies what action is expected for the coming appraisal period.

Once the interview has been conducted and feedback given to the employee, it is important to ensure that the focus on performance is not neglected until the next appraisal interview. The performance management cycle requires a continuous alignment of work targets with key business objectives and thus performance should be reviewed throughout the year. Expectations created at the appraisal interview, in terms perhaps of promotion prospects or training initiatives, should be acted upon to ensure the motivational aspects of performance appraisal are not disregarded. Above all, however, a genuine commitment to the process of performance management is required of all managers and employees if the process is to be effective.

THE ETHICS OF APPRAISAL

Banner and Cooke (1984), in their renowned contribution on ethical dilemmas in performance appraisal, suggest that despite the fact that performance appraisal involves the passing of a judgment on another individual using often rather subjective mechanisms, an organisation can morally justify the use of appraisal. This justification derives from the 'greater good' principle that positive outcomes for both the organisation and the appraisee can accrue from an engagement of the process. In their paper, the authors do point to a number of possible ethical dilemmas that may sometimes arise during the course of the appraisal process:

1. The problematic use of trait-oriented and subjective evaluation criteria.
2. Difficulties in the preparation and writing of performance standards and measurement indicators.
3. The deployment of different systems of performance appraisal within the same organisation.
4. Issues around how the results of the performance appraisal will subsequently be used.
5. Issues surrounding who actually determines the so-called objective standards.

Banner and Cooke conclude that, despite these issues, as long as the performance appraisal procedure is fair, consistent and evenly applied to all, it is a morally justified device and serves a legitimate function in advancing the objectives of the organisation and the individual.

Beyond the moral justification, and despite strong efforts to maintain a fair, objective and impartial approach in the preparation of appraisal assessments, errors of judgement do occur, where, as Grote (1996, 137) puts it, 'one individual observes and evaluates another'. Grote's extensive research and trawl of the extant literature has led him to identify nine common appraisal errors: contrast effect; first impression error; halo/horns effect; similar-to-me-effect; central tendency; negative and positive skew; attribution bias; recency effect; and stereotyping. Table 8.11, extracted from Grote's (1996) *Guide to Performance Appraisal*, defines and provides an example of each error.

Table 8.11 Common errors in the appraisal process

ERROR	DEFINITION	EXAMPLE
Contrast Effect	The tendency of a rater to evaluate people in comparison with other individuals rather than against the standards for the job.	Think of the most attractive person that you have known. Rate this individual's attractiveness on a scale of 1 to 10. Now think of your favourite glamorous movie star. Re-rate your acquaintance. If you have rated your friend lower the second time around, contrast effect is said to be at work.
First Impression Error	The tendency of a manager to make an initial positive or negative judgement of an employee and allow that first impression to colour or distort later information.	A manager new to a work group noticed one employee, who was going through a divorce, performing poorly. Within a month, the employee's performance had returned to its previously high level, but the manager's opinion of the individual's performance was adversely affected by the initial negative impression.
Halo/Horns Effect	Inappropriate generalisations from one aspect of an individual's performance to all areas of that person's performance.	Jeff was outstanding in his ability to get delinquent customers to pay up. His excellence in this most important area caused his manager to rate him highly in unrelated areas where his performance was actually mediocre.
Similar-to-me-Effect	The tendency of individuals to rate people who resemble themselves more highly than they rate others.	Carol, a single mother of four small children, had prevailed in her efforts to succeed and had been promoted to manager. She unwittingly rated several women who were also single mothers higher than their performance warranted.

➡

Table 8.11 Common errors in the appraisal process *(contd.)*

ERROR	DEFINITION	EXAMPLE
Central Tendency	The inclination to rate people in the middle of the scale even when their performance clearly warrants a substantially higher or lower rating.	Out of an erroneous belief that the law required all companies to treat all employees the same and a conscious desire to avoid confrontation, Harold rated all seven of the employees in his work group as 'Fully Meets Standard'.
Negative and Positive Skew	The opposite of central tendency: the rating of all individuals as higher or lower than their performance actually warrants.	Susan rates all of her employees higher than she feels they actually deserve, in the misguided hope that this will cause them to live up to the high rating that they have been given. Carlos sets impossibly high standards and expectations and is proud of never having met a subordinate who deserved a 'Superior Rating'.
Attribution Bias	The tendency to attribute performance failings to factors under the control of the individual and performance successes to external causes.	Harriet, a manager with a mixture of excellent and mediocre performers in her work group, attributes the successes of the former group to the quality of her leadership and the failings of the latter group to their bad attitudes and inherent laziness.
Recency Effect	The tendency of minor events that have happened recently to have more influence on the rating than major events of many months ago.	Victoria kept no formal records of the overall performance or critical incidents of her work group of twelve people during the course of the year. When she began writing their appraisal, she discovered that the only examples she could provide for either positive or negative performance had happened in the last two months.
Stereotyping	The tendency to generalise across groups and ignore individual differences.	Waldo is quiet and reserved, almost meek – about as far from the conventional cliché of a salesman as can be imagined. His sales record, however, is one of the best in the company. But his boss rated his performance lower than that of other salespeople since he didn't fit the mould, ignoring the results that Waldo had produced.

Source: Grote (1996, 138–9).

Knowing that many of these errors can and do occur, Longenecker and Ludwig (1990, 75) argue that the organisation has the right to demand accuracy in performance appraisal, but it also has a number of core obligations that it must observe and fulfil in order to improve accuracy and fairness in the process. Longenecker and Ludwig advance four such obligations that the organisation must meet:

1. The organisation must provide a sound procedure for managers to use in the execution of performance appraisal.
2. Training in performance appraisal must be provided for managers. This training should formally address the issue of intentional inaccuracy, and should deal not only with managers' ability, but willingness and motivation to execute accurate ratings.
3. Organisations must provide leadership from above. Middle and lower-level managers cannot be expected to provide accurate ratings if intentional inaccuracy is practised higher up in the organisation.
4. Like any procedure, the performance appraisal process must be audited to ensure the accuracy of the data generated and the overall integrity of the process.

PERFORMANCE APPRAISAL IN IRELAND

Empirical data on performance appraisal in Ireland is relatively scarce. Earlier evidence provided by McMahon and Gunnigle (1994) confirmed performance appraisal as a regular feature in most organisations. Among the key objectives for performance appraisal identified by this study were the improvement of future work performance, the provision of feedback on performance and the identification of training needs. The Cranet E./University of Limerick's Survey of HRM (1999/2000) supplies more recent evidence on performance appraisal in Ireland. The survey focused on three key areas: the existence of an appraisal system for management, professional/technical, clerical and manual employees; the contributors to the appraisal process; and finally the purpose for which the appraisal system is used.

Table 8.12 The existence of an appraisal system for employee categories (N=446)

	Yes	No	Missing
Managerial	62.6%	33.9%	3.5%
Professional/Technical	59.9%	35.2%	4.9%
Clerical	55.2%	39.9%	4.9%
Manual	38.6%	49.3%	12.1%

Source: Cranet E./University of Limerick Survey (2000).

The data from the survey reveal that managerial employees are covered by an appraisal system in 62.6 per cent of cases, as are nearly 60 per cent of professional employees. By comparison, it appears a relatively less common provision for manual employees. Just over one third of respondents indicate that they operate such a scheme for manual workers.

Turning to the issue of who is involved in the process, our survey asked HR managers to indicate who contributed directly to the performance appraisal process (see table 8.13).

Table 8.13 Direct contributors to the appraisal process (N=446)

	Yes	Missing/No
Immediate Superior	66.4%	33.6%
Next Level Superior	38.8%	61.2%
Employee	56.3%	43.7%
Subordinates	5.8%	94.2%
Peers	6.3%	93.7%
Customers	8.1%	91.9%

Source: Cranet E./University of Limerick Survey (2000).

Here the data portrays a relatively traditional picture of involvement and participation in the appraisal process. External stakeholder participation in the form of customer feedback is relatively uncommon, as is upward and lateral participation. In the majority of instances boss and individual appraisals dominate suggesting more limited support for multi-source/multi-rater schemes.

Table 8.14 Uses of the appraisal systems (N=446)

	Yes	Missing/No
Individual training needs	61.2%	38.8%
Organisational training needs	40.8%	59.2%
Promotion potential	49.3%	50.7%
Career development	52.9%	47.1%
Individual performance-related pay	39.9%	60.1%
Organisation of work	32.5%	67.5%

Source: Cranet E./University of Limerick Survey (2000).

Thus, in Ireland it emerges that data collected from appraisal systems routinely inform training, career development and promotion decisions. This confirms the dual remit of improved work performance and individual development and advancement.

This chapter has sought to provide an overview of the core dimensions of managing and measuring performance, and has focused on some aspects that are difficult to get right, as it were. Reference was made to the performance cycle, and useful detail was provided on the range of appraisal and assessment mechanisms that can be applied. Attention was drawn to critical aspects of appraisal that are especially prone to error and bias.

Hunt (1992, 11) argues that there are many potential problems with appraisal systems. They are, he notes, often poorly designed, over-ambitious, inadequately resourced, or any combination of these factors. Too often, he suggests, they consist simply of unstructured interviews, with neither party, appraiser nor appraisee, being fully aware of the purposes of the encounter. This is clearly unfortunate because the organisation that pays careful attention to the process of performance management and utilises a range of performance appraisal schemes to facilitate work performance will probably reap some dividends. However, with respect to ensuring that whatever system is put in place works, it must be seen to be 'procedurally fair and just' (Cropanzano 2001), and above all ethical (Longenecker and Ludwig 1990). Grote (1996) believes that performance appraisal done well, in an organisational context that takes the procedure seriously, can have a major and positive impact on the corporate culture. He notes that:

> The creation or renovation of a performance appraisal procedure can transform an enterprise from a best-effort environment to a results-driven climate. If a company is going to survive, let alone prevail, in the competitive climate that all face, performance appraisal, more than any other technique, has the power to generate incredible and sustained change throughout the organisation. More than any other action that management can take, the development or redevelopment of a performance appraisal procedure can focus the attention of every stakeholder on exactly those ends that must be achieved for the enterprise to survive . . . Do you want culture change? Serious and major change? Then look to your performance appraisal system. It can be the source of the most significant organisational redirection possible.
>
> Grote (1996, xi)

Given the requirement for high-performance work organisation (as described in chapter 6), one might have expected somewhat greater utilisation of performance appraisal systems. However, as the pressures for competitive functioning intensify, it is likely that organisations will pay more, rather than less, attention to performance management in the future.

9

Training and Development Policy and Context

A core objective of modern economies throughout the world today concerns how to create the conditions for rapid and sustained productivity growth and superior competitive advantage (see for example Kauppiner 2004; Morley 2004; Doyle and Young 2000; Porter 2000; Scarbrough *et al.* 1999; Leadbeater 1999; Boisot 1999; Prahalad and Hamel 1994). A nation's standard of living is ultimately determined by the productivity of its economy, which tends to be measured by the value of goods and services (products) produced per unit of the nation's human, capital, and natural resources. The recent upsurge in human capital research, preoccupied with the education and training of employees, lends support to the view that competitiveness is increasingly being built around strong investment in human resources (Nordhaug 2004). Indeed, Sappey and Sappey (1999) suggest that some industrialised societies may well have been impeding their own economic development by ignoring the necessity for a more skilled workforce. The importance of investment in national skills development was taken up by Horst Sieberg, President of the Kiel Institute of World Economics, at the World Economic Forum in 2000. He noted that the improvement of national systems for human capital formation was a major determinant of economic growth. The dimensions of human capital encompasses not only the level of education but also the work experience of the labour force and managerial expertise. Abramovitz and David (1996) suggest that the most rapidly growing factor of production has been human capital, while Baldwin *et al.* (1997) argue that in the new business reality, individuals need to be able to learn their way out of problems rather than try to apply known solutions to them. In this way learning and knowledge have emerged as essential competitiveness levers (Fulmer *et al.* 2000; Olian *et al.* 1998; Hallier and Butts 1998; Berry 1990) or indeed 'the new organisational wealth' (Sveiby 1997; Heraty and Morley 2003).

The last few years have witnessed considerable efforts to improve the national system of training and development in Ireland (Heraty and Morley 1998c; Tansey 1998; Walsh 1998). Since the mid-1960s, Government policy has focused on attracting foreign direct investment (FDI) to Ireland (using generous tax and financial incentives) and on building the physical and human capital support infrastructures. At the macro level, up until the mid-1990s the single greatest challenge facing the Irish economy was the need to effectively tackle the persistently high level of unemployment. Despite a pervasive feeling that the fundamentals of the Irish economy were sound (low inflation, stable currency, balance of payment surpluses, good industrial relations and solid GNP growth), the country had increasingly struggled to provide jobs for its young, well-educated workforce. However, since 1994 the Irish economy has experienced successive years of sustained economic performance (see earlier discussions in chapter 4). This growth has been reflected in considerable employment gains, impressive labour productivity growth, consistent decreases in the level of Government debt and positive trade surpluses (OECD 1999).

Much of the renewed focus on training and development in Ireland has been instigated not just by demand pressures associated with competitive market functioning, technological advancements and the emergence of skill gaps in certain industries, and renewed pressure to provide increased incentives for organisational level training. Rather, there is evidence of an altered policy focus towards active human capital investment as a critical driver of positive economic growth and development. The combined effect has been the dilution of the essentially voluntarist nature of the state's role in training and development towards a more interventionist approach. The various dimensions of training and development in Ireland are explored both in this chapter and in chapter 10. The frame of reference for this chapter is essentially policy-based: we examine training and development at a macro, national level, while organisational-level learning, training and development, focusing on procedures and practices, is discussed in the following chapter.

To start with, this chapter describes the evolution of the national system of training and vocational education in Ireland and provides a basic 'map' of Ireland's training framework. In particular it examines the historical development of Ireland's training infrastructure and highlights the major statutory and institutional reforms that have shaped the training system currently in operation. National policy decisions are analysed, critical commentaries expressed by various actors in the training arena are discussed, and the leading providers of training and development services in Ireland are reviewed. The chapter concludes with a discussion on the economic value of training and likely future developments of the national training system.

HISTORICAL OVERVIEW OF TRAINING AND DEVELOPMENT
The development of a national training and development framework can best be viewed as a series of distinct phases that originated with the guild system around the eleventh century and developed with considerable statutory reform in the last century. Table 9.1 provides a chronological overview of the stages in this development. In order to trace and fully understand the origins of the national training system in Ireland, it is necessary to consider the beginnings of vocational education, since it was from initiatives in this area that vocational education and training, as we now know it in Ireland, gradually evolved.

The Guild System
The history of training in Ireland can, like that in Britain, be traced back as far as the guild system. The Norman conquest of Britain in the eleventh century brought with it the guild system from mainland Europe, merchants settling in Britain used it to control and regulate trades. This system was also to follow the invaders into Ireland and commence the British influence on trade and training in this country.

The guilds became self-contained and self-perpetuating through a process of controlled apprenticeships, which provided each craft with a ready supply of trained craftsmen, but in numbers that left the power and control of each guild in the hands of a few. Training became an integral feature of these apprenticeships. The apprentice was viewed as his master's property, bound by contract to serve his master faithfully for seven years, while simultaneously learning his trade. The origins of craft apprenticeships may be traced to this era.

Table 9.1 Development of Ireland's national training infrastructure

1898	Agricultural and Technical Instruction (Irl) Act	First form of regulated apprenticeship in Ireland and specified that all training should be on-the-job.
1930	Vocational Education Act	Established VECs to provide a nationwide system of technical and continuing education with emphasis on vocational education.
1931	Apprenticeship Act	Set up apprenticeship committees to regulate apprenticeship training – including duration, wages, training courses.
1959	Apprenticeship Act	Established An Cheard Comhairle to co-ordinate and regulate the apprenticeship system.
1967	Industrial Training Act	Established AnCo to promote training and to assume responsibility for industry and commercial training including apprenticeships.
1970s and 1980s		Industrial expansion and development followed by recession.
1987	Labour Services Act	Evidence of change in policy direction. Established FÁS to provide, co-ordinate and promote training activities.
1988	Galvin Report	Highlighted the inadequacies of existing management development initiatives and the necessity for greater investment in such initiatives at organisational level.
1990	Culliton Report	Recommended the reorganisation of FÁS and the redirecting of resources to providing training for those at work and preparing for work.
1992	Apprenticeship re-examined	Apprenticeship system revisited and reorganised along the lines of competency based standards.
1997	Government White Paper on Human Resource Development	Focus on the State's role in assisting industry to create a learning environment with a view to upgrading the quality of Ireland's human resources.
1999	Qualifications (Education and Training) Act	Established the National Qualifications Authority of Ireland (NQAI) to develop a National Framework to incorporate accreditation of prior learning.
2000	White Paper on Adult Education	Focus on issues surrounding maintaining access to and participation in continuing education and training throughout life.

Source: Developed from Heraty *et al.* 2000

Industrial Development

The gradual decline of the guilds in mainland Europe and Great Britain coincided with the rise of the factory system of production in the late eighteenth century. Over time, this system of production was further developed through the application of scientific techniques for controlling and measuring work, which were aimed at eliminating inefficiency. A net result of such application lay in the introduction of the concept of division of labour, combined with the mechanisation of the production process. The rapid growth of industrialisation, and its increased utilisation of the division of labour, organised work into particular skills, crafts and tasks. It gave rise to a form of work classification that still exists today and is taken to be synonymous with the existing distribution and nature of occupational work categories. Groups within the labour force became broadly categorised as managerial, clerical, technical, skilled, semi-skilled and unskilled employees. These categorisations also reflected the growing organisation of trade unions around particular groups of workers, e.g. the skilled in craft unions, the semi-skilled and unskilled in general unions, clerical and technical staff in white-collar unions. In overall terms, a recognisable training entity was most associated with craft apprenticeships, and this system was to become the central focus of the earliest initiatives in vocational education and training.

Statutory Reform

In an attempt to formalise and regulate technical and scientific education, the City and Guilds of London was established in 1878. Through an examination system it initiated the development of courses and formulated recognised standards of attainment. Around this time, some significant developments had taken place in the large urban areas in Ireland such as Bolton Street College in Dublin and the Crawford Institute in Cork.

The British Government responded to this change of emphasis by enacting the Technical Instruction Act of 1891. This act made provision for funding by local authorities for technical education in schools, and was seen as a new departure towards satisfying the training needs of industry, which heretofore had been largely privately funded. This was soon followed in Ireland by the enacting of the Agricultural and Technical Instruction (Irl) Act of 1898, which introduced the first form of regulated apprenticeship in Ireland and specified that all training and instruction for apprentices should be given on the job.

Following the establishment of the Free State in 1922, it became clear that the system of apprenticeship training could be classified as aspirational in nature and was proving of little value to apprentices. Irish independence set the development of the Irish economy in motion, and a government-appointed Commission on Technical Education in 1926 was heavily critical of the educational system, particularly concerning its inability to meet the development needs of trade, industry and agriculture. In particular, major statutory reform was recommended to alleviate the inconsistencies of the previous system.

The Vocational Education Act 1930 introduced a new structure by establishing thirty-eight Vocational Education Committees (VECs), which were responsible for the provision of a suitable system of continuing education and technical education in committee areas. An emphasis was placed on vocational training, which was defined in terms of full-time, second-level training in literacy and scientific subjects, augmented by some concentration on manual skills. However, despite these new initiatives, the overall picture of apprenticeship training remained much the same, as there was no compulsion on the employer to send apprentices on any of the courses organised by the VEC, and many continued their practices unchanged.

Arising from the recommendations of the 1926 commission, the Apprenticeship Act 1931 attempted to achieve the reorganisation of the apprenticeship system. This represented the first systematic effort at regulating the Irish apprenticeship system. The main provisions of the Act centred around the formation of apprenticeship committees with responsibility for regulating apprenticeship training in the designated areas, e.g. construction, electrical, and so forth. These committees formulated rules governing the length of an apprenticeship, age limits for entry and educational requirements, wage levels, the number of working hours and the regulation of training courses. Employers were obliged by statute to release apprentices for these courses, providing such a course was held within three miles of the workplace and took place during normal working hours.

This Act is now perceived as being largely ineffective, as it merely laid down ground rules for the co-ordination of the apprenticeship system. There was evidence of considerable variation in the standard of training programmes available to apprentices and, in some cases, abuse of the apprenticeship system. To compound these difficulties, certain trades were in demand by industry, e.g. engineering and construction, while others were in decline. The organisation of apprenticeship schemes was very much scattered amongst the thriving industries, e.g. transport, steel, textiles and footwear, leaving other sections lagging behind.

In an effort to mitigate these problems, a new Government Commission on Youth Employment in 1943 recommended the establishment of a National Apprenticeship Committee to control and co-ordinate apprenticeship training at national level. Such a committee would have overall responsibility for all trades and so replace the existing committee system. There was general recognition that the origination of apprentices on a committee basis was ineffective and led to quality problems and other inconsistencies.

Statutory reform continued in the form of the Apprenticeship Act 1959, which attempted to address the problems caused by the multiple responsibilities allocated under the 1931 Act. Under its terms, a national apprenticeship board, An Cheard Comhairle, was set up to co-ordinate the apprenticeship system. This body was vested with the authority to examine the methods used by any trade for the recruitment and training of apprentices. It had a number of specific objectives including the setting down of appropriate education qualifications, ensuring the release of apprentices to technical colleges, providing on-the-job training, and establishing a system of examination on the practice and theory of each trade. While this board was successful to a large degree in its aims, outside the apprenticeship system, however, there was little recognition of the need for, or value of, training.

Economic Stagnation

The Irish economy about this time was inward-focused, with the policies adopted by Éamon de Valera and successive Fianna Fáil Governments concentrating on the imposition of trade barriers and the preservation of ownership of industry at national level. The manufacturing industry was still in its infancy when compared to agriculture and commerce, and it merited little attention in national planning terms. Indeed, foreign ownership of industry was barred, and there was little emphasis on export markets and foreign trade. With the exception of the statutory reform on the apprenticeship front, no coherent training policies were pursued at national level.

Ireland remained slow to recognise the need for training outside of the apprenticeship system. At national level, the Government adopted an essentially voluntaristic approach. Training was held to be the preserve of joint negotiation between both sides of industry, with the Government's role defined in purely advisory and facilitative terms. The Irish industrial sector was largely left to its own devices to provide the skills necessary for its growth and development. De Valera's philosophy of keeping Ireland for the Irish, with little emphasis on export markets and foreign trade, left marginal opportunity for the expansion of indigenous industry, and even less for the importing of new technologies and systems from abroad.

Ireland experienced a shortage of skilled labour in the early 1950s, especially in the engineering field. However, there was little coherent response at a policy level. By the end of the 1950s, there was no shortage of criticism of the training system in operation. Suggested reforms included direct financial aid from Government to companies, in respect of apprenticeship training, and the introduction of some system of statutory training levy, whereby companies that did not themselves train might contribute to the training costs of others.

Significantly, perhaps, this lack of progress towards reform was marked by the fact that neither side of industry was motivated to press for major change in the voluntarist structure of training provision. Employers, though pressed in some sectors by skill shortages, were prepared to pay the wages necessary to poach the skilled labour they required from their competitors. Trade unions concentrated on consolidating the apprenticeship system, following the logic that maintaining defensive control over conditions of entry led to skilled labour attracting a good price. The principle of voluntarism, and the maintenance of the status quo, therefore appeared to suit everybody.

Movement towards Institutional Reform

As the 1960s dawned it seemed increasingly clear that the voluntarist approach to training was failing to meet national needs. There were insufficient skilled workers and the lack of training outside the apprenticeship systems, combined with the narrow content of apprenticeship training itself, resulted in Ireland lagging behind most of her mainland European competitors in terms of the average skill levels and educational qualifications of her workforce. However, if the diagnosis of Ireland's training illness was clear, agreement on a possible cure was altogether more contentious. The Department of Labour and the educational establishments were somewhat more advanced than industry in recognising the need for reform. Employers and trade unions remained unconvinced and, to a large degree, unconcerned that there was a major problem with a voluntarist system that allowed both sides to pursue their different interests in relative harmony, through the apprenticeship framework. Skilled labour could attract a good price. Employers were left to train or not to train according to their short-term cost criteria, while negotiation between both sides of industry and the Government remained a purely facilitative one. Relative, if fragile, economic security allowed this complacency to flourish.

It was to take the perception of harsher economic conditions in the early 1960s, and a new determination on the part of the Government led by Seán Lemass, to inspire attempts at major reform. There is considerable agreement that this Government was responsible for dragging the Irish economy into the twentieth century. Ireland had joined the International Monetary Fund (IMF) in 1957 and the World Bank shortly afterwards. The Economic Development Report of 1958 added its impetus to the liberalisation of trade and commerce, and a more outward-looking economic focus began to emerge. Controls on foreign ownership of Irish industry were removed in 1963, import tariffs were removed over the period 1962–4, and in 1965 the Anglo-Irish Trade Agreement on Tariffs and Trades (GATT) was signed. These initiatives reflected Government policy aimed at creating a more open economy with the emphasis on attracting foreign investment to Ireland.

A cornerstone of this policy was the encouragement given to foreign companies to locate here, through tax incentives, capital investment grants, advance factories and so forth. With the arrival of these companies, vocational and skills training took on a new impetus, although the skill base remained very weak. It is worth noting that the influx of these multinational companies, many of whom espouse the training and development of employees as a fundamental priority investment, represents a landmark influence on training in this country, which has persisted to the present day.

Meanwhile, tourism and agriculture were also targeted for development with a view to reaching foreign markets. The Farm Apprenticeship Board was set up in 1963 to provide training for young farmers, and the Council for Education, Recruitment and Training (CERT) was established by the Tourist Board, to handle education and training in the tourist and hospitality sector. This change in economic policy led to a considerable slowdown in emigration and actually resulted in many emigrants returning to Ireland to work or to establish their own businesses.

In response to an International Labour Organisation (ILO) report on vocational education in 1962, a Dáil committee was set up in 1963 to tackle the problem of retraining the unemployed. The bulk of those unemployed were unskilled and in dire need of training so that the kind of workforce necessary for attracting foreign companies would be more readily available. The mid-1960s represented a watershed in national training policy, when the recognition of a number of significant issues was instrumental to the subsequent change of direction. The general conclusions reached were that:

- the voluntarist system facilitated the perpetuation and enhancement of familiar problems and allowed them to continue untackled;
- there was no effective national body to keep apprenticeship and other training activities under review;
- there was an insufficient number of skilled workers to meet the growing demands of the developing Irish economy;
- a small number of employers, e.g. Guinness and Bewleys, trained well, and their skilled workers were often poached by those who invested little in training;
- the state itself provided a poor example in this regard with inappreciable investment in training in the public sector;
- training methods were also poor, with few formal qualifications, and the training situation was in considerable need of improvement.

In response, the Government White Paper of 1965 adopted many of the recommendations of the ILO Report and set about establishing a national Industrial Training Authority.

The period from 1967 to 1980 is characterised by significant upheaval and reform of the training system at national and organisational level. The Industrial Training Act of 1967 repealed the 1959 Act and established An Comhairle Oilun – AnCo. This body was empowered by the Act to assume full responsibility for all industrial training, including apprenticeships, and its functions included the provision of training at all levels of industry and the provision, facilitation, encouragement, assistance, co-ordination and development of training initiatives. The activities of AnCo were organised into three key areas:

- *Training Advisory Service.* Through this service, trained advisors (including the ID, SFADCo, and Udaras na Gaeltachta) acted as consultants to industry. Their activities incorporated the assessment of company training needs, the drawing up of training plans and programmes and the sanctioning of grants to industry.
- *Training for Individuals.* Training centres were established to provide a range of courses aimed at unemployed or redundant workers, those seeking retraining for new skills, school leavers, and in assisting some community-based initiatives.
- *Apprenticeship Training.* AnCo was empowered to make detailed provisions for the training of apprentices: statutory designated areas included construction, engineering, metals, electrical, motor, furniture, printing and dental craft work.

AnCo was funded mainly by the Government, but the Act also allowed for the imposition of a levy/grant scheme to underwrite training costs and to heighten awareness of the economic benefits of investment in training. The scheme itself considered several factors, including company size, gross payroll levels, and the amount of training provided. The levy amounted to between 1 per cent and 1.25 per cent of annual gross payroll. Varying portions of the levy could be recovered, e.g. companies with fewer than fifty employees could claim back 90 per cent, while those employing between 51 and 500 could claim back between 50 per cent and 90 per cent. An upper limit of £50,000 (€63,487) was payable to any one company or £2,800 (€3,555) in respect of any one employer. The general purpose of the scheme was to tax prime industry into accepting its responsibility for its own training, while simultaneously fostering a systematic approach to training and development.

The 1967 Act represented a significant change in Government policy, reflecting an interventionist strategy aimed at sweeping away the concept of voluntarism. It also heralded an institutional role for a National Training Agency.

The early 1970s saw a considerable upsurge in economic activity in Ireland with the influx of foreign multinationals creating valuable employment for skilled and semi-skilled employees. This buoyancy was short-lived, however. The Irish economy drifted into crisis from the mid-1970s onwards due to the recession brought about by the oil price shocks and the resultant escalation of unemployment. High levels of Government borrowing for current expenditure led to a soaring foreign debt. Spending on education and training was severely curtailed during this period and companies, faced with rising costs and shrinking markets, cut back on non-essential spending. Consequently, training and development activities were severely curtailed.

The economic conditions of the late 1970s focused considerable attention on AnCo. The multiplicity of agencies seeking resources, paralleled by the growing scarcity of funds, was now a major problem. The perception of widespread duplication of functions precipitated severe criticisms of AnCo, the more salient of which were:

- Considerable doubt was expressed about the quality of the training and the competency of AnCo to provide such a wide range of training activities.
- There was considerable evidence to suggest an over-dependence on AnCo as a supporter of training.
- AnCo's concept of training was felt, by many employers, to be overly concerned with paperwork, which was seen to create a situation where training specialists were ultimately judged on their ability to recover the levy paid, rather than the innovativeness or the relevance of their training activities.
- Considerable resentment was building up over AnCo's access to European Social Fund monies. Accusations were made concerning the duplication of courses that were already available in many of the technical colleges; the redirection of funding away from education and towards AnCo; and the lack of any coherent, integrative policy on management training.
- The lack of a strategic focus, and the industry-based nature of training schemes militated against the development of an economy-wide strategy for training.

In 1985, in the midst of a sea of criticism, the Confederation of Irish Industry carried out a comprehensive analysis of the Irish training system and called for an extensive review of the levy scheme. Their main arguments are worth recording, and may be summarised as follows:

- In a period of rapid technological and market changes, education and training are crucial factors in the struggle to improve competitiveness and achieve further employment.
- The Government is responsible for ensuring the provision of basic education and transferable skills that are necessary for entering employment.
- Enterprises are responsible for the provision of relevant specialised training that is necessary for their economic development.
- Irish industry recognises the need to provide for retraining and the continuing education of its existing workforce, particularly in technical fields.
- Both employers and employees have a mutual interest in availing of education and training.
- Employees should be willing, in their own interests, to invest in further education and training, outside working hours if necessary.
- Recognition was given to the historical position of apprenticeship in Ireland in the sphere of education and training of craftspersons, and it was pointed out that the decreasing role of craftspersons within the manufacturing industry must be recognised, together with an increasing demand for technicians and skilled operatives.

White Paper on Manpower Policy (1986)
A White Paper on Manpower Policy, published in September 1986, examined the role of all actors involved in manpower policy and cited a number of proposals for action.

1. While the primary responsibility for providing training rested with employers, Government intervention was necessary to ensure that the quality and quantity of training available conformed to policy objectives.
2. The multiplicity of agencies responsible for training could be addressed through the amalgamation of a number of agencies into one authority.
3. The levy-grant scheme to be re-organised and based on a more selective approach (i.e. linked to approved company development plans and concentrated on key skill areas).
4. The apprenticeship system to be revised and modernised with a view to developing a system based on standards achieved, to ensure a satisfactory balance between supply and demand, and a reduced cost to the state while still maintaining quality.
5. Deficiencies in management training to be identified under the auspices of an advisory committee.

While the White Paper caused considerable consternation among the actors involved in training at the time, it also provided the impetus for the Government to make significant institutional reform and to streamline the national training system in Ireland.

Labour Services Act (1987)
The Government's response to the White Paper was the enactment of the Labour Services Act 1987, which represented the first attempt in twenty years, at state level, to reform the training system and bring it into alignment with economic objectives pursued by the Government. This Act provided for the establishment of FÁS (Foras Áiseanna Saothair), an amalgam of the National Manpower Service (NMS), AnCo and the Youth Employment Agency (YEA) into one body. CERT was excluded largely because of the tourism lobby who argued that because of the skill shortages, and the importance of tourism as an employment growth sector, CERT should remain independent and provide a specialised

service. The Act set out a number of important functions for FÁS, including the provision of training and retraining for industry and the management of particular employment schemes to assist in the reduction of unemployment in Ireland. Specifically, the mantra ascribed to FÁS was that it should adopt a customer-centred approach, regionalise its operations and give a high priority to meeting the needs of the long-term unemployed.

The Minister envisaged FÁS as a labour-intensive service, doing invaluable work for the economy and the community, and offering job satisfaction to its own employees. He did not, however, visualise any major dismantling of the existing services of the NMS, YEA or AnCo, but instead saw them being adapted over time to achieve a more regionally based and integrated service. His aspiration was for FÁS to move towards the provision of more effective services at local level. The period between 1987 and 1991 therefore represented a time of significant change for FÁS. In the immediate aftermath of the Act, a meaningful shift in its activities was seen, away from company-based facilitation activities towards an increase in community and youth employment-type training programmes.

Advisory Committee on Management Training (1988)

A review of statutory and institutional reform over the years highlights a consistent focus on apprenticeship training, youth employment schemes, training for the unemployed and so forth. However, little attention was given to management training and development and it was not until 1986 and the White Paper on Manpower Policy that explicit reference was made to the importance of management development. Under the direction of Paddy Galvin, the Advisory Committee on Management Development was set up to evaluate the quantity and quality of existing provision for the development of managers. The committee

Table 9.2 Summary findings of the advisory committee on management development

Issue to be addressed	Recommendations
Insufficient level of commitment and expenditure on management development initiatives	Increased commitment an urgent national priority; establish action group on management development to promote management training
Lack of understanding of what is involved, or what constitutes good practice, in management training and development	Develop a set of national guidelines on management development to be used as a code of practice
Lack of a common core of relevant business knowledge and skills	Adjustment of business education to reflect business needs; broadly common curriculum to be offered by providers of business education
Difficulties experienced by small businesses in implementing management development policies	Provision of incentives for small firms to draw up and implement management development programmes
The ambiguity and inconsistency of the state's role in funding post-experience management training	State funding to be redirected away from the providers of training and towards the users of training; closer alignment of utilisation of funds with economic policy
Separate training for public and private sector managers is not in the national interest	Merger of management training activities of the IMI and IPA

reported in 1988 and noted that economic performance is significantly influenced by the quality of organisational management. A number of key strengths of the management training and development system were identified including the quality of the main providers, the standard of general education, the wide choice of provision and experimentation with different delivery systems. The report further highlighted a number of specific weaknesses and made recommendations for action. The most salient finding concerning both the weaknesses identified and the recommendations made are summarised in table 9.2.

In particular, the committee reported that over one fifth of the top companies spent nothing on management development, while one half of them spent less than £5,000 (€6,349) on management development activities. In its recommendations, the committee highlighted the strategic importance of management training and development and stressed the necessity for it to be closely integrated with the strategic business objectives of the organisation. While the report was criticised on the basis that it was overtly prescriptive and that its case analysis was highly selective, it is recognised that its proposals represent a progressive development in highlighting the need for investment in training and development at all levels of the organisation.

NATIONAL TRAINING POLICY IN REVIEW

From about the mid-1990s there was a growing recognition that training policy, at national level, had resulted in a number of inconsistencies and had ill-supported the needs of industry generally. Over the years, a number of criticisms have been levelled at the national training system that probably served as the catalyst for a significant change in policy direction. A brief summative account of some of these is presented here.

The Culliton Report

The Culliton Report, published in 1992, made two specific recommendations about training and development at national level. First, it said that the provision for training at work was inadequate and new structures were urgently required to remedy the situation. It called for the institutional reorganisation of FÁS to reflect the sharp distinction between support activities for the unemployed and industry–relevant training. Second, it recommended that a greater proportion of FÁS resources and activities should be allocated to industry–relevant training directed towards those at work and preparing for work.

The recommendations of the Culliton Report clearly espoused an interventionist approach on the part of the state. The report pointed out that about 90 per cent of FÁS's budget was absorbed by activities that could not generally be described as training. Roche and Tansey (1992) argued that FÁS was a very complex organisation, with a set of multiple objectives both economic and social, coupled with a wide span of activities and programmes. They also suggested that FÁS was deserving of closer analysis due to its position and the national resources it has responsibility for managing.

IBEC's Analysis of Industrial Training (1994)

IBEC carried out a comprehensive review of industrial training in 1994, which identified a number of perceived weaknesses in our national training system. Specifically, it noted the following:

- National training policy was seen to be primarily driven by the state with the result that employers had only a consultative role and were not directly represented on important bodies.

- The training support scheme was held to be inadequate, with insufficient state support for industrial training.
- Training provision was overly fragmented between state agencies, educational institutions, consultancies, private training organisations and industrialists.
- Companies needed to invest more in training but the real problem in many small firms may be less to do with increasing their investment in training and more to do with the need to get a better return on any investment made.
- There was a major imbalance of resources allocated between support for training for the unemployed and training for those in employment. The report cited an expenditure figure of £280m for the unemployed and £1.8m for those in employment.

The report, while acknowledging the passive role played by employers to date and the consequent inadequate provision that resulted, concluded with a number of recommendations that would facilitate a greater contribution from employers.

Table 9.3 IBEC recommendations for industrial training

- The development of national training policy for the employed and the co-ordination of Government services to support industry.
- The researching of industry training needs to clearly articulate the training needed in key business growth areas to support business development. Direct consultation and the development of pilot projects would be a key part of this function.
- The promotion of truly effective and cost-efficient training that supports organisational objectives and improved performance.
- The development of a national framework of vocational qualifications both for off-the-job and in-company training.
- The generation of greater awareness of the contribution that well structured training can make to business competitiveness.
- The development of appropriate initiatives to satisfy the training and development needs of small business.
- The securing of direct financial support for training initiatives that meet criteria and standards laid down, with the actual training to be carried out by approved trainers, of whom FÁS would be one option. In this way, company-relevant training would receive a greater level of support.
- The improvement of the quality and design of training programmes for those in employment.
- The promotion and establishment of a quality training mark for companies with the objective of developing company accreditation as a requirement for the future availability of grant-aided training.
- The development of initiatives to meet gaps in training provisions particularly in the service sector.
- The representation of industry's interests on sectoral and educational bodies in the planning and organisation of education and training for industry.

Source: Garavan, Costine and Heraty (1995).

Trade Union Perspective on Training

During the 1990s it became more apparent that training and development was becoming an important item on the union agenda. For instance, ICTU highlighted the fact that in the area of raising the skill levels of existing employees, Irish firms lagged well behind their

European counterparts (Duffy 1993). In outlining an argument for improving this situation, Duffy referred to several deficiencies in the Irish training scene, including:

- the perceived lack of consultation with trade unions in the area of training and development;
- the focus on very job-specific training without any element of personal development;
- the tendency of firms to design their training with a view to maximising grant recovery, rather than focusing on the needs of individuals being trained;
- the absence of formal training agreements.

Duffy further classified training requirements into two broad categories: the need to continue upgrading existing skills, and the need to meet the challenges of a total change in work practices brought on by changes in technology. These general themes were also embraced in a report commissioned in 1993 by ICTU, entitled *New Forms of Work Organisation: Options for Trade Unions*, in which the need to ensure adequate skills training, as well as providing opportunities for personal development, is associated with the introduction of new work organisation strategies. In addition, Bill Attley (then Joint General President of SIPTU) stated his belief that the success of the Irish economy depends in large measure on high levels of skills and knowledge, and that it was the intention of trade unions to press for its vision of a highly skilled and flexible workforce.

Garavan *et al.* (1995) collated a number of generally perceived inconsistencies in the area of national training and development policy as follows:

- The state had handled its own training badly. It exhorted private enterprise to develop and implement corporate training plans, and yet the state itself did not operate such a process.
- During the previous ten years or so the Government had invested heavily in training, almost to the point where organisations had become dependent on such funding, with very uneven results. The cumulative effect of all state intervention had served to represent training to employers as something that is essentially provided by external agencies.
- Since the mid-1980s there had been a preoccupation in Ireland with training to reduce mass unemployment (particularly youth unemployment). This, in turn, had switched the emphasis of national training strategies away from the existing business enterprise and its needs, towards the creation of a network of non-business organisations. Because of this, the value of training for organisational improvement had been diminished in the eyes of many employers.
- With regard to providing the critically required impetus to the concept of continuing training in this country, the Labour Services Act (1987) seemed less than effective. It did not make a significantly positive statement about the role of training within organisations and the need to allocate more resources and commitment in this vital area.

White Paper on Human Resource Development

In response to continued criticism of the state's role in Ireland's training infrastructure, the Government produced a policy document entitled 'Human Resource Development White Paper' in May 1997. This White Paper represented a significant departure from the traditional programme-led interventions that had typified previous governmental responses, and which had resulted in ad hoc interventions that lacked overall strategic coherence. Instead, the emphasis was on clear objective-driven solutions and called for significant change in the approach to training and human resource development by business, individuals and the providers of training services. Three critical pillars of developing effective human resource development strategies were identified:

- the promotion of investment in the development of skills and knowledge of the workforce;
- the promotion of gainful employment by helping people to develop their knowledge and skills to their full potential;
- the achievement of high levels of efficiency, effectiveness and value for money in the delivery of state interventions, which yield permanent benefits to clients.

The White Paper further outlined a number of structural- and policy-based changes that were seen to be required if the Government were to achieve these strategic pillars. The more salient of these proposals included:

1. The 'Service to Industry' division of FÁS (including the regional advisory component) was to be transferred to a new body, Forbairt, while FÁS would retain responsibility for the delivery of training for those individuals who seek to enter or re-enter the labour market.
2. The development of a revitalised National Employment Service.
3. The development of a new training networks programme, to provide state support to encourage the development of best practice strategies.
4. The industrial training grants to be reviewed and grant-aid support maintained to those firms that provide the training necessary to enable newly recruited workers attain the requisite level of expertise and productivity.
5. The establishment of a Future Skills Identification Group, comprising representatives of business and trade unions, as well as representatives of Government, state development agencies and education and training providers, with a view to identifying skill needs and making recommendations for the education and training system.

Significant changes have occurred since 1997, many of which relate to the current operation of FÁS, and are documented towards the end of this chapter. However, there are many who argue that the changes have not been far-reaching enough and that considerably more needs to be done to support training for those at work if Ireland is to develop a truly knowledge-based economy. Tansey (1998) highlights the continuing importance of economic training to facilitate national competitiveness and encourages the delivery of high-quality training as a national priority. In particular, he highlights a number of core benefits that are seen to be associated with strategic economic training:

- It promotes national economic development by ensuring that the potential for national economic growth is maximised. Insufficient training, or a poor level of training, can lead to skill shortages that can inhibit the growth of the economy.
- Economic training improves individual productivity.
- Economic training has the potential to improve an industry's adaptability and its capacity to absorb changes in product and process technologies.
- Extensive economic training facilitates the introduction of more advanced physical capital.

- The existence of a pool of highly skilled labour at all levels is used as a mechanism for attracting foreign industry to Ireland.
- A skilled labour force becomes a significant differentiation factor within a single market.

National Qualifications Authority 2001

The National Qualifications Authority of Ireland (NQAI) was established by the Government in February 2001 as directed under the Qualifications (Education and Training) Act 1999. This act further provided for the establishment of two national awards councils that would come under the ambit of the NQAI but which are separate and independent from it. The role of the Authority includes the establishment of standards of awards and the determination of the procedures to be followed by the councils in the performance of their functions. The Further Education and Training Awards Council (FETAC) is the national awarding body for all further education and training in Ireland. This body makes awards previously made by four Irish awarding bodies, namely FÁS, the National Council for Vocational Awards, the National Tourism and Certification Board and Teagasc. HETAC (the Higher Education and Training Awards Council) is the qualifications awarding body for third-level education and training institutions outside the university sector (other than the Dublin Institute of Technology). It is the legal successor to the National Council for Educational Awards (NCEA).

A key role for the NQAI is the establishment of a national framework of qualifications that will include all awards in Ireland and will provide a mechanism for accrediting prior learning. Progress is continuing in this area at the time of writing, particularly with respect to access, transfer and progression through the various levels (1–10).

Expert Group on Future Skills Needs

Following one of the recommendations of the White Paper on HRD, the Expert Group on Future Skills Needs (EGFSN) was set up in 1997 to investigate and develop national strategies to tackle the issue of skills needs, human resource forecasting and training for business and education in Ireland. A clear remit of the EGFSN was to identify best practice in enterprise training, both nationally and internationally, and to commission sectoral studies of key skills needs into the future. A series of reports has been published by this body since 1997, some generally focused and others targeting specific sectors (e.g. the biotechnology sector report 2003 and the food processing sector report 2003), that detail a range of generic and employability and advanced skills training that are required for effective national competitiveness.

White Paper on Adult Education 2000

In 1997 the OECD Adult Literacy Survey noted that 25 per cent of the Irish population scored at the lowest level of literacy and that those with low skill levels were among those least likely to avail of any continuing education and training. These results fuelled an already heated debate concerning the lack of policy development with respect to adult and continuing education. The White Paper on Adult Education emerged in 2000 and describes adult education as systematic learning undertaken by adults who return to learning having concluded initial education or training. The White Paper highlighted the need to increase significantly the scale and flexibility of existing provision, to promote strategic shifts towards adult-friendly policies within existing educational institutions, to invest systematically in the development of core supporting services such as guidance and counselling, and childcare, and to provide for an increased role and funding for community education.

Report of the Task Force on Lifelong Learning (2002)

The Task Force on Lifelong Learning was set up in 2000 under the National Programme for Prosperity and Fairness to explore core issues surrounding the provision of learning for those in the workplace. Among the recommendations to Government were the development of more flexible delivery systems with regard to the opening hours of institutions, the move to modular courses and the potential of open and distance learning.

Forum on the Workplace of the Future (2005)

The Forum on the Workplace of the Future was established by the National Centre for Partnership and Performance (NCPP) at the request of the Government to assess how well Ireland's workplaces are equipped to meet the challenges that face us into the future. Following a lengthy consultation process, the Forum reported in 2005 and identified nine key attributes of a successful workplace in the future: agility, customer-centred, knowledge-intense, responsive to employee needs, networked, highly productive, participatory, continually learning and proactively diverse. A National Workplace Strategy, which was set down to help achieve these attributes, comprised 42 separate recommendations subsumed under five broad areas for action:

- Commitment to workplace innovation.
- Capacity for change.
- Developing future skills.
- Access to opportunities.
- Quality of working life.

A high-level implementation group has been established to develop and oversee the institutional arrangements needed for the successful implementation of this National Workplace Strategy. Full details on the Forum and related activities can be accessed on the NCPP website – www.ncpp.ie).

PROVISION OF TRAINING AND DEVELOPMENT SERVICES

As a result of many of the initiatives discussed earlier, the provision of training and development services has grown considerably in recent years. In this section we consider the role of the key actors currently operating in the Irish scene.

FÁS: The National Training Agency

FÁS activities are funded by the Irish Government, the National Training Fund and the European Union. While a considerable amount of FÁS's activities are still directed towards reducing unemployment and fostering community-based initiatives, some change has occurred recently with respect to its services to industry. These services operate on a regional basis (eight regions comprising twenty training centres and sixty-two employment offices), using a network of training advisors. There are also industry experts at national level who oversee the development of FÁS's activities in relation to the various industrial sectors.

FÁS, through its Services to Business Units, provides a broad range of training and company development programmes for businesses in Ireland. These programmes are available to all sectors of industry and commerce and all sizes and types of firm, whether indigenous or foreign. These programmes are categorised as:

- Services to business training courses.
- Small firms cluster programme.
- Excellence through people programme.
- Disability awareness training programme.
- Online training programmes from FÁS eCollege.

The Training Support Scheme (TSS) (1990–2002) was introduced by FÁS in 1990 to encourage and promote training (through funding support), particularly in small and medium-sized organisations – over half of the allocation for TSS was targeted at firms with fewer than fifty employees. However, this scheme was discontinued in 2002 and has been replaced by the Competency Development Programme.

The Competency Development Programme does not provide funding directly to companies; rather it commissions training (or sometimes supports training on the open market) from training organisations that are on the National Training Register (operated jointly by FÁS and Enterprise Ireland). This programme aims to target priority skills needs in particular occupations or sectors to ensure that the national stock of skills matches the national human resource requirements for continued economic growth. Specifically, it provides a training subsidy to enhance the competency of specific members of the company's workforce and enable those employees to cope with frequent and ongoing changes in work practices (see www.fas.ie for fuller details).

Responsibility for the promotion of training for certain companies (especially companies with export growth potential) was transferred from FÁS to Enterprise Ireland. EI provides training-related supports for its clients under a number of specific initiatives and programmes including R&D, mentoring and HRD more generally (www.enterprise-ireland.com).

In 1995, FÁS introduced its Training Awards Scheme and a new training quality standard, *Excellence Through People* (ETP), which is designed to reward and encourage high training standards and to demonstrate the link between training investment and improved business performance. The standard has two particular objectives:

- To act as a business improvement tool as well as being a driver for change and innovation.
- To promote employee learning, development and involvement in line with the organisation's goals.

At the end of 2004, 437 organisations, employing in excess of 150,000 people, had achieved the Excellence Through People standard.

The apprenticeship system operated today is competency-based. It combines both on-the-job and off-the-job training with the latter provided by a combination of FÁS and third-level institutes of technology. Apprentices who successfully complete the programme are issued with a National Craft Certificate, a qualification that is recognised not only in Ireland but also in other EU and non-EU countries. This competency-based or standards-based model of apprenticeship consists of seven distinct phases (there is one trade exception) and is based on the achievement of certain pre-set standards of skill and competence rather than on time served. This system facilities the progression of successful apprentices to further educational qualifications and to continue to technical level at a recognised national and international standard.

Participation in the apprenticeship system continues to be male dominated. FÁS operates a policy that is designed to promote and encourage the entry of women into apprenticeship and has established a number of measures to facilitate female participation in apprenticeships. One such measure sees FÁS offer a bursary to both private and public sector employers who recruit female apprentices under the Standards-Based Apprenticeship system in the currently designated trades. Up to £2,100 (€2,666) is paid to the employer for each female apprentice recruited. FÁS, in conjunction with the education system, further provides training for females where required to prepare them to train and work in what has been a traditionally male work environment.

The number of apprenticeships declined quite considerably in the 1990s. This decline in recruitment can be attributed both to demand constraints in terms of curbed public sector recruitment and industrial restructuring on the one hand, and to the increased incidences of sub-contracting and outsourcing on the other (*Labour Market Study: Ireland 1997*). However, since 1994 there has been renewed interest in apprenticeship as it becomes an increasingly popular career choice for school leavers in areas where recent economic buoyancy and increasing skill shortages have created significant opportunities for qualified craft and trade occupations. At the end of 2004, there were a total of 25,400 people registered in the apprenticeship system with 8,400 new recruits in 2004. A 1999 evaluation of the apprenticeship system (ESF Evaluation Unit) suggests that the educational profile of apprentices in recent years has demonstrated higher qualifications among participants than had hitherto been the case, again reflecting the growing attraction of craft qualifications in Ireland.

Complete details on the range of services provided by FÁS can be found on its website (www.fas.ie).

While FÁS has a strong institutional role to play in the provision of training services, both to industry and to the unemployed, there are numerous other actors involved in the training arena. The more widely recognised of these are listed below.

Irish Institute of Training and Development (IITD)
The IITD is a professional body that caters for those concerned with training and development in business, industry, consultancy and the community. Founded in 1969, the institute's mission is to provide for the growth of those involved in training and development and, by doing so, to become the Irish voice for the development of people at both organisational and individual level in Ireland. Membership of the institute currently stands at about 1,500 and members are organised through a national council and ten chapters around the country. It provides a range of services including local meetings, a bi-monthly journal (*Arena*), seminars and workshops, an annual conference and a mechanism for the representation of membership views to Government and other institutions. The IITD also runs its own certificate and diploma in training and development, and continuing professional development programmes at centres throughout the country. See the website (www.iitd.ie) for further information.

The Irish Management Institute (IMI)
The Irish Management Institute is a leading provider of management training in Ireland with a defined mission of providing leadership in the development of Irish management competence. Established in 1957, the IMI is a user-owned organisation (circa 1,400 corporate members and 700 individual members) that provides a range of advanced management and specialist programmes, both open and customised, which are dedicated to raising the level of corporate performance. Details on the range of services it provides can be found on its website (www.imi.ie).

Chartered Institute of Personnel and Development (CIPD)

The Chartered Institute of Personnel and Development is a professional body for those who work in the field of personnel management and development. Established in the UK, the CIPD now operates in a number of countries worldwide and has more than 100,000 members. CIPD Ireland is a branch member of CIPD UK and has about 5,000 members in Ireland. The CIPD operates an integrated education scheme that is designed to prepare individuals for a career in personnel/HR management. In Ireland, a number of universities, colleges and ITs around the country run programmes that are recognised as 'exempted' by CIPD. Students of these programmes, who opt to register with CIPD, are recognised as student (licentiate) members of CIPD (level of membership varies with the level of qualification achieved). Exempted programmes in Ireland have for the most part been undergraduate business (or related) degrees; diplomas in personnel/HR management and, for associate memberships, Certificate in Personnel Practice and Certificate in Training and Development. CIPD also provides an information and advisory service to members, arranges a number of conferences, workshops and seminars throughout the year, and publishes a range of journals (*People Management* in the UK and *CIPD News* in Ireland), books and monographs in the human resource management and human resource development fields. Further information can be found on its website (www.cipd.co.uk; www.cipd.ie).

Institute of Public Administration (IPA)

The Institute of Public Administration provides a range of education, training and development services that are designed to meet the changing demands on public servants in Ireland. In particular, it offers a wide range of courses on general business services, sectoral programmes for specific public sectors, and professional education services, including courses that are accredited by the HETAC, and programmes accredited by the institute itself.

Other Institutions

A considerable range of undergraduate, graduate and post-experience programmes are provided by the various universities, colleges and privately funded educational establishments throughout the country, and a number of institutes have been established that cater for professional development in select disciplines. The large growth in private-sector employment in recent years has also seen a considerable increase in the numbers of consultants who provide expertise in a range of training and development activities.

THE ROLE OF THE EUROPEAN UNION

A recent EU White Paper on the 'Learning Society' highlights the necessity of increasing investment in education and vocational training. It posits a number of critical short-term objectives that have application for member states, including the necessity to encourage the acquisition of new knowledge, to bring the school and the business sector closer together and to treat capital investment and investment in training on an equal basis.

Ireland has recorded significant gains from membership of the European Union; in recent years these gains have spilled over into the general areas of education and training provision. The EU Commission supports a number of specific initiatives that are designed to improve initial and continuing vocational education and training and to strengthen the links between the education and training systems and the enterprise and industry sectors. Four programmes, in particular, have relevance to the discussion here.

The first is the LEONARDO DA VINCI Vocational Training Programme. Its aim is to help member states devise national policies on vocational education through, for example, fostering university and industry co-operation, development of language skills, vocational guidance and improved access to education and training. Between 1995 and 1999 close to £12 million (€15 million) had been received to support Irish-led projects.

Second, the SOCRATES Programme focuses on improving the quality and relevance of education and supports initiatives, such as student and staff exchanges, a system of credit and mutual recognition of qualifications between member states, curriculum development, language training, open and distance learning. Between 1995 and 1999 it is estimated that Ireland received about £11 million (€14 million) under this programme.

Third, the EU EMPLOYMENT Initiative targets individuals with particular difficulties in relation to employment in the workplace, including people with disabilities, those who are disadvantaged, equal opportunities for women (NOW), and employment initiatives for young people from disadvantaged backgrounds. A total of £62 million (€79 million) has been made available over the lifetime of this programme.

Fourth, ADAPT is a Human Resources Community Initiative supported by the European Social Fund, which operated in all member states of the European Union (EU) until the end of 1999. A key objective of the ADAPT initiative was to heighten awareness of the need for industry to adapt swiftly to changing work environments. It was designed, therefore, to support innovative training and human resource development projects in organisations interested in introducing progressive human resource development practices and policies that will enhance the technical and skill levels and career development opportunities of their employees.

The cumulative effect of these programmes has been to heighten awareness of the critical link between education and economic and social wellbeing. It highlights the need for a more cohesive approach to developing education, vocational education and training systems that provide mutual gains to all stakeholders – students, participants, employees, employers, the economy and wider society. These EU-sponsored initiatives go some way towards fostering this learning society.

In this chapter we have endeavoured to provide the reader with a route map through Ireland's national system of training and development, past and present. In this regard we traced the historical development of Ireland's training infrastructure and set down the major statutory and institutional reforms that have shaped the training system that we see in operation today. In establishing the route map, we reviewed core national policy decisions in conjunction with the critical evaluations proffered by the actors in the training arena in Ireland on the direction that policy was and is taking.

Having established the nature of the enveloping national training framework, and the economic necessity of training and development, it remains to investigate training and development at the micro or organisational level. The following chapter discusses training and development at the level of the firm and examines the process by which organisations seek to achieve efficiency returns on their training investment.

10

Learning, Training and Development in Organisations

A series of social, organisational and technological developments over the last forty years has had a considerable impact on how organisations function and how they choose to manage and develop their workforce. In 1990 Block argued that strict controls, greater pressure, more clearly defined jobs and tighter supervision had run their course in their ability to give organisations the productivity gains required to compete effectively in the marketplace. Today, we live in the post-industrial era, the 'knowledge society' or the 'information age', each of which has likely implications for the array of knowledge, skills and abilities that are required to work in them. Here, DeGeus (1997, 28) postulates that 'within companies, our success depends on our skill with human beings: building and developing the consistent knowledge base of our enterprise'. While Iles (1994) cautions that the importance of people to an organisation's success is easily acknowledged in rhetoric, Walton (1999) argues that the way development activities are conducted and co-ordinated is a telling index of how an organisation views and values its staff.

This chapter examines the nature of learning, training and development (LT&D) in organisations. First, the rationale for increased attention to LT&D systems and processes is explored. Next, we present a process view of learning in organisations and highlight a number of important learning principles. Specific activities associated with career development and management development are outlined and discussed. In an effort to broaden the debate on the uitility of LT&D in organisations, two core frameworks are reviewed and their likely influence on LT&D provision are presented. The chapter concludes with a summary review of current learning, training and development practices in Ireland.

THE REQUIREMENT FOR LEARNING, TRAINING AND DEVELOPMENT

There is an ever-increasing volume of material that argues that effective learning, training and development is a core means of leveraging organisational competitiveness. Much of this literature suggests that heightened global competition, the internationalisation of business, borderless economies, and wide-scale technological advancements are leading to the realisation that the primary source of competitive advantage in the future is sharply focused on creating new knowledge that is disseminated through the company and which, in turn, leads to continuous innovation (Heraty 2004; Nordhaug, 2004; Nooteboom 1999; Probst and Buchel 1997; Nonaka and Takeuchi 1995; West 1994; Porter 1990; Senge 1990; Stata 1989). Porter (1990), in his prominent study on the competitiveness of nations, argued that to sustain competitive advantage an organisation must have a commitment to improvement, innovation and change. Important sources of these qualities, which cannot easily be replicated by competitors, are superior human resources and technical capability. As Gee *et al.* (1996, 19) suggest, 'gone are the workers hired from the neck down and simply told what to do'. Rather, as McEwan *et al.* (1988, 47) argue:

> If the people in the company are not mobilised to produce the right quality product or service, on time and every time, then the enterprise will fail. Thus people must be considered a factor of equal importance to finance, marketing, production and so forth in the business planning equation, because they are the medium through which plans are turned into successful reality.

Heraty (2004) notes that the 'fashionableness' of learning is evident across both the academic and policy literature, and that is especially widespread in Europe today. For example, 1996 was declared the 'European Year of Lifelong Learning'. Furthermore, at a European Council Summit meeting in Lisbon, Spain in 2000, it was the declared aim of the Heads of State and Government that European co-operation in education [thereafter termed the Lisbon Protocol] would be the route to ensure that 'the European Union becomes that most competitive knowledge-based economy in the world capable of sustainable economic growth and more and better jobs and greater social cohesion'. Concomitantly, the European Commission published an entire Memorandum in 2000 that considers lifelong learning a means of achieving not merely economic prosperity but also active citizenship. One of the key dilemmas expressed in the Memorandum concerns how individuals can be encouraged to assume responsibility for their own lifelong learning and how organisations, Governments and other partners can support them. In a recent report on lifelong learning in Europe (2001), one of the terms of the debate was to articulate the kind of environment that should be provided in order to ensure maximum development of people's skills potential. Specifically it queried what kind of action is needed for firms to develop ways of working that ensure that the skills and knowledge acquired are used, noting that a skill that is learnt and not applied is rapidly blunted (CEDEFOP, 2002, 12).

Some of the most recent organisational literature emphasises mechanisms – such as organisational restructuring, delayering, empowerment, flexibility and process re-engineering – that promote the development of learning and knowledge. Barrow and Loughlin (1992), for example, propose that organisations seek employees who:

- have the ability to learn new skills and adapt to changing circumstances;
- can conceptualise the contribution of their role to organisational effectiveness;
- are capable of working in flatter structures and without supervision;
- have the ability to manage the interface between customers and the organisation;
- possess capabilities such as problem-solving, creative thinking and innovativeness.

Saul (1997) makes that point that although work practices in many organisations still reflect hierarchical, fixed horizontal and vertical relationships, where many workers have narrowly defined job duties and responsibilities characteristic of Fordism; nevertheless, there is a movement towards teamwork and flatter hierarchies where workers at various levels participate in decision-making, and different backgrounds, experiences and perspectives are understood to enhance the productive potential of teams. The core of the argument is that organisations that can improve on their capability for learning (through increased knowledge, skill accumulation and application) are in a better position to compete. Boud and Garrick (1999, 4) effectively highlight the importance of this 'people' dimension thus:

> Distinctions between life and work, learning and production, community and enterprise are becoming less firm. No longer are the pools of knowledge and expertise acquired in initial education sufficient for the new work order . . . Modern organisations ignore learning at the cost of their present and future successes.

All of these requirements place considerable responsibility on the organisation's human resource department to ensure that employees are equipped to meet the demands required of them for this competitive agenda.

DEFINITION OF TERMS

There are a number of terms in common parlance within the field of LT&D: learning, training, development, education, knowledge, human resource development, strategic human resource development, employee development, competency development, organisational learning, knowledge management, the learning organisation. Much of these variations arise when different authors seek to focus on, or highlight, particular elements of the field of study, but it is probably true that some of the terms are used interchangeably. Some useful classification can be made relatively easily between, for example, education, learning, training and development, although learning, as a construct, underpins each activity (see table 10.1). Meaningful differentiation between some of the other terms is somewhat more problematic since it essentially comes down to a matter of interpretation, i.e. can organisations learn of themselves (the learning organisation) or is organisational learning anything more than the sum of individual learning that occurs in organisations? However, in an attempt to show the thinking behind them, a broad differentiation of each term is provided.

Table 10.1 Distinctions between learning, training, development and education

	Learning	Training	Development	Education Informal	Formal
Focus of activity	On values, attitudes, innovation, and outcome accomplishment	On knowledge, skills, ability, and job performance	On individual potential and future role in work-place	On personal development and the experience of life	On structured development of individual to specified outcomes
Clarity of objectives	May be vague and difficult to identify	Can be specified clearly	Objectives stated in general terms	Objectives are unique to individual and may not be clearly articulated	Objectives stated in general terms
Time-scale	Continuous	Short-term	Long-term	Lifelong	Specified period: e.g. ten years

➥

Table 10.1 Distinctions between learning, training, development and education *(contd.)*

	Learning	Training	Development	Education — Informal	Education — Formal
Values that underpin activity	Assumes continuous change; emphasises breakthrough	Assumes relative stability; emphasises improvement	Assumes continuous change; emphasises maximising potential	Assumes incremental change; emphasises improvements	Often assumes stability; emphasis on breakthrough
Nature of learning process	Instructional or organic	Structured or mechanistic	Instructional or organic	Instructional or organic	Structured or mechanistic
Content of activity	Learning how to learn, values, attitudes relevant to work	Knowledge, skills and attitudes relevant to specific job; basic abilities	Interpersonal, intrapersonal, and life skills	Life experience provides basis for education	Imposed and specified curriculums
Methods used	Informal learning methods, learner-initiated methods	Demonstration, practice, feedback	Coaching, counselling, guidance mentoring, peer learning	Experience, observation, experimentation, and reflection	Lectures, guided reading, debate, self-managed learning
Outcomes of process	Individuals learn how to learn and create own solutions	Skilled performance of tasks that make up job	Improved problem-solving, decision-making, intrapersonal, interpersonal competence	Personal outcomes internal to individual	External specified outcomes
Learning strategy used	Inductive strategies	Didactic, tutor-centred	Skill-building and inductive strategies	Inductive strategies	Combination of didactic, skill-building and inductive strategies
Nature of process	Inside-out: seeks to do for self	Outside-in: done by others	Combination of outside-in and inside-out	Inside-out: seeks to do for self	Largely outside-in: done by others
Role of professional trainer	To facilitate and guide	To instruct, demonstrate, and guide	To guide, instruct, coach, counsel, and mentor	Minimal: largely individual-directed	To act as expert, instruct, facilitate, and guide to learning resources
Document trainer philosophy	Existentialism; self-managed process	Instrumentalism: transferring knowledge using formal methods and measuring results	Existentialism: one-to-one learning, self-managed learning	Existentialism: totally self-managed	Combination of instrumentalism and existentialism
Type of need emphasised	Individual and organisational needs	Organisational needs	Organisational and individual needs	Individual needs	Institutional and individual needs

Table 10.1 Distinctions between learning, training, development and education *(contd.)*

	Learning	Training	Development	Education Informal	Formal
Process of evaluation	Continuous evaluation	Evaluation against specific job performance standards	Evaluation of skills and effectiveness	Evaluation against life goals and personal development	Evaluation in terms of pass v. fail levels
Link with corporate aims and strategies	Directly aligned with company's vision and requirements for success	Not necessarily linked to company's aims and goals	Directly aligned with company's aims and requirements for future but depends on type of development	No link to company's aims and goals	Not necessarily linked to company's aims and goals
Pay-back to company	Immediate and continuing	Almost immediate in form of skilled performance	Medium to long-term pay-back	No direct pay-back	Long-term at most

Source: Garavan, Costine, and Heraty (1995, 4–5).

Education. Educational objectives have traditionally been couched in general or abstract terms and are often perceived as person- rather than job-oriented. In its true sense, education refers to the assimilation of knowledge and understanding that can be far broader than the work context within which an individual may operate. When we speak of education, we typically refer to formal programmes of study, many of which are accredited, and which generally occur outside of a workplace. A core purpose of an education system, for example, is to provide and improve general skills (e.g. ability to read, to write and to reason).

Training. While no standard definition of training exists it is generally expressed in behavioural terms and, in a narrow sense, refers to the planned acquisition of knowledge, skills and attitudes (KSA) required to perform effectively in a given role or job. Each training intervention requires some change in performance and, for the most part, new performance requires some form of learning to occur. Training is vocationally based, i.e. its purpose is to improve specific skills or abilities that will (hopefully) result in better work performance.

Learning. For the most part learning is perceived as a process through which individuals assimilate new knowledge and skills that results in relatively permanent behavioural changes. Learning can be conscious or unconscious, formal or informal, and requires some element of practice and experience. Effective learning requires the ability to question habits and methods and to challenge one's assumptions. As learning underpins all LT&D activity in an organisation, it will be treated separately in the next section.

Development. By its nature development is a broad concept that is future-oriented and is concerned with the growth and enhancement of the individual. In organisational terms it refers to the acquisition of skills and abilities that are required for future roles in the organisation. In this way, development can be seen as a vehicle of career enhancement (career development), for succession planning (within an internal labour market – refer back to chapter 4), for determining managerial potential (management development/assessment centres) or for reasons of personal development (lifelong learning). To ensure commitment to the principles of development, individuals must recognise and understand the prerequisites and conditions for 'success' in their company, and how their contribution fits within this.

Human resource development. This concept has largely developed alongside the strategy literature (it first emerged at a conference in 1969) and generally refers to the development of a strategic organisational approach to managing LT&D at work. It advocates the strategic linking of training and development activities to corporate business objectives and a central role for line managers in developing employees. It refers to learning at the individual, group and organisational levels to enhance the effectiveness of human resource utilisation. It is the explicit link with strategy formulation and business objectives that serves to differentiate the term HRD from training and development more generally.

Competencies. While there is considerable confusion surrounding an overarching definition of competence or competencies, two streams of work can be identified. The first is vocationally based and it examines the competencies demanded by the job. Here the emphasis is on breaking the job into its various component parts and describing behavioural characteristics and standards of performance that need to be attained by the job-holder (Harrison 1997). The second focuses on the nature of the skills and abilities that the individual brings to the job (Boyatzis 1982). Organisations are increasingly adopting competency frameworks to help them identify the types of behaviours they wish to promote to assist the performance of individuals and organisations.

Knowledge management. Again, the origin of this term has a very recent pedigree, and was first used at a conference in 1996. Snyder (1996) suggests that an organisation's knowledge consists of three essential elements: skills, cognitions and systems. An organisation's skills include the technical, professional and social expertise of the organisation's members, i.e. the *know-how* of the organisation. Cognitions refer to the information, ideas, attitudes, norms and values shared by the organisation's members – including the *know-why* of the organisation. An organisation's systems include the structures, procedures, and policies related to performing tasks, co-ordinating resources and managing external relationships. All three components are inextricably interrelated and their configuration has variously been referred to in the management lexicon as core competencies (Pralahad and Hamel 1990), organisational capability (Ulrich and Lake 1991), knowledge or intellectual capital (Zeleny 1990), or strategic capability (Lenz 1980).

The learning organisation. The literature on the learning organisation as a distinct concept is relatively new, and again, while there is no agreement on what exactly constitutes a learning organisation, it is generally described as a participative learning system, which places an emphasis on the exchange of information and being open to enquiry and self-criticism. It promotes continuous development and improvement, a willingness to take risks and a work system that actively facilitates learning at work. A fuller description of the learning organisation and organisational learning is provided later in this chapter.

Finally, in recent years the term 'employee development' became increasing popular with both HR academics and students when the Chartered Institute of Personnel and Development (CIPD) used the term to refer to the specialist element of their professional programme that deals with the management of organised learning interventions at work. This term has now been replaced by CIPD with 'learning and development', but 'employee development' is still in common parlance. Within this text, we have connected the terms learning, training and development to form LT&D, which we now use to describe deliberate organisational interventions that seek to expand the range of knowledge, skills and competencies of individuals at work. In this way LT&D is broader than skills acquisition. Rather, it is about how, what and where individuals learn and how an organisation can facilitate this learning. It requires that we understand that individuals can and do learn outside the often narrow scope of their job; that individuals' contributions need not be bound within the confines of their job; and that the challenge for organisations is as much about creating work systems that facilitate and capture this, as it is about designing effective training interventions.

THE PROCESS OF LEARNING, TRAINING AND DEVELOPMENT IN ORGANISATIONS

All organisational activities, including training and development, involve some form of learning. Garavan *et al.* (1995) describe this learning as a complex process of acquiring knowledge, understanding, skills, and values in order to be able to adapt to the environment in which we live. This adaptation generally involves some recognisable change in behaviour, though this is not always the case. Barnett (1999) suggests that in our complex world today we are constantly challenged to reappraise or review the way we interpret the world and the underlying frameworks that we adopt to make sense of this world. He further notes that:

> The learning challenge that we all face at work requires not only that we learn new techniques, or new ideas or new practices. They require us to change or at least widen the frameworks through which we interpret the world. In this way we are being called upon to change who and what we are.

The process of learning, training and development is presented here as a series of key stages that commence at the strategic or business level of the organisation and work sequentially down from there. In practice, LT&D probably occurs much more intuitively and spontaneously than this sequence of activities suggests, but the sequencing is useful here to illustrate the interconnected nature of LT&D activity. In most organisations planned learning events are converted into training and/or development programmes and so, when we use the term training here (i.e. training policy, training needs analysis, training budget), it is to reflect this operationalisation of work-based learning.

Learning/Training Philosophies and Policies

A learning/training policy reflects the organisation's philosophy on LT&D and governs the priorities, standards and scope of its learning activities. As such it provides the framework within which all planned interventions take place. An organisation's LT&D philosophy can be expressed along a continuum where, on the one hand, training is viewed as an expense and occurs only as the need for it arises, and, on the other, employees are seen as a potential source of competitive advantage and so learning, training and development is a central organisational concern. In this respect, all organisations have an LT&D policy, whether explicit or implicit, positive or negative. The extent to which organisations develop explicit policies is contextually bound and influenced by a number of factors. The following are useful examples in this respect: prevailing employment legislation (e.g. equality, health and safety); state of the labour market (whether skilled labour is readily available, or can be contracted in or out); available resources that can be allocated to LT&D; prevailing views on the value of training (particularly at senior and strategic levels); nature of the product or service market; and, in some cases, the expectations of employees themselves.

Furthermore, organisations can differentiate themselves as 'desirable' employers by providing a range of employee and career development opportunities that are designed to attract and retain the required calibre of employee. Such an approach requires a high level of co-ordination between LT&D and the range of other human resource policy choices, such as recruitment and selection, performance appraisal, reward systems and employee relations.

Table 10.2 A comparative summary of employee development models

Model	Characteristics	Focus	Limitations
Unsystematic model	Unplanned approach; lack of training policies; individuals largely responsible for own development investment	Operational	Ad-hoc; reactive; training viewed as a cost rather than as an an investment
Problem-centred model	Identification and prioritisation of performance problems coupled with generation and evaluation of results	Operational	Highly reactive; high risk of inaccurate identification of priority problems
Systematic model	Grounded in systems theory; highly structured; rational means of directing resources; cyclical process from identification of needs through evaluation of outcomes	Operational	Very simplistic; low applicability in times of uncertainty; does not recognise individual differences; ignores context
Cycle of training model	Adopts a stakeholder approach; views training as a total organisational process; considers wider organisational implications	Semi-strategic	HR considerations not linked with business planning; does not consider line management role in training and development
Effectiveness improvement model	Advocates close relationship between line and staff managers; utilises performance audits as evaluation tool	Semi-strategic	No incorporation of HR considerations into strategic business planning; organisation's culture and role of top management not considered
Business focused strategic model	Related training needs to business requirements; identifies external triggers for change; highlights top and line management support	Strategic	Inadequate consideration of the training context; ignores nature of individual as learner

Source: Heraty (1992).

Within the extant training literature there exists a myriad of training models that have developed over the years ranging from the reactive, ad hoc varieties to those that seek to describe training and development in strategic terms. A select number of these models are presented in table 10.2, which illustrates the range of approaches that organisations can adopt towards LT&D.

The LT&D model adopted by an organisation presents a useful indication of its learning philosophy and thus the learning/training policy that it will employ. Moreover, in an organisation that adopts the unsystematic framework, one would expect little integration of employees' considerations into strategic decision-making or broader business issues. The converse holds true for organisations that adopt the more strategic models, where LT&D considerations play a critical role in the formulation of strategic business plans.

Once the learning/training policies have been developed the next step involves the organisation in translating these into specific objectives for action. At this stage a learning/training plan is drawn up that seeks to merge individual and organisational requirements into a clear course of action. A model of the learning/training process is presented in figure 10.1.

Figure 10.1 The learning, training and development process

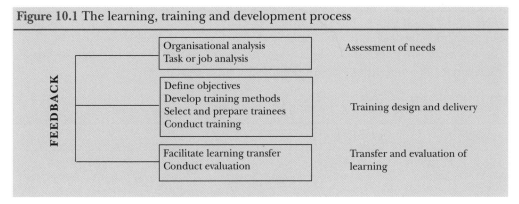

The process depicted here presents LT&D activities in an orderly and sequential manner: the reality may be quite different in organisations. What is most important to recognise is the interrelatedness of each feature, and the consequences of failing to consider certain stages of the process.

Identifying Learning/Training Needs

The first stage in the LT&D process is the identification of learning/training needs, often termed training needs analysis (TNA). Needs analysis is a central component of the training process as it ensures that learning, training and development occurs only where there is a valid need for it. Many organisations invest considerable resources in LT&D, but often fail to examine how effectively these can impact the business objectives.

In an organisational context, a need is a discrepancy or 'gap' between 'what is' and 'what ought to be', i.e. the distance between actual performance and desired/required performance. Thus, TNA refers to any shortfall between current knowledge, skills, attitudes etc. and the level required now, or in the future. This 'learning gap' is represented in figure 10.2.

Figure 10.2 The learning gap

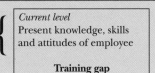

Source: Armstrong (1987).

Learning/training needs can be current, for the future, or both. Current needs arise where inconsistencies emerge in the present system and the organisation must act to remedy the situation, i.e. a new computer system has been introduced but no-one is trained to use it. Garavan *et al.* (1995) view this as a reactive needs analysis which usually provides a short-term solution. Future needs, on the other hand, arise from predicting organisational changes that are likely to occur and how they will impact learning requirements. They are prompted by internal and external factors such as strategy change, work restructuring, product or service diversification, introduction of new technology; skills' inventories matched against future requirements, and so forth. Such needs are usually more developmental in nature, and there can be a temptation to dismiss them and deal only with immediate needs. In such circumstances, however, it is difficult to envisage how LT&D can make a strategic contribution to effective organisational functioning.

Needs manifest themselves in a number of ways. Although there is much focus on identifying the needs of individual employees, needs occur at three levels (see table 10.3). There is a cascade effect at play here whereby organisational needs highlight needs for particular groups and thus carry implications for individual needs.

Table 10.3 Levels of learning/training needs analysis

LEVEL	CONCERN
Organisational	What does the organisation need to achieve its goals? Does it have the capability? Are there any strategic long-term objectives to consider?
Job or Occupational	Special skills, knowledge or attitude training needs for particular jobs
Individual	Where individual skills fall short of those required

Source: Boydell (1983).

As a first step it is recommended that an organisation-wide review of all learning/training needs and requirements is undertaken. Although hugely time-consuming, and expensive to complete, the information arising from this review can significantly influence a range of HR activities including performance management and reward, succession planning, job design and so forth. There are various sources of data that can be used to compile a needs analysis within an organisation (see table 10.4) and the choice of method to use and information to source is largely dependent on local circumstances. (How detailed does the review need to be? Who should be involved? What level of resources is available to collect and analyse data?) Wexley and Latham (1991) suggest that any organisational needs analysis should involve an examination of how it interfaces with the external environment, since the environment in which an organisation operates can be a critical factor in determining whether training and development should be conducted. Here, a first port of call for most organisations is to look at the business strategy and the core objectives that have been identified for the organisation for the next few years. This will give an indication of what changes are likely to occur, especially with respect to any new implementations (products, processes, people) that will be introduced to the organisation – these will usually have some learning/training dimension to them. Factors in the external environment (legislation, economic policies, taxation issues) will also affect organisational needs as they can influence the way employees do their jobs, how decisions are made and the types of skills and levels of flexibility required.

Table 10.4 Data sources for learning/training needs analysis

LEVEL	SOURCE	TRAINING NEED IMPLICATIONS
Organisational	Corporate objectives	emphasise direction training must take
	Manpower plans	current capability versus future needs
	Skills inventories	areas needing development
	Org. statistics (absenteeism, etc.)	identifies trends and problem areas
	System changes	new equipment/systems call for training
	Management requests	may apply in other areas too
	Exit interviews	may identify problems like poor supervision, etc.
Operational	Operational manpower plans	profiles future requirements, indications, etc.
	Job analysis/job description	indicates exact requirements of each job
	Task analysis	very detailed job analysis
	Person specifications	profiles skills/characteristics job holders need
	Training surveys	up to date information on needs
	Performing the job	shows trainer the needs of a new recruit
	Observe output	this may be delegated to line manager
	Review literature	journals, guidelines, approaches of other orgs.
	Ask questions	of the job holder, the supervisor, the manager
	Working groups	combine several viewpoints
	Analyse operating problems	differentiate environmental problems etc.
Individual Job	Appraisal, career development, etc., Interview	identifies weaknesses and development needs self-analysis involves the worker, increasing motivation
	Questionnaire	gives employee time to consider his needs
	Individual job analysis	compared with job description
	Tests	of knowledge, skill, achievement
	Attitude surveys	determining morale and motivation
	Training progress charts	up to date records
	Assessment centres	intensive assessment
	Manager's recommendation	the manager can identify individual needs

Source: Garavan, Costine and Heraty (1995).

Sparrow and Bognanno (1993) refer to the development of a competency profile for the organisation as a whole and suggest that there are four different categories of competency that an organisation needs to recognise.

1. Emerging competencies: those that will require greater emphasis as the organisation pursues its particular strategic path.
2. Maturing competencies: those that are becoming less relevant – perhaps due to technology or work restructuring.
3. Transitional competencies: those required of individuals during any change process such as a high tolerance of uncertainty or an ability to manage stress and conflict.
4. Core competencies: those that are central to an organisation's performance and so have persistent relevance.

By compiling a competency profile, the authors suggest that the organisation can attach a 'shelf life' to its existing range of skills, knowledge and abilities and can therefore estimate where learning/training gaps exist or are likely to emerge.

Organisational needs filter down into more specific departmental needs and these can then be translated into needs at the occupational or job level, e.g. the introduction of a new product will immediately impact the manufacturing department and sales and promotions, in terms of staff, skills, space etc. A comprehensive job analysis provides information about the duties required of, and the responsibilities attached to, various jobs. Here, for example, it is important to identify whether the job description on file is accurate and that it lists relevant knowledge, skills and competency levels for the job in question. This level of needs analysis allows priority areas for individual LT&D to be identified, i.e. to isolate the difference between current performance and what is required to do the job effectively, or to do a future identified job. Needs analysis at the individual level is usually conducted as part of a performance management system – through performance appraisal, 360-degree feedback, or self-appraisal, and should be available from an individual performance development/learning plan.

The value of a comprehensive needs analysis is worth re-stating – it forms the basis for the organisation's investment in learning and development activities and, as such, is the benchmark against which any return on investment can be evaluated. It allows the organisation to focus its investment on its core needs; the process of needs analysis helps to generate consensus and commitment to the principles of continuous learning, and the needs identified direct feed into the design of appropriate learning activities. It can also uncover system anomalies or problem areas that are adversely impacting performance (but are not learning/training-related) and need attending to.

Design and Implementation of Learning, Training and Development Activities

A key question for organisations during this phase of the LT&D process is 'how do we know what we want people to learn, and how will we help them to learn it?' Answering this question involves the organisation in four particular activities:

1. Specifying the core learning objectives.
2. Specifying the learning content.
3. Selecting the appropriate learning methods.
4. Structuring the learning event.

The 'what people need to learn' is relatively straightforward and can be read from the needs analysis just completed – though not quite so easy to address if no needs analysis has been undertaken. Following the needs analysis phase, the organisation can then start to prioritise these needs and to establish specific learning/training objectives and develop a learning/training plan – at departmental level and for each individual. Thus, for each learning/training event, a set of learning objectives can be identified, for example 'at the end of this session the learner should be able to/know about/describe . . .' Here it is also important to specify what performance standards may be required, e.g. is the learner expected to be completely proficient, or to be more skilled than before the learning/ training but still likely to make some mistakes? Three other issues are worth considering:

1. What will the learners expect to achieve from the learning event?
2. How will the learning be transferred?
3. How will you evaluate whether learning is being used?

Table 10.5 Learning, training and development methods

Method	Advantages	Disadvantages
On-the-Job Methods		
Sitting by Nellie; learn job from co-worker	Inexpensive; natural learning; high transfer of learning;	May pick up bad habits; often time-consuming; feedback may not be supportive/constructive
Coaching; supervisor guides and develops employee	Job relevant; facilitates succession planning and employee relations	Adversely affected by time constraints and work pressures; individual attention may be limited
Mentoring; manager guides, counsels and encourages development	Flexible; useful for socialisation, succession planning and management development	Contact may be infrequent; manager may not have the required mentoring skills or be committed to the process
Job rotation; range of placements within company	Relatively inexpensive; provides exposure to many situations; facilitates inter-departmental relations	May be unsettling; may lack direction; may be inconsistent; difficult to monitor
In-house courses	Can be tailored to meet specific organisational needs; range of techniques i.e cases, projects etc. can be based on real problems	High opportunity costs due to absence from work; participation may be quota based; can become an exercise in head count i.e quantity vs. quality of courses
Off-the-Job Methods		
External courses educational/skills-based	Exposure to broader range of knowledge and views; promotes networking; useful for specialised knowledge/skills acquisition	Learning transfer may be difficult; can be very expensive and time consuming; may raise employee expectations
Workshops, active discussion	Particularly suitable for managers; group-based approach facilitates problem solving; high learning transfer	Requires advance notification and preparation by participants; may be difficult to manage
Computer-based training	Individually focused; self-paced learning; performance is easily monitored; large numbers can be readily trained	Expensive to design; some employees may have a 'phobia' about computers; learning situation is contrived
Open/distant learning	Facilitates career development; useful for self-motivated employees; participants direct pace of learning	Very expensive; high drop-out rate; time consuming; can be difficult to balance work load and learning
External Placements	Provides useful external perceptions; builds external networks; facilitates attitudinal change	Learning transfer may be limited; can be very costly; may be perceived as a 'junket'; difficult to manage and control learning

Source: Adapted from Garavan *et al*. (1995) and Gunnigle and Flood (1990).

Reflecting on these will help in the development of learning content that is designed to fill the learning/training needs identified and will point to the most appropriate learning method for delivering this learning. A number of the more commonly used LT&D methods is presented in table 10.5 and, while this table is not exhaustive, it does highlight key characteristics of each approach that merit some consideration.

Recent developments in technology have had a significant influence on LT&D and we are increasingly witnessing the growth of e-learning as a feature of learning design. In essence, e-learning today involves delivering learning material electronically through the use of interactive multimedia and often via the internet through a web browser. Cole (2000) describes e-learning as a learning method that enables participants to undertake courses at their own pace and at their location of choice. This contrasts with traditional learning delivery, which imposes schedules for the learner. He argues that web-based pedagogy is seen as a freer form of instruction as it enables greater ease of use between the facilitator and learner and among learners, resulting in a learning environment developing where participants teach one another rather than 'enduring a passive, sender/receiver mode of learning'. Macpherson *et al.* (2004) identify two types of benefits associated with e-learning; those associated with costs and those relating to flexibility. Cost benefits include a reduction in training time, reduction in travel and time away from the office and the capability of e-learning to serve a large audience at one time, or over a period of time. Course fees are lower, travel-related expenses are removed. Flexibility benefits are described in terms of flexibility in delivery (to a large, geographically dispersed audience) and flexibility in the rate and distribution of learning. Questions remain concerning the efficacy of learner support, learning style and particularly the social dimension of learning and sharing knowledge that may have inhibited the adoption of e-learning more liberally. O'Donnell and Garavan (2003), in a survey on e-learning in Ireland, report that 44 per cent of responding organisations now use e-learning in some shape or other – the take-up is reportedly higher in larger organisations and in the public sector. However, while there is as yet insufficient evidence to suggest that e-learning will replace traditional learning delivery methods, it is a medium that more and more organisations are exploring with interest.

The choice of learning method is an important one since it can significantly impact the extent to which any useful learning actually occurs. However, for a variety of reasons (and most of these are probably reasonable enough), in many organisations the learning/ training method is chosen even before the individual participants are identified. While this may not cause undue concern in some quarters, problems can arise (and the net effect of the learning investment is reduced) when the particular methods chosen are inconsistent with the learning styles and preferences of the trainees. It is important, therefore, to at least give some thought to how individuals do learn, and especially how adults learn best in a work environment (which is, after all, the kind of learning that most concerns organisations).

Individual Learning

The field of individual psychology has informed much of what we know about individual learning. Early behavioural psychologists concentrated on cause-effect models of behaviour (stimulus-response) to demonstrate how learning can occur. Pavlov's experiments with dogs demonstrated how it was possible to prompt a reflexive, involuntary response through classic conditioning. Skinner's (1938) work focused on reinforcement (operant conditioning) and showed how more complex, voluntary behaviours could be shaped through the achievement of a desired reward, or the prevention of an undesired punishment. In an organisational scenario, the use of praise and encouragement by trainers or line managers can be seen as examples of promoting operant learning.

Further work by cognitive theorists focused on the 'thinking' part of human learning and is most closely associated with the process of experiential learning. Kolb's (1984) experiential learning cycle suggests that learning occurs in a sequential or cyclical manner. We experience something new (new information or knowledge), we reflect on that new experience and try to make sense of it, we generalise about it (i.e. what would happen if . . .) and then we test it out (try doing something new or adopt a different approach). The result of this experimentation leads us back to the start of the cycle, where this new result represents the something new or new experience that acts as a catalyst for further learning. Experiential learning suggests that learners must have time to experiment and try out new ideas if meaningful learning is to take place, i.e. practice or trial-and-error.

Bandura (1986) introduced a social dimension to learning and suggested that much of our experiences are picked up either directly, or indirectly, through observing other people. This social aspect to learning points to the necessity to have a supportive learning environment, which, in a work situation, would include superior or leader, work colleagues, or (outside work) friends and family.

Each of these theories of learning provides important starting points for LT&D systems. If we understand how individuals learn, we can build this into how learning/training courses and development programmes are designed and delivered. In this context of workplace learning, Revans' (1982) ideas on adult learning are worth noting. He suggests that adult learning is most effective where adults (learners):

1. Are motivated to learn of their own volition and not solely at the will of others – it must be something they want to achieve.
2. Can identify themselves with others who may not only share their needs, but who may also satisfy some of these needs – they seek support from their peers and colleagues and learn more effectively with this group support.
3. Can try out any new learning in actions of their own design – learning should be more than the acquiring of information but should involve some action.
4. Can, within a reasonable lapse of time, attain first-hand knowledge of the results of their trials – constant reinforcement and feedback on their performance.

Boud and Garrick (1999, 1) emphasise the critical importance of a thorough understanding of work-based learning and note that:

> In the complex enterprises of the new millennium, learning has moved from the periphery – from something that prepared people for employment – to the lifeblood which sustains them. There are few places left for employees at any level who do not continue to learn and improve their effectiveness throughout their working lives. There is no place for managers who do not appreciate their own vital role in fostering learning.

Arising from much of the theory of individual learning, it is possible to isolate a number of key learning principles that can be applied to the design and delivery of LT&D activities and events at work.

- *Motivation to learn.* The employee must want to learn and thus, in order to be committed to the process, must perceive that the learning event will result in the achievement of certain desired goals. There must be some tangible reward, e.g. they will be better at their job, or more employable for a better job.

- *Involvement of the learner.* The training or learning should be seen as an active, rather than a passive process. Adults learn more effectively when they are actively involved in the learning process. Getting individuals involved in discussing the course, what they hope to achieve from it, and seeking opinions and contributions throughout can make the learning more meaningful. Individuals need to 'own' the learning, i.e. if they are actively involved in coming up with solutions to problems or thinking up ideas the learning is internalised more easily. Where learning is off-the-job, the use of work problems and case studies workshops are useful means of creating ownership of learning.

- *Reinforcement of learning.* Employees should be given an opportunity to practise what they have learned. This facilitates continuous improvement and employees can engage in goal setting to heighten the learning process. In tandem with this, the training event must allow employees sufficient time both to absorb the material and practise or test new knowledge and skills.

- *Feedback.* Learners need constant and immediate feedback on their performance. This feedback should be both realistic and constructive if it is to reinforce behaviour or encourage further learning

- *Meaningfulness of the material.* The nature of the training/learning intervention must be seen to be relevant to the employee's work, i.e. it must be something that he/she can use or will be able to use sometime in the future. Wexley and Latham (1991) suggest that, to increase meaningfulness, learners should be provided with an overview of the material to be learned; the material should be presented using examples, concepts and terms familiar to the learner; the material should be sequenced in a logical manner; and simpler skills should be introduced as a basis for the attainment of more complex intellectual skills.

- *Communities of practice.* Communities of practice evolve as people united in an organisational setting develop a shared history as well as particular values, beliefs, ways of talking and ways of doing things. Since individuals both shape and are shaped by their social contexts, they bring to the workplace a variety of knowledge, experience and insights that can be capitalised upon. They learn to construct shared understanding amidst confusing and conflicting data and begin to rely on each other for mutual assistance. The context then within which LT&D is organised has a powerful influence on the learning that occurs and should be structured and managed in order to allow for information to be exchanged and applied.

There is a danger here of presenting an over-simplification of the learning process. Although it is argued that learning is as natural as breathing, it is also an inherently complex process. Work-based learning is particularly complex since individuals at work do not represent a homogenous group. They may share some common attributes, and work within a shared culture, but essentially employees represent a diverse group of individuals who just happen to be working in the same organisation. As such, each individual brings a unique set of experiences and expectations to the learning event that can shape the level of learning that takes place and the degree to which the learning becomes a significant aspect of subsequent behaviour. A number of pertinent factors have variously been posited (Garavan *et al.* 2003; Buckley and Caple 1992) as having a significant influence on learning. These factors include: the employee's age (which affects attitudes, motivations and interests), his/her levels of intelligence and ability (affects preferences for structured vs. unstructured learning events); his/her background and psychological disposition (predetermined perceptions of the value of training, previous experiences of training/schooling, concerns or anxieties surrounding learning); his/her learning style and preference (for reflective, practical or conceptual approaches); and finally his/her trainability or motivation to learn (affects aptitude for improved performance and expectations of training outcomes).

An understanding of learning styles is particularly important since the learning/training method chosen by an organisation must take cognisance of particular learning preferences that individual employees might express. For example, some individuals may learn more effectively in a structured learning/training environment using concrete examples that they can relate to, whereas others might prefer a more informal conceptual framework that draws on various scenarios that are not necessarily work based. Mumford (1986) suggests that a failure to take account of different learning styles can have seriously negative implications for the training process while Garavan *et al.* (1995) quoting Arment (1990) indicate that:

1. By the time we reach adulthood, each of us has developed our own method of learning, reflected in a unique and well-established learning style.
2. Trainers also have well-established learning styles and preferences.
3. The more compatible the style of learning with the approach to training adopted, the more likely it is that a positive learning experience will occur.

As indicated in table 10.5 above, the choice of learning methods available to organisations is considerable. When deciding on the most appropriate method to use, organisations must take cognisance of the principles of learning discussed earlier, the needs of the employees to be trained and the logistics of LT&D that affect every organisation, including available budget, time and expertise resources, physical resources and number of people requiring LT&D. All learning methods have their own particular strengths and can be modified to suit the organisation's requirements. The most important criterion in determining the choice of method is the extent to which it meets the particular objectives that have been established. Once the learning method and targeted learners/trainees have been identified, the organisation then delivers the learning event. Garavan *et al.* (2003) provide extensive guidelines and tips on how to deliver an effective learning activity, some of which are:

- Allowing sufficient time both for preparation and for delivery.
- Introducing the event – identifying learning objectives and learners' objectives, and use of an 'icebreaker' to help set the tone.
- Alternating theory/information with skill/practice sessions and giving constructive feedback throughout.
- Concluding with a review or summary of what has been achieved and pointers for applying the learning back to the job.

On completion of this stage of the LT&D process, the next phase involves the altogether more problematic phase of evaluating the impact of the learning itself.

Transfer of Learning

The term learning transfer refers to the extent to which skills and abilities acquired during a learning/training session are applied to the actual work situation or to the learning of a new, but related, skill. Reid *et al.* (1992) distinguish between two types of positive learning transfer: vertical and lateral. *Vertical transfer* occurs when one subject area acts as a basis for another, e.g. a foundation course in general business forms the basis upon which students or learners can progress to greater specialism or diversification, and where students can apply the general principles learned at foundation level. In training terms this involves the acquisition of additional knowledge or skills that build upon existing skills and abilities. *Lateral transfer* occurs where the same type of stimulus requires the same response. In this respect, training simulates a particular type of task and allows the learner an opportunity to practice in a 'safe' environment. Reid *et al.* (1992) use the example of training simulations that are used to train aircraft pilots. Buckley and Caple (1992) indicate that positive transfer will have taken place if the trainee is able to apply on the job what has been learned in training with relative ease (lateral), or is able to learn a new task more quickly as a result of earlier training on another task (vertical).

In some circumstances negative transfer occurs and this may be as a result of past learning experiences that contradict present practice, or perhaps the learning experience creates inhibitions that impede the acquisition of new skills. An illustration of the former might be where an individual who learns to drive on one side of the road might find it difficult to drive on the opposite side while abroad – this is particularly so in cases where the driver is distracted or stressed. In terms of the latter, the particular choice of learning method, style of trainer/facilitation, or indeed the learning situation might, individually or combined, serve to inhibit the learning process and thus result in negative learning transfer.

Gielen (1996) notes two further sets of work environment factors that may also play a part in determining the scope of learning transfer, namely work system factors and people factors. Work system factors include cultural factors such as communication, opportunity to use training (Ford *et al.* 1992) and willingness to use training. Latham and Crandall (1991) identify pay and promotion policies as key organisational variables that influence the level of learning transfer because they affect learning outcome expectations. This is directly related to our discussion earlier on learning principles and especially on the requirement that learners must be motivated to learn – they must see some benefit from participating in a learning event. Bandura (1986) suggests that trainees may believe that they are capable of performing a specific behaviour, but may choose not to do so because they believe it will have little or no effect on their status in the organisation. In terms of people factors, both peer group influence and supervisory support are seen to significantly impact the likelihood of transfer (Hawley and Barnard 2005; Ford *et al.* 1992). Garavan *et al.* (1995) indicate that peer interaction can provide support and reinforcement not only for learning but also for the application of learning to the job. Failure to achieve this support can result in alienation during and after the learning event. Supervisory support is a critical factor. Good supervisory support increases learner outcome expectations that the learning skills will be valued by the organisation.

Transfer of learning is thus a critical issue for organisations. The transfer of learning needs to be examined as part of the needs analysis process and specifically that the environment for learning be assessed to ensure the greater likelihood that learning actually gets used.

EVALUATION OF LEARNING

Evaluation of LT&D activities ensures that control is maintained over the learning process and allows for assessment of the outcomes, methods and overall impact of any learning, training and development programme. Buckley and Caple (1992) describe evaluation as the process of attempting to assess the total value of training, that is, the cost benefit and general outcomes that benefit the organisation as well as the value of the improved performance of those who have undertaken training. Easterby-Smith (1986) outlines three general purposes of learning/training evaluation:

- Summative – testing to determine whether training and development was effective and achieved its objectives.
- Formative – qualitative analysis of training as it is occurring to determine whether improvements or adjustments are required.
- Learning – assessing the extent to which the trainee can transfer the learning acquired back to his/her job performance.

The systems approach to learning/training evaluation as proposed by Kirkpatrick (1959) and later Hamblin (1974) delineates the contributions that learning can make at different levels within the organisation and requires that data be quantifiable and based on pre-determined objectives. Such models propose a hierarchy of evaluation where each level requires a different evaluation strategy and is seen as a measure of the progressive transfer and application of training content. This hierarchical approach to training evaluation is presented in table 10.6.

Table 10.6 Levels of learning/training evaluation

Level	Description	Methods	Assessment
1. Reaction	Seeks opinions of trainees	Questionnaires at end of training	Easy to collect; subjective; does not evaluate learning or learning transfer
2. Learning	Seeks knowledge, principles and facts learned by trainees before training	Tests, exams, projects, after training is completed	Evaluates level of learning; does not measure impact of learning on job performance
3. Behaviour	Seeks to determine positive changes in behaviour	Observation, measurement before start; after return to job	Objective assessment of impact of training on job performance; can be difficult to assess in some jobs
4. Results	Seeks to determine contribution to organisational objectives	General indicators (profits, turnover etc.) Specific indicators (absenteeism, accidents)	Evaluates return on investment of training expenditure; difficult to quantify

Evaluation constitutes the final stage in the learning, training and development process and, while difficult to measure, provides information that is critical to effective organisational functioning. Lack of evaluation can result in inappropriate training that is wasteful of both financial and human resources. The difficulty for most organisations lies in identifying a set of measurable criteria that can facilitate the effective evaluation of

LT&D interventions. In particular, many of the perceived key benefits of LT&D, such as improved morale, increased job satisfaction and improved employee relations, are, by their very nature, difficult to demonstrate in quantitative terms, and thus many organisations limit their activities to a level one (reaction) evaluation.

Learning, training and development is not solely limited to the provision of a number of formal training interventions. It is an ongoing process that spans the individual's employment with the organisation. For this reason, many organisations are developing a range of career development initiatives that can support an individual's lifelong learning experience. The dimension of career development, and of management development (as a particular career type) are discussed in the next sections.

CAREER DEVELOPMENT AND MANAGEMENT

There is little doubt that both organisations and individuals are paying increasing attention to the concept of career development and management. However, there is no complete agreement about what it is and, now more than ever before, careers are being described in perceptual terms. Greenhaus and Callanan (1994) describe the career as the pattern of work-related experiences that span the course of a person's life. From an employee's perspective this will encapsulate the sequence of jobs that individuals pursue throughout their working life. Traditional notions of a career and a career pathway have tended to focus on upward movement through a hierarchy acquiring additional salary and managerial responsibilities along the way. Adamson *et al.* (1998, 252) suggest that, 'It conjures up images of planned development, often of a hierarchical nature, and it suggests a logical sequence of work-related events and experiences.' Viewed in this way, a career is not simply a job but rather implies development and logical progression.

However, accelerated economic change, organisational de-layering and an increase in the use of outsourcing have combined to challenge the traditional perceptions not only of a job for life, but also of the existence of established, easily identifiable career paths within organisations.

More recent contributions to the career literature call for a paradigm shift with respect to how we understand a career today to offset the traditional view of a career as essentially managerially based, within a tall organisation hierarchy. Since the typical pyramid of progression leads to management positions (which are limited and exclusive in many organisations), traditional careers have largely been the remit of those with managerial ambitions. Contemporary career theories include the boundaryless career (Arthur and Rousseau 1996), the protean career (Hall and Moss 1998) and career concept model (Brousseau *et al.* 1996), and here a career can be conceptualised as a possibility for all employees across a variety of organisational settings. In an attempt to describe the dimensions of a career in the current business environment, Davies and Wilson (2002, 299) suggest that a career now represents 'the long term accumulation of education, skills and experience that an individual sells to an employer or employers, to try to provide the lifestyle that he or she wants for himself or herself and dependents'.

In organisational terms career management is a systematic process in which the organisation attempts to assist employees in the analysis of their abilities and interests and to guide their placement, progression and development while with the organisation (Arnold 1997). This may include activities such as learning/training and promotion, but also attempts to shape individuals' attitudes, opinions and emotions about their careers. Career management is defined as the ongoing process of preparing, implementing and monitoring career plans with the aim of meeting future organisational needs. For employees, a career can offer a sense of identity and purpose, and denote recognition within the system; and so can be understood in both subjective and objective terms. For organisations, supporting career development can be a key means of encouraging performance, and, increasingly, of retaining talent within the system.

The process of career development requires an understanding of both the stages of career development and the various careers that individual employees might pursue. Driver (1982) differentiates between four different types of career:

1. Steady state – a career choice represents a lifetime commitment to a particular occupation.
2. Linear – the employee moves 'up the ladder' in one particular occupation.
3. Spiral – the employee remains in a particular occupation for a lengthy period of time (7–10 years) and then chooses another occupation, which builds on acquired skills and abilities.
4. Transitory – the employee's choice of career changes frequently with each move signifying a change in direction.

Career development can further be understood in terms of an individual's life-cycle: as an individual progresses through the various stages in his/her life, different needs, concerns and aspirations take priority. Table 10.7 summarises the relationship between an individual's life stages and career cycle.

Table 10.7 Life and career stages

Stage	Characteristics
1. Childhood	Focus on ego-identification; development of concept of self; search for values and roles; formulation of interests and capabilities
2. Early adulthood (growth/ exploration)	Self-identification through role and occupational analysis; closer identification of needs, identification interests and capabilities; potential conflict between need to establish identity vs feeling of losing autonomy
3. Adulthood (establishment)	Focus on establishing self in work and life situations; clear career pattern; search for stability and personal security
4. Late adulthood (maintenance)	Emphasis on acceptance and consolidation of position; possible review and modification of life/work role; concern with providing for and guiding new generation
5. Maturity/Decline	Conclusion of career role; acceptance of life/career pattern; preparation for post-work challenges

Source: Gunnigle and Flood (1990).

Nicholson and West (1988) propose a transition cycle model of job change in organisations, and identify a set of strategies that organisations might adopt to facilitate the smooth transition from one job to another. They can include both the transition from education to work, and relocation within the organisation including transfers, promotions, and moves to group-based work design.

Figure 10.3 The transition cycle

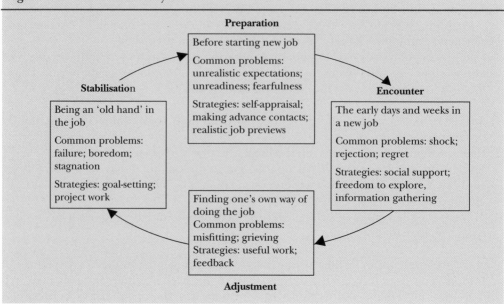

Source: Arnold, Robertson and Cooper (1995).

One major problem experienced by many organisations is the mismatch of employee expectations about the job and career prospects and the reality of the situation. This, in part, may explain the 'induction crisis' experienced by many organisations, when several new employees leave the organisation within the first six weeks of starting employment. Organisations can reduce this crisis by developing a 'realistic job preview', which attempts to describe the job and the company as seen by those who work there. In this way potential job applicants can self-match their skills, abilities and aspirations against the realistic job description provided.

Socialisation of employees in new work roles is critical and can be facilitated further through the establishment of informal support networks. Once employees become comfortable with their role and develop an understanding of the work environment, the organisation needs to concern itself with providing challenging work and feedback on performance. The danger exists that employees can become dissatisfied with the work or developmental opportunities available – for this reason career management is a central concern at every stage of the employment relationship.

Nicholson and Arnold (1989) identify four common shortcomings of organisational career development systems:

- Restricted: while some restrictions are inevitable, organisations can often create unnecessary ones such as non-promotional transfers between functions.
- Political: where career opportunities can be blocked by managers who perhaps seek to advance their own interests at the expense of individual employees.
- Mechanistic: where career moves are controlled by rules and procedures that do not allow for exceptions and fail to take account of changing circumstances.
- Neglected: where possible career paths are simply not identified and no one can see the way forward.

Several career development techniques have been identified over the years, the more salient of which are outlined in table 10.8.

Table 10.8 Career development techniques

Technique	Description
Succession Planning	The organisation identifies or 'earmarks' employees who are deemed suitable for key positions in the future and provides the necessary experiences, training and so forth to enable such employees to take up these positions.
Career Counselling	The organisation appoints an external counsellor (in some cases an internal manager may adopt the role) to assist individual employees to clarify their ideas about self and work. Psychometric tests are often used to identify career opportunities for individual employees.
Skills Inventories	The organisation develops detailed records on the skills, experiences, qualifications and expertise accumulated by each employee, coupled with information on individuals' career preferences and objectives.
Mentoring Programmes	The organisation develops systems whereby an older, more experienced worker acts as a role-model for a younger employee and supports, guides and counsels this employee through his/her time with the organisation.
Educational Opportunities	The organisations overtly promotes continuous development and provides information and financial support on both internal and external courses/training/conferences.

Both Mayo (1991) and Iles and Mabey (1993) note that the establishment of formal career management techniques is a useful managerial tool that can be used to build an effective internal labour market. Similarly it is of benefit to employees where the system takes cognisance of individual career aspirations and can try to ensure the creation of a range of opportunities that facilitates and encourages continuous development.

MANAGEMENT DEVELOPMENT

Managerial competence has been advanced as one of the keys to unlocking the potential of other core factors of production (Heraty and Morley 2003; Drejer 2001; Docherty and Nyhan 1997; Burack *et al.* 1997; Cappelli and Crocker-Hefer 1996; Hall and Foulkes 1991; Prahalad and Hamel 1990; Storey 1989) where the ability of managers is, to a great extent, what influences the return an organisation gets from its investment in human and material capital. Management development is now viewed as an 'enabler', which leverages organisational flexibility and efficiencies (Heraty and Morley 2003; O'Connell and Lyons 1995; Lippitt 1981) and builds competence among those responsible for formulating and implementing strategies and policies designed to manage the firm's resources effectively (Hales 1986; Hambrick 1987; Lees 1992; Baird *et al.* 1994; Black and Boal 1994; Cannon 1995; Sveiby 1997). However, as Kamoche (2000, 748) notes, while there seems to be some evidence that management training and development can positively impact on organisational performance, the 'difficulty of establishing such a linkage has led some to accept the value of management training and development as an act of faith'.

Definitions of management development abound, but the main difficulty with defining the concept lies in the debate on what exactly constitutes management and managerial work. Seminal work by Mintzberg (1973) reveals managerial work to be fragmented and disparate, conducted within complex social networks and with short time horizons.

There are various views on the rational for management development itself. Some theorists view management development as a means of engendering organisational change; as a tool in facilitating quality and excellence; or as a means of establishing core company values and strong corporate culture. As Cannon (1999) puts it:

> Management competence is without doubt a key factor in developing strategies to further an organisation's mission, in achieving an organisation's objectives and in improving performance, whether this means competitiveness in global markets or delivering a better public service. Developing that competence among managers whose daily routines are frequently fragmented and reactive has become a quest of Herculean proportions for companies and business schools alike in the increasingly unpredictable and often precarious environment of the modern organisation.

Similarly, Thompson *et al.* (2001, 1) note that:

> Without adequate development of the management cadre, it has been accepted by policy makers, companies, and perhaps most important of all, managers themselves, that a modern industrial economy cannot maintain its competitiveness, that organisations cannot be sufficiently flexible to respond to the rapidly changing circumstances of the late twentieth and early twenty-first centuries, and that managers cannot adjust to career patterns considerably removed from the expectations of their predecessors.

In defining management development, Mumford (1986) describes it as an attempt to improve managerial effectiveness through a planned and deliberate learning process, while Molander (1986) views it as 'a conscious and systematic process to control the development of managerial resources in the organisation for the achievement of goals and strategies'. Armstrong (1992) adopts a broader perspective in suggesting that management development incorporates any attempt to develop the effectiveness of the management pool and to equip managers to deal with change and future jobs requirements. In pulling together the various rationales underpinning management development, Mabey and Salaman (1995) outline what they perceive to be the dominant organisational 'agendas' for investing in management development. These are presented in table 10.9.

Storey (1995) differentiates between two divergent models of management development. The first model views management development as a highly structured, top-down event with a strong emphasis on structured training programmes, through which all managers must progress in order to rise up the ranks. The opposite approach, according to Storey, is far more decentralised and places the emphasis on self-development: the individual manager devises his/her own development plans and, in effect, owns the process. Within these two models, a variety of management development approaches may be adopted, ranging from educational programmes (the MBA route is most common in Ireland), through mentoring, coaching, action learning and natural learning.

Management development activities are based on the view that an organisation can develop and improve its managerial talent over time and thus a strong linkage with a performance appraisal system is essential to identify current levels of performance and

Table 10.9 The many agendas of management development

Type	Characteristic	Assumptions	Questions and problems
Functional-performance: 'a garage'	Knowledge, skills or attitudes to improve performance, bring about change, and increase national stock of managers	• Training needs can be objectively identified and matched against training	• Overlooks other factors influencing the impact of MD on performance
Political-reinforcement: 'a cascade'	MD acts as extension of company's political order	• Top team's perception of how organisational performance is to be improved is correct	• MD dogmas are frequently dependent on one or two key figures; what happens when they go?
	Programmes (e.g. culture change) propagate skills and attitudes believed by top team to be necessary to turn company around	• 'Recipe for success' can be translated into an MD programme and cascaded down the company	• Approach leaves little opportunity to be questioned, and career costs of doing so may be high; such a climate defies genuine commitment
Compensation: 'a reward'	MD activities are offered as compensation for deprivations of employment: e.g. • as welfare substitute • as alternative focus to alienating work-place • to promote self-development	• Such activities encourage employees to acquire a habit of learning	• This approach deflects attention from causes of alienation, offering a palliative instead • It is deceptive – and morally dubious – to 'use' education in this manner
Psychic defence: 'a displacement'	MD provides a safe situation in which to discharge anxieties by giving access to or participation in more strategic matters	• Managers need a social system for defending their psyche against persecutory anxiety arising from their competitive career drives • Apparently fair appraisal systems, target-setting and ordered management succession help reduce fear of disorder and chaos if latent competition were to leak out	• Would greater self-development and self-determination in the work-place necessarily lead to unbridled and selfish anarchy? • Only a few MD activities would typically provide an opportunity for such displacement

Source: Mabey and Salaman (1995, 147–8).

assess performance over time. Garavan *et al.* (1995) propose that the development of essential managerial qualities involves three main areas of learning:

1. The acquisition of knowledge, which includes professional, technical, organisational and business environment information that is required for all managerial tasks.

2. The acquisition of skills in areas such as problem-solving, communication, motivation and negotiation that are necessary for effective managerial functioning.
3. The development of aptitudes and attitudes, such as judgment, creativity, flexibility, initiative, self-reliance and respect for ethical standards that are required for high performance.

Clearly, then, a focus on managers is felt to be important, as managers with superior knowledge and skills can generate performance improvements. Doyle (2000) suggests that there is a growing commitment and a willingness to invest in the development of managers while Garavan *et al* (2001) note that organisations similarly and increasingly view the implementation of sophisticated workplace learning and development as important in responding to business needs.

FRAMEWORKS FOR MANAGING, LEARNING, TRAINING AND DEVELOPMENT AT WORK

Thus far our discussion has centred on learning, training and development at the individual level and the need for organisations to understand some of the guiding principles underpinning effective individual learning. However, the approach that the organisation adopts with respect to how it manages the range of human resource activities that underpin its activities will have an enormous influence on how LT&D is enacted, its role and function and, ultimately, its effectiveness. While there is a wide variety of organisational frameworks and approaches to choose from, for comparison and discussion purposes, we look here at two frameworks that have been widely debated in recent years and explore their likely implication for the management of LT&D within organisations. These frameworks include the *resource-based view of the firm* and the *learning organisation and organisational learning perspectives*. These approaches have a particular view on what is seen as permissible learning at work and what the underlying rationale for LT&D is – maximising resource potential or individual self-actualisation through lifelong learning, or perhaps a combination of both! It is important to note here that perspectives such as these are particularly useful in helping us to understand how the rationale for investment in learning and development, and the outcomes of that investment, can vary across organisations – it is not suggested that one approach is more favourable than the other.

The Resource-Based View of the Firm

The resource-based view (RBV) of the firm is rooted in an economic perspective of competitive functioning and it suggests that organisational assets that demonstrate a number of core characteristics allow a company to attain a sustainable competitive advantage. The RBV is most widely associated with Barney (1991), who argues that any number of a firm's attributes can be considered as resources, including all assets, capabilities, competencies, organisation processes, information and knowledge. However, only resources that meet the four criteria of value, rareness, inimitability and non-substitutability can deliver sustainable competitive advantage. The RBV essentially argues that an organisation's human resources can deliver sustainable competitive value provided that the organisation ensures that it delivers value; it is rare, it is difficult to imitate and cannot be easily substituted (Flood *et al.* 1996). Where an organisation adopts the RBV, we can envisage a number of core objectives for LT&D:

1. To ensure that human resources are valuable, i.e. add value to the organisation. Here LT&D would focus on activities that help to differentiate employees from others in the

competitive field in terms of their knowledge, skills and productivity levels. In chapter 4 we demonstrated how, over a period of time, internal labour markets can become highly differentiated; that investment in an organisation's specific, rather than general skills increases the value of employees to the one organisation (although this might not be as attractive to employees who seek general skills and therefore greater employability). Increased investment in specific skills that are non-transferable, but which are required by the organisation, can result in a highly differentiated workforce.

2. To ensure that human resources are rare. The extent to which a resource is rare depends on the quality and availability of that resource. This is somewhat more difficult to envisage unless there is a very tight labour market where needed skills are in short supply and difficult to source. It is plausible that economic growth in recent years has made some types of employees very rare indeed, i.e. those with particular expertise in software development, and some professional/knowledge workers more generally. However, it is also possible to argue that the nature of business today demands particular sets of abilities and behaviours (e.g. flexibility, adaptability and autonomy) and these attributes are not that readily available on the open market.

3. To ensure that human resources cannot be imitated. How an organisation manages its workforce is probably as much to do with serendipity as with conscious choice. An organisation's culture, values, ways of being, managerial style, co-worker relationships, communities of practice – each of these evolve over long periods of time and combine to make each organisation's environment unique. It is this combination of factors that make the calibre of human resources, and the human resource systems themselves, difficult to imitate. The LT&D system permeates all organisational knowledge systems and so directly contributes to the inimitableness of human resources.

4. To ensure that human resources are non-substitutable. In the long run it is doubtful whether any one individual cannot be replaced, either from the labour market or from other companies. However, substitution in the short-term can be more problematic, costly and risky, particularly where the skills or knowledge are valuable and rare. Moreover, as work processes are becoming team- and project-based, the breadth of knowledge required might not actually exist outside the company and so substitution might not be the most effective option.

The resource-based view suggests a broad canvas for LT&D within organisations. However, it is a strongly resource-oriented approach and it appears to suggest that organisations should be concerned most with resources that are capable of delivering sustainable competitive advantage. This approach could increase the pressure to deliver LT&D that is organisation-specific, that is immediately visible or that can demonstrably add value. It is difficult to determine whether there is any role for learning activities that have no immediate tangible or measurable results, but that might nevertheless be highly valuable. Furthermore, resources by their nature probably have a limited lifespan of sustainable competitive value – there is less clarity on what occurs to the human resource dimension in those circumstances.

The Learning Organisation and Organisational Learning
Conceptualising about and researching the dimensions of organisational learning and the learning organisation has become a significant academic activity in recent years (Heraty 2004; Popper and Lipshitz 2000; Goh 1998; Probst and Buchel 1997; Walton 1999; Heraty and Morley 1995). However, there is relatively little agreement on a definition of the

learning organisation other than it is an organisational process that seeks to highlight the supremacy of learning as a core competitive strategy. It has been described rather aspirationally as an organisation that facilitates the learning of all its members and consciously transforms itself (Pedler *et al.* 1989) or as a place where:

> . . . people continually expand their capacity to create the results they truly desire, where new and expansive patterns of thinking are nurtured, where collective aspirations are set free, and where people are continually learning how to learn together.
>
> Senge (1990)

Solomon (1999, 122) describes a learning organisation thus:

> While learning has always been a feature of working, learning at work has a new status in contemporary workforce discourse as learning is considered a part of everyday work. Learning becomes a cultural practice that is affirmed through the development of a mission and value statements, an identification of workers with corporate aims and the conceptualisation of an organisation as a site of ongoing learning.

Nonaka (1991) argues that a company is not a machine but a living organism and that the learning organisation represents a shared understanding of what the company stands for, where it is going, what kind of world it wants to live in, and most importantly, how to make that world a reality. More practically, Pedler *et al.* (1989) propose that a learning organisation is one that:

- has a climate in which individuals are encouraged to learn and develop to their full potential;
- extends its learning culture to include customers, suppliers and other significant stakeholders;
- makes human resource development strategy central to its business policy so that the process of individual and organisational learning becomes a major business activity.

The learning organisation literature suggests that, rather than interpreting the environment as a force to be reckoned with, organisations have the potential to shape and develop their environmental context. Calvert *et al.* (1994, 40) maintain that learning organisations use learning as a means of attaining their goals and create structures and procedures that facilitate and support continuous learning and development. They propose that:

- all organisations learn, hence learning is continuous;
- all organisations learn at different levels of proficiency and at different paces;
- to become a 'learning organisation' an organisation must find ways to make learning more intentional and more systematic, deliberate learning is more effective than learning that is left to chance.

There is an attempt made to link individual and organisational performance, which is often reflected in the reward choices made by the organisation. However, the process of becoming a learning organisation is not easily realised since it requires fundamental changes to how individuals think and interact and involves a comprehensive evaluation of deeply held assumptions and values. As with any change of process, the move towards adopting the learning mantle is often perceived with suspicion and mistrust by those who are averse to changing all that has traditionally been stable and consistent, and moving towards a situation where they are required to take responsibility for their continuous development and competency improvement.

Rather more recently, the term organisational learning has received considerable attention, perhaps as a means of offsetting some of the criticisms levelled at the learning organisation literature. While widely acclaimed for their seminal work on organisational learning, Argyris and Schön (1996, xvii) themselves note:

> Twenty or twenty-five years ago organisational learning was a rare species among ideas . . . With few exceptions . . . organisational learning was largely absent from the scholarly literature of organisational theory . . . Respected scholars . . . found the idea confusing and, in some ways, repugnant . . . Now, in the mid 1990s, it is conventional wisdom that business firms, governments . . . even whole nations . . . are all subject to a 'learning imperative', and in the academic as well as the practitioner world, organisational learning has become an idea in good currency.

Arguably, the tendency in this recent literature has been towards describing organisational learning in terms of organisational processes and structures such that learning is embedded in routines, policies and cultures (Heraty 2004; Cook and Yanow 1993; Huber 1991). Garvin (1993) acknowledges this process dimension to organisational learning and uses the term 'strategic learning' to describe the process by which an organisation can make sense of its environment in ways that broaden the range of objectives it can pursue or the range of resources and actions available to it for processing these objectives. Lundberg (1995) similarly proposes that individual learning must first be shared through communication and that institutional processes play a critical role in ensuring that organisational learning takes place. Specifically, institutional processes need to be developed that can support the transfer of what is learned by individuals to the organisation, and also be capable of storing and accessing what is learned. Tompkins (1995) describes this as collective learning: the diffusion of knowledge and/or skills from individuals to members of the collective, which increases the organisation's capacity to take effective action.

Without question some of the literature on the learning organisation is overtly prescriptive and aspirational, since, by definition, organisations never reach the stage at which they can be said to have fulfilled the criteria required to become a learning organisation. Notwithstanding this, the principles upon which the concept is founded represent a set of ideals to which most organisations would aspire: the creation of an organisational climate that facilitates continuous development, a system that rewards continuous improvement, and a structural design that promotes ongoing learning.

It is possible to identify a range of LT&D systems and activities that would fit within the learning organisation paradigm. For example, the promotion of learning for the sake of learning (not tied to specific jobs or roles within the organisation); the development of facilitative structures that would promote learning and development, such as mentoring and coaching arrangements; identified developmental pathways through the organisation for career progression; a commitment to the principles of lifelong learning in whatever guise they present themselves.

LEARNING, TRAINING AND DEVELOPMENT PRACTICES IN IRELAND

The final section of this chapter examines the nature of training and development practices in Ireland. Chapter 9 demonstrated how institutional actors such as the national educational system, professional associations, government interventions in labour market skill formation and trade unions shape the environment within which organisations do business and ultimately impact on the nature of their LT&D activities. The challenge facing Irish organisations, as with their counterparts in the European Union, is the mobilisation of human resources as a necessary prerequisite for the tight, efficient and productive operation of business strategies. The question is: to what extent are Irish organisations actively meeting this challenge? Here we draw on evidence from two data sources: recent evidence on learning, training and development in Ireland from successive CIPD (Ireland)-sponsored surveys (Heraty and Garavan 2001; Garavan *et al.* 2003; O'Donnell and Garavan 2003); and on management development from the 1999/2000 Cranet E. Survey on International Human Resource Management (see Heraty and Morley 2003). For the purposes of this chapter, five key pieces of evidence are drawn from that survey: the forces that trigger learning activity among Irish organisations, the level of expenditure on learning, training and development activity, the volume of learning activity undertaken, the methods utilised to identify learning/training needs and the evaluation strategies employed.

Learning Triggers

Respondents to the CIPD survey (2001) identified a wide range of factors that they perceived to be influencing learning, training and development in their organisation. Three factors in particular were considered to be significant triggers: the requirement to ensure the effective utilisation of human resources, the use of LT&D to facilitate the implementation of new technology, and organisational change. Other organisational-level triggers reported included the development of an appropriate organisational culture, the implementation of multi-skilling strategies, and the maintenance of quality standards. It also emerged that LT&D investment may also be used to achieve a number of human resource type objectives, including the retention of employees, the attraction of high-quality candidates to the organisation, the management of employee career expectations and the psychological contract.

In relation to the issue of expenditure on training and development, unlike some of their European counterparts, Irish companies are not required to invest a minimum proportion of annual turnover on updating the skills and knowledge of their employees, nor are they obliged to declare the amount they spend annually on learning, training and development function (Heraty and Morley 1994). Fox (1987) argues that problems continuously arise in drawing up statistics on training and development as organisations have differing perceptions of what constitutes learning and training, and since many companies tend to rely on informal training strategies and mechanisms, the problem of quantifying training expenditure is further compounded. In the 2001 survey, 78 per cent or 174 organisations provided details of their expenditure on training as a percentage of their total payroll (see table 10.10).

Average annual expenditure (for companies employing more than 50 people) was calculated at 3.85 per cent of payroll with the median expenditure standing at 2.8 per cent. In 2003, this figure stood slightly lower at 3.55 per cent. A ballpark percentage figure of training expenditure is useful to the extent that it allows for comparison and illustrates trends in expenditure over time, but it is a rather crude measure of investment since it does not take into account either spread or quality of investment efforts.

Table 10.10 Factors influencing or driving the provision of training and development in organisations

Factor	Mean	Std. Dev.	N.
To ensure the effective utilisation of human resources	4.02	1.07	207
Facilitation of the implementation of new technology	3.96	0.94	213
Facilitation of the implementation of organisational change	3.88	0.86	208
Meet employee career expectations and demands for learning	3.71	0.92	210
Foster the development of an appropriate organisational culture	3.70	0.97	206
Meet statutory requirements such as health and safety	3.70	1.05	212
A strategy to foster employee commitment to business objectives	3.65	0.89	205
Create a work environment that encourages individuals to learn	3.67	0.93	206
Enhance establishment ability to attract good candidates	3.64	1.07	204
Enhance the retention of employees	3.51	1.11	213
Facilitate the implementation of multi-skilling strategies	3.45	1.07	203
Secure or retain international quality standards	3.23	1.36	208
Facilitate product innovation and development	3.16	1.29	201
Improve the market share of the business	3.13	1.30	198
Manage the employee psychological contract	2.96	1.08	198

Source: Heraty and Garavan (2001).

Table 10.11 Training and development expenditure as a percentage of payroll

Training Expenditure	%	No.
No details provided	21	47
< 0.5%	8	17
0.5 – 1%	9	19
> 1% – < 2%	26	57
> 2% – < 4%	26	57
> 5%	10	24
Total	100	221
Average	3.85	
Median	2.8	

Source: Heraty and Garavan (2001).

Turning then to the spread of investment, the 2001 survey asked respondents to estimate the number of days' training per employee per annum that they provided. Their responses are presented in table 10.12 by occupational category.

Table 10.12 Number of days formal training provided per employee

Occupational Category	AVERAGE NUMBER OF DAYS TRAINING						
	None	< 1 day	1–3 days	4–7 days	8–12 days	12+ days	Total
Semi-skilled/Unskilled	4.05	5.78	36.99	40.46	10.40	2.31	173
Supervisors	3.80	12.50	38.04	36.96	6.52	2.17	184
Craft/Technician	6.08	6.08	42.57	36.49	6.76	2.03	148
Clerical/Admin.	3.09	4.64	40.72	39.69	9.79	2.06	194
Senior Management	4.37	12.62	35.92	35.44	7.28	4.37	206

Source: Heraty and Garavan (2001).

The data is interesting in a number of respects. Very few organisations indicated that they provide no training at all to employees. They were more likely to provide learning and training for senior management personnel than for any other employee category. The mean number of days' training for manager grades was reported at 5.25 days. Establishments are less likely to provide training and development for professional and technical job categories. Only a small percentage of establishments provide more than eight days of formal training per employee in any one year. Almost 4.5 per cent of establishments indicated that they provide twelve days' or more training. The mean number of days' training for all job categories was 5.61 days. Results from the 2003 survey suggest that relatively little has changed overall. Although there is some variation within each category, the figures depict a small decrease in the overall mean number of days' training from 5.61 to 5.35.

Needs analysis is considered a central component of the learning, training and development process, primarily because it helps ensure that an appropriate LT&D solution is selected to match the identified needs. Clearly, survey, case study and anecdotal evidence exists to suggest that organisations in Ireland invest considerable resources in LT&D activities, and the evidence here confirms a high level of awareness of the necessity to systematically identify training and development needs before investing in LT&D. Four out of every five organisations indicate that they regularly conduct a systematic learning/training needs analysis (81 per cent in 2001; 83 per cent in 2003). This figure suggests that training and development needs identification is a well established and common practice in Irish-based companies.

A broad range of methods is used to identify training and development needs (see table 10.13).

Table 10.13 Methods used by Irish-based companies to identify learning, training and development needs

Method Used	Weighted Score
Line manager requests	913
Data from performance management appraisal systems	840
Employee requests for training	662
Training and development audits	625
Performance training	249
Competency profiling	206
360° feedback processes	143
Psychological testing	57
Work study processes	54
Work sample tests	44

Source: Heraty and Garavan (2001).

The data reveals that respondents tend to rely on what may be described as the more traditional methods to identify training and development needs. In order of usage these are: line manager requests; data from performance management appraisal systems; employee requests for training; and the use of training and development audits – these are used by more than 80 per cent of all respondents. The 2003 survey reveals no change in this respect. There is some evidence to indicate an increased use of more progressive and innovative identification methods of training needs, but the data from both the 2001 and 2003 surveys suggests that these are more commonly utilised by larger organisations.

The evaluation of training and development is considered a critical component of the LT&D cycle since it provides an indication of the extent to which learning has occurred. Two questions were included in the surveys to derive a snapshot of current learning, training and development evaluation practices in Irish-based companies. Table 10.14 presents the data from the 2001 survey – there was no significant change from this reported in 2003.

A total of 78 per cent of respondents indicated that they evaluated training and development activities while 22 per cent suggested that they do not have any evaluation systems in place. Organisations tend to utilise a broad range of quantitative and qualitative criteria to evaluate the effectiveness of their learning, training and development initiatives. Some of the more quantitative criteria used include the total number of days' training undertaken per period, the level of exam pass rates for certified programmes and measured job performance both immediately and some months after training. Seventy-seven percent of establishments indicated that they utilise informal feedback of line managers as a key source of evaluation information. This is ranked the second most important criterion used by establishments. The highest ranked criterion, that of meeting the objectives set out in the training and development plan, is a rather narrow one and is more akin to training validation rather than training evaluation *per se*.

Table 10.14 Ranked criteria used by Irish establishments to evaluate learning, training and development activities

Criterion	% used	No.	Priority Weighting	Rank
Informal feedback from line managers	77	127	162	2
Meeting the objectives set out in the training and development plan	75	124	183	1
Informal feedback from employees	64	104	102	4
Measured job performance some months after training	50	83	108	3
Total number of days training per period	39	65	72	5
Exam pass rates for certified programmes	39	64	36	7
Measured job performance immediately after training	36	59	56	6
Enhanced promotability of employees	26	43	35	8

Source: Heraty and Garavan (2001).

Seventy-five per cent of respondents indicated that they evaluate learning and training in terms of whether it meets the objectives set out in their learning, training and development plan. The majority of the criteria utilised by organisations tend to be job-specific or tied to dimensions of the training programme itself. However, 26 per cent of establishments indicated that they consider the enhanced promotability of employees to be an important criterion, but this is accorded the lowest priority of all the evaluation criteria reported by establishments. This is potentially a useful evaluation criterion, especially in view of our discussion earlier concerning career development and management.

Turning finally to the issue of management development in Ireland, Heraty and Morley (2003) report a considerable increase in the number of days' training provided per manager per year over the period 1992–2000. The mean number of management development days provided was 4.5 days in 1999/2000, which is broadly in line with the volume reported in many European countries, and is in stark contrast to the gloomy picture of management development activity portrayed both in the Government-commissioned Galvin report (1988) and the Culliton report (1992). Irish data from the Cranet E surveys since 1992 reflect an increasing propensity to invest in LT&D more generally, and management development in particular. While it is not possible to say with absolute certainty why organisations in Ireland are investing in management development to a greater extent now than in the past, they argue that consistent and concerted messages from national learning stakeholders continue to highlight the development of knowledge and learning as key strategic imperatives for Government action, for policy development and for organisational performance.

In summary, this chapter has focused on learning, training and development within organisations. It has been highlighted that recent social, organisational and technological developments have combined to heighten the overall significance of LT&D in organisational life. Building and continuously developing the knowledge base of the enterprise has gained a strong currency in the armoury of competitiveness, globally and locally (Tregaskis *et al.* 2001).

We have sought to unpack some of the arguments being advanced for according a 'new status' to LT&D and set down the typical systems being established by organisations in the learning/training domain. We have reviewed some of the core reasons for the increased attention being paid to LT&D systems, examined learning processes and outlined some of the conditions necessary for effective learning to take place. We have also presented the core aspects of the cycle of training and reviewed particularly important initiatives beyond that cycle, namely career development and management development. Two particular organisational perspectives were presented, namely the resource-based view of the firm and the learning organisation/organisational learning framework, and core LT&D processes associated with them were outlined. Finally, drawing upon recent survey evidence, we have provided a contemporary portrait of organisational-level learning, training and development in Ireland.

11

Employee Relations: Institutions and Actors

Employee relations is one of the most significant aspects of the HR role in organisations. Indeed, in the past the traditional role of the average HR (or 'personnel') manager in Ireland could perhaps more appropriately be described as 'industrial relations' or 'employee relations' manager, given their primary concern with collective bargaining and trade union interactions. While the past two decades has undoubtedly witnessed considerable diminution of this employee relations emphasis and a concomitant broadening of the HR role, employee relations remains a critical area of HR activity.

This chapter sketches the nature of employee relations, describes the Irish context, and considers the parties involved in employee relations interactions. Particular focus is placed on the role of trade unions and state institutions in employee relations. The role of employers and employer organisations in employee relations is discussed in chapter 12.

THE NATURE OF EMPLOYEE RELATIONS

As has often been noted, the very nature of employee relations is a source of some confusion (Tiernan *et al.* 2001). Traditional definitions have focused on the concept of *industrial* rather than *employee* relations. Such an approach reflected an emphasis on the formal regulation of the employment relationship through collective bargaining between *organised employees* and employers. This perspective remains significant as employers, trade unions and Government seek to develop processes and agreements at various levels (e.g. enterprise or national level). However, as the nature of employment has changed, the term 'employee relations' has achieved increased prominence. The concept of employee relations is seen as embracing a broader scope than *industrial relations*. In this text the term *employee relations* is used as a generic term to embrace all employer, employee and state interactions on employment matters. It focuses on the nature of the relationship between the parties to the labour process, embraces both collectivist and individualist approaches and encapsulates state, organisational and intermediary level arrangements. It primarily involves the following issues:

1. collective bargaining;
2. communications policy and practice;

3. employee involvement and participation;
4. grievance handling;
5. discipline administration;
6. the management of change;
7. aspects of social responsibility.

In most of these issues trade unions may play an important role. However, they are not a prerequisite and employee relations is a critical HRM concern in non-union as well as in unionised organisations.

EMPLOYEE RELATIONS IN IRELAND

Employee relations practice in the great majority of medium and large organisations in the Republic of Ireland has traditionally been associated with a strong collectivist emphasis. In this model, employee relations considerations rarely concern strategic decision-makers; relations between management and employees are grounded in the pluralist tradition with a primary reliance on adversarial collective bargaining:

> Over a wide range of industries and services, employers and unions have conducted their relations on the basis of the premise that their interests were in significant respects different and in opposition . . . These differences of interest were reconciled on an ongoing basis through what is sometimes known in the academic literature as 'collective bargaining pure and simple'.
>
> Roche (1990, 22)

This 'pluralist tradition' is predicated on relatively high levels of union density, a heavy reliance on collective bargaining in handling employee relations issues, and employee relations as the key role of the specialist HR function (Gunnigle and Morley 1993).

As was the case in many developed countries, the 1980s witnessed considerable change in the environment and practice of employee relations in Ireland (see chapter 1). From an employer's perspective, economic recession lessened the emphasis on hitherto core workforce management activities, such as recruitment and, particularly, employee relations. Trade union membership fell significantly and industrial unrest also declined. At the same time, many companies sought to establish competitive advantage through improvements in quality, service and performance. Consequently, we witnessed considerable change and innovation in employee relations practice, particularly in areas such as work systems, rewards, management-employee communications and employee development (Murray 1984; Flood 1989).

In terms of Government approaches to employee relations, a number of significant issues emerge. Traditionally, the approach of successive Governments to employee relations has been grounded in the 'voluntarist' tradition. This meant that employers and employees (or their representative bodies) were largely free to regulate the substantive and procedural terms of their relationship with a minimum of intervention from Government or its agencies (Hillery 1994; Breen *et al.* 1990; Roche 1997b). However, this 'voluntarist' tradition has undoubtedly been diluted somewhat over the years, particularly as a result of the increase in individual employment legislation and its impact in regulating many aspects of employee relations (e.g. in relation to individual employment rights).

An important aspect of public policy in employee relations is the constitutional support for freedom of association. Article 40.6.1. of the Irish Constitution supports the right of individuals to form or join associations or unions. However, there is no statutory provision for trade union recognition in Ireland. This means that although workers have constitutional support to join trade unions, there is no legal obligation for employers to recognise or deal with trade unions. The issue of trade union membership and recognition is addressed later in this chapter.

Another important aspect of public policy relates to approaches to industrial development. Since the late 1950s Government policy has actively encouraged foreign direct investment (FDI) in Ireland. In chapter 1 we noted the large numbers of foreign-owned multinational corporations (MNCs) operating in Ireland, which now employ approximately 130,000 people, with a particular focus on financial services, information and communication technologies (ICT), health care and pharmaceuticals. We also saw that the US is the main source of FDI, while the UK and Germany are also important sources. The period since the late 1980s saw significant growth in the scale of FDI into Ireland (OECD 1999), while more recent data shows that in period 2001–2003 Ireland attracted the fourth highest level of inward FDI in the world (UNCTAD 2004).

In regard to employee relations it certainly appears that MNCs have been a source of innovation in management practices, particularly in the application of new HR and employee relations approaches and in expanding the role of the specialist HR function (Gunnigle *et al.* 1999; Gunnigle and McGuire 2001). However, it would also seem that MNCs pose unique challenges in the sphere of employee relations. In particular, their ability to switch the locus of production and also to adopt employee relations styles that challenge the traditional pluralist model, most particularly in regard to union avoidance (Gunnigle 1995; Gunnigle *et al.* 1997; Gunnigle *et al.* 2005; Kelly and Brannick 1988b; McGovern 1988).

A critical initial step in grappling with the study of employee relations in Ireland is an appreciation of the range and nature of the actors and institutions involved in our employee relations system. The key parties or 'actors' involved in employee relations include individual workers, trade unions, worker representatives, employers, managers, Government and Government agencies. The interaction of these parties in employee relations will be heavily influenced by context so that economic conditions, historic and political factors, and developments in technology and markets will significantly influence employee relations activities. Figure 11.1 outlines the main parties involved in employee relations. In employee relations terms the critical parties are employers and employees, both of whom may seek to form and use associations to represent their interests (i.e.

Figure 11.1 Employee relations: the main parties

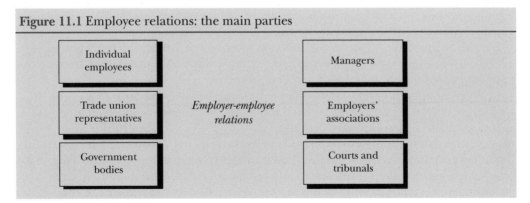

Source: Gunnigle, Garavan and Fitzgerald (1992).

employer associations and trade unions). The state also plays a critical role in employee relations. The respective roles of trade unions and state are reviewed below while employers' approaches are considered in the next chapter. Before this, we briefly consider the main means through which employers and unions and sometimes Government interact in employee relations, via collective bargaining.

COLLECTIVE BARGAINING

Collective bargaining has traditionally been seen as the primary means of regulating interactions between unions, employees and employers in Ireland (see chapter 13). It refers to the process through which agreement on pay, working conditions, procedures, and other negotiable issues are reached between organised employees and management representatives. Collective bargaining represents a mechanism through which divergent interests of employees and employers can be reconciled through an orderly process involving negotiation and compromise. Its principal feature is that employees do not negotiate with their employers on their own behalf, but do so collectively through representatives, and that various aspects of a worker's contract of employment are determined not individually but collectively (Wallace *et al.* 2004).

For collective bargaining to operate effectively a number of conditions are necessary. Workers must have the freedom to join together in trade unions, which are not in any way under the control or influence of employers (i.e. freedom of association), while employers must be prepared to recognise and deal with trade unions for collective bargaining purposes (see chapter 13 for more detail). Additionally, we have also noted that the Irish 'system' of collective bargaining is essentially voluntary. There is no legal obligation on trade unions and employers to engage in collective bargaining on pay or any other issue at any level. The system relies on the moral commitment of the participants, with collective agreements regarded as being 'binding in honour only'. The Report of the Commission of Inquiry on Industrial Relations (1981) noted that the Irish system reflects the view that collective bargaining, not the law, should be the primary source of regulation in the employment relationship, based on the assumption by all parties that recourse to the law will be avoided.

While collective bargaining has been the primary means of managing employee relations in most industrialised nations, it is not the only method of dealing with issues such as pay and working conditions. Indeed, even where collective bargaining predominates, it generally operates concurrently with other mechanisms, including individual bargaining between employer and employee, regulation by the state (especially through legislation), the unilateral imposition of terms of employment by employers or, similarly – if much less likely – the imposition of unilateral terms by trade unions.

Individual bargaining refers to the situation whereby individual workers negotiate on a one-to-one basis with their employer to arrive at an 'individual contract' that sets outs the terms and conditions of each individual's employment.

Collective bargaining may take place at differing levels (see figure 11.2). The most obvious, of course, is bargaining between union and management representatives at the level of the individual workplace or establishment, i.e. *establishment-level bargaining*. However, we also know that many organisations, such as banks, restaurant chains and manufacturing firms, have multiple establishments. Thus, collective bargaining may also take place between unions representing workers from a number of establishments and corporate level management, i.e. multi-establishment level bargaining. Both establishment level and multi-establishment level bargaining are focused on one employer. However, employers with common interests may also choose to form employer associations. Often these common interests come from operating in the same industrial sector or geographical region and, consequently, such an employer grouping may seek to bargain with trade unions representing workers in the relevant industrial sector or region, i.e. multi-employer bargaining. In Ireland, for example, this has occurred in sectors such as the construction industry, where the Construction Industry Federation (representing employers) and a grouping of trade unions (representing workers in the construction sector) have regularly concluded collective agreements dealing with pay and working conditions. Over recent decades we have also seen that *national-level bargaining* involving representatives of employers, Government and trade unions, has become the principal means of dealing with pay, in addition to numerous other aspects of economic and social affairs, in Ireland.

This tendency towards so-called 'centralised bargaining' essentially refers to institutionalised negotiations between trade unions (via the Irish Congress of Trade Unions), employers' associations (primarily the Irish Business and Employers Confederation, and some other employers' associations, see next chapter), Government and certain other societal groupings (e.g. farming organisations, the community and voluntary sector) over wages and various other economic and social issues.

Figure 11.2 Levels of collective bargaining

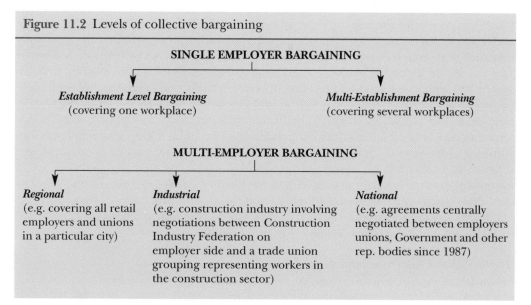

Since Ireland achieved independence in 1922, collective bargaining has oscillated between national and establishment level bargaining (including levels in between), with a general trend towards centralised (national) bargaining over recent decades. Since 1970 pay determination has predominantly been decided through some form of centrally bargained agreement between employer associations and the trade union movement (except for the years 1982 to 1986). Since 1987 there have been six major agreements involving unions, employers and Government. Greater detail on these agreements is provided in chapter 13.

Even in the presence of centralised bargaining, however, collective bargaining may still take place at various other levels. This is particularly the case in regard to workplace bargaining. National agreements generally set out agreed broad national level guidelines for wage increases and other related issues, while also allowing scope for supplementary bargaining between unions and employers in individual firms, such as on issues of productivity, organisational change and working time.

We now turn to the role of trade unions in employee relations.

TRADE UNIONS

As we saw in chapter 1, the historical development of HRM is inextricably linked to the growth of organised labour through the trade union movement. Modern trade unionism has its roots in the 'factory system' and the dramatic changes brought about by the industrial revolution, which began in Britain in the eighteenth century and later spread to Europe and North America. The growth of the factory system heralded a change from a largely peasant society based on agriculture and craft production to an industry-based society characterised by new social divisions, where people worked together in much larger numbers and relied on wages for their existence (Wallace *et al.* 2004). In the face of authoritarian management styles and poor working conditions, these new factory workers were poorly positioned, lacking in economic and political power. It was not until the growth of organised labour, through the trade union movement, that employee concerns could command the attention and action of factory owners and management.

Despite Ireland's relatively recent history of industrialisation, trade unions were well established in many industries in Dublin, Belfast and Cork by the early 1900s (McNamara *et al.* 1988; Wallace *et al.* 2004). The development of trade unionism in Britain profoundly influenced events in Ireland. The passing of the Trade Disputes Act of 1906, often referred to as the 'Bill of Rights for Workers', provided legal immunity for unions involved in strike activity and authorised peaceful picketing. Increased conflict between employer and trade union interests characterised this period and eventually came to a head in the Dublin lockout of 1913 (*see* Yeates 2000). An important effect of this turbulent period was that it served to encourage the organisation of employees into trade unions and employers into employers' association. It also served to increase employers' emphasis on employee relations as an increasingly significant management task. Over time, the fledgling union movement was reluctantly accepted and employers began to take initial steps to accommodate its role. This was often achieved through multi-employer bargaining via employers' association, and through the employment of labour relations officers to deal with HR and employee relations matters in organisations.

Trade Union Objectives and Legal Status

Essentially, unions are organisations that aim to unite workers with common interests, while seeking to define those interests, express them, safeguard and advance them through their interactions (particularly collective bargaining) with individual employers, employers' association, Government, Government agencies and other parties (Wallace *et al.* 2004). A trade union's basic strength rests with its ability to organise and unite workers. Through joining trade unions, it is argued, workers provide themselves with the collective means to redress the imbalance in bargaining power that would otherwise exist between individual workers and employers. While workers may join trade unions for numerous reasons, the most common reasons include a desire to influence pay claims, to have protection against management actions, and because of an ideological belief in the role that trade unions play in a democratic society (Tiernan *et al.* 2001). The Webbs (1920, 1), who wrote the first comprehensive history of trade unions and early collective bargaining, came up with what was long accepted as the most comprehensive definition of a trade union:

A continuous association of wage earners with the objective of improving or maintaining conditions of employment.

Although this definition accurately embraces the workplace role of trade unions, it does not capture their broader societal role in advancing worker interests in the political arena (Salamon 1998; Wallace *et al.* 2004). Thus, trade unions may be most appropriately viewed as permanent associations of organised employees whose primary objectives are to:

- Replace individual bargaining by collective bargaining, thereby redressing the balance of bargaining power in favour of employees and reducing management prerogative in employment-related matters.
- Facilitate the development of a political system where worker interests have a greater degree of influence on political decisions resulting in an economic and social framework which reflects the interests of wage earners.
- Achieve satisfactory levels of pay and conditions of employment and provide members with a range of services.

The main legislation dealing with the formation and operation of trade unions in Ireland are the Trade Union Acts of 1941 and 1971 and the Industrial Relations Act 1990. Trade unions are defined under the 1941 Trade Union Act as bodies carrying out negotiations for fixing wages or other conditions of employment. This legal definition of trade unions is very broad ranging and extends to employer organisations (Kerr 1997; Kerr and Whyte 1985). This legislation stipulates that, apart from certain 'excepted' bodies, only 'authorised' trade unions holding negotiating licenses are permitted to engage in collective bargaining on pay and working conditions. The legislation also specifies the conditions that a trade union must fulfil before it will be issued with such a licence. Trade unions may only be granted a negotiating licence when they register with the Registrar of Friendly Societies and meet specified criteria, particularly the following:

- *Notification.* Unions must notify the Minister for Enterprise, Trade and Employment and the Irish Congress of Trade Unions at least eighteen months before applying for a license.
- *Membership.* A minimum of 1,000 members.
- *Financial deposit.* Ranging between €25,395 and €76,184, depending on membership numbers.

It should be noted that financial deposits are not required when a new trade union is formed as a result of the amalgamation of two or more unions. Furthermore, while trade unions with headquarters outside the Republic of Ireland are not required to adhere to these requirements, they must be legally recognised trade unions in their country of origin and meet some prescribed guidelines in relation to their controlling authority. Otherwise such unions must meet the notification, membership and deposit requirements set out above.

The legislation also provides for the operation of a number of 'excepted' bodies. These excepted bodies are not required to hold a negotiating licence to engage in collective bargaining and include work-place ('staff' or 'house') associations and unions, some civil service associations and teachers' associations (Kerr and Whyte 1985). Examples of excepted bodies include the Irish Hospital Consultants Association and the Irish Dental Association. A number of organisations that now hold a negotiation licence and operate as a trade union were originally 'excepted bodies', such as the Irish Nurses Organisation.

The major piece of legislation governing trade union operation is the Industrial Relations Act 1990, and its main provisions in relation to trade disputes are noted in chapter 13.

Trade Union Types

Irish trade unions are normally organised on an occupational basis. This means that workers tend to join a particular union because of the particular job or trade in which they are employed. Trade unions in Ireland have traditionally been grouped into three broad categories: craft unions, general unions and white-collar unions. It should be noted that it is extremely difficult to categorise unions as 'purely' craft, general or white-collar, since many unions deviate from a tight definition of their union category on some dimension. For example, general unions may have white-collar and craft workers in membership; not all 'craft' unions operate an 'exclusive' membership system based on the completion of a recognised apprenticeship programme. Thus, the categorisation of trade unions as craft, general or white-collar should be interpreted as broadly indicative of union types in Ireland. In other countries they may be characterised by different classifications. In Japan, for example, one finds a proliferation of so-called 'enterprise unions'. These are company-based unions comprised of different employee categories (manual, administrative etc.) whose sole membership comes from the enterprise in which they operate. Even in the UK, which has a similar union classification to Ireland, Turner (1962) suggested that a more appropriate categorisation of union types is one based on whether union membership is 'open' to employees regardless of occupation or 'closed' to all employees except those working in a defined trade requiring a prescribed apprenticeship or training period. However, the craft, general, white-collar categorisation provides a convenient benchmark by which to analyse Irish trade unions.

CRAFT UNIONS

Craft unions cater for workers who possess a particular skill in a trade where entry is restricted to workers who have completed a prescribed apprenticeship programme or equivalent. Prominent examples of occupational categories organised in craft unions are electricians and fitters. Craft unions probably represent the earliest form of union organisation and have their origins in the early unions, which emerged in Britain at the start of the nineteenth century. These 'model' unions, as they became known, confined their membership to skilled categories such as printers and carpenters who had served a recognised apprenticeship in their particular trade. The first British craft union to organise in Ireland was the Amalgamated Society of Engineers, which established branches in the early 1850s (Boyd 1972). While the early craft unions represented only a small proportion of the labour force, the organisation of workers into craft unions was critical in establishing trade unions as legitimate institutions representing worker interests to employers and Government.

Craft unions have traditionally sought to protect their trades by ensuring that full members of the relevant craft union are allowed to carry out particular types of skilled work. This is the basis of the concept of 'demarcation', which relates to the delineation of skilled work among different craft categories. It is suggested that craft unions, by controlling entry to the craft, have traditionally held considerable negotiating power. This strategy is often criticised as being a source of restrictive work practices and demarcation disputes. Increased mechanisation and consequent de-skilling has had a detrimental impact on the membership and power of craft unions. Indeed, some older craft unions have ceased to exist, their traditional craft being rendered obsolete by developments in technology and work practices.

However, craft unions remain an important part of Ireland's employee relations landscape. In recent years this was made apparent by the number of disputes by craft workers in the construction industry. Figures from the Irish Congress of Trade Unions (ICTU) suggest that the two main engineering craft unions – the Technical, Electrical and Engineering Union (TEEU) and the National Union of Sheet Metal Workers of Ireland (NUSMWI) – have almost 5 per cent of ICTU members. The former Allied Electrical and Engineering Union (AEEU), now known as AMICUS-AEEU, had approximately 8,000 members in the Republic before it merged with AMICUS. The major building unions, the Union of Construction and Allied Trades and Technicians (UCATT), the Building and Allied Trades Unions (BATU) and the Operative Plasterers and Allied Trades Society of Ireland (OPATSI) account for just under 4 per cent of total ICTU membership.

GENERAL UNIONS

Unlike the restrictive recruitment strategies of craft unions, general trade unions adopt a more open approach, taking into membership all categories of worker, broadly regardless of skill or industry. Despite this open recruitment approach, however, general unions have traditionally catered for semi-skilled and unskilled workers. In more recent years, some general unions have attracted white-collar and some craft categories into membership.

The origins of general trade unions are rooted in the increased number of unskilled or general workers employed in the large factories and other major organisations that characterised late nineteenth- and early twentieth-century Britain. These new unions tended to be more militant than the more traditional craft unions of the period. They initially organised categories of workers such as general labourers and dockers and were noted for both their aggressive bargaining style in attempting to improve pay and working conditions of their members, and for their greater political consciousness in attempting to advance working class interests.

Whereas general unions catering for unskilled workers such as labourers and dockers existed in Ireland from the 1860s, they came to play a more active role in Irish industrial and political life in the early 1900s (Wallace *et al.* 2004). A major development was the establishment in 1909 of the Irish Transport and General Workers Union (ITGWU) led by Jim Larkin. The ITGWU and some other general unions organised categories such as dockers, carters and railway workers and became engaged in a series of disputes culminating in the Dublin lockout of 1913. While this dispute initially dealt a severe blow to the general unions they slowly recovered and reorganised and by the early 1920s membership had recovered dramatically (Boyd 1972; McNamara *et al.* 1988).

In 2004, general unions were typically the largest union type and were commonly found in all types of organisations and industrial sectors. The best-known general union in Ireland is the Services, Industrial, Professional and Technical Union (SIPTU), which has a membership of 206,871 (ICTU 2004). SIPTU is by some way the country's largest union, accounting for almost 30 per cent of ICTU membership and 40 per cent of total trade union members. It was created in 1990 as a result of the merger of the then two largest trade unions in the country, the ITGWU and the Federated Workers Union of Ireland (FWUI). Other prominent examples of general unions in Ireland include the Amalgamated Transport and General Workers Unions (ATGWU) and the Marine Port and General Workers Union (MPGWU).

WHITE-COLLAR UNIONS

White-collar unions primarily cater for professional, supervisory, technical, clerical and managerial categories. These unions have experienced significant growth in membership since the late 1960s. In the period 1966–76 white-collar unions increased their membership by 71 per cent as compared to an overall growth of 30 per cent in union membership over that period (Roche and Larragy 1989). The dramatic growth in employment in the services sector (particularly the public sector) was a significant factor contributing to increased white-collar unionisation. However, Kelly (1975) identifies a number of factors that served to increase the propensity of white-collar workers to unionise. In particular, he noted the impact of negative circumstances at work, especially poor job design and general quality of working life, as important factors encouraging white-collar unionisation. One can also point to changing attitudes of white-collar workers to trade unions, a development accelerated by the emergence of unions designed to cater for the specific needs of white-collar workers. The British-based Association of Scientific Technical and Managerial Staffs (ASTMS) attracted a large number of Irish insurance workers and other professional staff into its membership. The Irish Transport and General Workers Union became the first general union explicitly to develop a white-collar section under the current Labour Party leader Pat Rabitte TD.

Another significant factor in white-collar unionisation was the significant advances in pay and conditions secured by blue-collar unions, which encouraged hitherto more conservative white-collar workers to unionise. White-collar categories thus represented a relatively 'greenfield' opportunity for union membership drives in the 1960s and 1970s.

In evaluating union membership statistics it is difficult to differentiate between white-collar and blue-collar workers. However, the major areas of concentration of white-collar workers are the public sector and financial and professional services. Recent figures from the Irish Congress of Trade Unions (ICTU) suggest that the five largest public sector unions (the Irish Municipal Public and Civil Trade Union (IMPACT), the Communications Workers Union (CWU), the Irish Nurses Organisation (INO), the Civil and Public Services Union (CPSU) and the Public Services Executive Union (PSEU)) account for over 17 per cent of ICTU members, while two of the major teachers' unions (the Irish National Teachers Organisation (INTO) and the Teachers Union of Ireland (TUI)) account for almost 6 per cent of ICTU members. The third major teachers' union, the Association of Secondary Teachers, Ireland (ASTI) is not affiliated to ICTU and has over 16,000 members. Turning to the financial services sector we find that the Irish Bank Officials Association (IBOA) accounts for another 2.5 per cent of ICTU membership. The former Manufacturing Science and Finance Union (MSF) merged with AMICUS to form AMICUS-MSF, which has almost 25,000 members. As noted earlier, many white-collar workers are also members of general unions such as SIPTU.

Trade Union Structure

Turning to the actual operation of trade unions in Ireland, three different levels may be identified: (i) workplace level, (ii) branch level and (iii) national level. This structure is illustrated in figure 11.3. The ultimate decision-making authority in a trade union is vested in the membership and executed through resolutions passed at the Annual Delegate Conference (ADC). It is the responsibility of the union executive to carry out policy decisions reached at the ADC. The primary role of the trade union official is to carry out the operational aspects of the union's role, servicing the membership through assistance and advice.

Figure 11.3 Trade union structure

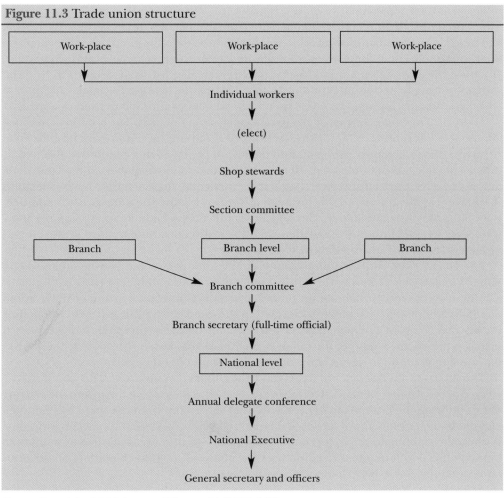

Source: Gunnigle, McMahon and Fitzgerald (1999, 120).

The *shop steward* is the key trade union representative in the workplace. They are selected by fellow trade union members at elections, which normally take place once a year. A number of shop stewards may be elected to represent different sections within the workplace. The shop steward's role is to represent the interests of union members on workplace issues, liaise with union officials, and to keep members well-informed about union affairs. Salamon (1998, 175) describes the role of the shop steward as 'an employee who is accepted by management and union as a lay representative of the union and its members with responsibility to act on their behalf in industrial relations matters at the organisational level'.

Shop stewards may become involved in workplace bargaining involving local grievances or disputes. On more major issues, their role is to support the trade union official and give feedback to the membership. Shop stewards are also employees of the organisation and, as such, must perform their normal job. It should be noted that the code of practice (under the Industrial Relations Act 1990) issued in 1993 in respect of Employee Representatives states that such representatives should be afforded 'reasonable' time off to perform their representative duties. Equally, trade union representatives are charged with representing their members in a fair and equitable manner. It has become the custom and practice in a number of organisations for shop stewards to be given time off to perform their union role and to have access to requisite facilities (e.g. secretarial and telephone). However, these are often minimal and it is extremely rare for shop stewards to be given substantial leave to perform their union duties. This may be because the small scale of most Irish organisations does not facilitate such resources being afforded to shop stewards.

The *section committee* consists of group of elected shop stewards. The section committee allows stewards representing various sections or groupings in the organisation to meet regularly, discuss common problems and decide on policy. Such a committee is generally called a Shop Stewards Committee. All of the shop stewards are members of the same trade union. However, one can also have a section committee of shop stewards who are members of different trade unions. In this instance it is called a Joint Shop Stewards Committee. Joint Shop Stewards Committees can regulate conflict between unions, and support and – if necessary – sanction individual stewards. They also constitute a more powerful and unified body for negotiating with management.

The *branch* is the basic organisational unit in a trade union and may be organised on either a geographic (catering for several companies) or establishment basis (Gunnigle *et al.* 1995). In Ireland, a trade union branch normally comprises a group of trade union members from different companies located in the same geographic area. Occasionally, a branch may comprise union members from one large business enterprise. A union branch manages the internal affairs of the union in their particular area or constituency and strives for improvements in the terms and working conditions of branch members.

The affairs of the branch are managed by the branch committee. This committee is elected at the Annual General Meeting of the branch, which is also the forum for electing delegates from the branch to attend the ADC of the union. Both the branch committee and the branch members are served by a branch secretary. In larger unions, this individual is normally a permanent employee of the union. If so, they are described as a full-time branch official, whose role is to administer the affairs of the branch and negotiate terms and conditions for all branch members with management.

At *national level*, the election of union officers takes place at the ADC. It is here that motions concerning trade union policy are discussed and voted upon. Such motions usually emanate from branch level. If approved by the ADC a motion then becomes a resolution of the conference and ultimately union policy. The ADC comprises branch delegates and the union's National Executive. The National Executive is responsible for carrying out the decisions of the ADC and appointing branch officials and other union staff. The General Officers of the union are usually full-time union employees and normally consist of a General President, a General Secretary, a General Vice President and a General Treasurer.

Irish Congress of Trade Unions (ICTU)

The Irish Congress of Trade Unions (ICTU) is the central co-ordinating body for the Irish trade union movement. It is estimated that some 90 per cent of Irish trade unionists are in membership of one of the forty-five unions affiliated to Congress. However, important unions not affiliated to the ICTU are the National Bus and Rail Workers Union (NBRU), the Psychiatric Nurses Association (PSA), the Dairy Executives Association (DEA) and ASTI.

Although Congress acts as the representative of the collective interests of the Irish trade union movement, individual unions retain a large degree of autonomy and the ICTU relies on the co-operation of affiliated unions in promoting its overall goals (Wallace *et al.* 2004). The ICTU plays an extremely important role at national level, representing union views to Government and other institutions. The ICTU role is particularly significant in centralised pay negotiations. Along with the other social partners (i.e. Government, employer, farming and voluntary sector representatives), it is party to national negotiations on pay and other aspects of social and economic policy. It is the vehicle through which trade unions decide on participation in centralised pay bargaining, approve any agreement thus concluded, and ensure affiliated unions adhere to the terms of such agreements. The ICTU also represents trade unions on several national bodies and provides union nominees for conciliation and arbitration services.

Ultimate decision-making power within Congress is vested in the ADC, where delegates from affiliated unions consider various resolutions presented by union delegates. Those adopted become ICTU policy. The executive is responsible for policy execution as well as general administration. A number of important committees operate under the auspices of the ICTU. A Disputes Committee deals with inter-union disputes in relation to union membership. The Demarcation Tribunal deals with inter-union disputes in relation to work boundaries. The Industrial Relations Committee has the particularly important responsibility of granting an 'all-out picket' in industrial disputes. An 'all-out picket' requires that all union members employed in the organisation with which the dispute exists, do not pass the picket (provided that the picket is peaceful, at the place of work of the employer and 'in contemplation or furtherance of a trade dispute'). Furthermore, a secret ballot of all union members must be held and the aggregate majority must be in favour of such industrial action. Individual unions can only sanction a 'one union picket', whereby only members of the union in dispute are obliged not to pass.

Trade Union Membership

A major indicator of the role of trade unions in a country is the level of trade union membership. In 2004 Ireland had some forty-five trade unions catering for a membership of over 521,000 people. The most commonly used indicator of trade union penetration is *trade union density*, which gauges the proportion of 'unionisable' workers currently in membership of trade unions. It is normally based on two measures:

1. *Workforce density:* this measures the percentage of the total civilian workforce (i.e. including those employed and those seeking employment) who are trade union members.
2. *Employment density:* this measures the percentage of civilian employees in the labour force (excluding the self-employed, security forces and assisting relatives) who are trade union members.

Table 11.1 outlines trends in trade union density in Ireland over the period 1925–90. This data indicates that aggregate trade union membership increased, more or less progressively, from the 1930s right up to 1980 (for a detailed review of trends in trade union membership in Ireland see Roche 1997b; Roche and Ashmore 2002). There was then a significant decline in union membership from 1980. This decline in union membership is principally attributed to macro-economic factors: economic depression, increased unemployment, changes in employment structure involving the decline or stagnation of employment in traditionally highly unionised sectors (such as areas of the public sector and 'traditional' manufacturing, e.g. textiles) and growth in sectors traditionally more union-averse, such as private services and areas of 'high-technology' manufacturing such as electronics (Roche 1997b; Roche and Larragy 1989; Roche and Ashmore 2002). In addition to these factors, it is also likely that developments at enterprise level also contributed to this decline, most notably changes in management approaches to industrial relations. Of particular significance in this respect was the growth in union avoidance strategies on the part of employers (Gunnigle, O'Sullivan and Kinsella 2002; McGovern 1989a).

Table 11.1 Trends in trade union density 1925–90

Year	Membership	Employment Density %	Workforce Density %
1925	123,000	21.2	18.7
1930	99,450	20.0	20.0
1935	130,230	22.6	18.6
1940	151,630	26.2	23.0
1945	172,340	27.7	25.3
1955	305,620	45.7	41.6
1965	358,050	52.4	48.8
1975	449,520	60.0	53.2
1980	527,960	62.0	55.3
1985	485,040	61.3	47.5
1990	474,590	57.1	45.0

Source: Derived from UCD DUES Data Series

Table 11.2 outlines more detailed data on trends in trade union membership, for the period 1994–2004.[1] Union membership increased from almost 433,000 in 1994 to over 521,000 in 2004. This increase in membership clearly reflects the progressive and significant increase in employment levels over this period. However, when we look at trends in trade union density we find a much less positive picture. In 1994 employment density was 45.8 per cent but this had fallen to 34.6 per cent by 2004. Historically, employment growth has positively impacted on trade union density in Ireland. Clearly this has not been the case in the boom years since the mid-1990s and represents a very worrying trend for Irish trade unions. Taking a longer-term perspective, the 2004 figure for employment density represents a fall of over 27 percentage points since the high point of 1980, when employment density reached 62 per cent.[2] It should be noted that the union membership figures supplied by the CSO and outlined in table 11.2 are much lower than those previously available from the Department of Enterprise, Trade and Employment (DETE) and used in previous publications (cf. Wallace *et al.* 2004).[3]

1. Note that the data from tables 11.1 and 11.2 come from different sources. The former draws on University College Dublin's DUES data series, while the latter is based on the latest CSO Quarterly National Household Survey and indicates a lower level of union density than previously estimated.
2. As the data on union density for 1980 and 2004 are from different sources, the drop of 27.4 percentage points is an estimate.
3. For example, the DETE quoted a membership figure of 641,600 for 2003 whereas the equivalent CSO figure was 555,500. Dobbins (2005a) accounts for the difference by the fact that the DETE figures are based on negotiating license returns at the end of each year, and are likely to include large numbers of lapsed, inactive or retired union members.

Table 11.2 Trade union density 1994–2004

Year	Membership	Employment Density (%)
1994	432,900	45.8
1995	446,900	44.7
1996	468,600	44.5
1997	463,600	42.3
2001	534,900	38.0
2002	521,400	36.1
2003	555,500	37.6
2004	521,400	34.6

Note: Figures on union membership and density for the years 1998–2000 are not available from the CSO.

Source: CSO Quarterly National Household Survey

In comparison to other countries however, we find that levels of union density in Ireland are in the middle to lower range. As illustrated in table 11.3, the level of trade union density in Ireland compares favourably with union density in a number of Eastern European countries, Spain and the US. It is somewhat lower than union density in Austria and Slovenia and considerably lower than Nordic and Scandinavian countries, Romania, Malta, Italy and Cyprus.

Table 11.3 International trade union density 2004

Density Rate Categories (%)	Countries
Over 90	Romania
80–89	Belgium, Denmark, Finland, Sweden
70–79	Italy, Norway
60–69	Cyprus, Malta
50–59	Luxembourg
40–49	Austria, Slovenia
30–39	Hungary, Ireland, Portugal
20–29	Bulgaria, Germany, Greece, the Netherlands, Slovakia, the UK; New Zealand, Japan
10–19	Estonia, Latvia, Poland, Spain, United States

Source: Figures for Europe from http://www.eiro.eurofound.eu.int/2004/03/update/tn0403105u.html; Figures for USA, Japan and New Zealand from Wallace *et al.* 2004

When we look at the distribution of trade union membership in Ireland by size of union we find considerable imbalance as illustrated in table 11.4. At one extreme, a small number of large unions account for the majority of union membership in Ireland, while at the other we find a large number (twenty-seven) of small unions that together cater for just under 10 per cent of total union membership in Ireland. This may be a vindication of Government policy in the Industrial Relations Act 1990 to encourage the reduction of small unions (see discussion below on trade union mergers).

Table 11.4 Trade union membership by size of union 2004

No. of Members	No. of Unions	% of Total Membership
Under 1,000	11	0.8
1,000–4,999	13	5.1
5,000–9,999	3	3.5
10,000–19,999	8	19.3
20,000 or over	6	71.2

Note: there were 45 unions registered in 2004 but four did not make returns to the Department of Enterprise, Trade and Employment

Source: Department of Enterprise, Trade and Employment

A related and important development in regard to Irish trade union structure over recent decades has been the increase in trade union merger activity. This relates to situations where two or more unions join together. The aggregate number of trade unions in the Republic of Ireland has declined dramatically in recent years, falling from eighty-six unions in 1980 to forty-five unions in 2004 (see table 11.5). The merger of the two largest trade unions in the country in 1990 to form SIPTU was probably the most significant trade union merger in Ireland.

Table 11.5 Number of trade unions in Ireland 1980–2004

Year	Number of Unions	Year	Number of Unions	Year	Number of Unions
1980	86	1994	56	2000	46
1985	77	1995	56	2001	46
1990	67	1996	56	2002	46
1991	62	1997	55	2003	46
1992	59	1998	47	2004	45
1993	59	1999	46		

Source: Department of Enterprise, Trade and Employment

TRADE UNION MEMBERSHIP AT ORGANISATION LEVEL

While national statistics provide us with an overall picture of trade union density, it is necessary to look at union membership levels at organisation level to gain insights into the operational role and impact of trade unions. The levels of trade union membership and the extent of trade union recognition are key indicators of the nature of enterprise level employee relations.

The Cranfield-University of Limerick (CUL) study[4] conducted in 1992, 1995 and 1999 investigated HRM and industrial relations practices in large and medium-sized Irish

---

4. The Cranfield-University of Limerick (CUL) Study of Human Resource Management in Ireland forms part of the Cranfield Network (Cranet) on International HRM, first established in 1989 and currently involving twenty-six participating countries. The Irish node of this study is located at the Employment Relations Research Unit at the University of Limerick and is directed by Michael Morley, Patrick Gunnigle and Tom Turner. For a summary of data emanating from the international study see Brewster and Hegewisch (1994); for a review of the 1992 Irish data see Gunnigle, Flood, Morley and Turner (1994), and for the 1995 data see Gunnigle, Morley, Clifford and Turner (1997).

organisations. Respondents were asked to indicate the proportion of the workforce in their organisation that was in membership of a trade union. These findings are summarised in figure 11.4. If we take a point-in-time perspective, one might argue that this data indicates that union density levels among larger organisations in Ireland are reasonably high: in 1999 over half the organisations reported that 50 per cent or more of their employees were trade union members. However, it should be noted that the CUL study covers organisations with fifty or more employees and thus only provides insights into employee relations and HRM among larger organisations in Ireland. Turning to levels of union density, we find a pattern of progressive decline. In the first survey (1992), two thirds of organisations reported that 50 per cent or more of their workforce were trade union members: by 1999 this had fallen by some 13 per cent.

Figure 11.4 Proportion of workers in membership of a trade union

Source: Cranfield-University of Limerick (1992, 1995, 1999).

As in the previous phases of the CUL survey, the 1999 data reveals that levels of union density remain particularly high in the public sector. The difference in union density is clearly outlined in figure 11.5, which compares union membership levels in private and

Figure 11.5 Proportion of workers in membership of a trade union: private versus state sector state or semi-state organisations. These findings are in line with previous studies; for example, in 1996 Hourihan estimated that union density in the public service was approximately 80 per cent but only around 36 per cent in the private sector. Using more CSO data, Dobbins (2005a) argues that the level of private sector density is now much lower, estimating private sector employment density at between 21 and 23 per cent, while the equivalent public sector level is in the approximate range of 75 to 80 per cent.

Trade Union Recognition

Trade union recognition represents a critical barometer of 'collectivism' in industrial relations. This is particularly the case in Ireland, which has no mandatory legal procedure for dealing with union recognition claims (see the discussion later in this chapter). As we noted earlier, while the Irish Constitution supports the right of workers to join trade unions, there is no legal obligation on employers to recognise or bargain with such unions, with the exception of the Protection of Employment Act 1977, in cases of collective redundancies. Thus the granting of recognition remains largely an issue to be worked out voluntarily between employers and trade unions and ultimately depends on whether or not employers agree to recognise and bargain with a trade union representing all or a proportion of its workforce. In addition to data on trade union density, therefore, trends in regard to trade union recognition thus provide another important indicator of trade union penetration.

Salamon (1998, 175) defines trade union recognition as:

> . . . the process by which management formally accepts one or more trade unions as the representative(s) of all, or a group, of its employees for the purpose of jointly determining terms and conditions of employment on a collective basis.

He further describes such recognition as:

> . . . perhaps the most important stage in the development of an organisation's industrial relations system . . . it confers legitimacy and determines the scope of the trade union's role.

By securing recognition an employer acknowledges the right of a trade union to represent and protect their members' interests in the workplace and to become jointly involved in regulating key aspects of the employment relationship. As Torrington and Hall (2005, 492) specifically comment, trade union recognition represents 'an almost irrevocable movement away from unilateral decision making by management'.

Turning to empirical evidence, data from the 1999 CUL study finds what at first might seem a reasonably healthy picture of trade union recognition in Ireland (see table 11.6). Some 69 per cent of participating organisations recognised trade unions for collective bargaining purposes. However, when we look at the trend in regard to trade union recognition, we find that the proportion of organisations that recognise trade unions fell from 83 per cent in the first survey (1992), to the current level of 69 per cent, a fall of 14 per cent over a seven-year period. We should again add the important caveat that the CUL study covers only larger organisations, excluding those with fewer than fifty employees. Moreover, we also know that much of Ireland's business activity takes place among small firms employing fewer than fifty workers. It is well established in the literature that union penetration is lower in smaller organisations; consequently, union recognition in the small firm sector is likely to come in well below the CUL figures presented in table 11.6.

Table 11.6 Trade union recognition in larger organisations 1992–99

Trade Union Recognition	1992	1995	1999
Yes	83% (186)	80% (205)	69.2% (296)
No	17% (38)	20% (50)	30.8% (132)

N.B. Actual numbers in parentheses.

Source: Cranfield-University of Limerick (1992, 1995, 1999).

By and large, the national statistics and data from the CUL study present a mixed picture of trade union penetration in Ireland. Looking at trends in regard to aggregate levels of trade union density we find a picture of steady decline since 1980. A similar picture emerges from our review of trade union membership levels within organisations. However, while there is some decline in the numbers of workers in membership, the evidence also indicates that most of the larger organisations are characterised by reasonably high levels of union penetration. In the 1999 CUL study, seven in ten organisations recognised trade unions for collective bargaining purposes, while over one third report that 75 per cent or more of their workforce are trade union members. Thus, whilst the evidence indicates a decline in union penetration, the case remains that reasonably high levels of trade union recognition and density characterise most of Ireland's larger organisations. We have already seen that union penetration tends to be strongest in the public service and in 'traditional' manufacturing. It is therefore useful to look outside these sectors to better inform our understanding of trade union penetration.

Some of the most interesting evidence on trends in trade union recognition emerges from research on more recently established companies. In reviewing developments in Ireland we can draw on survey and interview data from a representative sample of firms in the manufacturing and internationally traded services sectors, which were established at greenfield sites over a ten-year period 1987–97.[5] Given the profile of the greenfield site population and, particularly, the prevalence of both US and 'high-technology' firms, one would anticipate a high incidence of non-union firms. As can be seen from figure 11.6, this was indeed the case with over 65 per cent of firms not recognising trade unions. This evidence is indicative of significant growth in union avoidance among large greenfield start-ups in Ireland. Given that the incidence of non-union approaches was significantly higher in the second phase of the study, the findings also reflect the progressive diminution of union penetration in greenfield firms over the ten-year period studied (91 per cent of firms were non-union in the second phase while the corresponding figure for the first phase was 53 per cent).

Non-unionism is clearly most prevalent amongst multinationals of US origin in high-technology industries. This factor is commonly attributed both to the prevalence of a unitarist managerial ideology among US-owned companies and to the competitive nature of the technology sector and the consequent managerial preference for maintaining high levels of numerical and functional flexibility (Roche and Gunnigle 1997; Toner 1987).

---

5. The study excluded firms with fewer than 100 employees and was gathered in two distinct phases. Phase 1 covered all qualifying greenfield site firms established in the period 1987–92, while the second phase covered those established in the period 1993–97. Altogether, the greenfield site data set draws on information from seventy-six greenfield firms (fourty-four US, thirteen Irish, ten European, nine 'other foreign'). For more details, see Gunnigle 1995; Gunnigle, Morley and Turner 1997; Gunnigle, MacCurtain and Morley 2001.

Figure 11.6 Trade union recognition in greenfield sites by ownership 1987–97

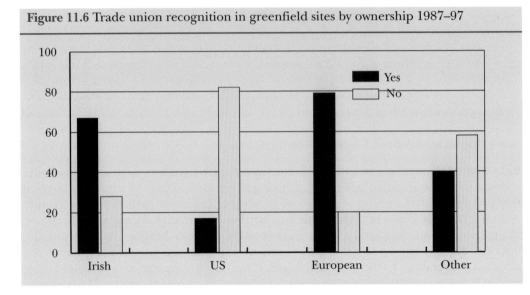

Looking at the longitudinal pattern of union recognition in greenfield sites, it appears that non-union approaches began to take off in the early 1980s, became significantly more commonplace as the decade progressed, and are now characteristic of the great majority of greenfield site firms in the manufacturing and internationally traded services sector in Ireland (Gunnigle 1995; Gunnigle *et al.* 2001). While the early non-union firms were predominantly US-owned and located primarily among 'high-tech' firms (mostly electronics, software and internationally traded services), more recent evidence from the early 1990s points to the broader diffusion of union avoidance to embrace both Irish and other foreign-owned firms, and a broader range of industrial sectors (Gunnigle *et al.* 2005). It is all the more revealing that this decline in union penetration in new firms has occurred during an era when the trade union movement has exerted significant influence in shaping economic and social policy and when economic growth and employment creation have been exceptionally high.

Alternatives to Trade Unions

Before completing our discussion of trade unions, it should be noted that while trade unions have been the most conspicuous means of representing employee interests, there are a number of alternative approaches that workers may adopt.

Workers may deal with employers on an individual basis (*individual bargaining*). This may be attractive to workers who are in a strong bargaining position, especially those in possession of particular skills or knowledge that is highly valued by employers. This may particularly be the case when certain categories of labour are in short supply and where workers in such categories and possessing valued skills can command favourable terms and conditions of employment through direct dealings with employers. Individual bargaining may also be attractive in organisations where management place a high priority on individual employee needs and provide attractive pay and conditions of employment. More generally, however, it is felt that individual workers are at a severe disadvantage in bargaining terms vis-à-vis employers and, consequently, individual bargaining is not an optimal approach for most workers. Indeed, this has been a traditional selling point of trade unions: that collective employee representation through trade unions serves to counter-balance employer bargaining power and thus redresses the perceived bargaining disadvantage of the individual worker.

Another alternative for workers is to form work-based staff associations or groups to represent their interests to employers. Company-based *staff associations* usually represent employee interests through consultation with senior management on employee relations issues. They have traditionally been associated with white-collar grades, particularly professional and managerial categories, who are not trade union members. The use of staff associations is often seen as an improvement on individual bargaining. By joining together, it is argued, workers can present a more united front to employers. An important consideration, particularly among some employers, is that staff associations provide for a modicum of collective employee representation without the introduction of a 'third party' (a trade union) into management-employee relations.

Employees may also prefer to join staff associations on occasion. For example, the traditional perception of trade unions as catering for blue-collar workers may create a 'snob' value that encourages employees to join or remain in staff associations. Employers may also perceive staff associations as less difficult to deal with and less likely to engage in confrontational or adversarial employee relations approaches. Employers may thus see staff associations as 'easier' bargaining partners. However, work-based staff associations have been criticised because of their lack of independence from the organisation. Another disadvantage is the absence of an external organisational structure and resources with which to provide bargaining expertise or legal advice.

Table 11.7 Trade unions and staff associations: contrasts

	Trade Unions	**Staff Associations**
Objectives	1. Replace individual bargaining with collective bargaining 2. Pay and employment conditions 3. Political objectives	1. Similar but less ideological commitment 2. Yes 3. No
Controlling authority	Union headquarters; normally strong role for ICTU	No external authority
Rules/ Procedures	Detailed constitution often with strong political dimension	None or brief constitution; oriented to firm
External resources	Access to external expertise and resources. Influence on national issues (e.g. via centralised agreements on pay and other social/economic issues)	None except by contracting in external expertise. No explicit means of influence on national issues.
Methods	Collective bargaining, often with adversarial orientation	More consultative orientation
Use of sanctions	Prepared to use strike weapon	Most unlikely
Services to members	May have range of services	None or limited range

✳Traditional trade unionists generally take a cynical view of staff associations, viewing them as a poor apology for real trade union organisation. These factors may often combine to limit the bargaining power of staff associations in their interactions with management. Some of the major contrasts between trade unions and staff associations are summarised in table 11.7. It is important to note that these generalisations may not characterise all trade unions or staff associations.

ROLE OF THE STATE

This section considers the role of the state in Irish employee relations. It focuses on the four main methods by which the state may intervene in employee relations:

1. in terms of overall employee/industrial relations policy;
2. as a provider of dispute resolution machinery;
3. as a legislator; and
4. as an employer.

Policy: State Approaches to Employee Relations

Before reviewing the Irish context let us first consider the range of options that Governments may pursue in the employee relations sphere. Crouch (1982) provides a useful framework of four policy alternatives or approaches which may be pursued by the state, namely: (i) market individualism, (ii) liberal collectivism, (iii) corporatism and (iv) bargained corporatism. Crouch sees these alternative approaches as expressions of the inter-relationship between the dominant political and economic ideology vis-à-vis employee relations, the relative power and autonomy of trade unions and the nature of employer-employee relations (see table 11.8).

Table 11.8 State approaches to employee relations			
	Political ideology	**Trade unions**	**Employer-employee relationships**
Market individualism	laissez-faire	weak and regulated	exploitative or paternalistic
Liberal collectivism	liberal	strong and autonomous	voluntarist, free collective bargaining
Corporatism	corporatist	weak and regulated	subordinated and controlled, trade unions agents of control
Bargained corporatism	interventionist	strong and autonomous	voluntarist and tripartite

Source: Adapted from Rollinson (1993).

With *market individualism* the dominant political and economic philosophy is that of laissez-faire. This philosophy sees the market forces of supply and demand as the ultimate arbitrator of the competitive interests of capital and labour. Labour is seen as a commodity to be bought or sold at a price to be determined by the market mechanism. Trade union interventions in the form of collective bargaining are seen as distorting the operation of the market and are treated with open hostility by employers favouring such a strategy. The laissez-faire option means mitigating trade union strength other than by means of compromise and agreements, typically by increased legislation aimed at placing legal limitations on trade union freedoms. Hence trade unions under market individualism tend to be weak and regulated. Thus, as Crouch (1982) points out, market individualism subordinates employees to the control and authority of the owner and the relationship between them is at best paternalistic but at worst exploitative. In keeping with the laissez-faire doctrine, direct involvement by the state in employee relations matters is avoided. Roche (1997b) refers to this state approach as a 'market control' strategy, which sees the Government's role as supporting the re-construction of competitive labour markets and controlling inflation and hence wage settlements by managing the money supply.

Liberal collectivism describes a framework in which a liberal political ideology co-exists with the development of strong autonomous trade unions. Such an accommodation sees the acceptance (by management) of autonomous trade unions that represent, bargain and reconcile conflicting interests with management through the collective bargaining process. However, as Salamon (1998) points out, the dominant interests of management are protected through the establishment of a boundary between issues to be decided by collective bargaining and issues to be determined by managerial prerogative. The concepts of 'voluntarism' and 'pluralism' are central to this state approach. In this approach the parties to employee relations insist on settling their own affairs without state interference. Roche (1997b) classifies this state approach as 'auxiliary state control'. The role of the state is primarily facilitative, confined to providing dispute resolution institutions to aid the reconciliation of conflicts of interests that arise, and legislating to provide employees with a 'floor of rights' or minimum standards, which of course can be improved upon through collective bargaining between employers and trade unions.

Corporatism as an employee relations concept has its origins in a broader model of society, whereby the state functions in co-operation with organised social interest groups. As such it was intended to chart a middle ground between liberal capitalism and state totalitarianism. Roche (1989) defines corporatism:

> . . . as a strategy or model of public policy-making in which the state seeks to co-opt the leadership of social interest groups into policy formulation in return for assurances that the latter will seek to deliver their respective constituencies when it comes to the implementation or execution of policies developed in central talks or agreements.

Lehmbruch *et al.* (1982) attribute the following characteristics to a full corporatist system:

1. Interest organisations are strongly co-opted into governmental decision making.
2. Large interest organisations (in particular unions) are strongly linked to political parties and take part in policy formation.
3. Most interest organisations are hierarchically structured and membership tends to be compulsory.
4. Occupational categories are represented by non-competitive organisations enjoying a monopoly.
5. Industrial relations are characterised by strong concentration of unions and employers' associations with the government involved.

Two types of corporatism have been identified: (i) state corporatism; and (ii) bargained corporatism. *State* or *pure corporatism* is facilitated by a concentration of powers in government, monopoly forms of capital, the absence of associations of labour and political systems with a single party. This form of corporatism either involves massive state coercion or sufficient societal unity to make coercion unnecessary. In particular a unity of view must exist among employers, the state and the trade union leadership. The corporate state is one that is often associated with totalitarian regimes of fascist Italy and Germany in the 1930s and 1940s, and countries of the former Soviet bloc.

Bargained corporatism, often referred to as societal or liberal corporatism, describes a state approach to employee relations that evolves in the presence of a dominant interventionist political ideology and strong autonomous trade unions. It represents the outcome of centrally organised interest groups and of open political systems. Such an approach involves increased Government consultation, negotiation or political exchange with both employers' associations and organised labour through established tri-partite corporatist forums at national level. This approach involves the Government, in effect, becoming a third party to the collective bargaining process interposed between the trade union movement and employers' association. It is the voluntary nature of bargained corporatism and the consequent lack of compulsion and independence of trade unions that differentiates it from pure corporatism.

State Approaches in Ireland: a Summary Overview

The dominant state approach to industrial relations in Ireland at the beginning of this century was market individualism. However, the increased 'collectivisation' of employee relations, specifically increased worker organisation into trade unions, prompted a change to liberal collectivism or what Roche (1997b) terms 'auxiliary state control'. This is in line with our earlier observation that Government approaches to employee relations in Ireland were traditionally grounded in the so-called 'voluntarist' tradition. This is generally taken to indicate an approach in which the role of the state in employee relations was restricted to the establishment of legislative ground rules and the provision of mediation and arbitration machinery, leaving employers and employers' association and employees and trade unions free to develop procedures and terms and conditions to suit particular organisational contexts.

Therefore, Governments tended to adopt a 'hands off' approach in regard to interactions between employers and workers or trade unions, who were then left comparatively free to engage in collective bargaining and come to their own agreements on issues such as pay increases and working conditions. The state tended to become involved only when conflict occurred (e.g. by providing conciliation services) or when one party was in a dominant power position (e.g. by laying down basic terms and conditions of employment in a particular industrial sector where trade union organisation was weak: see discussion on Joint Labour Committees below). This approach was largely a historical legacy of the British voluntarist tradition.

In discussing state strategies towards employee relations in the post-World War II period, Roche (1989) argues that there has been a drift from auxiliary state control to attempts at greater corporate control. He argues that this has occurred in two fairly distinct phases. The first phase, which occurred during the 1960s, saw trade unions becoming involved in a number of largely consultative bodies such as the Employer Labour Conference and the National Industrial and Economic Council. Throughout this period, however, liberal collectivism and 'collective bargaining remained inviolate' with any attempt by the state to intervene in pay determination being perceived as hostile by the trade unions, who used the threat of withdrawing from these consultative bodies as a means of repelling such corporatist advances. Roche suggests that it was during this phase that the strategic and institutional basis for further state intervention in employee relations was established.

The second phase involved the negotiation of a series of National Wage Agreements and two tri-partite National Understandings beginning in 1970 and continuing into the early 1980s. This period was characterised by more active state involvement in the process of collective bargaining, together with trade union participation in the process of government. Liberal collectivism or the auxiliary state re-surfaced for a short period between 1982 and 1986 with a return to decentralised bargaining. However, as we saw earlier, 1987 saw the negotiation of the first in a series of national agreements (the Programme for National Recovery (PNR)), which have continued to the most recent agreement, Sustaining Progress. In evaluating this growth in bargained corporatism in Ireland some background is useful, specifically in relation to developments since the turn of the 1980s.

We have already noted the voluntary tradition of employee relations in Ireland and its roots in the British voluntary framework. Consequently the Irish approach closely reflected the British context. However, by the turn of 1980s it was clear that Government approaches to employee relations in both the UK and Ireland had begun to follow quite different trajectories. In the UK, Conservative Governments took progressive steps, both legislative and otherwise, to reduce union power, lessen the coverage of collective bargaining, and ensure that wage levels and other employee relations outcomes were determined by market forces.

In Ireland, the voluntarist tradition also became increasingly diluted over the period. One important source of this dilution has been the increase in employment legislation and its impact in regulating many aspects of employee relations (see chapter 13). Another key factor impacting on the overall employee relations systems has been the increased level of centralisation, particularly in regard to pay and other aspects of economic and social policy (Roche 1989; 1997b). We have already noted that over the period 1970–82 Ireland had a series of national agreements and understandings on pay and related employment issues. These were initially heralded as important vehicles in delivering wage restraint, reduced industrial conflict and low inflation. However, these agreements failed to deliver, and the period was characterised by high levels of inflation and industrial conflict. Central agreements were abandoned by the somewhat disillusioned social partners (particularly employers) and there was a brief return to decentralised bargaining in the 1982–86 period. With the country locked in a deep recession, the Fianna Fáil administration revived central agreements through the Programme for National Recovery (PNR) in 1987. This period was characterised by very moderate wage increases and increased economic growth. We have since had a series of centralised agreements on pay and aspects of economic and social policy covering issues such as welfare provision, employment creation and tax reform, involving negotiations between the 'social partners' (principally Government, trade unions, employers' association and farming organisations).

This period saw unprecedented levels of economic growth and employment creation (see chapters 1 and 4). Much of the credit for such success has been attributed to centralised agreements, although it is plausible to argue that much of this period would have been characterised by low pay increases and low levels of industrial conflict regardless of whether pay was negotiated centrally or locally. Clearly a range of factors, many related to developments in the world economy, have combined to contribute to Ireland's strong economic performance over this period and one cannot simply attribute this economic success to centralised agreements. Many other contributory factors were mentioned in chapter 1 (such as the growth in foreign direct investment (FDI)), while others, such as monetary and fiscal policy, and the impact of the European Union, are beyond the scope of this text (see, for example, Gray 1997; Tansey 1998). Since the turn of the millennium we have seen increased debate on the effectiveness and stability of centralised agreements, particular in the context of high economic growth such as that experienced in the mid- to late 1990s. As Frawley (2000, 15) observed,

> [there is] an uncomfortable feeling among unions and employers alike that the type of partnership arrangements which have helped build the economy over the last twelve years, structurally cannot handle the demands of an economy growing at the speed with which ours is at the moment.

Despite such concerns, centralised bargaining has continued to date. Over recent years certain groups of public sector employees, in particular, indicated their disappointment at being 'left out of the loop' of economic prosperity. Notable examples of such groups include nurses and teachers. Indeed, the basis for the pay demands of ASTI are indicative of the feelings of other public sector employees. These include a fair share in the current economic prosperity and compensation for increases in the cost of living (ASTI website, www.asti.ie). Such sentiments in 1999 led to the highest number of working days lost since 1990, after an eight-year period of relatively low strike activity. Some observers have been highly critical of the wealth distribution effects of 'social partnership' with Allen (2000) claiming that three traditional linkages involving pay (pay and profit, pay and productivity, and pay and inflation) have been removed. Despite such criticisms, and the pressures brought by a slowing down of the economy and the introduction of benchmarking (see below), national wage agreements have continued and 'social partnership' has remained an integral part of the Irish industrial relations landscape (see chapter 13).

The State as a Provider of Dispute Resolution Machinery

In the area of dispute resolution the state provides a number of specific agencies to address employee relations matters: the Labour Relations Commission, the Labour Court, rights commissioners, Employment Appeals Tribunal, Equality Authority and Equality Tribunal. The passing of the Industrial Relations Act 1990 into legislation introduced a new framework under which some of these institutions must operate.

THE LABOUR RELATIONS COMMISSION

The Labour Relations Commission was established under the Industrial Relations Act 1990. It is a tri-partite body with employer, trade union and independent representation and has been charged with the general responsibility of promoting 'good industrial relations'. The Commission provides a comprehensive range of services designed to help prevent and resolve disputes. The main functions provided by the Labour Relations Commission (LRC) are as follows:

- the conciliation service;
- the advisory service;
- preparation of codes of practice relevant to industrial relations after consultation with unions and employers organisations, and the provision of guidance on such codes of practice;
- selection and nomination of persons for appointment as rights commissioners;

- commissioning research into matters relevant to industrial relations;
- reviewing and monitoring developments in the area of industrial relations;
- assisting joint labour committees and joint industrial councils in the exercise of their functions.

A critical aspect of the work of the Labour Relations Commission is its conciliation service. This service was formerly provided by the Labour Court. The role of conciliation is to assist resolution of cases referred to them by parties in dispute. These are normally issues where the parties have failed to reach agreement or compromise at local level. The relocation of the conciliation service to the Commission in 1991 was designed to give a new impetus to the role of conciliation and to encourage the conflicting parties to take more responsibility for the resolution of disputes. It was hoped that this would encourage the resolution of disputes at the earliest possible stage of the dispute-settling machinery rather than having issues progress almost automatically to a full Labour Court investigation. The normal pattern for an issue to be processed to conciliation and, possibly, to full Labour Court investigation is outlined in figure 11.7.

Figure 11.7 Labour Court referral procedure

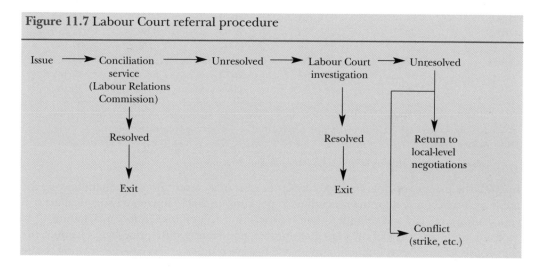

The conciliation process involves an industrial relations officer (IRO) presiding over a meeting of the parties in dispute. Having listened to the parties involved, the IRO may hold separate meetings ('side conferences') with both to get a better idea of the basis for the dispute and what is required to resolve the issue. The IRO can then attempt to guide the parties towards an acceptable solution. Conciliation is essentially voluntary with the IRO acting as a facilitator in the search for an acceptable solution. Success rates in resolving issues at conciliation have fluctuated over the years and there have been frequent criticisms of both the employers and the unions abusing the system through their unwillingness to settle at conciliation. However, conciliation generally has a good track record in resolving disputes, as demonstrated in table 11.9.

Table 11.9 Conciliation service referrals 1971–2004

Year	No. of disputes in which conciliation conferences were held	No. of disputes settled at conciliation (% in parentheses)	Year	No. of disputes in which conciliation conferences were held	No. of disputes settled at conciliation (% in parentheses)
1971	628	429 (68)	1988	1,571	1,064 (68)
1972	713	443 (62)	1989	1,450	1,019 (70)
1973	855	487 (56)	1990	1,552	1,143 (74)
1974	951	646 (68)	1991	1,880	1,598 (85)
1975	1,108	576 (52)	1992	1,935	1,451 (75)
1976	1,071	581 (54)	1993	1,844	1,309 (71)
1977	1,175	638 (54)	1994	1,551	1,028 (66)
1978	1,288	651 (51)	1995	1,692	1,184 (70)
1979	1,301	633 (49)	1996	1,487	1,204 (81)
1980	1,375	693 (50)	1997	1,588	1,318 (83)
1981	1,582	766 (48)	1998	1,563	1,286 (82)
1982	1,855	927 (50)	1999	1,923	1,615 (84)
1983	2,090	1,114 (53)	2000	1,899	1,614 (85)
1984	1,750	1,037 (59)	2001	1,815	1,507 (83)
1985	2,021	1,355 (67)	2002	1,693	1,371 (81)
1986	1,892	1,268 (67)	2003	1,597	1,310 (82)
1987	1,787	1,151 (64)	2004	1,806	1,445 (80)

Note: For the years 1993 and 1996–2003, the number of disputes settled at conciliation are approximations as they have been calculated from the rounded percentage figure.

Source: Labour Court and Labour Relations Commission Annual Reports.

In 2004, the private sector accounted for 52 per cent of all referrals to conciliation while the public sector accounted for the remaining 48 per cent. In 2003,[6] the main issues dealt with at conciliation were pay and remuneration, restructuring and rationalisation and staffing.

While the main focus of the conciliation service is dealing with immediate disputes, the role of the advisory, development and research service (advisory service), according to the LRC (2003, 23), is to assist employers and employees in building and maintaining positive working relationships and to work with them 'to develop and implement ongoing effective problem-solving mechanisms'. Its services include performing industrial relations audits, chairing joint working parties, providing preventative mediation/facilitation and advice, monitoring usage of the Commission's services and drafting codes of practice. While codes of practice are set in a statutory framework they are not directly enforceable in that a breach of the code will not attract any civil or criminal sanction. The codes of practice are intended to give guidance to employers and trade unions on particular issues and are intended to have strong moral authority. To date eight codes of practice have been prepared, on:

1. Disputes procedures, including procedures in essential services.
2. Duties and responsibilities of employee representatives and the protection and facilities to be afforded to them by their employer.

---

6. The LRC Annual Report 2004 does not give details of the issues dealt with at conciliation.

3. Disciplinary and grievance procedures.
4. Compensatory rest periods.
5. Sunday working in the retail trade.
6. Voluntary dispute resolution.
7. Victimisation.
8. Procedures for addressing bullying in the workplace.

Other functions of the LRC are to undertake or commission research, monitor developments in the general employee relations arena and assist *Joint Industrial Councils* (JICs) and *Joint Labour Committees* (JLCs) in the discharge of their functions. In regard to JICs and JLCs, the LRC's main role is to provide industrial relations officers to act as chairpersons of a number of them.

Joint Industrial Councils are permanent voluntary negotiating bodies whose task is to facilitate collective bargaining at industry level in certain industrial sectors. They are composed of representatives of employers and trade unions from within the relevant industrial sector. Joint Industrial Councils may be registered with the Labour Court. At present there are three registered JICs: for footwear, construction and the Dublin wholesale fruit and vegetable trade. There are a number of other JICs, which are not registered with the Labour Court, but only a small number are active. In 2004, meetings took place of one registered JIC (Construction Industry) and of five unregistered JICs (State Industrial Employees, Electrical Contracting Industry, Woollen and Worsted, Hosiery and Knitwear, and Printing) (Labour Court 2004).

Joint Labour Committees are statutory bodies comprised of employer and trade union representatives and independent members which set minimum wages and conditions of employment in areas where collective bargaining is poorly established. The JLC submits proposals to the Labour Court for fixing minimum wage rates or for regulating conditions. If the Court accepts the proposals then it promulgates them in the form of an Employment Regulation Order (ERO), giving statutory effect to the proposals. Employment Regulation Orders are enforced by labour inspectors, appointed by the Minister for Enterprise, Trade and Employment. There are currently nineteen Joint Labour Committees (JLCs) in existence. Joint Labour Committees exist in respect of the following industries: aerated waters, agriculture, brush and broom, catering (excluding Dublin), catering (County Borough of Dublin and Dun Laoghaire), contract cleaning (Dublin), contract cleaning (outside Dublin), hairdressing (Cork), hairdressing (Dublin), handkerchief and household goods, hotels (excluding Dublin and Cork), hotels (Dublin), law clerks, provender milling, retail grocery, security, shirtmaking, tailoring and women's clothing and millinery. JLCs set minimum wages and conditions alongside the National Minimum Wage (NMW) and other statutory employment legislation (Wallace and O'Sullivan 2004). The mid-term review of Part Two of Sustaining Progress provided that a review of JLCs be undertaken and it remains to be seen what effect, if any, such a review will have on JLC operation.

THE LABOUR COURT

The Labour Court is the principal institution in Ireland that facilitates the resolution of trade disputes (Gunnigle *et al.* 1995). It was established under the terms of the Industrial Relations Act 1946 and amended by the Industrial Relations Acts of 1969 and 1976. The Industrial Relations Act of 1990 assigned many of the functions previously held by the Labour Court to the Labour Relations Commission (most notably the conciliation service). The Court has a number of key functions:

- investigating and issuing recommendations on cases referred to it by parties in dispute;
- the registration and variation of certain agreements;
- the establishment and servicing of Joint Labour Committees and the ratification of conditions of employment by these Committees;
- the provision of secretaries for Joint Industrial Councils;
- hearing appeals against a rights commissioner's recommendations and appeals against an equality officer's decision.

The principal role of the Labour Court is to investigate and make recommendations on cases referred to it by parties in dispute. These are normally issues where the parties have failed to reach agreement or compromise at local level. The Industrial Relations Act 1990 provides that the Court may normally investigate a dispute only in one of the following situations:

- if it receives a report from the LRC that no further efforts on its part will help resolve the dispute; or
- if it is notified by the Chairman of the LRC that the LRC has waived its function of conciliation in the dispute. In both of the above cases, the parties to the dispute must also request the Court to investigate the dispute.

The Court may also investigate a dispute:

- if it is hearing an appeal in relation to a recommendation of a rights commissioner or of an equality officer; or
- if it decides, after consultation with the LRC, that the exceptional circumstances of the case warrant a Labour Court investigation;
- if referred to it under Section 20 of the Industrial Relations Act 1969.

In addition the Court may investigate a dispute at the request of the Minister for Enterprise, Trade and Employment.

The Labour Court currently comprises a chairman, two deputy chairmen and six ordinary members. While all these appointments are made by the Minister, ordinary members are nominated for appointment by organisations representing trade unions and employer interests. To facilitate speed of operation, the Labour Court normally sits by *division*. A division of the Court comprises of an independent chairman (chair or deputy chair of the Court) and an employer and union representative. A Labour Court hearing is normally presided over by such a division. Hearings are generally held in private, involve written and oral submissions by the parties, and some element of cross-examination. When the Court feels it has adequately investigated the case it will conclude the hearing and set about issuing a recommendation. The recommendations of the Court are generally not legally binding on the parties to the dispute. Consequently such recommendations may be accepted or rejected by the parties. However, there are some important instances where decisions of the Court are legally binding:

1. Where the Court hears an appeal of the decision of a rights commissioner or an equality officer.
2. Where workers or their trade unions refer a dispute to the Court for investigation under section 20.1 of the Industrial Relations Act 1969 (i.e. where the trade union refers the dispute on its own and agrees to be bound by the Court's recommendation).

3. Disputes under Sustaining Progress.
4. In certain instances under the Industrial Relations (Amendment) Act 2001 and Industrial Relations (Miscellaneous Provisions) Act 2004.

Decisions by the Court on disputes taken under the Industrial Relations (Amendment) Act 2001 are binding with regard to terms and conditions of employment and dispute resolution and disciplinary procedures. It is useful to consider some context in relation to this Act and its linkages to our earlier discussion in regard to trade union recognition. Traditionally, the role of the Labour Court, as the primary dispute resolution body, was to issue non-binding recommendations in union recognition cases that came before it. A trade union also had the option of taking a case to the Labour Court, under section 20.1 of the Industrial Relations Act 1969, whereby any recommendation made would be binding on the union but not the employer. This was used as an attempt to pressure an employer into recognising the union. The lack of statutory provision in relation to trade union recognition has not been a major problem in Irish industrial relations as most medium-sized and large employers have traditionally recognised and concluded collective agreements with trade unions.

However, we saw earlier that the issue of trade union recognition has in recent years become an extremely contentious issue, due to the fall in trade union density throughout the 1980s and 1990s, and to a number of high-profile disputes between unions and employers, such as Pat the Baker and Ryanair. To address the concerns of trade unions, and the Irish Congress of Trade Unions in particular, a high-level group was established under Partnership 2000 to examine the issue. The group issued two reports in 1997 and 1999. The reports culminated in a Code of Practice on Voluntary Dispute Resolution, promulgated in 2000 by the Minister for Enterprise, Trade and Employment, and an Industrial Relations (Amendment) Act 2001. Under the new arrangements it is intended that a voluntary process would be given precedence in a union recognition dispute (as outlined in the code of practice). Under the provisions of the code, the employer and union would negotiate the issue voluntarily with the assistance of the LRC. If this does not resolve the dispute, or bargaining arrangements are non-existent, the provisions of the Industrial Relations (Amendment) Act would come into effect. Under the Act, the Labour Court may investigate the case and issue a non-binding recommendation. Should this, and a subsequent short-term determination, fail to resolve the dispute, the Court may issue a second binding determination. It is important to note that the recommendations and determinations of the Court will not decide on union recognition but on terms and conditions of employment, dispute resolution and disciplinary procedures. Two criticisms of the 2001 Act were that it did not include any provisions on anti-victimisation and there were no time limits on the procedures. To address these issues, the Industrial Relations (Miscellaneous Provisions) Act 2004 and an enhanced Code of Practice on Voluntary Dispute Resolution were introduced. The code of practice sets a target of twenty-six to thirty-four weeks to process cases under the 2001 Act and original code of practice on Voluntary Dispute Resolution. Should the timeframe be breached or exhausted, the 2004 Act allows the Labour Court to investigate such cases. Dobbins (2004a) notes that this timeframe is intended to protect against delaying tactics by employers or a failure to observe the code of practice in good faith. The 2004 Act also reduced the number of steps in the procedural process: for example, it removed the Labour Court's role of reviewing a determination before seeking enforcement of it in the Circuit Court. In relation to anti-victimisation, the 2004 Act states that no employer, employee, trade union or excepted body shall victimise another employee because they are/are not a member of a trade union. Complaints of victimisation may be made to the rights commissioner. Dobbins (2004a, 20) argues that the 2004 Act is 'unlikely to quell the overall furore surrounding trade union recognition, which remains something of a "blot" on the social partnership landscape'.

The 2001 and 2004 Acts also provided for an enhanced role for the Labour Court and involved a further departure from the Court's traditional voluntary position. In spite of the generally non-binding nature of Labour Court recommendations, it has had a very satisfactory record: Kevin Duffy, chairman of the Labour Court, estimates that around three-quarters of its recommendations are accepted by both parties (*Industrial Relations News* 2004, 22). Indeed, even where Labour Court recommendations are rejected, their terms may often form the basis for a solution on return to local level negotiations.

The Labour Court was seen to depart from its broad role of promoting collective bargaining and resolving industrial conflict when it was given the role of the determinant of disputes under the employment equality legislation, notably the Anti-Discrimination (Pay) Act 1974, Employment Equality Act 1977 and, more recently, the Employment Equality Act 1998 (Fennell and Lynch 1993; Wallace *et al.* 2004). Table 11.10 summarises the range of cases that the Labour Court was involved in during 2004.

Table 11.10 Cases completed by the Labour Court in 2004	
Industrial Relations	588
Equality	37
Organisation of Working Time	59
National Minimum Wage	5
Part-time Work	10
Total	**699**

Source: Labour Court Annual Report

THE RIGHTS COMMISSIONER

The appointment and functions of the rights commissioner were approved under the terms of the Industrial Relations Act 1969. The rationale underpinning the establishment of the rights commissioner service was to reduce the workload of the Labour Court and to provide a speedy service to parties in dispute over 'less major industrial relations issues' (Kelly 1989). The rights commissioner service is now attached to the LRC. However, rights commissioners operate independently in the performance of their functions. Rights commissioners are appointed by the Minister for Enterprise, Trade and Employment from a panel submitted by the LRC and, under the terms of the Industrial Relations Act 1969, may investigate a trade dispute provided that:

- it is not a dispute connected with the rates of pay, hours or times of work, or annual holidays of a body of workers;
- it is not a dispute concerning persons who do not have access to the Labour Court;
- a party to the dispute does not object in writing to such an investigation (only available under Industrial Relations Acts and Unfair Dismissals Acts);
- the Labour Court has not made a recommendation about the dispute.

Rights commissioners operate individually and meet the parties in dispute. They are available to parties in dispute provided both agree to such a hearing and agree to accept the commissioner's decision. In practice, rights commissioners mostly investigate disputes concerning individual employees (e.g. discipline or demarcation issues). Hearings are held in private with rights commissioners examining each case on its merits and issuing a written recommendation. A great advantage of this service is its flexibility and accessibility, providing a quick and efficient mechanism for dealing with problems that have proved intractable at local level. An objection to an investigation by a rights commissioner must be notified in writing to the Commissioner within three weeks of the date of notification (by post) that a dispute has been referred. (Only available under Industrial Relations Acts/Unfair Dismissals Acts.)

There are currently five rights commissioners in office. Their role has significantly expanded since 1969 with the enactment of further employment legislation giving them additional functions. They now have a statutory role in investigating cases under a variety of acts, as shown in Table 11.11. A recommendation by a rights commissioner is not legally binding but in practice they tend to be observed by employers and trade unions. However, disputes heard under the Industrial Relations Act 1969 may be appealed to the Labour Court, which can result in a binding order on the parties in the dispute. An appeal against a rights commissioner's recommendation must be notified in writing to the Labour Court within six weeks from the date of the recommendation. Cases in relation to the other acts in which they have a role can be appealed to the Employment Appeals Tribunal. Similarly, an appeal against the recommendation of the rights commissioner under these acts must be made within six weeks. Table 11.11 summarises the work of the rights commissioner service in 2004. It indicates that while rights commissioners deal with a significant number of pieces of legislation, much of their workload is accounted for by four areas: industrial relations, payment of wages, working time and unfair dismissals. In general, the rights commissioner service has been received favourably by all sides of industry (Kelly 1989; O'Leary 2000; Wallace *et al.* 2004).

Table 11.11 Cases Referred under legislation to the Rights Commissioners 2004

Legislation	Number	Percentage of Referrals
Payment of Wages Act 1991	1,538	32.40
Industrial Relations Acts 1969–2001	1,171	24.70
Unfair Dismissal Acts 1977–1993	808	17.00
Organisation of Working Time Act 1997	611	12.90
Terms of Employment Information 1994	245	5.20
Protection of Employees (Fixed Term Work) Act 2003	119	2.50
Protection of Employees (Part Time Work) Act 2001	85	1.80
EC (Safeguarding of Employees Rights on Transfer of Undertakings) (Amendment) Regulations 2003	66	1.40
National Minimum Wage Act 2000	63	1.30
Parental Leave Act 1998	24	0.51
Maternity Protection Act 1994	8	0.17
Industrial Relations (Miscellaneous Provisions) Act 2004	7	0.15
EC (Protection of Employment) Regulations 2000	4	0.08
Carers Leave Act 2001	0	0
Protection of Young Persons (Employment) Act 1996	0	0
Protection of Person Reporting Child Abuse Act 1998	0	0
Adoptive Leave Act 1995	0	0
Competition Act 2002	0	0
Total	**4,749**	**100**

EQUALITY INSTITUTIONS

The Employment Equality Act 1998 made some changes to the structure of the state dispute resolution machinery. It provided for a body, the Equality Authority, to replace the Employment Equality Agency. The functions of the Equality Authority are:

- to work towards the elimination of discrimination in relation to employment;
- to promote equality of opportunity in relation to matters covered under the Act;
- to review the working of the Pensions Act 1990 as regards the principle of equal treatment.

The Equality Authority (www.equalityauthority.ie) fulfils these functions by providing information, undertaking research, drafting codes of practice, conducting equality reviews on companies and providing free legal assistance to claimants in a small number of cases with strategic importance.

Prior to 1998, equality officers, under the auspices of the Labour Relations Commissions, dealt with issues relating to discrimination on the grounds of sex or marital status arising under the terms of the equality legislation (previously the Anti-discrimination (Pay) Act 1974 and the Employment Equality Act 1977). The Employment Equality Act 1998 created the office of the Director of Equality Investigations (ODEI) in the Department of Justice, Equality and Law Reform to act as the main locus for redress under the Employment Equality Act. Under the Employment Equality Act 2004 the ODEI was renamed the Equality Tribunal. Employment equality cases are generally referred to the Equality Tribunal in the first instance. Cases on grounds of gender may initially be referred to the Circuit Court instead of the Tribunal. The Equality Act 2004 removed the Labour Court's previous role of hearing dismissals cases under employment equality legislation. Thus, dismissals cases that the Labour Court commenced investigating prior to July 2004 remain under Labour Court jurisdiction. Any dismissals cases claimed under equality legislation since July 2004 are referred to the Equality Tribunal in the first instance.

The Equality Tribunal assists in resolving equality cases through two services: mediation and investigation. Complaints made under the Employment Equality Acts must be made within six months of an incident, except in the case of equal pay. If the Director of the Equality Tribunal finds that complaints are made in bad faith, frivolous, vexatious, relating to a trivial matter, or misconceived, they may be dismissed (Employment Equality Act 2004). If the Tribunal receives a complaint which it thinks could be resolved by mediation, then it will ask the complainant and respondent to indicate in writing whether they have any objection to trying mediation (Equality Tribunal Annual Report 2003). Mediations are conducted by equality mediation officers. Mediations are conducted in private and any settlements are not published. Once the parties have signed a settlement, it is legally binding and may be enforced through the Circuit Court. Table 11.12 shows the mediation activity of the Equality Tribunal for the years 2002–2003.

Table 11.12 Mediation case referrals to Equality Tribunal 2002 and 2003

	2003		2002	
	Cases	**Claimants**	**Cases**	**Claimants**
Single	52	52	51	51
Multiple	1	2	4	11

If the mediation is unsuccessful, or either party objects to it, a complaint may proceed to investigation. Investigations are quasi-judicial processes that are carried out by tribunal equality officers. Each party makes a submission to the equality officer before a hearing. The equality officer then makes legally binding, published decisions. Where discrimination is found to have taken place, redress options open to an Equality Officer are compensation, equal treatment, equal pay, arrears of equal pay, an order that the respondent take a specified course of action, and an order for re-instatement or re-engagement with or without compensation. A decision of an equality officer can be appealed to the Labour Court within forty-two days or to the High Court on a point of law. The Labour Court's decision can also be appealed to the High Court on a point of law. Enforcement of a decision of an equality officer or the Labour Court is through the Circuit Court. Table 11.13 shows the number of individual and grouped claims made under each discriminatory ground in 2003. In total, sixty decisions were made by Equality Officers, the results of which were: forty-two were in favour of the respondent and fifteen were in favour of the claimant. In two cases, the Tribunal decided that it had no jurisdiction and there was a split decision in one case (Equality Tribunal Annual Report 2003).

Table 11.13 Claims made under Employment Equality Acts to Equality Tribunal 2003

Discriminatory Ground	Individual claims	Grouped claims
Gender	107	61
Age	32	32
Disability	36	31
Race	85	35
Traveller Community	3	3
Marital Status	2	2
Family Status	8	4
Sexual Orientation	4	4
Religion	1	1
No grounds	7	7
Multiple Grounds	76	64
Total	**361**	**244**

The Employment Appeals Tribunal

The Employment Appeals Tribunal (EAT) was originally established as the Redundancy Appeals Tribunal under the terms of the Redundancy Payments Act 1967. The Minimum Notice and Terms of Employment Act 1973 extended the jurisdiction of the Tribunal to claims brought under that Act by dismissed employees for compensation or loss sustained by them by reason of their employer's failure to give them the statutory period of notice. It was later renamed the EAT under the terms of the Unfair Dismissals Act 1977, which further extended its work to incorporate claims for redress for unfair dismissals. The EAT currently adjudicates upon and interprets a number of other Acts, including the Maternity Protection Act 1994, Protection of Employees (Employers Insolvency) Acts 1984–91, the Payment of Wages Act 1991, the Worker Protection (Regular Part-time Employees) Act 1991, the Parental Leave Act 1998 and the Organisation of Working Time Act 1997. The EAT may also hear appeals of the decisions of rights commissioners. In 2002, 6,259 referrals (direct claims and appeals) were made to the EAT. Over 63 per cent of those referrals were made under the Minimum Notice and Terms of Employment Acts. A significant percentage was also made under the Unfair Dismissals Acts (21 per cent).

The EAT comprises a chairman, who must be a practising barrister or solicitor, and twenty-two vice-chairmen, all appointed by the Minister for Enterprise, Trade and Employment. It also includes a panel of thirty employer members and twenty-eight (with two vacancies) employee members. These members are nominated by employers' associations and the Irish Congress of Trade Unions respectively. The EAT normally sits in divisions. Each division consists of a chairman or vice-chairman and one member from the employer and trade union sides. A clerk, whose function is to offer mainly administrative support to the tribunal, attends each EAT hearing.

Applications to the EAT are made on special forms available from the tribunal or the Department of Enterprise, Trade and Employment. Applicants to the EAT may present their case in person, may be represented by counsel or a solicitor or by a representative of a trade union or employer's association (Fennell and Lynch 1993). Of the 1,222 cases heard by the EAT in 2002, 963 employees (78.8 per cent) were represented (348 by trade unions, 578 by solicitor and/or counsel and 37 by other persons) and 695 employers (56.9 per cent) were represented (82 by employer organisations, 448 by solicitor and/or counsel and 165 by other persons) (Employment Appeals Tribunal 2002). Employees must observe the time limits specified by the Act under which they apply – otherwise they may lose their right to bring a claim.

The procedures adopted by the EAT follow court procedures to a certain degree, but there is a greater amount of informality. Under the various regulations it is possible for parties at an EAT hearing to make an opening statement, call witnesses, cross-examine any witnesses called by any other party, give evidence and address the tribunal at the close of the evidence. Evidence is normally given under oath. Hearings of the EAT are usually held in public, but may be held *in camera* (in private) at the request of either party. The decision ('determination') of the EAT can be given at the close of the hearing, but is more usually issued some time later in written form. Should an employer fail to carry out the terms of an EAT determination, proceedings may be taken by the Minister for Enterprise, Trade and Employment to the Circuit Court in order to ensure compliance. For applicants under the unfair dismissals legislation, the EAT issues determinations that may be appealed to the Circuit Court within six weeks. At the Circuit Court the case is heard *de nova*, i.e. there is a full re-hearing of the case. Appeals in relation to the other acts such as redundancy, protection of employees, minimum notice and part-time workers, falling under the jurisdiction of the EAT, can only be made to the High Court on a point of law.

RECENT DEVELOPMENTS IN DISPUTE INSTITUTIONS

As is evident from this review, there is a range of dispute institutions dealing with a multitude of employment rights legislation. Indeed, there has been growing criticism that the structure and functions of the institutions is too complex, with seven bodies dealing with 25 Acts concerned with employment rights and industrial relations. Arising from such concern, a Review Group on the Functions of the Employment Rights Bodies was established in 2003, as provided for in the Programme for Government 2000–7. The Review Group focused its attention on the rights commissioners service, the EAT, the Labour Court, the Equality Tribunal and the Employment Rights Enforcement Unit of the Department of Enterprise, Trade and Employment (not examined in this chapter). The Group issued its report in April 2004 and its main recommendations are listed in figure 11.8.

Following the Group's report, Kevin Bonner, former Secretary General of the Department

> **Figure 11.8** Main recommendations of the Review Group on the Functions of the Employment Rights Bodies
>
> - The establishment of an Implementation Group to drive the change process.
> - The establishment of Working Groups in each institution to improve service delivery.
> - A single point of contact for all institutions reviewed.
> - Provision of mediation service by the rights commissioners.
> - Rights commissioner service and Equality Tribunal to be bodies of first reference.
> - Amalgamation of EAT and Labour Court.

of Enterprise, Trade and Employment, was appointed to assess the degree of support for the recommendations. He recommended that the proposal to have rights commissioners provide a mediation service be dropped due to lack of support. He also recommended that the EAT and Labour Court should not be merged. There was a concern that, should they merge, the Labour Court would evolve into a quasi-judicial body (Fitzgerald, 2005). Instead, Bonner recommended that the EAT should only hear appeals of cases and not cases in the first instance.

In May 2005, the Minister for Labour Affairs, Tony Killeen, announced that a programme of action had been agreed by the Government. The programme outlines that an Employment Rights Group (ERG) will be established and will have a number of functions. It will consider how best to simplify and streamline the complaint, appeal and enforcement procedures across all dispute institutions and examine the possibility of creating a single point of contact for the Labour Court, EAT, LRC and rights commissioners. A significant change to the institutional division of functions, included in the programme, is that the EAT will become an appellate body only and any cases currently heard by the EAT in the first instance will be referred to the rights commissioners. It remains to be seen whether a larger number of cases can be resolved by the rights commissioners or whether it will be used as a stepping stone for parties who may only accept the decision of the EAT. The review of the institutions is being undertaken in conjunction with the consolidation of employment rights legislation, which is also planned by the Government.

THE STATE AS AN EMPLOYER – EMPLOYEE RELATIONS IN THE STATE SECTOR

Apart from its legislative and facilitative functions, the state plays a significant role as the country's major employer. It accounts for approximately one third of all employees in a range of areas, principally composed of the civil service proper, education, local authorities, security forces, and state-sponsored bodies. Trade unions or staff associations represent the bulk of these state-sector employees. In some public sector areas distinctive employee relations features have developed. However, as the Commission on Industrial Relations (1981) noted, personnel and employee relations issues in the public and private sectors are largely similar, and differences that tend to occur are largely in the area of procedural responses (Cox and Hughes 1989).

In relation to the negotiation of pay and conditions of employment, a notable distinction may be drawn between those public sector areas subject to agreed conciliation and arbitration schemes and those that fall within the scope of the Labour Court and the LRC. Conciliation and arbitration (C and A) schemes date from the 1950s. Currently, different schemes operate for categories such as the (non-industrial) civil service, teachers, gardai and the Vocational Educational Committees. A unique feature of the civil service scheme is the network of staff panels that evaluate any claims from recognised unions or staff associations before these are forwarded to conciliation. Conciliation consists of joint councils of management and employee representatives, which consider claims before them and issue an agreed report. The composition and specific role of conciliation councils differ between individual schemes and only specific issues may be referred to conciliation. These generally include pay, allowances, working hours, overtime, grading, and policy on recruitment, promotion, discipline, pensions and sick pay. Most schemes exclude issues relating to individual employees.

The vast majority of issues are resolved at conciliation, but those that are not may proceed to arbitration, provided they are arbitrable under the appropriate C and A scheme. An Arbitration Board normally consists of an agreed chairman (often legally qualified) and two representatives from both the management and staff side. Both sides make detailed written submissions, supplemented by oral submissions, and witnesses may be called as appropriate. The findings of the Board are sent to the Minister for Finance and the other appropriate Minister, who have one month to either approve the report or submit it to the Government. It has the option of accepting the report or moving a Dáil motion to reject or amend it. This latter route is normally seen as an exceptional one. The local authority and health board scheme differs from the above format in that the management or staff side have the option of rejecting the decision of arbitration.

Wallace *et al.* (2004) note that, in recent years, some C and A schemes have been abolished (health services, local authorities and Teachers Union of Ireland (TUI) (academic staff of institutes of technology)) and others have been revised. The schemes were abolished in favour of using the Labour Court and Labour Relations Commission due to their greater flexibility and pragmatism (Frawley 2002).

A notable characteristic of public sector employee relations is the key role of the Department of Finance. It acts as the Government's adviser on matters relating to public sector pay and employment related matters. It will critically review pay claims, lay down appropriate policy guidelines and oversee their implementation through direct and indirect negotiations. The Department represents the state as employer at the Employer-Labour Conference and is involved in many of the conciliation and arbitration hearings. Another important actor on the management side in the public sector is the Local Government and Staff Negotiations Board (LGSNB) whose role is to assist local authorities and health boards in employee relations. Representatives of the board act on behalf of management on the appropriate conciliation and arbitration scheme and in major negotiations with non-officer grades.

A significant development in the state's role of employer was the introduction of benchmarking. Under the Programme for Prosperity and Fairness (PPF), a Public Service Benchmarking Body (PSBB) was established with the task of examining the pay of public service employees against that of comparable private sector employees. It looked at the pay of most public sector employees, with the exception of high-level posts, which were analysed by the Review Body on Higher Remuneration in the Public Sector. The PSBB issued its report in July 2002 and recommended a wide range of pay increases: for example, the basic nursing grade was awarded 8 per cent, top civil servants were awarded 14 per cent and the defence forces 4 per cent. Twenty-five per cent of benchmarking awards was agreed to be paid from December 2001, even before the PSBB issued its report. Under Sustaining Progress, five Performance Verification Groups (PVGs) were established to assess whether affected employees delivered industrial peace and modernisation in exchange for payment of benchmarking payments (Dobbins 2004b). Following rulings from the PVGs, many public servants received a further 50 per cent of benchmarking payments from 1 January 2004. The final 25 per cent of payments was due from 1 July 2005. Under Sustaining Progress, there is a commitment to undertake a second benchmarking review exercise in late 2005. Benchmarking has been one of the most controversial aspects of Irish industrial relations in recent years. Some of the issues under debate have been the difference in increases awarded to public sector groups, the level of modernisation implemented by public sector workers and the impact of payments on public finances.

CONCLUSION

This chapter has considered the nature of employee relations with particular focus on the Irish context. It also considered the role of trade unions and Government in employee relations. The next chapter considers the role of employers and management in employee relations.

12

Employer and Management Approaches to Employee Relations

This chapter focuses on the role of employers and management in employee relations.[1] It initially considers employers' objectives in employee relations. The role of employers' associations is then addressed with particular emphasis on the Irish context. Finally, the chapter considers management approaches to employee relations and reviews some contemporary developments.

EMPLOYERS' OBJECTIVES IN EMPLOYEE RELATIONS

The primary concern for organisations operating in a competitive environment is to maximise organisational performance and generate satisfactory returns for the owners and stakeholders of the enterprise (Wallace *et al.* 2004). Such returns are often expressed in terms of cost effectiveness and, for the commercial organisation, profitability. Thus, the primary goal of the management is to organise the factors of production, including labour, to achieve these objectives. It is difficult to assess the degree to which employers have specific employee relations objectives or adopt related workplace strategies (Thomason 1984; Gunnigle 1995). Organisations vary greatly and a particular organisation's approach to employee relations (and HRM more generally) will be influenced by a range of environmental factors such as historical development and market conditions (see chapter 2). Nevertheless, it is worthwhile considering some general beliefs common among employers. Thomason (1984) identifies the following employer beliefs or objectives in employee relations:

1. *Preservation and consolidation of the private enterprise system.* This has larger political overtones and relates to the concerns of employers to preserve an environment conducive to achieving business objectives at enterprise level. They will be particularly concerned that principles such as private ownership, the profit motive and preservation of managerial authority and control are maintained.

---

1. For a more detailed examination of many of the issues covered in this chapter see chapters 6 and 15 of Wallace, Gunnigle and McMahon, *Industrial Relations in Ireland* (2004).

2. *Achievement of satisfactory returns for the owners.* This relates directly to the organisation's primary business goals. For commercial organisations to survive in the long term, satisfactory profit levels must be achieved. Consequently, managerial approaches and strategies will always be influenced by this primary concern. Non-profit making organisations will be equally concerned with cost-effectiveness and quality.

3. *Effective utilisation of human resources.* An organisation's workforce represents a key management resource and its effective utilisation is central to the management process.

4. *Maintenance of control and authority in decision-making.* Employers will strive to ensure effective control and authority in executing its management role particularly in strategic decision-making.

5. *Establishment and maintenance of satisfactory management-employee relations.* Employers will also strive to maintain good working relations with employees but this must be achieved within the operational constraints of the organisation. The scope to agree attractive remuneration levels and conditions of employment will vary according to the organisation's market position and profitability as well as its HRM philosophy. Good employee relations will be a priority since they are an important ingredient in ensuring the organisation achieves its primary business goals as well as being laudable in itself.

THE ROLE OF EMPLOYERS' ASSOCIATIONS

To help achieve the employer and managerial objectives listed above it is clear that employers are likely to combine collectively for purposes associated with employment and labour matters (Traxler *et al.* 2001). This is especially the case in many European countries where employer associations play a very prominent role. In particular they are seen as a key 'social partner' at EU level, specifically in regard to their involvement in the development of EU social policy (Traxler 2004). This contrasts with the US experience, where 'employers' organisations as a means of advancing employer interests are largely negligible' (Behrens and Traxler 2004, 1).

The major impetus for the growth of employer organisation was the perceived need to react to, and deal with, the 'new unionism'. This helps distinguish employers' associations, whose *raison d'être* was to deal with labour matters, from those associations where trade and commercial reasons are the major focus and which are normally referred to as trade associations. Behrens and Traxler (2004, 1) describe employer associations as '. . . bodies designed to organise and advance the collective interests that employers have in the labour market'. They identify three main types of 'business interest associations':

1. *'Pure' employers' associations,* which specialise in representing only interests related to the labour market and employee relations issues.

2. *'Pure' trade associations,* which represent only product market interests.

3. *'Dual' associations,* which combine the representation of labour market and product market interests. Our focus in this chapter embraces only 'pure' and 'dual' employer associations.

Oechslin (1985) provides a long-standing definition of employers' associations that deal with labour market issues as:

> . . . formal groups of employers set up to defend, represent or advise affiliated employers and to strengthen their position in society at large with respect to labour matters as distinct from commercial matters.

A particular and traditional reason why employers have formed representative associations is to prevent harmful economic competition with each other, particularly in relation to pay, and to counter the power of trade unions. Another reason for the development of such associations was the increasingly complex nature of collective bargaining and employment legislation. Employers' associations also provide a forum for the exchange of views among employers (Thomason 1984; Gunnigle *et al.* 1995; Traxler *et al.* 2004). The main role of employers' associations is to represent employers' views in employee relations and their objectives may be categorised as political, social, economic and employee relations (see figure 12.1).

Figure 12.1 Objectives of employers' associations

1. Political: To effectively represent employers' views to Government, the general public and other appropriate bodies so as to preserve and develop a political, economic and social climate in which business objectives can be achieved.

2. Economic: To create an economic environment that supports the free enterprise system and ensures that managerial prerogative in decision-making is protected.

3. Social: To ensure any social or legal changes best represent the interests of affiliated employers.

4. Employee Relations: To ensure a legislative and procedural environment which supports free collective bargaining and to co-ordinate employers' views and approaches to employee relations matters and provide assistance to affiliated employers.

Employers' associations assume a significant role in representing the interests of employers on national issues. They provide a mechanism through which Governments can solicit the opinions of employers on areas such as labour legislation and are important vehicles for influencing public opinion on more general political matters. This political role is most clearly associated with the desire to influence broad economic decision-making. Employers' organisations will generally support what could be termed conservative economic policies, which serve to protect the interests of employers and ensure freedom from an excess of state intervention in business. In the area of social policy the approach of employers' associations will largely be pragmatic. On the one hand they will generally attempt to prevent, or at least lessen, the effects of protective labour or social legislation such as legal moves towards extending industrial democracy or information disclosure. On the other hand, they will accept some degree of social and legislative reform, provided its perceived effects on the interests of business are not adverse. In their analysis of the role of employer associations in Europe, Behrens and Traxler (2004, 16) conclude that:

> . . . employers' associations play a crucial role in a variety of fields. [They] . . . have an essential function in multi-employer collective bargaining and in bargaining coordination, they pursue political lobbying in a variety of fields, and through their involvement in numerous statutory bodies they participate in shaping various aspects of social and economic life.

With regard to the political influence of employers' associations in Europe, Traxler (2004) finds that it varies according to the collective bargaining system, suggesting that they have much greater involvement in public policy determination in countries where multi-employer and/or national-level bargaining is common (e.g. Ireland and Germany) as compared to systems where single employer bargaining prevails (e.g. the UK).

An outline of the objectives of Ireland's largest employers' association, the Irish Business and Employers' Confederation (IBEC), is outlined in its mission statement in figure 12.2.

Figure 12.2 Mission Statement – Irish Business and Employers' Confederation

IBEC will vigorously promote the interests of Irish business and employers by working to create and sustain a competitive business environment that encourages enterprise and growth.

As the recognised independent voice of business, IBEC is dedicated to meeting member needs by providing leadership and excellent services through its team of professional and committed staff.

The specific role of employers' associations in employee relations may be categorised into four broad areas as follows (Wallace *et al.* 2004).

1. *Exchange of views.* Employers' associations provide a useful forum for opinion exchange and discussion. However, employers may also use associations to develop and agree common policies and strategies in employee relations.
2. *Represent employers' views to Government and its agencies.* Employers' associations provide an important means through which employers may represent their views to Government. For example, they may seek to influence labour legislation and Government policy generally so that the position of affiliated employers is adequately protected. In Ireland this role is executed by the major employers' associations, particularly IBEC, in representing business and employer views. They represent employers' opinions on bodies such as: the National Economic and Social Council, which was established by the Government as a forum for the discussion of the principles relating to the economy; FÁS, the training and employment authority; the National Authority for Occupational Safety and Health, which controls the operation and enforcement of occupational health and safety legislation in Ireland; and the Equality Authority, which is the statutory authority with responsibility for the elimination of discrimination and promotion of equality in employment. Employers' associations also provide representatives of employers' interests for appropriate bi-partite or tri-partite bodies such as arbitration councils, Government commissions, international organisations. In Ireland, IBEC plays the lead role in nominating employers' representatives to such bodies as the Labour Court, the Labour Relations Commission and the Employment Appeals Tribunal.
3. *Representation of Employer Interests to the General Public.* Employers' associations are also involved in representing employers' opinions to the general public on relevant issues such as forthcoming employment legislation.
4. *Provision of Specialised Services to Members.* A major role of employers' associations is the provision of a range of employee relations services to their membership. Sisson (1983) suggests the main employee relations services provided by employers' associations are: (i) negotiation of pay and conditions of employment; (ii) operation of disputes procedures; (iii) advisory and consultancy services; and (iv) representation. This key role is discussed later in this chapter.

EMPLOYERS' ASSOCIATIONS IN IRELAND

As indicated above, employers' organisations in Ireland are classified into two categories, namely *employers' associations* and *trade associations*. While both of these are required to register with the Registrar of Friendly Societies, only employers' associations are involved in employee relations and are required to hold a negotiating license under the terms of the Trade Union Act 1941. In 2004 there were some ten registered employers' associations in Ireland as defined in table 12.1.

Table 12.1 Employers' associations in Ireland 2004

NAME OF ASSOCIATION	MEMBERSHIP
Construction Industry Federation	2,435
Cork Master Butchers' Association	16
Irish Business and Employers' Confederation	3,485
Irish Commercial Horticultural Association	332*
Irish Hotels' Federation	939
Irish Master Printers' Association	40
Irish Pharmaceutical Union	1,605
Irish Printing Federation	48*
Licensed Vintners' Association	750
Society of the Irish Motor Industry	1,817
Total	**11,467**

* Figures are for 2003 as these organisations did not make returns for 2004

Source: Department of Enterprise, Trade and Employment

While the number of employers' associations in Ireland is considerably less than their trade union counterparts, there is clearly a considerable diversity in membership composition. For example, table 12.1 provides examples of traditional masters' associations, industry-based associations and a general association that is national in scope.

The Irish Business and Employers' Confederation (IBEC)
The Irish Business and Employers' Confederation (IBEC) is the largest employers' association in Ireland. Using Behrens and Traxler's (2004) categorisation noted earlier, IBEC is a 'dual' association, combining the representation of the labour market and trade/product market interests. It was formed in 1993 as a result of the merger of the then Federation of Irish Employers (FIE) and Confederation of Irish Industry (CII). IBEC represents business and employers in all matters relating to employee relations, labour and social affairs. It provides services to some 3,500 member businesses and organisations. As the country's major representative of business and employers, IBEC seeks to shape national policies and influence decision-making in a way that protects and promotes the interests of its members. Unlike its predecessors, IBEC's role is not confined solely to employee relations. Rather, it seeks to represent industry in all matters of economic and social policy. A major role of IBEC is to represent employers' interests to Government, other 'social partners' and the general public. It also provides employers' representatives for various national and international bodies. The organisational structure of the Irish Business and Employers' Confederation is outlined in figure 12.3.

Other Employers' Associations in Ireland
The Construction Industry Federation (CIF) is Ireland's second largest employers' association. Unlike IBEC, the CIF is essentially an industry-based association dealing with both trade

and employee relations affairs on behalf of employers in the construction industry. According to 2004 figures, the CIF had a membership of almost 2,500 firms. In the employee relations sphere, the CIF offers advice, information and support on rates of pay, bullying and harassment, data protection and email usage and all employment-related matters. It also represents members at the Labour Court, Employment Appeals Tribunal etc. Most of the remaining employers' associations in Ireland are primarily concerned with trade and commercial issues. However, some also have a strong employee relations dimension.

The *Irish Hotels' Federation* represents employers' interests on the Hotels (excluding Cork and Dublin) Joint Labour Committee and Hotels (Dublin) Joint Labour Committee and provides general employee relations advice to members. However, it does not involve itself in local bargaining.

The *Society of the Irish Motor Industry* provides advice and assistance on HRM and employee relations matters to affiliated members.

The *Licensed Vintners' Association* represents Dublin-based publicans on the Catering (Dublin) Joint Labour Committee and in negotiations on pay and working conditions with the Irish National Union for Vintners and Allied Trades Assistants. It also provides members with a HRM advisory service.

The *Chambers of Commerce of Ireland* (CCI) is an umbrella body for fifty-nine business associations and its main function is to lobby the Government on issues affecting competitiveness and business. Unlike other employer organisations mentioned, the CCI does not hold a negotiation licence and so does not engage in collective bargaining on terms and conditions of employment (and thus is not included in table 12.1). However, in 2004, it set up its own twenty-four-hour HR service in response to 'a growing need from our members for skilled advice and guidance in the increasingly complex area of personnel and employment law' (www.peninsula-uk.com). The service is aimed at small employers who do not have their own HR manager. Among the services provided by 'ChamberHR' is indemnification against representation costs and unfair dismissal and unlawful discrimination awards.

Higgins (2005, 6) argues that this development by CCI 'appears to be a significant challenge to the services provided by other employer bodies, particularly IBEC'. This is in line with Behrens and Traxler's (2004) finding that competition among employer associations in Europe is on the increase and that this is most intense in regard to representing small and medium-sized enterprises (SMEs). The Irish experience certainly bears this out. In 1994 a number of small firm affiliates left IBEC to form a separate representative body for SMEs, the Irish Small and Medium Enterprises Association (ISME). Although this body is currently not a registered employer association, it also provides a range of HR advisory services to members, similar to those of IBEC and the ICC. It is likely that competition in regard to the SME sector will increase over future years.

Other Groups of Employers

It is important to note that employers may establish and combine in less formal groupings for purposes associated with employee relations. Such groups are generally used by employers as a forum for the exchange of views and information on employee relations/HRM matters. They may also facilitate co-ordination of employers' approaches in dealing with particular employee relations issues. Such associations may be organised by industrial sector or region and may meet either on a semi-permanent basis or only when a significant issue arises. The Chartered Institute of Personnel and Development (CIPD) in Ireland, which is the major professional association for HRM practitioners, may also act as a forum for representing employers' interests in employee relations.

Figure 12.3 The Irish Business and Employers' Confederation: structure of organisation

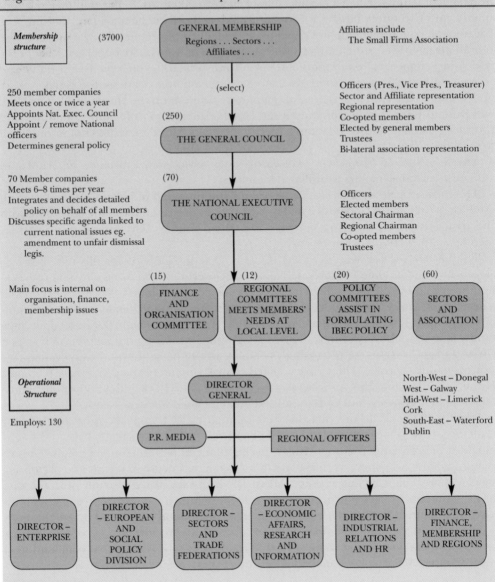

EMPLOYERS' ASSOCIATIONS' SERVICES

Our earlier discussion alluded to the range of employee relations services provided by employers' associations in areas such as collective bargaining, research and advice. These services are discussed below.

Research and Advisory Services

In commenting on developments in Britain, Sisson (1983) found that the greatest area of growth in the work of employers' associations was in the provision of research and advisory services. These services fall into three broad categories: (i) legal; (ii) pay; and (iii) specialist consultancy. The growth of labour legislation in Ireland since the 1970s has led to a significant increase in employers' demands for specialist legal advice in areas such as dismissals, employment conditions and employment equality. Many larger employers' associations provide a specialist legal section to advise and assist member companies. They may also publish and disseminate guidelines on legislation for their membership. A more traditional service involves the provision of information and advice to members on wage rates and levels of wage increases. Many of them provide surveys of wage levels and fringe benefits for differing occupations, regions and size of organisation. Consequently they are able to provide members with up-to-date information on local, regional and national pay trends and advise such firms on reward issues. Some employers' associations also provide members with specialist advice and assistance. These might include issues such as performance management, productivity schemes and recruitment. In an Irish pilot study, Butler (1985) found that advisory and consultancy services are seen by members as the most useful function of the associations and found that those dealing with legislation, pay and redundancy were most widely utilised.

Collective Bargaining

Historically, one of the most important services provided by employers' associations was that of assisting employers in collective bargaining with trade unions. Such bargaining might be of a multi-employer (regional, industry or national) or single employer nature. Multi-employer bargaining on an industry or, more commonly, national basis has traditionally meant a key role for employers' associations in conducting negotiations on pay and related matters on behalf of affiliated employers.

In Ireland, they have been particularly prominent in periods of centralised pay bargaining. IBEC plays a significant role in the Irish context, being the key representative of employers' opinions to the other 'social partners'. Behrens and Traxler (2004, 15–16) observe that 'IBEC has seen its role in national bargaining gradually expand under successive social partnership agreements'.

However, the Irish experience indicates that even where the locus of collective bargaining moves to the enterprise level, employers' associations still play an important role in advising and assisting management in the bargaining process. This role may incorporate: co-ordination of policy on pay and employment related issues; formulating general guidelines for affiliated employers; supplying research data and information for use in negotiations; and providing expert personnel either to conduct the negotiations or to advise and assist local management (Wallace *et al.* 2004). Such involvement may comprise direct participation in employee relations negotiations, but would also cover research and specialist advisory services as well as assistance with the preparation of employment agreements, consultation on particular HRM issues and the provision of premises and facilities for consultation and negotiation.

A particularly important role for employers' associations in collective bargaining is that of *representing affiliated members* in face-to-face negotiations or during third-party referrals. They may represent members in enterprise level negotiations with trade unions. They may also represent employers' interests in industry or national level bargaining. An increasingly significant aspect of this representational role applies to mediation and arbitration. Here, officials from employers' associations may represent affiliates in tribunal hearings, conciliation meetings and arbitration hearings such as the Labour Court, Labour Relations Commission or Employment Appeals Tribunal.

Education and Training

An increasingly important service provided by larger employers' associations relates to the provision of education and training programmes for affiliated members. Such provision is often aimed at keeping member firms *au fait* with current developments in employee relations such as employment law, working conditions and EU-level matters. They may also focus on developing managerial capacity among members' firms by providing training programmes for HRM practitioners in areas such as negotiating skills and employment legislation.

MEMBERSHIP OF EMPLOYERS' ASSOCIATIONS

In analysing the factors impacting on membership of employers' associations, Thomason (1984) notes the impact of *corporate form*. In particular, Thomason (1984) differentiates between entrepreneurs who essentially own and run their businesses and abstract corporate entities that are run by professional management. The corporate business firm has replaced the older entrepreneurial type firm as the prevalent type of organisation in membership of employers' associations. Thomason argues that the change in composition of membership from entrepreneurial owner-managers to corporate business firms run by professional management partly explains the changing role of employers' associations. There is also evidence that *country of ownership* may influence the membership of employers' associations. In Ireland a study of newly established companies found that US-owned firms were less likely to join employers' associations than other foreign-owned companies (Gunnigle 1995). This may be related to the corporate approach to trade unions and collective bargaining. Where this involves a preference for non-union status, such organisations may be reluctant to join an employers' association (Purcell and Sisson 1983; Oechslin 1985).

The issue of *public sector organisations* becoming members of employers' associations is a relatively recent phenomenon. While initially it might seem incompatible for public sector organisations to join employers' associations (traditionally a bastion of free enterprise), many have adopted a pragmatic approach by utilising their services in certain areas (Oechslin 1985). In Ireland the Department of Finance and the Local Government Staff Negotiations Board play a role in assisting and advising management on employee relations issues in many parts of the public sector. However, some public sector organisations, and particularly those in the semi-state sector, have increasingly taken up membership.

It has also been argued that an *organisation's size* is an important factor impacting on membership and patterns of utilisation of employers' associations. It is sometimes suggested that small firms have more to gain by joining them for reasons related to cost and resource considerations (ILO 1975). When a small organisation becomes involved in formalised collective bargaining it may be particularly attracted to joining an employers' association. A small organisation may not be in a position to employ HRM specialists; the owner or managers of such firms may not have either the necessary time or expertise to handle such matters effectively. Since the cost of joining such an association is generally related to size and/or profitability, it may be relatively inexpensive for small firms to join. However, despite the apparent validity of this line of argument, there is no conclusive evidence to support the view that small firms are more likely to join employers' associations (Government Social Survey, UK 1968; Gunnigle 1995). In fact the research evidence indicates that employers' associations are not more frequently used by smaller organisations (Brown 1981; Daniel and Millward 1983). Indeed, it seems that larger firms are more likely to join and utilise the services of employers' associations and that membership is positively correlated with the organisation's size, trade union recognition, and the presence of a specialist HR function.

Important influences on organisational decisions about whether or not to join employers' associations are the perceived advantages and disadvantages of such membership. Clearly these perceptions will be influenced by issues specific to the individual organisation, such as management's desired approach to employee relations. Broader contextual and environmental factors such as industrial sector, size, product market performance and ownership will also be influential (Thomason 1984). Figure 12.4 summarises some of the generally perceived advantages and disadvantages of employer association membership. Clearly the relative significance of these will vary between organisations and across industrial sectors.

Figure 12.4 Advantages and disadvantages of membership of employers' associations

ADVANTAGES	DISADVANTAGES
• Collective approaches and uniform policy	• Cost of membership
• Advice on trade union matters	• Loss of autonomy
• Technical advice and information	• Loss of flexibility
• Skilled negotiators	• Comparisons with other firms
• Expert advisory and consultancy services	• Greater acceptance of role for trade unions
• Standardised pay and employment conditions	• Greater formalisation in employee relations
• On par with regional/industry norms	
• Assistance in employee relations difficulties	
• Influence on Government, national affairs	

Source: Gunnigle, McMahon and Fitzgerald (1999).

The range of employee relations services provided by employers' associations, considered in the preceding section, correlate closely with the perceived advantages of membership of employers' associations (as outlined in figure 12.4). It is therefore appropriate to consider here some reasons why organisations may choose not to join employers' associations.

A common argument for not joining an employers' association is the potential reduction of *managerial autonomy* in decision-making. As in any formal association or club, employers' associations will be keen to ensure that members adhere to commonly agreed polices in areas such as pay and conditions of employment. These policies and related guidelines normally reflect the needs of the general membership. However, it is a decision for the individual organisation to assess whether such norms are appropriate to its particular needs.

The issue of *comparability with other firms* is also an important consideration. By joining an association comprised of numerous other companies, a particular firm's pay and conditions will be compared to that pertaining across the general membership. Trade unions often use the terms of collective agreements struck with some member firms as 'leverage' to secure similar terms with other member organisations. Another important consideration impacting on membership of employers' associations is the impact of a firm's desired *employee relations/HRM style*. As we have seen, the legal definition of employers' associations means that they are, in a legal context, trade unions of employers. Traditionally they have had a preference for dealing with their employee counterparts, trade unions, through collective bargaining. However, it is also clear that many firms now pursue

311

employee relations 'styles' which seek to avoid trade union recognition (Gunnigle and Brady 1984; McGovern 1989a). Some of these firms place a strong emphasis on dealing with employees on a more individual basis (Gunnigle, Morley and Turner 1997). For such firms, membership of an employers' association (i.e. a trade union of employers) would be totally incompatible with a management approach based on direct contact with the individual.

A more pragmatic reason for non-membership is related to the *cost of membership*. Normally firms pay the full cost of membership regardless of services used. This contrasts with the situation in relation to the use of management consultants where firms normally only pay a fee related to services used. The subscription fee paid to IBEC is normally based on a company's total salaries/wages paid in a financial year, but a turnover scale may apply where a company has a high turnover to labour costs ratio (data supplied directly by IBEC). The subscription paid is the higher of the two scales (data supplied directly by IBEC). A selection of IBEC subscription rates are detailed in table 12.2, according to total salaries and wages.

Table 12.2 Selection of IBEC subscription rates 2005

Total salaries and wages (€)	Subscription (€)
0–906,300	1,923.63
2,797,501–3,195,900	7,939.80
7,311,701–8,043,000	18,899.26
15,673,501–17,240,800	40,503.45
36,651,501–40,316,400	86,847.87
167,373,401–251,053,200	165,744.26
Over 251,053,201	175,199.73

Source: Data supplied by IBEC

At a European level, Behrens and Traxler (2004, 17) found no evidence of a weakening of employer willingness to join employer associations. Rather they found that in most countries employer association membership was fairly stable. They also suggest that in regard to the public role of employer associations, 'there is little indication of any general questioning of their representativeness'. This contrasts with the experience of trade unions, where we have seen evidence of significant falls in union density and representativeness.

MANAGEMENT APPROACHES TO EMPLOYEE RELATIONS

While employers' associations clearly play an important role in employee relations, individual employers are primarily responsible for the development and implementation of employee relations policies and practices within their individual organisations and workplaces. The remainder of this chapter addresses the role of management in enterprise-level employee relations and reviews contemporary research on management approaches to employee relations.

Managerial Frames of Reference

In his seminal work, Fox (1968) argues that management approaches to employee relations are largely determined by the frame of reference adopted by managers. A frame of reference is defined by Thelen and Withall (1979) as 'the main selective influences at work as the perceiver supplements, omits and structures what he notices'. Fox (1968) suggests that a manager's frame of reference is important because:

1. it determines how management expects people to behave and how it thinks they should behave (i.e. values and beliefs);
2. it determines management reactions to actual behaviour (i.e. management practice); and
3. it shapes the methods management choose when it wishes to change the behaviour of people at work (e.g. strategies/policies).

Fox identified two alternative frames of reference to help evaluate management approaches to employee relations. These were termed (i) the unitarist and (ii) the pluralist frame of reference. The key features of these two approaches are summarised in figure 12.5.

Figure 12.5 Unitarist and pluralist frames of reference

Unitarist	Pluralist
Emphasises the dominance of common interests. Everyone – management and employees – should strive to achieve the organisation's primary business goals since everyone will benefit	The organisation is viewed as composed of different interest groups with different objectives but linked together instrumentally by their common association with the organisation
There is only one source of authority (management) and it must command full loyalty	Management's role is to achieve some equilibrium satisfying the various interest groups thus helping achieve the organisation's goals
Anyone who does not share these common interests and does not accept managerial authority is viewed as a dissenter/agitator	A certain amount of conflict is inevitable since the objectives of the parties will clash on occasion
Since dissenters endanger organisational success they must either fall into line, appreciate the overriding importance of corporate goals and accept managerial authority, or risk elimination from the organisation	Management must expect and plan for conflict so that it can be handled successfully and not endanger the achievement of the organisation's primary objectives
	Management should not seek to suppress conflicting interests, but rather aim to reconcile them in the organisation's interests.

Source: Fox (1968).

These contrasting frames of reference represent the dominant employee relations orientations that may be adopted by management. In practice one finds that managers do not strictly adhere to one of these approaches but may adopt different approaches in different situations and/or change their approaches over time. Nevertheless, the frames of reference approach provides a useful framework for evaluating management approaches to employee relations at enterprise level. For example, Marchington's (1982) analysis considered how management approaches to employee relations might differ depending on the particular frame of reference adopted. In evaluating management approaches to trade unions, Marchington (1982) argues that managers holding a unitary perspective would see no role for trade unions. Such managers would see unions as 'encroaching on management's territory', making unreasonable demands, prohibiting change, flexibility, and, therefore, competitiveness (Gunnigle *et al.* 1999). As a consequence, trade unions would be viewed as an externally imposed force that introduces conflict into the organisation and prohibits the development of 'good' employee relations. Furthermore, workers associated with the promotion of trade unionism would be seen as 'disloyal', 'agitators' or 'troublemakers'. In contrast, managers adopting a pluralist perspective would see a legitimate role for trade unions in representing and articulating employees' views in the workplace.

A second area where Marchington (1982) identified different approaches was in relation to managerial prerogative. Managerial prerogative refers to areas of decision-making where management see themselves as having sole decision-making authority. Marchington (1982) suggests that managers adopting a unitary frame of reference would be unwilling to accept any reduction of management prerogative as a result of trade union organisation. They would see management as the legitimate decision-making authority. On the other hand, managers adopting a pluralist frame of reference would acknowledge the legitimacy of other interest groups, such as trade unions, in the organisation. They would also accept the need to allow trade unions a role in decision-making and consequently accept some reduction in managerial prerogative.

The final area where management approaches may differ is in relation to industrial conflict. Marchington (1982) suggests that managers adopting a unitary frame of reference would view the enterprise very much along 'team'/'family' lines with everyone working together to achieve company objectives. In this context conflict is seen as something of an aberration, only occurring as a result of a breakdown of communications or the work of troublemakers. By contrast, managers adopting a pluralist frame of reference would accept that some degree of industrial conflict is inevitable because the interests of management and labour will clash on occasion. Since the pluralist perspective accepts the legitimacy of conflict, managers adopting this frame of reference will tend to plan for it by, for example, agreeing to grievance disputes and disciplinary procedures.

The Concept of Management Styles

Moving beyond Fox's unitarist-pluralist dichotomy, several commentators have attempted to develop categorisations of management styles in employee relations to explain differences in organisational approaches to employee relations. One of the most widely used management styles typologies is that of Purcell and Sisson (1983), who developed a five-fold categorisation of 'ideal-typical' styles of employee relations management. Their typology, outlined in figure 12.6, was based on differing management approaches to trade unions, collective bargaining, consultation and communications.

Despite the apparent attractiveness of management style typologies, it appears that in reality it is difficult to categorise organisations into neat 'ideal-typical' groupings (Deaton 1985; Gunnigle 1995). Using data from some 1400 UK organisations Deaton (1985) sought to empirically evaluate the appropriateness of Purcell and Sisson's (1983) typology. He firstly attempted to classify management styles in unionised companies as either 'sophisticated' or 'standard modern'. However, Deaton (1985) found it difficult to distinguish between these two types of management styles, suggesting that it is rather tenuous to classify firms recognising trade unions into either of these groupings. Deaton (1985) also attempted to categorise management styles in non-union companies into 'paternalist', 'anti-union', and 'sophisticated paternalists'. Here Deaton (1985) found greater evidence of organisations conforming to Purcell and Sisson's (1983) 'ideal-typical' style typologies. He found that 'sophisticated paternalists' and 'anti-union' organisations emerged as 'polar opposites' while 'paternalist' organisations took the middle ground (having some characteristics common to both 'anti-union' and 'sophisticated paternalist' organisations). Deaton (1985) concluded that attempts to classify firms into a small number of ideal styles were problematic and that, while the distinction between organisations that recognise trade unions and those that do not is crucial, it may not be possible to sub-divide styles further in organisations where unions are recognised. However, Deaton (1985) felt that there was a greater tendency in organisations that do not recognise trade unions to adopt the 'identikit' styles suggested above.

Figure 12.6 Management styles in employee relations

Management Style	Characteristics
Traditionalist	'Orthodox unitarism': oppose role for unions; little attention to employee needs
Sophisticated Paternalist	Emphasise employees' needs (training, pay, conditions etc.); discourage unionisation; demand and facilitate employee loyalty and commitment.
Sophisticated Modern	Accept trade unions' role in specific areas; emphasis on procedures and consultative mechanisms; Two variations: (i) Constitutionalists: emphasise codification of management–union relations through explicit collective agreements; (ii) Consultors: collective bargaining established but management emphasises personal contact and problem-solving, playing down formal union role at establishment level.
Standard Modern	Pragmatic approach: unions' role accepted but no overall philosophy or strategy developed; 'Fire-fighting'/reactive approach.

Source: Adapted from Purcell and Sisson (1983).

Using more anecdotal evidence to examine variations in managerial styles in employee relations, Poole (1986) suggested that the evidence points to the existence of 'a progressively rich array' of hybrid styles, rather than any convergence towards particular predominant styles or patterns.

INDIVIDUALISM AND COLLECTIVISM AS DIMENSIONS OF MANAGEMENT STYLES

More recent analyses of management styles in employee relations have tended to focus on key dimensions of management styles rather than 'ideal-typical' style categorisations. Purcell (1987) provides us with two widely accepted dimensions of management styles in employee relations, namely individualism and collectivism.

Collectivism in employee relations incorporates the extent to which management acknowledges the right of employees to collective representation and the involvement of the collective in influencing management decision-making (Purcell 1987; Sisson 1994;

Storey and Sisson 1983). This dimension addresses both the level of democratic employee representative structures and the extent to which management legitimise their representational and bargaining role. Thus conceived, the collectivist dimension spans a continuum from a unitarist perspective incorporating management opposition to employee representation, through a middle ground of adversarial or reluctant collectivism, to a co-operative perspective (Purcell 1987; Marchington and Parker 1990). Thus, high collectivism is manifested in the establishment recognition and incorporation of mechanisms for employee representation, particularly trade unions, as a vehicle in the conduct of establishment-level employee relations, while at the other extreme low collectivism is manifested in managerial opposition to collective employee representation (see figure 12.7).

Figure 12.7 Collectivism as a dimension of management styles in employee relations

HIGH COLLECTIVISM ——— Pluralist/ Co-operative

LOW COLLECTIVISM ——— Unitarist/Little/No co-operation

Source: Adapted from Purcell (1987).

Individualism as a dimension of management style in employee relations incorporates the degree to which management adopts an essentially individualist focus in employee relations management (Purcell and Gray 1986; Purcell 1987; Marchington and Parker 1990). Purcell (1987, 536) describes individualism thus:

> . . . the extent to which the firm gives credence to the feelings and sentiments of each employee and seeks to develop and encourage each employee's capacity and role at work . . . Firms which have individualistically-centred policies are thus expected to emphasise employees as a resource and be concerned with developing each person's talents and worth.

Purcell argues that high individualism is characterised by management recognising the resource value of employees and adopting comprehensive employee development policies. In contrast, low individualism conceives of employees in utility terms within the overriding goal of profit maximisation. Here the management emphasis is on tight management control, minimisation of labour costs and little concern for broader human resource issues such as job satisfaction, employment security or employee commitment (see figure 12.8).

Figure 12.8 Individualism as a dimension of management styles in employee relations

HIGH INDIVIDUALISM ——— Employees as a resource; comprehensive employee development emphasis

LOW INDIVIDUALISM ——— Employees as commodities; no employee development

Source: Adapted from Purcell (1987).

The contemporary literature identifies an increased management emphasis on the development of an individualist orientation in management-employee interactions as a significant development in changing patterns of employee relations (Beaumont 1985, 1991; Beaumont and Townley 1985; Kochan *et al.* 1986; Guest 1989; Storey 1992; Bacon and Storey 1993; Gunnigle, MacCurtain and Morley 2001; Roche 2001). However, we also saw earlier that high levels of collectivism, and specifically trade union recognition, membership and influence, are integral to the traditional pluralist model, and are considered characteristic of employee relations in Ireland (Roche 1989, 1997b; Brewster and Hegewisch 1994; Roche and Turner 1994; Hillery 1994). Thus, findings on the levels of collectivism and individualism are seen as critical indicators of change in management styles in employee relations (Beaumont 1985).

The so called 'soft' HRM approach has been associated with a move from collectivism to individualism via sophisticated recruitment, rewards and employee development policies (Guest 1987, 1989). However, Purcell (1987) argues that individualism need not necessarily counterpoise collectivism, so that managements can develop policies to increase individualism whilst retaining established collectivist structures, including trade union recognition. Marchington and Parker (1990) suggest that this interpretation makes the dimensions of management style more 'dynamic', allowing organisations to alter their positions along these dimensions over time. In a study of recently established ('greenfield') companies in Ireland, Gunnigle *et al.* (1997) attempted to evaluate management approaches to employee relations on the dimensions of collectivism and individualism (see, for example, Gunnigle, Morley and Turner 1997; Gunnigle, Turner and D'Art 1998). To this end a number of indicators were developed to evaluate the relative management emphasis on individualism and collectivism. These indicators are summarised in figure 12.9.

Figure 12.9 Indicators of collectivism and individualism

MEASURES OF INDIVIDUALISM

1. *Sophistication of the employment and socialisation system:* measured through an evaluation of the degree of sophistication and relative emphasis on individualism in the management of human resource 'flows'.
2. *Communications:* based on an analysis of the level, nature and sophistication of management-employee communications.
3. *Performance-related pay:* measured through an analysis of the incidence of performance-related pay systems and the utilisation of formal performance appraisals to aid performance-related pay decisions among manual/operative grades.
4. *Employee involvement:* measured through an analysis of the extent to which management utilises explicit techniques to facilitate employee involvement in decision-making.
5. *Employee autonomy:* measured through an analysis of the extent to which management seek to facilitate/promote employee autonomy.

MEASURES OF COLLECTIVISM

1. *Trade union presence:* measured through an analysis of levels of trade union recognition and trade union density.
2. *Pattern of trade union organisation:* measured though an examination of the nature of trade union recognition and impact of trade unions on workplace employee relations
3. *Role of trade unions and other employee representative bodies:* measured though an examination of role of trade unions and other employee representative bodies in management-employee communications/interactions
4. *Employers' association membership and utilisation:* measured through an examination of the extent to which greenfield companies are in membership of employers' associations and of the patterns of utilisation of employer association services.

These measures were used to evaluate management styles in a number of Irish organisations on the dimensions of collectivism and individualism. While the findings only apply to recently established firms, they provide some interesting insights into management approaches to employee relations in Ireland (Gunnigle 1995; Gunnigle, Morley and Turner 1997).

Probably the most significant finding of the greenfield-site study was the powerful evidence of changing management approaches to collectivism as a means of managing workplace employee relations. Such a trend was evidenced by policies designed to mitigate attempts to achieve trade union recognition or, where unions are recognised, to prescribe tightly their role in workplace employee relations. As noted in the preceding chapter, this evidence points to a severe erosion in levels of trade union recognition and density in newly established firms (cf. Gunnigle, Collings and Morley 2005; Gunnigle, MacCurtain and Morley 2001; Roche 2001). While it might be argued that this differential may be explained by the relative immaturity of greenfield companies, it is important to note that pre-production closed-shop agreements have traditionally characterised large industrial start-ups in Ireland (see, for example, O'Hara 1981; Murray 1984; McGovern 1989a). It appears that this is no longer the case and that greenfield companies are increasingly and consciously choosing the non-union alternative rather than pre-production agreements. More recent research by Gunnigle, Collings and Morley (2005) on MNCs in Ireland has identified the practice of 'double breasting'. This is the practice whereby MNC subsidiaries with a tradition of union recognition and collective bargaining had recently established new plants in Ireland on a non-union basis. The trend emerging in greenfield sites indicates a shift from collectivism to individualism. While this development does not mean that collectivist structures are abandoned, it does appear that the strong collectivist traditions characteristic of Irish employee relations are being diluted.

The second critical characteristic of emergent patterns of employee relations management was a greater emphasis on individualist approaches to employee relations. This study found that the most significant indicators of high levels of individualism were performance-based pay systems tied to individual employee appraisals and greater direct communications with employees. An increased management focus on more extensive and direct communications with individual employees was an important feature of employee relations management in many of the companies studied, and predominantly so among the non-union companies. In particular, many companies put an especially strong emphasis on communicating information on company performance to employees. In many of these companies, such information was used to emphasise issues such as market volatility, intensity of competition and requirements for high-quality and low-cost production and service. However, it appears that the rationale for such communications was largely based on utilitarian objectives of facilitating improved employee performance and flexibility, rather than on more altruistic motives such as enhanced employee involvement.

The other key indicator of individualism identified in the greenfield study was the extent of utilisation of performance-related pay (PRP) systems based on formal appraisals of individual employee performance (Gunnigle 1995; Gunnigle, Turner and D'Art 1998; Roche 2001). This study found significant differences between greenfield and longer established ('brownfield') companies in the extent of utilisation of PRP systems based on formal appraisals among non-managerial/white-collar grades. The role of appraisal in aiding PRP decisions among non-managerial and white-collar grades is a crucial differentiating factor since the use of more 'traditional' PRP systems among manual grades is nothing new (Clegg 1979; Mooney 1980).

However, such PRP systems (e.g. measured day work) were based on quantitative evaluations of employee performance and were normally the subject of collective bargaining. As such, quantitative PRP systems were very much integral to the collectivist tradition of Irish employee relations (Mooney 1980; Grafton 1988; Armstrong and Murlis 1994).

By contrast, performance appraisal is essentially an individualist management tool (Beer *et al.* 1984). By linking performance appraisals to incremental pay decisions, managements in greenfield sites are posing a challenge to collectivism in employee relations. The collectivist tradition implies that incremental pay decisions are achieved through collective bargaining and, once agreed, apply 'across the board' to all relevant employee categories. In contrast, PRP decisions based on performance appraisal are normally the subject of a management review of individual employee performance. Consequently, incremental pay decisions are made by management rather than through collective bargaining and vary according to individual appraisals rather than applying equally to all through a collective agreement. Thus, individualism replaces collectivism at two critical phases: (i) the process of appraisal is individualist rather than collectivist (individual appraisal rather than collective bargaining); and (ii) the outcome takes the form of varying PRP decisions among individual employees rather than a fixed amount that applies equally to all employees.

Some commentators have suggested that PRP does not necessarily have negative implications for collectivism, and specifically trade unions (Heery 1992). This argument is based on evidence that PRP systems may co-exist alongside collective bargaining on pay (Casey *et al.* 1992). The evidence from Irish greenfield sites does not support this argument. In these companies, individualism tends to counterpoise collectivism. Furthermore, the strongest component of individualism in greenfield sites is the use of PRP systems based on individual performance appraisals among non-managerial and white-collar grades (Collings *et al.* 2006; Roche 2001). The evidence on greenfield sites identifies company ownership and trade union recognition as the major factors impacting on the adoption of PRP systems based on individual performance appraisals. Such systems were predominantly used in non-union and US-owned companies and were largely absent in unionised companies (Roche 2001). As mentioned above, these findings indicate that individualism tends to counterpoise rather than complement collectivism in terms of management styles in employee relations.

Another indicator of increased individualism identified in the literature is the adoption of sophisticated and highly individualist employment systems to effectively manage 'human resource flows', particularly in the areas of selection and employee development (Foulkes 1980; Beer *et al.* 1984). A further important indicator of high individualism in the extant literature is the incidence of extensive mechanisms to facilitate employee autonomy and involvement (Lawler 1978, 1982; Beer *et al.* 1984). It was interesting that Gunnigle's study of Irish greenfield companies did not find widespread evidence of sophisticated employment systems or mechanisms to facilitate employee involvement or autonomy in the majority of greenfield companies studied (Gunnigle 1995).

In considering these results it can be argued that while individualism appeared to be an important and significant management strategy in employee relations in greenfield companies, this did not necessarily imply that managements in greenfield companies adopt a 'resource perspective' of employees (Purcell 1987). This Irish study found little evidence of a shift from a utility perspective to a resource perspective in greenfield companies. The aggregate evidence suggests that, while there is a greater emphasis on individualism in greenfield companies than has traditionally been the case with longer-established companies, this does not equate to high levels of individualism. Rather it appears that managements in greenfield sites are adopting more individualist approaches in selected aspects of employee relations but are not moving towards a wholly individualist approach equating to the 'soft' HRM model (Beer *et al.* 1984; Guest 1989; Storey 1989).

This chapter has reviewed employers' organisations and approaches to employee relations. It has placed particular emphasis on the role of employers' associations in Ireland. The chapter also considered the issue of management styles in employee relations and reviewed some recent research evidence on developments in management styles in employee relations. The next chapter focuses more specifically on employee relations practice at the level of the workplace.

13

Employee Relations Practice

This chapter considers key aspects of employee relations practice. Particular emphasis is placed on those employee relations activities undertaken at enterprise level such as collective bargaining, grievance handling, discipline administration and employee participation.[1]

COLLECTIVE BARGAINING

We have seen that employee relations is primarily concerned with how issues such as pay, conditions of employment, workplace relations, workplace rules and other such issues are dealt with by employers and employees. In chapter 11 we noted that a key institution of employee relations is collective bargaining, whereby pay, conditions of employment, and other employment-related issues are regulated between organised employees and management. We further noted that collective bargaining provides a means for the orderly resolution of divergent employer and worker interests. A key feature of collective bargaining is that employees do not negotiate with employers on their own behalf, but rather collectively through representatives (normally trade unions, but also through staff associations or employee councils/committees). We also noted the necessary pre-conditions for collective bargaining to function effectively, as follows:

1. Employees must have the freedom to associate, enabling workers to join together in trade unions or other associations which are not in any way under the control or influence of employers.
2. Employers must be prepared to recognise such trade unions and associations and accept the constraints placed upon their ability to deal with employees on an individual basis.

We further observed that collective bargaining is not the only method of regulating employment matters. Even in countries where it is widely used, such as Ireland, it usually operates alongside other mechanisms such as individual bargaining between employer and

---

1. Students will find greater detail on these issues in chapters 8, 10, 11 and 13 in Wallace *et al.* 2004.

employees, regulation by the Government (legislation) and the unilateral imposition of terms of employment by management or by trade unions. The International Labour Organisation (ILO) has long argued that collective bargaining offers a number of advantages, which make it the most appropriate method of regulating labour issues and which explain its widespread utilisation (ILO 1975; also see Donovan 1968). These include the following:

1. It is seen as more flexible than other methods (e.g. regulation by the state).
2. It helps redress the disparity in bargaining power between the individual employee and his/her employer.
3. It allows workers an opportunity to participate in decisions on the conditions of employment under which they operate.
4. It provides an orderly mechanism for identifying and handling grievances and differences of opinions through negotiation aimed at securing eventual agreement.

The normal end product of the collective bargaining process is a collective agreement. However, this objective does not preclude situations in which negotiation breaks down and a strike or other form of industrial action results, provided of course there was a genuine attempt to reach agreement.

Collective agreements are frequently regarded as covering two different kinds of arrangement, namely those that deal with substantive issues and those that are procedural in nature. The scope of substantive agreements will obviously vary widely from company to company, but substantive terms incorporate the 'hard' terms of collective agreements, such as those dealing with levels of wage increases, hours of work and holidays. In contrast, procedural issues are concerned with the ways (procedures) in which terms and conditions of employment are arrived at and how differences over the application of agreed terms and conditions are settled. Such procedural arrangements normally prescribe how wage claims, disciplinary issues, grievances, disputes and related matters are to be processed or handled by the parties.

Levels of Collective Bargaining
We have seen that collective bargaining requires collective action on the part of employees. However, employers may engage in collective bargaining on an individual basis or collectively through, for example, employers' associations. Thus, trade unions or other representative employee bodies may bargain with one employer, a group of employers, or with representatives of employer associations. As a consequence the locus of collective bargaining may vary between organisations and over time. It can occur at a multi-employer or single-employer level (see discussion on levels of collective bargaining in chapter 11, especially figure 11.2).

Multi-employer bargaining normally involves the representation of employers' interests by employer associations and may take place at national, regional or industry level. *Single-employer bargaining* can also take place at a number of levels depending on the structure of the organisation. A particular organisation may be involved in bargaining at establishment level (largely referred to as workplace bargaining) and at a multi-establishment level (if the organisation is a multi-site operation). In addition, collective bargaining at the level of the single employer might involve negotiations either with an individual union or, in a multi-union environment, with representatives from a group of unions.

In Ireland we have seen that the primary locus of collective bargaining in recent years has been at the national level, primarily involving negotiations between representatives of trade union interests (ICTU), employers' interests (primarily IBEC) and Government representatives. Such national level bargaining normally operates alongside supplementary workplace level bargaining on company level issues, such as work practices and productivity. Several commentators have noted the pros and cons of bargaining on either a single- or multi-employer basis. For example, it is suggested that employers may prefer multi-employer bargaining because it removes the need to deal with annual wage negotiations at company level and leaves the management team free to devote their time to other aspects of organisational management. It is also suggested that the standardisation of pay levels and working conditions helps to avoid wage competition between employers, regulating an important aspect of the competitive market. It has also been suggested that organisations in comfortable trading positions may see multi-employer bargaining as a relatively painless way of dealing with employee relations. On the other hand, multi-employer bargaining may have disadvantages for employers. For example, bargaining on a single-employer (individual) basis may allow management greater scope to ensure that wage levels and other conditions of employment more closely reflect their competitive position. This may be achieved by linking concessions on wage levels and working conditions to union and worker commitments to increase productivity, or contribute to other cost reductions in a way that may be more difficult to achieve through multi-employer bargaining.

Collective Bargaining in Ireland

In chapter 11 we saw that collective bargaining has traditionally been the major activity area for HRM practitioners in Ireland, and especially so among larger organisations. We further noted that the Irish system of collective bargaining is grounded in voluntary principles, relying on the moral commitment of the participants to adhere to agreements achieved through the bargaining process. A key characteristic of collective bargaining in Ireland over recent decades is a tendency towards high levels of centralisation in the level of bargaining.

As noted earlier, centralised bargaining essentially describes institutionalised negotiations between representatives of trade union confederations and employers' associations about wages and other issues. Although the first attempts at centralised pay bargaining took place in 1948 and led to a series of 'wage rounds', it was not until the 1970s that the first (of seven) National Wage Agreements was negotiated. In addition to dealing with basic wage increases these national agreements included arrangements for moving towards equal pay for equal work, for special anomaly claims, for incentive schemes and productivity bargaining and for dispute resolution procedures.

These early national agreements did not encompass direct Government involvement as a separate party to the negotiations (however, the Government was involved in its role as an employer). Towards the end of the 1970s, as it became clear that national pay bargaining was closely linked to Government's economic and social policy, Government became directly involved in negotiations on national agreements in its own right (and not simply as an employer). The result was the more ambitious National Understandings, of which two were negotiated in 1979 and 1980. These National Understandings embraced policies not just on employment and pay, but also issues such as taxation, education, health and social welfare.

The sequence of centralised agreements ceased at the expiry of the second National Understanding in 1982. The period from 1982 to 1987 witnessed a short period of decentralised bargaining. During this period it appeared that viability and economic performance became key criteria in shaping levels of wage increases. Settlement levels varied between industries and industry sectors, with little convergence towards a wage round norm (see McGinley 1989a and b). The Government at times sought to impose a norm through pay guidelines but these were largely ignored by private sector negotiators and, as Von Prondzynski (1985) argues, were best seen as the Government's opening position in public sector pay negotiations. A notable feature of this period was the reduction, over the rounds, in the number and range of supplementary cost-increasing claims. Irish wage costs rose by only 7 per cent between 1980 and 1985, compared to an average of 37 per cent in competing countries (Hardiman 1988).

The major factor contributing to a return to centralised bargaining in 1987 was, undoubtedly, the growing crisis in the public finances. The national debt represented 148 per cent of Gross National Product (GNP) in 1986, while unemployment had risen dramatically and contributed to an apparently disastrous economic outlook. A critical Government concern was the need to control the public sector pay bill. The newly elected Government, led by Fianna Fáil, announced a number of measures to improve the public finances, including restrictive measures in relation to public sector pay. The Government also indicated its interest in attaining a three-year pay agreement. The ICTU and some prominent union leaders also indicated interest in discussing a national plan for growth and economic recovery. Negotiations for a new agreement eventually concluded towards the end of 1987, culminating in the Programme for National Recovery (1987–91). Since then, five further such agreements were negotiated, the Programme for Social and Economic Progress (1991–4), the Programme for Competitiveness and Work (1994–7), Partnership 2000 for Inclusion, Employment and Competitiveness (1997–2000), the Programme for Prosperity and Fairness (2000–3) and Sustaining Progress (2003–6).

A summary of the sequence of centralised wage agreements in Ireland since 1970 is outlined in table 13.1, while tables 13.2 and 13.3 summarise the detailed provisions of the most recent programme, Sustaining Progress.

Table 13.1 Centralised wage agreements 1970–2006

Seven National Wage Agreements 1970–1978	
1st National Wage Agreement	1970
2nd National Wage Agreement	1972
3rd National Wage Agreement	1974
4th National Wage Agreement	1975
5th National Wage Agreement	1976
6th National Wage Agreement	1977
7th National Wage Agreement	1978
Two National Understandings 1979 and 1980	
1st National Understanding	1979
2nd National Understanding	1980
Programme for National Recovery (PNR)	1987–1990
Programme for Economic and Social Progress (PESP)	1991–1994
Programme for Competitiveness and Work (PCW)	1994–1997
Partnership 2000	1997–2000
Programme for Prosperity and Fairness (PPF)	2000–2003
Sustaining Progress (SP) (Parts One and Two)	2003–2006

Note: no centralised agreements in the period 1982–7.

Table 13.2 Sustaining Progress 2003–6: pay terms for the private sector

First 18 months	Phase 1 (first 9 months) 3% of basic pay	Phase 2 (second 6 months) 2%	Phase 3 (next 3 months) 2%
Second 18 months	Phase 1 (first 6 months) 1.5% or 2%*	Phase 2 (second 6 months) 1.5%	Phase 3 (next 6 months) 2.5%

* 2% applies to employees with an hourly rate of €9 or less on commencement of the first phase of the second 18-month period

Table 13.3 Sustaining Progress 2003–6: pay terms for the public service

First 18 months	**First 6 months** Pay freeze	**Phase 1 (from 1 January 2004)** 3%	**Phase 2 (From 1 July 2004)** 2%	**Phase 3 (From 1 December 2004** 2%
Second 18 months	**Phase 1 (from 1 June 2005)** 1.5% or 2%*	**Phase 2 (from 1 December 2005)** 1.5%	**Phase 3 (from 1 June 2006)** 2.5%	

*2% applies to employees who earn €351 per week (€18,315 per annum) or less

NEGOTIATING IN EMPLOYEE RELATIONS

A fundamental element of collective bargaining is the negotiations process. Negotiations in employee relations involve discussions and interactions between representatives of employers and employees over some divisive issues with the objective of reaching agreement. Walton and McKersie (1965) identify two dominant forms of such negotiations:

- 'Distributive' bargaining involves negotiations over pay and conditions of employment, which tend to be characterised as distributive because they involve bargaining or haggling over issues where a favourable settlement for one party means an element of loss for the other. This 'win-lose' approach represents an adversarial model of collective bargaining, where each party pursues its own specific objectives and hopes to concede minimal concessions to the other party. It is most obvious in pay negotiations where concessions by management inevitably represent both a quantifiable cost and a reduction in profits/dividends.
- 'Integrative' (or 'co-operative') bargaining involves a more joint problem-solving approach, which occurs where both parties are concerned with finding a jointly acceptable solution resulting in benefits for both sides (i.e. a 'win-win' approach).

In practice, employee relations negotiations normally involves a combination of both approaches.

Phases in the Negotiations Process

Formal employee relations negotiations normally involve one party submitting a claim to the other party and then entering discussions on this claim or issue. Subsequent interactions generally involve the parties bargaining and haggling over the divisive issues and reporting back to their respective constituents. Such negotiations may conclude either by reaching a mutually acceptable agreement or, possibly, failure to agree, resulting in a breakdown of negotiations. Such an impasse may be addressed through further discussion, use of third party mediation or the use of sanctions, such as industrial action. Whether or not the negotiating process reaches a successful conclusion depends on a number of factors. Most importantly, factors such as willingness to compromise, bargaining skills (including persuasive abilities) and, ultimately, the balance of power between parties will influence the final outcome of the negotiations (Hawkins 1979).

It is important to note that negotiating is an ongoing process not limited to one particular issue or time. The parties will generally be concerned with the establishment of enduring and stable relations. The long-term relationship between both parties is often considered more important than the particular issue upon which a single set of negotiations is focused: thus the maintenance of this relationship may take precedence over achieving a short-term 'victory' (Gunnigle *et al.* 1999).

It should be noted that employee relations negotiations may also occur at a more informal level involving line management and employees and/or their representatives. Such negotiations normally concern more minor and/or individual issues, such as individual grievances or minor disciplinary matters. The negotiating process itself will generally follow a number of predictable phases, namely (i) preparation; (ii) bargaining; and (iii) follow-up. See Figure 13.1.

Figure 13.1 Phases in the negotiations process

PHASE	ACTIVITIES
1. PREPARATION	Agree objectives and mandate Assess relative bargaining power Conduct relevant research Choose negotiating team/develop skills Make appropriate administrative arrangements
2. BARGAINING	Discover positions Expectation structuring Compromise and movement
3. POST-NEGOTIATION	Document agreement/disagreement Clarify Agree action plans Communicate Review

Source: Gunnigle *et al.* (1999).

PREPARATION
As with all types of managerial activity, careful preparation is an important prerequisite for success in employee relations negotiations. Such preparation requires that negotiators be familiar with the details of the case and have a clear idea of their objectives and mandate before entering the bargaining arena. This means that negotiators should clarify what they want to achieve, both from the collective bargaining process in general, and each set of negotiations in particular. Specific objectives tend to vary according to the issue at hand

and should involve specific targets, trade-off options and resistance points. Flexible objectives are generally more appropriate than rigid ones, since information may be uncovered during negotiations that may alter the substance of either party's case. It is important that each party's objectives are clearly articulated and approved by constituents, particularly top management on the employer side, and trade union members on the union side (Gunnigle *et al.* 1999).

A central issue in agreeing negotiating objectives involves establishing a bargaining range, including the limits within which each party is prepared to reach agreement. In practice this often means establishing an *ideal settlement point, a realistic settlement point* and a *fall-back position,* beyond which a party is not prepared to enter agreement.

Figure 13.2 Management-trade union bargaining range (example of pay negotiations)

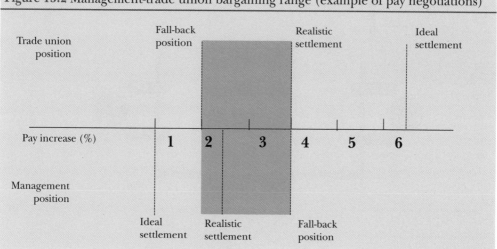

Source: Gunnigle, Garavan, and Fitzgerald (1992).

These various positions are illustrated in figure 13.2 in the context of hypothetical negotiations on wage increases between a trade union and employer. Here the process of establishing bargaining parameters facilitates the identification of bargaining objectives, deciding on trade-offs and concessions, and provides a benchmark against which to evaluate progress. In this particular instance, it is clear that agreement between the management and trade union teams is only possible where resistance points (fall-back positions) overlap, that is in the 2–4 per cent pay range (see figure 13.2). A settlement is not possible outside this range unless one of the parties alters its position. If this does not happen then the parties are in conflict over the issue and third party referral or industrial action may be used to help resolve this impasse.

An important aspect of effective preparations is adequate research. This helps focus negotiations on facts rather than discussing opinions or value judgements (Fisher *et al.* 2003). Preparatory research might also incorporate an evaluation of the repercussions of likely settlement options and 'knock-on' effects of different potential outcomes, including industrial action. Effective preparation also involves ensuring that appropriate administrative arrangements are made in relation to timing, location and support facilities. The size and composition of the negotiating team largely depends on the issue(s). It is generally suggested that, with the exception of quite minor issues, a negotiating team should comprise a minimum of two people to facilitate case presentation, record keeping and evaluation of progress (Nierenberg 1968). In larger organisations the HR manager will normally represent management in employee relations negotiations. However, line managers may often handle more minor issues or assist the HR manager during major negotiations.

BARGAINING

Figure 13.3 outlines the typical phases involved in the actual bargaining process: (i) opening; (ii) expectation structuring; (iii) offer, concession, movement; (iv) agreement/disagreement; and (v) close.

Figure 13.3 Stages in the bargaining process

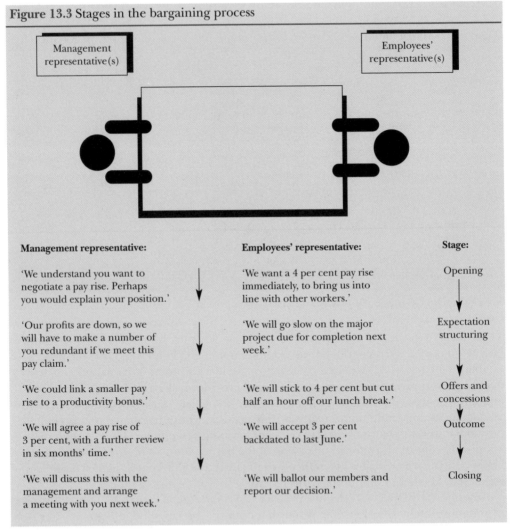

Management representative:		Employees' representative:	Stage:
'We understand you want to negotiate a pay rise. Perhaps you would explain your position.'	↓	'We want a 4 per cent pay rise immediately, to bring us into line with other workers.'	Opening
'Our profits are down, so we will have to make a number of you redundant if we meet this pay claim.'	↓	'We will go slow on the major project due for completion next week.'	Expectation structuring
'We could link a smaller pay rise to a productivity bonus.'	↓	'We will stick to 4 per cent but cut half an hour off our lunch break.'	Offers and concessions
'We will agree a pay rise of 3 per cent, with a further review in six months' time.'	↓	'We will accept 3 per cent backdated to last June.'	Outcome
'We will discuss this with the management and arrange a meeting with you next week.'		'We will ballot our members and report our decision.'	Closing

Source: Gunnigle, Garavan and Fitzgerald (1992).

The *opening phase* normally involves both parties articulating their respective positions. At this stage both parties normally attempt to find out more about each other's positions and assess the degree to which movement and concession is possible.

The next phase of bargaining often involves what is termed *expectation structuring*, where each party attempts to convince the other of the logic of their own position and their depth of commitment to that position. The parties may also highlight what are seen as deficiencies in the other party's position. Each party to the negotiations thus attempts to structure or influence the other party's expectations and tries to convince them to accept whatever concessions are offered. For example, during pay negotiations employers often refer to factors such as increased competition, or the need for re-investment, in an attempt to reduce employee or union expectations.

The *offer, concession, movement* phase generally follows the process of expectation structuring. This stage involves some initial offers and concessions by either party. This is a crucial phase in the overall negotiating process. It is felt that correct timing is absolutely crucial in making offers or concessions and it is normally advisable to take some time before making any major concessions. If such concessions are made too early in negotiations, the other party may press for more during subsequent bargaining. Any movement or offer from a team's opening position should be carefully weighed up in terms of its long- and short-term implications. During this phase adjournments are often used to allow the parties to evaluate their options and progress to date.

After some time both parties will be in a position to evaluate the likelihood of reaching *agreement* or, possibly, the extent and implications of a *breakdown* in negotiations. In the event of a breakdown, it is important that neither party walks away from the bargaining table without at least some agreement as to how communication will be re-initiated and by whom. Again, the idea that long-term relations may be more important than the issue(s) at hand is an important principle for both parties to keep in mind. For this reason the parties should be keen to avoid damaging conflict or breakdowns and be prepared to compromise on certain issues for the benefit of that longer-term perspective.

Both parties will normally recognise and anticipate the *closing phase* in the bargaining process. This phase normally involves the following: finalising the agreement, issues for further negotiation, procedures for interpretation of the agreement or details of breakdown.

POST-NEGOTIATION PHASE

At the end of the negotiations, the parties involved will usually report back on the outcome, the employee or union side reporting back to the workers they represent, and the management team reporting back to senior and, possibly, line management. This post-negotiation phase normally involves reviewing the implementation of any agreement reached and, possibly, a general evaluation of the implications of the negotiations and agreement.

INDUSTRIAL CONFLICT

Given the potential differences of interest that can arise on employment matters, it is not surprising that some degree of conflict is inevitable in employee relations. There are numerous explanations as to why industrial conflict occurs. In the preceding chapter, the pluralist and unitarist frameworks were posited as useful models for explaining employee relations interactions and industrial conflict (Fox 1968, 1974; Marchington 1982; Wallace *et al.* 2004).

In the pluralist framework, organisations are seen as comprising a range of individuals and groups with different interests and priorities. It suggests that the interaction of these competing interests and groups necessitates the development of institutional arrangements, which help manage these competing interests and achieve a level of bargained compromise that allows the organisation to conduct its normal business. Thus, the pluralist framework accepts that conflict is inherent in organisations because the needs and objectives of various interest groups will clash on occasion.

The unitarist framework provides a different explanation for industrial conflict. The unitarist approach is based on the premise that organisations are essentially cohesive and harmonious units and that all members of the organisation (management and employees) should share common goals. Within the unitarist framework there is only one source of authority, namely management (Fox 1968, 1974; Marchington 1982). Management and employees are seen as having the same interests with conflict occurring only as a result of misunderstandings or due to the efforts of troublemakers. Thus, within the unitarist model industrial conflict is not inevitable and consequently there is no perceived need for institutional arrangements to deal with conflict.

In practice it would seem that some degree of conflict is inherent in employee relations and that differences will arise between management and workers. These differences are not necessarily harmful and need not necessarily lead to industrial conflict. Where conflict does occur it can also have decidedly positive effects by, for example, leading to positive changes in management practice.

Industrial conflict is normally categorised into two broad forms: (i) explicit and organised industrial conflict, and (ii) unorganised and more implicit industrial conflict (Bean 1976; Wallace *et al.* 2004). Explicit, overt forms of industrial conflict represent organised and systematic responses and include strikes, go-slows and overtime bans. Implicit reactions include absenteeism, labour turnover, and poor performance and may often reflect low levels of employee satisfaction and morale.

Strike Activity in Ireland

The most visible way in which workers can demonstrate industrial conflict is to go on strike. Strike action can take different forms and arise for a variety of reasons.

A number of critical factors which impact on the level and pattern of strike activity have been identified such as the level of economic activity (business cycle), unemployment (tightness/looseness of the labour market), industrial development, inflation (earnings), and unionisation (Brannick and Doyle 1994). Three key measures are normally used in evaluating the extent of strike activity: (i) strike frequency (number of strikes); (ii) workers involved (number of workers participating in strikes); and (iii) working days lost (number of working days lost due to strike activity). Using these indicators, the pattern of strike activity in Ireland over the period 1922–2004 is summarised in figures 13.4, 13.5 and 13.6 and table 13.3. This evidence indicates a clear upward trend in strike activity in Ireland during the 1960s and 1970s, followed by a significant decline in strike activity for much of the 1980s and 1990s. The number of strikes in the years 2000–4 was the lowest number ever recorded. The number of workers involved and working days lost in the years 2001–4 has also been extremely low compared with previous years.

In the 1980s, Kelly and Brannick (1983) identified two key trends in the pattern of strike activity in Ireland: (i) the disproportionate effect of a few large strikes on Irish strike statistics; and (ii) the different patterns of strike activity between the public and private sectors. In relation to the former, Kelly and Brannick note that over the period 1960–79, 43 strikes (2 per cent of total strikes in the period) accounted for 57 per cent of all days lost due to strike activity and comment thus:

> Clearly, the Irish strike pattern is extremely sensitive to this comparatively small number of large strikes and it has been an enduring feature over the 20-year period. Indeed should these be removed from the Irish strike quantum the result would be a record which would show a comparatively strike-free nation in terms of workers involved and total man-days lost.

Wallace *et al.* (2004) have noted a more accentuated pattern in recent years. They highlight that in the years 1995–2002, the top two strikes accounted for 75 per cent of all working days lost and 78 per cent of workers involved in strikes.

Figure 13.4 Strike activity in Ireland: strike frequency 1922–2004

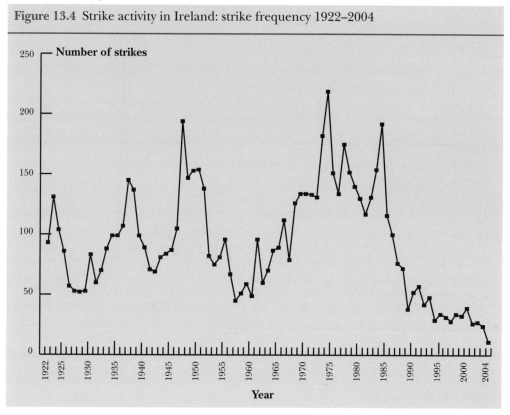

Note. Figures from the CSO are subject to minor fluctuations due to factors such as the carry-over of strikes from one year to another and variations in the numbers of workers participating in strike activity over the period of a particular strikes. However, these minor variations do not affect overall trends in the pattern of strike activity.

Source. UCD Database of Strike Statistics; CSO

In evaluating patterns of strike activity in the public and private sectors, Kelly and Brannick (1988c) found that the private sector was the most strike-prone sector in the period 1960–86. However, their study indicated that the proportion of strike activity accounted for by the private sector was greatest during the 1960s but has been declining since then. This development has paralleled a marked increase in the proportion of strike activity accounted for by the public sector over the period 1970–89. In the period 1990–5, there was not much difference between the public and private sectors with regard to the number of strikes. The private sector accounted for the greatest proportion of working days lost while the public sector accounted for the greatest proportion of workers involved. Again, in the period 1996–2002, the public sector accounted for more workers involved. Wallace *et al.* (2004: 227) comment that:

> The larger number of workers involved is the main contributor to the public sector strike record and is reflective of the larger size of public organisations.

Figure 13.5 Strike activity in Ireland: workers involved, 1922–2004

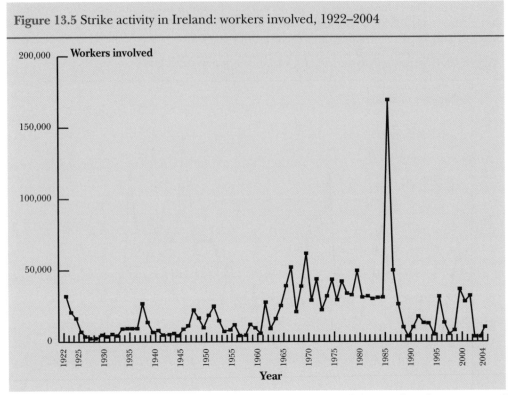

Note: Figures from the CSO are subject to minor fluctuations due to factors such as the carry-over of strikes from one year to another and variations in the numbers of workers participating in strike activity over the period of a particular strikes. However, these minor variations do not affect overall trends in the pattern of strike activity.

Source: UCD Database of Strike Statistics; CSO

In contrast to previous periods since the 1960s, the public sector also accounted for the greatest proportion of working days lost over the years 1996–2002. However, Wallace *et al.* (2004) argue that when the strike indices are standardised for levels of employment the public sector has not become more strike-prone since the 1980s.

Table 13.4 Strike activity in the public and private sectors (in per cent)

	Strike frequency		Workers involved		Working days lost	
	Public sector	Private sector	Public sector	Private sector	Public sector	Private sector
1960–1969	17.9	82.1	36.5	63.5	24.2	75.8
1970–1979	18.3	81.7	22.6	67.4	37.9	62.1
1980–1989	29.1	70.9	68.9	31.1	37.7	62.3
1990–1995	47.0	53.0	61.0	39.0	27.0	73.0
1996–2002	45.1	54.9	75.0	25.0	58.7	41.3

Source: 1960–95 data from Brannick *et al.* 1997; 1990–2002 from data supplied directly by the CSO

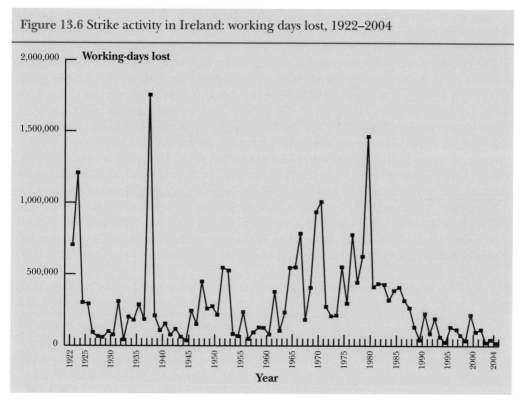

Figure 13.6 Strike activity in Ireland: working days lost, 1922–2004

Note: Figures from the CSO are subject to minor fluctuations due to factors such as the carry-over of strikes from one year to another and variations in the numbers of workers participating in strike activity over the period of a particular strikes. However, these minor variations do not affect overall trends in the pattern of strike activity.

Source: UCD Database of Strike Statistics; CSO

However, management strategies and practice also influence levels of industrial conflict and strike activity. The range of factors that may influence patterns is illustrated in Kelly and Brannick's (1988a, 1988b, 1988c, 1989, 1991) analysis of strike patterns among multinational companies (MNCs) in Ireland from the 1960s to the 1980s. In comparing patterns of strike activity in British and US-owned MNCs, Kelly and Brannick found that US companies were the most strike-prone during the 1960s. However, levels of strike activity in US companies declined dramatically from the 1970s to a stage where US-owned MNCs had a low incidence of strike activity. In evaluating the improvement of the strike record of US companies during this period, Kelly and Brannick offer two reasons.

1. The changed industrial composition of US MNCs: most were by then primarily high technology companies in the 'newer' industrial sectors, particularly electronics and chemicals (as opposed to labour intensive companies producing standardised products in the 1960s).
2. US MNCs were predominantly based in the electronics sector, which had been at the forefront in developing what are seen as innovative and proactive employee relations and HR strategies and policies.

In contrast, the strike record of British companies deteriorated dramatically over the period. Kelly and Brannick attribute the increase in strike activity to product market difficulties encountered by British-owned companies in Ireland resulting from increased competition.

The relative impact of official and unofficial strikes is another important issue affecting patterns of strike activity. 'Official' strikes are defined as those that have been fully sanctioned by the union executive. Such strikes normally occur after negotiations have failed to resolve the issue and when all due procedures have been exhausted (Gunnigle *et al.* 1995). In contrast, 'unofficial' strikes are those that have not been sanctioned by the trade union. Such strikes tend to be quite reactive in nature and are often sparked off by a particular event or incident at workplace level, such as the dismissal or suspension of a worker. Unless subsequently granted official approval by the trade union, unofficial strikes normally last for a shorter time and involve fewer workers than official strikes (Wallace and O'Shea 1987; Wallace 1988a and 1988b). In their study of unofficial strikes in Ireland, Wallace and O'Shea (1987) found that there has been a dramatic reduction in unofficial strikes since the mid-1970s (see table 13.4). Wallace *et al.* (2004) note that the percentage of strikes that were unofficial fell from 42 per cent in the 1980s to 27 per cent in the 1990s

Table 13.5 Official and unofficial strikes in Ireland (percentage share in parentheses)

	Unofficial strikes	Official strikes	Working days lost, unofficial strikes	Working days lost, official strikes
1980	81 (61.4)	51 (38.6)	184,000 (45.6)	219,500 (54.4)
1981	61 (52.1)	56 (47.9)	131,000 (30.0)	305,000 (70.0)
1982	55 (42.0)	76 (58.0)	74,000 (16.9)	363,000 (83.1)
1983	58 (38.4)	93 (61.6)	58,000 (18.6)	253,000 (81.4)
1984	75 (39.3)	116 (60.7)	51,000 (14.0)	313,000 (86.0)
1985	45 (39.1)	70 (60.9)	43,000 (9.8)	394,000 (90.2)
1986	38 (38.0)	62 (62.0)	20,500 (6.5)	295,500 (93.5)
1987	22 (28.9)	54 (71.1)	25,000 (9.6)	235,000 (90.4)
1988	26 (36.1)	46 (63.9)	6,500 (5.0)	123,500 (95.0)
1989	13 (31.7)	28 (68.3)	11,600 (28.0)	29,800 (72.0)
1990	16 (31.4)	35 (68.6)	6,800 (3.3)	196,900 (96.7)
1991	13 (25.0)	39 (75.0)	9,300 (11.2)	73,600 (88.8)
1992	11 (26.8)	30 (73.2)	2,800 (1.5)	186,800 (98.5)
1993	9 (18.8)	39 (81.3)	4,800 (7.3)	60,600 (92.7)
1994	5 (15.6)	27 (84.4)	3,800 (14.9)	21,700 (85.1)
1995	7 (19.4)	29 (80.6)	900 (0.7)	129,700 (99.3)
1996	6 (18.8)	26 (81.3)	3,000 (2.6)	111,600 (97.4)
1997	6 (21.4)	22 (78.6)	1,000 (1.3)	73,500 (98.7)
1998	15 (44.1)	19 (55.9)	8,600 (23.0)	28,800 (77.0)
1999	16 (50.0)	16 (50.0)	27,100 (12.6)	188,500 (87.4)
2000	12 (30.8)	27 (69.2)	12,000 (12.4)	85,000 (87.6)
2001	6 (23.1)	20 (76.9)	5,637 (4.9)	108,976 (95.1)
2002	2 (8.3)	22 (91.7)	1,110 (5.9)	17,731 (94.1)
2003	3 (13.6)	19 (86.4)	213 (0.6)	36,490 (99.4)
2004	1 (9.1)	10 (90.9)	5,887 (28.3)	14,897 (71.7)

Note: The following have been excluded from the above figures: in 2003, two strikes with 779 working days lost, which were not categorised as being official or unofficial; in 2000, one strike which was classified jointly (i.e. official and unofficial) and one unclassified strike; in 2002 one strike which was classified jointly and two unclassified strikes.

Source: Department of Enterprise, Trade and Employment and data supplied directly by the CSO.

and 23 per cent between 2000 and 2002. Looking at the distribution of working days lost, we see an even more dramatic decrease in the impact of unofficial strikes. Unofficial strikes accounted for 19 per cent of working days lost in the 1980s but only 6 per cent in the 1990s and 9 per cent for the period 2000–2004, so that they now account for a very small proportion of working days lost due to strike activity.

Other Forms of Industrial Action

Other forms of action, such as overtime bans and working to rule (that is, working to the letter of written terms and conditions of employment) are actually more common than strikes themselves. These other forms of overt action can provide an effective means of achieving bargaining goals, while not entailing the potential hardships of strike action. In particular, actions such as go-slows or overtime bans can place considerable pressures on employers to move towards resolution while not jeopardising employees' income and job security to as great a degree as might be the case as result of strike action (Gunnigle *et al.* 1995). A far less obvious result of poor employee relations is a lack of commitment to the organisation and lack of trust in management. This can have far-reaching long-term effects: for example, changes in work practices may be bitterly resisted; if other jobs are available, labour turnover may be high; recruitment may be difficult; productivity may fall and absences may be high. It is important that employers are aware of such long-term consequences and have a clear and fair policy on employee relations.

Finally, it is important to note that employers may also instigate industrial action. The major form of industrial action undertaken by management is normally a lockout. A lockout by management involves preventing the workforce from attending at work and is the equivalent of strike action by employers.

CONFLICT RESOLUTION: DEALING WITH DISPUTES IN EMPLOYEE RELATIONS

At the level of the enterprise, all parties involved in employee relations have an important role to play in conflict handling and resolution. Line managers, employee representatives and workers have a key role in handling disputes and grievances that arise at shop-floor level. Senior management has overall responsibility for the development of effective policies and procedures to handle employee relations and industrial conflict. Where a specialist HRM function exists, it will normally have responsibility for advising top management on optimal employee relations strategies and developing appropriate procedures and practices. It may also provide training, advice and guidance to line management in handling workplace issues. Trade unions undertake a similar role on the employee side. As mentioned above, industrial conflict should not be viewed as having a necessarily negative impact on employee relations. Industrial conflict can have certain positive effects, allowing employees to highlight and pursue issues of concern, and thus facilitate change and development in the nature of employee relations.

Possibly the most widespread response to conflict in the workplace has been the development of joint mechanisms to discuss and resolve issues of difference (Gunnigle *et al.* 1995). Such institutionalisation of conflict is primarily characterised by the development of procedures to facilitate conflict resolution. This institutionalisation of conflict reflects an implicit acceptance that issues of conflict will arise and is characteristic of the pluralist approach to employee relations discussed earlier.

In creating institutions (such as collective bargaining) and procedures for handling employee relations and industrial conflict, the parties involved seek to create a framework through which the parties can interact, argue, disagree and agree, while allowing for the ongoing operation of the business.

Grievances, disputes and disciplinary procedures are a characteristic feature of Irish employee relations and represent an important means of dealing with employee relations and industrial conflict at the level of the enterprise (see, for example, Wallace 1989). We now consider these issues.

Grievance Handling

In employee relations, the term 'grievance' is normally used to describe a formal expression of employee dissatisfaction. Given the nature of industrial organisation, it is inevitable that employees, either individually or in groups, will have grievances that they want management to address. The great majority of such grievances normally involve minor complaints related to the immediate work environment. As such, these grievances can normally be handled at shop-floor level by line management and employees and/or employee representatives. It is suggested that managers should pay particular attention to effective grievance handling and its contribution to the promotion of good employee relations in the workplace. It is also suggested that management should handle employee grievances promptly, since the non-handling of grievances may give rise to frustration which can permeate through to other employees and promote an uneasy working environment in which disputes and poor employee relations can arise. Some summary guidelines for managers involved in grievance handling are outlined in figure 13.7.

An important dimension in grievance handling is the establishment and application of grievance procedures. Such procedures normally outline the stages and approaches to be followed in handling grievances in the workplace. The main advantages associated with such procedures include the following: (i) increased clarity in employee relations interactions; (ii) prevention of misunderstandings and arguments over interpretation; (iii) ease of communication; and (iv) increased fairness and consistency in application.

Figure 13.7 Management checklist for grievance handling

- Management should make every effort to understand the nature of, and the reasons for, disputes and grievances.
- All levels of management should be aware of the key influence which grievance handling has on industrial and company performance generally.
- Management should establish a policy, which sets out an orderly and effective framework for handling disputes/grievances.
- Line management, particularly first level supervision, must be aware of their key role in effective grievance handling.

The main aim of grievance procedures is to ensure that issues raised by employees are adequately handled and settled fairly and as near as possible to their point of origin. Such aims are based on the premise that, operated effectively, grievance procedures embrace a strong preventative dimension in helping thwart the escalation of grievance issues into more serious industrial disputes. Most problems or complaints raised by employees should, ideally, be handled by the immediate supervisor without recourse to a formal grievance procedure.

However, issues that warrant more thorough consideration, may be more appropriately handled through a formal, written and agreed procedure. Grievance procedures should normally be in writing, simple and easy to operate, and aim to handle disputes and grievances fairly and consistently. Formal procedures generally follow an upward path from one hierarchical level to the next. A sample grievance procedure in a unionised organisation is outlined in figure 13.8.

Figure 13.8 Sample grievance procedure

STAGE Nature of Grievance	Procedural Level	
	Management	Employees/Trade Union
1. Issue involving local work rules or employment conditions affecting an individual or small work group.	Immediate supervisor	Employee(s)/concerned.
2. (a) Any issue which has remained unresolved at stage 1. (b) Grievance or claim where the issue has direct implications for a group of workers on a departmental or section basis.	Department manager (with relevant supervisor as appropriate)	Employee(s) concerned and shop steward or employee representative.
3. (a) Any issue which has remained unresolved from stage 2. (b) Grievance or claim with company wide implications.	HR manager and line manager(s)	Employee(s) concerned and/or shop steward/ employee reps. (inc. union official)
4. An unresolved issue that has been through the appropriate lower stages and remains unresolved.	Third party investigation: rights commissioner, Labour Relations Commission	
5. Any issue which remains unresolved after stage 4.	Labour Court Investigation: Employment Appeals Tribunal	

Since it is not always possible to resolve all grievances at firm level, it is generally necessary to make provision for referral of issues to an independent third party for mediation and/or arbitration. The main third party agencies involved in employee relations were outlined earlier in chapter 11. Grievance procedures normally contain a provision that no form of industrial action should be taken by either party until all stages of the procedure have been exhausted, and an agreed period of notice has expired before industrial action is initiated. Effectively operated, this ensures both parties have ample opportunity to settle issues either through direct discussion, or by opting for third party referral.

Handling Disciplinary Issues

Inevitably, situations will also arise in organisations where management seeks to take disciplinary action against employees. Most organisations will seek to establish and maintain what they consider are acceptable rules, standards or norms in areas such as performance, attendance and conduct at work. Should employees breach such standards management will normally seek to take some form of disciplinary action. Such disciplinary action may range from relatively minor rebukes to more serious forms such as formal warnings, suspension or dismissal.

An important aspect of discipline administration in organisations is the establishment of acceptable rules and standards and the utilisation of disciplinary procedures to deal with breaches of such rules/standards. *Disciplinary rules* set out the standards of acceptable behaviour expected from employees within an organisation and the consequences of not meeting these standards. *Disciplinary procedures* constitute the administrative machinery for applying these rules and executing any resulting action.

A critical concern in the area of discipline administration is the legal context within which discipline should be administered in organisations. In particular, the common law concept of natural justice requires that:

1. There should be a basic understanding of what constitutes a transgression, therefore company rules and standards should be clearly outlined and communicated.
2. The consequences of breaching such rules/standards should be clear.
3. Employees not achieving the required standards should be so informed and given opportunity to improve where possible.
4. Employees alleged to have breached discipline should be entitled to fair and consistent treatment, including an opportunity to state their case, have access to representation, and a right to appeal to a higher authority.

These principles combined with the legislative framework surrounding discipline administration mean that organisations should have some formal disciplinary procedure in operation, ensure employees are familiar with its contents, and apply this procedure in a reasonable fashion. The legal context for discipline administration is summarily outlined in chapter 14.[2] The most significant legislative development affecting discipline administration is the unfair dismissals legislation (1977, 1993) which provides guidelines as to what constitutes fair and unfair dismissal, and provides a mechanism for dealing with claims of unfair dismissal and for deciding upon redress for those found to be unfairly dismissed.

A disciplinary procedure is an important aspect of effective discipline administration. It is suggested that disciplinary procedures serve to establish an explicit *modus operandi* for bringing alleged offences to the notice of employees, allow employees an opportunity to respond to such charges, and facilitate the imposition of disciplinary action as necessary. A critical initial step in establishing a disciplinary procedure is to outline company rules and standards, and the form of disciplinary action associated with breaches of these rules and standards.

The establishment of explicit workplace rules helps ensure consistency in the treatment of employees. Such an outline of rules and standards should indicate: (i) those rules and standards where breaches may lead to dismissal in the first instance (e.g. theft or violence at work); and (ii) those rules and standards where breaches would lead to the operation of a standard disciplinary procedure (e.g. lateness, absenteeism and inadequate work performance). To facilitate the effective administration of disciplinary procedures the golden rules would seem to suggest that such procedures should be *agreed* between management and employees, *fair*, *understood* by management and employees and *applied consistently*. A sample disciplinary procedure is outlined in figure 13.9.

---

2. This text provides only a summary overview of the legal context of discipline administration and is not a legal interpretation thereof. Readers requiring more comprehensive insights into the legal context of discipline administration might refer to Fennel and Lynch 1993, Meenan 1999, and Lynch-Fannon and Connolly.

Figure 13.9 Sample disciplinary procedure

Preamble

The following disciplinary procedure will be used to deal with all breaches of company rules and standards except where the offences or transgression constitute gross misconduct.

The primary aim of this procedure is to help employees whose conduct or performance falls below company requirements to achieve the necessary improvements. It is desirable both in contributing to company success and the fair treatment of employees. It is company policy to apply this procedure as reasonably as possible and to ensure consistency and order in its application. It will apply to all breaches of company rules or standards not constituting gross misconduct that may typically include, but are not limited to the following:

- bad timekeeping
- unacceptable work performance
- unauthorised absence
- poor attendance
- lack of co-operation
- breaches of safety regulations

Disciplinary Procedure

1. In the first instance the individual will be asked to attend a counselling interview by his supervisor, where the employees' transgression will be made clear, the standard of performance required outlined and the employee verbally reprimanded.
2. In the second instance the employee will receive a verbal warning at a formal meeting with his supervisor and department manager, where details of the misdemeanour and the consequences of further offences will be outlined.
3. In the third instance the employee will receive a final written warning from the HR manager at a meeting with the HR manager, the department manager and, if appropriate, the supervisor. The employee will be informed of the details of the offence, future performance standards required and that further offences will lead to suspension or dismissal.
4. In the last instance the employee will either be suspended without pay or dismissed (depending on the offence). Notice of this will be given to the employee at a meeting with the general manager, when the offence will be outlined both verbally and in writing and the employee advised of his/her right of appeal.

Gross Misconduct

Gross misconduct is conduct of such a serious nature that the company could not tolerate keeping the employee in employment and it is hoped that such instances will not occur. However, for the mutual protection of the company and its workforce, any employee found guilty of gross misconduct may be dismissed summarily. Examples of gross misconduct include:

- violation of a criminal law
- consumption or possession of alcohol or illegal drugs
- threats or acts of physical violence
- theft from another employee or from the company
- malicious damage to company property
- falsifying company records (including clock cards)

Before any action is taken the company will thoroughly investigate the case, during which time the employee will be suspended. After such investigations the employee will attend a meeting with company management where he will have an opportunity to state his case and be advised of his right of appeal. Should the company still feel the employee was guilty of gross misconduct he will be dismissed and given a letter outlining the nature of the offence and reasons for dismissal.

An important aspect in ensuring procedural fairness and equity in discipline administration is the employee's right to adequate representation (by either a fellow employee or trade union representative as appropriate). Management should also ensure that accurate records are maintained in disciplinary cases.

It is important to note that the unfair dismissals legislation places the burden of proof primarily on the employer. Consequently management must be able to substantiate their case with adequate documentary evidence. Much of this work will be the responsibility of the specialist HR function. In disciplinary cases there is an onus on management to thoroughly investigate the circumstances and establish the facts of the case. If, after a thorough investigation, management decide that disciplinary action is merited a meeting is normally arranged with the employee(s) concerned. The purpose of such *disciplinary interviews* is to assess culpability, decide on appropriate action and attempt to effect the desired change in employee behaviour. The disciplinary interview also provides the employee(s) with an opportunity to present their point of view. In disciplinary cases, employees should be given a reasonable opportunity to explain their position.

Only after a thorough investigation and disciplinary meeting is management in a position to decide on appropriate action. Should the investigation and disciplinary meeting point to a need for disciplinary action, management's position should be explained to the employee(s), who should be made fully aware of their shortcomings and management's concern. The precise nature of any improvement required and the means for its achievement should be outlined, as should the consequences of future transgressions.

There is an onus on management to ensure that employees fully understand the discipline imposed and the right of appeal. After the interview, the details should be accurately recorded and a copy given to the employee(s) concerned (and their representative as necessary). Any commitments entered into should be carried out promptly.

In the longer term, the total process should be monitored from a number of viewpoints (e.g. impact on employee behaviour, trends in disciplinary incidents and effectiveness of various forms of discipline). The area of discipline administration should be approached by management in a positive vein with the overall objective being to change employees' behaviour. The HR function has an important role to play in establishing disciplinary policy and related procedures and in monitoring their application throughout the organisation. Two key factors, which need to be kept in mind, are the need for reasonableness and consistency in undertaking disciplinary action.

PARTNERSHIP AND ADVERSARIALISM IN IRISH EMPLOYMENT RELATIONS

Much of the preceding discussion on employee relations practice, and particularly that concerning collective bargaining, is grounded in what is characterised as 'adversarialism'. The adversarial system, based on the premise that the interests of management and labour conflict, relies primarily on bargaining interactions between these parties to achieve 'mutually acceptable compromises'.

As noted earlier, employee relations in Ireland is characterised by a strong adversarial tradition. This system has come in for increasing criticism in recent years, both in Ireland and abroad. A general criticism has been the perceived dominance of distributive bargaining with its emphasis on dividing limited resources (Fisher *et al.* 2003). It is argued that this approach leads the parties to develop adversarial positions believing that any gains can only be made by inflicting losses on the other side. Distributive bargaining reflects the very essence of the traditional adversarial employee relations model: claims, offers, bluff, threats, compromise, movement, agreement or conflict.

However, it is suggested that approaches based on more integrative and co-operative bargaining represent a more attractive alternative with their emphasis on a collaborative approach, exploring common ground and seeking solutions of mutual benefit to both parties. The so-called 'partnership approach' to employee relations is grounded in such thinking, suggesting that employers, workers and their representative associations should seek to address employee relations problems jointly and to develop mutually beneficial solutions (cf. Kochan and Osterman 1994; Beaumont 1995a).

Based on recent analyses of industrial change, it is widely argued that there is a need for a new 'partnership' model of employee relations that incorporates a strong trade union role (cf. McKersie 2002). This need emerges from the argued weakness of a traditional employee relations system based on adversarial collective bargaining. It is further argued that this new model allows both sides to break out of the traditional adversarial relationship through the adoption of a new model based on 'mutual gains' principles. The essential 'deal' is that employers and trade unions enter into a set of mutual commitments as follows:

1. Employers recognise and facilitate worker rights to information, consultation and involvement.
2. Workers and trade unions commit themselves actively to productivity improvements.
3. The gains of productivity improvements are shared between employers and workers.
4. Productivity improvements do not result in redundancies but rather employers actively seek new markets to keep workers gainfully employed.

In essence the mutual gains argument is that workers and trade unions actively pursue, with management, solutions to business problems and appropriate work re-organisation, in return for greater involvement in business decisions and in the process of work re-organisation.

In evaluating the merits of developing such a new relationship with workers and their trade unions, it appears that both sides face a fundamental choice on the nature of management-employee relations. Should worker/trade union involvement be confined to joint consultation or be extended to joint regulation? From a worker/trade union perspective, joint consultation initiatives run the risk of remaining essentially 'symbolic', whereby workers/trade unions have no real influence but become associated with decisions where they possess no right to veto. Employers may be equally reticent to enter into joint regulation initiatives because it may lead to a slowing in the decision-making process.

Some of the difficulties in developing partnership approaches, in the conduct of enterprise-level employee relations, are apparent in recent debates.

As noted earlier, a criticism of patterns of social partnership in Ireland is that its operation is restricted to the most senior levels of employer and trade union interests, with little diffusion into enterprise-level employee relations (see Roche 1995). At the enterprise level, a critical aspect of the partnership debate is that concerning employee participation.

EMPLOYEE PARTICIPATION

Partnership approaches to employee relations are invariably associated with initiatives designed to facilitate greater employee participation. Employee participation may be broadly interpreted as incorporating any mechanisms designed to increase employee input into managerial decision-making. Increased employee participation is an important aspect of many recent initiatives in the areas of work organisation (ICTU 1993; Kochan *et al.* 1986; Kochan and Osterman 1994).

Employee participation can take numerous forms and can range from the relatively superficial level, such as management informing employees of decisions that affect them, to consultation with employees on certain decisions or joint participation in the actual decision-making process. Such initiatives may result in a variety of institutional arrangements to facilitate employee participation, such as suggestion schemes, joint consultative committees, works councils, quality circles and board-level participation. Employee participation can also be facilitated through collective bargaining, which attempts to lessen the sphere of managerial prerogative and make more issues subject to joint negotiation and agreement.

In particular, we can point to a difference between *direct* and *indirect* forms of employees' influence. With the former approach, workers are directly involved in the decision-making process. Often captured under the rubric of *employee involvement*, direct employee participation may take a variety of forms, such as quality circles, consultative meetings and possibly the most commonly used example, namely team-working.

In contrast, indirect forms rely on the use of employees' representatives to articulate the views and claims of the larger body of employees and therefore is often termed *representative participation*. Common examples include trade unions (through collective bargaining) and works councils. Representative participation seeks to reduce the extent of management prerogative and effect greater employee influence on areas of decision-making that have traditionally been the remit of senior management.

It is possible to identify four different forms of participation, each varying in both the level and nature of participation (see figure 13.10): (i) task participation; (ii) equity participation; (iii) representative participation; and (iv) participation through collective bargaining. Variations in approaches to employee participation may stem from a variety of reasons, such as the structure and development of collective bargaining, the attitude of trade unions or the political philosophy of Government. The variety of institutional arrangements adopted in different countries and by different organisations may also reflect different philosophies and approaches to employee participation. Participation may be supported by the law or may be established through collective agreements and may be minimal or extensive.

It is often suggested that all parties in employee relations can benefit from increased employee participation (Beer *et al.* 1984). For example, it is suggested that employers need a flexible and committed workforce that will respond to change and perform at high levels of productivity, with minimum levels of supervision and that this can be achieved through employee involvement and participation initiatives. From the employees' perspective, it is suggested that the achievement of an input into decisions that affects their working lives is a very legitimate goal, allowing them greater control and discretion in their jobs (Hackman and Oldham 1980). Even at the macro level, the state and the community at large may benefit from positive workplace relations based on trust, open communications, and employees' satisfaction (Beer *et al.* 1984).

A significant aspect of the debate on employee participation in Ireland concerns the role of trade unions. Traditionally, the Irish trade union movement did not seem particularly committed to representative forms of employee participation, such as worker-directors or works councils (Morrissey 1989). Reactions to participation though equity participation have been mixed, and no discernible trend is evident. Indeed, apart from support for greater disclosure of information, the traditional trade union approach to employee participation has been marked by a considerable degree of apathy. Such apathy has strong links with the doubts many trade unionists harbour about the implications of representative participation for the union's role in collective bargaining.

> **Figure 13.10** Forms of employee participation
>
> *Task Participation:* This encompasses various initiatives to design jobs and work systems, which allow for greater employee involvement in decisions affecting their jobs and immediate work environment. Such initiatives may take a variety of forms such as autonomous work groups, quality circles and consultative meetings and committees.'
>
> *Equity Participation:* This involves the adoption of mechanisms through which employees can gain an equity share in their organisations through various profit-sharing and share-ownership schemes. Some schemes may have the broad-based objective of increasing employee loyalty, commitment and morale through the closer identification of employee interests with those of the organisation. However, equity participation by itself will not normally allow for a substantial increase in employees' influence, as employees will generally represent a minority of the shareholders. Organisations such as the John Lewis Partnership in the UK and Donnelly Mirrors in Ireland have long been known for their policy of sharing profits with employees, and many companies now offer share options or some other form of profit-sharing.
>
> *Representative Participation:* This has been the focus of most attention and applies to institutionalised arrangements that give employees input into management decision-making, sometimes with statutory support. The most obvious example is provision for the election of worker-directors to the boards of management. It also applies to lower-level participation, such as joint consultative committees and works councils. The passing of the Worker Participation (State Enterprises) Act 1977 introduced board-level participation to seven semi-state companies and these provisions were extended to a number or other state organisations under the terms of the Worker Participation (State Enterprises) Act 1988. However, board-level representation has largely been confined to the semi-state companies covered by the legislation.
>
> *Participation through Collective Bargaining:* This has been the most traditional approach to effecting higher levels of employee participation. The growth of workplace bargaining has greatly facilitated this process with trade unions being the key mechanism for representing and extending employees' rights at workplace level. However, as discussed in the text, this approach is seen as essentially adversarial in nature and as such has attracted the criticism that it is not an effective means of promoting a joint problem-solving approach to employee relations issues.

However, the trade union position seems to have altered during the 1990s. The ICTU policy documents, *New Forms of Work Organisation* and *Managing Change*, argued that trade unions needed to take a more proactive role in influencing the planning and implementation of new workforce management strategies (ICTU 1993, 1995). These reports place a particular focus on task participation at enterprise level. They note the importance for trade unions of developing, and actively participating in, employee involvement initiatives at workplace level. They also identify important aspects of employee participation that unions need to address, particularly the joint monitoring of participation initiatives at workplace level, involvement of trade unions in the internal communications processes of organisations, access to and understanding of business information and involvement in high-level business decision-making.

A more recent significant development in the area of employee participation has been the Employees (Provision of Information and Consultation) Bill 2005 which has been drafted to comply with the EU Information and Consultation Directive. The deadline for transposing the directive was 23 March 2005 but Ireland did not meet this deadline. This Bill means that, for first time in Ireland, there may be a general right to information and consultation for employees, though it only applies to undertakings with at least fifty employees, and certain procedures may have to be met beforehand. Dobbins (2005b) comments that the Bill will not give workers an automatic right to information and consultation and argues that the Bill's provisions appear to constitute a rather 'minimalist' interpretation of the EU directive. Under the Bill, negotiations to set up an information and consultation structure will be initiated only as a result of a written request from 10 per cent of a company's workforce, subject to a minimum of fifteen and a maximum of 100 employees. This so-called 'opt-in' process, whereby the onus is on employees to trigger information and consultation initiatives, contrasts with an 'opt-out' approach, whereby the Government could have placed the onus on employers to trigger information and consultation structures, unless employees did not want them. Information and consultation structures can be created through a negotiated agreement between the employer and workers or through Standard Rules, depending on the circumstances. The Standard Rules include the establishment of an Information and Consultation Forum. The ICTU and certain unions (e.g. SIPTU) have been critical of the Bill's provisions, particularly in regard to the absence of protection for employees who wish to exercise the information and consultation provisions. The ICTU Assistant General Secretary, Bill Bunting, argued that the Bill will 'do nothing to aid workplace consultation or representation' (www.ictu.ie). The only real criticism IBEC had was the delay in publishing the Bill (www.ibec.ie). There has been a mixed response to the Bill from US MNCs. Dobbins (2005c) comments that Hewlett Packard have started to establish an information and consultation forum in order to pre-empt the provisions of the Bill, while other MNCs, such as Intel, have opposed indirect collective representation and indicated their preference for direct interactions with employees. The National Centre for Partnership and Performance (NCPP) considers the EU directive a potential catalyst for diffusing enterprise partnership more widely (Dobbins 2005d). However, Dobbins also advises caution with regard to how effective a catalyst the directive will be.

CONCLUSION
This chapter reviewed key aspects of employee relations practice with particular emphasis on collective bargaining, grievance handling, discipline administration and employee participation. It also considered the impact of employee involvement initiatives. The next chapter considers an area of particular interest to HR practitioners, namely that of employment law.

14

Employment Law

This final chapter provides an overview of Irish employment law, but is not a legal interpretation thereof.[1]

It explores the legal framework within which human resource management (HRM) takes place. There are two particular aspects of employment or labour law that concern us.

1. Individual labour law, which concentrates on the relationship between the individual worker and the employer.
2. Collective labour law, which is concerned with regulating the relationship between employers and groups of employees – normally trade unions.

The primary emphasis in this chapter is on documenting the various legislative provisions that have particular relevance to the practice of HRM in Ireland. We begin with a brief introduction to the sources of law with implications for the employment relationship. The formation of a contract of employment is then examined and various statutes affecting employment are discussed. The chapter concludes with a brief discussion on the reform of collective labour law. We have previously considered the area of employee relations and aspects of 'collective' labour law in chapter 11.

SOURCES OF IRISH LAW
The Irish legal system comprises of a number of sources of law, namely the Constitution, statute law and common law.

- The *Constitution* is essentially divided into two distinct parts. First, that which sets down fundamental personal rights that are guaranteed to every Irish citizen and that the state is obliged to protect. Second, that which directs the structures and establishment of various institutions such as the Oireachtas, Government and judiciary.

---

1. For detailed information readers should refer to the particular Act or consult with the Department of Enterprise, Trade and Employment (www.entemp.ie). Readers requiring a more detailed treatment of Irish employment law should refer to, for example, Fennell and Lynch (1993) or Meenan (1999).

- *Statute law* consists of the various acts that have been passed over the years, collectively referred to as legislation. After the Constitution, statute law is the most important source of law. It can be broadly classified according to its subject matter: family law, company law, land law, criminal law, labour law and so forth. A number of pertinent employment statutes are reviewed later in this chapter.
- *Common law* is an unwritten system that has evolved over the centuries. Often called 'judge-made' law, it consists of the decisions made by the judiciary when cases are decided. In practice, this means that judges refer to similar cases when making their decisions; this is commonly known as following a precedent and it provides for some element of consistency in the interpretation of the law. Common law implies a number of duties into the contract of employment. Employers' duties specify that all employers must reimburse employees for legitimate expenses and must provide a duty of care, a safe place of work, a safe system of work, safe machinery and competent co-workers. As the employment relationship is a contract of service, it is implied that employees will perform the job personally, work co-operatively, obey all reasonable instructions, give fidelity to the employer, employ reasonable care and skill and avoid conflicts of interest.

FORMATION OF A CONTRACT OF EMPLOYMENT

The contract of employment is the legal basis of the employment relationship and is central to the interpretation and application of statutory rights. As with the basic law of contract, it requires that there must be 'offer and acceptance'; the offer being made by the employer and the acceptance by the employee when he/she agrees to work for the employer. There must also be 'consideration' or remuneration from the employer for work done, and both parties must intend to create legal relations, that is, both parties must recognise that they have particular rights and obligations that must be observed. The contract of employment may be made either orally or in writing.

Common law attempts to distinguish between a contract *of* service and a contract *for* service. An employee is someone who is employed under a contract of service; this is distinct from an independent contractor who is employed under a contract for services. The distinction is a vital one, for a variety of reasons, not least of which is that only 'employees' can benefit from much of the modern employment legislation granted to workers (Fennell and Lynch 1993). Three tests have been developed to differentiate between contracts of and for service:

1. *The Control Test.* This is based on the principle that the employer has the right to control how work is done. In other words, the employer not only tells the employee what to do but also how to do it. However, this test is difficult to administer in practice, particularly where many contracts of service (employees) have considerable discretion over the work that they do.
2. *The Integration Test.* This is based on the view that an employee is a person whose work is integrated into the business, whereas independent contractors merely work for the business. This test is also difficult to apply today since it fails to take account of work practices such as home working, which can give the appearance of self-employment and thus might be construed as contracts for service.
3. *The Multiple or Economic Reality Test.* Under this test, the entire arrangement between employer and worker is reviewed to determine whether the worker is an employee or an independent contractor. Thus the court would seek information concerning:

- whether wages, sick and holiday pay are provided and who pays them;
- whether income tax and social security are deducted under the PAYE and PRSI schemes by the company;
- whether the worker shares in the profits or losses of the company;
- whether tools and equipment for the job are provided by the company;
- whether there are specific provisions relating to termination of employment; and finally
- whether the employer is entitled to exclusive service.

If the person is free to work for other companies, provides his or her own equipment, sets his or her own work pace, and can sub-contract the work to others, then it might generally be assumed that he or she is an independent contractor.

However, despite the variety of issues that can be examined in dealing with this question, Fennell and Lynch (1993) suggest that a certain amount of confusion exists about what test should be applied. Table 14.1 outlines the key differences that can be seen to exist between a contract of service and a contract for service.

Table 14.1 Key differences between contracts of service and contracts for service

CONTRACTS OF SERVICE	CONTRACTS FOR SERVICE
Employer-employee relationship	Employer-contractor relationship
Usually a continuous relationship	A relationship based on a one-off-piece of work
Duty of care owed to employees	Duty of care arising from occupier's liability
Generally liable for the vicarious acts of employees, e.g. any wrong or injury done by an employee while in the course of his or her work	Generally not liable for the vicarious acts of independent contractors
Protective legislation applies to contract	Protective legislation does not apply (apart from Safety, Health and Welfare at Work Act 1989)
Wage or salary payment	Fee payment
Subject of contract is to carry on continuous work	Subject of contract is one-off

Source: Gunnigle, Garavan and Fitzgerald (1992).

EMPLOYMENT LEGISLATION

There is a considerable body of employment protection legislation in Ireland that provides a basic floor of rights for individual employees. This legislation is marked by several inconsistencies, particularly with respect to the differing periods of service required to qualify, and the different adjudicating mechanisms employed (see chapter 11). Several important Acts have been passed since the 1970s that have increased the number of rights that employees can expect from the employment relationship. A summary of employment legislation and its main provisions is given in Table 14.2.

It is important to note that certain categories of employees are excluded from the protection of some pieces of employment legislation, e.g. the defence forces, gardai, FÁS trainees, those working for a close relative in the home, certain public sector categories and anyone engaging in illegal employment. It is important to consult the particular Act for precise details in relation to excluded categories.

Table 14.2 Summary of employment legislation in Ireland

INDIVIDUAL EMPLOYEE LEGISLATION
Terms and conditions of employment

Terms of Employment (Information) Act 1994	Provision of a written statement to employees setting out particulars of their conditions of employment
Organisation of Working Time Act 1997	Hours of work; rest periods; annual leave; public holidays
Protection of Employees (Part-time Work) Act 2001	Extends the benefits of employment legislation to part time workers
Protection of Young Persons (Employment) Act 1996	Conditions for employing young persons
Payment of Wages Acts 1979–91	Payment by cheque; deductions from pay
National Minimum Wage Act 2000	Right to minimum rate of pay
Protection of Employees (Fixed-Term Work) Act 2003	Limits the amount of fixed-term contract an employee may have
Pensions Acts 1990–2003	Rights in relation to pensions

Employment Equality

Maternity (Protection of Employees) Acts 1981–2004	Maternity pay and job security, right to health and safety, and paternal leave in certain circumstances
Adoptive Leave Act 1995	Rights of an adopting mother and a sole male adopter are outlined
Parental Leave Act 1998	Rights of parents to leave for the purpose of caring for their child
Carers Leave Act 2001	Rights of employees to leave to care for person requiring full-time care
Employment Equality Acts 1998–2004	Outlaws 9 areas of discrimination; establishes Equality Authority and Equality Tribunal

Termination of Employment

Minimum Notice & Terms of Employment Act 1973	Notice and provisions regarding termination of employment
Unfair Dismissals Acts 1977–2001	Protection against unfair dismissal
Protection of Employment Act 1977	Consultation prior to group redundancies
Redundancy Payments Acts 1967–2003	Payment of lump sum on redundancy

Health and Safety at Work

Safety, Health and Welfare at Work Acts 1989–2005	Duties on employers, employees and others regarding health and safety issues
Safety, Heath and Welfare at Work Regulations 1993	Specific procedures and regulations for employers

COLLECTIVE EMPLOYEE LEGISLATION

Industrial Relations Acts 1946–2004	Outlines rights and procedures regarding regulation of trade disputes and industrial relations issues
Transfer of Undertakings Regulations	Right to employment security, seniority and continuity of service on the transfer of a business

INDIVIDUAL EMPLOYEE LEGISLATION

The following is a brief summary of the main individual rights of employees. Most of the statutory rights (i.e. those granted under the various acts) are only available to those who have had a specific period of continuous employment with their company or organisation. Legally, this is known as the 'qualifying period', but unfortunately there is little consistency from one Act to another as differing periods of service apply.

Terms and Conditions of Employment

WRITTEN PARTICULARS OF TERMS OF EMPLOYMENT

A contract of employment comes into force as soon as a job offer is made and accepted, whether orally or in writing, and appropriate conditions related to contract formation are adhered to. The Terms of Employment (Information) Act 1994, implements a European Union Directive that requires employers to provide a written statement setting out particulars of the employee's terms of employment within twenty-eight days or to direct employees to where they can find details of their employment. The Act also repeals sections nine and ten of the Minimum Notice and Terms of Employment Act 1973, as those sections were overtaken by the provisions of this Act.

Information to be included in the written statement includes:

- the full names of the employer and employee;
- the address of the employer in the state or, where appropriate, its principal place of business, or the registered address of the employer as registered with the Companies Registration Office;
- the place of work or, where there is no main place of work, a statement that the employee is required or permitted to work at various places;
- the job title or nature of the work;
- the date of commencement of employment;
- if the contract is temporary, the expected duration of employment;
- if the contract is for a fixed term, the date on which the contract expires;
- the rate of remuneration or method of calculating remuneration;
- whether remuneration is paid weekly, monthly or otherwise;
- terms or conditions relating to hours of work (including overtime);
- terms or conditions relating to paid leave (other than paid sickness leave);
- terms or conditions relating to incapacity for work due to sickness or injury;
- terms or conditions relating to pensions and pensions schemes;
- periods of notice which the employee is entitled to receive and required to give on termination of employment; where this cannot be indicated when the written statement is given, the written statement must give the method for determining the period of notice;
- a reference to any collective agreements that affect the terms of employment: where the employer is not a party to the agreement, the written statement must indicate the bodies or institution that made the agreement.

CONDITIONS OF EMPLOYMENT

The entitlement of employees to holidays, rest periods and the determination of hours of work is governed by the Organisation of Working Time Act 1997. It repeals the Conditions of Employment Acts 1936 and 1944, the Holidays (Employees) Act 1973, and a range of other acts covering working conditions in shops and bakeries. It provides that employees shall not work more than an average of forty-eight hours in each seven-day period. Such an average is calculated over a four-month period, but in certain specified cases, a six-month period is permissible.

The Act contains very specific provisions in relation to rest periods, Sunday working and night working. An employee is entitled to at least eleven consecutive hours of rest in each period of twenty-four hours worked. They are also entitled to a rest period of fifteen minutes for working four hours and a rest period of thirty minutes if the working period is six hours. A weekly rest period of twenty-four consecutive hours is also provided for in the Act. This weekly rest period must include a Sunday, unless otherwise provided for in the employee's contract of employment. Where an employee is required to work on Sunday and this does not form part of the employment contract, the employee is entitled to compensation. This may take the form of the following: time off in lieu, payment of a special allowance, increase in the employee's rate of pay or a combination of these items. Night work is defined under the Act as work carried out between midnight and 7 a.m. A night worker is defined as an employee who works at least three hours of their daily working period during night-time and where the number of hours worked during night-time represents at least 50 per cent of the total hours worked during the year. In order to comply with the Act, employees must ensure that night workers do not work more than an average of eight hours per night, averaged over a two-month period. The Act also sets out quite extensive provisions relating to zero-hour contracts.

In relation to holidays, an employee is entitled to paid annual leave equal to the greater of:

• four working weeks in a leave year in which 1,365 hours are worked;
• one third of a working week for each month in a leave year in which 117 hours are worked;
• eight per cent of the hours worked in a leave year (to a maximum of four working weeks).

This ensures that all employees (full-time and part-time) are entitled to annual leave/ holiday entitlements. In the case of public holidays, employees are entitled to one of the following:

• a paid day off on that day;
• a paid day off within a month of that day;
• an additional day of annual leave;
• an additional day's pay.

At present, there are nine public holidays:

• New Year's Day
• St Patrick's Day
• Easter Monday
• May Public Holiday (first Monday in May)
• June Public Holiday (first Monday in June)
• August Public Holiday (first Monday in August)
• October Public Holiday (last Monday in October)
• Christmas Day
• St Stephen's Day

In addition, the Act states that part-time employees must have worked at least forty hours during the five weeks prior to the public holiday to be entitled to the public holiday.

PART-TIME EMPLOYEES

The Protection of Employees (Part-Time Work) Act 2001 repealed the Worker Protection (Regular Part-time Employees) Act 1991, which only extended labour law protection to part-time employees who worked more than eight hours a week and who had an appropriate period of service with the same employer. The 2001 Act was introduced to provide labour law protection to all part-time workers, though many employment laws still only cover employees with an appropriate level of service. For example, an employee must have one year's service to bring an unfair dismissals claim under the Unfair Dismissals Acts 1977–2001. However, if the dismissal relates to trade union matters, the period of service required under the Act falls to thirteen weeks.

Contract Work

The Protection of Employees (Fixed-term Work) Act 2003 was introduced to comply with an EU Directive, which was to be implemented into Irish law by July 2001. The aim of the Act is to prevent people being employed for years on fixed-term contracts, without being offered a permanent position. The Act contains different regulations regarding contracts depending on their commencement date. For employees on fixed-term contracts which commenced prior to the passing of the Act (14 July 2003), the following provisions apply:

- once they complete/have completed three years' continuous employment, the employer may renew the contract for a fixed term on one occasion only;
- that renewal may be for a period of no longer than one year.

For employees on a fixed-term employment contract that commenced after the passing of the Act, the following applies:

- where they are employed on two or more continuous fixed-term contracts, the aggregate duration of those contracts may not exceed four years.

However, the Act states that the rules do not apply where there are objective grounds justifying the renewal of a contract of employment for a fixed term only.

Employment of Young People

The Protection of Young Persons (Employment) Act 1996 repeals the Protection of Young Persons (Employment) Act 1977, and lays down a number of conditions for the employment of young people. A child is defined under the Act as a person under sixteen years of age, whereas a young person is regarded as a person between sixteen and eighteen years of age.

The Act prohibits the employment of children. Young people are allowed to work a maximum of forty hours per week or eight hours in any one day. They must receive a maximum rest period of twelve hours in each twenty-four hour period and a rest period of two days in each seven-day period.

The Act creates exemptions in relation to the employment of close relations of the employer. Specific provisions are also laid down in the Act in relation to rest periods, rates of pay and the complaints procedure to the rights commissioner. Neither children nor young people are permitted to be engaged in night work.

PAY

The Payment of Wages Act 1991 repeals the Payment of Wages Act 1979 and the Truck Acts 1831 to 1896, and provides that no deductions can be made from an employee's wages without their explicit consent. The Act obliges employers to furnish an employee with an itemised pay statement setting out any deductions from the employee's wages and explaining the nature and amount of the deductions. The Act also allows for the payment of wages in modes other than cash, provided the employee consents to such arrangements.

The National Minimum Wage Act 2000 introduced a legislative framework establishing the right of employees to a legally enforceable minimum rate of pay for their labour.

Significantly, the provisions of the Act do not apply when the employee is related to the employer, or when the employee is an apprentice. Specific provisions and calculations are also set out under the Act for individuals entering employment for the first time upon reaching the age of eighteen, as well as for individuals undergoing a course of training or study authorised by their employer. However, the provisions of the Act also extend to individuals employed under a contract for services.

The Act also contains detailed provisions to ensure ease of compliance with the Act and ease of determination of employee remuneration, taking into account employee working hours and issues of 'reckonable' and 'non-reckonable' pay.

The national minimum wages, which were determined in conjunction with the Programme for Prosperity and Fairness (Section 12), were as follows:

- £4.40 (€5.59) per hour from 1 April 2000
- £4.70 (€5.97) per hour from 1 July 2001
- £5.00 (€6.35) per hour from 1 October 2002

Under the subsequent national wage agreement, Sustaining Progress, the social partners agreed that the rate would be increased to €7 per hour from February 2004; and that the Labour Court would be asked to review the minimum wage. In February 2005, the Labour Court proposed that the minimum wage be increased to €7.65 per hour and this was subsequently sanctioned by the Minister for Labour Affairs, Tony Killeen. The new national minimum wage rate took effect from 1 May 2005.

PENSIONS

The Pensions Act 1990 and the Pensions (Amendment) Act 1996 regulate the operation of occupational pension schemes in Ireland. The 1990 Act is a lengthy and complex piece of legislation establishing a legal framework for the regulation and beneficial tax treatment of pension schemes established by employers for the benefit of employees. It provides that members who have the appropriate length of service and who lose their employment before retirement age are entitled to a preserved benefit. The Act also contains provision for a transfer payment for eligible members and lays down specific provisions relating to the disclosure of information in relation to pension schemes and provisions for the equal treatment of men and women in occupational benefit schemes. Furthermore, the 1990 Act establishes the Pensions Board to carry out the following functions:

- to monitor and supervise the operation of the Act and pensions developments;
- to advise the relevant minister on pensions matters;
- to issue guidelines on the duties and responsibilities of pension scheme trustees and establish codes of practice;

- to encourage the provision of appropriate training facilities for pension su
- to publish reports (including an annual report);
- to perform other tasks at the minister's request.

In 2002, a Pensions (Amendment) Act was introduced, which provided for the
duction of Personal Retirement Savings Accounts (PRSAs) and a Pensions Ombudsn.
The function of the Pensions Ombudsman is to investigate and decide complaints
involving occupational pension schemes and the PRSAs (www.pensionsombudsman.ie).

Employment Equality
MATERNITY PROTECTION AND MATERNITY LEAVE
The Maternity Protection Act 1994 was amended and extended by the Maternity Protection
(Amendment) Act 2004. The main purpose of the Acts is to provide protection for all
pregnant employees and those who have recently given birth or who are breast-feeding.
They do this by giving them certain legal rights, the main ones being:

- the right to eighteen weeks' paid maternity leave;
- the right to up to eight weeks' additional unpaid maternity leave;
- the right to return to work;
- the right to paid time off for one set of ante-natal classes, except for last three classes,
  for expectant mothers;
- the right to paid time off for fathers to attend the last three ante-natal classes;
- where breastfeeding facilities are available, the right to breastfeeding breaks for up to
  one hour per day;
- where no breastfeeding facilities are available, the right to reduced hours of work by up
  to one hour per day for breastfeeding purposes;
- the right to health and safety leave in certain circumstances;
- the right to protection of their jobs during maternity leave, additional maternity leave,
  father's leave, health and safety leave and time off for ante-natal and post-natal care;
- the right to improvement in pay and conditions to which the employee would have been
  entitled if they were not absent from work;
- the right not to be dismissed for any pregnancy-related reason, from the beginning of
  pregnancy until the end of maternity leave;
- the right to postpone part of the maternity and/or additional leave should the child be
  hospitalised;
- the right of the father to certain leave entitlements in the event of the death of the
  mother.

The Act entitles female employees to a period of maternity leave of at least eighteen weeks,
if notice is given to the employer in writing at least four weeks before the expected date of
birth, together with a medical certificate establishing the fact of pregnancy. There is no
qualifying service in order to secure the right. The exact dates of the maternity leave can
be chosen by the employee, but the period must cover the two weeks before and the four
weeks after the birth.

During the period of maternity leave there is no break in the continuity of employee's
service. She is entitled to return to her job after the birth, provided she notifies the
employer in writing of her intention at least four working weeks before the expected date
of return. Strict compliance with these requirements is essential.

In the event of the death of the mother within sixteen weeks of the birth of a living child, the father of the child is entitled to leave until the end of the sixteenth week. The father is also entitled to 'further leave' of eight weeks. In the event of the death of the mother after sixteen weeks but before twenty-four weeks, the father is entitled to leave up until end of the twenty-fourth week.

ADOPTIVE LEAVE

Under the Adoptive Leave Act 1995, an adopting mother or a sole male adopter who is in employment is entitled to:

- a minimum of ten consecutive weeks' leave from work, beginning on the day of placement of the child, and
- up to four weeks' additional leave.

The ten-week period of adoptive leave will attract a social welfare benefit in the majority of cases.

PARENTAL LEAVE

The Parental Leave Act 1998 gives an employee fourteen working weeks' unpaid leave for the purpose of caring for his/her child. The provisions of the Act apply to the natural or adoptive parents of a child, and both the mother and the father of the child qualify for the leave concerned. In addition, one period of leave may be taken in respect of each natural or adopted child of the employee. However, the Act stipulates that periods of leave are not transferable between parents. To qualify for the full period of parental leave, the employee must have completed one year's continuous service with the employer from whom the leave is to be taken.

Employees wishing to take parental leave must give notice in writing to their employer at least six weeks before the commencement of the period of leave. An employer may postpone parental leave for a period of six months where the taking of parental leave would have a substantial adverse effect on the employer's business.

The Act also makes provision for *force majeur* leave, when an employee may avail of paid leave where their immediate presence at home or elsewhere is indispensable because of urgent family reasons owing to the injury or illness of certain persons. Such leave should not exceed three days in any twelve-month period or five days in any thirty-six-month period.

CARER'S LEAVE

The Carer's Leave Act 2001 provides an opportunity to employees with twelve months' continuous service of taking sixty-five weeks' unpaid leave for the purpose of providing full-time care and attention to a person requiring it. It applies to situations where the person involved has a disability that requires the continual supervision and frequent assistance of the employee throughout the day in connection with normal bodily functions or in order to avoid danger to themselves. To avail of carer's leave, an employee must apply to the relevant minister for a decision by a specially appointed deciding officer. Notice of the intention to take carer's leave must be given in writing to the employer at least six weeks before the commencement of such leave. The notice must state:

- the proposal to take carer's leave;
- that an application for carer's leave has been made to the deciding officer;
- the proposed date of commencement of the carer's leave.

The Act also specifies a set of provisions under which an employee may apply for consecutive period of carer's leave.

EMPLOYMENT EQUALITY ACT

The Employment Equality Acts 1998–2004 have become the cornerstone of Irish employment equality law. They repealed the Anti-Discrimination Pay Act 1974 and the Employment Equality Act 1977. The Employment Equality Acts 1998–2004 define discrimination as 'the treatment of a person in a less favourable way than another person is, has been or would be treated in a comparable situation on any of the [nine] grounds', which are:

- Gender
- Marital status
- Family status
- Sexual orientation
- Religious belief
- Age
- Disability
- Race
- Membership of the Travelling Community.

Discrimination is prohibited in the following areas:

- An employer shall not discriminate against an employee, prospective employee or agency worker in relation to access to employment, conditions of employment, training or experience for or in relation to employment, promotion or regrading or classification of posts.
- Discrimination is outlawed in collective agreements and with regard to equal pay for like work.
- Advertising in relation to employment is prohibited where it indicates (or may be reasonably understood to indicate) an intention to discriminate.
- An employment agency shall not discriminate against any person availing of their services or guidance.
- Instructors or providers of vocational training shall not discriminate in terms of any course offered or provided.
- Professional or trade organisations or vocational bodies shall not discriminate against any person in relation to membership or entry to that profession, vocation or occupation.

The Acts reaffirm the principle that employers are responsible for the actions of their employees taken in the course of their employment, regardless of whether the employer knew or approved of the actions. The Acts also require an employer to take appropriate measures to accommodate the needs of employees with disabilities, unless the measures would impose a disproportionate burden on the employer.

In terms of equality between men and women, the basic principle that men and women should receive equal pay for like work is underlined.

In relation to the other grounds of discrimination, the Acts provide that each contract of employment shall be deemed to include a non-discriminatory equality clause. This means that employees are entitled to the same rate of remuneration, despite differences

status, sexual orientation, religious belief, age, disability, race and
elling community, provided they are engaged in like work for the
loyer.

on is prohibited under the Acts. This relates to a situation where
visions, put a group of persons at a particular disadvantage
ups of persons, for example a height requirement for a job would
ntage women than men. Harassment and sexual harassment are
Harassment is defined as 'any form of unwanted conduct related
to any of the discriminatory grounds which has the purpose or effect of violating a person's
dignity and creating an intimidating, hostile, degrading, humiliating or offensive
environment for the person' (Equality Act 2004). The definition for sexual harassment is
the same as harassment, but the former emphasises that unwanted verbal, non-verbal or
physical conduct is of a sexual nature. Harassment or sexual harassment may take the form
of acts, requests, spoken words, gestures or the production, display or circulation of written
words, pictures or other material. An employer will be held responsible for acts of sexual
harassment carried out on employees by other employees, clients, customers or other
business contacts, regardless of whether the acts take place inside or outside the work
environment. Therefore an employer must take 'all reasonable steps' to ensure a
harassment-free workplace. Significantly, no remedy is provided under the Acts for same-
sex harassment. Claims under the Employment Equality Acts 1998–2004 are generally
referred to the Equality Tribunal, as noted in chapter 11.

TERMINATION OF EMPLOYMENT

Section 14 (1) of the Unfair Dismissals Act 1977 provides that within twenty-eight days of
offering employment, an employer must give the employee a notice in writing setting out
the procedure the employer will observe before and for the purpose of dismissing the
employee. If an employee is dismissed, the employer must give a written statement of the
reasons within two weeks of the date of dismissal.

It is wise to send all such statements by recorded delivery and where related previous
correspondence exists – such as warning letters, dismissal letters – to include copies of these
as well. Although all such earlier incidents or warnings should have been properly recorded
and the employee given copies at the time that they occurred, it is advisable to include
copies and refer to them again in the final written reasons for dismissal. An employee may
take a case before the Employment Appeals Tribunal if written reasons are refused or if
the reasons are perceived to be inadequate.

Notice of Termination

Both the employer and the employee are normally entitled to a minimum period of notice,
although either employer or employee may accept pay in lieu of notice. Under Section 4
(1) of the Minimum Notice and Terms of Employment Act 1973, an employee who has
thirteen weeks' continuous service is entitled to a statutory minimum notice. Section 4 (2)
of the Act sets out the periods of minimum notice to which employees covered by the Act
are entitled: see table 14.3.

These are *minimum* periods: if a contract of employment gives entitlement to a longer
period, the longer period will apply.

Under Section 6 the employer in turn is entitled to a period of notice of not less than
one week from an employee who has been in continuous employment for thirteen weeks

Table 14.3 Periods of minimum notice

Continuous Service of Employee	Minimum Notice
Less than 2 years	1 week
More than 2 years but less than 5	2 weeks
More than 5 years but less than 10	4 weeks
More than 10 years but less than 15	6 weeks
15 years or more	8 weeks

or more. This period does not increase in line with the length of service; however, the contract of employment may specify a period of notice that is required by the employer.

The Employment Appeals Tribunal has stated that the notice given by the employer must be sufficiently certain and precise, leaving no room for ambiguity or uncertainty. The precise expiry date (date of dismissal) must be clearly specified in writing and the period of notice given must be not less than the minimum statutory period or the formal contractual period of notice. Employees to whom the notice provisions apply are entitled to the same rights during the minimum notice period as they would enjoy but for the notice. Failure by an employer to give notice correctly can affect the effective date of dismissal and therefore the eligibility of an employee's claim of unfair dismissal to be heard by the Employment Appeals Tribunal.

If the employer fails to give the employee the proper period of notice, the employee may claim breach of contract through the courts (common law remedy) or, if he/she is covered by the Minimum Notice and Terms of Employment Act, through an action to the Employment Appeals Tribunal. Categories of workers not covered by these provisions include the Garda Siochana, defence forces, local authority employees and civil servants.

Unfair Dismissal

Under the Unfair Dismissals Act 1977, once an employee has been continuously employed for one year he/she has a right of action if he/she is unfairly dismissed. If an employee has been dismissed and perceives it as being unfair he or she can bring a case to the Employment Appeals Tribunal or a rights commissioner within six months of the date of dismissal. The Unfair Dismissals (Amendment) Act 1993, provides that, in exceptional circumstances, the time frame within which a case may be brought may be extended to within twelve months of the date of dismissal. The date of dismissal is taken to be the date on which notice of the termination of contract expires. When prior notice is not given, the date of dismissal is taken to be the date on which such notice would have expired if it had been given. (The Employment Appeals Tribunal and rights commissioners are discussed in chapter 11.)

The following categories of employees are not eligible to submit a claim for unfair dismissal:

- employees who have less than one year's continuous service with the same employer. (If it is shown that a dismissal resulted wholly or mainly from the employee's membership, or proposed membership, of a trade union, or from their activities on behalf of a trade union the requirement of one year's continuous service does not apply; a woman who claims she was dismissed because of pregnancy may bring her unfair dismissal claim even though she does not have a year's continuous service with her employer.);

- those over the normal retiring age;
- close relations of the employer who are members of his or her household and work in a private dwelling house;
- members of the Garda Siochana and defence forces;
- those employed by or under the state;
- those serving apprenticeships with FÁS;
- officers of local authorities, health boards and vocational educational committees.

Dismissal is automatically unfair where it is shown that it resulted wholly or mainly from any of the following causes:

- taking part in a strike or other industrial action;
- following a lockout;
- the employee's trade union membership or activities;
- religious or political opinion;
- involvement in legal proceedings against the employer;
- the age of the employee;
- the race or colour of the employee;
- the sexual orientation of the employee;
- the pregnancy of the employee;
- the employee's membership of the travelling community;
- unfair selection for redundancy.

In general, where a dismissal is contested, the burden of proving that the dismissal is fair rests firmly with the employer. However, in constructive dismissal cases, where the employee terminates the employment contract because of the employer's conduct or because conditions in the organisation make it impossible to stay, the onus is on the employee.

The decision to dismiss must be taken carefully, as the penalties that may be incurred if a dismissal is ruled as unfair by the Employment Appeals Tribunal are severe. It is important, therefore, that one should know the conditions under which an employee may be fairly dismissed. The Unfair Dismissals Acts were updated in 2001 to take into account changes introduced by the Protection of Employees (Part-time Work) Act 2001.

DISMISSAL FOR MISCONDUCT

The issue of reasonableness has great significance in the context of dismissal for misconduct. The Employment Appeals Tribunal (EAT) will consider general industrial standards. There is no absolute definition of reasonableness since it depends on individual circumstances within the company. The EAT has emphasised that misconduct must be measured in the context of the employee's actions and not just the consequences or potential consequences of that behaviour to the employer. It has further decided that in misconduct cases, the employer must, before taking the decision to dismiss, consider whether there were mitigating circumstances, such as a record of good service or personal difficulties experienced by the employee.

In the case of minor misconduct – such as persistent lateness – an employer must show that all of the stages in the disciplinary procedure have been followed and, having exhausted these, have given written warning that further infringements would lead to dismissal. To prove that the employer had acted properly it is necessary to have kept a written record of all the procedures that had gone through in the case.

If the misconduct were more serious – such as fighting, breaking a works rule, or sleeping on duty – going through every stage of the procedure might be unnecessary. However, the employer would need to observe the rules of natural justice, which are:

- the employee has a right to be told the facts of the case against him/her;
- the employee has the right to a hearing (to tell his/her side of the story);
- the employee has the right to representation of his/her choice;
- the employee has the right to appeal to a higher level of his/her choice within the company.

Failure to comply with the rules of natural justice may render a dismissal unfair.
An employer should also:

- Enquire into the matter to find out what really happened. If fact-finding is going to take some time it may be necessary to suspend the employee on full pay.
- Interview the employee to get his/her side of the story, advising him/her of the right to be represented if appropriate.
- Decide on the basis of the information what action is reasonable in the circumstances. Did the employee know the rule that was broken? Was he/she aware of its significance? Would a clearly stated warning of dismissal for repetition be more reasonable than dismissal for a first time offence? How have similar cases been treated in the past, i.e. is the employer being consistent with previous 'custom and practice'?
- Make clear to the employee what action is to be taken and how he/she can appeal against the decision if the procedure allows this.

CAPABILITY, COMPETENCE OR QUALIFICATIONS

Section 6 (4) (a) of the Unfair Dismissals Act 1977 provides that a fair basis for dismissal relates to the capability, competence or qualifications of the employee for performing work of the kind he/she was employed by the employer to do. While it may be fair to dismiss someone for incapability, if a complaint were made an employer would need to convince a tribunal that they had a valid reason for dismissing the person, and that they had acted reasonably in treating that reason as a sufficient cause for dismissal.

Capability, as determined by EAT, usually relates to dismissals arising from illness, injury or similar inadequacy. The question of whether the employee was to blame for the illness or incapacity is irrelevant. In the case of capability the Tribunal has introduced a number of exceptions:

1. Where an employee who is incapacitated due to injury or illness could be given lighter work that he would have been able to perform, the dismissal may be unfair.
2. Where an employee is absent it is up to the employer to try to find out why. It is not reasonable to assume, without further investigation, that the absence is due to illness that might justify dismissal.

INCAPABILITY BECAUSE OF ILL-HEALTH

Dismissals resulting from incapacity due to ill health may arise in cases of persistent short-term absenteeism or cases of long-term absence caused by prolonged illness or injury. In both instances, an employer needs to ask how reasonable it is to dismiss an employee who has been off work for an extended period of time. Reasonable action would again consist of being seen to follow fair procedures and securing the fullest possible information. Evidence of fair procedure might include the following:

- visiting the employee (perhaps on more than one occasion) to find out how likely it is that they will be returning to work, and to make clear to them how long the company can wait;
- if the company cannot wait any longer, obtaining an independent medical report, which would be a useful element in making a decision;
- considering whether alternative work could be made available;
- advising the employee of the decision.

In the case of dismissal due to illness-related absence, the High Court has set out the following grounds placing an onus on employers to prove that the dismissal is fair by showing:

1. it was the employee's ill-health that was the reason for the dismissal;
2. this was the substantial reason;
3. the employee received fair notice that the question of their dismissal for incapacity was being considered;
4. the employee was afforded an opportunity of being heard.

INCAPABILITY BECAUSE OF INCOMPETENCE

Competence issues arise when an employee is alleged to have demonstrated a poor work performance, for example failure to meet reasonable targets set by the employer. To act fairly in dismissing someone for this reason, an employer must detail evidence of the alleged incompetence, and must have discussed this with the employee. An employer would also need to establish that they did not contribute to the incompetence by failing to make requirements clear, or by not providing the necessary facilities to allow the job to be done competently.

A warning might be appropriate. If so, it should clearly state what is required of the employee within set time limits. In such instances, an employee must be given a reasonable time period within which to effect such improvement and a reasonable work situation within which to concentrate on their work defects. In the case of long-serving employees, it might be more reasonable to consider whether a less arduous job could be found.

As with misconduct, warnings are not necessary if an employer believes they serve no purpose, but the employer might have to convince a tribunal of this. A case will obviously be much easier to make if an employee has been given warnings and a chance to improve with as much reasonable help from the employer as possible.

INCAPABILITY BECAUSE OF QUALIFICATIONS

The concept refers primarily to the absence of formal qualifications that are essential to the job, which is another fair reason for dismissal under certain circumstances. This category might include the case of an accountant losing their professional qualifications, or the case of an employee who misled an employer into thinking they had certain qualifications or experience on joining, but in fact did not. It might also arise where the employee did not have the qualifications on joining, has agreed to take steps to obtain them, but who seems unable to obtain them despite repeated attempts and every assistance from the company.

Reasonable dismissal in this category would depend on how critical the qualification was to the job and the duties of the employee in question, and how long the situation was likely to continue. As in other cases, an employer would need to consider whether an alternative job could be offered for which the person was qualified.

BREAKING ANOTHER STATUTE

It is fair for an employer to dismiss an employee who could not continue to work without breaking another law. The sales representative who loses his driving licence is a clear example. As usual, however, an employer would need to consider alternatives to dismissal. Could the employer offer alternative work? Could other arrangements be made for the period?

INDUSTRIAL ACTION

Section 5 (1) of the Unfair Dismissals Act 1977 provides that the dismissal of an employee by way of lockout is fair if the employee is offered reinstatement or re-engagement from the date of resumption of work. Section 5 (2) provides that the dismissal of an employee for taking part in a strike or other industrial action is unfair if any other employee or employees who took part in the strike were reinstated or re-engaged. Where an employer dismissed all the employees who took part, the onus is still on them to prove that they had fair grounds under one of the previous headings or on other substantial grounds. If they cannot do so the dismissal will be unfair.

OTHER SUBSTANTIAL GROUNDS

An employer may succeed even if a dismissal does not fall under any of the previous headings if they can claim that it qualifies on 'other substantial grounds'. This heading has not been used very often and furthermore there is little consistency in the decisions of the Employment Appeals Tribunal.

Redundancy

The Redundancy Payments Act 1991 provides that a dismissal resulting from a redundancy of an employee is not unfair. Redundancy is basically defined as dismissal caused by either the fact that the employer has ceased their business, or that they no longer require the work carried out by the particular employee, or they are reducing the scope of their workforce. The onus is on the employer to prove the existence of redundancy. They cannot simply claim that a situation of redundancy exists; they must produce substantial evidence.

Even where there is a genuine redundancy not all dismissals will necessarily be fair. A number of qualifications have been introduced.

1. Where an employee was selected in contravention of a procedure that has been agreed between the employer and the employee or trade union or that was established by custom and practice and no special reasons are produced for departing from this procedure, then the dismissal will be unfair.
2. If the employer had an ulterior motive in selecting the particular employee, then the dismissal will be unfair even if there was a genuine redundancy.

An employer should not use arbitrary criteria in selecting employees for redundancy. The Employment Appeals Tribunal examines all aspects of an employee's conduct, including the observance of statutory obligations such as the Protection of Employment Act 1977 (this Act allows for consultation and information relating to mass redundancies). Not only must an employer use proper criteria, but they must also be applied in a fair manner.

REDUNDANCY PAYMENTS

Under the Redundancy Payments Acts 1967–2003, employees under a contract of employment or apprenticeship who have had at least two years' continuous service and are aged between 16 and 66, are entitled to a redundancy payment in the event of being made redundant. The Redundancy Payment Act 2003 significantly altered the statutory payment, which is calculated as follows:

- two weeks' pay per year of service;
- one week's pay (the bonus week).

There is a ceiling on the amount of weekly pay to be used when calculating the redundancy, which is €507.90. Employees are not entitled to a redundancy payment if they unreasonably refuse an offer of suitable alternative employment with their own employer, or with another company in the same group where continuity of employment can be maintained, provided the alternative employment does not involve a significant reduction in status or conditions.

LEGAL REGULATION FOR REDUNDANCY

Redundancy legislation is very complex, containing many detailed provisions and rules. As a general classification the Acts fall into two categories:

- Legislation dealing with collective redundancies; this lays down procedural regulations to be observed by employers, and bestows a number of rights on unions.
- Legislation on what constitutes redundancy, the right to a redundancy payment and the calculation of continuous service.

The Protection of Employment Act 1977 lays down procedural obligations in the case of collective redundancies. There are a number of specific provisions that a manager will need to be aware of:

1. The Act applies to a situation where in a period of thirty days a number of employees are dismissed for redundancy. The minimum number required varies, depending on the size of the total workforce.
2. The main obligation on employers is consultation and notification. If a company has a collective redundancy then the Minister for Enterprise, Trade and Employment must be notified at least thirty days before the final dismissal. The employer must also send a copy of this notice to the employees' representatives.
3. At least thirty days before the dismissal, the employer must enter into consultation with the employee's representatives with a view to reaching agreement on issues such as the numbers to be made redundant, alternative courses of action and the implementation of the redundancies. The Act does not specify what happens in the event of an agreement not being reached.
4. Employers are also obliged to provide the employees with certain information relating to the redundancy. Examples include the reasons for the redundancy, the number of employees affected and the period during which it is to take place.
5. Employers are also obliged to keep adequate records of the situation.

In the event of a redundancy taking place, the individual employee's situation is governed by the Redundancy Payments Acts 1967–2003. Under Section 7 of the 1967 Act as amended, redundancy is defined as follows: '. . . an employee who is dismissed shall be taken to be dismissed by reason of redundancy if the dismissal is attributable wholly or mainly to one of the following':

- where the employer has ceased or intends to cease to carry on business for the purpose of which the employee was employed;
- where the requirements of the business do not require the particular type of work which the employee has to offer;
- where the employer decides to carry on the business with fewer employees;
- where the employer decides that the work which the employee does is to be done in a different manner;
- where the employer decides that the work done by the particular employee should from now on be done by a person who is capable of doing other work for which the employee is not sufficiently qualified to do.

Other important provisions include the following:

- The entitlement to a redundancy payment cannot be waived and any term in a contract of employment that purports to do so is invalid.
- The employer must give notice in writing to the employee of the proposed dismissal and must send a copy to the Minister for Enterprise, Trade, and Employment thirty days in advance. The employer must also furnish the employee with a redundancy certificate.
- The Acts allow the employee time off to try out the alternative job to test its suitability. The employee has four weeks in order to test its suitability.
- Employees eligible for redundancy pay are entitled to reasonable time off work, with pay, to look for another job. An employer may in such circumstances seek evidence that the employee is actually using the time off in the intended manner. If an employer refuses to allow time off, the employee may bring the matter to the EAT.
- Furthermore, an employee who is under notice does not have to work this notice if it is agreed that he should receive any due payment in lieu.

However, where the employer terminates the contract, it is also important that they give notice correctly, as this could affect the effective date of dismissal and therefore the eligibility of an employee's claim of unfair dismissal to be heard by the Employment Appeals Tribunal. The effective date of dismissal should be made very clear (in writing) to the employee and any period of notice given must not be less than the minimum statutory period or the formal contractual period of notice.

HEALTH AND SAFETY AT WORK[2]

Both common law and statute law lay down a number of provisions concerning health and safety in the workplace. A useful classification of the relevant statutes is as follows:

- those that deal exclusively with the safety and health of workers;
- those concerned with the regulation of hours of work;
- those not designed exclusively as worker protection measures, but that nevertheless provide varying degrees of protection;

---

2. Readers requiring more detailed information on safety, health and welfare at work regulations should consult with the Health and Safety Authority (www.hsa.ie) or Garavan (2002).

- those on the border line between issues of general environmental pollution and occupational health and safety.

Common Law

Outside all the legislation (statute law) that exists on health and safety at work, an employer may also incur liability at common law. The position is that an employer is legally responsible for any injuries or diseases that occur on the job. Case law has clearly laid down that an employer must exercise reasonable care towards employees and must guard them against any likely injury or disease. If an employer fails to live up to this obligation, then liability for negligence will occur if an employee is injured. However, it is important to remember that liability will only arise when an employer's negligence actually caused or contributed to an employee's injury or disease. Furthermore, the incident that occurs must be reasonably foreseeable. The reason for this is simple – common law is not concerned with anticipating damages or setting standards of good behaviour in order to prevent accidents, it only comes into play after the event, and its main function is to compensate employees for any injuries they receive while at work.

As well as laying down a general principle of employers' liability for injuries, the courts have gone further and have specified different elements of the employers' duties. This is directly relevant and provides a useful framework within which to evaluate a company's safety effort. The four duties are worth considering in detail.

1. SAFE PLANT AND EQUIPMENT

This duty covers machinery, raw materials, tools etc. However, employers will not incur liability if they obtain supplies from a reputable company and had no reason to suspect that they were faulty.

Employers must also keep up to date with the potential dangers of new processes and machinery. They will have observed their duty of care if they keep up to date with information that is already known to exist: no liability will arise against a hazard that scientific knowledge is not yet aware of.

2. COMPETENT FELLOW WORKERS

Employers are expected to take reasonable steps to ensure that employees are able to do their jobs. This involves clarifying the personal qualities and skills required to do the particular job, ensuring that one has a systematic recruitment and selection procedure and providing the necessary training to do the job and special remedial training where necessary.

For an employee to succeed in an action under this heading he/she would have to show two things:

1. That the other worker was unsuitable for the job.
2. The employer had not been sufficiently careful in appointing or retraining the other worker.

If an employee exhibits quite unpredictable behaviour that causes injury to a fellow employee, the employer will not be held responsible, unless there has been a history of an employee exhibiting such behaviour.

3. Provision of Safety Equipment and Effective Supervision

Employers are under an obligation to provide employees with the necessary protective equipment and clothing required to do the job without exposing them to risk or injury. Proper instructions should also be issued. The courts have also clearly stated that it is not enough for the employer to inform the employee that the equipment is available; they must take reasonable measures to see that the employee uses it. This could include issuing formal warnings for not wearing such personal protective equipment (PPE).

4. Safe Premises and System of Work

Employers must take great care in the way work is laid out and organised. They must not expose employees to risks that could easily be avoided by more careful organisation. They are also expected to maintain their premises in a reasonable state of repair and orderliness.

The courts have held that this duty extends to a customer's premises. If an employee is injured while working on a customer's premises they may have a claim against the employer. The employer's responsibility will be less, however, than if it was on the employer's premises. Employers will be liable to their employees for injuries that arise out of defects in the customer's premises that were apparent and that the employer should have taken reasonable precautions against.

Employers will not be liable, as a general rule, for employees on their way to and from work. However, if employers provide a company bus for transporting staff, they must have a competent driver and must ensure that the bus is properly maintained. Furthermore, if an employer allows their employees onto the premises outside working hours, reasonable steps must be taken to ensure that the premises is safe. The law further indicates that employers are vicariously liable for any damage or injury caused by their employees while in the course of their employment. Should a driver employed by a company injure a member of the public whilst driving in the course of their job, the employer may be found liable for the injury to the member of the public.

The Safety, Health and Welfare at Work Act 2005

The Safety, Health and Welfare at Work Act 2005 repealed the Safety, Health and Welfare at Work Act 1989. The primary focus of the 2005 Act is on the prevention of workplace accidents, illnesses and dangerous occurrences and the provision of significantly increased fines and penalties aimed at deterring those who continue to flout health and safety laws.

The Health and Safety Authority

The 1989 Act established the National Authority for Occupational Safety and Health and the 2005 Act changed its name to the Health and Safety Authority (HSA). The Authority comprises a chairman and eleven ordinary members (three nominated by employee organisations, three nominated by employer organisations and five nominated by the Minister for Enterprise, Trade and Employment). Its functions include the following:

- to enforce the Health, Safety and Welfare at Work Act;
- the provision of advisory services;
- to promote a 'safety culture';
- to provide education and training in health, safety and welfare of persons at work;
- to conduct research on matters relating to its functions;
- to monitor and make recommendations to the Minister the implementation of, and compliance with, the legislation and best practice on health, safety and welfare at work.

Duties Imposed by the Safety, Health and Welfare Act 2005

A number of general and specific duties are imposed by the Act on both employers and employees.

Employers

1. To ensure the health, safety and welfare at work of all employees (Section 8). The Act gives examples of some areas that must be considered:
   (a) design, provision and maintenance of the place of work;
   (b) safe means of access to and exit from the place of work;
   (c) the provision and maintenance of machinery without risk;
   (d) safe systems of work;
   (e) the provision of information, instruction, training and supervision;
   (f) where hazards exist that cannot be controlled or eliminated, the provision and maintenance of suitable protective equipment;
   (g) adequate and current emergency plans;
   (h) ensuring safety with regard to articles or substances in use;
   (i) the provision and maintenance of welfare facilities;
   (j) the use of specialist services to provide for health, safety and welfare of the workforce.
2. To ensure that those not in their employment who may be affected are not exposed to risks to their safety or health (Section 12).
3. To prepare a safety statement (Section 19). The safety statement must:
   - Specify the manner in which health, safety and welfare shall be secured.
   - Be based on an identification of hazards and an assessment of risks.
   - Include arrangements made and resources provided.
   - Specify the co-operation required from employees.
   - Specify the names of the persons responsible.
   The safety statement must be brought to the attention of all those who are affected by it.
4. To consult employees. Employers must consult their employees so that they can initiate and maintain effective measures; they can co-operate in promoting and developing measures to ensure health and safety; that the effectiveness of their arrangements can be ascertained.
5. To take account of employees' views (Section 26). Not only must there be consultation, but employers must take account of representations made by the workforce.

Employees

Section 13 details the general duties of employees while at work.

1. They must take reasonable care for their own safety and that of any other person who may be affected.
2. They must co-operate with their employer to such an extent that all relevant statutory provisions are complied with.
3. They must report any problems of which they become aware, or that might have an effect on safety, health or welfare.
4. They must not be under the influence of an intoxicant (drugs or alcohol) at the workplace to the extent that they are likely to endanger their own, or another person's, safety, health and welfare.

5. They may be required by their employer to submit reasonable tests for intoxicants by, or under the supervision of, a medical practitioner.
6. They must attend such training and assessment as required by their employer.
7. They must not engage in improper conduct or behaviour.
8. They may be required to undergo a medical assessment of their fitness to perform work activities, which give rise to serious risks to health and safety.

A controversial part of the Act concerns the possible testing of employees for intoxicants. The purpose of this part of the Act is to make alcohol and drug testing company policy in safety-critical industries, particularly the construction, transport and pharmaceutical industries. Regulations will be introduced to govern this process but it is unlikely to occur in the near future due to the need for the HSA to consult widely with interested groups, including social partners, before formulating the regulations. It is anticipated that, in certain circumstances or sectors, regulations may specify that an employee, if required by their employer, must 'submit to independent tests by a competent person which are appropriate, reasonable and proportionate' (Department of Enterprise, Trade and Employment website, www.entemp.ie).

Complaints by Employees

The 1989 Act conferred quite specific rights on employees. They have the right to make representations to, and to consult their employers on matters of safety, health and welfare in their place of work. The 2005 Act expands on employee rights provided for in the 1989 Act. Employees and safety representatives now have the right to make a complaint to a rights commissioner if they believe they have been penalised for the following:

- acting in compliance with the legislation;
- being a safety representative;
- making a complaint to the safety representative or employer regarding health, safety and welfare at the workplace;
- leaving a workplace or refusing to return to work while a serious and imminent danger persisted.

Penalisation can include suspension, lay-off, dismissal, demotion, loss of promotion opportunity, transfer of duties, coercion and intimidation. If a rights commissioner finds that a complaint is well-founded, they may require the employer to take a specific course of action and/or require the employer to pay compensation to the employee. Appeals of rights commissioners' decisions may be made to the Labour Court.

The Safety Representative and Safety Committee

Employees are entitled to appoint a safety representative whose functions may include the following:

1. To investigate accidents and dangerous occurrences.
2. To investigate complaints relating to health, safety and welfare at work.
3. To accompany an inspector carrying out an inspection of a place of work, not related to an accident.
4. At the discretion of an inspector, to accompany them carrying out an inspection of a place of work related to an accident.

5. At the discretion of an inspector, and at the request of an employee, to attend an interview of an employee by an inspector.
6. To make representations to the employer.
7. To make representations to an inspector on health and safety matters, including the investigation of accidents.
8. To receive advice and information from inspectors.

Employees are also entitled to appoint a safety committee, for the purposes of assisting employers and employees in relation to the legislation. A committee shall consist of not less than three people and not more than one for every twenty people employed or ten, whichever is the less.

Joint Safety and Health Agreements
A new feature introduced by the Safety, Health and Welfare at Work Act 2005 is that a trade union of employers and a trade union of employees can negotiate a joint safety and health agreement, which provides practical guidance with respect to safety, health and welfare at work. The parties can then apply to the Health and Safety Authority to approve the agreement and an approved agreement can be taken into account when enforcing the Act.

The Safety, Health and Welfare at Work Regulations
Since the inception of the Safety, Health and Welfare at Work Act 1989, a series of regulations has emerged to make explicit and operational the provisions implicit in the Act. While numerous sets of regulations have been enacted covering areas such as construction, signage, carcinogens, biological agents, night work and shift work, the most prominent of these regulations have been the Safety, Health and Welfare at Work (General Applications) Regulations (S.I. No. 44 of 1993; S.I. No. 188 of 2001). They provide detailed information on safety management, particularly in relation to accident-reporting requirements, training, first aid, manual handling and PPE. The Safety, Health and Welfare at Work (Pregnant Employees) Regulations 2000 (S.I. No. 218 of 2000), which repeals the Safety, Health and Welfare at Work (Pregnant Employees) Regulations 1994 (S.I. No. 446 of 1994) obliges employers to carry out a risk assessment of the workplace to ensure the safety and health of employees during pregnancy and breastfeeding. Furthermore, it contains specific provisions regarding night working and supplying employees (or their safety representative) with information on the results of the risk assessment and the measures to be taken concerning the employees' safety. The Safety, Health and Welfare at Work (Explosive Atmosphere) Regulations 2003 (S.I. No. 258 of 2003) provides health and safety rules for workplaces where an explosive atmosphere is likely to be present and specify classifications of explosive atmospheres. The Health, Safety and Welfare at Work (Confined Spaces) Regulations, 2001 (S.I. No. 218 of 2001) concerns safety and emergency rescue procedures in workplaces with confined spaces such as diving or mining.

COLLECTIVE LEGISLATION
Collective labour law establishes the legal framework for employee/industrial relations, and is distinguished from individual labour law in that it is concerned with regulating the relationship between employers and collectivises of employees – normally trade unions (see chapter 11).

Industrial Relations

The Industrial Relations Act 1990 is the definitive piece of legislation governing relations between employers and employees and their representatives. The Act is the most comprehensive revision of the law governing trade unions, trade disputes and industrial relations generally. The provisions of the Act can be broadly divided between trade union law and industrial relations law.

TRADE UNION LAW

Trade Disputes

The approach adopted in the area of trade disputes law was to repeal the Trade Disputes Acts of 1906 and 1982 and to reintroduce the main provisions of these Acts with amendments. The main features of the provision relating to trade disputes are as follows:

1. *Individual disputes.* The Act withdraws immunities from one-person disputes where agreed procedures have not been followed.
2. *Secondary action.* This is now restricted unless the union can show that the secondary employer directly sought to frustrate the aims of the dispute.
3. *Picketing.* Workers may now picket only their own employer at the employer's place of work.
4. *Immunities.* The Act places limitations on the blanket immunity that existed under Section 4 of the Trade Dispute Act 1906 in respect of tortuous acts (acts for which a civil action for damages could be brought). The immunity now exists only for acts 'committed in contemplation or in furtherance of a trade dispute'.
5. *Worker v. worker dispute.* These no longer fall within the definition of a trade dispute.
6. *Injunctions* (an order issued by a court to a party to an action, to refrain from some act). In trade dispute situations where a secret ballot has been held and one week's notice given, the granting of injunctions to employers, especially *ex-parte* injunctions, is restricted.

Secret Ballots

Union rules must contain provisions for the holding of secret ballots before any form of industrial action can be taken. No injunction will be granted to an employer in the event of a secret ballot being held.

Trade Union Rationalisation

The Act makes a number of amendments to existing trade union law designed to encourage mergers and to discourage formation of new or breakaway unions. The Act essentially increases the minimum membership required for trade unions to secure a negotiating licence (to 1,000) and the sum of money required to be held on deposit with the High Court (between €25,395 and €76,184, depending on membership numbers). The Act also amends the Trade Union Act 1975 by offering grants towards the expenses incurred in a two-year period prior to a merger attempt even if the attempt fails.

INDUSTRIAL RELATIONS LAW

The Industrial Relations Act 1990 provides for the establishment of the Labour Relations Commission and divides functions between it and the Labour Court. Previously, the Labour Court had two primary functions – a conciliatory and an investigative function – and a number of secondary functions, such as those of joint industrial councils, joint labour committees, rights commissioners. Under the Act a number of functions of the Labour Court were transferred to the Labour Relations Commission, the most important being the conciliation service and the rights commissioners service (see chapter 11).

The Industrial Relations (Amendment) Act 2001 introduced additional provisions for promoting harmonious relations between employers and employees. It outlined a set of criteria allowing trade unions to petition the Labour Court to investigate a particular trade dispute. In such instances, the Court may make a recommendation, giving its opinion on the matters under dispute. Where the matter is not resolved, the Court may be asked by the trade union to make a determination. Such determinations are legally enforceable by court order. The Industrial Relations (Miscellaneous Provisions) Act 2004 extended the provisions of the 2001 Act by cutting down on the number of steps provided for in the 2001 Act and providing a time frame for the remaining steps.

Transfer of Undertakings

The Transfer of Undertakings Regulations (S.I. No. 487 of 2000 and S.I. No. 131 of 2003) provide employees with a series of rights on the transfer of a business. A transfer under the 2003 Regulations means the transfer of an economic entity that retains its identity. Under such circumstances, the employment rights, seniority, continuity of service and representation rights of employees are protected and employers are obliged to consult with their employees in the event of a proposed transfer. An employee may not be dismissed solely by reason of the transfer. The regulations also outline a set of sanctions in the event of non-compliance by employers with the provisions contained therein. Complaints under the 2003 Regulations may be made by an employee, trade union, staff association or excepted body to the rights commissioner with a right of appeal to the Employment Appeals Tribunal.

Bibliography

Abramovitz, M., and David, P. (1996), 'Technological change and the rise of intangible assets: the U.S. economy's growth path in the twentieth century', *Employment and Growth in the Knowledge-based Economy*, Paris: OECD, 35–61.

Adams, J. (1965), 'Inequity in social exchange', in L. Berkowitz (ed.), *Advances in Experimental Social Psychology*, vol. 2, London: Academic Press.

Adamson, S., Doherty, N., and Viney, C. (1998), 'The meanings of career revisited: implications for theory and practice', *British Journal of Management*, December, 251(9).

Adkins, C., Russell, C., and Werbel, J. (1994), 'Judgements of fit in the selection process: the role of work value congruence', *Personnel Psychology*, 47 (3), 605–24.

Aldag, R., and Brief, A. (1979), *Task Design and Employee Motivation*, New York: Scott, Foreman and Company.

Alderfer, C. (1972), *Existence, Relatedness and Growth*, New York: The Free Press.

Alexander, L. (1985) 'Successfully implementing strategic decisions', *Long Range Planning*, vol. 18, no.3, 91–7.

Allen, K. (2000), *The Celtic Tiger: The Myths of Social Partnership*, Manchester: Manchester University Press.

Allen, R. (2001), 'Aligning reward practices in support of total quality management', *Business Horizons*, May.

Anastasi, A. (1982), *Psychological Testing*, London: Macmillan.

Anderson, L., and Wilson, S. (1997), 'Critical incident technique', in D. Whetzel and G. Wheaton (eds), *Applied Measurement Methods in Industrial Psychology*, Palo Alto, CA: Davies-Black Publishing.

Anderson, N. (1992), 'Eight decades of employment interview research: a retrospective meta-review and prospective commentary', *European Work and Organisational Psychologist*, 2, 1–32

Anderson, N., Born, M., and Cunningham-Snell, N. (2001), 'Recruitment and selection: applicant perspectives and outcomes, in N. Anderson, D. Ones, H. Sinangil and C. Viswesvaran (eds), *Handbook of Industrial, Work and Organizational Psychology*, London and New York: Sage, vol. 1, 200–18.

Anderson, N., and Shackleton, V., (1986) 'Recruitment and selection: a review of developments in the 1980s', *Personnel Review*, vol. 15, no. 4.

Anderson, N., and Shackleton, V. (1993), *Successful Selection Interviewing*, Oxford: Blackwell.

Appelbaum, S., and Shapiro, B. (1991), 'Pay for performance: implementation of individual and group plans', *Journal of Management Development*, vol. 10, no. 7.

Applebaum, E., Bailey, T., Berg, P., and Kalleberg, A. (2000), *Manufacturing Advantage: Why High Performance Work Systems Pay Off*, Washington, D.C.: Economic Policy Institute.

Applebaum, E., and Batt, R. (1994), *The New American Workplace: Transforming Work Systems in the United States*, Ithaca, NY: ILR Press.

Argyris, C., and Schön, D. (1978), *Organisational Learning: A Theory-in-Action Perspective*, Reading, MA: Addison Wesley.

Arment, L. (1990), 'Learning and training: a matter of style', *Industrial and Commercial Training*, vol. 22, no. 3, 16–21.

Armstrong, M. (1987) 'Human resource management: a case of the emperor's new clothes', *Personnel Management*, vol.19, no. 8, 30–5.

Armstrong, M. (1992), *Human Resource Management: Strategy and Action*, London: Kogan Page.

Armstrong, M. (1995), *A Handbook of Personnel Management Practice*, London: Kogan Page.

Armstrong, M. (1999), *A Handbook of Human Resource Management Practice* (7th edn), London: Kogan Page.

Armstrong, M., and Baron, A. (1995), *The Job Evaluation Handbook*, London: Institute of Personnel and Development.

Armstrong, M. and Murlis, H. (1988, 1994, 1998), *Reward Management: A Handbook of Remuneration Strategy and Practice* (various edns), London: Kogan Page/Institute of Personnel Management.

Armstrong, P. (1988), 'The personnel profession in the age of management accountancy', *Personnel Review*, vol. 17, no. 1, 25–31.

Armstrong, P. (1994), 'Accountancy and HRM' in J. Storey (ed.), *Human Resource Management: A Critical Text*, London: Routledge.

Arnold, J. (1997), *Managing Careers into the 21st Century*, London: Paul Chapman Publishing.

Arnold, J., Robertson, I.T., and Cooper, C. (1995), *Work Psychology: Understanding Human Behaviour in the Workplace*, London: Pitman.

Arthur, J. (1992). 'The links between strategy and industrial relations systems in American steel minimills', *Industrial and Labor Relations Review*, 45, 488–506.

Arthur, J. (1994), 'Effects of human resource systems on manufacturing performance and turnover', *Academy of Management Journal*, 37, 3, 670–87.

Arthur, M., and Rousseau, D. M. (eds) (1996), *The Boundaryless Career: a New Employment Principle for a New Organisational Era*, New York: Oxford University Press.

Ashton, D. (1986), 'Current issues in line/staff relationships', *Management Education and Development*, 10, 2, 105–18.

Atkinson, A. (1984), *Flexible Manning: The Way Ahead*, London: Institute of Manpower Studies.

Atkinson, J., and Meager, N. (1986), 'Is flexibility just a flash in the pan?', *Personnel Management*, September, 26–9.

Attwood, M. (1989), *Personnel Management*, London: Macmillan.

Avery, R., Miller, H., Gould, R., and Burch, P. (1987), 'Interview validity for selecting sales clerks', *Personnel Psychology*, 40, 1–12

Bacon, N. and Storey, J. (1993), 'Individualization of the employment relationship and the implications for trade unions', *Employee Relations*, vol. 15, no. 1, 5–17.

Bain, G. (1970), *The Growth of White Collar Unionism*, Oxford: Clarendon Press.

Baird, L., Briscoe, J., Tuden, L., and Rosansky, L. (1994), 'World class executive development', *Human Resource Planning*, 17, 1–16.

Baldwin, T., Danielsen, C., and Wiggenhorn, W. (1997), 'The evolution of learning strategies in organizations: from employee development to business redefinition', *Academy of Management Executive*, 11, 4, 47–58.

Balkin, D., and Gomez-Mejia, L. (1987), *New Perspectives on Compensation*, New York: Prentice Hall.

Bandura, A. (1986), *Social Foundations of Thought and Action*, Englewood Cliffs, NJ: Prentice Hall.

Banner, D., and Cooke, R. (1984), 'Ethical dilemmas in performance appraisal', *Journal of Business Ethics*, 3, 327–33.

Barber, A. (1998), *Recruiting Employees: Individual and Organizational Perspectives*, Thousands Oaks, CA: Sage.

Barnett, R. (1999), 'Learning to work and working to learn', in D. Boud and J. Garrick (eds), *Understanding Learning at Work*, London: Routledge.

Barney, J. (1991), 'Firm resources and sustained competitive advantage', *Journal of Management*, 17, 99–120.

Barney, J. (1995), 'Looking inside for competitive advantage', *Academy of Management Executive*, 9, 49–81.

Barney, J. (1997), *Gaining and Sustaining Competitive Advantage*, Addison-Wesley.

Barrow, M., and Loughlin, H. (1992), 'Towards a learning organisation: 1. the rationale', *Industrial and Commercial Training*, 24, 1, 3–7.

Barry, F. (2002), 'FDI and the host economy: a case study of Ireland', unpublished paper presented at Department of Management, National University of Ireland, Galway, 8 November.

Bean, R. (1976), 'Industrial reactions' in E. Cohen and G. Studdard (eds), *The Bargaining Context*, London: Arrow.

Beardwell, I., and Holden, L. (1997), *Human Resource Management: A Contemporary Perspective*, London: Pitman.

Beardwell, I., and Holden, L. (2001), *Human Resource Management: A Contemporary Perspective* (3rd edn), London: Pearson Publishing.

Beattie, R., and McDougall, M. (1998), 'Inside or outside HRM? Locating lateral learning in two voluntary sector organisations', in Mabey, C., Skinner, D., and Clark, T. (eds), *Experiencing Human Resource Management*, London: Sage, 218–35.

Beaumont, P. (1980), 'The success of white collar recognition claims', *Employee Relations*, vol. 2, no. 4.

Beaumont, P. (1985), 'New plant work practices', *Personnel Review*, vol. 14, no. 5, 15–19.

Beaumont, P. (1991), 'Trade unions and HRM', *Industrial Relations Journal*, vol. 22, no. 4, 300–8.

Beaumont, P. (1993), *Human Resource Management: Key Concepts and Skills*, London: Sage.

Beaumont, P. (1995a), *The Future of Employment Relations*, London: Sage.

Beaumont, P. (1995b), 'The European Union and developments in industrial relations' in P. Gunnigle, and W. Roche (eds), *New Challenges to Irish Industrial Relations*, Dublin: Oak Tree Press.

Beaumont, P., and Harris, R. (1994), 'Opposition to unions in the non-union sector in Britain', *International Journal of Human Resource Management*, vol. 5, no.2, 457–71.

Beaumont, P., and Townley, B. (1985), 'Greenfield sites, new plants and work practices', in V. Hammond (ed.), *Current Research in Management*, London: Frances Pinter.

Bechet, T., and Walker, J. (1995), 'Aligning staffing with business strategy', *Human Resource Planning*, 16, 2, 1–16.

Becker, B., and Gerhart, B. (1996), 'The impact of human resource management on organizational performance: progress and prospects', *Academy of Management Journal*, 39, 4, 779–801.

Becker, B., and Huselid, M. A. (1998), 'High performance work systems and firm performance: A synthesis of research and managerial implications', in G. R. Ferris (ed.), *Research in Personnel and Human Resource Management*, vol. 16, 53–101, Greenwich, CT: JAI Press.

Becker, B., Huselid, M., Pickus, P., and Spratt, M. (1997), 'HR as a source of shareholder value: research and recommendations', *Human Resource Management*, vol. 36, no. 1, 39–47.

Becker, G. (1964), *Human Capital*, New York: Columbia Press.

Beer, M., Spector, B., Lawrence, P., Mills, D., and Walton, R. (1985), *Human Resource Management: A General Manager's Perspective*, New York: The Free Press.

Beer, M., Spector, B., Lawrence, P., Quinn-Mills, D. and Walton, R. (1984), *Managing Human Assets: The Groundbreaking Harvard Business School Program*, New York: The Free Press.

Behrens, M., and Traxler, F. (2004), 'Employers' organisations in Europe', European Industrial Relations Observatory on line, www.eiro.eurofound.eu.int/2003/11/study/tn0311101s.htm.

Bell, D. (1974), *Planning Corporate Manpower*, London: Longman.

Benchley, R. (2001), 'The value of human capital', *Chief Executive*, February.

Bendix, R. (1956), *Work and Authority in Industry: Ideologies of Management in the Course of Industrialization*, New York: Wiley.

Benge, E. (1944), *Job Evaluation and Merit Rating*, Washington DC: US National Foreman's Institute.

Bennet, R. (1991), *Management*, London: Pitman.

Berg, A. (1989), 'Part-time employment: a response to economic crisis', in Rosenberg, S. (ed.), *The State of the Labour Market*, New York: Plenum.

Berggren, C. (1990), 'Det nya bilarbetet' ['The new automobile employment'], PhD Dissertation, University of Lund, Sweden.

Berridge, J. (1992), 'Human resource management in Britain', *Employee Relations*, vol. 14, no. 5, 62–92.

Berry, J. (1990), Linking Management Development to Business Strategies, *Training and Development Journal*, vol. 44, no. 8, 20–22.

Bevan, S., and Thompson, M. (1992), 'How are companies interpreting performance management?', *Personnel Management*, November.

Biddle, D., and Evenden, R. (1989), *Human Aspects of Management*, London: Institute of Personnel Management.

Birchall, A. (1975), *Job Design: Planning and Implementation Guide for Managers*, London: Gower Press.

Black, J., and Boal, K. (1994), 'Strategic resources – traits, configurations and paths to sustainable competitive advantage', *Strategic Management Journal*, 15, 131–48.

Blackwell, J. (1990), 'The changing role of part-time work in Ireland and its implications', Labour Market Review, Issue 1, June.

Blennerhassett, E. (1983), *Work Motivation and Personnel Practices: A Study of Civil Services Executive Staff*, Dublin: Institute of Public Administration.

Blennerhassett, E., and Gorman, P. (1986), *Absenteeism in the Public Service: Information Systems and Control Strategies*, Dublin: Institute of Public Administration.

Block, P. (1990), *The Empowered Manager*, San Francisco: Jossey Bass.

Bloom, M., and Milkovich, G. (1998), 'Relationships Among Risks, Incentive Pay and Organizational Performance', *Academy of Management Journal*, 41, 3.

Blyton, P., and Morris, J. (eds) (1991), *A Flexible Future: Prospects for Employment and Organisation*, Berlin: De Gruyter.

Blyton, P., and Morris, J. (1992), 'HRM and the limits of flexibility', in P. Blyton and P. Turnbull (eds), *Reassessing Human Resource Management*, London: Sage.

Blyton, P., and Turnbull, P. (eds) (1992), *Reassessing Human Resource Management*, London: Sage.

Blyton, P., and Turnbull, P. (1994), *The Dynamics of Employee Relations*, London: Macmillan.

Boerlijst, G., and Meijboom, G. (1989), 'Matching the individual and the organisation', in P. Herriot (ed.), *Assessment and Selection in Organisations: Methods and Practice for Recruitment and Appraisal*, Chichester: John Wiley.

Boisot, M. (1999), *Knowledge Assets: Securing Competitive Advantage in the Information Economy*, Oxford: Oxford University Press.

Boud, D., and Garrick, J. (eds) (1999), *Understanding Learning at Work*, London: Routledge.

Bowey, A. (1975), Installing Salary and Wage Systems, in Bowey, A. (ed.) (1982), *Handbook of Salary and Wage Systems*, London: Gower.

Bowey, A., and Thorpe, R. (1986), *Payment Systems and Productivity*, London: Macmillan.

Boxall, P. (1992), 'Strategic human resource management: beginnings of a new theoretical sophistication, *Human Resource Management Journal*, 2, 3, 60–79.

Boxall, P. (1996), 'The strategic HRM debate and the resource-based view of the firm', *Human Resource Management Journal*, 6, 3, 59–75.

Boxall, P., and Purcell, J. (2000), 'Strategic human resource management: where have we come from and where are we going?', *International Journal of Management Reviews*, 2, 2, 183–203.

Boxall, P., and Purcell, J. (2003), *Strategy and Human Resource Management*, Basingstoke: Palgrave Macmillan.

Boyatzis, R. (1972), *The Competent Manager: A Model for Effective Performance*, New York: Wiley.

Boyd, A. (1972), *The Rise of Irish Trade Unions: 1729–1970*, Tralee: Anvil.

Boyer, R. (ed.) (1988), *The Search for Labour Market Flexibility*, Oxford: Clarendon Press.

Brannick, T., and Doyle, L. (1994), 'Industrial conflict', in T. Murphy and W. Roche (eds), *Irish Industrial Relations in Practice*, Dublin: Oak Tree Press.

Brannick, T., Doyle, L., and Kelly, A. (1997), 'Industrial Conflict', in T. Murphy and W. Roche (eds), *Irish Industrial Relations in Practice*, Dublin: Oak Tree Press.

Bratton, J., and Gold, J. (1999), *Human Resource Management: Theory and Practice*, Basingstoke: Macmillan Press.

Braverman, H. (1974), *Labour and Monopoly Capital: The Degradation of Work in the Twentieth Century*, London,: Monthly Review Press.

Breaugh, J., and Starke, M. (2000), 'Research on employee recruitment: so many studies, so many remaining questions', *Journal of Management*, vol. 26, 405–34.

Breen, R., Hannon, D., Rottman, D. and Whelan, C. (1990), *Understanding Contemporary Ireland: State, Class and Development in the Republic of Ireland*, Dublin: Gill and Macmillan.

Brewster, C. (1990), 'Flexible working and strategic HRM in Europe: research data', Brussels: MCE Industrial Relations Conference, November.

Brewster, C., and Hegewisch, A. (eds) (1994), *Policy and Practice in European Human Resource Management*, London: Routledge.

Brewster, C., Hegewisch, A., Lockhart, T., and Mayne, L. (1993), 'Flexible working patterns in Europe', *Issues in People Management*, no. 6, London: Institute of Personnel Management.

Brewster, C., Mayrhofer, M., and Morley, M. (2000), 'The concept of strategic European human resource management', in C. Brewster, W. Mayrhofer and M. Morley (eds), *New Challenge for European Human Resource Management*, 3–33.

Brooks, I. (1999), *Organisational Behaviour: Individuals, Groups and the Organisation*, London: Financial Times/Pitman Publishing.

Brousseau, K., Driver, M., Eneroth, K. and Larsson, R. (1996), 'Career pandemonium: realigning organisations and individuals', *Academy of Management Executive*, 10, 4, 52–66.

Brown, J. (1994), 'The juridification of the employment relationship', Aldershot: Aylesbury.

Brown, W. (1981), *The Changing Contours of British Industrial Relations*, Oxford: Blackwell.

Buchanan, D. (1979), *The Development of Job Design Theories and Techniques*, London: Saxon House.

Buchanan, D. (1994), 'Principles and practice of job design' in K. Sisson (ed.), *Personnel Management: A Comprehensive Guide to Theory and Practice in Britain*, Oxford: Blackwell.

Buchanan, D., and McCalman, J. (1989), *High Performance Work Systems: The Digital Experience*, London: Routledge.

Buckley, M., Ferris, G., Bernardin, H., and Harvey, M. (1998), The disconnect between the science and practice of management', *Business Horizons*, 41, 31–8.

Buckley, R., and Caple, J. (1992) *The Theory and Practice of Training*, London: Kogan Page.

Buller, P., and Napier, N. (1993), 'Strategy and human resource management integration in fast growth versus other mid-sized firms', *British Journal of Management*, 4, 2, 77–90.

Burack, E., Hochwarter, W., and Mathys, N. (1997), 'New management development paradigm', *Human Resource Planning*, 20, 14–22.

Butler, J. E. (1988), 'Human resource management as a driving force in business strategy', *Journal of General Management*, 13, 4, 88–102.

Butler, P. (1985), 'Employer organisations: a study', unpublished BBS final-year project, University of Limerick.

Byrne, T. (1988), 'IPM in Ireland 1937–1987', *IPM News*, vol. 3, no. 2.

Cairns, N., and Thompson, J. (1988), 'Manpower Planning in Northern Ireland', *Irish Business and Administrative Research*, vol. 9, 38–45.

Calvert, G., Mobley, S., and Marshall, L. (1994), 'Grasping the learning organisation', *Training and Development*, June.

Campion, M., Purcell, E., and Brown, B. (1988), 'Structured interviewing: raising the psychometric properties of the employment interview', *Personnel Psychology*, 41, 25–42.

Cannon, F. (1995), 'Business driven management development', *Journal of European Industrial Training*, 19, 26–31.

Cannon, T. (1999), Foreword, in J. Winterton and R. Winterton, *Developing Managerial Competence*, London: Routledge.

Cappelli, P. (1995), 'Rethinking employment', *British Journal of Industrial Relations*, 33, 4, 563–602.

Cappelli, P. (1999), *The New Deal at Work: Managing the Market Driven Workforce*, Cambridge: Harvard Business School Press.

Cappelli, P., and Crocker-Hefer, A. (1996), 'Distinctive human resources are a firm's core competencies', *Organizational Dynamics*, 28, 2, 7–21.

Carey, A. (1967), 'The Hawthorne studies: a radical criticism' *American Sociological Review*, June.

Carnoy, M. (1999), 'The family, flexible work and social cohesion at risk', *International Labour Review*, vol. 138, 4, 411–23.

Cascio, W. (1986), *Managing Human Resources: Productivity, Quality of Work Life, Profits*, McGraw-Hill.

Casey, B., Lakey, J., and White, M. (1992), *Payment Systems: A Look at Current Practice* (Research Series, no.5), Department of Employment, London: Policy Studies Institute.

CEDEFOP (2002), *National Actions to Implement Lifelong Learning in Europe*, Brussels: European Commission.

Central Bank of Ireland (2000), *Winter Bulletin*, Dublin: Central Bank of Ireland.

Central Statistics Office (2004a), *Statistical Yearbook of Ireland 2004*, Dublin: Government Publications Office.

Central Statistics Office (2004b), *Population and Labour Force Projections 2006–2036*, Dublin: Government Publications Office.

Chadwick, C., and Cappelli, P. (1999), 'Alternatives to generic strategy typologies in strategic human resource management', in P. Wright, L. Dyer, J. Boudreau, and G. Milkovich (eds), *Research in Personnel and Human Resources Management*, supplement 4, 11–29, Greenwich, CT: JAI Press.

Chandler, A. (1962), *Strategy and Structure: Chapters in the History of the Industrial Enterprise*, Cambridge, MA: MIT Press.

Chartered Institute of Personnel and Development (2004), *Recruitment, Retention and Turnover Survey*, London: CIPD.

Cherns, A., and Davis, L. (1975), *The Quality of Working Life*, London: Macmillan.

Chubb, B. (ed.) (1992), *FIE: Federation of Irish Employers 1942–1992* Dublin: Gill and Macmillan 1992.

Clarke, P. (1989), 'Payment by result schemes: a review of trends', *Industrial Relations News*, no. 8, 23.

Clegg, H. (1979), *The Changing System of Industrial Relations in Great Britain*, Oxford: Blackwell.

Cole, A. (2000), *Issues in Web Based Pedagogy: A Critical Primer*, London: Greenwood Press.

Cole, G. (1988), *Personnel Management: Theory and Practice*, London: DP Publications.

Collings, D., Gunnigle, P., and Morley, M. (2006), 'American multinational subsidiaries in Ireland: changing the nature of employment relations?' in G. Boucher and G. Collins (eds) *Working in Contemporary Ireland* (in press), Dublin: Liffey Press.

Commission on Industrial Relations (1972). 'Employers' Organisations and Industrial Relations' Study no. 1, London: H.M.S.O.

Commission of Inquiry on Industrial Relations (1981). *Report of the Commission of Inquiry on Industrial Relations*, Dublin: The Stationery Office.

Confederation of Irish Industry (1981), 'Jobs and the Workforce' Business Report no. 11.

Conner, K., and Prahalad, C. (1996), 'A resource based theory of the firm: knowledge versus opportunism', *Organization Science*, 7, 477–501.

Conway, E. (2004), 'Relating career stage to attitudes towards HR practices and commitment: evidence of interaction effects?' *European Journal Of Work And Organisational Psychology*, 13, 4, 417–46.

Conway, E., and McMackin, J. (1997), 'Developing a culture for innovation : what is the role of the HR system?', Dublin City University Business School Research Paper no. 32, Dublin: Dublin City University.

Conyon, M., Peck, S., and Read, L. (2001), 'Performance pay and corporate structure in UK firms', *European Management Journal*, 19, 1, 73–82.

Cook, J., and Crossman, A. (2004), 'Satisfaction with performance appraisal systems: a study of role perceptions', *Journal of Managerial Psychology*, 19, 5, 526–41.

Cook, S., and Yanow, D. (1993), 'Culture and organizational learning', *Journal of Management Enquiry*, 2, 4, 373–90.

Cowling, A., and Walters, M. (1990), 'Manpower planning – where are we today?', *Personnel Review*, 19, 3, 3–8.

Cox, B., and Hughes, J. (1989), 'Industrial relations in the public sector' in *Industrial Relations in Ireland: Contemporary Issues and Developments*, Dublin: University College Dublin.

Coyle-Shapiro, J., Kessler, I., and Purcell, J. (2004), 'Exploring organizationally directed citizenship behaviour: reciprocity or "it's my job"', *Journal of Management Studies*, 41, 1, 85–105.

Cradden, T. (1992), 'Trade unionism and HRM: the incompatibles', *Irish Business and Administrative Research*, vol. 13, 37–48.

Cranet E./University of Limerick (1992), *Study of HR Practices in Ireland*, Limerick's Employment Relations Unit, University of Limerick.

Cranet E./University of Limerick (1995), *Study of HR Practices in Ireland*, Limerick's Employment Relations Unit, University of Limerick.

Cranet E./University of Limerick (1999), *Study of HR Practices in Ireland*, Limerick's Employment Relations Unit, University of Limerick.

Cronshaw, M., Davis, E., and Kay, J. (1994), 'On being stuck in the middle or good food costs less at Sainsbury's', *British Journal of Management*, 5, 1, 19–32.

Cropanzano, R. (2001), *Justice in the Workplace: From Theory to Practice*, New Jersey: Lawrence Erlbaum Associates.

Cross, C., and Turner, T. (2005), 'Irish workers' perceptions of the impact of immigrants: a cause for concern?', paper to the Irish Academy of Management, Galway, September.

Crouch, C. (1982), *Trade Unions: The Logic of Collective Action*, London: Fontana.

Culliton, J. (1992), *A Time for Change: Industrial Policy for the 1990s*, report of the Industrial Policy Review group, Dublin: Stationery Office.

Curson, C. (1986), *Flexible Patterns of Work*, London: IPM.

Dale, M. (1995), *Successful Recruitment and Selection: A Practical Guide for Managers*, London: Kogan Page.

Daniel, W., and Millward, N. (1983), *Workplace Industrial Relations in Britain: The DE/PSI/ESRC Study*, London: Heinemann.

D'Art, D. (2002), 'Managing the employment relationship in a market economy', in D. D'Art and T. Turner (eds), *Irish Employment Relations in the New Economy*, Dublin: Blackhall Press.

D'Art, D., and Turner, T. (2002), 'Corporatism in Ireland: a view from below', in D. D'Art and T. Turner (eds), *Irish Employment Relations in the New Economy*, Dublin: Blackhall Press.

Dastmalachian, A., Blyton, P., and Adamson, R. (1991), *The Climate of Workplace Relations*, London: Routledge.

Datta, D., Guthrie, J., and Wright, P. M. (2005), 'Human resources management and labour productivity: does industry matter?', *Academy of Management Journal*, 48, 1, 135–46.

Davies, G., and Wilson, T. (2002), 'Implications for reflective HRD practitioners of the influence of life experience on managerial career decisions', in J. McGoldrick, J. Stewart and S. Watson (eds), *Understanding Human Resource Development: A Research Based Approach*, London: Routledge.

Davis, L. (1966), 'The design of jobs', *Industrial Relations*, 6, 1.

Davis, T., and Landa, M. (1999), 'A contrary look at employee performance appraisal', *Canadian Manager*, 24, 3,18–21.

Deaton, D. (1985), 'Management style and large scale survey evidence', *Industrial Relations Journal*, vol. 16, no. 2, 67–71.

De Cieri, H., and Dowling, P. (1999), 'Strategic human resource management in multinational enterprises: theoretical and empirical developments' in *Research in Personnel and Human Resources Management*, supplement 4, 304–26, Greenwich, CT: JAI Press.

DeGeus, A. (1997), *The Living Company: Growth, Learning and Longevity in Business*, London: Nicholas Brealey.

Delaney, J., and Huselid, M. (1996), 'The impact of human resource management practices on perceptions of organisational performance', *Academy of Management Journal*, vol. 39, 4, 949–69.

Delbridge, R., and Turnbull, P. (1992), 'Human resource maximization: the management of labour under just in time manufacturing systems' in P. Blyton and P. Turnbull (eds), *Reassessing Human Resource Management*, London: Sage.

Delery, J., and Doty, D. (1996), 'Modes of theorising in strategic human resource management; tests of universalistic, contingency, and configurational performance predictions, *Academy of Management Journal*, 39, 4, 802–35.

Department of Enterprise and Employment (1993), *Duties and Responsibilities of Employee Representatives and the Protection and Facilities to be Afforded them by their Employer*, Dublin: Department of Enterprise and Employment.

Dessler, G. (2001), *A Framework for Management*, New Jersey: Prentice Hall.

Dineen, D. (1987), 'Employment development in the Irish Economy since 1979', paper presented to the International Conference on 'The Changing Nature of Employment: New Forms and New Areas', Paris: BIPE.

Dineen, D. (1992), 'Atypical work patterns in Ireland: short term adjustments or fundamental changes', *Administration*, vol. 40, no. 3, Autumn.

Dobbins, T. (2004a), 'New Act bars victimisation of both non-union and union workers', *Industrial Relations News*, 9, 20–21.

Dobbins, T. (2004b), '2004: the year in review', *Industrial Relations News*, 48, 16–20.

Dobbins, T. (2005a), 'Union density decline driven by global economic forces', *Industrial Relations News*, 35, 18–21.

Dobbins, T. (2005b), 'Onus will be on workers to "trigger" consultation rights', *Industrial Relations News*, 5.

Dobbins, T. (2005c), 'US Chamber leaves indelible stamp on Employee Consultation Bill', *Industrial Relations News*, 30.

Dobbins, T. (2005d), 'Consultation law seen as catalyst for "high-road" industrial relations', *Industrial Relations News*, 27.

Dobson, P. (1989), 'Reference reports' in P. Herriot (ed.), *Assessment and Selection in Organisations*, John Wiley.

Docherty, P., and Nyhan, B. (1997), *Human Competence and Business Development: Emerging Patterns in European Companies*, London: Springer-Verlag.

Doeringer, P., and Piore, M. (1971), *Internal Labour Markets and Manpower Analysis*, New York: Lexington Books.

Donnelly, E. (1987), 'The training model: a time for change?', *Industrial and Commercial Training*, May/June, 3–6.

Donovan, Lord (Chairman) (1968), Royal Commission on Trade Unions and Employers' Associations, 1965–1968, Cmnd 3623, London: HMSO.

Downes, D. (1986), 'Manpower planning in Ireland: A survey of current practice in the Mid-West region', unpublished final-year project (BBS–Personnel), NIHE, Limerick.

Doyle, W., and Young, J. (2000), 'Management development: making the most of experience and reflection, *Canadian Manager*, Fall, 18–20.

Drejer, A. (2001), 'How can we define and understand competencies and their development?', *Technovation*, 21, 135–46.

Driver, M. (1982), 'Career concepts: a new approach to career research' in R. Katz (ed.), *Career Issues in Human Resource Management*, Englewood Cliffs: Prentice Hall.

DuBrin, A. (1978), *Human Relations: A Job Oriented Approach*, Virginia: Reston Publishing Company.

Duffy, K. (1993), 'Training: why we lag behind our Euro partners', *Irish Independent*, Business and Recruitment Supplement, 18 March, 3.

Duggan, D., Hughes, G., and Sexton, J. (1997), 'Occupational employment forecasts 2003', *FÁS/ESRI Manpower Forecasting Studies*, Report no. 6, November, Dublin: FÁS/Economic and Social Research Institute.

Easterby-Smith, M. (1986), *Evaluation of Management, Training and Development*, Aldershot: Gower.

Economist, The (1988), 'A survey of the Republic of Ireland. Poorest of the rich', *The Economist*, vol. 306, no. 7533, 1–26.

Economist, The (1997), 'Green is good – advantages of Ireland as a host for FDI', 17 May, vol. 343, no. 8017, 21–4.

Economist Intelligence Unit (EIU) (1999), 'Country profile: Ireland', London: Economist Intelligence Unit.

Edwards, M., Ewen, A., and O'Neal, S. (1995), 'Using multisource assessment to pay people not jobs', *ACA Journal*, Summer, 4–17.

Edwards, P., and Wright, M. (2001), 'High-involvement work systems and performance outcomes: the strength of variable, contingent and context-bound relationships', *International Journal of Human Resource Management*, vol. 12, no. 4, 568–85.

Eichel, E., and Bender, H. (1984), *Performance Related Pay: A Study of Current Techniques*, American Management Association.

Elger, T. (1991), 'Flexible futures? New technology and the contemporary transformation of work', *Work, Employment and Society*, vol. 1, no. 4.

Elkington, J. (1997), *Cannibals with Forks: The Triple Bottom Line of 21st Century Business*, Oxford: Capstone.

Elliott, R. (1990), *Labour Economics – A Comparative Text*, Berkshire, UK: McGraw Hill.

Elloy, D., and Smith, C. (2003), 'Patterns of stress, work-family conflict, role conflict, role ambiguity and overload among dual-career and single-career couples: an Australian study', *Cross Cultural Management*, 10, 1, 55–66.

Employment Appeals Tribunal (2000), *The Employment Appeals Tribunal Thirty-Second Annual Report 1999*, Dublin: The Employment Appeals Tribunal.

Employment Appeals Tribunal (2003), *The Employment Appeals Tribunal Thirty-Fifth Annual Report 2002.* Dublin: Employment Appeals Tribunal.

Equality Authority (2001), *The Equality Authority Annual Report 2000*, Dublin: The Equality Authority.

European Commission (1997), *Labour Market Studies: Ireland*, Series No. 1, Brussels: European Commission.

European Foundation for the Improvement of Living and Working Conditions (EFIWLC) (1997), *New Forms of Work Organisation: Can Europe Realise its Potential?* Dublin: European Foundation for the Improvement of Living and Working Conditions.

European Foundation for the Improvement of Working and Living Conditions (EFIWLC) (1999), *EPOC: Direct Employee Participation in the Public Services*, Dublin: European Foundation for the Improvement of Living and Working Conditions.

European Industrial Relations Review (1992) 'Lean production – more of the same or revolution', *European Industrial Relations Review*, no. 223, August.

Evenden, R., and Anderson, G. (1992), *Management Skills: Making the Most of People*, Wokingham: Addison-Wesley.

Farnham, D. (1984), *Personnel in Context*, London: Institute of Personnel Management.

Farnham, D., and Pimlott, J. (1990), *Understanding Industrial Relations*, London: Cassell.

FÁS (1998), *Labour Market Updates*, Dublin: FÁS.

FÁS (2000), *Review of Labour Market Trends in 2000 and Outlook to 2001*, Labour Market Updates 4/2000, www.fas.ie

FÁS (2005), *Labour Market Updates*, Dublin: FÁS.

Feldman, D., and Doerpinghaus, H. (1992), 'Missing persons no longer: managing part-time workers in the 1990s', *Organizational Dynamics*, vol. 21, no. 1, 59–73.

Fennell, C., and Lynch, I. (1993), *Labour Law in Ireland*, Dublin: Gill and Macmillan.

Ferris, G., Hochwarter, W., Buckley, M., Harrell-Cook, G., and Frink, D. (1999), 'Human resources management: some new directions', *Journal of Management*, 25, 3, 385–427.

Field, L., and Ford, B. (1995), *Managing Learning Organisations*, Melbourne: Longman.

Fierro, F. (2001), 'Global human resource management: stock options in remuneration programs', *Market Reporter*, 16 July.

Finn, G., and Morley, M. (2001), 'Expatriate Selection: The Case of an Irish MNC', in M. Linehan, M. Morley and J. Walsh (eds), *International HRM and the Expatriate Transfers: Irish Experiences*, Dublin: Blackhall Press.

Fisher, R., Ury, W., and Bruce, B. (2003), *Getting to Yes: Negotiating Agreement Without Giving In*, New York: Random House.

Fitzgerald, K. (2005), 'Cautious welcome for revamp of employment rights bodies', *Industrial Relations News*, 23, 26–7.

Fitzgerald, T. (1971), 'Why motivation theory doesn't work', *Harvard Business Review*, July–August, 12–19.

Flamholtz, E., and Lacey, J. (1981), *Personnel Management: Human Capital Theory and Human Resource Accounting*, Los Angeles: Institute of Industrial Relations, UCLA.

Flanagan, J. (1954), *The Critical Incident Technique*, Psychological Bulletin, 41, 236–358.

Flanders, A. 1968. *Trade unions*, London: Hutchinson.

Fletcher, C., and Williams, R. (1985), *Performance Appraisal and Career Development*, London: Hutchinson.

Fletcher, C., and Williams, R. (1992), *Performance Management in the UK: An Analysis of the Issues*, London: Institute of Personnel and Development.

Flood, P. (1989), 'Human resource management: promise, possibility and limitations', unpublished research paper, University of Limerick.

Flood, P. (1990), 'Atypical employment: core-periphery human resource strategies- the implications for corporate culture', *Industrial Relations News*, nos. 9 and 10.

Flood, P., Fong, C.-M., Smith, K., O'Regan, P., Moore, S., and Morley, M. (1997), 'Top management teams and pioneering: a resource based view', *International Journal of Human Resource Management*, 8, 3, 291–306.

Flood, P., Gannon, M., and Paauwe, J. (1996), *Managing without Traditional Methods: International Innovations in International Human Resource Management*, Wokingham: Addison Wesley.

Foley, A. (1990), 'Indigenous manufacturing', in Foley, A., and Mulreany, M. (eds), *The Single European Market and the Irish Economy*, Dublin: Institute of Public Administration.

Foley, K., and Gunnigle, P. (1994), 'The personnel/human resource function and employee relations' in Gunnigle, P., Flood, P., Morley, M. and Turner, T. *Continuity and change in Irish employee relations*, Dublin: Oak Tree Press 1994.

Foley, K., and Gunnigle, P. (1995), 'The personnel function: change or continuity' in T. Turner and M. Morley, *Industrial Relations and the New Order*, Dublin: Oak Tree Press.

Foley, K., Gunnigle, P., and Morley, M. (1994), 'Financial rewards and company ownership: an examination of reward practices in the Republic of Ireland', *The International Executive*, vol. 36, no. 5, 575–99.

Foley, K., Gunnigle, P., and Morley, M. (1996), 'Personnel management in Ireland: a new epoch?', *International Journal of Employment Studies*, vol. 4, no. 2, 1–25.

Fombrun, C. (1986), 'Structural dynamics within and between organizations', *Administrative Science Quarterly*, 31, 403–21.

Fombrun, C., Tichy, N., and Devanna, M. (1984), *Strategic Human Resource Management*, New York: Wiley.

Ford, J., Quinones, M., Sego, D., and Sorra, J. (1992), 'Factors affecting the opportunity to perform trained tasks on the job', *Personnel Psychology*, 45, 511–27.

Foulkes, F. (1980), *Effective Personnel Policies: A Study of Larger Non-Union Enterprises*, Englewood Cliffs, NJ: Prentice Hall.

Fowler, A. (1988), 'New directions in performance pay', *Personnel Management*, November, 30–34.

Fowler, A. (1991), 'Performance related pay', *Personnel Management Plus*, June.

Fowler, A. (1996), 'How to: pick a job evaluation system', *Personnel Management*, 8 February, 42–3.

Fox, A. (1966), 'Management ideology and labour relations', *British Journal of Industrial* Relations, vol. 4.

Fox, A. (1968), 'Industrial sociology and industrial relations', Research Paper no. 3, Royal Commission on Trade Unions and Employers' Associations, London: HMSO.

Fox, A. (1974), *Beyond Contract: Work, Power and Trust Relations*, London: Faber.

Fox, R. (1987), *Training of the Employed: Statistics for Ireland*, AnCO, October.

Fox, R., and O'Reilly, A. (1979), *Corporate Manpower Planning in Ireland*, Dublin: AnCO.

Frawley, M. (2000), 'Year 2000 – partnership signed, broken and rescued?', *Industrial Relations News*, 48, 15–17.

Frawley, M. (2002) 'Technology teachers latest group to switch to LRC, Labour Court', *Industrial Relations News*, 24, 14–15.

Fulmer, R., Gibbs, P., and Goldsmith, M. (2000), 'Developing leaders: how winning companies keep on winning', *Sloan Management Review*, 42, 49–59.

Furnham, A. (1997), *The Psychology of Behaviour at Work: The Individual in the Organization*, London: Psychology Press.

Galbraith, J., and Nathanson, D. (1978), *Strategy Implementation: The Role of Structure and Process*, New York: West Publishing.

Galvin, P. (1988), *Managers for Ireland: The Case for Development of Irish Managers*, Dublin: Advisory Committee on Management Training, Department of Labour.

Garavan, G., Costine, P., and Heraty, N. (1995), *Training and Development in Ireland: Context, Policy and Practice*, Dublin: Oak Tree Press.

Garavan, T. (1991), 'Strategic human resource development', *Journal of European Industrial Training*, vol.15, no. 1, 17–31.

Garavan, T. (2002), *The Irish Health and Safety Handbook*, Dublin: Oak Tree Press.

Garavan, T., Collins, E., and Brady, S. (2003), *Training and Development in Ireland*, Dublin: Chartered Institute of Personnel and Development.

Garavan, T., Morley, M, and Flynn, M. (1997), '360 degree feedback: its role in employee development', *Journal of Management Development*, vol. 16, no. 2, 134–48.

Garavan, T., Morley, M., Gunnigle, P., and Collins, E. (2001), 'Human capital accumulation: the role of human resource development, *Journal of European Industrial Training*, 25, 2/3/4, 48–68.

Garvin, J. (1993), 'Building learning organizations', *Harvard Business Review*, July/August, 78–91.

Gatewood, R., and Fields, H. (1998), *Human Resource Selection*, Fort Worth, TX: Dryden Press.

Geary, J. (1994a), 'Task participation: employee's participation – enabled or constrained' in K. Sisson (ed.), *Personnel Management: A Comprehensive Guide to Theory and Practice in Britain*, Oxford: Blackwell.

Geary, J. (1994b) 'New forms of work organisation: implications for employers, trade unions and employees', working paper no. 9, Graduate School of Business, University College Dublin.

Geary, J. (1995a) 'Working at teamwork: lessons from Europe', working paper, Graduate School of Business, University College Dublin.

Geary, J. (1995b) 'World class manufacturing and the implications for industrial relations' in P. Gunnigle amd W. Roche (eds), *New Challenges to Irish Industrial Relations*, Dublin: Oak Tree Press in association with the Labour Relations Commission.

Geary, J. (1998), *New Work Structures and the Diffusion of Teamworking Arrangements in Ireland*, paper presented at the Sixth Annual John Lovett Memorial Lecture, University of Limerick, 2 April.

Gee, J., Hull, G., and Lankshear, C. (1996), *The New Work Order: Behind the Language of the New Capitalism*, Sydney: Allen and Unwin.

George, J., and Jones, G. (1992), *Organizational Behaviour*, New Jersey: Prentice Hall.

Gerhart, B., and Rynes, S. (2003) *Compensation: Theory, Evidence, and Strategic Implications*, Thousand Oaks, CA: Sage Publications.

Gielen, E. (1996), 'Transfer of training in a corporate setting: testing a model', proceedings of the Academy of Human Resource Development.

Gill, D. (1977), *Appraising Performance: Present Trends and the Next Decade*, London: IPM.

Gilliland, S. (1993), 'The perceived fairness of the selection system: an organisational perspective', *Academy of Management Review*, 18, 694–734.

Gladstone, A. (1984), 'Employers' associations in comparative perspective: functions and activities' in J. Windmuller and A. Gladstone (eds), *Employer's Associations and Industrial Relations: A Comparative Study*, Oxford: Clarendon.

Gleeson, J. (1998), 'A consensus approach to policy making: the case of the Republic of Ireland' in I. Finlay, S. Niven and S. Young (eds) (1998), *Changing Vocational Education and Training: An International Comparative Perspective*, London: Routledge.

Godard, J., and Delaney, J. (2000), 'Reflections on the "high performance" paradigm's implications for industrial relations as a field', *Industrial and Labour Relations Review*, 53, 482–502.

Goffee, R., and Scase, R. (1986), 'Are the rewards worth the effort? Changing managerial values in the 1980s', *Personnel Review*, vol. 15, no. 4.

Goh, S. (1998), 'Towards a learning organization: the strategic building blocks', *SAM Advanced Management Journal*, 63, 2, 15–21.

Goldstein, I. (1986), *Training in Organizations: Needs Assessment, Development and Evaluation*, Pacific Grove, CA: Brooks/Cole.

Gooderham, P., Morley, M., Brewster, C., and Mayrhofer, W. (2004), 'Human resource management: a universal concept?' in C. Brewster, M. Mayrhofer and M. Morley (eds), *Human Resource Management in Europe: Evidence of Convergence?*, Oxford: Butterworth-Heinemann.

Goold, M., and Campbell, A. (1987), *Strategies and Styles: The Role of the Centre in Managing Diversified Corporations*, Oxford: Blackwell.

Goss, D. (1994), *Principles of Human Resource Management*, London: Routledge.

Government Publications Office (1997), *White Paper on Human Resource Development* (Pn. 3381), Dublin: Government Publications Office, May.

Government Publications Office (1998), *Green Paper on Adult Education in an Era of Lifelong Learning*, Dublin: Government Publications Office, November.

Government Publications Office (2000), *White Paper on Adult Learning*, Dublin: Government Publications Office.

Government Social Survey (UK) (1968), *Workplace Industrial Relations* (SS40Z), London: HMSO.

Grafton, D. (1988), 'Performance related pay: securing employee trust', *Industrial Relations News*, no. 44, 11–12, 17 November.

Graves, L., and Karren, R. (1996), 'The employee selection interview: a fresh look at an old problem', *Human Resource Management*, 35, 2, 163–80.

Gray, A. (ed.) (1997), *International Perspectives on the Irish Economy*, Dublin: Indecon Economic Consultants.

Green, F., Krahn, H., and Sung, J. (1993), 'Non-standard work in Canada and the United Kingdom', *International Journal of Human Resources*, vol. 14, no. 5, 70–86.

Greenhaus, H., and Callanan, G. (1994), *Career Management* (2nd edn), Forth Worth, TX: Dryden Press.

Griffin, R. (1987), 'Toward an integrated theory of task design', *Research in Organizational Behaviour*, 9, 79–120.

Griffin, R., and McMahan, G. (1994), 'Motivation through job design' in J. Greenberg (ed.), *Organizational Behaviour: The State of the Science*, Hillsdale: Lawrence Erlbaum.

Grote, D. (1996), *The Complete Guide to Performance Appraisal*, New York: American Management Association.

Grundy, T. (1997), Human resource management: a strategic approach', *Long Range Planning*, 30, 4, 507–17.

Gubman, E. (1994), 'HR strategy and planning: from birth to business results', *Human Resource Planning*, 27, 1, 13–23.

Gubman, E. (2004), 'From engagement to passion for work: the search for the missing person', *Human Resource Planning*, 27, 3, 42–7.

Guest, D., (1983) 'Personnel Management Strategies, Procedures and Techniques', in Guest, D. and Kenny, J., *A Textbook of Techniques and Strategies in Personnel Management*, Institute of Personnel Management.

Guest, D. (1987), 'Human resource management and industrial relations', *Journal of Management Studies*, vol. 24, no. 5, 503–21.

Guest, D. (1989), 'Human resource management: its implications for industrial relations and trade unions', in Storey, J. (ed.), *New Perspectives on Human Resource Management*, London: Routledge.

Guest, D. (1990), 'Human resource management and the American dream', *Journal of Management Studies*, vol. 27, no. 4, 377–97.

Guest, D. (1992), 'Right enough to be dangerously wrong: an analysis of the in search of excellence phenomenon' in G. Salaman (ed.), *Human Resource Strategies*, London: Sage/Open University Press.

Guest, D. (1997), 'Human resource management and performance: a review and research agenda', *International Journal of Human Resource Management* 8, 3, 263–76.

Guest, D. (1998), 'Combine harvest', *People Management*, 29 October.

Guest, D. (2001a), 'Human resource management: when research confronts theory', *International Journal of Human Resource Management*, 12, 76, 1092–106.

Guest, D. (2001b), 'Perspectives on the study of work-life balance', discussion paper for the ENOP Symposium, Paris, 29–31 March.

Guion, R. (1998), *Assessment, Measurement, and Prediction for Personnel Decisions*, Mahwah, NJ: Lawrence Erlbaum Associates.

Gunnigle, P. (1989), 'Management approaches to industrial relations in the small firm', in *Industrial Relations in Ireland: Contemporary Issues and Developments*, Dublin: University College Dublin.

Gunnigle, P. (1991), 'Determinants and nature of personnel policy choice: the context for human resource development', *Journal of European Industrial Training*, vol. 15, no. 3, 22–31.

Gunnigle, P. (1992a), 'Changing management approaches to employee relations in Ireland', *Employee Relations*, vol. 14, no. 5, 40–51.

Gunnigle, P. (1992b), 'Human resource management in Ireland' *Employee Relations*, vol. 14, no. 5, 5–22.

Gunnigle, P. (1993), 'Multinational companies and labour relations: a perspective on the experience of the Republic of Ireland', paper presented to OECD/Hungarian Ministry of Labour Seminar, 'Labour–Management Relations in Foreign Enterprises in Hungary', Organisation for Economic Co-operation and Development (OECD), Budapest, June.

Gunnigle, P. (1995), 'Collectivism and the management of industrial relations in greenfield sites', *Human Resource Management Journal*, vol. 5, no.3, 24–40.

Gunnigle, P. (1998a), 'Human resource management and the personnel function' in W. Roche, K. Monks and J. Walsh (eds), *Human Resource Management Strategies: Policy and Practice in Ireland*, Dublin: Oak Tree Press.

Gunnigle, P. (1998b), 'More rhetoric than reality: enterprise level industrial relations partnerships in Ireland', *Economic and Social Review*, vol. 28, no. 2, 179–200.

Gunnigle, P., and Brady, T. (1984) 'The management of industrial relations in the small firm', *Employee Relations*, vol.6, no.5, 21–4.

Gunnigle, P., Collings, D. and Morley, M. (2005), 'Exploring the dynamics of industrial relations in US multinationals: evidence from the Republic of Ireland', *Industrial Relations Journal*, 36, 3, 241–56.

Gunnigle, P., and Daly, A. (1992), 'Craft integration and flexible work practices: training implications', *Industrial and Commercial Training*, vol. 24, no. 10, 10–18.

Gunnigle, P., and Flood, P. (1990), *Personnel Management in Ireland: Practices, Trends and Developments*, Gill and Macmillan.

Gunnigle, P., Flood, P., Morley, M., and Turner, T. (1994), *Continuity and Change in Irish Employee Relations*, Dublin: Oak Tree Press.

Gunnigle, P., Foley, K., and Morley, M. (1994), 'A review of organisational reward practices', in P. Gunnigle, P. Flood, M. Morley and T. Turner, *Continuity and Change in Irish Employee Relations*, Dublin: Oak Tree Press.

Gunnigle, P., Garavan, T., and Fitzgerald, G. (1992), *Employee Relations and Employment Law in Ireland*, Limerick: University of Limerick/Plassey Management and Technology Centre.

Gunnigle, P., MacCurtain, S., and Morley, M. (2001), 'Dismantling pluralism: industrial relations in Irish greenfield sites', *Personnel Review*, vol. 30, no. 3, 263–79.

Gunnigle, P., and McGuire, D. (2001), 'Why Ireland? A qualitative review of the factors influencing the location of US multinationals in Ireland with particular reference to the impact of labour issues', *Economic and Social Review*, 32, 1, 43–67.

Gunnigle, P., McMahon, G., and Fitzgerald, G. (1999), *Industrial Relations in Ireland: Theory and Practice* (revised edn), Dublin: Gill and Macmillan.

Gunnigle, P., and Moore, S. (1994), 'Linking business strategy and human resource management: issues and implications', *Personnel Review*, vol. 23, no.1, 63–84.

Gunnigle, P., and Morley, M. (1993), 'Something old, something new: a perspective on industrial relations in the Republic of Ireland', *Review of Employment Topics*, vol. 1, no. 1, 114–43.

Gunnigle, P., Morley, M., Clifford, N., and Turner, T. (1997), *Human Resource Management in Irish Organisations: Practice in Perspective*, Dublin: Oak Tree Press.

Gunnigle, P., Morley, M., and Foley, K. (1995), 'Human Resource Management in Ireland', in I. Brunstein (ed.), *Human Resource Management in Western Europe*, Berlin: De Gruyter.

Gunnigle, P., Morley, M., and McDonnell, M. (eds) (2002), *The John Lovett Lectures: A Decade of Developments in Human Resource Management*, Dublin: Liffey Press.

Gunnigle, P., Morley, M., and Turner, T. (1994), 'Developments in industrial relations and HRM in the Republic of Ireland', *Irish Business and Administrative Research*, vol. 15, 76–92.

Gunnigle, P., Morley, M., and Turner, T. (1997), 'Challenging collectivist traditions: individualism and the management of industrial relations in greenfield sites', *Economic and Social Review*, vol.28, no. 2, 105–34.

Gunnigle, P., O'Sullivan, M. and Kinsella, M. (2002), 'Organised labour in the new economy: trade unions and public policy in the Republic of Ireland' in D. D'Art and T. Turner (eds), *Irish Employment Relations in the New Economy*, Dublin: Blackhall Press.

Gunnigle, P., and Roche, W. (eds) (1995), *New Challenges to Irish Industrial Relations*, Dublin: Oak Tree Press/Labour Relations Commission.

Gunnigle, P., Turner, T., and D'Art, D. (1998), 'Counterpoising collectivism: performance-related pay and industrial relations in greenfield sites', *British Journal of Industrial Relations*, vol. 36, no. 4, 565–79.

Gunnigle, P., Turner, T., and Morley, M. (1998), 'Strategic integration and industrial relations: the impact of managerial styles', *Employee Relations*, vol. 20, no. 2, 115–31.

Hacker, C. (1997), 'The cost of poor hiring decisions . . . and how to avoid them', *HR Focus*, 74, 10, 13–16.

Hackman, J. (1977), 'Work Design', in J. Hackman and J. Suttle (eds), *Improving Life at Work*, Santa Monica: Goodyear.

Hackman, J. (1987), 'The design of work teams', in J. Lorsch (ed.), *Handbook of Organizational Behavior*, New Jersey: Prentice Hall.

Hackman, J., and Oldham, G. (1980), *Work Redesign*, New York: Addison Wesley.

Hackman, J., Oldham, G., Janson, R., and Purdy, K. (1975), 'A new strategy for job enrichment', *California Management Review*, 17, 51–71.

Hakim, K. (1991), 'Cross national comparative research on the European Community: the EC labour force surveys', *Work, Employment and Society*, vol. 5, no. 1, 1991, 101–17.

Hales, C. (1986), 'What do managers do? A critical review of the evidence', *Journal of Management Studies*, 23, 88–115.

Hall, D., and Foulkes, F. (1991), 'Senior executive development as a competitive advantage', *Advances in Applied Business Strategy*, 2, 183–203, JAI Press.

Hall, D., and Moss, J. (1998), 'The new protean career contract', *Organizational Dynamics*, Winter, 22–38.

Hallier, J., and Butts, S. (1998), 'Employer's discovery of training: self-development, employability and the rhetoric of partnership', *Employee Relations*, 21, 1, 80–94.

Hamblin, A. (1974), *Evaluation and Control of Training*, Maidenhead: McGraw-Hill.

Hambrick, D. (1987), 'The top management team: key to strategic success', *California Management Review*, 30, 88–107.

Hannan, D. (1998), *Trading Qualifications for Jobs: Over-education and the Irish Youth Labour Market*, Dublin: Oak Tree Press.

Hannaway, C. (1987), 'New style collective agreements: an Irish approach', *Industrial Relations News*, no. 13, 16–22.

Hannaway, C. (1992), 'Why Irish eyes are smiling', *Personnel Management*, May, 38–41.

Hannigan, K. (1999), 'Survey of MNCs in Ireland: Results of the Second Annual Survey of Competitiveness', Dublin: Irish Management Institute.

Hannigan, K. (2000), 'Ireland's economic performance: A view from the MNCs', *Irish Business and Administrative Research*, vol. 21, no. 1, 69–83.

Hardiman, N. (1988), *Pay, Politics and Economic Performance in Ireland 1970–1987*, Oxford: Clarendon Press.

Hardy, S., and Adnett, N. (2002), 'The parental leave directive: towards a family-friendy social Europe?', *European Journal of Industrial Relations*, 8, 2, 157–72.

Harker, L. (1996), 'The family friendly employer in Europe', in S. Lewis and J. Lewis (eds), *The Work/Family Challenge: Rethinking Employment*, London: Sage Publications.

Harrell-Cook, G. (2002), 'Human resources management and competitive advantage: A strategic perspective', in G. Ferris, M. Buckley and D. Fedor (eds) *Human Resource Management: Perpectives, Context, Functions and Outcomes*, Upper Saddle River, New Jersey: Prentice Hall.

Harrison, R. (1997), *Employee Development*, London: IPD.

Hart, T. (1993), 'Human resource management: time to exorcize the militant tendency', *Employee Relations*, 15, 3, 29–36.

Haughton, J. (2000), 'The historical background: from Independence to 1973', in J. O'Hagan (ed.), *The Economy of Ireland*, Dublin: Gill and Macmillan.

Hawkins, K. (1979), *A Handbook of Industrial Relations Practice*, London: Kogan Page.

Hawley, J., and Barnard, J. (2005), 'Work environment characteristics and implications for training transfer: a case study of the nuclear power industry', *Human Resource Development International*, 8, 1, 65–80.

Hay Associates (1975), *Survey of Human Resource Practices*, London: Hay Associates.

Heery, E. (1992), 'Divided we fall? Trade unions and performance related pay', paper presented to London School of Economics/Trade Union Congress Seminar, London School of Economics, 19 March.

Heffernan, M. (2004), 'High performance work systems and employee outcomes – rebalancing the debate', paper presented at Seventh Irish Academy of Management Conference, Trinity College Dublin, 2–3 September.

Heffernan, M. and Dundon, T. (2004), 'High performance work systems and employee outcomes – an organisational justice perspective', HRM Study Group Working Paper Series, International Industrial Relations Association, September.

Hegewisch, A., and Bruegel, I. (1992), 'Flexibilisation and part-time work in Europe', BSA 92 Conference, Canterbury, April.

Hendry, C. (1995), *Human Resource Management: A Strategic Approach to Employment*, Oxford: Butterworth Heinemann.

Hendry, C., and Pettigrew, A. (1992), 'Patterns of strategic change in the development of human resource management', *British Journal of Management* 3, 3, 137–56.

Hequet, M. (1995), 'Not paid enough? You're not alone', *Training*, vol. 32, no. 11, 44–55.

Heraty, N. (1992) 'Training and development: a study of practices in Irish based companies', MBS thesis (unpublished), University of Limerick.

Heraty, N. (2004), 'Towards an architecture of organization-led learning', *Human Resource Management Review*, 14, 4, 449–73.

Heraty, N., and Garavan, T. (2001), *Training and Development in Ireland*, Dublin: Chartered Institute of Personnel and Development.

Heraty, N., and Morley, M. (1994), 'Human resource development in Ireland: position, practices and power', *Administration*, 42, 3, 299–319.

Heraty, N., and Morley, M. (1995), 'A review of issues in conducting organisational level research with reference to the learning organisation', *International Journal of the Learning Organization*, 2, 4, 27–36.

Heraty, N., and Morley, M. (1998a), 'In search of good fit: policy and practice in recruitment and selection in Ireland', *Journal of Management Development*, 17, 9, 662–86.

Heraty, N., and Morley, M. (1998b), 'Recruitment and selection practices', in W. Roche, K. Monks, K. and J. Walsh (eds), *Human Resource Strategies: Policy and Practice in Ireland*, 109–47.

Heraty, N., and Morley, M. (1998c), 'Training and development in the Irish context: responding to the competitiveness agenda', *Journal of European Industrial Training*, vol. 22, nos. 4 and 5, 190–204.

Heraty, N., and Morley, M. (2003), 'Management development in Ireland: The new organisational wealth?', *Journal of Management Development*, 22, 1, 60–82.

Heraty, N., Morley, M., and McCarthy, A. (2000), 'Vocational education and training in the Republic of Ireland: institutional reform and policy developments since the 1960s', *Journal of Vocational Education and Training*, 52, 2, 177–98.

Heraty, N., Morley, M. and Turner, T. (1994), 'Trends and developments in the organisation of the employment relationship', in P. Gunnigle, P. Flood, M. Morley and T. Turner (eds), *Continuity and Change in Irish Employee Relations*, Dublin: Oak Tree Press, 82–102.

Herriot, P. (1989), *Recruitment in the 90s*, London: Institute of Personnel Management.

Herzberg, F. (1968), 'One more time: how do you motivate employees', *Harvard Business Review*, January/February, 115–25.

Higgins, C. (1992), 'Executive search – an essential requirement for the 1990s', *Industrial Relations News*, 38, 8 October.

Higgins, C. (2005), '"Chambers HR" service offers insurance against losing employment cases', *Industrial Relations News*, 4, 20 January.

Highhouse, S., and Hoffman, J. (2001), 'Organizational attraction and job choice', in C. Cooper and I. Robertson (eds), *International Review of Industrial and Organizational Psychology*, Chichester: Wiley, vol. 16, 37–64.

Hill, J., and Trist, E. (1955), 'Changes in accidents and other absences with length of service', *Human Relations*, 8 May.

Hillery, B. (1989), 'An overview of the Irish industrial relations system' in University College Dublin, *Industrial Relations in Ireland: Contemporary Issues and Developments*, Dublin: University College Dublin.

Hillery, B. (1994), 'The institutions of industrial relations' in T. Murphy and W. Roche (eds), *Irish Industrial Relations in Practice*, Dublin: Oak Tree Press.

Hoevemeyer, V. (1989), 'Performance based compensation: miracle or waste', *Personnel Journal*, July.

Hofer, C., and Schendel, D. (1978), *Strategy Formulation: Analytical Concepts*, St Paul, Minneapolis MN: West Publishing.

Horwitz, F. (1999), The emergence of strategic training and development: the current state of play', *Journal of European Industrial Training*, 23, 4/5, 1–10.

Hourihan, F. (1996), 'The Labour Court – fifty years on', *Industrial Relations News*, March, 12, 21.

Hourihan, F. (1997), 'The European Union and industrial relations' in T. Murphy and W. Roche (eds), *Irish Industrial Relations in Practice* (revised and expanded edn), Dublin: Oak Tree Press.

Huber, G. (1991), 'Organizational learning: the contributing processes and the literatures', *Organizational Science*, 2, 88–115.

Hucznyski, A., and Buchanan, D. (1991), *Organizational Behaviour: An Introductory Text*, Hemel Hempstead: Prentice Hall.

Hunt, N. (1992), *How to Conduct Staff Appraisals*, Plymouth: How To Books.

Hunter, J., and Hunter, R. (1984), 'Validity and utility of alternative predictors of job performance', *Psychological Bulletin*, 96, 72–98.

Hunter, L., and McInnes, J. (1992), 'Employers and labour flexibility: the evidence from case studies', *Employment Gazette*, June, 307–15.

Huselid, M. (1995), 'The impact of human resource management practices on turnover, productivity, and corporate financial performance', *Academy of Management Journal*, 38, 3, 635–72.

Huselid, M., and Becker, B. (1996), 'Methodological issues in cross-sectional and panel estimates of the human resource-firm performance link', *Industrial Relations*, vol. 35, 3, 400–22.

Huselid, M., Jackson, S., and Schuler, R. (1997) 'Technical and strategic human resource management effectiveness as determinants of firm performance', *Academy of Management Journal*, vol. 40, 171–88.

Huseman, R., Hatfield, J., and Miles, E. (1987), 'A new perspective on equity theory: the equity sensitivity construct', *Academy of Management Review*, vol. 12, 222–34.

Hutchinson, S., and Purcell, J. (2003), *Bringing Policies to Life: The Vital Role of Front Line Managers in People Management*, London: Chartered Institute of Personnel and Development.

Hyman, J., and Summers, J. (2004), 'Lacking balance? Work-life employment practices in the modern economy', *Personnel Review*, 33, 4, 418–29.

Ichniowski, C. (1992), 'Human resource practices and productive labour-management relations', in D. Lewin, O. Mitchell and P. Sherer (eds), *Research Frontiers in Industrial Relations and Human Resources*, Madison, WI: Industrial Relations Research Association, 239–71.

Ichniowski, C., Kochan, T., Levine, D., Olson, C., and Strauss, G. (1996), 'What works at work: overview and assessment', *Industrial Relations*, vol. 35, 299–333.

IDA Ireland (2001), *IDA Ireland Annual Report*, Dublin: IDA Ireland

IDA Ireland (2002), *IDA Ireland Annual Report*, Dublin: IDA Ireland.

IDA Ireland (2003), 'Cautious optimism for 2003', press release, 6 January, Dublin: IDA Ireland.

IDA Ireland (2005), *IDA Ireland Annual Report*, Dublin: IDA Ireland.

Iles, P. (1994), 'Developing learning environments: challenges for theory, research and practice', *Journal of European Industrial Training*, 18, 3.

Iles, P. (1999), *Managing Staff Selection and Assessment*, Buckingham: Open University Press.

Iles, P., and Mabey, M. (1993), *Strategic Human Resource Management*, London: Blackwell.

Iles, P., and Robertson, I. (1997), 'The impact of personnel selection procedures on candidates', in N. Anderson and P. Herriot (eds), *International Handbook of Selection and Assessment*, Chichester: Wiley, 543–66.

Industrial Relations News (2001), 'Nortel: severance deal nears completion', 25 October.

Industrial Relations News (2004), 'New Labour Court chair would like major overhaul of employment law', 5, 21–3.

International Labour Organisation (1975), *Collective Bargaining in Industrialised Market Economies*, Geneva: International Labour Organisation.

International Labour Organisation (1998), *Industrial Relations, Democracy and Social Stability* (World Labour Report 1997–98), Geneva: International Labour Organisation.

Internet Business Network (IBN) (1999), 'Electronic recruiting index: the industry matures', www.interbiznet.com, Road Mill Valley, CA: IBN.

Irish Business and Employers Confederation (IBEC) (various), *IBEC Annual Reviews*, Dublin: IBEC.

Irish Business and Employers Confederation (IBEC) (1993) *IBEC: An Introduction*, Dublin: IBEC.

Irish Business and Employers Confederation (IBEC)(1998), *Survey of Reward/Payment Schemes*, Dublin: IBEC.

Irish Business and Employers Confederation (IBEC) (2004), 'Employee absenteeism – a guide to managing absence', Dublin: IBEC.

Irish Congress of Trade Unions (1993), *New Forms of Work Organisation: Options for Unions*, Dublin: ICTU.

Irish Congress of Trade Unions (ICTU) (1995), *Managing Change*, Dublin: ICTU.

Irish Congress of Trade Unions (ICTU) (2004) *Annual Report*, Dublin: ICTU.

Irish Industrial Relations Review (1993), 'Trade union organisation in the Republic', vol. 2, no.7, July.

Jackson, M. (1982) *Industrial Relations: A Textbook*, London: Kogan Page.

Jacobs, J., and Gerson, K. (2001), 'Overworked individuals or overworked families: explaining trends in work, leisure and family time', *Work and Occupations*, 28, 1, 40–63.

Jacobsen, D., and Andreosso, B. (1990), 'Ireland as a location for multinational investment' in A. Foley and M. Mulreanny (eds), *The Single European Market and the Irish Economy*, Dublin: Institute of Public Administration.

Janson, R. (1979), 'Work redesign: a results oriented strategy that works', *S. A. M. Advanced Management Journal*, 44, 1, 21–4.

Kakabadse, A. (1990), 'Top people, top teams', paper presented to the Annual Conference of the Irish Institute of Training and Development, Limerick.

Kamoche, K. (2000), 'Developing managers: the functional, the symbolic, the sacred and the profane', *Organization Studies*, 21, 4, 747–74.

Kaplan, R., and Norton, D. (1996), *The Balanced Scorecard: Translating Strategy into Action*, Boston, MA: Harvard Business School Press.

Kauppiner, T. (2004), 'The puzzle of the knowledge society', paper to the Irish Presidency Conference, *Foresights for Innovations: Shaping and Aligning Policies*, Dublin: 14–15 June.

Keenoy, T. (1990), 'HRM: A case of the wolf in sheep's clothing?' *Personnel Review*, vol. 19, no. 2, 3–9.

Kelly, A. (1975), 'Changes in the occupational structure and industrial relations in Ireland', *Management*, no. 2.

Kelly, A. (1989), 'The worker director in Irish industrial relations', *Industrial Relations in Ireland: Contemporary Issues and Developments*, Dublin: University College Dublin.

Kelly, A., and Brannick, T. (1983), 'The pattern of strike activity in Ireland, 1960–1979: some preliminary observations', *Irish Business and Administrative Research*, vol. 5, no.1, 65–77.

Kelly, A., and Brannick, T. (1985), 'The strike-proneness of public sector organisations', *Economic and Social Review*, vol. 16, no. 4, 251–71.

Kelly, A., and Brannick, T. (1986), 'The changing contours of Irish strike patterns: 1960–1984', *Irish Business and Administrative Research*, vol. 8, no. 1, 77–88.

Kelly, A., and Brannick, T. (1988a), 'Explaining the strike proneness of British companies in Ireland', *British Journal of Industrial Relations*, vol. 26, no. 1. 37–57.

Kelly, A., and Brannick, T. (1988b), 'The management of human resources: new trends and the challenge to trade unions', *Arena: Journal of Irish Institute of Training and Development*, August, 11–15.

Kelly, A., and Brannick, T. (1988c), 'Strike trends in the Irish private sector', *Irish Business and Administrative Research*, vol. 9, 87–98.

Kelly, A., and Brannick, T. (1989), 'Strikes in Ireland: measurement, indices and trends', *Industrial Relations in Ireland: Contemporary Issues and Developments*, Dublin: University College Dublin.

Kelly, A., and Brannick, T. (1991), 'The impact of new human resource management policies on US MNC strike patterns' (unpublished), Department of Business Administration, University College Dublin.

Kelly, A., and Monks, K. (1997a), 'Performance related pay: what makes a successful scheme?', *Research Paper Series*, Dublin: Dublin City University Business School.

Kelly, A., and Monks, K. (1997b), 'View from the bridge and life on deck: contrasts and contradictions in performance related pay', in T. Clark, C. Mabey and D. Skinner (eds), *Experiencing Human Resource Management*, 113–28, London: Sage.

Kelly, J. (1980), 'The costs of job redesign: a preliminary analysis', *Industrial Relations Journal*, vol. 11, no. 3.

Kerr, A. (1997), 'Collective labour law' in T. Murphy and W. Roche (eds), *Irish Industrial Relations in Practice*, Dublin: Oak Tree Press.

Kerr, A., and Whyte, G. (1985), *Irish Trade Union Law*, Abington: Professional Books.

Kessler, I., and Purcell, J. (1992), 'Performance related pay: objectives and application', *Human Resource Management Journal*, vol. 3, no. 2.

Keynes, J. (1936), *The General Theory of Employment, Interest and Money*, London: Macmillan.

Kikoski, J. (1999), 'Effective communications in the performance appraisal interview: face-to-face communication for public managers in the culturally diverse workplace', *Public Personnel Management*, 28, 301–23.

Kilibarda, P., and Fonda, N. (1997), 'Random Selection', *People Management*, December, 36–9.

Kirkpatick, D. (1959), 'Techniques for evaluating programmes', *Journal of the American Society for Training Directors*, 13.

Klein, B., Crawford, R., and Alchian, A. (1978), 'Vertical integration, appropriate rents and the competitive contracting process', *Journal of Law and Economics*, 21, 297–326.

Klein, J. (1989), 'The human costs of manufacturing reform', *Harvard Business Review*, March–April, 60–6.

Kochan, T., Katz, H., and McKersie, R. (1986), *The Transformation of American Industrial Relations*, New York: Basic Books.

Kochan, T., and Osterman, P. (1994), *The Mutual Gains Enterprise*, Cambridge, MA: Harvard Business School Press.

Kohn, A. (1993), 'Why incentive plans cannot work', *Harvard Business Review*, September–October, 54–63.

Kolb, D. (1984), *Experiential Learning – Experience as a Source of Learning and Development*, New Jersey: Prentice Hall.

Kopelman, R. (1985), 'Job redesign and productivity: a review of the evidence', *National Productivity Review*, Summer, 237–55.

Kuhn, M., and Yockey, M. (2003), 'Variable pay as a risky choice: determinants of the relative attractiveness of incentive plans', *Organizational Behaviour and Human Decision Processes*, 90, 2, 323–41.

Labour Court (various), *Labour Court Annual Reports*, Dublin: Labour Court

Labour Relations Commission (2001), *Labour Relations Commission Annual Report 2000*, Dublin: Labour Relations Commission.

Labour Relations Commission (2003), Editorial, *LRC Review: The Journal of the Labour Relations Commission*, 2, May.

Labour Relations Commission (2004), *Labour Relations Commission Annual Report 2003*, Dublin: Labour Relations Commission.

Labour Relations Commission (2005), *Labour Relations Commission Annual Report 2004*, Dublin: Labour Relations Commission.

Laffan, B. (1984), 'The youth employment scheme in Ireland', University of Strathclyde: Strathclyde Papers.

Lane, C. (1988), 'Industrial change in Europe: the pursuit of flexible specialisation in Britain and West Germany', *Work, Employment and Society*, vol. 12, no. 2, 1988, 141–68.

Latham, G., Almost, J., Mann, S., and Moore, C. (2005), 'New developments in performance management', *Organizational Dynamics*, 34, 1, 77–87.

Latham, G., and Crandall, S. (1991), 'Organisational and social influences affecting training effectiveness' in J. Morrison (ed.), *Training for Performance*, Chichester: Wiley.

Lawler, E. (1977), 'Reward systems', in J. Hackman and J. Suttle (eds), *Improving Life at Work: Behavioural Science Approaches to Organisational Change*, New York: Goodyear.

Lawler, E. (1978) 'The New Plant Revolution', *Organisational Dynamics*, Winter 1978, 3–12.

Lawler, E. (1982), 'Increasing worker involvement to enhance organisational effectiveness', in P. Goodman (ed.), *Change in Organisations*, San Francisco: Jossey Bass.

Lawler, E. (1986), *High Involvement Management: Participative Strategies for Improving Organizational Performance*, San Francisco: Jossey-Bass.

Lawler, E. (2000), *Rewarding Excellence*, San Francisco: Jossey-Bass.

Lawler, E. (2003), 'Reward practices and performance management system effectiveness', *Organizational Dynamics*, 32, 4, 396–404.

Lawler, E., Mohrman, S., and Ledford, G. (1995), *Creating High Performance Organizations, Practices and Results in Employee Involvement and Total Quality Managemenr in Fortune 1000 Companies*, San Francisco: Jossey-Bass.

Leadbeater, C. (1999), *The Knowledge Driven Economy*. Association for Management Education and Development Conference, August, Cranfield.

Leddin, T., and Walsh, B. (1994), *The Macro Economy of Ireland*, Dublin: Gill and Macmillan.

Lees, S. (1992), 'Ten faces of management development', *Management Education and Development*, 23, 89–105.

Legge, K. (1989), 'Human resource management: a critical analysis', in J. Storey (ed.), *New Perspectives on Human Resource Management*, London: Routledge.

Legge, K. (1995), *Human Resource Management: Rhetoric and Realities*, London: Macmillan.

Legge, K. (2000), 'Personnel management in the lean organisation', in S. Bach and K. Sisson (eds), *Personnel Management: A Comprehensive Guide to Theory and Practice*, Oxford: Blackwell, 43–69.

Legge, K. (2005), *Human Resource Management: Rhetorics and Realities*, Basingstoke: Palgrave Macmillan.

Lehmbruch, G., Schmitter, F., and Philippe, C. (1982), *Patterns of Corporatist Policy Making*, London: Sage.

Lengnick-Hall, C., and Lengnick-Hall, M., (1988), 'Strategic human resources management: a review of the literature and a proposed typology', *Academy of Management Review*, 13, 454–70.

Lenz, R. (1980), 'Strategic capability: a concept and framework for analysis', *Academy of Management Review*, 5, 225–34.

Lepak, D., and Snell, S. (1999), 'The human resource architecture: toward a theory of human capital allocation and development', *Academy of Management Review*, 24, 31–48.

Lepak, D., and Snell, S. (2002), 'Examining the human resource architecture: the relationship among human capital, employment, and human resource configurations', *Journal of Management*, 28, 517–43.

Lepak, D., Takeuchi, R., and Snell, S. (2003), 'Employment flexibility and firm performance: examining the interaction effects of employment mode, environmental dynamism, and technological intensity', *Journal of Management*, 29, 681–703.

Lewin, D. (2001), 'Low Involvement Work Practices and Business Performance', Proceedings of the 53rd Annual Meeting, Industrial Relations Research Association January 3–5, 275–292.

Lewis, C. (1984), 'What's New in Selection?', Personnel Management, January.

Lievens, F., van Dam, K., and Anderson, N. (2002), 'Recent trends and challenges in personnel selection', *Personnel Review*, vol. 31, no. 5, 580–601.

Lippitt, G. (1981), 'Management development as the key to organisation renewal', *Journal of Management Development*, 1, 34–40.

Litwin, G., and Stringer, R. (1968), *Motivation and Organizational Climate*, Boston: Harvard University Press.

Locker, A., and Teel, K. (1977), Survey of human resource practices', *Personnel Practices Journal*, March.

Lockett, J. (1992), *Effective Performance Management: A Strategic Guide to Getting the Best from People*, London: Kogan Page.

Long, P. (1986), *Performance Appraisal Revisited*, London, IPM.

Long, P. (1988), 'A review of approved profit sharing (trust) schemes in Ireland and the UK', unpublished dissertation, Dublin Institute of Technology.

Longenecker, C., and Ludwig, D. (1990), 'Ethical dilemmas in performance appraisal revisited', *Journal of Business Ethics*, 9, 961–69.

Lowery, C., Petty, M., and Thompson, J. (1996), 'Assessing the merit of merit pay: employee reactions to performance based pay, *Human Resource Planning*, vol. 19, no. 1.

Lundberg, C. (1995), 'Learning in and by organizations: three conceptual issues', *International Journal of Organizational Analysis*, 3, 1, 10–23.

Lundy, A., and Cowling, A. (1996), *Strategic Human Resource Management*, London: Routledge.

Luoma, M. (2000), 'Investigating the link between strategy and HRD', *Personnel Review*, 29, 6, 769–90.

Lupton, T. (1976), 'Best fit in the design of organisations' in E. Miller (ed.), *Task and Organisation*, New York: John Wiley.

Lynch-Fannon, I. and Connolly, U. (forthcoming) *Labour Law in Ireland*, Dublin: Gill and Macmillan.

Mabey, C., and Salaman, G. (1995), *Strategic Human Resource Management*, Oxford: Blackwell.

MacDuffie, J. (1995), 'Human resource bundles and manufacturing performance: organisational logic and flexible production systems in the world auto industry', *Industrial and Labour Relations Review*, 48, 2, 197–221.

Mackay, L., and Torrington, D. (1986), *The Changing Nature of Personnel Management*, London: Institute of Personnel Management.

Macon, T., and Dipboye, R. (1988), 'The effects of interviewers' initial impressions on information gathering', *Organisational Behaviour and Human Decision Processes*, 42, 364–87.

Macpherson, A., Elliot, M., Harris, T., and Homan, G. (2004), 'E-learning: reflections and evaluation of corporate programmes', *Human Resource Development International*, 7, 3, 295–313.

Magee, C. (1991), 'Atypical work forms and organisational flexibility', paper presented to the Institute of Public Administration Personnel Management Conference, Dublin, 6 March.

Makin, P., and Robertson, I.T. (1986), 'Selecting the best selection technique', *Personnel Management*, November.

Marchington, M. (1982), *Managing Industrial Relations*, London: McGraw-Hill.

Marchington, M. (1990), 'Analysing the links between product markets and the management of employee relations', *Journal of Management Studies*, vol. 27, no. 2, 111–32.

Marchington, M., and Grugulis, I. (2002), '"Best practice" human resource management: perfect opportunity or dangerous illusion', in P. Gunnigle, M. Morley and M. McDonnell (eds), *The John Lovett Lectures: A Decade of Developments in Human Resource Management*, Dublin: Liffey Press.

Marchington, M., and Parker, P. (1990), *Changing Patterns of Employee Relations*, Hemel Hempstead: Harvester Wheatsheaf.

Marginson, P. (1991), 'Continuity and change in the employment structure of large firms', in A. Pollart (ed.), *Farewell to Flexibility*, Oxford: Blackwell.

Marsden, D. (1986), *The End of Economic Man? Custom and Competition in Labour Markets*, New York: St Martin's Press.

Marsh, A. (1973), *Managers and Shop Stewards*, London: Institute of Personnel Management.

Marshall, A. (1928), *Principles of Economics* (8th edn), London: Macmillan.

Martin, J. (2001), *Organizational Behaviour*, London: Thomson Learning.

Maslow, A. (1943), 'A theory of human motivation', *Psychological Review*, vol. 50, no. 4.

Mathis, R., and Jackson, J. (1994), *Human Resource Management* (7th edn), St Paul, Minneapolis MN: West Publishing Company.

Matthews, J., and Candy P. (1999), 'New dimensions in the dynamics of learning and knowledge' in D. Boud and J. Garrick (eds), *Understanding Learning at Work*, London: Routledge.

Mayo, A. (1991), *Managing Careers: Strategies for Organisations*, Wimbledon: IPM.

Mayrhofer, W., Brewster, C., and Morley, M. (2000), 'The concept of strategic European human resource management' in C. Brewster, W. Mayrhofer and M. Morley (eds), *New Challenges for European Human Resource Management*, London: Macmillan, 3–31.

McBeath, G., and Rands, N. (1989), *Salary Administration*, (4th edn), London: Gower.

McCarthy, A., and Pearson, J. (2000), 'Performance feedback is coming full circle', *CIPD News*, vol. 1, no. 2, 12–14.

McCarthy, A., and Pearson, J. (2001), '360° feedback in the global HRM arena and the expatriate management process' in M. Linehan, M. Morley and J. Walsh (eds), *International Human Resource Management and Expatriate Transfers: Irish Experiences*, Dublin: Blackhall Press.

McCarthy, C. (1977), 'A review of the objectives of the national pay agreements 1970–1977' *Administration*, vol. 25, no. 1.

McCarthy, W., O'Brien, J., and Dowd, V. (1975), *Wage Inflation and Wage Leadership*, Dublin: Economic and Social Research Institute.

McClelland, D. (1961), *The Achieving Society*, New York: Van Nostrand.

McClelland, D., and Boyatzis, R. (1982), 'Leadership motive pattern and long term success in management', *Journal of Applied Psychology*, vol. 67, no. 2.

McEwan, N., Carmichael, C., Short, D., and Steel, A. (1988), 'Managing organisational change: a strategic approach', Long Range Planning, 21, 6, 71–8.

McGinley, M. (1989a), 'Pay increases in the 1980s: the issue of control' *Industrial Relations News*, no. 30, August.

McGinley, M. (1989b), 'Pay increases between 1981 and 1987', *Personnel and Industrial Relations Directory*, Dublin: Institute of Public Administration.

McGovern, P., (1988), 'Increasing opposition to unionisation in the 1980s', *Industrial Relations News*, no. 45, 24 November, 15–18.

McGovern, P. (1989a), 'Union recognition and union avoidance in the 1980s' in *Industrial Relations in Ireland: Contemporary Issues and Developments*, Dublin: University College Dublin.

McGovern, P., (1989b), 'Trade union recognition – five case studies', *Industrial Relations News*, no. 6, 9 February, 12–16.

McGrath, P., and Geaney, C. (1998), 'Managing organisational change', in W. Roche, K. Monks and J. Walsh (eds), *Human Resource Strategies: Policy and Practice in Ireland*, Dublin: Oak Tree Press, 311–48.

McGregor, A., and Sproull, A. (1992), 'Employers and the Flexible Workforce', *Employment Gazette*, May, 225–34.

McGregor, D. (1960), *The Human Side of Enterprise*, New York: McGraw Hill.

McKersie, R. (2002), 'Labour-management partnerships: U.S. evidence and implications for Ireland', in P. Gunnigle, M. Morley and M. McDonnell (eds). *The John Lovett Lectures: A Decade of Developments in Human Resource Management in Ireland*, Dublin: Oak Tree Press.

McLagan, J. (1989), *Models of HRD Practice*, Alexandria: ASTD.

McLagan, P. (1989) 'Models for HRD practice', *Training and Development Journal*, September, 49–59.

McMahon, G. (1988), 'Personnel selection in Ireland: scientific prediction or crystal ball gazing', *IPM News*, vol. 3, no. 3, 20–3.

McMahon, G. (1989), 'The joint labour committee system' in *Industrial Relations in Ireland: Contemporary Issues and Developments*, Dublin: University College Dublin.

McMahon, G. (2001), 'Special feature on web recruitment', *Irish Times*, May.

McMahon, G., and Gunnigle, P. (1994), *Performance Appraisal: How to Get it Right*, Dublin: Productive Personnel Ltd in association with IPM (Ireland).

McMahon, G., Neary, C., and O'Connor, K. (1988), 'Multinationals in Ireland three decades on', *Industrial Relations News*, no. 6, 11 February.

McMahon, J. (1994), 'Employee relations in small firms' in P. Gunnigle, P. Flood, M. Morley and T. Turner, *Continuity and Change in Irish Employee Relations*, Dublin: Oak Tree Press.

McMahon, J. (1996) 'Employee relations in small firms in Ireland: an exploratory study of small manufacturing firms', *Employee Relations*, vol. 5, no. 5, 66–80.

McNamara, G., Williams, K., and West, D. (1988), *Understanding Trade Unions: Yesterday and Today*, Dublin: O'Brien Educational Press.

Meenan, F. (1999), *Working within the Law*, Dublin: Oak Tree Press.

Menagh, M. (1999), 'IT costs per hire: finding net (and other) savings', *Computerworld*, 18 January, 44.

Merrick, N. (1997), 'Broadbanding not a corporate quick fix', *People Management*, 20 February, 16.

Meulders, P., and Tytgat, B. (1989), 'The emergence of atypical employment in the European Community' in G. Rodgers and J. Rodgers (eds), *Precarious Jobs in Labour Market Regulation: The Growth of Atypical Employment in Western Europe*, Geneva: International Labour Office.

Meyer, H. (1975), 'The pay for performance dilemma', *Organisational Dynamics*, vol. 3, no. 1.

Miles, R., and Snow, C. (1978), *Organizational Strategy, Structure and Process*, New York: McGraw Hill.

Miles, R., and Snow, C. (1984), 'Designing strategic human resources systems', *Organisational Dynamics*, Spring, 36–52.

Milkovich, G., and Newman, J. (2002), *Compensation* (7th edn), Boston, MA: McGraw-Hill Irwin.

Miller, D., and Lee, J. (2001), 'The people make the process: commitment to employees, decision making and performance', *Journal of Management*, March.

Millmore, M. (2003), 'Just how extensive is the practice of strategic recruitment and selection?', *Journal of Management*, vol. 29, 87–108

Mintzberg, H. (1978), 'Patterns in strategy formulation', *Management Science*, vol. 24, May, 934–48.

Mintzberg, H. (1987), 'The strategy concept I: five Ps for strategy', *California Management Review*, 30, 1, 11–24.

Mintzberg, H. (1988), 'Opening up the definition of strategy' in J. Quinn, H. Mintzberg and R. Rames (eds), *The Strategy Process: Concepts, Contexts and Cases*, New Jersey: Prentice-Hall.

Mintzberg, M. (1973), *The Nature of Managerial Work*, New York: Harper and Row.

Molander, C. (1986), *Management Development*, Bromley: Chartwell-Bratt.

Mondy, R., and Noe, R. (1984), *Personnel: The Management of Human Resources*, Allyn and Bacon.

Monks, K. (1992), 'Personnel management practices: uniformity or diversity? Evidence from some Irish organisations', *Irish Business and Administrative Research*, vol. 13.

Monks, K. (1993), 'Models of personnel management: a means of understanding the diversity of personnel practices?', *Human Resource Management*, 3, 2, 29–41.

Monks, K. (2001), 'The role of the corporate human resource function in Irish international firms', in M. Linehan, M. Morley and J. Walsh (eds), *International Human Resource Management and Expatriate Transfers: Irish Experiences*, Dublin: Blackhall Press.

Monks, K., and McMackin, J. (2001), 'Designing and aligning an HR system', *Human Resource Management Journal*, 11, 2, 57–62.

Montgomery, C. (1996), 'Organization fit as a key to success', *HRM Magazine*, January, 94–6.

Mooney, P. (1980), *An Inquiry into Wage payment Systems in Ireland*, Dublin: Economic and Social Research Institute/European Foundation for the Improvement of Living and Working Conditions.

Mooney, M. (1988), 'From industrial relations to employee relations in Ireland', unpublished PhD thesis, Trinity College, Dublin.

Moorhead, G., and Griffin, R. (1989), *Organizational Behaviour*, New York: Houghton Mifflin Company.

Morley, M. (1994), 'A team approach to job design', *Irish Business and Administrative Research*, 15, 1, 20–34.

Morley, M. (2004), 'Contemporary debates in European human resource management: context and content', *Human Resource Management Review*, 14, 4, 353–64.

Morley, M., and Garavan, T. (1993), 'The new organisation – its implications for training and development', paper read to the Irish Institute of Training and Development National Conference, Galway, April.

Morley, M., Garavan, T., Gunnigle, P., and Collins, E. (2001a), 'Human capital accumulation: the role of human resource development', *Journal of European Industrial Training*, vol. 25, nos. 2–4, 48–68.

Morley, M., and Gunnigle, P. (1993), 'Trends in flexible working patterns in Ireland' in P. Gunnigle, P. Flood, M. Morley and T. Turner (eds), *Continuity and Change in Irish Employee Relations*, University of Limerick.

Morley, M., Gunnigle, P., and Heraty, N. (1999), 'Constructing the reward package: the extent and composition of change in wage and non wage increases in Ireland', *International Journal of Employment Studies*, vol. 7, no. 2, 121–50.

Morley, M., Gunnigle, P., Heraty, N., and Garavan, T. (guest eds) (2001b), 'Human resource development: sectoral and intervention level evidence of human capital accumulation', *Journal of European Industrial Training*, 25, 2/3/4, 48–229.

Morley, M. and McCarthy, A. (1999), 'The management of rewards', in P. Gunnigle (ed.), *The Irish Employee Recruitment Handbook: Finding and Keeping a High Quality Workforce*, Dublin: Oak Tree Press.

Morley, M., Moore, S., Heraty, N., and Gunnigle, P. (1998), *Principles of Organisational Behaviour: An Irish Text*, Dublin: Gill and Macmillan.

Morrissey, T. (1989), 'Employee participation at sub-board level' in *Industrial Relations in Ireland: Contemporary Issues and Developments*, Dublin: University College Dublin.

Moss Kanter, R. (1983), *The Change Masters*, London: Unwin.

Mowday, R. (1987), 'Equity theory predictions of behaviour in organisations', in R. Steers and L. Porter, *Motivation and Work Behaviour*, New York: McGraw Hill.

Mowday, R., Porter, L., and Steers, R. (1982), *Employee-Organization Linkages: The Psychology of Commitment, Absenteeism and Turnover*, New York: Academic Press.

Muchinski, P. (1986), 'Personnel selection methods' in C. Cooper and I. Robertson (eds), *International Review of Industrial and Organisational Psychology*, John Wiley.

Mumford, A. (1986), 'Learning to learn for managers', *Journal of European Industrial Training*, 10, 2, 1–22.

Munns, V. (1968), 'The functions and organisation of employers' associations in selected industries' in Employers Associations' Research Paper no. 7, Royal Commission on Trade Unions and Employers Associations, London: HMSO.

Munro-Fraser, J. (1954), *A Handbook of Employee Interviewing*, London: McDonald and Evans.

Murphy, K., Cleveland, J. (1991), *Performance Appraisal: An Organizational Perspective*, Needham Heights, MA: Allyn and Bacon.

Murphy, T., and Roche, W. (eds) (1997), *Irish Industrial Relations in Practice* (revised and expanded edn), Dublin: Oak Tree Press.

Murray, B., and Gerhart, B. (1998), 'An empirical analysis of a skill-based pay program and plant performance outcomes', *Academy of Management Journal*, vol. 41, no. 1.

Murray, S. (1984), *Employee Relations in Irish Private Sector Manufacturing Industry*, Dublin: Industrial Development Agency (IDA).

National Economic and Social Forum (NESF) (1995) *Jobs Potential of the Services Sector*, Forum Report no. 7, Dublin: National Economic and Social Forum.

Nevin, E. (1963), *Wages in Ireland*, Dublin: Economic and Social Research Institute.

Newell, S. (1995), *The Healthy Organization: Fairness, Ethics and Effective Management*, London: Routledge.

Newell, S. (2000), 'Selection and assessment in the "knowledge" era' (editorial), *International Journal of Selection and Assessment*, 8, 1, 1–6.

Nicholson, N., and Arnold, J. (1989), 'Graduate early experience in a multinational corporation', *Personnel Review*, 18, 4, 3–14.

Nicholson, N., and West, N. (1988), *Managerial Job Changes: Men and Women in Transition*, Cambridge: Cambridge University Press.

Nierenberg, G. (1968), *The Art of Negotiating*, New York: Cornerstone.

Nilsson, F., and Kald, M. (2002), 'Advances in performance management: the Nordic case', *European Management Journal*, 20, 3, 235–45.

Nilsson, F., and Rapp, B. (1999), 'Implementing business unit strategies: the role of management control systems', *Scandinavian Journal of Management*, 15, 65–88.

Nilsson, F., and Rapp, B. (2002), 'Creating competitive advantage: the importance of strategic congruence and integrated control' in B. Rapp, Y. Merkuryev and G. Merkuryeva (eds), *From Strategy to Operations in Production and Logistics*, Consa Report no. 5, Linköping: Linköping University.

Niven, M., (1967), *Personnel Management 1913–1963*, London: Institute of Personnel Management.

Nolan, P., and O'Donnell K. (1995), 'Industrial relations and productivity' in P. Edwards (ed.), *Industrial Relations* Oxford: Blackwell.

Nollen, S., and Gannon, M. (1996), 'Managing without a complete full-time workforce', in P. Flood, M. Gannon and J. Paauwe (eds), *Managing Without Traditional Methods: International Innovatism in Human Resource Management*, Wokingham: Addison-Wesley.

Nonaka, I. (1991), 'The knowledge creating company', *Harvard Business Review*, vol. 69, 96–104.

Nonaka, I., and Takeuchi., H. (1995), *The Knowledge-Creating Company: How Japanese Companies Create the Dynamics of Innovation*, Oxford: Oxford University Press.

Nooteboom, B. (1999), 'Innovation, learning and industrial organisation', *Cambridge Journal of Economics*, 23, 127–50.

Nordhaug, O. (1994), *Human Capital in Organizations*, New York: Oxford University Press.

Nordhaug, O. (2004), 'Contributions towards an economic theory of human resource management', *Human Resource Management Review*, 14, 4, 383–95.

Nowack, K. (1993), '360 degree feedback: the whole story', *Training and Development*, 47, 1, 69–73.

O'Brien, G. (1998), 'Business strategy and human resource management', in Roche, W., Monks, K. and Walsh, J., *Human Resource Strategies: Policy and Practice in Ireland*, Dublin: Oak Tree Press.

O'Brien, J. (1981), 'A study of national wage agreements in Ireland', paper no. 104, Economic and Social Research Institute, Dublin.

O'Brien, J. (1989), 'Pay determination in Ireland' in *Industrial Relations in Ireland: Contemporary Issues and Developments*, Dublin: University College Dublin.

O'Connell, P., and Lyons, M. (1995), *Enterprise Related Training and State Policy in Ireland: The Training Support Scheme*, Economic and Social Research Institute.

O'Connor, E. (1995), 'World class manufacturing in a semi-state environment' in P. Gunnigle and W. Roche (eds), *New Challenges to Irish Industrial Relations*, Dublin: Oak Tree Press in association with the Labour Relations Commission.

O'Connor, K. (1982), 'The impact of the Unfair Dismissals Act 1977 on personnel management and industrial relations', *Irish Business and Administrative Research*, vol. 5, no. 2.

O'Donnell, D., and Garavan, T. (2003), *eLearning in Irish Organisations: A Study of eLearning in the Republic of Ireland*, Dublin: Chartered Institute of Personnel and Development.

Oechslin, J. (1985), 'Employers' organisations' in R. Blanpain (ed.), *Labour Law and Industrial Relations*, Deventer: Kluwer.

O'Leary, A. (2000), 'Rights Commissioners: what methods of third party intervention do they adopt?', unpublished MBS thesis, University of Limerick.

Olian, J., Durham, C., Kristoff, A., Brown, K., Pierce, R., and Kunder, L. (1998), 'Designing management training and development for competitive advantage: lessons from the best', *Human Resource Planning*, 21, 20–30.

O'Hara, B. (1981), *The Evolution of Irish Industrial Relations: Law and Practice*, Dublin: Folens.

O'Higgins, E. (2002), 'Government and the creation of the Celtic Tiger: can management maintain the momentum?', *Academy of Management Executive*, 16, 3, 104–20.

O'Mahony, D. (1958), *Industrial Relations in Ireland*, Dublin: Economic Research Institute.

O'Malley, E. (1983), 'Late industrialisation under outward looking policies: the experience and prospects of the Republic of Ireland' unpublished PhD thesis, University of Sussex.

O'Neill, G., and Lander, D. (1994), 'Linking employee skills to pay: a framework for skill-based pay plans', *ACA Journal*, Winter, 14–27.

Organisation for Economic Co-operation and Development (1996): *Education at a Glance*, Paris: OECD.

Organisation for Economic Co-operation and Development (1997), *Economic Surveys: Ireland*, Paris: OECD.

Organisation for Economic Co-operation and Development (1999), *Economic Surveys: Ireland*, Paris: OECD.

Organisation for Economic Co-operation and Development (2000), *International Direct Investment Statistical Yearbook*, Paris: OECD.

Organisation for Economic Co-operation and Development (2005), *Education at a Glance*, Brussels: OECD.

Ost, E. (1990), 'Team based pay: new wave incentives', *Sloan Management Review*, Spring.

O'Sullivan, C. (1996), 'Time ripe for the Irish annual hours contract?', *IR Data Bank*, vol. 14, February, 21–3.

O'Sullivan, M. (2005), 'The joint labour committee system – a public policy examination of its operation, relevance and future', unpublished PhD thesis, Kemmy Business School, University of Limerick.

Ouchi, W. (1981), 'Theory Z: how American business can meet the Japanese challenge', Reading MA: Addison-Wesley.

Papalexandris, N., and Kramar, R. (1997), 'Flexible working patterns: towards reconciliation of family and work', *Employee Relations*, 19, 6, 581–95.

Pearse, J. (1987), 'Why merit pay doesn't work: implications for organisations theory' in D. Balkin and L. Gomez-Mejia (eds), *New Perspectives on Compensation*, New York: Prentice Hall.

Pedler, M., Boydell, T., and Burgoyne, J. (1989), 'Towards the learning company', *Education and Development*, vol. 20, part 1.

Penrose, E. (1959), *The Theory of the Growth of the Firm*, Oxford: Blackwell.

Perry, B. (1984), *Enfield: A High Performance System*, Bedford, MA: Digital Equipment Corporation, Educational Services Development and Publishing.

Personnel Standards Lead Body (1993) *A Perspective on Personnel*, London: Personnel Standards Lead Body.

Peters, T., and Waterman, R. (1982), *In Search of Excellence: Lessons from America's Best Run Companies*, New York: Harper and Row.

Pettigrew, P., Hendry, C., and Sparrow, P. (1988), 'Linking strategic change, competitive performance and human resource management: results of a UK based empirical study', University of Warwick.

Pettinger, R. (1994), *Introduction to Management*, London: Macmillan.

Pfeffer, J. (1994), *Competitive Advantage through People*, Boston: Harvard Business School Press.

Pfeffer, J. (1998a), 'Seven practices of successful organizations', *California Management Review*, 40, 96–124.

Pfeffer, J. (1998b), *The Human Equation: Building Profits by Putting People First*, Boston: Harvard Business School Press.

Pfeffer, J., and Viega, J. (1999), 'Putting people first for organizational success', *Academy of Management Executive*, 13, 37–48.

Phelps-Brown, H. (1986), *The Origins of Trade Union Power*, Oxford: Oxford University Press.

Philpott, L., and Sheppard, L. (1993), *Managing for Improved Performance*, London: Kogan Page.

Pil, F., and MacDuffie, J. (1996), 'The adoption of high-involvement work practices', *Industrial Relations*, 35, 3, 423–55.

Plumbley, P. (1985), *Recruitment and Selection*, London: Institute of Personnel Management.

Poelmans, S., Chinchilla, N., and Cardona, P. (2003), 'The adoption of family friendly HRM policies: competing for scarce resources in the labour market', *International Journal of Management*, 24, 2, 128–47.

Poelmans, S., and Sahibzada, K. (2004), 'A multi-level model for studying the context and impact of work–family policies and culture in organizations', *Human Resource Management Review*, 14, 4, 409–31.

Pollert, A. (1988), 'The flexible firm: fact or fixation?', *Work, Employment and Society*, vol. 2, 3, 281–316.

Pollert, A. (ed.) (1991), *Farewell to Flexibility*, Blackwell, Oxford.

Pollock, H., and O'Dwyer, L. (1985), *We Can Work it Out: Relationships in the Workplace*, Dublin: O'Brien Educational Press.

Poole, M. (1986), 'Managerial strategies and styles in industrial relations: a comparative analysis', *Journal of General Management*, vol. 12, no. 1, 40–53.

Popper, M., and Lipshitz, R. (2000), 'Organizational learning: mechanisms, culture and feasibility', *Management Learning*, 31, 2, 181–96.

Porter, M. (1980), *Competitive Strategy: Techniques for Analysing Industries and Competitors*, New York: Free Press.

Porter, M. (1985), *Competitive Advantage: Creating and Sustaining Superior Performance*, New York: Free Press.

Porter, M. (1987), 'From competitive advantage to corporate strategy', *Harvard Business Review*, May–June, 43–59.

Porter, M. (1990), *The Competitive Advantage of Nations*, New York: Free Press.

Porter, M. (2000), in *Global Competitiveness Report 2000*, Geneva: World Economic Forum.

Prahalad, C., and Hamel, G. (1990), 'The core competencies of the corporation', *Harvard Business Review*, 68, 79–91.

Prahalad, C., and Hamel, G. (1994), 'Strategy as a field of study: why search for a new paradigm?', *Strategic Management Journal*, 15, 5–16.

Probst, G., and Buchel, B. (1997), *Organisational Learning: The Competitive Advantage of the Future*, London: Prentice Hall.

Pulakos, E. (1997), 'Ratings of job performance' in D. Whetzel and G. Wheaton (eds), *Applied Measurement Methods in Industrial Psychology*, Palo Alto CA: Davies-Black Publishing.

Purcell, J. (1987), 'Mapping management styles in employee relations', *Journal of Management Studies*, vol. 24, no. 5, 533–48.

Purcell, J. (1989), 'The impact of corporate strategy on human resource management', in J. Storey (ed.), *New Perspectives on Human Resource Management*, London: Routledge.

Purcell, J. (1999), 'The search for best practice and best fit in human resource management; chimera or cul de sac?', *Human Resource Management Journal*, 9, 3, 26–41.

Purcell, J. (2004), 'The HRM-performance link: why, how and when does people management impact on organisational performance?', paper presented at the Twelfth Annual John Lovett Memorial Lecture, University of Limerick, March.

Purcell, J., and Gray, A. (1986), 'Corporate personnel departments and the management of industrial relations: two case studies in ambiguity', *Journal of Management Studies*, vol. 23, no. 2, 205–23.

Purcell, J., Kinnie, N., Hutchinson, S., Rayton, B., and Swart, J. (2003), *Understanding the People and Performance Link: Unlocking the Black Box*, London: Chartered Institute of Personnel and Development.

Purcell, J., and Sisson, K. (1983), 'Strategies and practice in the management of industrial relations' in G. Bain (ed.), *Industrial Relations in Britain*, Oxford: Blackwell.

Quinn, J. (1992), *Intelligent Enterprise*, New York: Free Press.

Quinn Mills, D. (1991), *Rebirth of the Corporation*, New York: John Wiles and Sons.

Raghuram, S., and Arvey, R. (1996), 'Business strategy links with staffing and training practices', *Human Resource Planning*, 17, 3, 55–73.

Randell, G. (1994), *Performance Appraisal in Personnel Management: A Comprehensive Guide to Theory and Practice in Britain*, Oxford: Blackwell.

Rao, P. (2002), *The Economics of Transaction Costs: Theories, Methods and Applications*, London: Palgrave.

Recardo, R., and Pricone, D. (1996), 'Is skill based pay for you?', *SAM Advanced Management Journal*, 61, 4, 16–22.

Redman, T., and Mathews, B. (1995), 'Trends in recruitment: a ten year retrospective view', *International Journal of Career Management*, 7, 2, 10–16.

Regalia, I. (1995), *Humanize Work and Increase Productivity*, Dublin: European Foundation for the Improvement of Living and Working Conditions.

Reid, M., Barrington, M., and Kenney, J. (1992), *Training Interventions: Managing Employee Development*, London: Institute of Personnel Management.

Reilly, P. (1996), 'Human resource planning: an introduction', Institute for Employment Studies Report 312, Brighton: IES.

Reilly, R., and Chao, G. (1982), 'Validity and fairness of some alternative selection procedures', *Personnel Psychology*, 35.

Reilly, R., and Warech, M. (1993), 'The validity and fairness of alternatives to cognitive tests', in L. Wing (ed.), *Employment Testing and Public Policy*, Boston: Kluwer.

Revans, R. (1982), 'Action learning: the skills of diagnosis', *Management Decision*, 21, 2, 46–52.

Reynaud, J. (1978), 'Problems and prospects for collective bargaining in the EEC member states', Document no. V/394/78-EN, Brussels: Commission of the European Community.

Ricardo, R., and Pricone, D. (1996), 'Is skill based pay for you?', *SAM Advanced Management Journal*, 61, 4, 16–22.

Ridgely, P. (1988), 'How relevant is the FUE?', *Irish Business*, February.

Robbins, S. (2001), *Organizational Behaviour*, New Jersey: Prentice Hall.

Roberts, K., and Glick, W. (1981), 'The job characteristics approach to task design: a critical review, *Journal of Applied Psychology*, vol. 66, no. 2, 193–217.

Robertson, I., and Makin, P. (1986), 'Management selection in Britain: a survey and critique', *Journal of Occupational Psychology*, 59.

Roche, W. (1988), 'Ireland: trade unions in Ireland in the 1980s', *European Industrial Relations Review*, no. 176.

Roche, W. (1989), 'State strategies and the politics of industrial relations in Ireland since 1945' in *Industrial Relations in Ireland: Contemporary Issues and Developments*, Dublin: University College Dublin.

Roche, W. (1990), 'Industrial relations research in Ireland and the trade union interest', paper presented to the Irish Congress of Trades Unions Conference on Joint Research between Trade Unions, Universities, Third-Level Colleges and Research Institutes, Dublin.

Roche, W. (1992), 'Modelling trade union growth and decline in the Republic of Ireland', *Irish Journal of Business and Administrative Research*, vol. 14, no. 1, 87–103.

Roche, W. (1995), 'The new competitive order and employee relations in Ireland: challenges and prospects', paper presented to the Irish Business and Employers Confederation Conference, 'Human Resources in the Global Market', Dublin, November.

Roche, W. (1997a), 'The trend of unionisation' in T. Murphy and W. Roche (eds), *Irish Industrial Relations in Practice* (revised and expanded edn), Dublin: Oak Tree Press.

Roche, W. (1997b), 'Pay determination, the state and the politics of industrial relations', in T. Murphy and W. Roche (eds), *Irish Industrial Relations in Practice* (revised and expanded edn), Dublin: Oak Tree Press.

Roche, W. (1999), 'In search of coherent commitment-oriented human resource policies and the conditions which sustain them', *Journal of Management Studies*, 36, 5, 653–78.

Roche, W. (2001), 'The individualisation of Irish industrial relations?', *British Journal of Industrial Relations*, 39, 2, 183–206.

Roche, W., and Ashmore, J. (2002), 'Irish unions in the 1990s: testing the limits of social partnership', in P. Fairbrother and G. Griffin (eds), *Changing Prospects for Trade Unionism: Comparisons between Six Countries*, London/New York: Continuum, 137–76.

Roche, W., and Geary, J. (1994), 'The attenuation of host-country effects? Multinationals, industrial relations and collective bargaining in Ireland', Working Paper, Business Research Programme, Smurfit Graduate School of Business, University College Dublin.

Roche, W., and Gunnigle, P. (1997), 'Competition and the new industrial relations agenda' in T. Murphy and W. Roche (eds), *Irish Industrial Relations in Practice* (revised and expanded edn), Dublin: Oak Tree Press.

Roche, W., and Larragy, J. (1989), 'The trend of unionisation in the Irish Republic' in *Industrial Relations in Ireland: Contemporary Issues and Developments*, Dublin: University College Dublin.

Roche, W., and Tansey, P. (1992), *Industrial Training in Ireland: Report Submitted to Industrial Policy Review Group*, Dublin: Department of Industry and Trade.

Roche, W., and Turner, T. (1994), 'Testing alternative models of human resource policy effects on trade union recognition in the Republic of Ireland', *International Journal of Human Resource Management*, vol. 5, no. 3, 721–53.

Rodger, A. (1952), *The Seven Point Plan*, London: National Institute of Industrial Psychology.

Roethlisberger, F., and Dickson, W. (1939), *Management and the Worker*, Harvard University Press.

Rollinson, D. (1993), *Understanding Employee Relations: A Behavioural Approach*, Wokingham: Addison-Wesley.

Ross, J. (1981), 'A definition of HRM', *Personnel Journal*, 60, 10, 781–83.

Roth, S. (1993), 'Lean production in German motor manufacturing', *European Participation Monitor*, no. 5. 35–9.

Rothwell, S. (1995), 'HRP' in J. Storey (ed.), *Human Resource Management: A Critical Text*, London: Routledge.

Russo, G., Rietveld, P., Nijkamp, P., and Gorter, C. (1995), 'Issues in recruitment strategies: an economic perspective', *International Journal of Career Management*, 7, 3, 3–13.

Salaman, G. (1992), *Human Resource Strategies*, London: Sage/Open University Press.

Salamon, M. (1998), *Industrial Relations: Theory and Practice*, Hemel Hempstead: Prentice Hall.

Sandico, C., and Kleiner, B.(1999), 'How to hire employees effectively', *Management Research News*, 22, 12, 33–7.

Sanfilipo, F., and Weigman, G. (1991), 'A compensation strategy for the 1990s', *Human Resource Professional*, vol. 4, no. 1, Fall.

Sappey, R., and Sappey, J. (1999), 'Different skills and knowledge for different times: training in an Australian retail bank', *Employee Relations*, 21, 6, 577–89.

Sargent, A. (1990), *Turning People On: The Motivation Challenge*, London: Institute of Personnel Management.

Saul, R. (1997), *The Unconscious Civilisation*, Melbourne: Penguin.

Scarbrough, H., Swan, J., and Preston, J. (1999), *Knowledge Management: A Literature Review*, Wimbledon: Chartered Institute of Personnel and Development.

Schermerhorn, J., Hunt, J., and Osborn, R. (1985) *Managing Organizational Behaviour*, New York: Wiley.

Schneider, B., and Schmitt, N (1986), *Staffing Organisations*, Illinois: Waveland.

Schuler, R. (1987), 'Personnel and human resource management choices and organizational strategy', *Human Resource Planning*, vol. 10, no. 1, 1–17.

Schuler, R. (1989), 'Strategic human resource management', *Human Relations*, vol. 42, no. 2, 157–84.

Schuler, R. (1992), 'Strategic human resource management: linking the people with the strategic needs of the business', *Organisational Dynamics*, vol. 21, no. 1, 18–31.

Schuler, R. (1995), *Managing Human Resources* (5th edn), St Paul, Minneapolis MN: West Publishing Company.

Schuler, R., Dowling, P., and De Cieri, H. (1993), 'An integrative framework of strategic international human resource management', *International Journal of Human Resource Management*, 4, 4, 717–64.

Schuler, R., Galante, S., and Jackson, S. (1987), 'Matching effective HR practices with competitive strategy', *Personnel*, September, 18–27.

Schuler, R., and Jackson, S. (1987a), 'Linking competitive strategies with human resource management practices', *Academy of Management Executive*, vol. 1, no. 3, August, 209–13.

Schuler, R., and Jackson, S. (1987b), 'Organizational strategy and organizational level as determinants of human resource management practices', *Human Resource Planning*, vol. 10, no.3. 125–41.

Schuler, R., and Jackson, S. (1996), *Human Resource Management: Positioning for the 21st Century*, St Paul, Minneapolis MN: West Publishing Company.

Schuler, R. and Jackson, S. (1999), *Strategic Human Resource Management*, Malden: Blackwell Publishers.

Scott-Lennon, F. (1995), *The Appraisals Pocketbook*, Alresford: Management Pocketbooks Limited.

Searle, R. (2003), *Selection and Recruitment: A Critical Text*, Milton Keynes: Open University/Palgrave Macmillan.

Senge, P. (1990), *The Fifth Discipline*, New York: Doubleday.

Sexton, J., Canny, A., and Hughes, G. (1996), *Changing Profiles in Occupations and Educational Attainment*, FÁS/ESRI Manpower Forecasting Studies, Report no. 5, November, Dublin: FÁS/Economic and Social Research Institute.

Sexton, J., Hughes, G., McCormick, B., and Finn, C. (2001), *Estimating Labour Force Flows, Job Openings and Human Resource Requirements 1990–2005*, Dublin: FAS/ESRI Manpower Forecasting Studies.

Sheehan B. (1997), 'Broadbanding pay system encourages sideways movement', *Industrial Relations News*, no. 6, 17 February.

Shivanath, G. (1987), 'Personnel practitioners 1986: their role and status in Irish industry', unpublished MBS thesis, University of Limerick.

Simons, R. (1995), *Levers of Control: How Managers Use Innovative Control Systems to Drive Strategic Renewal*, Boston: Harvard Business School Press.

Sisson, K. (1983), 'Employers' organisations' in Bain, G. (ed.) *Industrial Relations in Britain*, Oxford: Blackwell.

Sisson, K. (1989), *Personnel Management in Britain*, Oxford: Blackwell.

Sisson, K. (1994), 'Workplace Europe. Direct participation in organisational change: introducing the EPOC Project', presented to the International Industrial Relations Association Fourth European Regional Congress, 'Transformation of European Industrial Relations: Consequences of Integration and Disintegration', Helsinki.

Sisson, K. (1997), 'Towards new forms of work organisation – can Europe realise its potential? An interim report of the results of the EPOC questionnaire survey of direct employee participation in Europe', Luxembourg: European Foundation/Office for the Official Publication of the European Communities.

Sisson, K., and Storey, J. (2000), *The Realities of Human Resource Management*, Buckingham: Open University Press.

Sisson, K., and Timperley, S. (1994), 'From manpower planning to strategic human resource management' in K. Sisson (ed.), *Personnel Management: A Comprehensive Guide to Theory and Practice in Britain*, Oxford: Blackwell.

Skinner, B. (1938), *The Behaviour of Organisations*, New York: Appleton-Century-Cross.

Skrovan, D. (1983), *Quality of Work Life*, Reading, MA: Addison-Wesley.

Smith, A. (1970), *The Wealth of Nations*, London: Pelican.

Smith, I. (1992), 'Reward management and HRM' in Blyton, P. and Turnbull, P. (eds), *Reassessing Human Resource Management*, London: Sage.

Smith, M., and Robertson, I. (1986, 1993), *The Theory and Practice of Systematic Staff Selection*, London: Macmillan.

Smith, M., Gregg, M., and Andrews, D. (1989), *Selection and Assessment – A New Appraisal*, London: Pitman.

Smith, P., and Kendall, L. (1963), 'Retranslation of expectations: an approach to the construction of unambiguous anchors for rating scales, *Journal of Applied Psychology*, 47, 149–55.

Snell, S. (2005), 'HR strategy and organizational learning: extending the architecture in an era of competitive potential', Thirteenth Annual John Lovett Memorial Lecture, University of Limerick, April.

Snell, S., and Dean, J., Jr. (1992), 'Integrated manufacturing and human resource management: a human capital perspective', *Academy of Management Journal*, 35, 467–504.

Snell, S., and Youndt, M. (1995), 'Human resource management and firm performance: testing a contingency model of executive controls', *Journal of Management*, 21, 711–37.

Snell, S., Youndt, M., and Wright, P. (1996), 'Establishing a framework for research in strategic human resource management: merging resource theory and organizational learning' in G. Ferris (ed.), *Research in Personnel and Human Resources Management*, Greenwich, CT: JAI Press.

Snyder, W. (1996), 'Organizational learning and performance: an exploration of the linkages between organizational learning, knowledge and performance', unpublished doctoral thesis, University of Southern California. Source: Dale (1995).

Solomon, N. (1999), 'Culture and difference in workplace learning', in D. Boud and J. Garrick (eds), *Understanding Learning at Work*, London: Routledge.

Sparrow, P. (1996), 'Too good to be true?', *People Management*, 5 December, 22–7.

Sparrow, P. (2002), 'Globalisation as an uncoupling force: internationalisation of the HR process' in P. Gunnigle, M. Morley and M. McDonnell (eds), *The John Lovett Lectures: A Decade of Developments in Human Resource Management*, Dublin: Liffey Press.

Sparrow, P., and Bognanno, M. (1993), 'Competency requirements forecasting: issues for international selection and assessment', *International Journal of Selection and Assessment*, vol. 1, no. 1, 50–8.

Sparrow, P., and Hiltrop, J. (1994), *European Human Resource Management in Transition*, London: Prentice Hall.

Stata, R. (1989), 'Organisational learning: the key to management innovation', *Sloan Management Review*, vol. 30, no. 3, Spring.

Steers, R., and Mowday, R. (1987), 'Employee turnover in organisations' in R. Steers and L. Porter (eds), *Motivation and Work Behaviour*, New York: McGraw-Hill.

Steers, R., and Porter, L. (1987), *Motivation and Work Behaviour*, New York: McGraw Hill Publishing Company.

Steers, R., and Rhodes, S. (1978), 'Major influences on employee attendance: a process model', *Journal of Applied Psychology*, 63, 391–407.

Stewart, A. (1991), 'Performance appraisal' in Prior, J. (ed.), *Handbook of Training and Development* (2nd edn), Aldershot: Gower.

Stiles, P., and Kulvisaechana, S. (2003), *Human Capital and Performance: A Literature Review*, Judge Institute of Management, University of Cambridge.

Storey, J. (1989), 'Management development: a literature review and implications for future research part 1', *Personnel Review*, 18, 2–15.

Storey, J. (1992), *Developments in the Management of Human Resources*, Oxford: Blackwell.

Storey, J. (ed.) (1995, 2001), *Human Resource Management: A Critical Text*, London: Thomson Learning.

Storey, J. and Sisson, K. (1983), *Managing Human Resources and Industrial Relations*, Buckingham: Open University Press.

Strachan, G., and Burgess, J. (1998), 'The "family-friendly" workplace: origins, meaning and application at Australian workplaces', *International Journal of Manpower*, 19, 4, 250–65.

Strauss, G., and Sayle, L. (1972), *Personnel: The Human Problems of Management*, London: Prentice Hall.

Stredwick, J. (2000), 'Aligning rewards to organisational goals – a multinational's experience', *European Business Review*, 12, 1, 9–18.

Sugarman, L. (1986), *Life Span Development*, London: Methuen.

Suttle, S. (1988), 'Labour market flexibility', *Industrial Relations News*, vol. 38, no. 6, 13–16.

Sveiby, K. (1997), *The New Organizational Wealth: Managing and Measuring Knowledge Based Assets*, San Francisco: Berrett-Koehler.

Sweeney, P. (1998), *The Celtic Tiger: Ireland's Economic Miracle Explained*, Dublin: Oak Tree Press.

Tansey, P. (1998), *Ireland at Work: Economic Growth and the Labour Market 1987–1997*, Dublin: Oak Tree Press.

Taylor, F. (1911), *The Principles of Scientific Management*, New York: Harper and Row.

Taylor, F. (1947), *Scientific Management*, New York: Harper and Row.

Taylor, S. (1998), *Employee Resourcing*, London: IPD.

Teague, P. (1995), 'Pay determination in the Republic of Ireland: towards social corporatism?', *British Journal of Industrial Relations*, vol. 333, no. 2, 253–73.

Terpstra, D. (1996), 'The search for effective methods (employee recruitment and selection)', *HR Focus*, 17, 5, 16–18.

Terpstra, D., Mohamed, A., and Kethley, R. (1999), 'An analysis of federal court cases involving nine selection devices', *International Journal of Selection and Assessment*, 7, 1, 26–34.

Thelen, H., and Withall, J. (1979), 'Three frames of reference: the description of climate', *Human Relations*, vol. 2, no. 2, 159–76.

Thomas, S., and Ray, K. (2000), 'Recruiting on the Web: hi-tech hiring', *Business Horizons*, 43, 3, 43–61.

Thomason, G. (1984), *A Textbook of Industrial Relations Management*, London: Institute of Personnel Management .

Thompson, A., Mabey, C., Storey, J., Gray, C., and Iles, P. (2001), *Changing Patterns of Management Development*, Oxford: Blackwell.

Thompson, P. (1983), *The Nature of Work – an Introduction to Debates on the Labour Process*, London: Macmillan.

Thurley, K., and Wood, S. (1983), *Industrial Relations and Management Strategy*, Cambridge: Cambridge University Press.

Tiernan, S., Morley, M., and Foley, E. (1996, 2001), *Modern Management* (2 edns), Dublin: Gill and Macmillan.

Toegel, G., and Conger, J. (2003), '360-degree assessment: time for reinvention', *Academy of Management Learning and Education*, 2, 297–311.

Tomlinson, J. (1993), 'Human resources: partners in change', *Human Resource Management*, 32, 4, 545–54.

Tompkins, T. (1995), 'Role and diffusion in collective learning', *International Journal of Organizational Analysis*, 3, 69–85.

Toner, B. (1987), 'Union or non-union employee relations strategies in the Republic of Ireland', unpublished PhD thesis, London School of Economics.

Torrington, D., and Hall, L. (2005), *Human Resource Management*, Hemel Hempstead: Prentice Hall.

Traxler, F. (2004), 'The metamorphoses of corporatism: from classical to lean patterns', *European Journal of Political Research*, 43, 571–98.

Traxler, F., Blaschke, S., and Kittel, B. (2001), *National Labour Relations in Internationalised Markets. A comparative Study of Institutions, Change and Performance*, Oxford: Oxford University Press.

Tregaskis, O., Hearty, N., and Morley, M. (2001), 'HRD in multinationals: the global/local mix', *Human Resource Management Journal*, 11, 2, 34–56.

Turner, H. (1962), *Trade Union Growth, Structure and Policy*, London: Allen and Unwin.

Turner, T. (1988), 'Wage bargaining in Ireland: future strategies', *Industrial Relations News*, no. 27, July.

Turner, T. (1994), 'Unionisation and human resource management in Irish companies', *Industrial Relations Journal*, 25, 1, 39–51.

Turner, T., and Morley, M. (1995), *Industrial Relations and the New Order*, Dublin: Oak Tree Press.

Tyler, K. (1998), 'Compensation strategies can foster lateral moves and growing in place', *HR Magazine*, vol. 43, no. 5, 64–71.

Tyson, S. (1985), 'Is this the very model of the modern personnel manager?', *Personnel Management*, May.

Tyson, S. (1987), 'The management of the personnel function', *Journal of Management Studies*, vol. 24, no. 5, 523–32.

Tyson, S. (1992), 'Business and human resource strategy', *Irish Business and Administrative Research*, vol. 13, no. 1, 1–5.

Tyson, S. and Fell, A. (1986) *Evaluating the Personnel Function*, London: Hutchinson.

Tyson, S., Witcher, M., and Doherty, N. (1994), *Different Routes to Excellence*, Human Resource Research Centre, Cranfield University School of Management.

Ulrich, D. (1997), *Human Resource Champions*, Cambridge: Harvard Business School Press.

Ulrich, D., and Lake, D. (1991), 'Organizational capability: creating competitive advantage', *Academy of Management Executive*, 7, 77–92.

Umstot, D. (1988), *Understanding Organisational Behaviour* (2nd edn), St. Paul, Minneapolis: West Publishing.

United Nations Commission for Trade and Development (UNCTAD) (2004), *World Investment Report*, Geneva: United Nations Publications.

Vaill, P. (1982), 'The purpose of high performing systems', *Organizational Dynamics*, Autumn, 23–39.

Vogeley, E., and Schaeffer, L. (1995), 'Link employee pay to competencies and objectives', *HR Magazine*, vol. 40, no. 10.

Von Prondzynski, F. (1985), 'The death of the pay round', *Industrial Relations News*, no. 43, November.

Von Prondzynski, F. and McCarthy, C. (1984), *Employment Law in Ireland*, London: Sweet and Maxwell.

Von Prondzynski, F., and Richards, W. (1994), *European Employment and Industrial Relations Glossary: Ireland*, London: Sweet and Maxwell/Luxembourg: Office for Official Publications of the European Communities.

Vroom, V. (1964), *Work and Motivation*, New York: Wiley.

Wagner, R. (1949), 'The employment interview: a critical summary', *Personnel Psychology*, 2, 17–46.

Waldman, D., Atwater, L., and Antonioni, D. (1998), 'Has 360 degree feedback gone amok?', *Academy of Management Executive*, vol. 12, no. 2, 86–94.

Walker, C. and Guest, R. (1952), *The Man on the Assembly Line*, Boston: Harvard University Press.

Walker, J. (1980), *Human Resource Planning*, New York: McGraw-Hill.

Wall, T. (1982), 'Perspectives on job redesign', in J. Kelly and C. Clegg (eds), *Autonomy and Control at the Workplace: Context for Job Redesign*, London: Croom Helm.

Wall, T. and Wood, S. (2005), 'The romance of human resource management and business performance, and the case for big science', *Human Relations*, 58, 4, 429–62.

Wallace, J. (1988a), 'Unofficial strikes in Ireland', *Industrial Relations News*, no. 8, 15 February.

Wallace, J. (1988b), 'Workplace aspects of unofficial strikes', *Industrial Relations News*, no. 9, 3 March.

Wallace, J. (1989), 'Procedure agreements and their place in workplace industrial relations' in *Industrial Relations in Ireland: Contemporary Issues and Developments*, Dublin: University College Dublin.

Wallace, J., (1991) 'The Industrial Relations Act 1990 and other developments in labour law', paper presented to the Mid-West Chapter of the Institute of Personnel Management, University of Limerick.

Wallace, J. (2003), 'Unions in 21st century Ireland – entering the Ice Age?', paper presented at the *Industrial Relations News Conference*, University College Dublin, 27 February.

Wallace, J., and Clifford, N. (1998), *Collective Bargaining and Flexibility in Ireland*, Geneva: International Labour Office.

Wallace, J., Dineen, D., and O'Sullivan, M. (2001), 'The contribution of the services sector to the Irish employment miracle' in J. Dølvik (ed.), *At your Service: Comparative Perspectives on Employment and Labour Relations in the European Private Services Sector*, Brussels: PIE-Peter Lang.

Wallace, J., Gunnigle, P., and McMahon, G.V. (2004), *Industrial Relations in Ireland*, Dublin: Gill and Macmillan.

Wallace, J., and O'Shea, F. (1987), *A Study of Unofficial Strikes in Ireland*, Dublin: Stationery Office.

Wallace, J., and O'Sullivan, M. (2004), 'Employment protection in Ireland', *International Employment Relations Review*, 10, 1, 53–66.

Walsh, B. (1999) 'The persistence of high unemployment in a small open labour market: the Irish case' in F. Barry (ed.), *Understanding Ireland's Economic Growth*, London: MacMillan Press.

Walsh, J. (1998), 'Managing human resource development' in W. Roche, K. Monks and J. Walsh (eds), *Human Resource Strategies: Policy and Practice in Ireland*, Dublin: Oak Tree Press.

Walton, J. (1999), *Strategic Human Resource Development*. London: Prentice Hall.

Walton, R. (1973), 'Quality of working life: what is it?', *Sloan Management Review*, vol. 15, Fall, 11–21.

Walton, R. (1985), 'From control to commitment in the workplace', *Harvard Business Review*, 63, 57–74.

Walton, R., and Lawrence, P. (1985), *Human Resource Management – Trends and Challenges*, Harvard, MA: HBS Press.

Walton, R., and McKersie, R. (1965), *A Behavioural Theory of Labor Negotiations*, New York: McGraw-Hill.

Ward, P. (1995), 'A 360 degree turn for the better', *People Management*, February, 20–2.

Wareing, R. and Stockdale, J. (1987), 'Decision making in the promotion interview: an empirical study', *Personnel Review*, 16, 4.

Way, S., and Johnson, D. (2001), 'The evaluative process model: a multiple stakeholder framework for strategic human resource management research', paper read to the Washington meeting of the Academy of Management, August.

Webb, S., and Webb, B. (1920), *The History of Trade Unionism*, Harlow: Longman.

Webster, B. (1990), 'Beyond the mechanics of HRD', *Personnel Management*, 22, 3, 44–7.

Webster, E. (1964), *Decision Making in the Employment Interview*, Quebec: Eagle Publishing.

Werner, S. and Ward, S. (2004), 'Recent compensation research: an eclectic review', *Human Resource Management Review*, 14, 2, 201–27.

Wernerfelt, B. (1984), 'A resource based view of the firm', *Strategic Management Journal*, 5, 171–80.

West, P. (1994), 'The learning organisation: losing the luggage in transit?', *Journal of European Industrial Training*, vol. 18, no. 11.

Westwood, R. (1992), *Organisational Behaviour*, London: Longman.

Wexley, K., and Latham, G. (1991), *Developing and Training Human Resources in Organisations*, New York: HarperCollins.

Whelan, C. (1982), 'Worker priorities, trust in management and prospects for worker participation', Paper 111, Dublin: Economic and Social Research Institute.

White Paper on Education (1995), *Charting our Education Future*, Pn 2009, Dublin: Government Publications Office, April.

White Paper on Human Resource Development (1997), Pn. 3381, Dublin: Government Publications Office.

Whittington, R. (1993), *What is Strategy and Does it Matter?* London: Routledge.

Wickham, J. (1993), *New Forms of Work in Ireland: An Analysis of the 'New Forms of Work and Activity' Data Set*, Working Paper no. WP/93/31/EN, Dublin: European Foundation for the Improvement of Living and Working Conditions.

Wiesner, W., and Cronshaw, S. (1988), 'A meta-analytic investigation of the impact of interview format and degree of structure on the validity of the employment interview', *Journal of Occupational Psychology*, 61, 275–90.

Wilkinson, A., Godfrey, G., and Marchington, M. (1997), 'Bouquets, brickbats and blinkers: total quality management and employee involvement in practice', *Organization Studies*, 18, 5, 799–819.

Williams, M., and Dreher, G. (1992), 'Compensation system attributes and applicant pool characteristics', *Academy of Management Journal*, vol. 35, no. 3, 571–96.

Williamson, O. (1978), *Markets and Hierarchies: Analysis and Anti-trust Implications*, Glencoe: Free Press.

Williamson, O., and Masten, S. (eds) (1999), *The Economics of Transaction Costs*, New York: Edward Elgar.

Windmuller, J. (1984), 'Employers associations in comparative perspective; organisation, structure and administration' in J. Windmuller and A. Gladstone (eds), *Employer Associations and Industrial Relations*, Oxford: Clarendon.

Wood, S. (1995), 'The four pillars of HRM; are they connected?', *Human Resource Management Journal*, 5, 5, 49–59.

Wood, S. (1999), 'Human resource management and performance', *International Journal of Management Reviews*, 1, 4, 367–413.

Wood, S., and Albanese, M. (1995), 'Can we speak of a high commitment management on the shop floor?', *Journal of Management Studies*, vol. 32, 2, 215–47.

Wood, S., and de Menezes, L. (1998), 'High commitment management in the UK: evidence from the workplace industrial relations survey and employers' manpower and skills practices survey', *Human Relations*, 51, 485–515.

Womack, J., Jones, D., and Roos, D. (1990), *The Machine that Changed the World*, New York: Rawson Associates.

Wright, P., Dunford, B., and Snell, S. (2001), 'Human resources and the resource-based view of the firm', *Journal of Management*, 27, 701–21.

Wright, P., and McMahon, G. (1992), 'Theoretical perspectives for strategic human resource management', *Journal of Management*, 18, 2, 295–320.

Wright, P., and Snell, S. (1991), 'Toward an integrative view of strategic human resource management', *Human Resource Management Review*, 1, 203–25.

Wright, P., and Snell, S. (1998), 'Toward a unifying framework for exploring fit and flexibility in strategic human resource management', *Academy of Management Review*, 23, 756–72.

Wright, V., and Brading, L. (1992), 'A balanced performance', *Total Quality Magazine*, October.

Yeates, P. (2000), *Lockout: Dublin 1913*, Dublin: Gill and Macmillan.

Zeleny, M. (1990), 'Knowledge as capital/capital as knowledge', *Human Systems Management*, 9, 129–30.

Index